Making Sense

A Real-World Rhetorical Reader

SECOND EDITION

Making Sense

···●

A Real-World Rhetorical Reader

Cheryl Glenn
PENN STATE UNIVERSITY

BEDFORD/ST. MARTIN'S

Boston ◆ New York

For Bedford/St. Martin's

Developmental Editor: John Elliott
Senior Production Editor: Shuli Traub
Production Supervisor: Jessie Markland
Senior Marketing Manager: Rachel Falk
Art Director/Cover Designer: Lucy Krikorian
Text Design: Anna Palchik
Copy Editors: Wendy Polhemus–Annibell/Sally Scott
Picture Research: Alice Lundoff
Cover Art: Tony DeBlasi, "It Ain't Necessarily So," Acrylic on Wood
Composition: Pine Tree Composition, Inc.
Printing and Binding: R. R. Donnelley & Sons Company

President: Joan E. Feinberg
Editorial Director: Denise B. Wydra
Editor in Chief: Nancy Perry
Director of Marketing: Karen Melton Soeltz
Director of Editing, Design, and Production: Marcia Cohen
Managing Editor: Erica T. Appel

Library of Congress Control Number: 2004108137

Manufactured in the United States of America.

0   9   8   7   6   5
f   e   d   c   b   a

For information, write:
Bedford/St. Martin's
75 Arlington Street
Boston, MA 02116   (617–399–4000)

ISBN: 0–312–41311–4

EAN: 978–0–312–413–11–8

Preface

··· ●

Why This Book?

Making Sense: A Real-World Rhetorical Reader is based on the kinds of reading, thinking, and writing we all—teachers and students alike—do every day. Every day, in conversations, emails, letters, memos, notes to colleagues, and many other forms of discourse, we describe, define, tell stories, classify groups of people or things, provide examples, make comparisons, analyze processes, analyze causes and consequences, and argue. Therefore, everyday language—yours and your students'—provides a foundation for the teaching you will be doing and the reading and writing your students will be doing for this course. Using *Making Sense,* your students will simply build on what they already know and already do fairly well.

What we English teachers have traditionally called the "modes of discourse" aren't just for English teachers or writing classes; these are nine rhetorical methods everyone uses to make sense of the world: the ways we work out problems, make decisions, and come to understandings. And these methods have a long, well-documented history. In fact, Aristotle wrote about them over two thousand years ago when he described them as operations of the human mind, operations that help us solve various kinds of rhetorical problems. Thus, these methods serve as sources of information, places we can go to begin thinking through a specific problem or writing assignment. Whether we're teachers or

v

students, we can use them as strategies of invention, ways of shaping an entire essay or of invigorating just one paragraph.

Making Sense takes these time-tested traditional rhetorical methods in exciting new directions by revealing how they underlie a surprising range of daily real-world discourse—both verbal and visual, in print and online. In doing so, the book links the kinds of reading and writing students do for school to the ways they encounter and use language and images. A thematic focus on literacy helps them think critically about the meaning and importance of reading and writing both in their own lives and in a wider cultural context. And to help them put all these insights into practice, the extensive prompts and other assignments get students writing sooner and more often than other rhetorical readers, and frequently in collaboration with others.

What's Special about This Book?

- **A focus on "real-world" examples.** Dozens of brief examples of specific rhetorical methods in the chapter introductions include a postcard to the author, an online want ad, a letter to Dear Abby, handwritten directions for heating up pizza, amazon.com reviews of a Stephen King book, bilingual and pictorial instructions for installing drywall, and many other kinds of nonacademic writing, often drawn from online sources or incorporating visuals. These examples, one of which opens each chapter, help students see how they are already familiar with—and comfortable using—the nine classic rhetorical methods, whether to solve a problem, tell a story, question an answer, or explain a process.

- **Engaging contemporary readings.** The seventy-three textual readings, including one student essay in each chapter, have been chosen with an eye toward stimulating student interest and offering instructors more options outside the "canonical" range of most other rhetorical readers. Along with traditional favorites by writers like N. Scott Momaday, Annie Dillard, Maya Angelou, and E. B. White, each chapter includes recent pieces by newer or lesser-known authors on topics such as student excuses for turning assignments in late (Carolyn Foster Segal's "The Dog Ate My Disk and Other Tales of Woe"), the ordeal of being a teenage oboe prodigy (Meghan Daum's "Music Is My Bag"), and a ban on marriages between heterosexuals who aren't masculine or feminine enough (George Saunders's "My Amendment").

- **Sustained attention to visual rhetoric.** More than seventy-five photographs, drawings, ads, product labels, cartoon, computer screen shots, and other images—at least six per chapter—feature prominently in chapter introductions, as accompaniments to text readings, and as readings in themselves. (The last reading in each chapter is a visual selection.) Study questions, along with advice provided in the introduction to the book and to each chapter, help students learn to analyze visual elements critically and see how they can use them in their own writing.

- **More opportunities for writing and collaboration than any other rhetorical reader.** Going beyond the usual questions and assignments that accompany readings, *Making Sense* provides activities throughout each chapter introduction that stimulate students to begin writing as soon as they are introduced to the rhetorical method. Beginning with one about the chapter–opening example, these activities focus on issues of literacy, visual analysis, and the different purposes for using the chapter's method. Many questions and assignments in each chapter call on students to work with one or more classmates, and each chapter introduction ends with a revision checklist to help students analyze their own drafts or those of their peers in terms of the chapter's guidelines.

- **A thematic emphasis on literacy.** Building on my own research interests, the book brings home to students the centrality of reading and writing in their lives both in and out of the classroom. Each chapter begins with a writing prompt to focus students' attention on some issue of literacy and includes at least one selection on a literacy–related topic, from a narrative about learning a new language to an exploration of why students aren't reading.

- **An introduction focusing on the reading–writing connection.** The first chapter gets students thinking about their own literacy development and shows them how active reading can contribute to skilled, purposeful writing. Among other features, it introduces students to strategies for critical reading (previewing, annotating, summarizing) and invention (freewriting, brainstorming, clustering) and includes a model analysis of an essay excerpt and a visual "text." The introduction also traces the development of a model student essay from invention activities to peer analysis of a draft to revisions and choice of illustrations for a final draft.

- **Help with research and documentation.** An appendix extends this discussion of the reading–writing connection by helping students understand how to use and incorporate source materials (their reading) into their writing and provides guidelines and examples for citing sources in MLA style. To provide additional examples and practice in these skills, several of the readings (including one of the new student essays) include source citations, and a number of the writing assignments invite or require research.

What's New in the Second Edition?

- **Twenty–seven new contemporary, classic, student, and visual selections.** Constituting almost 40 percent of the total, the new selections include four classic essays in the argument chapter (including Martin Luther King Jr.'s "Letter from Birmingham Jail" and H. L. Mencken's "On the Penalty of Death"), an additional well–known essay in four other chapters (including Stephanie Ericsson's "The Ways We Lie" and Suzanne Britt's "Neat People vs. Sloppy People"), and three new student essays. There are also more of the lively contemporary essays and visuals that made the first edition so distinctive. For instance, Bob Costas compares Muhammad Ali and Michael Jordan in their historical contexts; Laura Sessions Stepp uses Darwinian terminology to classify teenaged girls into three categories; and Ted Allen of *Queer Eye for the Straight Guy* lays down the laws of fashion for men, with pointed verbal and visual examples.

- **Two timely new casebooks in the argument chapter.** Besides the existing casebook on college athletics and the four added classic argument essays, this chapter now offers new groups of essays on vegetarianism and on the military draft and national service, which provide a variety of perspectives on two topics with national and global implications as well as immediate personal ones for many students.

- **More guidance for critical reading.** To help students build the reading skills they need to become more successful writers, a new "How Do You Read?" section in each chapter introduction advises students on how to approach a text that uses the chapter's method, pointing out the main features to look for and the ways in which a text can succeed or fail in fulfilling its intended rhetorical purpose for a specific audience.

- **More guidance and practice in analyzing and using visuals.** A new section at the end of each chapter introduction, "'Reading' and Using Visuals," analyzes a sample visual to help students learn how to judge the rhetorical effectiveness of images both as readers and as writers. In addition, a number of the prompts at the end of the chapter introductions, the readings, and the chapter now ask students to incorporate visuals into their own writing.

- **A new two-color design.** Adding a second color to the book's interior design makes it easier to find the writing prompts and other assignments as well as such features as checklists and the MLA documentation guidelines.

What Comes with the Book?

Besides all the writing activities built into the text, the accompanying instructor's manual (which is bound in with the text in the Instructor's Edition) offers you further ideas for your class: ideas for student presentations and assignments; prompts for helping your students write and evaluate essays; ways to interconnect the essays, modes, and authors in the book; guides for helping you and your students tap the resources of the Web; background information on authors, historical events, and the teaching of writing; as well as a selection of essays and articles regarding ways to teach college-level writing. The author of the manual, Jessica Enoch of the University of New Hampshire at Durham, also wrote most of the text for the book's Web site, <bedfordstmartins.com/makingsense>, which offers further ideas for your class: helpful and explicit grading standards; additional writing assignments that incorporate and combine the rhetorical methods; suggestions for a step–by–step approach to student writing that incorporates freewriting exercises, essay proposals, and peer reviewing sessions; and links for your students to other sites that may be helpful in writing essays on topics related to those in the readings.

Who Helped?

Making Sense was reinvigorated during a meeting with wise and creative Joan Feinberg, who continues to guide Bedford/St. Martin's with unparalleled grace and success; the smart and conscientious Nancy Perry, whose ability to put together the perfect publishing team is unmatchable; marketing specialist Jimmy Fleming and executive editor Steve Scipione, whose expert opinions were essential in shaping the revision and especially in updating the table of contents and choosing the new argument casebooks; and John Elliott, my constant intellectual companion and editor extraordinaire, whose gentlemanly tone makes granting his requests for more (and more) writing and rewriting almost a pleasure. Together, John and I worked closely with Joelle Hann, who helped locate readings and supervise the new student writers; Alice Lundoff, who again carried out the art research, carefully selecting images that complement the featured essays; Kristy Bredin, who took care of a multitude of clerical chores, mailings, and research threads and ravelings; Laura King, who edited the instructor's manual; Sandy Schechter, who oversaw the huge task of chasing down permissions; and project editor Shuli Traub, who took over the manuscript where John left off, carefully overseeing the copyediting, typesetting, and proofreading. I remain smitten with Anna Palchik's artistic sense and am delighted that she designed the interior of this second edition of *Making Sense*; thanks also to Lucy Krikorian, who handled the individual designs of the new chapter openers and the sizing and cropping of the visuals. Although I never thought I'd love a cover more than that of the first edition, Lucy also managed to design my current favorite cover, which features another of artist Tony DeBlasi's fabulous creations, "It Ain't Necessarily So" (from his Energy One Series). Without the help, support, and prodding of these remarkably gifted people and friends, I simply could not have revised *Making Sense*.

In addition to all the contributing members of the Bedford/St. Martin's editorial and marketing teams, I want to thank my teaching colleagues who took the time out of their already busy lives to review the first edition of *Making Sense*, offering me their insights and advice for shaping the revision: Joel R. Brouwer, Montcalm Community College;

Alan Brown, University of West Alabama; Ken A. Bugajski, Rogers State University; Rosalyn Collings, Penn State University; Vikki Dykstra, Kalamazoo Valley Community College; Ernest Enchelmayer, Troy State University; Linda G. Foss, Centralia College; Ellen Foster, Slippery Rock University; Kristen L. Hague, Mesa State College; Mary Hurst, Cuyahoga Community College; Richard Kyer, Fairmont State College; Donna J. Long, Fairmont State College; Ann M. Marlowe, Missouri Southern State College; Troy D. Nordman, Butler County Community College; Craig Payne, Indian Hills College; Tony Perrello, Angelo State University; John S. Prince, Ball State University; Lisa Schifano, Penn State University; Lauren Servais, Cascadia Community College; Greta Skogseth, Montcalm Community College; Kathryn Lyn Skulley, Front Range Community College; Mary Ann Tighe, Troy State University; Shannon Walters, Penn State University; Justin George Watson, Holy Cross College; Scott Andrew Wible, Penn State University; and Hui Wu, University of Central Arkansas.

I remain ever-grateful to Jess Enoch for once again contributing her scholarly and pedagogical expertise to the ancillary materials and, especially, for her friendship. She continues to teach, write, and research with enthusiasm, success, and a remarkable measure of joy. I'm especially grateful to Jon Olson, who makes my everyday life better in every way, and to Eddie and Helen, who make every day of the future look brighter.

Cheryl Glenn

Contents

....●

3 Narration 131

4 Exemplification   *203*

GRETEL EHRLICH, *About Men*   223

Responding to what she calls mistaken stereotypes of the cowboy, Ehrlich offers a list of well-supported examples that complicate any simple definitions of what it means to be a man.

BRENT STAPLES, *Just Walk on By: A Black Man Ponders His Power to Alter Public Space*   229

Staples's moving examples illustrate his stark point about the ways that African American males affect the emotional temperature of the public spaces they inhabit.

EVA PAYNE, *Handy*   [STUDENT ESSAY]   234

A student whose physical dexterity has long been recognized sets out to demonstrate her intellectual "handiness" as well.

MICHELLE STACEY, *All You Can Eat*   237

Using a series of vivid examples to support her points, a magazine writer argues that portions in American restaurants are too big.

DIANE RAVITCH, *The Language Police: How Pressure Groups Restrict What Students Learn*   242

Ravitch provides a long list of examples to argue that "bias and sensitivity reviewers" have gutted textbooks and standardized tests of anything interesting to children.

JONATHAN KOZOL, *The Human Cost of an Illiterate Society*   254

With a series of touching examples, a prominent social critic measures the penalties imposed on those who can't read.

TED ALLEN, *The Laws of Fashion*   [VISUAL]   263

Starting with the fundamental rule "Know yourself, *then* get dressed," the *Queer Eye for the Straight Guy* star lists some fashion laws that every man should follow, with witty verbal and visual examples.

Additional Suggestions for Writing   *267*

5 Classification and Division   *269*

7 Process Analysis   *427*

chapter **1**

INTRODUCTION:
THE READING-WRITING
CONNECTION

Reading a book is like re-writing it for yourself. . . . You bring to a novel, anything you read, all your experience of the world. You bring your history and you read it in your own terms. — ANGELA CARTER

Read, read, read. Read everything—trash, classics, good and bad, and see how they do it. — WILLIAM FAULKNER

Writing is an exploration. You start from nothing and learn as you go. — E. L. DOCTOROW

Writing saved me from the sin and inconvenience of violence. — ALICE WALKER

*E*very day you read and write in order to make sense of the world around you. You might get online to find—to read about—solutions to your problems, whether they have to do with eliminating a computer virus, locating a quotation, or finding the cheapest airline fare. And when you're online, you're often writing as well, whether you're jotting down instructions, keyboarding in an eBay bid, or writing out a quotation you've found. When you're offline, you're reading and writing, too. From browsing through catalogues and skimming the back of the cereal box to sending birthday cards and taking notes in class, your days are filled with the reading and writing that enrich your life as a literate human being. In fact, most of us do so much reading and writing each day that we hardly think about what we're doing—we just do it.

Making Sense invites you to look at how you're using all this reading and writing, to think about your own **literacy**—but not just in terms of your basic ability to read, write, and see. Rather, this book helps you imagine your literacy in a much broader sense: how you react to and interpret verbal and visual language in particular ways, and how you produce and use language to achieve certain kinds of goals. Thus the book provides you opportunities for reading and writing experiences—literacy experiences—that will not only seem familiar and everyday to you but will also help prepare you for making sense of the assignments you'll encounter in your first-year writing class and in the college coursework (and working life) that follow.

To those ends, *Making Sense* introduces you to nine basic methods of communication we all rely on: description, narration, exemplification, classification and division, comparison and contrast, process analysis, cause-and-consequence analysis, definition, and argument. Each of these nine methods is **rhetorical** in that it uses language for a specific purpose in a way that leads to the creation of knowledge. These are the **rhetorical methods** we've all used since we were young, whether we're explaining, working out problems, making decisions, coming to an understanding, or making a case. In fact, you already bring to this course a good deal of rhetorical skill: you already know how to gauge the way you perceive and produce verbal and visual language according to the particular **rhetorical situation**—the intended audience, the purpose, the topic, the medium (oral, written, electronic), the time and place. You may not always gauge perfectly; your perception may not always be accurate and your production may not always be successful, but you often interpret and choose language in ways that are appropriate to the rhetorical situation. You already know how to use language to make sense.

Building on the rhetorical knowledge you already have and regularly use, *Making Sense* will guide you as you create, select, and organize information in ways that describe an issue, narrate an entertaining story, explain a complex process, analyze your options, explore the consequences of a decision, or prove a point. *Making Sense* will help you become more conscious of exactly how words help you think through these kinds of language situations.

Whether you're expected to read critically in preparation for class discussion, keep a journal, respond to someone else's rough draft, or plan and submit a formal academic essay, *Making Sense* will help you all the way, building on the literacy skills and rhetorical experiences you have spent your whole life developing. No matter what the assignment, when you use *Making Sense* you'll be reading, writing, thinking, and talking about it—tapping your literacy background and your rhetorical skills—from beginning to end, from process to product.

Looking at Your Own Literacy When you read and write, where do you start—on a computer or on paper? Write for five minutes, making four lists: the kinds of reading you do online, the kinds you do on paper; the kinds of writing you do on a screen, and the kinds you do on paper. What did you learn from your own lists? Be prepared to share your findings with the rest of your class.

What's Reading Got to Do with Writing?

Why read in a class on writing?

Reading and writing are the basic components of literacy—as well as of contemporary rhetorical skills. Good readers are most often good writers, and vice versa, so you'll want to be both, in college and after. If you're like most first-year students, you're no doubt interested in improving in every way to meet the challenges of your new college curriculum. Most likely you'll find yourself doing twice—if not three times—as much reading as you did in high school, and your writing obligations will be triple as well. Plus, you'll be expected to read and write more skillfully, making careful observations and asking many questions. Therefore *Making Sense* offers you innumerable opportunities to read and analyze models of good writing, to explore visual images and the ways they relate to verbal texts, to practice thinking about your own writing, and to respond to thought–provoking questions and assignments.

I hope that you'll come to see your literacy development (that is, your development as a reader and writer) as an unfolding, ever-improving process of growth and understanding—each time you analyze and discuss the readings, write to crystallize your thinking, share and discuss your drafts, and revise them until your words take the form that best articulates your intended meaning.

important
intensley
criticize

❋Reading Actively and Critically

Look at the picture on p. 6 of the father and child reading together. Although the baby cannot decode the printed page, he is nevertheless *reading actively.* How do we know? First of all, the book is predominantly in the baby's lap, not the father's. The baby seems to know instinctively to hold his hands and arms out of the way of the book so he and his father can see the words and pictures. But the most compelling evidence that this baby is reading actively is that he is "talking," reading aloud, so to speak, just like his father. This baby has already entered the active world of literacy, and he is learning how to inhabit—to "get into"—a text in ways that are productive and appropriate to his age.

When you read actively, you read productively, efficiently, and in age–appropriate ways as well. You no longer sit on a parent's lap to read, but you still might catch yourself reading aloud in order to make sense of a difficult text. You also might like to talk with someone else about what you're reading—just like the baby does. Your reading strategies are every bit as age–appropriate, then, as the baby's.

Reading actively means constantly interacting with the text as though you are in conversation with it. You start out by looking at an accompanying image, if there is one. Then, you read the introductory materials and try to make sense of the rhetorical situation: the connections among the author, the text itself, and the audience for the text. That is, you start out by asking questions like these:

What do I know about this author?

What else has she written?

Why is he writing about this subject?

Who is the intended audience?

What does the title mean? Does it announce the intended subject, or is it intended to arouse interest?

How does the image connect with the text?

Reading actively means looking over the headings, taking the time to figure out the meanings of unfamiliar words and references by using a dictionary or examining the context. It means considering where and when
the piece appears (and where and when it was first published, if necessary)
and what that context means for your full understanding. Finally, reading
actively means bringing your own observations to the text, connecting it
with other reading you've done and the experiences you've had.

Active readers are critical readers; they approach the text inquisitively and carefully, with an eye toward judging its strengths and weaknesses. Active readers ask questions like these:

- What is the gist of this text?
- What's important in it?
- How does it compare, contrast, or connect in some other way with other pieces I've read on the same subject?
- Does it hold my attention? How easy is it to follow?
- Are terms clearly defined? Does the author provide enough details and examples?
- What does the author think, and why does she hold that opinion?
- What do *I* think, and why do *I* hold my opinion?
- What are the key points the author makes or the main impression he creates?
- Do the points or impression seem convincing, given the information the author provides?
- Do the points or impression seem convincing, given my own knowledge about the subject?

To answer questions like these, active readers make sense of the text by inhabiting it in earnest, writing in the margins, underlining, adding checkmarks and asterisks. In short, active readers are engaged readers, raising significant questions and making significant connections between the text itself and the broader rhetorical situation.

Practical Reading Strategies

Reading actively and critically involves skills that people are not born with or casually develop. Often one person in particular (a teacher, a parent, a relative) took the time to teach a young reader these skills and then practiced with the reader until the skills became automatic. The following reading strategies form the basis for reading well—and they can be acquired, practiced, and perfected at any age.

Preview   Stop, look, and, yes, listen to a text before reading it in earnest. Like the baby in the picture, hold the reading close to you, taking in the title, the author, the headings, the introduction. Look to see what the text might be trying to tell you. Read aloud if you care to. Just as the baby might choose his favorite book by its familiar cover and pictures, you can use visuals to become familiar with a text as well. Locate the parts of the text the visuals relate to, and glance over the captions. Consider, too, when and where the piece first appeared. Readers—even baby readers— who have a good idea of where they're heading rarely get lost along the way.

✳ *Annotate*   Don't just listen to the text—talk back to it as well, just as the baby is doing. As you read, pose questions in the margins of the text, drawing arrows to connect supporting or opposing ideas. When the text pushes in a certain direction, push back, jotting down your questions, disagreements, and comments. If the text is online, most word-processing systems offer annotating capabilities that invite you to respond on the screen.

Summarize   Learn to perform one of the toughest but most rewarding reading tasks of all—summarizing the main points of what you read or see. Establish the author's purpose, audience, main point, and support. The better your reading skills, the better your summarizing skills. And vice versa.

✳ *Connect*   Most important is to connect with what you read—whether emotionally or intellectually. In other words, you have to find a relation-ship with the text (through some facet of your personality, interests, or life experience) in order to hear it—and then to talk back to it. You may find yourself connecting with the author, specifically with the ways he or she has kept your attention, taught, pleased, or moved you. Or you may connect immediately with a visual for reasons you'll want to analyze. If you find yourself disagreeing strongly with the text or being completely bored by it, think about what features or passages make you feel discon-nected to it.

✳ *Respond*   Respond to the text: talk back, write back. You might respond on the actual text itself, or you might record your responses elsewhere—in a journal or on a class listserv. Or you might get together with class-mates to talk about the reading, responding among yourselves. If the text is in a public, nonacademic setting like a newspaper or an online magazine or discussion forum, you might send a letter to the editor or post a comment.

Review   When you're finished reading, go back to the top, reconsidering the title, the author, the headings, the introduction and conclusion. By doing so, you'll recover a better sense of their importance to the full text. When you review a visual, you'll see how the parts work together to cre-ate an impact.

Here's an excerpt from *Where We Stand: Why Class Matters*, in which the writer bell hooks describes her memories of her childhood in Kentucky. If we apply the preceding reading strategies to this excerpt, the text might look something like this:

In the backyard vegetables grew. Scarecrows hung to chase away

Scarecrows, a field—this must have been a big backyard!

birds who could clear a field of every crop. My task was to learn

how to walk the rows without stepping on growing things. Life was

everywhere, under my feet and over my head. The lure of life was everywhere in everything. The first time I dug a fishing worm and

watched it move in my hand, feeling the sensual grittiness of min-
This image is so vivid that even someone who's never dug up a worm can identify with it.
gled dirt and wet, I knew that there is life below and above—always
This is the second sentence in a row she's said "life is everywhere"—let's move on!
life—and it lures and intoxicates. The chickens laying eggs were

such a mystery. We laughed at the way they sat. We laughed at the
Why not describe the chickens and their sounds?
sounds they made. And we relished being chosen to gather eggs.

One must have tender hands to hold eggs, tender words to soothe

chickens as they roost. *This repetition of "tender hands, tender words" gives a soothing sensation.*

Making Sense of Visuals

We are constantly surrounded by visual images, from the photographs and cartoons in the morning paper and the nightly reruns of situation comedies to magazine advertisements for khakis and sports shoes and Web pages for companies, organizations, and individuals. Whether these visuals narrate stories, describe a scene or person, compare and contrast two things, explain the steps in a process, define a concept, or argue a point, they use rhetorical methods just like those used in verbal texts. And as with spoken or written words, their overall success depends on how well they balance considerations of purpose, audience, and situation.

Because contemporary life has become increasingly a visual as well as a verbal one, *Making Sense* helps you develop the necessary skills for looking at—really seeing—and responding to visuals, for "reading" them actively and critically. At a time when the golden arches alone have helped sell billions of hamburgers; when Michael Jordan promotes sales of long-distance programs, men's underwear, and shoes of every kind; when photographs of abuse of prisoners can change the course of a war, it's time for all of us to develop our visual literacy. Therefore *Making Sense* uses visuals as "texts" for study and analysis, both as complements to written selections and as examples of various rhetorical methods in and of themselves. You'll find questions and writing assignments that ask you to consider how a particular visual works to fulfill its rhetorical goal. (You'll also learn how to use visuals to enhance your own verbal texts, as discussed on p. 27.) Just as you analyze the components of a verbal text, you'll analyze visual texts in terms of their rhetorical properties, asking questions like these:

- What is the overall purpose of the visual? How well does it achieve this purpose?

- Who is the intended audience? How does the visual appeal to this audience?
- Who or what company is the "author" of the visual? Is the author clearly identified?
- How is the visual arranged? What elements of it are emphasized—and de–emphasized? What is not shown? How effective is the arrangement?
- Which smaller or more subtle elements of the visual support or extend the overall purpose?
- Is the visual accompanied by verbal text? If so, what is said? What goes unsaid? How are the visual and the text related?

You bring to this course a good deal (years, in fact) of successful experience in making sense of visuals. Some of you may have even had a special course in visual literacy. Regardless of your background in this area, no matter how expert or amateur you think you may be, you can build on your experiences as you make sense of this textbook and this course, improving your visual literacy and rhetorical capacities along the way.

The Readings and Visuals in Making Sense

As I've said repeatedly, reading and writing are literacy skills that are impossible to separate; thus the verbal and visual selections in this text–book are so closely linked to the writing activities that it's hard to talk about one without the other. But I'll try.

The readings and visuals have been selected on the basis of their familiarity to you in some cases and their newness to you in others, but they have also been selected in terms of their rhetorical situation, including the author, subject, intended audience, purpose, and method of development. Every reading and visual is meant to provoke your interest, critical thinking, and response—in both speech and writing. In other words, none of these readings or visuals serves as *the* perfect model that you should admire and try to imitate; instead, all the readings and visuals promote work on your own thinking and writing as soon as possible. (I'll talk more about the individual and group writing activities in the following section.)

As you look through this book, you'll see the names of professional writers that you might already know: Malcolm X, Terry McMillan, Jerry Seinfeld, Amy Tan, Dr. Martin Luther King Jr., Dave Barry, and William Shakespeare, for example. You'll also find examples from professional and student writers that you don't yet know. Many of the essays and examples are taken from sources that are familiar to you (*Consumer Reports, Elle, Esquire,* the *New York Times, Latina, Rolling Stone, Seventeen, Sunset,* and *USA Today*), whereas other excerpts and examples come from the kinds of sources you'll continue to encounter in and after college (urban newspapers, novels, academic writing, autobiography, American ethnic literatures, creative nonfiction, Web–based journals, and so on). You'll also come across visuals, some that you've seen on billboards, in magazines and newspapers, on the World Wide Web, or in other textbooks, and others that are new to you. For instance, you'll see a daily newspaper's "Five–Day Weather Forecast" and charts that represents golfers' play histories. You'll also find online reader reviews of Stephen King's *On Writing* and news articles from online magazines.

Whether familiar or not, all the readings and visuals were selected especially for the ways they can help you develop your literacy skills as first–year college students and later as college graduates. Each chapter opens with a visual or a short reading that provides an immediate, familiar, nonacademic example of the rhetorical method of the chapter. Whether the chapter opens with an advertisement, a postcard, instructions, or a dictionary definition, it moves on to a full explanation of the rhetorical method at hand, including more verbal and visual examples. As you read the explanation, you are asked to reflect on your own literacy, to begin analyzing the method, and to try your own hand at using it. Following the introductory explanation are eight or nine (sometimes more) reading selections, including one focusing on a visual, one written by a college student, and sometimes one that is a poem or piece of fiction. These selections show the chapter's method (as well as other methods) at work in different ways, and each one is followed by questions and assignments that ask you to focus on particular aspects of the reading and apply what you've learned to essays of your own.

I'll show you how the readings work in *Making Sense* by using the following excerpt, which is followed by the same kinds of questions and writing assignments you'll find throughout this book:

I was eight years old. At that moment in my life, nothing was more important to me than baseball. My team was the New York Giants, and I followed the doings of these men in the black-and-orange caps with all the devotion of a true believer. Even now, remembering that team — which no longer exists — I can reel off the names of nearly every player on the roster. Alvin Dark, Whitey Lockman, Don Mueller, Johnny Antonelli, Monte Irvin, Hoyt Welhelm. But none was greater, none more perfect nor more deserving of worship than Willie Mays, the incandescent Say Hey kid.

That spring, I was taken to my first big-league game. Friends of my parents had box seats at the Polo Grounds, and one April night a group of us went to watch the Giants play the Milwaukee Braves. I don't know who won, I can't recall a single detail of the game, but I do remember that after the game was over my parents and their friends sat talking in their seats until all the other spectators had left. It got so late that we had to walk across the diamond and leave by the center-field exit, which was the only one still open. As it happened, that exit was right below the players' locker rooms.

Just as we approached the wall, I caught sight of Willie Mays. There was no question about who it was. It was Willie Mays, already out of uniform and standing there in his street clothes not ten feet away from me. I managed to keep my legs moving in his direction and then, mustering every ounce of my courage, I forced some words out of my mouth. "Mr. Mays," I said, "could I please have your autograph?"

He had to have been all of twenty-four years old, but I couldn't bring myself to pronounce his first name.

His response to my question was brusque but amicable. "Sure, kid, sure," he said. "You got a pencil?" He was so full of life, I remember, so full of youthful energy, that he kept bouncing up and down as he spoke.

I didn't have a pencil, so I asked my father if I could borrow his. He didn't have one, either. Nor did my mother. Nor, as it turned out, did any of the other grownups.

The great Willie Mays stood there watching in silence. When it became clear that no one in the group had anything to write with, he turned to me and shrugged. "Sorry, kid," he said. "Ain't got no pencil, can't give no autograph." And then he walked out of the ballpark into the night.

I didn't want to cry, but tears started falling down my cheeks, and there was nothing I could do to stop them. Even worse, I cried all the way home in the car. Yes, I was crushed with disappointment, but I was also revolted at myself for not being able to control those tears. I wasn't a baby. I was eight years old, and big kids weren't supposed to cry over things like that. Not only did I not have Willie Mays' autograph, I didn't have anything else, either. Life had put me to the test, and in all respects I had found myself wanting.

After that night, I started carrying a pencil with me wherever I went. It became a habit of mine never to leave the house without making sure I had a pencil in my pocket. It's not that I had any particular plans for that pencil, but I didn't want to be unprepared. I had been caught empty-handed once, and I wasn't about to let it happen again.

If nothing else, the years have taught me this: if there's a pencil in your pocket, there's a good chance that one day you'll feel tempted to start using it. As I like to tell my children, that's how I became a writer.

— PAUL AUSTER, "Why Write?"

Of course, becoming a writer is more complicated than just remembering to carry a pencil. Still, Auster's story is charming and effective. Now take a few minutes to do the following:

1. Underline one phrase, sentence, or passage in Auster's piece that seemed familiar to you. In the margin, jot down the main reason it is familiar.

2. Circle one phrase, sentence, or passage that feels "foreign" to you. In the margin, write out the reason why. You might not know who Willie Mays is; you might be bored by all sports; you might not be interested in

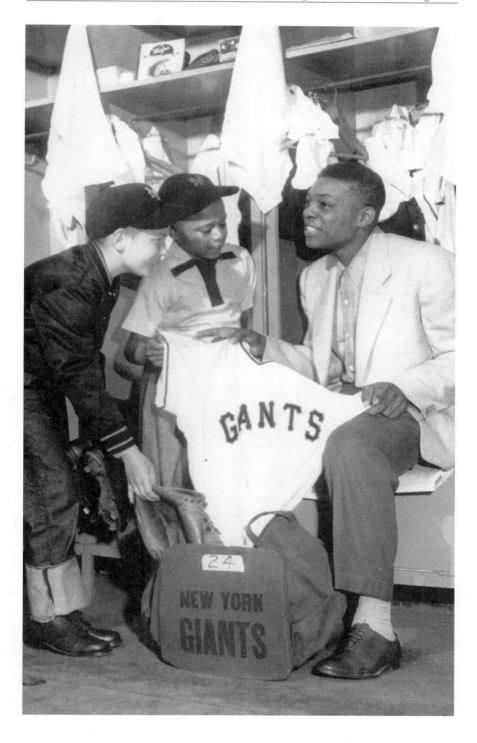

writing. Whatever you write, try to tell the truth about yourself and your reaction.

3. Compare the information provided by the visual and the text.

4. On a separate piece of paper, write for five minutes about a particular disappointment, challenge, or success you've had as a writer. Concentrate on one event, if you can, the way Auster does.

5. Share your writing with two or three classmates. Among your group, decide what your stories have in common and how they differ. Prepare a short report to share with the rest of the class.

6. Draft a two- to three–page essay based on the preceding in-class writing in which you connect a specific incident in your life with your development as a writer. Or, if you'd rather, draft a two- to three–page essay in which you connect your development as a reader with your development as a writer.

Writing Well

You've been writing since you were a small child. Maybe you and your parents *thought* it was scribbling or coloring, but all those scribbles were nothing more or less than writing. The urge to make one's mark is a

primitive urge, one that nearly every human being embraces early on. In fact, small children usually "write" before they read. Think back on all the "writing" you did as a child: in coloring books, on chalkboards and side-walks, on sides of buildings, on walls and windows. The baby in the photo on p. 14 cannot "write," but still he wants to get out his crayons and put his marks on a surface. These are his first steps toward develop-ing his writing life, the writing part of his literacy.

Now that you're in college, you'll be putting your mark on many paper surfaces — and electronic interfaces — as you continue to develop your college literacy. Essays, reports, bibliographies, exams, summaries, proposals, analyses, e-mail, abstracts, articles, memos, résumés, letters, questions, journals: these are just *some* of the things you'll have occasion to write in college (and, most likely, at work). *Making Sense* will help you learn some of the basic organizational patterns of thinking and writing that you'll need to use in producing them. The examples, explanations, reading and writing questions, and guidelines will help prepare you for a lifetime of writing well.

But instead of explaining how this textbook will promote your de-velopment as a writer, a topic I'll return to eventually, right now I'd like to ask you a few questions about that same subject: your writing and the way you do it. Take out a piece of paper, and write out short answers to the following questions:

1. How do you typically go about preparing for a writing assignment? De-scribe the steps you take, including rereading the assignment, asking questions about it, talking to instructors or friends, jotting down ideas, gathering information, and so on. How far in advance of the due date do you usually begin working on the assignment?

2. What would be your ideal place to write? Would it be solitary and silent, or would it provide background noise? Describe the place(s) you'll actu-ally be doing your writing for this course, and then discuss its suitability for you. Do you begin on paper or on the screen?

3. Describe your typical drafting or writing process. Do you finish a draft in one sitting, or do you need to take breaks? When you get stuck, what do you do to get moving again? Is your process efficient? Are there specific steps you could take to improve your efficiency?

4. What does revising mean to you? Do you ever revise, and if so, what specifically do you do when you revise (insert, delete, move around in-formation; check punctuation; proofread for typos and misspellings)? Why do you revise?

5. Finally, how do you respond to the evaluation of your writing? What do you read first — the grade itself or the teacher's comments? Do you want an explanation for your grade immediately, or do you understand how you earned that grade? Do you refer back to your teacher's comments on previous assignments as you work on your current assignment?

After you answer all these questions, you might want to draft a short essay (three to four pages) in which you describe yourself as a beginning college writer. You may discover details about your writing life that you have never been aware of before.

What's Rhetoric Got to Do with Writing?

As I said earlier in this chapter, rhetoric is purposeful language that leads to the creation of knowledge, and the most effective language is always appropriate language. In other words, it's always gauged according to the rhetorical situation (the audience, the purpose, the context for meaning). Your goal in this course is to learn how to compose written assignments that are purposeful, appropriate, and effective. The following rhetorical considerations will help develop successful writing strategies.

● Understanding the Writing Task

Start by making sense of your overall rhetorical situation. Are you putting together a job application? writing out directions to your home? reviewing a movie? asking for money? placing an order through a Web site? Have you been assigned to keep the minutes of a meeting? write up lab results? describe a painting? analyze an essay? We all face many daily writing tasks, some self-initiated, some assigned by others. Whichever it is, you have to figure out an effective way to handle the task.

Try Your Hand   In order to begin using *Making Sense* in the way it is intended, stop now and consider the answer you gave for question 1 (see p. 15). Break into groups of two or three, and discuss your original answers. What do you all do the same? How is each of you different in your preparation? What do your classmates do that you forgot to mention? How might you improve your preparations by learning from one of your classmates? Now revise your original response, adding to, deleting from, or rearranging the answer you wrote out. Try again: How *do* you typically prepare for a writing assignment? Break into groups of two or three, and compare your revised responses. Then prepare to share your group's responses with the rest of the class.

Now that you're actively thinking about your own process of writing and considering the strategies of your classmates, you'll have an easier time improving on the writing you do for college, no matter how strong the skills you bring to this course and this textbook. In fact, you're probably already self-conscious about your strengths as a writer.

Try Your Hand   Write for three or four minutes, responding to the following questions:

1. What part of your writing process are you most efficient and effective at?
2. What is the most enjoyable part of the process?
3. What is the least effective part of your writing process?
4. What is the least enjoyable part?

Break into groups of two or three, and compare your answers. What did you learn from one another about the similarities and differences of your writing processes? How can you individually benefit from this knowledge? Be prepared to share your group's responses with the rest of the class.

You may already know that when you are faced with a specific writing assignment, you'll need to read that assignment carefully and talk back to it before beginning to carry it out. But you might not realize that you'll want to watch for particular words of guidance, such as *inform, explain, describe, define, entertain, persuade, prove, compare,* or *argue.* These words signal what you should do and help you focus on your purpose; sometimes they even tell you which organizational method to follow.

More often, though, your writing assignments will provide you little — if any — specific purpose or direction. They may include only a subject and the vaguest of directions: "Write about your first week in college"; "Write a research paper focusing on the reasons diversity requirements are important — or inappropriate"; or "Describe the labor that your most recent job entailed." In these writing situations, you'll need to figure out a way to transform the assignment into one you can and want to write about: "What information about that job might interest my audience?" "Do I want to entertain the audience or just inform them?" "What organizational pattern might work best in describing the job?" "Is there a story I can tell to help explain it?" Once you figure out your angle, you'll feel as though it's your topic rather than one generated by your instructor.

Try Your Hand   In preparation for making sense of your college–level writing assignments, take a minute to write out what each of the following terms means to you:

inform	describe	entertain	analyze	define
persuade	prove	compare	argue	explore
convince	evaluate	propose	formulate	classify
observe	report	explain		

Working with one or two classmates, compare your answers. Discuss your group's response with the rest of the class. You may be surprised by the range of definitions you and your classmates give these important academic terms.

● Focusing on Your Purpose, Audience, and Subject

Why are you writing? Did you initiate this writing, or was it assigned by your instructor, your boss, or someone else? Are you writing to provide information about something for someone? to entertain someone? to urge someone to do something? And who is this "someone" you are writing for and this "something" you are writing about?

Knowing your purpose is important because if you have only a vague idea (or no idea) of what you want to accomplish, it's easy to achieve the wrong purpose—one you definitely didn't intend—or to leave your readers bored or confused. For example, if your economics professor asks you to analyze how the political systems of Mexico and the United States influence those countries' economies, you probably should not focus on trying to prove that the U.S. political system is better than that of Mexico, or vice versa. Your professor has asked you to explain something, not to make an argument, and may be annoyed if (without asking) you write with a different purpose. But even if the writing task is flexible enough to allow you to choose your own purpose or to combine different purposes, like the assignments about your first week in college or your most recent job, you need to think about purpose in order to guide your writing and avoid just stringing together random ideas about the subject. Once you have a good idea of your overall purpose, you can start thinking more specifically: Would a humorous or a serious approach be more likely to achieve your purpose of persuading your classmates that the student activity fee is unfair? Do you need just to give readers a general understanding of what your job involved, or is it important that you explain all the details?

If you're applying for a job, you have a pretty good idea who will read your application (your audience). If you're sending an e-mail or writing a letter to your mom and dad, you know, too. In the first situation, you're more than likely writing for a general audience of personnel directors, but in the second case, you're writing for a specific audience, people you know by name and face. Sometimes, though, when you're writing for an academic assignment, it's harder to decide who (besides your instructor) your audience really is. Should you write directly to your instructor, who may know more about the subject than you do? Should you address your classmates, who may be working with the same materials? Or should you assume a more general audience of readers who may be interested in your topic but have little expertise in it? If you're writing for a class, ask your instructor what audience you need to assume and address.

When you have a sense of who your readers are, then think about what they are like. How old, what sex, how educated are they? What are their values and beliefs? What do they already know about your topic? What do they want to know more about? What is their attitude toward the topic? toward you as a writer? Do they know anything about you? Do they have expectations about you or the topic that you need to fulfill?

Answering these questions will help you decide which tone to take, information to include, terms to use, and points to make. The audience is a crucial element of the rhetorical situation—and connecting with it is crucial to all successful writing.

Try Your Hand   Working with a classmate, discuss the role that audience has played in your writing.
1. What specific audience have school assignments asked you to address? the instructor? classmates? others?
2. How much thought do you give to the audience as you write? Can either of you remember an experience of writing with particular attention to a specific audience?
3. Does your audience affect your choice of writing by hand or using a computer?
4. Prepare a joint report for the rest of the class.

When your instructor offers you a writing topic as broad as a temporary job, the first week of school, or the sociology of the family, your job is to narrow down the subject to one that interests you (at the same time that you're considering a purpose for your writing and imagining a specific audience). You might start this subject-focusing process by asking a series of questions:

What is it?
What caused it?
What are its consequences?
What is it like?
What is it a part of?
What are its parts?
Who is involved in it?

Looking at a topic or piece of writing from a variety of perspectives.

Questions like these help you think about your subject in a variety of ways. Your answers will bring to the fore various features of the larger subject that you might want to concentrate on. (Your answers might also help you get a foothold on a purpose and an imagined audience.) Imagine that Paul

Auster (p. 11) took the general subject of "sports" before narrowing it down to "professional baseball." From there, he might have moved on to "my first major–league game," before finally focusing on Willie Mays and then a lowly pencil. At last, Auster had a topic he wanted to work with.

You might also decide to freewrite on one of those smaller subjects (see p. 23 for an explanation of freewriting) or talk with one of your classmates about it — just to see what comes forth. But focusing on your subject cannot be separated from focusing on your purpose, which means that you may have to work simultaneously to tweak the assignment, narrowing or stretching it to suit your interest, experience, and knowledge. Auster focused his subject down to the much–needed pencil. And he decided that his purpose would be to explain how he became a writer. So, don't be afraid to ask your instructor if you may customize your assignment to fit your own situation or preferences; after all, one size does *not* fit all. Besides, you're going to be writing for the rest of your life, so you might as well learn now how to imagine the kind of writing you *want* to do.

If you have been assigned to write about your first week at college, for example, you might decide to give advice (a specific purpose) to seniors in high school (a specific audience) on how best to prepare for — or to survive — the first week (a specific subject). If the assignment is about your job experience, you might choose to describe your nannying position briefly but focus most of your rhetorical energy on the consequences of holding that job: you now realize rich families are not necessarily happy families; you want to move rapidly into a "real" career; you are more grateful than ever for the way your own parents raised you.

Try Your Hand   Now that we're discussing your individual interests and life as a writer, take a minute or two to consider the following questions:
1. What have you been taught about writing, either directly or indirectly, that has helped or hindered your development as a writer?
2. How has your writing improved over the years? Why has it improved?
3. What kinds of writing do you expect to do in the future?
4. What kinds of writing do you hope to do? do you want to learn how to do?
5. What kinds of writing do you hope to avoid?

Prepare to share your responses with the rest of the class.

Practical Writing Strategies

Once you have an overview of your rhetorical situation, you can move on to practical strategies for accomplishing each of the steps to successful writing.

● Generating Ideas

Where do ideas come from? Some of your best ideas will come from your own experience and observation; others will come from conversation with others or from your reading and research. To tap those sources, you might want to try some of the following activities.

Journal writing may be the most familiar of all the invention activities. Many instuctors ask students to record their ideas, thoughts, and feelings about their composition class or about topics they might want to write on. Other instructors ask you to keep a reading journal, a response to your class assignments. But besides offering up subjects and purposes for writing and responses to other people's writing, journal writing has another significance: keeping a journal can change your feelings about writing, forever, for the better! Because a journal is a record of your *reac-tions*, not your actions, you can let your thoughts flow. If you allow yourself to record your thoughts, rather than your body and its movements, if you read some excerpts of good journals kept by writers like Francisco Urondo, Rita Valdivia, Virginia Woolf, or Anne Frank, you'll soon see that a journal can be every bit as interesting and thought-provoking as good fiction. For example, in preparation for writing an essay about a job, Jennifer Favorite, one of my students at Penn State, wrote the following journal entry:

> My time in Connecticut as a nanny for a wealthy family was like nothing else I'd ever experienced, yet it fit all the stereotypical descriptions of nannying. I learned so much about the damage that wealth can do to people and their families. The experience forced me to reexamine how much I valued my upbringing just as much as I cultivated my desire to dissect the people I lived with for a year. The children I worked with had lots of qualities that shocked me at first: they were disrespectful, rude, ill mannered, and highly competitive, especially with each other. Their parents bought them almost anything they wanted and were incredibly lazy when it came to discipline. It was as if the parents wanted children, but only for bragging rights. They seemed to want nothing to do with the ins and outs of actually teaching children to be good people. Even so, the children were not necessarily complete monsters. They are all incredibly bright and talented, especially in sports. But it was what they *lacked* that made them so difficult to manage.

Some instructors ask students to keep a double-entry notebook, writing down notes of fact on one side of the page and personal responses on the other side. Favorite's journal writing could easily be organized that way, because she so clearly thinks that the parents themselves are responsible for "difficult" children.

Brainstorming requires only that you jot down all the ideas that come to mind, as they come. As Favorite worked to get a foothold on how she might write about her nannying job, she brainstormed and came up with the following ideas:

family dynamics	spoiled children	Connecticut
parental discipline	socialization	child care
middle class	upper class	societal expectations
parental neglect	emotional development	overachieving
overscheduled	pretension	executive lifestyle
idea of the elite	overspending	maintaining a façade
mother-daughter rivalry	father-son rivalry	sense of entitlement
class nights	parental expectations	child stress
exclusivity	sibling rivalry	

Sometimes just doing as Favorite has done, putting random thoughts on paper (or on a screen), can get you started on the assignment by provid–ing details you can develop.

Clustering is a way to map out your ideas visually. Write your subject or a phrase about it in the center of a piece of paper and circle it, the way Favorite has done here with the word *nannying*. Then think of other ideas related to the central idea, write them around it, circle them, and draw lines to show the connections, as Favorite has done with *kids*, *child care*, and *parents*. Then think of ideas related to these ideas and repeat the process. As one idea leads to another, as various ideas radiate outward from the nucleus idea and its associations, you'll see patterns and details emerging that can provide you with a structure and support for your

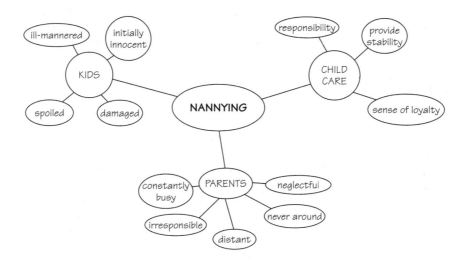

writing task. Or you may discover that you want to focus on just one part of the cluster that is especially interesting or important.

Freewriting is the easiest exercise of all, because all you do is write — without stopping — on whatever comes to your mind. You'll want to start out by writing down the topic you're considering — but then let your mind and hand go, writing for five minutes or so nonstop. NONSTOP — that's the key. (And nonstop means that you might get off the subject.) You'll be surprised at how many ideas pop into your mind within those five minutes. And when you reread what you've written, you may discover insights into your subject that you never expected.

Here's what Favorite freewrote about her nannying job:

> Sometimes I hated the kids I worked with in Connecticut, but most of the time I felt sorry for them. Their parents were never around, their mother has some kind of self-image disorder, their father is distant and overbearing at the same time, and the only real connection they have to some sort of real-world thinking is me — their nanny, who can barely stand the thought of sticking out the one year she's signed up for. I wonder if these kids have a hard time attaching to a yearly nanny and then detaching. It seems as though the process has left them armored, less reachable as human beings. The youngest son didn't even say goodbye to me when I left. He told me he was glad I was leaving because now he wouldn't be grounded from the computer anymore. He's going to be the most screwed up of the three children, I feel sure. And it's very sad. But after a year of nannying these kids, I'm pretty sure that the damage has already been done and is cemented in their psychological makeup. Sad but true. What's saddest of all, though, is that the parents don't even think of spending time with their kids to try to undo some of the damage or to change their behavior. As soon as school gets out in the summer, the children are off to camp for eight weeks straight. And as soon as camp is over, school starts again within a week or two. I asked the little girl if she'd rather go to camp or spend the time with her parents, and she said camp was more fun. I'm not sure these kids even realize that their parents are neglectful. I think they will, though, someday, when they're older. And that knowledge might be the most damaging thing of all.

In freewriting, Favorite discovered her sympathy for the children as well as her ability to identify the reasons for their unpleasant behavior.

Looping combines freewriting and clustering. First freewrite for five minutes on a subject. As you read over what you've written, circle the dominant idea or the best idea, the one you want to develop. Then loop back, freewriting for five minutes on that idea only and then again circling an idea you want to pursue further. Keep going with this exercise, maybe even giving yourself a break of an hour or so, until you land on an idea that might serve as the purpose and subject of your essay.

Here's how Favorite used looping to think and write about her job as a nanny:

> I see the children as damaged goods. That's what they are. Every child is essentially a blank slate, and it's up to the parents to fill the slate with good ideas. But since these parents are too lazy to segregate the good from the bad, these children have absorbed more of the latter than the former. They've adopted the bad language they hear in R-rated movies; they act toward one another with spite and hatred, just as they've seen adults act on television; they are completely ignorant of proper table manners in general since their parents never reinforced these ideas. They are damaged in an almost tragic way because they have had so little to do with their own damage. And since they live such a privileged lifestyle, the damage seems to be magnified because they don't have any excuses, like no money, no social life, no education, no opportunity. These kids have everything — everything material, that is. They do not know the meaning of saving for an item; instant gratification is all they know. They feel entitled to all they desire, be it an ice cream cone or a new computer or a sleepover with friends. They are damaged in that they do not know how to process negative responses from others. It is a foreign concept to them and instead of reacting logically, they react in a primitive way through screaming and anger. Their development as emotionally maturing human beings is stunted.

After writing this paragraph, Favorite looked over it and realized that her dominant idea was "damage." Later she returned to freewriting, starting with this dominant idea and expanding on it.

Questioning is another useful exercise for getting started. You may have heard of the classic questions a news story should answer: "Who?" "What?" "When?" "Where?" "Why?" and "How?" Those are still good places to start. You can think about your subject and ask questions such as "What happened/is happening/will happen?" "Who or what did/does/will do it?" "Where and when did/does/will it happen?" "How and why did/does/will it happen?" The following questions and answers are Favorite's:

Who? Rich people who have children they're too busy (or rich) to bother with.

What? The result is bratty children and a hired child–wrangler.

When? One year, when I was 22 and the kids were 9, 10, and 11.

Where? and **Why?** I wanted to live in the East, with rich people who traveled and did interesting things. These rich people needed someone they could pay to spend time with their wild children.

How? I applied to a nanny agency where the children's mother worked.

Coming up with ideas about your subject can be easy if you try one or more of the preceding activities. In fact, taking the time to do so will help you move from a general subject to a specific topic and a purpose for writing.

● **Deciding on a Tentative Thesis**

Spending time on generating ideas can also help you formulate a tentative **thesis,** the main idea you will develop in your writing. Usually your final thesis will appear in your introduction as a **thesis state-ment;** but even if the tentative thesis ends up changing drastically or the final thesis ends up being implied rather than stated directly, you need to formulate a thesis for yourself at an early stage to serve as a guide in or-ganizing and drafting. As you move through several invention exercises, you might find yourself returning to one idea that seems to control your writing and thinking—that's probably the basis for your thesis. In addi-tion, these activities may help you determine which thesis you can most easily support with the details that you've come up with while you're generating material about your subject.

Looking over the ideas she had generated, Jennifer Favorite decided on the tentative thesis "My year as a nanny for an extremely wealthy, ex-tremely dysfunctional family showed me that the ways parents act—or fail to act—toward their children can make them very damaging models for the children's development." If you look at her final draft on p. 36, you can see that she has essentially stayed with this thesis in her intro-ductory paragraph, moving the information in the first part of the thesis into different sentences and ending up with the thesis statement in the last sentence: "And the moral you take away will be that children learn from their parents, especially those lessons that cause lifelong damage."

● **Organizing Your Ideas**

Some 2,000 years ago, Aristotle announced that every argument must include a beginning, a middle, and an end—advice that still holds true for all writing. *Making Sense* provides models of many good ways to organize an essay, from chronological and emphatic (p. 59) to inductive and deductive (see Chapter 10), depending on the overall purpose for your writing. Just as reading and writing go together, purpose and organization do, too.

One of the most common ways to organize information involves the outline. *Scratch outlining* offers you a quick way to begin organizing your in-formation (and it simultaneously supports the generation of more mate-rial). Favorite scratched out the following outline as she was experimenting with ways she might divide up and approach the subject of nannying:

Nannying

I. Parents
  —Responsibilities
      socialization
      nurturing
      providing good examples
      commitment to good development

    — Failures
        reliance on others to socialize, nurture, all of the above
        seldom around the children
        force children into too many activities
        unwilling to change children's behavior
  II. Children
    — Strengths
        intelligent
        well provided for
        talented
        athletic
    — Weaknesses
        stubborn
        lack strong emotional health
        lack of manners
        unaware of how to respond properly to a challenge

Favorite's scratch outline helped her narrow and begin to organize her topic. She found that by analyzing the responsibilities and failures of the parents and the strengths and weaknesses of the children, she could better understand and explain the nature and outcome of their family dynamics. When you read Favorite's first and final drafts (see pp. 30 and 36), though, you'll see that she eventually decided to organize the body of her essay largely by describing each of the family members in terms of his or her individual strengths and (mostly) weaknesses.

Generally speaking, you need to familiarize yourself with four patterns of organization, any of which can be used as the organizing principle of an outline: (1) chronological, in order of time; (2) spatial, in order of location; (3) emphatic, in order of importance or interest; and (4) level of detail, from general to specific. Some organizational patterns naturally unfold from the rhetorical method you're using, and you'll see just how such connections play out when you read the following chapters. For instance, when you're writing *descriptions*, you'll probably use spatial organization most often. Most *narratives* or stories are arranged chronologically, but you might find yourself using flashbacks to events that took place before the time of the narrative and flashforwards to later events as well. Writing that uses *exemplification* usually moves from general assertion to specific example(s), and sometimes vice versa; and you'll often want to arrange the examples themselves in chronological, emphatic, or some other kind of purposeful order. You'll also organize a *classification and division* according to a general principle before classifying your information into specific categories or breaking it down into specific parts; similarly, a *comparison and contrast* will establish a general basis for comparing two or more subjects and then present specific points of comparison between them, either whole-by-whole or part-by-part. A *process analysis* will use a strict chronological organization, whereas in an *analysis of causes and*

consequences you'll choose between presenting the causes or the consequences of the event in chronological or emphatic order. Whenever you
write a *definition*, though, you'll link your organizational pattern to your
purpose, following any one of the preceding patterns for a description,
process, comparison, exemplification, or definition. Finally, *argument* requires you to pay careful attention to the ordering of material. You might
call on all the general organizational patterns as you introduce your argument, refute opposing arguments, and draw your conclusion.

Because most of the rhetorical methods offer options rather than
strict requirements for organization, and because almost any essay uses
more than one method, only you can decide if your entire essay or just a
certain section of it would benefit from any one organizational pattern in
particular. No matter which overall pattern you choose, you'll want to be
sure that you include an introduction that engages your readers' interest,
a clear and purposeful thesis (usually in the form of an explicit statement), plenty of supporting or illustrative details, and a conclusion that
extends your thesis by answering the question "So what?" *Making Sense*
will give you lots of practice in fulfilling all these features of a successful
piece of writing.

● Drafting

When you've organized your ideas in the way that seems best, you're
ready to begin drafting. Often you'll be able to lift passages directly from
your freewriting or journal entries; at other times you'll find yourself inspired by what you've written while generating ideas and will easily be
able to translate it into essay-quality material. In the first draft of
Favorite's essay, which appears on p. 30, you can see how she drew from
her generating exercises and then moved ahead with her draft.

● Using Visuals

With technology making it easy to download images from the Web
and scan them into word-processing programs (and with college writing
increasingly being submitted online instead of on paper), more and more
students are including visuals in their essays. Each chapter of *Making
Sense* offers guidelines for choosing visuals for writing that follow the
chapter's rhetorical method. In general, if you are considering using visuals, think about the following questions as you do so:

1. Will your instructor object to visuals? Some may prefer that you make
   your points with words alone.
2. What kind of visuals would most enhance your essay? photographs? cartoons? bar or line graphs? pie charts? diagrams or other drawings?
   screen shots?

3. What purpose do you want the visuals to serve? Do you want them to strengthen your argument? help explain a complex process? set a mood?

4. Can the visuals stand on their own, or do you need to include labels, captions, or references to the visuals within the text?

Often a visual can help you focus your subject or your purpose. As you can see on p. 30, in her first draft Jennifer Favorite used a scanned photograph from a magazine to set up an implicit contrast between her own unpleasant experience as a nanny and the world of the television show *The Nanny*, in which the nanny becomes the beloved center of a motherless family. For Favorite, the popular TV show represented exactly what her life as a nanny was not. As she wrote, she was continually influenced by that particular visual. With her final draft (p. 36), Favorite used two visuals: the photograph and a cartoon, downloaded from the Web, that suggested an experience more like her own.

If you know that you want to include visuals, you may find that it's more efficient to locate several possibilities as you draft and revise so that when you're finished you can choose among them. If you put off looking for the visuals until the very end, you may not find any that really fit what you've written. It's better to let the visuals and the writing work together from an early stage.

If you want to use visuals that you did not create yourself and your essay is going to be posted or distributed on the Internet, you should request permission from the creator or owner to use them, because visuals are often protected by copyright laws. You don't need to request permission if your essay will be submitted only to your instructor and classmates and only in print form. In either case, though, you should mention the sources of the visuals in the main text, in a caption or label, or perhaps (if the visuals are just intended to set a mood) in a note at the beginning or end of the essay. If you look at Jennifer Favorite's final draft, you can see that she identified the source of the photograph in a caption and the source of the cartoon in the text. Your instructor may also want you to include the sources in a Works Cited list at the end of your essay (see the Appendix). Favorite's instructor didn't require such a list because her essay didn't include any outside sources other than visuals. In *Making Sense* you will see that many of the visuals include captions or labels, others are referred to in the text, and still others stand on their own, but the sources of those that were not created by the author or the publisher are credited starting on p. 790.

● Collaborating

Many of the things you read on a daily basis are the direct result of collaborations — between writers, between writers and editors, among writers and editors and publishers, among writers and their coworkers, among writers and their family members and friends. Every newspaper, textbook, novel, cookbook, guidebook, Web site, scientific proposal, and MasterCard or Visa statement is a collaboration of some sort. When you're writing, you will want to take advantage of the same opportunities that professional writers regularly use to talk with other people about their writing and work with others to strengthen it, asking and answering questions that will lead to your best work. *Making Sense* offers you many opportunities to learn how to collaborate on projects where you are individually responsible for producing a final draft and those where a group creates it. It offers you daily opportunities to talk with the people in your class, to meet in pairs or small groups to compare your responses to the reading selections, to help one another with your reading and writing tasks. Step–by–step, then, you'll work together to read and respond to essays, generate ideas, evaluate rough drafts, and polish up almost–final drafts. Every chapter includes guided activities for reading, writing, and revising that help make peer evaluations successful and rewarding, and you'll soon see how much better you read and write when you have a group of friends to help you.

Guidelines for Group Work. Successful collaboration is not hard to achieve; the general guidelines are as follows:

1. Whether your instructor assigns you to a group or you form your own, try to keep it small, for the sake of convenience.
2. Arrange for regular places and times to meet, whether online or in a coffee shop. Attend all the meetings — your group needs you.
3. Set specific tasks for each meeting, and review them at the end of the meeting to make sure you haven't forgotten anything.
4. When you meet, stay on task, no matter how tempting it is to talk about the latest football game or sorority party. When you know you'll accomplish your goals, you'll look forward to your group meetings.
5. Divide up duties in order to make your meetings efficient as well as effective. Let one group member keep the time schedule, the amount of time you spend on each person's essay. Assign another member to keep everyone on task, whether you're focusing on organizing, support, or final editing.
6. Take time to evaluate group dynamics, concentrating on what *you* can do to improve the collaboration.

A Response to a Draft. After Jennifer Favorite drafted her essay, she asked one of her classmates, Rey Saavedra, to respond to her draft. As you can see, he annotated the text to highlight what he saw as its strong points as well as places where she needed to revise or add or delete material. He also summarized his reaction to the draft in a few paragraphs on p. 34.

I Played the Nanny

*Great opening; right away you're inviting
readers to identify with you.*

Walk a while in my shoes: you've just finished a year–long job as a nanny for three children aged 9, 10, and 11. You cannot believe the things you experienced and saw; in fact, you like to refer to your time in this extremely wealthy, extremely dysfunctional family as a

*What sorts of things? You might mention some of the
worst of them right now, in order to hook your reader.*

sociological experiment of sorts. You also acknowledge it was

This sounds awkward.

as if being an observer and ancillary member of a living theater, a

*I'm getting confused by all the comparisons to experiments,
acting, being a spectator — maybe settle on just one?*

human spectacle that is fit to be explored.

Any character study of the household dynamic in this spectacle would be best begun by examining the patriarch of the family. Father is a high–ranking executive for a major television network who is home two to three days per week, on average. This character is the

What's a rogue horse, and what does it have to do with a theater?

rogue horse of this living theater. He frequently enters chomping

This is quite a vivid image — very effective!

on a gigantic cigar and bellowing for his childrens' affections.

Brash, pompous and rude are his most redeeming qualities. He

claims to love his children, but will describe his daughter to you as

"a little bitch." Father frequently professes undying adoration for his

wife, loudly, in front of you, yet careful observation and pricked–up

ears will tell you he's most certainly carrying on with his ex–wife.

The role of Mother is played by a polite yet vacant woman who

exhibits momentary displays of caring but seems always to be

This opening topic sentence seems stronger and more
focused than the one in the previous paragraph.   complications — or contradictions?
focused on other tasks.ˆShe is her own little gem of complications.ˆ

Fifteen years younger than Father, Mother lives on a steady diet of

Does the age difference make a big difference? (By the way, how old
is the ex-wife?) What point do you want to make about her diet?
popcorn, yogurt, and vanilla ice cream.ˆYou are frequently woken

around six in the morning to the sound of the Stairmaster motor

churning below you, alerting you to Mother's first round of exercise

This essay has great sound effects!
for the day.ˆRounds two and three will be completed while Mother

is at work for her nanny agency (yes, the very same one that

What connections do you want to make between her diet and her
exercise schedule? And her age? I'm unclear about her role at the nanny agency. Is she
an executive there? Your sentence sounds
almost like Mother works as a nanny, and I know you don't mean that.
employs you).ˆMother has also dabbled in chewing tobacco at one

time, most certainly for the purpose of helping her to purge her

Mother was bulimic? How do you know? Did she tell you, as though you weren't even im-
portant enough to be private in front of? Or were you supposed to be her nanny as well?
Her confidante? "Vittles" sounds too informal, as if you're trying for humor — it doesn't
seem to fit in with your overall tone of disgust and amazement.
vittles.ˆ

The three child members of this troupe can be grouped into

in?
Sons and Daughter. Elder Son and Younger Son are atˆconstant

battle. Their years competing in myriads sports have cultivated

their battle skills to the point where Younger Son's coaches plead

with Mother and Father to curb his ruthlessly competitive

Why do you think the Sons become more competitive instead of bored or exhausted? Do
they earn extra points with their parents by being competitive on the sports field and
with each other? Also, you need an example or two of the Younger's "ruthlessly competi-
tive nature."

nature.ˬThe Sons share an unhealthy obsession with online in-

stant messaging, exploding with beast–like behavior when asked

to leave the computer to complete homework or eat a meal. Each

Son tells you on numerous occasions to "shut up," and neither

avoid?

Son takes seriously any warning to <u>arrest the use</u>ˬof offensive

Do you want to connect this verbal behavior with the competition
idea? Or is there an idea that arches over both of them?

language in your presence.ˬYounger Son is positively brilliant, yet

These kids sound simply repulsive. Is there any way you could shape your
paragraph in terms of all of their material and intellectual advantages ver-
sus their emotional disadvantages? I think the "bleak future" idea is an im-
portant point. In fact, these kids have a pretty bleak present, if you ask me.

his lack of decorum and emotional depth betray a bleak future.ˬ

Both Sons take glee in torturing Daughter, who is the middle

Would this sentence sound better at the beginning of the
next paragraph? Here it just seems to trail off at the end.

child in this cast of characters.ˬ

   Daughter is pleasant and darling to look at, but can exhibit the

What makes her darling?

cunning and insincerity of a well–seasoned politician.ˬShe has been

hardened by years of pummeling by the Sons and will assert herself

brothers? parents? nanny?

forcefully in any argument against any opponent.ˬThe other side of

Daughter's personality sees herself adopting you as her newest con–

fidante and permanent playmate as soon as you come on stage in

So like Mother, Daughter is a bundle of contradictions?

The Sons sound like their sneaky, aggressive Father.

this family drama.ˬLike the Sons, Daughter is overbooked with

sports and other activities, and struggles to live the life of a normal

What would that normal life be like? How do bright
and personable equate with dramatic? What do you
want the topic sentence of this paragraph to be?   *best actor?*

ˬten–year old. She is bright and personable, the trueˬ<u>dramatic</u> of the

family. However, it troubles you to know that Daughter refuses to

sleep in her own bed at night, preferring instead to occupy the floor

Why does it trouble you? Why does she claim to want to sleep there?
Why do the parents let her? What do the brothers do about this?
next to the marital bed in the master bedroom. ‸
I love the idea of the nanny as wrangler. That might be another option for your opening.
  Your role in this living theater will be to act as a sort of wrangler. ‸

Part referee, part instructor, part exorcist to the demons ~~living~~ inside

each child, you must be as athletic as the children themselves,
What do you mean by this phrase?
constantly juggling activities, <u>playing both defensive and ‸offensive</u>

<u>positions</u>. The stresses are considerable, and the victories are hard–

won. You have an occasional moment of camaraderie with the

Children, be it watching them thrill with delight at a cartoon

beheading or gingerly answering Elder Son's wild inquiries into the

nature of sex. You must also play the part of chef extraordinaire,
They're not "tots," they're closer to teenagers. Also, this sentence seems out of place
here unless you mean your performance in the chef role was one of your victories.
catering to the divergent palates of each temperamental tot. ‸Overall,

this role is one of many highs and lows, and you are careful to assert

yourself and to keep your equanimity. You are determined to fulfill
There seem to be lots of things left unsaid in this paragraph.
But your perseverance comes across very clearly.
your contract with this theater to its completion. ‸

   Near the end of your run in the living theater of this family, you
You need to explain this "existential" idea
has been?   more if you're going to introduce it here.
realize the entire experience <u>to ‸be</u> an existential ‸one: what are the
put up?
effects of the actions you took, of the defenses you <u>played</u>; ‸ did you
Is this the right word?
in fact <u>affect</u> ‸any lasting change in the lives of these children? It is

nearly impossible to tell, although the family's reactions to you near

the end leave you feeling vindicated. Father has acknowledged your

talents, Mother has thanked you for your resolve, Elder Son has
Are the commas OK in this sentence? (I always have trouble remembering the rules.)
turned to you for life advice, ‸Daughter has admitted her fondness

for you, Younger Son has laughed at your attempts at humor. The show has not ended badly, but the family characters will remain

This sentence seems too upbeat, given the "bleak" picture you've painted.

steadfast in their roles. ˄As the outsider, you take your final bow. You

are finished now. You close the curtain on this play and raise the

curtain to another, a play far removed from the world of a nanny, a

It isn't an actor who closes and raises the curtain, is it? Maybe try a different theater idea — but the end of the sentence is great!

play with you perhaps in the starring role. ˄

Here are Rey Saavedra's comments:

Jen,

First of all, I think you've got lots of good information to work with already, especially statements that just need to be developed in more detail. I've marked the places that I think need more explanation. Second, I'd be careful with the theater metaphor. I'd keep it — that's for sure. I'd just be careful that I was using all the comparisons correctly and being consistent. (I think Maria is a theater major; she'd probably be able to help you.) If you keep the theater metaphor, try to connect it more clearly with an overall purpose and thesis — at the end of the introduction it's not very clear where you're going.

Third, I think you need to strengthen your opening. As I read over your title and looked at the picture (it's the cast from *The Nanny*, right?), I couldn't help thinking about the TV show and how different your experience was from Fran Drescher's. Her nanny character moves in with a dysfunctional rich family and soon becomes the moral center of it. The children adore her; the butler criticizes her but has a soft spot for her; and she ends up running the entire family operation. I wonder if you might compare your experience with the show, which idealizes what a nanny can do. Doing that might hook your readers. And if you did that, you might have better luck introducing the characters in the way you've set up your essay. Or if you didn't want to do anything like that, you might give some statistics on the number of nannies that are advertised for yearly in the U.S. I also found myself wondering what kind of families hire nannies. In other words, how different was your experience from the typical experience?

Last, I want to tell you that the second-person approach you used is terrific. I was really impressed how easily you used "you." I haven't read very many essays that do that — it's unusual.

If you'd like, I'll read your revision,

Rey

● Revising, Editing, and Proofreading

Getting responses to your draft, as important as they are, is only part of the work you need to do for the last steps in getting your essay into its final, polished form: revising, editing, and proofreading. All three of these steps involve making changes in your draft, and they usually over-lap to a considerable extent. But it's still useful to think about them sepa-rately as three different ways in which you need to read your own draft actively and critically, asking the same kinds of questions that others re-sponding to it did, or that you would in reading something written by someone else. If you deliberately try to focus on each step at some point, it will help keep your attention from straying into other areas and pre-vent you from forgetting some things you need to do.

Essentially, these three steps just involve focusing on three different levels of your rhetorical task. **Revising,** which literally means "seeing again," deals with the broadest issues: how well your draft achieves your purpose; how successfully you've addressed your specific audience; how clear your thesis is; whether you've met the requirements of the overall rhetorical method you're using; how effective your organization, introduc-tion, and conclusion are; whether you've included too little or too much detail. *Making Sense* can give you a lot of help with this part of the writing process, because each chapter includes a checklist that summa-rizes the kinds of things you need to pay attention to in writing using that chapter's rhetorical method. (For example, look at the one on "Checking Over Descriptive Writing" on p. 61.) You can use these questions not only in revising your own draft but also in reviewing a classmate's.

In **editing,** you focus on issues that are smaller in scale but equally important (some of which are also covered in the chapter checklists): the length, structure, and variety of your paragraphs and sentences; your choice of words; the transitions between your ideas; the effectiveness and accuracy of your punctuation. Finally, **proofreading** focuses on the kinds of surface-level problems that are so important to the first visual impression your writing makes on readers: typos, misspellings, word spacing. The spell checkers in most word-processing programs can help with proofreading, although they don't catch everything; you'll still need to go through what you hope will be your final draft to check for these kinds of problems. (For editing, on the other hand, grammar checkers are themselves more often wrong than right in identifying "errors.")

To see what Jennifer Favorite did in these steps, compare her first draft with the final draft on p. 36. She followed through on several sug-gestions Rey Saavedra had provided her for large-scale revisions, the most important being improvement of her use of the theater metaphor and strengthening of her introduction. She also changed a number of individual words and phrases he had questioned and re-sponded to his questions about commas and the visual by changing the commas to semicolons and adding a caption. Favorite herself realized that she needed to add more details about the family members and to include a new, stronger thesis statement that was more like her original tentative thesis and more clearly achieved her purpose of conveying the sadness of the situation she had been a part of.

Saavedra's remark about one of her topic sentences led her to look at all of them more closely and edit them to tie them into the thesis. And her spell checker corrected *childrens'* to *children's* in the second paragraph. As I mentioned earlier, she also decided to add a second visual, a cartoon.

Although this book shows only Favorite's first draft and her final essay, you'll often need to work through multiple drafts before you achieve something that makes perfect sense to you, your instructor, your classmates, and whoever else will be reading your writing. (For example, this book went through four or five drafts on its way to publication.) The good news is that computers have made revising, editing, and proof-reading physically faster and easier than ever before. In fact, it's often impossible to tell when one "draft" ends and another begins—you can keep cutting and pasting, tinkering with words and sentences, asking classmates for a response until you're ready to submit the essay, without ever stopping to create and re-create a "hard copy."

I Played the Nanny

The Nanny, Mary Poppins, The Sound of Music—all productions with nannies in starring roles. If you are like I was a year ago, when I applied for a position as a nanny, this is the kind of role that you imagine for yourself. You imagine the supporting cast as well: one or two loving (if distant) parents and several good-hearted (if mischievous) children. But life doesn't resemble show business, you soon discover—or rather, in this case it looks and feels less like a situation comedy than a Shakespearean tragedy (without the physical fatalities). In your year caring for three children aged 9, 10, and 11, you find that the plot and characters in this real-life production are nothing like you expected. You are, for the most part, sharing the set with cold and inaccessible parents and with ill-mannered and permanently defiant children. Although such a situation is not what the nanny agency had described throughout the application and interview process, it does turn out to be the sad norm among all the other nannies you met. You were all assured that you'd be part of a family, but you come to realize that families can be dysfunctional in ways you'd never dreamed of. You end up feeling less like Julie

In this publicity photograph from the television show *The Nanny,* Fran Drescher's smile reveals that the title character will overcome initial suspicions to win the loyalty and love of a motherless family. From what I've experienced and heard about, happy endings like these are rare in families that hire nannies.

Andrews than like Juliet's nurse. Cast in what you hoped would be a major role, you turn out with a part that's even more demanding than you'd bargained for—but much less rewarding. At the same time, since you've joined a show already long in its run, you also watch the plot unfold from the perspective of the audience, becoming an appalled onlooker at a human spectacle. And the moral you take away will be that children learn from their parents, especially those lessons that cause lifelong damage.

Perhaps the most damaging lessons are those taught by the patriarch of the family. A high-ranking executive for a major television network who is home two to three nights each week, on average, Father is the "stage hog" of this domestic drama. He frequently enters chomping on a gigantic cigar and bellowing for his children's affections. Brash, pompous, and rude are his most redeeming qualities. Although he announces that he loves his children, he tells you privately that his daughter is "turning into a little bitch." When he's around, the children compete for his attention, however brief, and his favor, vying for the role of most–loved offspring. Father encourages this sibling rivalry by pushing them to excel in sports and academics and conducting overbearing lectures when any child challenges or falters in his or her assigned role. He particularly likes proving his children wrong and arguing them down like the attorney he was trained to be. (When Father is onstage, your role is to stand to the side and silently watch the drama unfold.) When his company's photographer wants the family to pose, Father grabs his wife and children around him and roars that *this* is a family! Publicly and loudly, Father frequently assures you (and everyone else) that he adores his current, much–younger wife. Yet it doesn't take long for you to figure out that he seems to have an undying adoration for his former wife as well.

The role of Mother is played by a polite, rather vacant woman, who occasionally can emote maternal feelings. Despite Father's alleged adoration of her, the two exchange very little affection or even dialogue. In fact, Mother is focused on herself most of the time and seems happiest when Father is absent. If you venture any inquiry into Mother's tastes or personal history, she gives you banal and terse responses. If you say anything about your own life, Mother rarely responds at all, let alone acknowledges your statement with a question. But despite her seemingly placid emotional life, your observation reveals that she is truly complicated. Mother lives on a steady diet of dry popcorn, low–fat yogurt, and premium vanilla ice cream. You are frequently awakened around six in the morning to the sound of the Stairmaster motor churning below you, alerting you to Mother's first round of exercise for the day. Rounds two and three will be completed during breaks from her job as owner of a nanny agency (yes, the very same one that employs you). And at night, she will be back into the ice cream. Well, exercise is undoubtedly better than bulimia, which Mother used to rely on, using chewing tobacco as her purgative. What gives Mother pleasure besides her slim figure? Not her children. Like Father, she is rarely around the house or the children, preferring instead to let you act as chauffeur and role model for the younger generation while she naps behind the scenes, alone. Sometimes, though, she comes on stage to applaud or threaten the children, depending on their performances and her mood.

Among the junior members of this troupe, Elder Son and Younger Son wage constant battle. Their years of rigorous, elite training both at home and in myriad sports have cultivated their combat skills to the point where Younger Son's coaches plead with Mother and Father to help him curb his ruthlessly competitive nature. A basketball game between the Sons will soon dissolve into a screaming fisticuffs where you, the intervener, are faced with insult (and, on occasion, injury). Elder Son refuses defeat by his just as capable brother and retaliates with unmitigated violence whenever his tenuous dominance is threatened. The Sons' shared obsession with online instant messaging further fuels their competition, as they argue over the one computer relegated to the children. When you ask your so-called charges to leave the computer to complete homework or eat a meal, the Sons explode with bestial nastiness. Both feel free to tell you to "shut up," and neither thinks of avoiding offensive language in your presence. You believe the Sons have learned much of their behavior from the violent and vulgarity-filled television programs they have been allowed to watch and from their parents' own practices. Younger Son is brilliant, yet his lack of personal control and emotional depth foretell a bleak future. Elder Son can display occasional moments of warmth, but his superior attitude eradicates any hope of lasting improvement. In spite of all the material advantages heaped upon them by Mother and Father, the Sons remain unappreciative of these advantages and absolutely resistant to any accompanying social lessons. When their ever–changing cast of friends visit, the Sons invariably get into a grim fight. As a result, those who visit rarely return.

Despite the pleasure they take in fighting each other, the Sons take special satisfaction in torturing Daughter, the middle child and unequivocally the most gifted performer on this living stage. Daughter is darling to look at, a young beauty who wears the finest clothes a child can own. Outsiders and Father, in particular, praise her freely for her beauty and people–pleasing personality. While displaying intelligence and charm in public, however, she privately exhibits the cunning and insincerity of a cynical politician. Hardened by years of brotherly abuse, she asserts herself forcefully in any disagreement, with child or adult. And the lies she regularly tells are delivered with bright steady eyes and a cheerful sweet voice. Her uglier activities are usually reserved for backstage performances. To your face, she wheedles you to be her newest confidante and playmate, at least for the duration of your one–year run. During that run, Daughter steals most scenes, dazzling you and her parents with her dancing, singing and joke–telling abilities, exhausting herself to win over her audiences. Like the Sons, she is too busy attracting attention and participating in too many sports and lessons to live the life of a regular ten–year–old. Instead of sleepovers, Daughter attends late–night piano lessons, acting courses, and soccer practices. Instead of riding bikes with girls her own age, she rides in the car with her nanny to the next of her closely booked activities. Daughter seems confident and capable to all her public audience, but you know that privately she fights her insecurities. Her constant struggle to please Father and Mother, to get their attention and approval, has resulted in a deep–seated self–doubt. And you know that she slips into bed every single night with Mother, or both her parents when Father is at home. There is no resistance to this practice, and Mother and Father do nothing to help her overcome her fears and insecurities. Interestingly, the most time Daughter ever gets to spend with either of her parents is when she is sleeping with them.

Although it's tempting to (try to) perform the role of healer in this fractured family, you are forced instead into the less rewarding role of wrangler. Part referee, part instructor, part exorcist to the demons coursing through each child, you must be as aggressively athletic as the children themselves, constantly cross–training, switching off between defensive and offensive positions, regardless of the sport or activity. After all, Mother and Father have consistently removed themselves from most duties of a director; preoccupied with their own performances, they've abandoned you to a position of sole responsibility for the junior members of the cast (just like the nanny in Robert Mankoff's cartoon from the *New Yorker* on the next page). Your authority is challenged endlessly, and you must just–as–endlessly justify your responsibility, experience, and knowledge to these argumentative and perpetually resistant children. Any attempt on your part to undo an offensive behavior results immediately in an argument: "We don't have to do what you say; Mom and Dad let us (just fill in the blank)." In the meantime, Mother and Father continually pledge their support to your efforts, while doing nothing concrete to assist you. You're on your own, no speaking lines already written or assigned. In addition, you find you've had to develop new skills in lie–detection and surveillance to look after these children. (After all, their parents have always participated in elaborate schemes designed to fool, from Father's devotion to two wives to Mother's eating disorders.) No homework sheet or written assignment can go unchecked. You must also play the part of chef extraordinaire, catering to the unique palate of each demanding charge. Whatever the scene, the mental and physical stresses are intense, and the victories hard–won. Your role demands that you develop your survival skills, for you're determined to fulfill your contract.

Near the end of your run, you wonder how successful your performance has really been. What will be the effects of the actions you took, of the efforts you made; did you in fact achieve any lasting change in the lives of these children? It is nearly impossible to tell, although the family's reactions to you near the end leave you feeling vindicated, if only momentarily. Father has sparingly acknowledged your talents; Mother has thanked you for your resolve; Elder Son has turned to you for advice about life; Daughter has admitted a fondness for you; Younger Son has laughed at your attempts at humor. The show has not ended in disaster, but the family actors still seem all too typecast in their roles. The damage that was done before you arrived will remain—

"They can't see you right now—would you like a bottle while you're waiting?"

but not for your lack of persistence. As the outsider, the good nanny, the supporting character who's had to offer far too much support, you take your final bow. You exit the stage of this drama and step onto another, a stage on which you really are the star.

Favorite's finished essay is a descriptive one: she moves from describing one character to the next. Yet within her overall description she taps the rhetorical power of narration, cause-and-consequence analysis, comparison and contrast, and exemplification, mixing the rhetorical methods. Her organization is emphatic overall, ending with a description of herself because the nanny is the most important character in her description. But within the individual paragraphs she moves from emphatic to chronological to spatial patterns of organization.

Favorite opens the essay with a "hook," mentioning the three shows that feature nannies in starring roles, three shows with happy endings. In her introduction she compares these fictional nannies with the actual nannies she knows (including herself), few of whom have managed to achieve such happy endings in the families they serve. In fact, Favorite's thesis statement is that the parents, no matter how neglectful or negative their behavior, are the role models the children emulate. Each of the remaining paragraphs now opens with a focused topic sentence that extends the thesis statement. And each paragraph includes details of various kinds (stories, examples, comparisons and contrasts) that bring the topic sentence to life. Favorite closes her essay with a question that grows out of her thesis statement: Has she been able to compensate to any significant extent for the parents' faults? She concludes that she has done the best job she can but that if she wants a role where she can thrive, rather than merely survive, she'll have to star in a show of her own making.

Making Sense with Your Writing

Now that you've seen the steps and strategies a writer needs to work through to achieve a rhetorical purpose—to create knowledge by making sense of a subject—let me return to my explanation of how this book will help you do this. In each chapter, *Making Sense* asks you to question the readings and your own writing in ways that will help you define a purpose and audience, decide on a thesis, develop supporting details, organize them into a series of related, purposeful paragraphs, choose an appropriate vocabulary and style, and write strong introductions and conclusions. As I mentioned earlier, every chapter also offers you help for revising; after you've drafted a text, you can turn to the checklist, respond to the questions, and apply your responses to your writing. You can also use these questions to respond to your classmates' writing or to have them respond to yours. In fact, a great many of the activities and assignments in *Making Sense* ask you to work with one or more classmates, giving you practice in the collaboration that's often so crucial to writing successfully. And each chapter offers suggestions for thinking about how to use specific kinds of visuals to enhance your writing and help you achieve your rhetorical goals.

As I hope you will see, the emphasis of *Making Sense* is on *your* development as a college-level reader, writer, and thinker—and sometimes a speaker as well. It includes many opportunities for in-class writing, speaking, and conversation as well as for self-evaluation, peer evaluation, and group evaluation of your writing. In every case you will be working toward improving your literacy and your rhetorical skills; you'll also be improving your essays for your instructor's evaluation. But *Making Sense* isn't teacher-centered; it's student-centered, focused on improving your writing process as well as your written products.

Try Your Hand   To reflect one more time on your feelings about writing, take a few minutes to write out answers to the following questions:

1. What does it mean to be a writer?
2. Do you think of yourself as a writer (or a particular kind of writer)? If so, when did you first begin to think of yourself that way?
3. Have you ever described yourself to others as a writer (or a particular kind of writer)? Can you remember the first time you did so?
4. Do you think of yourself as part of a community (or multiple communities) of writers? Who makes up your community or communities?
5. Does your writing include visuals?

Finally

I hope you have some fun using *Making Sense*. The readings, visuals, questions, writing assignments, and group work are all intended to help you continue to develop your verbal and visual literacy skills as a college student and a working adult. My greatest hope is that you become more self-conscious and confident about your own thinking, reading, and writing as you work your way through this text and make sense of the world beyond it. Best of luck in college—and let me know how I can help you.

Cheryl Glenn < cjg6@psu.edu >

jobcenter
"When can you start?"

The most jobs in DFW from The Dallas Morning News, plus jobs employers!

JOB CATEGORIES: Multiple selections are allowed.

```
All
Accounting/Bookkeeping
Advertising
```

KEYWORDS: Enter keywords that describe your skills, experiences and/or i separate words with spaces.

Search   ▶ Advanced Job Finder

joblink

Wa

Click here for your online interview!
▶ GO!

For Job Seekers

MyJobCenter
Job Search
Post a Resume
JobCenter JobLink
JobClips
Company Profiles
Salary Wizard
Need Help?
Job Hunting Tips

chapter **2**

DESCRIPTION

▶Member Login
▶JobCenter Dem
▶JobCenter TV D
▶Products
▶Post a Job

▶Career Events
▶Education / Tra
▶Jobs at Belo

Job Profile

SUBMIT RÉSUMÉ | SEND TO A FRIEND | RESULTS LIST | ALL JOBS | VIEW PROFILE

COMPANY: **Dallas Morning News** *
JOB TITLE: Copywriter
LOCATION: Dallas, TX 75202

PUBLICATION:
Dallas News

JOB DESCRIPTION (Reference No. Copywriter)
Copywriter
Ideal opportunity for news-loving night owl writer seeking four-day work week.
In-house creative group seeks copywriting professional whose primary responsibility is to communicate the value and relevance of news content to readers through the use of intriguing and compelling promotional messages. Candidates with print media familiarity and experience are strongly preferred.

The copywriter will interact with key personnel within the company on a daily basis. A primary responsibility of this position is to incorporate keen consumer insights into effective communication messages about the product, its features and benefits across a variety of media.

The copywriter must build and maintain relationships with marketing and creative department management and staff to ensure consistency and continuity of the message.
The ideal candidate will have a passion for news and reporter-like tenacity when it comes to getting the story. Must be self-directed, proactive, intuitive and a mature, confident, responsible individual capable of making key strategic decisions on-the-fly. Must anticipate and quickly react to changing conditions and still produce a quality product. Must also be a strategic thinker with both big-picture vision and attention to detail. Accuracy and consistency are a must.

SKILLS

- Outstanding written and verbal communication skills are required. The position demands impeccable working knowledge of grammar and the AP Stylebook.
- A bachelor's degree in journalism, communications or related field and 3–5 years of experience are required.
- Proficiency retrieving electronic images for placement with copy in formatted Quark and templates is strongly preferred.

EXPERIENCE
3–5 Yrs Exp

STATUS
Full-time

TRAVEL
No Travel Specified

SKILL CONCEPTS
- Detail
- Image
- Journalism
- Marketing
- Media
- Placement
- Print Media
- Proactive
- Promotional
- Quark
- Relationships
- Self-Directed
- Verbal Communications Skills
- Vision

*E*xamine the online want ad on the facing page, and notice how specific details paint a verbal picture not only of the employer ("in–house creative group," "key personnel") but also of the ideal employee ("news-loving night owl," "print media familiarity and experience," "passion for news and reporter–like tenacity," "self–directed, proactive, intuitive," "mature, confident, responsible"). In particular, the description of the successful job candidate gives an overall sense of the newspaper's expectation and the impression candidates must make: "responsible individual capable of making key strategic decisions on–the–fly," "big–picture vision and attention to detail." Visually, this want ad has impact as well. "Skill Concepts" related to the job are listed in the right margin, and below the job description are a list of key skills and other headings that make it easy for people skimming the want ads to see quickly whether the job fits their needs and experience.

The details in the ad help job seekers decide whether to apply for this position and, if they apply, what details of their experience and education to highlight in their application. The ad describes the job; those applying for it will then use the clues in the ad to describe themselves in a way that they hope will persuade the personnel director to grant them an interview.

Looking at Your Own Literacy   Have you ever created an advertisement? If so, what was it for, and which parts did you create? What do you think are the specialized characteristics of copywriting? Would you like to write ads for a living? What would you need to know about reading and specialized writing to succeed at the job advertised in the opening of this chapter? Take a few minutes to write about your familiarity with copy-writing and why you might qualify — or not — for this position.

What Is Description?

Every day, we use **description** to depict in words the details of what we see, hear, smell, taste, touch, or sense in some less physical way — or in our imagination. Description is such an indispensable element in our daily thinking and conversation that we often use it unconsciously. Just think of the descriptions you encounter in textbooks and assignments at school, the memos and e-mails you read at work, and the newspaper articles and television programs that tell you about the day's events. When you're alert to descriptions, to the ways writers and speakers try to appeal to your five senses, you'll realize how prevalent description really is.

Sometimes an entire piece of writing is devoted to description, but more often a writer uses description, visuals, and other kinds of writing to fulfill a broader purpose. Explanatory descriptions, for example, lead us through a process or help us make decisions. Repair manuals are

filled with descriptions, as are gardening guides, bird-watching hand-
books, and much advertising. Some particularly lush descriptions, such
as those of national parks, museums, or other tourist attractions, persuade us to visit a place. Other descriptions of people or places simply
entertain us, like a good story does. Whether you are explaining your
pet's symptoms to the veterinarian, sending a postcard from a vacation
spot, writing up a lab report, or compiling your birthday wish list, you
have reasons every day to describe something.

When you are writing descriptions, your job is to transfer your own
perceptions into a lasting image or impression for the reader. One way to
create these images and impressions is to write with vivid details: either
sensory details that appeal to the physical senses (sight, hearing, smell,
taste, and touch), or details that appeal to your reader's emotional, physical, or intellectual **sensibilities** (such as prudence, nostalgia, empathy,
kindness, and aesthetic taste). Writers create such sensations in descriptions all around you, from the "hot new colors" for athletic wear and the
"refreshing citrus scents" in a new shampoo to the "bacteria-fighting
power" of a mouthwash and the "natural crunch" of a breakfast cereal.
On items as mundane as the label of your shampoo bottle or the packaging of your toothbrush, descriptions help you perceive the product in
the way the writer wants you to perceive it.

Thinking about Description

1. Reread the classified advertisement at the beginning of the chapter.
   As you read, underline all the descriptive phrases. What sensibilities
   of potential applicants is the ad writer appealing to with each descriptive phrase? What sensibilities of undesirable job candidates
   are being rejected or discouraged?
2. What might be the purpose for describing a toothbrush (to inform,
   to entertain, to persuade)? Choose three words or phrases from the
   description of a toothbrush above. Indicate which sense or sensibil-
   ity each word or phrase appeals to.

Why Use Description?

The three most common purposes of description are to inform, to
entertain, and to argue a point. If you are writing a description, you will
need to decide on your purpose (or purposes, if you have more than one)
and then choose those details that best help you achieve that purpose.

Every day, descriptions that inform help you make decisions, even small ones such as which coat to wear. For example, you might look at the forecast in the weather section of the morning paper: "Today, intervals of clouds, snow, and high wind. High 36, low 24." These descriptive details provide you the information you need to decide whether to wear a winter coat, a raincoat, or a light jacket. You might also use these details to describe the weather in an e-mail message to a friend who is coming to visit. By conveying details about the weather to him, you will provide him with the information he needs for packing.

Good informative descriptions are loaded with details. In the following paragraph from a *New Yorker* profile of Harvard theologian Peter Gomes, details inform the reader about Gomes's distinctive appearance and voice:

> Gomes, now fifty-four, is . . . a Baptist minister with "an Anglican oversoul," who was named one of America's "star" preachers by *Time*. He is a former Secretary of the Pilgrim Society and an honorary fellow of Emmanuel College, Cambridge, and his mien owes as much to nineteenth-century England as it does to twentieth-century America. When he is not in clerical garb, he favors three-piece charcoal-gray suits, rep ties, a pocket watch and fob, and a starched white handkerchief, which he tucks into his left coat sleeve. He alternates between pipes and cigars and is rarely seen outdoors without a hat. His rich baritone is three parts James Earl Jones, one part John Houseman. From Freshman Sunday to the benediction at commencement, his is the first and last official voice that every Harvard student hears, and one of the few whose words are likely to be remembered.   — ROBERT BOYNTON, "God and Harvard"

The rich details about Gomes's clothing and voice — and reputation — build an overall impression of an appealing, memorable man.

Try Your Hand   Look at the syllabus for this class, noting the information your instructor has included about the amount of required reading, the number of written assignments, how grades are calculated, and so on. Then write a paragraph for one of your classmates describing the course requirements. Compare your paragraph with your classmate's. How were your descriptions alike? In what ways did they differ?

Perhaps the most familiar kinds of descriptions are those intended to entertain. Whether they are found in the opening lines of a novel or essay, a radio announcer's play-by-play of a sports event, or a travel guide's account of exotic scenery, descriptive details give us pleasure. For instance, when D. H. Lawrence settled in northern New Mexico, he entertained his readers with vivid details of the landscape that nourished his soul and his writing:

> For a *greatness* of beauty I have never experienced anything like New
> Mexico. All those mornings when I went with a hoe along the ditch to the
> Cañon, at the ranch, and stood, in the fierce, proud silence of the Rock-
> ies, on their foothills, to look far over the desert to the blue mountains
> away in Arizona, blue as chalcedony, with the sage-brush desert sweep-
> ing grey-blue in between, dotted with tiny cube-crystals of houses, the
> vast amphitheatre of lofty, indomitable desert, sweeping round to the
> ponderous Sangre de Cristo mountains on the east, and coming up flush
> at the pine-dotted foothills of the Rockies! What splendour! Only the
> tawny eagle could really sail out into the splendour of it all.... It had a
> splendid silent terror, and a vast far-and-wide magnificence which made
> it way beyond mere aesthetic appreciation. Never is the light more pure
> and overweening than there, arching with a royalty almost cruel over the
> hollow, uptilted world. For it is curious that the land which has produced
> modern political democracy at its highest pitch should give one the great-
> est sense of overweening, terrible proudness and mercilessness: but so
> beautiful, God! so beautiful.   —D. H. LAWRENCE, "NEW MEXICO"

Lawrence's description of the New Mexico landscape is moving and
spiritual: "the fierce, proud silence of the Rockies"; "the blue mountains
away in Arizona, blue as chalcedony"; "the sage–brush desert sweeping
grey–blue." The pleasure we take in the details of his description helps
us not only envision the beauty he sees but also better understand his
state of mind, his excitement and wonder, toward the last years of his
life.

If you are writing a description of a person or a place, you will discover that providing your own response to details about physical appearance and personality as well as the details themselves creates a well-
rounded portrait. Like Lawrence, you should include expected details
("blue mountains away in Arizona"; "pine–dotted foothills") as well as unexpected details ("a splendid silent terror"; "light more pure and overweening") to make your description memorable.

> **Try Your Hand**   Think of a special family member—a grandmother,
> cousin, nephew, parent, or sibling. What makes this relative special? Is
> he or she admirable? successful? good–looking? hardworking? kind
> and generous? funny? talented? In a paragraph or two, to be read by
> one of your classmates, describe this relative using rich details that
> make him or her come alive in an entertaining way.

Description can often seem to be just a sensory rush of seemingly
objective details that transports a reader into the presence of a person or
a place—of Peter Gomes or New Mexico, for example. But description
can also be used as argument. In writing and in conversation, the emotional charge of a few well–chosen descriptive details can change the

opinions or actions of our readers or listeners. Consider this excerpt from a flyer intended to discourage smoking:

> When a smoker takes a typical long drag on a cigarette, he follows with a deep inhalation that pulls the smoke into the farthest recesses of the lungs. It is as if every one of the hundreds of thousands of air sacs is clamoring to be filled with the tar-bearing, nicotine-laden, gaseous mixture.
>
> In this process, the sticky tar with many chemical constituents, including several cancer-causing agents, is deposited on the mucous membrane of the entire bronchial system — air passages of the lungs.
>
> —AMERICAN CANCER SOCIETY

The passage goes on to trace the physiological process by which the elements in cigarette smoke lead to the development of lung cancer. It is the descriptive details in the opening sentences, though, that catch readers' attention and perhaps cause them to change their actions by appealing to—or offending—all their physical senses. Details ranging from sight (the images of a smoker taking a drag and of tar being deposited on mucous membranes) to smell and taste and even sound ("clamoring" air sacs) and touch ("sticky" tar) work together to persuade readers of the direct correlation between smoking and illness.

Try Your Hand   Think of the descriptive details that teachers, parents, community leaders, advertisements, and health books have used to try to persuade you not to smoke, binge drink, engage in unprotected sex, or participate in other potentially harmful activities. Or if you are a parent, think of details you have used with your children. Choose one of these potentially harmful activities, and make a list of vivid sensory details that describe its dangers. Draft a descriptive paragraph using details that might persuade one of your classmates not to engage in the activity.

How Do You Read a Description?

In order to write effective descriptions, you'll first need to learn to read descriptive writing closely and critically. Reading critically means analyzing, evaluating, and questioning as you read in order to determine the techniques that contribute to a successful piece of writing (and the problems that can work against success), no matter which rhetorical method of development you're considering. As the next section of this chapter introduction explains, in the case of description, the sensory details of the writing should work together to give a clear overall impression that is appropriate for the intended purpose and audience. For example, if the description is intended to be mainly informative, is it clear?

Or does it seem confusing, contradictory, incomplete, or perhaps too de-tailed or not detailed enough for the intended readers? If the purpose is to entertain, is the description vivid or flat? And if it's meant to be argu-mentative, will the audience find the details believable, or might they seemed biased or too skimpy?

To achieve a critical understanding of the piece under review, start out by considering the title (if it has one) and how that title orients you to what follows and how it might suggest its purpose. Robert Boynton's title, "God and Harvard" (p. 49), for example, provides you a point of ref-erence — although not an especially helpful one in this case — for the de-scription of Harvard theologian Peter Gomes. In a longer piece, such as Boynton's entire essay, you'd need to evaluate the contributions of the introduction and conclusion to the description, locating the author's the-sis and main points to see what part each of these features plays in re-vealing and supporting the overall purpose. You'd then need to read through the body of the text again, this time more closely, to see how (or whether) the use of descriptive details creates an overall impression that fulfills the purpose.

Boynton's description, for example, is informative as well as enter-taining and includes a number of sensory details that contribute to a clear overall impression of Gomes. Notice that many of the details as-sume an audience of well-educated, often sophisticated readers who would appreciate the references to James Earl Jones and John Houseman and know what a rep tie, a watch fob, and a nineteenth-century English mien are. English writer D. H. Lawrence's entertaining description of New Mexico (p. 50) was aimed at a literary audience, many of the same Euro-peans and Americans who had been reading his fiction before he immi-grated to the American Southwest. Given this readership, Lawrence could assume that his audience would understand a sentence such as "Never is the light more pure and overweening than there, arching with a royalty almost cruel over the hollow, uptilted world." Notice that in comparison with Boynton's, his description seems to reveal both the writer's perspec-tive as an outsider in the United States and his personal emotional reac-tion to what he describes: "For it is curious that the land which has pro-duced modern political democracy at its highest pitch should give one the greatest sense of overweening, terrible proudness and mercilessness: but so beautiful, God! So beautiful."

Finally, assess every description in terms of not only what the author says, but what is unsaid as well. Sometimes, details that are not men-tioned (what Gomes looks like, how his nineteenth-century English mien comes off among Harvard students; Lawrence's attitude toward his home country, his reaction to the people as opposed to the landscape of New Mexico) can be just as important to the overall impression as those that are, so you'll always want to try to imagine what could be missing and why.

Try Your Hand   Working with another classmate, look over D. H. Lawrence's description of New Mexico on p. 50 and then answer the following questions. Be prepared to share your answers with the rest of the class.

1. What words or passages appeal specifically to your physical senses?
2. How does the author seem to want you to feel about this landscape?
3. What information might be left unsaid? Why?
4. How successfully does Lawrence achieve his overall purpose? Be specific in identifying words or phrases that succeed or fail in supporting that purpose.

How Do You Write a Description?

Whether its purpose is to inform, to entertain, to argue, or to achieve some combination of these goals, a description must create a dominant impression by using the right amount of detail, effective descriptive language, and an appropriate organizational pattern. In choosing details, language, and organizational pattern, a writer also needs to think about the audience—the knowledge, expectations, and attitudes of those who will be reading the description.

● Determining Your Purpose

You will need to think about whether your description will fulfill one or multiple purposes and whether it will be the main focus of your essay or play a smaller part in a larger piece of writing. These factors may influence, for example, how many or which details you choose to include. For instance, if you're writing an essay–length description with an informative purpose, you might follow the example of Trudier Harris, when she writes about how she and her siblings joined forces to help their mother, Miss Unareed, maintain her standards of grooming and dress during her last years in a nursing home:

> Within the nursing home and to regular visitors, my mother was known for her appearance. First, her hair. It was always shampooed, cut, curled, and permed — none of those weeklong hairstyles that many women in nursing homes are left to endure. Never did Ann allow Momma's hair to look raggy just because she was in a nursing home. The same was true of her clothes. She had closet upon closet full of clothing . . . and was changed into clean outfits as often as three and four times a day . . .
>   Miss Unareed's beautiful — and always beautifully clean — outfits were accessorized with earrings and breast pins and, early on, makeup

and sometimes a bracelet or rings. Her outfits were topped off with the cologne my brother Husain provided from his store, Husain's Fashions, to go along with the earrings and pins he donated. He also regularly contributed new clothing, as did other family members. Ann shopped for the rest and became known as one of the expert locators of sales in Tuscaloosa and the surrounding areas. Momma was therefore always dressed to the nines, sweet smelling, and perfectly coifed. Several folks thought that we kept her dressed so well because we were keeping up her identity as a former schoolteacher. They were surprised to learn that this woman who won nursing home beauty contests had been the wife of a cotton farmer and had also worked as a domestic, a janitor, and a cook.   —TRUDIER HARRIS, "NURSING HOME"

This descriptive passage uses vivid sensory details to engage and entertain readers, but notice that Harris is also making an implicit argument that older people should be supported in their efforts to keep up appearances, even when they live in a nursing home.

Even short descriptions can be used to fulfill a smaller purpose in a larger piece of writing. Consider the brief descriptions of items on a menu or in a catalogue, for example. Under the guise of being informative, these kinds of brief descriptions can be entertaining as well as persuasive, arguing, as they do, for you to choose the item to which they refer.

● Considering Your Audience

Closely tied to your purpose is your audience. Even if you don't know your readers by sight or name, you'll still need to consider the characteristics of the person(s) who will read your description and how these should influence the details you include (or leave out). For instance, the audience for Trudier Harris's essay might include academics who already know Harris by scholarly reputation, general nonfiction lovers, people interested in the life experiences of African Americans, or readers who are caring for elderly relatives.

When Penny Wolfson wrote about Ansel Adams's series of black-and-white photographs entitled *Moonrise, Hernandez, New Mexico,* her audience was made up of the well-educated readers of the *Atlantic Monthly:*

In *Moonrise* two-thirds of the space is usurped by a rich black sky; a gibbous moon floats like a hot-air balloon in an other-worldly — and yet absolutely southwestern — landscape. A gauzy strip of low clouds or filtered light drifts along the horizon; distant mountains are lit by waning sun or rising moon. Only in the bottom third of the photo, among scrubby earth and sparsely scattered trees, does human settlement appear: a small collection of modest adobe houses and one larger adobe church. Around the edge of the village white crosses rise from the ground at many angles; at first glance they resemble clotheslines strung with sheets or socks, but on more-careful examination it is obvious that they mark graves.

The prints differ greatly in quality from the reproductions one usually sees, and also differ slightly from one to another: here we see a more defined darkness, burnt in by the photographer, there a variation in exposure, a grainier texture. But that does not change the essential meaning of the photograph, a meaning one never forgets in the Southwest: nature dominates. Human life is small, fragile, and finite. And yet, still, beautiful. —Penny Wolfson

Notice that Wolfson assumes her audience not only has seen reproductions of the photo she's describing but also understands such vocabulary as *usurped, gibbous, waning,* and *finite.* If she had been writing for a different audience, she might have chosen not to compare the prints to reproductions or to use different language, such as *taken up* for *usurped* or *limited* instead of *finite.*

Creating a Dominant Impression

The **dominant impression** you want a description to make on your readers is the quality of the subject that you want to convey to them or the attitude toward it that you want them to share. To create such an impression, you need to choose details that are directed to your specific audience, details that can "show" rather than just "tell" those readers exactly what you mean. In addition, you need to organize your description in a way that strongly reinforces the dominant impression.

Often, you will state that dominant impression in a **thesis,** a one-sentence declaration of the main idea of your description. A thesis — which can refer to a paragraph, a longer passage, or an entire essay — sums up your subject, the perspective you're taking on the subject, and your purpose in writing the description.

In her memoir, Rebecca Wells describes the following scene, which creates a dominant impression of lovingly prepared regional food:

> With her first bite of crayfish *étouffée,* Sidda could see her mother in the kitchen at Pecan Grove. She saw Vivi first melting butter in a large cast-iron skillet, then slowly stirring flour into the butter, and cooking the roux until it became a chestnut brown. She smelled the onions, celery, and green peppers as Vivi added them to the roux. She saw the dish change color as Vivi added the crayfish tails, along with fresh parsley, cayenne pepper, and generous shakes of the ever-present Tabasco bottle. With each bite, Sidda tasted her homeland and her mother's love.
> —Rebecca Wells, *The Divine Secrets of the Ya-Ya Sisterhood*

As she describes the memory of making crayfish *étouffée,* Wells uses sensory details such as colors, smells, and tastes to evoke emotions and create the dominant impression. The chronological organization (arranged according to a sequence in time), following each step of the recipe, helps build the impression that culminates in the thesis: "With each bite, Sidda tasted her homeland and her mother's love."

Although every description should have a clear sense of subject and purpose, not every one needs an explicit thesis. Sometimes an **implied thesis** can convey the description's mood or overall impression as well as its purpose—but not directly. Instead, the thesis is suggested by means of the selection, organization, focus, and force of the descriptive details. For example, the antismoking flyer excerpted on p. 51 contains no explicit thesis, but the main idea behind the description is perfectly clear: smoking cigarettes starts a chain of events that can lead to lung cancer.

One other important consideration in creating a dominant impression is deciding how much descriptive detail to include. Because you're already familiar with the subject you're describing, you may tend either to include every single bit of information about it or to provide too few details. It's hard to figure out the right amount of detail by yourself, so don't hesitate to ask a friend or classmate to read your draft and tell you where you go overboard on detail and where you need to add more.

Using Descriptive Language

Descriptive writing calls for descriptive language, either objective or subjective. **Objective description** tells about something (an event, person, place, animal, inanimate object) without evaluating it or revealing the writer's personal feelings about it. Writers who want to emphasize the accuracy and trustworthiness of their writing—most journalists, scientists, technical writers—rely on objective description. In turn, objective description relies on **denotative language,** words that sound neutral and do not carry any emotional associations. **Subjective description,** on the other hand, shifts the emphasis from the facts to the writer's reactions and responses to those facts. It often uses **connotative language,** words that suggest evaluations and emotional responses. For example, an urban neighborhood might be described either with the denotative label *low-income* or the connotative label *slum,* a word that carries associations not just of low incomes but also of crime, decay, and squalor. Writers often choose the type of descriptive language according to their particular purpose and audience. A political scientist, for example, might use *low-income* in an article for a scholarly journal about her latest research project, an article intended to inform an audience of other political scientists. But she might use *slum* in a letter to the editor of the local newspaper in which she tries to persuade a more general audience that the city government should provide better housing or police protection for the neighborhood's residents.

In fact, rarely is a description purely objective or subjective. It is almost impossible to be totally objective, to let "the facts speak for themselves." At the same time, even the most subjective description needs to be grounded in objective facts in order to make sense, to be meaningful to readers. To write a successful description, a writer often needs to use both types so that the overall description stands the test of (objective) reality or (subjective) meaning. In choosing whether to use objective or subjective description, or both, and how much of each, you will have to identify your purpose and the relationship you want to establish with your readers.

Using both objective and subjective description, for example, *Rolling Stone* writer Mark Kemp describes musician Vic Chesnutt:

> When Vic Chesnutt heard that Madonna would be singing one of his songs on the *Sweet Relief II* benefit compilation, he wasn't so much elated as he was dubious. "I thought, 'No way!'" the 31-year-old singer/songwriter says, scrunching up his bony shoulders like a boy and smiling mischievously. " 'That won't happen.'" Chesnutt, a two-day shadow on his face, leans forward in his ragged wheelchair and reaches for another Camel Light. He's parked in the living room of his Athens, Ga., home on a stormy summer afternoon, wearing baggy beige pants, a coffee-stained long-sleeved T-shirt and a baseball cap emblazoned with EASTERN AIRLINES — the company for which his father worked for 20 years as a baggage handler until deregulation left him jobless.   —MARK KEMP, "Famous by Association"

The objective details inform readers that Chesnutt is 31 years old, sits in a wheelchair, smokes Camel Lights, lives in Athens, Georgia, and is wearing beige pants, a long–sleeved T–shirt, and an Eastern Airlines baseball cap. But Kemp includes subjective details as well: he describes Chesnutt as "scrunching up his bony shoulders like a boy and smiling mischievously." Kemp also includes connotative language: "ragged," "emblazoned," "jobless," and so on. The interplay of objective and subjective details and denotative and connotative language provides a tantalizing opening to a biographical sketch of a young man who plays music and smokes cigarettes more often than he shaves.

Descriptive language also often includes **figurative language,** a type of subjective language that departs from the denotative meaning of a word or phrase for the sake of emphasis. Most often, figurative language involves a comparison between two unlike things. To describe Peter Gomes's voice (p. 49), the author writes: "His rich baritone is three parts James Earl Jones, one part John Houseman." Gomes's voice is not literally three–fourths Jones and one–fourth Houseman, but the **metaphor,** the indirect comparison of one thing to another, suggests a certain sound to readers. Mark Kemp's description of Vic Chesnutt above includes the metaphor of a "two–day shadow on his face," and D. H. Lawrence's description of New Mexico (p. 50) includes a number of metaphors ("cube–crystals of houses"; "the vast amphitheatre of lofty, indomitable desert"). A **simile,** on the other hand, is a direct comparison

"Reading" and Using Visuals in Description

Many times, writers use visuals to anchor their descriptions. Photographs, drawings, or other kinds of images can strengthen the dominant impression of the descriptive writing, provide an organizational format (particularly a spatial one), and help the writer keep the point of view consistent. If you want to use visuals in writing for an academic assignment, it is a good idea to check with your instructor beforehand. You also need to consider whether to include labels or captions (if the visuals do not already include them) and whether to refer to the visuals in your written text or to let them stand on their own.

To use visuals effectively in descriptive writing, you'll need to learn how to "read" them critically in the same way that you do written descriptions—to judge what their intended purpose and audience

connecting two unlike things with the word *like, as,* or *than.* The excerpt from the antismoking flyer (p. 51) contains an especially striking simile: "It is as if every one of the hundreds of thousands of air sacs is clamoring to be filled." When Marjorie Garber describes dogs (p. 59) she includes the similes "the Chinese cresteds ... looked like tiny but determined cheerleaders" and "[t]he Maltese ... traversed the diagonal runway like little Miss Americas in training." Whenever you write a description, consider whether metaphors or similes can make it more effective.

● Organizing Your Description

Because descriptive writing generally focuses on visual details, it most often follows some variation on a **spatial organizational pattern,** with the details arranged according to their location. By arranging your description spatially, you are ordering information from a particular physical **point of view** (the assumed eye and mind of the writer). Charlotte Hogg uses spatial order to describe her hometown library:

> The library looked the same that day as it has every day since. To the
> right of the door are magazine racks, to the left, the librarian's desk. To

are, how well they achieve this purpose for this audience, and why. Consider for a moment the accompanying visual. Photographs of prolific Native American (Kiowa) writer N. Scott Momaday often accompany announcements of his lectures and other appearances — but to what purpose? What descriptive details can you glean from this visual representation of the literary figure?

Considered a foremost authority on the native peoples and cultures of the American Southwest, Momaday's appearance complements his reputation. His sports coat, plaid shirt, and necktie suggest that he (or perhaps his publisher or publicity agent) wants to present a combination of respectability and informality; notice the difference between the way he's dressed and Robert Boynton's description of Peter Gomes's clothing (p. 49). Momaday's pose, with his hand on his chin, is a traditional visual way to suggest intellect and shows off his large silver-and-turquoise bracelet and ring, reminders of the American Indian heritage that is the focus of his writing. Whenever you look at a visual that seems intended as a description — and especially if you're thinking of using it as part of a written description — carefully consider its details and how well they work together to achieve a particular purpose for the intended audience.

the left of that is the children's section, its own little square area of books, but not quite separate, since volunteer librarians like my grandma watch from the desk.

Spatial order is not the only possibility, however. When Rebecca Wells lists the details for making crayfish *étouffée* (p. 55), she uses a **chronological organizational pattern** to reflect the steps of the recipe: "first melting butter"; "then slowly stirring flour into the butter"; then adding onions, celery, green peppers, crayfish tails, fresh parsley, cayenne pepper, and "generous shakes of the ever-present Tabasco bottle." When Marjorie Garber describes "orders" of dogs, she uses an **emphatic organizational pattern;** she includes details that move from large dogs to small ones, for she has decided to concentrate on size:

An owner of big dogs myself, I was inclined at first to admire the large ones above the small. The giant Schnauzers, an improbable and handsome crew; the Briards, with stuffed-toy good looks in a jumbo size; the all-white Great Pyrenees and the all-black Newfies. To me the Chinese cresteds, hairless except for strategic poufs, looked like tiny but determined cheerleaders, with pompoms at foot and head. The Maltese all seemed to be *en femme,* with bow in hair and silky coats brushing the ground, and they traversed the diagonal runway like little Miss Americas in training. But some small breeds proved unexpectedly endearing; I fell in love with the border terriers, a breed I'd never noticed in the flesh (or the fur?) before.   —MARJORIE GARBER, *Dog Love*

Garber names all the big dogs she likes at the beginning of the paragraph, and then she catalogues the small dogs she doesn't much like. Finally, though, she moves to the small dogs she finds herself admiring: "But some small breeds proved unexpectedly endearing." By organizing her description according to size, Garber builds up to a surprise, something unexpected for her as well as for her readers: she loves border terriers.

The Garber passage is a good reminder that just as in choosing your descriptive details and language, in deciding on an organizational pattern you may want to take into account not only your purpose but also your audience. You might consider an order that reflects the audience's physical or mental point of view rather than your own, moving from most familiar (to them) to least familiar, from most remote (from them) to closest, from least persuasive (to them) to most persuasive. Whatever organizational method you use, be sure to remain consistent to one point of view, as Garber does—unless, of course, you are deliberately recording multiple viewpoints of the same subject. Finally, a brief description, such as the ones of Chesnutt and Gomes, might not need an explicit organizational pattern.

Understanding and Using Description

Analyzing Description

1. **Together with another classmate,** reread the description of Peter Gomes on p. 49, underlining every word and phrase that helps evoke a specific image of him. Next, writing individually, write one sentence expressing what Gomes may be trying to "say" with his clothing. Read your sentences first to each other and then to two or three other classmates, comparing your findings. Did you and your classmates arrive at the same conclusion about Gomes?

2. Why might a writer want to inform readers about Gomes? Is Boynton trying to convey a quality of the man or an attitude toward him? In other words, what seems to be his purpose? What details support your answers?

3. Reread D. H. Lawrence's description of New Mexico on p. 50 and Penny Wolfson's description of *Moonrise* on p. 54. Are they primarily objective or subjective descriptions? What words or phrases from the descriptions support your answer? Write out the figurative phrases Lawrence and Wolfson use—the metaphors or similes.

4. Who is the audience for the antismoking flyer excerpted on p. 51? Is the audience composed of potential smokers, nonsmokers, or smokers? Is the writer being objective or subjective in describing the consequences

of smoking? Which descriptive details will get the most attention from the audience?

Planning and Writing Descriptions

1. Write a brief description of what you're wearing today. Try to be as objective as possible; don't evaluate your clothes, shoes, jewelry, backpack, or handbag—just describe them. Then, after rereading the descriptions of Vic Chesnutt (p. 57), Peter Gomes (p. 49), and Miss Unareed (p. 53), write a paragraph on how your attire represents the type of person you want to appear to be. Is there a discrepancy between what you're wearing today and the type of person you want people to think you are? Write another paragraph about this discrepancy, if there is any. If there's no discrepancy, then write a paragraph about your ability to represent yourself by what you wear.

2. Refer to your answer to question 2 under "Analyzing Description." Again, reread Lawrence's and Wolfson's descriptions (p. 50 and 54), as well as bell hooks's description of her childhood backyard (p. 8), as the basis for your own description of a place. You might want to walk out the front door of the place where you live and look around, or glance out your window, or go somewhere that seems especially beautiful to you. Try to convey as much information as you can by taking down descriptive details of this place. Choose an audience and purpose before writing. Is your description more objective or subjective, or is it a balance of the two? **Share your first draft with a classmate** who is also drafting a description of a physical place. What do your drafts tell each other about your purposes and your audiences?

3. Do you wish you had more time for one particular activity—such as writing letters or e-mail, visiting relatives, studying more diligently, working longer hours, watching television, or browsing the Web? Draft a three- to four-page essay in which you describe your current lifestyle in order to explain why you do not engage more frequently in that activity. Be sure to refer to the following guidelines for checking over descriptive writing.

4. Write a quick description of the place where you now sleep. You don't have to write complete sentences; just jot down every detail you can think of. Then freewrite for five minutes, describing your sleeping place and making connections between that space and the person you are right now. You might decide to use this freewriting as the basis for a full-length essay of two to three pages. **Working with a classmate,** read over your description, using the following guidelines for checking over descriptive writing.

✓ Checking Over Descriptive Writing

1. What is the main purpose of your description—to inform, to entertain, or to persuade? How well does your description fulfill that purpose?

2. Who is the audience for your description? Have you taken the audience into account in choosing details, language, and organizational pattern?

3. What quality or atmosphere of your subject do you want to convey to your readers, or what attitude toward it do you want them to share? Does the dominant impression of your draft convey that quality or at- mosphere or encourage that attitude? Do you need more descriptive de- tails? fewer? Do any of the details you do provide contradict (or distract from) the impression you intend to convey? Does your description in- clude an explicit thesis? If not, would an explicit thesis strengthen the dominant impression?

4. Is your description intended to be primarily objective (emphasizing the person or thing you're describing) or subjective (emphasizing your own opinions and response), or a combination of both? What details did you use to achieve this goal, and how well did you succeed? Do you need to add or substitute more neutral, denotative language? more emotional, connotative language?

5. Which details did you include that appeal to each of the senses: smell, taste, sight, touch, sound? Which details appeal to emotional or intellec- tual sensibilities, such as compassion or a desire for adventure? Are there other senses or sensibilities you might appeal to?

6. Have you used appropriate comparisons (similes and metaphors)? Where else might a comparison enliven your description?

7. How have you organized your description? Does the organizational pat- tern contribute to the dominant impression you intended, or might an- other pattern work better? What is your viewpoint? Is it consistent?

8. If you're using visuals, what specific details in them help fulfill your overall purpose? Do you need to add labels, captions, or references in the written text?

READINGS

GAVIN REMBER
Closing Doors

Gavin Rember wrote the following essay as an undergraduate at the University of Denver, where he was majoring in mass communication and hoping to pursue a career in photojournalism. Rember's purpose is to inform his readers about the realities of the Denver Department of Social Services, both as a physical place and as a benefactor. Rember has no positive memories of the Social Services office, yet he and his mother relied on its benefits for a number of years.

Preview As you read, consider what the title, "Closing Doors," has to do with the essay.

A lonely child screams for her mother. A couple bickers in Spanish; the   1
woman begins to sob. I sit in silence, trying to drown out the noise. These sights and sounds represent the instability of my childhood. Years later, in the sanctuary of my bedroom, I recall the discomfort of the welfare office.

The Denver Department of Social Services office was located in a   2
strip mall, behind a Vietnamese Market and a restaurant called The Organ Grinder. Skydeck Liquors, Kim Hong Jewelry, and Plaza Mexico Salon Eldorado, and other small businesses scattered the mall. A vast asphalt parking lot sat ominously before the strip mall, which sprawled nearly half the length of a city block. Hideous shrubs grew near the entrance — an attempt at landscaping gone horribly awry. The exterior façade was all glass. It had a reflective coating, which gave an effect similar to that of a two-way mirror. White metal railings rose from the steps and ancient rust stained the sidewalk at their base.

Inside the building, everything seemed inconsistent. The waiting area   3
was filthy, unorganized and overcrowded. Plastic chairs awaited the welfare-hopefuls, after they took a number. A large indicator above the

counter would tell which number the overworked staff was serving, a dismal reminder of the crying, throbbing, aching mass of humanity yet to be served. The carpet, a dingy blue, clashed with its surroundings. The blandness of the building and its furnishings radiated with the blandness of government. The one exception could be found in the walls, which were painted a bright white and a gaudy purple. These flashy colors gave the impression that the social services facility was child-friendly.

However, the Department of Social Services was not child-friendly.   4
Perhaps that's one of the reasons I hated it so much. A sign in the waiting room read: "PARENTS PLEASE SILENCE YOUR CHILDREN." Another demanded, "PLEASE KEEP CHILDREN OFF COUNTER TOPS." The government offered no day care services of any kind. Parents brought their children to the office, making them sit for hours waiting to see a caseworker. Fortunately I had to visit only a few times.

The visions of people I encountered there remain clear in my mind.   5
The office was always full of people, many of whom were Hispanic or Vietnamese immigrants who spoke little if no English. The screams of infants and cries of toddlers echoed throughout the building. Out of view of the social workers, abusive parents with few parenting skills would rebuke, spank, or hit their children.

The caseworker assigned to my mother and me was a middle-aged   6
white woman. She wore a red nylon jacket with red-and-white striped cuffs, brown pants, and a white shirt. Perhaps she held a second job driving a bus, I guessed from her clothing. Her lifeless gaze told a sad story. She hated her job, but years of it had desensitized her from its depressing reality.

I hated this place. To me, it symbolized the height of my family's instabilities.   7
It shrouded me in embarrassment: not only having to visit the office, but the humiliation of having to use food stamps at the grocery store. By using them, I felt we were telling everyone that we were a family of limited means, that we were poor.

I know my mother didn't want to take me along. She resented what I   8
had to go through by being there. She had little choice. I'm an only child of a single mom. My mother's an artist; her work often reflects crucial parts of her life, and in turn, a great deal of it reflects me. She's painted all of her life, and she is extremely talented. However, like many artists, her income fluctuates dramatically. One year we relied on food stamps, and the next we traveled to Europe.

Because my mother's income was so inconsistent, we moved around   9
quite a bit. In all, I've gone to over 10 different schools and lived in just as many houses. Despite the moving, I had a good childhood. After I was born (at St. Luke's Hospital in Denver), we moved in with my great aunt in Greeley. Shortly after, we went west to Rifle, a small ranching town an hour east of the Utah-Colorado border. My mom painted, and I attended school. We lived in several houses in Rifle and then moved to Glenwood

Springs in 1985. We lived there for several years, moving from place to place many times.

In 1988, rent rose so high that we were forced to move again. We 10 lived in a tent for two months that summer until we found a house in New Castle, a small town on the Colorado River, located about 150 miles west of Denver. My mother had no success with her art there and felt that moving to the city was the best choice. We had only lived in New Castle for a year and had no real reason to stay. We packed up our two dogs, three cats, and the rest of our belongings and left for Denver.

We found a house for rent in north Denver and moved in. I started 11 school that September, and we started our life over once again. Because of financial instability, we were forced to go on food stamps. Every month, my mom and I would go to the Denver Department of Social Services to pick them up. The Social Services office was the most depressing place I have ever been in my life.

Through all of this, my bedroom was a place of refuge. The safety of 12 my room always welcomed me. There I could be alone, far from the screaming children and chaos of the Social Services office. But it wasn't until we bought our first house in 1991 that I had a true sanctuary. Previous houses weren't homes; they were temporary places to stay for a year or less. The house we bought on Adams Street was permanent. I could live there without the threat of leaving looming above me.

Recently, I went back to the Social Services office on Alameda and 13 Federal. I parked and walked to the building. Above the entrance, the sign still reads: "Denver Department of Social Services." Posted on the inside of a door, a piece of paper reads: "DENVER HUMAN SERVICES DEPARTMENT WILL BE CLOSED AT THIS LOCATION PERMANENTLY."

The railing leading to the stairs rattled with icy gusts of wind. The 14 once-prominent bushes dwindled in the chilly September sun. Old dry hoses snaked their way between the dying plants. I moved toward the window. The reflective covering peeled inward from the edges, allowing me to see into sections of the glass. Inside, the blue carpet remained. Dark spots on the floor revealed where desks and other large furnishings had once been. In one of the rooms, a solitary wooden chair faced outward towards the window. The chair, like many other artifacts inside, seemed out of place. A dusty yellow computer monitor sat sideways beside the chair, its power cord intertwined with unused phone cords.

Back in my car, I sat in silence—with no noise to drown out my 15 thoughts. In the distance, a young boy ran across the parking lot. I watched as he disappeared behind a building. I looked back at the Social Services office. The doors weren't simply closed on the outside. For me they had closed a chapter that signified the instability of my life. My hatred for this place had diminished. The uneasiness I had once felt was replaced with a sense of tranquility. It was the tranquility I needed to find peace in my life.

Reading Closely

1. How does Rember connect his description of the Denver Department of Social Services office with the supposed values of that office?
2. Rember recounts his experiences in this office as representing the "instability" of his childhood. What details does he provide at the beginning of the essay that lead you to think in terms of instability?
3. What—if anything—do you learn about the writer as you read his essay? What is your dominant impression of him? What words or phrases contribute to this impression? **With another classmate,** compare your findings.

Considering Larger Issues

1. Whether stated or implied, what is the thesis of Rember's essay?
2. What is the purpose of this essay? What details and information help you grasp the purpose? Who might be the audience? What does Rember assume the audience already knows about the Department of Social Services? about the (child–*unfriendly*) atmosphere of a Social Services office? How are purpose and audience connected in this essay?
3. How does Rember organize his essay? Try outlining it or mapping it out. What other organizational patterns could he have used? Which pattern do you think would be the most effective? Why? **Working with one or two classmates,** discuss your findings and prepare a group response to share with the rest of the class.
4. COMBINING METHODS. Rember's essay provides not only descriptive details but also a *comparison and contrast* between periods of instability and stability in his life. Mark those passages of comparison and contrast. What other subjects does he compare and contrast? Prepare to discuss your findings with the rest of the class.

Thinking about Language

1. **Working with a classmate,** use the context of the essay and your dictionary to define any of the following words you do not know. How does Rember's use of these words contribute to the dominant impression of the essay?

sanctuary (1)	desensitized (6)	artifacts (14)
ominously (2)	fluctuates (8)	intertwined (14)
dingy (3)	refuge (12)	instability (15)
gaudy (3)	chaos (12)	tranquility (15)

2. Reread Rember's essay, and circle or list all the evaluative (subjective) words or phrases he uses. What types of things does he evaluate?
3. Write out a list of all the comparisons (metaphors or similes) that Rember uses. What effect does this language have on his essay?

4. How does Rember use transitional words or phrases to help you understand the time elements of his essay? Underline all the transitions. Does he use transitions to signify space as well? Which ones accomplish this?

Writing Your Own Descriptions

1. Watch a television program—any program—that is at least 30 minutes long. As you watch the program, write down details of dialogue, setting, characters, facial expressions, and so on. As you take notes, try to begin placing your responses and descriptions into various categories (dialogue, setting, and so on). As soon as the program is over, turn the television off. Review and organize your notes into categories of description; think about the ways the details in each category help create a dominant impression. Finally, draft a two- to three-page review of the program you watched; introduce the dominant impression early on in your review, and then demonstrate how the various elements of the program contributed to that impression. Refer to the guidelines for checking over descriptive writing (p. 61) as you draft and revise.

2. Rember's essay is about moving beyond an initial feeling. Think back to your own early impressions of a person you're currently living with or a person you're close to. Try to remember what happened during your first encounter. Describe these events and your perceptions of this person in as much detail as possible. Draft without stopping to edit—not yet, anyway. Read over your writing, checking to see if the details you have included convey a dominant impression. Can you translate that dominant impression into a thesis statement and then into a two- to three-page descriptive essay? **Consider working with a classmate** as you revise your draft, relying on the guidelines for checking over descriptive writing on p. 61.

SUSAN ORLEAN

The American Man, Age Ten

Susan Orlean (b. 1955) is a staff writer for the *New Yorker* and has also written for *Rolling Stone, Outside, Vogue,* and *Esquire* magazines. In addition, she has written several books, including *Saturday Night* (1990); *The Orchid Thief* (2000), which was made into the Academy Award–winning movie *Adaptation; Homewrecker* (2004); and *The Bullfighter Checks Her Makeup* (2001), from which the following essay is taken.

Preview   What does the title mean to you? What are you expecting from the essay?

If Colin Duffy and I were to get married, we would have matching super- 1
hero notebooks. We would wear shorts, big sneakers, and long, baggy T-shirts depicting famous athletes every single day, even in the winter. We would sleep in our clothes. We would both be good at Nintendo Street Fighter II, but Colin would be better than me. We would have some homework, but it would never be too hard and we would always have just finished it. We would eat pizza and candy for all of our meals. We wouldn't have sex, but we would have crushes on each other and, magically, babies would appear in our home. We would win the lottery and then buy land in Wyoming, where we would have one of every kind of cute animal. All the while, Colin would be working in law enforce-ment—probably the FBI. Our favorite movie star, Morgan Freeman, would visit us occasionally. We would listen to the same Eurythmics song ("Here Comes the Rain Again") over and over again and watch two hours of television every Friday night. We would both be good at foot-ball, have best friends, and know how to drive; we would cure AIDS and the garbage problem and everything that hurts animals. We would hang out a lot with Colin's dad. For fun, we would load a slingshot with dog food and shoot it at my butt. We would have a very good life.

Here are the particulars about Colin Duffy: He is ten years old, on the 2
nose. He is four feet eight inches high, weighs seventy-five pounds, and appears to be mostly leg and shoulder blade. He is a handsome kid. He has a broad forehead, dark eyes with dense lashes, and a sharp, dimply smile. I have rarely seen him without a baseball cap. He owns several, but favors a University of Michigan Wolverines model, on account of its pleasing colors. The hat styles his hair into wild disarray. If you ever managed to get the hat off his head, you would see a boy with a nimbus of golden-brown hair, dented in the back, where the hat hits him.

Colin lives with his mother, Elaine; his father, Jim; his older sister, 3
Megan; and his little brother, Chris, in a pretty pale blue Victorian house

on a bosky street in Glen Ridge, New Jersey. Glen Ridge is a serene and civilized old town twenty miles west of New York City. It does not have much of a commercial district, but it is a town of amazing lawns. Most of the houses were built around the turn of the century and are set back a gracious, green distance from the street. The rest of the town seems to consist of parks and playing fields and sidewalks and backyards—in other words, it is a far cry from South-Central Los Angeles and from Bedford–Stuyvesant and other, grimmer parts of the country where a very different ten–year–old American man is growing up today.

There is a fine school system in Glen Ridge, but Elaine and Jim, who are   4 both schoolteachers, choose to send their children to a parents' cooperative elementary school in Montclair, a neighboring suburb. Currently, Colin is in fifth grade. He is a good student. He plans to go to college, to a place he says is called Oklahoma City State College University. OCSCU satisfies his desire to live out west, to attend a small college, and to study law enforcement, which OCSCU apparently offers as a major. After four years at Oklahoma City State College University, he plans to work for the FBI. He says that getting to be a police officer involves tons of hard work, but working for the FBI will be a cinch, because all you have to do is fill out one form, which he has already gotten from the head FBI office. Colin is quiet in class but loud on the playground. He has a great throwing arm, significant foot speed, and a lot of physical confidence. He is also brave. Huge wild cats with rabies and gross stuff dripping from their teeth, which he says run rampant throughout his neighborhood, do not scare him. Otherwise, he is slightly bashful. This combination of athletic grace and valor and personal reserve accounts for considerable popularity. He has a fluid relationship to many social groups, including the superbright nerds, the ultra–jocks, the flashy kids who will someday become extremely popular and socially successful juvenile delinquents, and the kids who will be elected president of the student body. In his opinion, the most popular boy in his class is Christian, who happens to be black, and Colin's favorite television character is Steve Urkel on *Family Matters*, who is black, too, but otherwise he seems uninterested in or oblivious to race. Until this year, he was a Boy Scout. Now he is planning to begin karate lessons. His favorite schoolyard game is football, followed closely by prison dodgeball, blob tag, and bombardo. He's crazy about athletes, although sometimes it isn't clear if he is absolutely sure of the difference between human athletes and Marvel Comics action figures. His current athletic hero is Dave Meggett. His current best friend is named Japeth. He used to have another best friend named Ozzie. According to Colin, Ozzie was found on a doorstep, then changed his name to Michael and moved to Massachusetts, and then Colin never saw him or heard from him again.

He has had other losses in his life. He is old enough to know people   5 who have died and to know things about the world that are worrisome. When he dreams, he dreams about moving to Wyoming, which he has visited with his family. His plan is to buy land there and have some sort of ranch that would definitely include horses. Sometimes when he talks about this, it sounds as ordinary and hard–boiled as a real estate appraisal; other times it can sound fantastical and wifty and achingly naive, informed by the last inklings of childhood—the musings of a balmy real estate appraiser assaying a wonderful and magical landscape that erodes from memory a little bit every day. The collision in his mind of what he understands, what he hears, what he figures out, what popular culture pours into him, what he knows, what he pretends to know, and what he imagines makes an interesting mess. The mess often has the form of what he will probably think like when he is a grown man, but the content of what he is like as a little boy.

He is old enough to begin imagining that he will someday get mar- 6
ried, but at ten he is still convinced that the best thing about being married will be that he will be allowed to sleep in his clothes. His father once observed that living with Colin was like living with a Martian who had done some reading on American culture. As it happens, Colin is not especially sad or worried about the prospect of growing up, although he sometimes frets over whether he should be called a kid or a grown–up; he has settled on the word *kid-up*. Once, I asked him what the biggest advantage to adulthood will be, and he said, "The best thing is that grown-ups can go wherever they want." I asked him what he meant, exactly, and he said, "Well, if you're grown up, you'd have a car, and whenever you felt like it, you could get into your car and drive somewhere and get candy."

Colin loves recycling. He loves it even more than, say, playing with little 7
birds. That ten–year–olds feel the weight of the world and consider it their mission to shoulder it came as a surprise to me. I had gone with Colin one Monday to his classroom at Montclair Cooperative School. The Co-op is in a steep, old, sharp–angled brick building that had served for many years as a public school until a group of parents in the area took it over and made it into a private, progressive elementary school. The fifth–grade classroom is on the top floor, under the dormers, which gives the room the eccentric shape and closeness of an attic. It is a rather informal environment. There are computers lined up in an adjoining room and instructions spelled out on the chalkboard — BRING IN: (1) A CUBBY WITH YOUR NAME ON IT, (2) A TRAPPER WITH A 5–POCKET ENVELOPE LABELED SCIENCE, SOCIAL STUD-IES, READING/LANGUAGE ARTS, MATH, MATH LAB/COMPUTER; WHITE LINED PAPER; A PLAS-TIC PENCIL BAG; A SMALL HOMEWORK PAD, (3) LARGE BROWN GROCERY BAGS — but there is also a couch in the center of the classroom, which the kids take turns occupying, a rocking chair, and three canaries in cages near the door.

It happened to be Colin's first day in fifth grade. Before class began, 8
there was a lot of horsing around, but there were also a lot of conversations about whether Magic Johnson had AIDS or just HIV and whether

someone falling in a pool of blood from a cut of his would get the disease. These jolts of sobriety in the midst of rank goofiness are a ten–year–old's specialty. Each one comes as a fresh, hard surprise, like finding a razor blade in a candy apple. One day, Colin and I had been discussing horses or dogs or something, and out of the blue he said, "What do you think is better, to dump garbage in the ocean, to dump it on land, or to burn it?" Another time, he asked me if I planned to have children. I had just spent an evening with him and his friend Japeth, during which they put every small, movable object in the house into Japeth's slingshot and fired it at me, so I told him that I wanted children but that I hoped they would all be girls, and he said, "Will you have an abortion if you find out you have a boy?"

At school, after discussing summer vacation, the kids began choosing   9
the jobs they would do to help out around the classroom. Most of the jobs are humdrum — putting the chairs up on the tables, washing the chalkboard, turning the computers off or on. Five of the most humdrum tasks are recycling chores — for example, taking bottles or stacks of paper down to the basement, where they would be sorted and prepared for pickup. Two children would be assigned to feed the birds and cover their cages at the end of the day.

I expected the bird jobs to be the first to go. Everyone loved the birds;   10
they'd spent an hour that morning voting on names for them (Tweetie, Montgomery, and Rose narrowly beating out Axl Rose, Bugs, Ol' Yeller, Fido, Slim, Lucy, and Chirpie). Instead, they all wanted to recycle. The recycling jobs were claimed by the first five kids called by Suzanne Nakamura, the fifth–grade teacher; each kid called after that responded by groaning, "Suzanne, aren't there any more recycling jobs?" Colin ended up with the job of taking down the chairs each morning. He accepted the task with a sort of resignation — this was going to be just a job rather than a mission.

On the way home that day, I was quizzing Colin about his world-   11
views.

"Who's the coolest person in the world?"   12
"Morgan Freeman."   13
"What's the best sport?"   14
"Football."   15
"Who's the coolest woman?"   16
"None. I don't know."   17
"What's the most important thing in the world?"   18
"Game Boy." Pause. "No, the world. The world is the most important   19
thing in the world."

Danny's Pizzeria is a dark little shop next door to the Montclair Coopera-   20
tive School. It is not much to look at. Outside, the brick facing is painted muddy brown. Inside, there are some saggy counters, a splintered bench, and enough room for either six teenagers or about a dozen ten–year–olds

who happen to be getting along well. The light is low. The air is oily. At Danny's, you will find pizza, candy, Nintendo, and very few girls. To a ten–year–old boy, it is the most beautiful place in the world.

One afternoon, after class was dismissed, we went to Danny's with 21 Colin's friend Japeth to play Nintendo. Danny's has only one game, Street Fighter II Champion Edition. Some teenage boys from a nearby middle school had gotten there first and were standing in a tall, impenetrable thicket around the machine.

"Next game," Colin said. The teenagers ignored him.   22

"Hey, we get next game," Japeth said. He is smaller than Colin, scrappy, 23 and, as he explained to me once, famous for wearing his hat backward all the time and having a huge wristwatch and a huge bedroom. He stamped his foot and announced again, "Hey, we get next game."

One of the teenagers turned around and said, "Fuck you, *next game*," 24 and then turned back to the machine.

"Whoa," Japeth said.   25

He and Colin went outside, where they felt bigger.   26

"Which street fighter are you going to be?" Colin asked Japeth.   27

"Blanka," Japeth said. "I know how to do his head–butt."   28

"I hate that! I hate the head–butt," Colin said. He dropped his voice a 29 little and growled, "I'm going to be Ken, and I will kill you with my dragon punch."

"Yeah, right, and monkeys will fly out of my butt," Japeth said.   30

Street Fighter II is a video game in which two characters have an ex– 31 plosive brawl in a scenic international setting. It is currently the most pop-ular video arcade game in America. This is not an insignificant amount of popularity. Most arcade versions of video games, which end up in pizza parlors, malls, and arcades, sell about two thousand units. So far, some fifty thousand Street Fighter II and Street Fighter II Championship Edition ar-cade games have been sold. Not since Pac–Man, which was released the year before Colin was born, has there been a video game as popular as Street Fighter. The home version of Street Fighter is the most popular home video game in the country, and that, too, is not an insignificant thing. Thirty–two million Nintendo home systems have been sold since 1986, when it was introduced in this country. There is a Nintendo system in seven of every ten homes in America in which a child between the ages of eight and twelve resides. By the time a boy in America turns ten, he will almost certainly have been exposed to Nintendo home games, Nintendo arcade games, and Game Boy, the handheld version. He will probably own a sys-tem and dozens of games. By ten, according to Nintendo studies, teachers, and psychologists, game prowess becomes a fundamental, essential male social marker and a schoolyard boast.

The Street Fighter characters are Dhalsim, Ken, Guile, Blanka, 32 E. Honda, Ryu, Zangief, and Chun Li. Each represents a different country, and they each have their own special weapon. Chun Li, for instance, is from China and possesses a devastating whirlwind kick that is triggered if you push the control pad down for two seconds and then up for two seconds, and then you hit the kick button. Chun Li's kick is money in the bank, because most of the other fighters do not have a good defense against it. By the way, Chun Li happens to be a girl—the only female Street Fighter character.

I asked Colin if he was interested in being Chun Li. There was a long 33 pause. "I would rather be Ken," he said.

The girls in Colin's class at school are named Cortnerd, Terror, 34 Spacey, Lizard, Maggot, and Diarrhea. "They do have other names, but that's what we call them," Colin told me. "The girls aren't very popular."

"They are about as popular as a piece of dirt," Japeth said. "Or, you 35 know that couch in the classroom? That couch is more popular than any girl. A thousand times more." They talked for a minute about one of the girls in their class, a tall blonde with cheerleader genetic material, who they allowed was not quite as gross as some of the other girls. Japeth said that a chubby, awkward boy in their class was boasting that this girl liked him.

"No way," Colin said. "She would never like him. I mean, not that he's 36 so . . . I don't know. I don't hate him because he's fat, anyway. I hate him because he's nasty."

"Well, she doesn't like him," Japeth said. "She's been really mean to 37 me lately, so I'm pretty sure she likes me."

"Girls are different," Colin said. He hopped up and down on the balls 38 of his feet, wrinkling his nose. "Girls are stupid and weird."

"I have a lot of girlfriends, about six or so," Japeth said, turning con– 39 templative. "I don't exactly remember their names, though."

The teenagers came crashing out of Danny's and jostled past us, so 40 we went inside. The man who runs Danny's, whose name is Tom, was leaning across the counter on his elbows, looking exhausted. Two little boys, holding Slush Puppies, shuffled toward the Nintendo, but Colin and Japeth elbowed them aside and slammed their quarters down on the machine. The little boys shuffled back toward the counter and stood gawking at them, sucking on their drinks.

"You want to know how to tell if a girl likes you?" Japeth said. "She'll 41 act really mean to you. That's a sure sign. I don't know why they do it, but it's always a sure sign. It gets your attention. You know how I show a girl I like her? I steal something from her and then run away. I do it to get their attention, and it works."

They played four quarters' worth of games. During the last one, a 42 teenager with a quilted leather jacket and a fade haircut came in, pushed his arm between them, and put a quarter down on the deck of the machine.

Japeth said, "Hey, what's that?"   43

The teenager said, "I get next game. I've marked it now. Everyone   44
knows this secret sign for next game. It's a universal thing."

"So now we know," Japeth said. "Colin, let's get out of here and go   45
bother Maggie. I mean Maggot. Okay?" They picked up their backpacks
and headed out the door:

Psychologists identify ten as roughly the age at which many boys experi-   46
ence the gender–linked normative developmental trauma that leaves
them, as adult men, at risk for specific psychological sequelae often manifest as deficits in the arenas of intimacy, empathy, and struggles with
commitment in relationships. In other words, this is around the age
when guys get screwed up about girls. Elaine and Jim Duffy, and probably most of the parents who send their kids to Montclair Cooperative
School, have done a lot of stuff to try to avoid this. They gave Colin dolls
as well as guns. (He preferred guns.) Japeth's father has three motorcycles
and two dirt bikes but does most of the cooking and cleaning in their
home. Suzanne, Colin's teacher, is careful to avoid sexist references in her
presentations. After school, the yard at Montclair Cooperative is filled
with as many fathers as mothers — fathers who hug their kids when they
come prancing out of the building and are dismayed when their sons
clamor for Supersoaker water guns and war toys or take pleasure in
beating up girls.

In a study of adolescents conducted by the Gesell Institute of Human   47
Development, nearly half the ten–year–old boys questioned said they
thought they had adequate information about sex. Nevertheless, most
ten–year–old boys across the country are subjected to a few months of
sex education in school. Colin and his class will get their dose next
spring. It is yet another installment in a plan to make them into new, improved men with reconstructed notions of sex and male–female relationships. One afternoon I asked Philip, a schoolmate of Colin's, whether he
was looking forward to sex education, and he said, "No, because I think
it'll probably make me really, really hyper. I have a feeling it's going to
be just like what it was like when some television reporters came to
school last year and filmed us in class and I got really hyper. They stood
around with all these cameras and asked us questions. I think that's what
sex education is probably like."

At a class meeting earlier in the day: 48

Colin's teacher, SUZANNE: Today was our first day of swimming class,   49
and I have one observation to make. The girls went into their locker
room, got dressed without a lot of fuss, and came into the pool area. The
boys, on the other hand, the *boys* had some sort of problem doing that
rather simple task. Can someone tell me what exactly went on in the
locker room?

KEITH: There was a lot of shouting.   50

SUZANNE: Okay, I hear you saying that people were being noisy and 51 shouting. Anything else?

CHRISTIAN: Some people were screaming so much that my ears were 52 killing me. It gave me, like, a huge headache. Also, some of the boys were taking their towels, I mean, after they had taken their clothes off, they had their towels around their waists and then they would drop them really fast and then pull them back up, really fast.

SUZANNE: Okay, you're saying some people were being silly about 53 their bodies.

CHRISTIAN: Well, yeah, but it was more like they were being silly about 54 their pants.

Colin's bedroom is decorated simply. He has a cage with his pet parakeet, 55 Dude, on his dresser, a lot of recently worn clothing piled haphazardly on the floor, and a husky brown teddy bear sitting upright in a chair near the foot of his bed. The walls are mostly bare, except for a Spider-man poster and a few ads torn out of magazines he has thumbtacked up. One of the ads is for a cologne, illustrated with several small photographs of cowboy hats; another, a feverish portrait of a woman on a horse, is an ad for blue jeans. These inspire him sometimes when he lies in bed and makes plans for the move to Wyoming. Also, he happens to like ads. He also likes television commercials. Generally speaking, he

likes consumer products and popular culture. He partakes avidly but not indiscriminately. In fact, during the time we spent together, he provided a running commentary on merchandise, media, and entertainment:

"The only shoes anyone will wear are Reebok Pumps. Big T–shirts are 56 cool, not the kind that are sticky and close to you, but big and baggy and long, not the kind that stop at your stomach."

"The best food is Chicken McNuggets and Life cereal and Frosted 57 Flakes."

"Don't go to Blimpie's. They have the worst service."   58

"I'm not into Teenage Mutant Ninja Turtles anymore. I grew out of 59 that. I like Donatello, but I'm not a fan. I don't buy the figures anymore."

"The best television shows are on Friday night on ABC. It's called 60 TGIF, and it's *Family Matters, Step by Step, Dinosaurs,* and *Perfect Strangers,* where the guy has a funny accent."

"The best candy is Skittles and Symphony bars and Crybabies and 61 Warheads. Crybabies are great because if you eat a lot of them at once you feel so sour."

"Hyundais are Korean cars. It's the only Korean car. They're not that 62 good because Koreans don't have a lot of experience building cars."

"The best movie is *City Slickers,* and the best part was when he saved 63 his little cow in the river."

"The Giants really need to get rid of Ray Handley. They have to get 64 somebody who has real coaching experience. He's just no good."

"My dog, Sally, costs seventy–two dollars. That sounds like a lot of 65 money but it's a really good price because you get a flea bath with your dog."

"The best magazines are *Nintendo Power,* because they tell you how to 66 do the secret moves in the video games, and also *Mad* magazine and *Money Guide*—I really like that one."

"The best artist in the world is Jim Davis."   67

"The most beautiful woman in the world is not Madonna! Only 68 Wayne and Garth think that! She looks like maybe a . . . a . . . slut or something. Cindy Crawford looks like she would look good, but if you see her on an awards program on TV she doesn't look that good. I think the most beautiful woman in the world probably is my mom."

Colin thinks a lot about money. This started when he was about nine 69 and a half, which is when a lot of other things started—a new way of walking that has a little macho hitch and swagger, a decision about the Teenage Mutant Ninja Turtles (con) and Eurythmics (pro), and a persistent curiosity about a certain girl whose name he will not reveal. He knows the price of everything he encounters. He knows how much college costs and what someone might earn performing different jobs. Once, he asked me what my husband did; when I answered that he was a lawyer, he snapped, "You must be a rich family. Lawyers make $400,000 a year." His preoccupation with money baffles his family. They are not struggling, so this is not the anxiety of deprivation; they are not rich, so he is not responding to an elegant, advantaged world. His allowance is five dollars a week. It seems sufficient for his needs, which consist chiefly of quarters for Nintendo and candy money. The remainder is put into his Wyoming fund. His fascination is not just specific to needing money or having plans for money: It is as if money itself, and the way it makes the world work, and the realization that almost everything in the world can be assigned a price, has possessed him. "I just pay attention to things like that," Colin says. "It's really very interesting."

He is looking for a windfall. He tells me his mother has been notified 70 that she is in the fourth and final round of the Publisher's Clearinghouse Sweepstakes. This is not an ironic observation. He plays the New Jersey lottery every Thursday night. He knows the weekly jackpot; he knows the number to call to find out if he has won. I do not think this presages a future for Colin as a high-stakes gambler; I think it says more about the powerful grasp that money has on imagination and what a large percentage of a ten-year-old's mind is made up of imaginings. One Friday, we were at school together, and one of his friends was asking him about the lottery, and he said, "This week it was $4 million. That would be I forget how much every year for the rest of your life. It's a lot, I think. You should play. All it takes is a dollar and a dream."

Until the lottery comes through and he starts putting together the 71 Wyoming land deal, Colin can be found most of the time in the backyard. Often, he will have friends come over. Regularly, children from the neighborhood will gravitate to the backyard, too. As a technical matter of real-property law, title to the house and yard belongs to Jim and Elaine Duffy, but Colin adversely possesses the backyard, at least from 4:00 each afternoon until it gets dark. As yet, the fixtures of teenage life—malls, video arcades, friends' basements, automobiles—either hold little interest for him or are not his to have.

He is, at the moment, very content with his backyard. For most in- 72 tents and purposes, it is as big as Wyoming. One day, certainly, he will grow and it will shrink, and it will become simply a suburban backyard and it won't be big enough for him anymore. This will happen so fast that one night he will be in the backyard, believing it a perfect place, and by the next night he will have changed and the yard as he imagined it will be gone, and this era of his life will be behind him forever.

Most days, he spends his hours in the backyard building an Evil 73 Spider-Web Trap. This entails running a spool of Jim's fishing line from every surface in the yard until it forms a huge web. Once a garbageman picking up the Duffys' trash got caught in the trap. Otherwise, the Evil Spider-Web Trap mostly has a deterrent effect, because the kids in the neighborhood who might roam over know that Colin builds it back there. "I do it all the time," he says. "First I plan who I'd like to catch in it, and then we get started. Trespassers have to beware."

One afternoon when I came over, after a few rounds of Street Fighter 74
at Danny's, Colin started building a trap. He selected a victim for inspira‐
tion—a boy in his class who had been pestering him—and began wrap‐
ping. He was entirely absorbed. He moved from tree to tree, wrapping;
he laced fishing line through the railing of the deck and then back to the
shed; he circled an old jungle gym, something he'd outgrown and aban‐
doned a few years ago, and then crossed over to a bush at the back of
the yard. Briefly, he contemplated making his dog, Sally, part of the web.
Dusk fell. He kept wrapping, paying out fishing line an inch at a time. We
could hear mothers up and down the block hooting for their kids; two
tiny children from next door stood transfixed at the edge of the yard,
uncertain whether they would end up inside or outside the web. After a
while, the spool spun around in Colin's hands one more time and then
stopped; he was out of line.

It was almost too dark to see much of anything, although now and 75
again the light from the deck would glance off a length of line, and it would
glint and sparkle. "That's the point," he said. "You could do it with thread,
but the fishing line is invisible. Now I have this perfect thing and the only
one who knows about it is me." With that, he dropped the spool, skipped
up the stairs of the deck, threw open the screen door, and then bounded
into the house, leaving me and Sally the dog trapped in his web.

Reading Closely

1. If Orlean had omitted Colin's age, how would we know that she's writing about a ten‐year‐old boy?
2. What details capture the "American" part of the title? Write a few minutes about how Orlean relates being ten, a boy, a man—*and* an American.
3. Write one paragraph summarizing this essay. **Trade paragraphs with a classmate,** and annotate your partner's paragraph with information from the essay that you've gleaned but your partner hasn't. Then work together to prepare a brief, unified report for the rest of the class.
4. What is Orlean's purpose in writing this description?

Considering Larger Issues

1. Does Orlean's essay have a one‐sentence thesis? If so, what is it? If her thesis is implied, write out what it might be.
2. Who is Orlean's audience for this story? How might it fit within a collec‐ tion of essays entitled *The Bullfighter Checks Her Makeup?*
3. What is the dominant impression of this essay? Mark the specific de‐ scriptive details that enhance or fulfill this dominant impression. Which

words, phrases, or events seem to adhere to a ten–year–old boy's sensibilities? to those of a "man"? Be prepared to share your answers with the rest of the class.

4. What specific details in the visual enhance Orlean's description of this "man"? of this ten–year–old?

5. **COMBINING METHODS.** How does Orlean use *exemplification* to enhance her description? In other words, how does she assert a point and back it up with many examples? Which passages are more concerned with providing examples than with describing?

Thinking about Language

1. Using the context of the essay and your dictionary, define any of the following terms that are unfamiliar to you. Be prepared to share your answers with the rest of the class.

nimbus (2)	sobriety (8)	avidly (55)
bosky (3)	prowess (31)	indiscriminately (55)
rampant (4)	normative (46)	windfall (70)
valor (4)	trauma (46)	deterrent (73)
wifty (5)	sequelae (46)	contemplated (74)
musings (5)	partakes (55)	transfixed (74)

2. The essay ends, "With that, he dropped the spool, skipped up the stairs of the deck, threw open the screen door, and then bounded into the house, leaving me and Sally the dog trapped in his web." What is the overall effect of ending the essay this way?

Writing Your Own Descriptions

1. Think about a ten–year–old (or fifteen–year–old or twenty–year–old) you've known or the ten–year–old you once were. Using "The American Man, Age Ten" as a model, draft a two- to three-page description of that person. As you begin drafting this essay, consider the various ways you might arrange the information. List descriptive details, keeping in mind the dominant impression that all the details suggest. What aspects of the dominant impression can you develop? Can you arrange those aspects from least to most important? Is there a chronology to the details? Would a spatial organization best serve your purpose? Write out a thesis statement. As you draft, be sure to refer to the guidelines for checking over descriptive writing on p. 61.

2. **Working with a classmate who is writing about someone the same age,** trade your drafts. Write out the dominant impression of your classmate's essay, underlining words or phrases that bring the impression into focus. Number the descriptive details in the order your classmate has placed them, and decide if rearranging them would strengthen the essay's overall effect. Discuss the effectiveness of the thesis as well. After the two of you have worked together, revise your own essay, referring to the guidelines for checking over descriptive writing on p. 61.

N. SCOTT MOMADAY
The Way to Rainy Mountain

Writer, teacher, and painter N(avarre) Scott Momaday writes eloquently about American Indian life in the United States. Born in 1934 of Kiowa ancestry, Momaday grew up in Lawton, Oklahoma, where he attended Native American schools. He graduated from the University of New Mexico in 1958, received his Ph.D. from Stanford University in 1963, and currently teaches English and creative writing at the University of Arizona. Momaday's books include the Pulitzer Prize–winning *House Made of Dawn* (1968), *The Way to Rainy Mountain* (1969), *The Man Made of Words: Essays, Stories, Passages* (1997), *In the Bear's House* (1999), and several collections of poetry. The following essay is excerpted from the introduction to *The Way to Rainy Mountain*, an entertaining book that has an informative purpose: to help readers understand the American Indians' connection to the land. As you read the first paragraph, pay careful attention to the way Momaday uses specific details to lead up to its final phrase: "this . . . is where Creation was begun."

Preview   What do you know about American Indians' connection to the land?

A single knoll rises out of the plain in Oklahoma, north and west of the   1
Wichita Range. For my people, the Kiowas, it is an old landmark, and they gave it the name Rainy Mountain. The hardest weather in the world is there. Winter brings blizzards, hot tornadic winds arise in the spring, and in summer the prairie is an anvil's edge. The grass turns brittle and brown, and it cracks beneath your feet. There are green belts along the rivers and creeks, linear groves of hickory and pecan, willow and witch hazel. At a distance in July or August the steaming foliage seems almost to writhe in fire. Great green–and–yellow grasshoppers are everywhere in the tall grass, popping up like corn to sting the flesh, and tortoises crawl about on the red earth, going nowhere in the plenty of time. Loneliness is an aspect of the land. All things in the plain are isolate; there is no confusion of objects in the eye, but *one* hill or *one* tree or *one* man. To look upon that landscape in the early morning, with the sun at your back, is to lose the sense of proportion. Your imagination comes to life, and this, you think, is where Creation was begun.

I returned to Rainy Mountain in July. My grandmother had died in   2
the spring, and I wanted to be at her grave. She had lived to be very old and at last infirm. Her only living daughter was with her when she died, and I was told that in death her face was that of a child.

I like to think of her as a child. When she was born, the Kiowas were   3
living that last great moment of their history. For more than a hundred years they had controlled the open range from the Smoky Hill River to the Red, from the headwaters of the Canadian to the fork of the Arkansas

and Cimarron. In alliance with the Comanches, they had ruled the whole of the southern Plains. War was their sacred business, and they were among the finest horsemen the world has ever known. But warfare for the Kiowas was preeminently a matter of disposition rather than of survival, and they never understood the grim, unrelenting advance of the U.S. Cavalry. When at last, divided and ill-provisioned, they were driven onto the Staked Plains in the cold rains of autumn, they fell into panic. In Palo Duro Canyon they abandoned their crucial stores to pillage and had nothing then but their lives. In order to save themselves, they surrendered to the soldiers at Fort Sill and were imprisoned in the old stone corral that now stands as a military museum. My grandmother was spared the humiliation of those high gray walls by eight or ten years, but she must have known from birth the affliction of defeat, the dark brooding of old warriors.

→ came and tried to take over by the trail of tears. pushing them west, and U.S killed everything that could be helpful to live.

Her name was Aho, and she belonged to the last culture to evolve in North America. Her forebears came down from the high country in western Montana nearly three centuries ago. They were a mountain people, a mysterious tribe of hunters whose language has never been positively classified in any major group. In the late seventeenth century they began a long migration to the south and east. It was a long journey toward the dawn, and it led to a golden age. Along the way the Kiowas were befriended by the Crows, who gave them the culture and religion of the Plains. They acquired horses, and their ancient nomadic spirit was suddenly free of the ground. They acquired Tai-me, the sacred Sun Dance doll, from that moment the object and symbol of their worship, and so shared in the divinity of the sun. Not least, they acquired the sense of destiny, therefore courage and pride. When they entered upon the Southern Plains, they had been transformed. No longer were they slaves to the simple necessity of survival; they were a lordly and dangerous society of fighters and thieves, hunters and priests of the sun. According to their origin myth, they entered the world through a hollow log. From one point of view, their migration was the fruit of an old prophecy, for indeed they emerged from a sunless world.

4

→ A lot of cities have a large mix of cultures. sharing of food and way of 5 doing things.

Although my grandmother lived out her long life in the shadow of Rainy Mountain, the immense landscape of the continental interior lay like memory in her blood. She could tell of the Crows, whom she had never seen, and of the Black Hills, where she had never been. I wanted to see in reality what she had seen more perfectly in the mind's eye, and traveled fifteen hundred miles to begin my pilgrimage.

Yellowstone, it seemed to me, was the top of the world, a region of deep lakes and dark timber, canyons and waterfalls. But, beautiful as it is, one might have the sense of confinement there. The skyline in all directions is close at hand, the high wall of the woods and deep cleavages of shade. There is a perfect freedom in the mountains, but it belongs to the eagle and the elk, the badger and the bear. The Kiowas reckoned their

6

stature by the distance they could see, and they were bent and blind in the wilderness.

Descending eastward, the highland meadows are a stairway to the [7] plain. In July the inland slope of the Rockies is luxuriant with flax and buckwheat, stonecrop and larkspur. The earth unfolds and the limit of the land recedes. Clusters of trees and animals grazing far in the distance cause the vision to reach away and wonder to build upon the mind. The sun follows a longer course in the day, and the sky is immense beyond all comparison. The great billowing clouds that sail upon it are shadows that move upon the grain like water, dividing light. Farther down, in the land of the Crows and Blackfeet, the plain is yellow. Sweet clover takes hold of the hills and bends upon itself to cover and seal the soil. There the Kiowas paused on their way; they had come to the place where they must change their lives. The sun is at home in the plains. Precisely there does it have the certain character of a god. When the Kiowas came to the land of the Crows, they could see the dark lees of the hills at dawn across the Bighorn River, the profusion of light on the grain shelves, the oldest deity ranging after the solstices. Not yet would they veer southward to the caldron of the land that lay below; they must wean their blood from the northern winter and hold the mountains a while longer in their view. They bore Tai-me in procession to the east.

A dark mist lay over the Black Hills, and the land was like iron. At [8] the top of a ridge I caught sight of Devil's Tower upthrust against the gray sky as if in the birth of time the core of the earth had broken through its crust and the motion of the world was begun. There are things in nature that engender an awful quiet in the heart of man; Devil's Tower is one of them. Two centuries ago, because they could not do otherwise, the Kiowas made a legend at the base of the rock. My grandmother said:

> Eight children were there at play, seven sisters and their brother. Suddenly the boy was struck dumb; he trembled and began to run upon his hands and feet. His fingers became claws, and his body was covered with fur. Directly there was a bear where the boy had been. The sisters were terrified; they ran, and the bear after them. They came to the stump of a great tree, and the tree spoke to them. It bade them climb upon it, and as they did so, it began to rise into the air. The bear came to kill them, but they were just beyond its reach. It reared against the tree and scored the bark all around with its claws. The seven sisters were borne into the sky, and they became the stars of the Big Dipper.

From that moment, and so long as the legend lives, the Kiowas have kinsmen in the night sky. Whatever they were in the mountains, they could be no more. However tenuous their well-being, however much they had suffered and would suffer again, they had found a way out of the wilderness.

My grandmother had a reverence for the sun, a holy regard that now is all but gone out of mankind. There was a wariness in her, and an ancient awe. She was a Christian in her later years, but she had come a long way about, and she never forgot her birthright. As a child she had been to the Sun Dances; she had taken part in those annual rites, and by them she had learned the restoration of her people in the presence of Tai-me. She was about seven when the last Kiowa Sun Dance was held in 1887 on the Washita River above Rainy Mountain Creek. The buffalo were gone. In order to consummate the ancient sacrifice — to impale the head of a buffalo bull upon the medicine tree — a delegation of old men journeyed into Texas, there to beg and barter for an animal from the Goodnight herd. She was ten when the Kiowas came together for the last time as a living Sun Dance culture. They could find no buffalo; they had to hang an old hide from the sacred tree. Before the dance could begin, a company of soldiers rode out from Fort Sill under orders to disperse the tribe. Forbidden without cause the essential act of their faith, having seen the wild herds slaughtered and left to rot upon the ground, the Kiowas backed away forever from the medicine tree. That was July 20, 1890, at the great bend of the Washita. My grandmother was there. Without bitterness, and for as long as she lived, she bore a vision of deicide. [9]

Now that I can have her only in memory, I see my grandmother in the several postures that were peculiar to her: standing at the wood stove on a winter morning and turning meat in a great iron skillet; sitting at the south window, bent above her beadwork, and afterwards, when her vision had failed, looking down for a long time into the fold of her hands; going out upon a cane, very slowly as she did when the weight of age came upon her; praying. I remember her most often at prayer. She made long, rambling prayers out of suffering and hope, having seen many things. I was never sure that I had the right to hear, so exclusive were they of all mere custom and company. The last time I saw her she prayed standing by the side of her bed at night, naked to the waist, the light of a kerosene lamp moving upon her dark skin. Her long, black hair, always drawn and braided in the day, lay upon her shoulders and against her breasts like a shawl. I do not speak Kiowa, and I never understood her prayers, but there was something inherently sad in the sound, some merest hesitation upon the syllables of sorrow. She began in a high and descending pitch, exhausting her breath to silence; then again and again — and always the same intensity of effort, of something that is, and is not, like urgency in the human voice. Transported so in the dancing light among the shadows of her room, she seemed beyond the reach of time. But that was illusion; I think I knew that I should not see her again. [10]

Reading Closely

1. In what ways is Momaday's experience different from his grandmother's experience? Draw a line down the center of a piece of paper and record the experiences of the narrator on one side, the grandmother on the other. Be prepared to present your findings to the rest of the class.

2. On a sheet of paper, make five columns, one for each of the senses: sight, smell, hearing, touch, taste. Then list all the words and phrases in this essay that evoke each sense. For which sense do you find the largest number of descriptive words and phrases? Which sense does Momaday rely on most heavily in this essay?

Considering Larger Issues

1. What is Momaday's thesis? Is it implied or explicitly stated?

2. Descriptive essays may have several purposes. The main purpose of Momaday's essay is to entertain; his secondary purpose is to inform. Make a list of the specific words, phrases, and organizational strategies that Momaday uses to fulfill his dual purposes.

3. Who is the intended audience for this essay? How does the author's main purpose intersect with the knowledge and interests of this target audience? Write out your answers to these questions, and then **compare them with those of one or two classmates.** Prepare a small group report to share with the rest of the class.

4. What part does Momaday's use of myth (the children, bear, and stars) play in his essay?

5. What is the dominant impression of Momaday's essay? **Working with two or three classmates,** write a one-page report stating the dominant impression and listing the descriptive strategies Momaday has used to achieve this impression.

6. COMBINING METHODS. In which passages does Momaday move from an emphasis on descriptive detail to an emphasis on *narration*, on storytelling? Mark those passages.

Thinking about Language

1. Use the context of the essay and your dictionary to define the following terms. Be prepared to share your answers with the rest of the class.

knoll (1)	forebears (4)	caldron (7)
writhe (1)	nomadic spirit (4)	upthrust (8)
headwaters (3)	luxuriant (7)	engender (8)
preeminently (3)	lees (7)	tenuous (8)
disposition (3)	profusion (7)	deicide (9)
pillage (3)	solstices (7)	postures (10)

2. What specific descriptive language does Momaday use to evoke loneliness? Write out the comparisons or connotative language that conveys this feeling.

3. What specific language does Momaday use to describe his grandmother? Write out the denotative and connotative language about her. How do the connotations provide an emotional element to the description?

Writing Your Own Descriptions

1. Freewrite for five minutes about a familiar place—either one that you'd like to return to just once more, or one that you want never to experience again. Using this writing as a starting point, draft a three- to four-page essay in which you describe the sensations you experience when you think about returning to that familiar place. What smells, textures, sights, sounds, and tastes does that place call to mind? What emotional or intellectual sensibilities does it evoke? If you've gone there regularly over a long period, your feelings about it now might be very different from your earlier ones. Recalling those early memories and sensory impressions might help enrich your current feelings about that familiar place. Guidelines for checking over descriptive writing can be found on p. 61.

2. Drawing on your previous freewriting about a familiar place, draft a three- to four-page essay in which you describe this place both from your point of view and from the point of view of someone who has different feelings about the place. You and your mother, for instance, might have markedly different memories of a camping spot: you may remember a carefree scene in the woods, whereas she may have worried about the family's safety or may have felt overworked with camp chores. Or the situation might be reversed: even though you might dread visiting your childhood home because it has changed so much, your children might be thrilled to hunt for treasure in the dusty and damp, cluttered basement. You could start the essay with one point of view and then move to the other; or the points of view could interweave and overlap. In other words, your organizational pattern may vary.

    Consider asking a classmate to read your draft, marking all the sections that express your point of view, the sections that convey the other person's point of view, and the sections in which the two views overlap.

    As you revise your draft, concentrate on strengthening the dominant impression. Make sure the essay fulfills your main purpose, whether it is to inform, to entertain, or to persuade. Refer to the guidelines for checking over descriptive writing on p. 61.

3. If you've enjoyed visiting online places or communities such as MOOs, MUDs, or computer game sites, you might want to write about one. Freewrite for five to ten minutes about this cyberplace, and then decide on a purpose for writing about it. Be sure to connect your purpose with a specific audience. As you draft and revise your three- to four-page essay, refer to the guidelines for checking over descriptive writing on p. 61.

MEGHAN DAUM

Music Is My Bag

● Meghan Daum (b. 1970) has become one of the most celebrated and widely recognized essayists of her generation. Praised by reviewers as "fresh," "provocative," and "witty," her essays reveal the hidden landscapes of American culture. Daum grew up in New Jersey, graduated from Vassar College, and earned a master of fine arts degree at Columbia. Since then, she has published articles and essays in the *New Yorker*, the *New York Times Book Review*, *GQ*, *Vogue*, and *Self*. She is a regular contributor to *Harper's Bazaar* as well as to National Public Radio's *This American Life* and *Morning Edition*. Her first novel, *The Quality of Life Report*, was published in 2003. Daum currently lives in Lincoln, Nebraska. "Music Is My Bag" first appeared in *Harper's* magazine and was reprinted in a collection of Daum's essays, *My Misspent Youth* (2001).

> **Preview** Do you know what the phrase "Music Is My Bag" refers to? If not, what does the phrase suggest to you?

The image I want to get across is that of the fifteen-year-old boy with the beginning traces of a mustache who hangs out in the band room after school playing the opening bars of a Billy Joel song on the piano. This is the kid who, in the interests of adopting some semblance of personal style, wears a fedora hat and a scarf with a black-and-white design of a piano keyboard. This is the kid who, in addition to having taught himself some tunes from the *Songs from the Attic* sheet music he bought at the local Sam Ash, probably also plays the trombone in the marching band, and experienced a seminal moment one afternoon as he vaguely flirted with a not-yet-kissed, clarinet-playing girl, a girl who is none too popular but whose propensity for leaning on the piano as the boy plays the opening chords of "Captain Jack" gives him a clue as to the social possibilities that might be afforded him via the marching band. 1

If the clarinet-playing girl is an average student musician, she carries her plastic Selmer in the standard-issue black plastic case. If she has demonstrated any kind of proficiency, she carries her Selmer in a tote bag that reads "Music Is My Bag." The boy in the piano-key scarf definitely has music as his bag. He may not yet have the tote bag, but the hat, the Billy Joel, the tacit euphoria brought on by a sexual awakening that, for him, centers entirely around band, is all he needs to be delivered into the unmistakable realm that is Music Is My Bagdom. 2

I grew up in Music Is My Bag culture. The walls of my parents' house were covered with framed art posters from musical events: The San Francisco Symphony's 1982 production of *St. Matthew's Passion*, The Metropolitan Opera's 1976 production of *Aida*, the original Broadway production of *Sweeney Todd*. Ninety percent of the books on the shelves were about 3 music, if not actual musical scores. Childhood ceramics projects made by my brother and me were painted with eighth notes and treble clef signs. We owned a deck of cards with portraits of the great composers on the back. A baby grand piano overtook the room that would have been the dining room if my parents hadn't forgone a table and renamed it "the music room." This room also contained an imposing hi-fi system and a $300 wooden music stand. Music played at all times: Brahms, Mendelssohn, cast recordings of Sondheim musicals, a cappella Christmas albums. When my father sat down with a book, he read musical scores, humming quietly and tapping his foot. When I was ten, my mother decided we needed to implement a before-dinner ritual akin to saying grace, so she composed a short song, asking us all to contribute a lyric, and we held hands and sang it before eating. My lyric was, "There's a smile on our face and it seems to say all the wonderful things we've all done today." My mother insisted on harmonizing at the end. She also did this when singing "Happy Birthday."

Harmonizing on songs like "Happy Birthday" is a clear indication of the Music Is My Bag personality. If one does not have an actual bag that reads "Music Is My Bag"—as did the violist in the chamber music trio my mother set up with some women from the Unitarian Church—a $300 music stand and musical-note coasters will more than suffice. To avoid confusion, let me also say that there are many different Bags in life. Some friends of my parents have a $300 dictionary stand, a collection of silver

4

bookmarks, and once threw a dinner party wherein the guests had to dress up as members of the Bloomsbury Group.* These people are Litera- ture Is My Bag. I know people who are Movies Are My Bag (detectable by key chains shaped like projectors, outdated copies of *Halliwell's Film Guide*, and one too many T-shirts from things like the San Jose Film Festival), people who are Cats Are My Bag (self-explanatory), and, perhaps most annoyingly, Where I Went To College Is My Bag (Yale running shorts, plastic Yale tumblers, Yale Platinum Plus MasterCard, and, yes, even Yale screensavers—all this in someone aged forty or more, the perennial con- tributor to the class notes).

Having a Bag connotes the state of being overly interested in some-   5 thing, and yet, in a certain way, not interested enough. It has a hobbyish quality to it, a sense that the enthusiasm developed at a time when the enthusiast was lacking in some significant area of social or intellectual life. Music Is My Bag is the mother of all Bags, not just because in the early 1980s some consumer force of the public radio fund-drive variety distributed a line of tote bags that displayed that slogan, but because its adherents, or, as they tend to call themselves, "music lovers," give off an aura that distinguishes them from the rest of the population. It's an aura that has to do with a sort of benign cluelessness, a condition that, even in middle age, smacks of that phase between prepubescence and real adolescence. Music Is My Bag people have a sexlessness to them. There is a pastiness to them. They can never seem to find a good pair of jeans. You can spot them on the street, the female French horn player in con- cert dress hailing a cab to Lincoln Center around seven o'clock in the evening, her earrings too big, her hairstyle unchanged since 1986. The fifty-something recording engineer with the running shoes and the shoulder bag. The Indiana marching band kids in town for the Macy's Thanksgiving Day Parade, snapping photos of each other in front of the Hard Rock Cafe, having sung their parts from the band arrangement of *Hello Dolly* the whole way on the bus, thinking, *knowing*, that it won't get better than this. Like all Music Is My Bag people, they are a little too in love with the trappings. They know what their boundaries are and load up their allotted space with memorabilia, saving the certificates of partic- ipation from regional festivals, the composer-a-month calendars, the Mostly Mozart posters. Their sincerity trumps attempts at snideness. The boys' sarcasm only goes a fraction of the way there, the girls will never be great seducers. They grow up to look like high school band direc- tors even if they're not. They give their pets names like Wolfgang and Gershwin. Their hemlines are never quite right.

---

   * **Bloomsbury Group:** In early twentieth-century London, a group of brilliant bo- hemian thinkers, writers, and artists collaborated, worked, and loved together. Among this antipuritanical clique were Virginia Woolf and her sister, Vanessa Bell, Clive Bell, Roger Fry, John Maynard Keynes, Lyntton Strachey, and Leonard Woolf.

I played the oboe. This is not an instrument to be taken lightly. The oboist 6
runs a high risk of veering into Music Is My Bag culture, mostly because to
get beyond the entry level is to give oneself over to an absorption with
technique that can make a person vulnerable to certain vagaries of a subcategory, the oboe phylum. This inevitably leads to the genus of *wind ensemble* culture, which concerns itself with the socio–political infrastructure
of the woodwind section, the disproportionate number of solo passages, a
narcissistic pride in sounding the A that tunes the orchestra. Not many
people play the oboe. It's a difficult instrument, beautiful when played
well, horrifying when played poorly. I was self–conscious about playing the
oboe, mostly because so many people confuse it with the bassoon, its much
larger, ganglier cousin in the double–reed family. The act of playing the
oboe, unlike the graceful arm positions of the flute or the violin, is not a
photogenic one. The embouchure puckers the face into a grimace; my
childhood and adolescence is documented by photos that make me look
slightly deformed—the lipless girl. It's not an instrument for the vain.
Oboe playing revolves almost entirely around saliva. Spit gets caught in
the keys and the joints and must be blown out using cigarette rolling paper
as a blotter (a scandalous drugstore purchase for a twelve–year–old). Spit
can accumulate on the floor if you play for too long. Spit must constantly
be sucked out from both sides of the reed. The fragile, temperamental reed
is the player's chronic medical condition. It must be tended to constantly. It
must be wet but never too wet, hard enough to emit a decent sound, but
soft enough to blow air through. The oboist must never stray far from
moisture; the reed is forever in her mouth, in a paper cup of water that
teeters on the music stand, being doused at a drinking fountain in Parsip-
pany High School at the North Jersey Regional Band and Orchestra Audi-
tion. After a certain age, the student oboist must learn to make her own
reeds, build them from bamboo using knives and shavers. Most people
don't realize this. Reed–making is an eighteenth–century exercise, something that would seem to require an apprenticeship before undertaking
solo. But oboists, occupying a firm, albeit wet, patch of ground under the
tattered umbrella of Music Is My Bag, never quite live in the same era as
everyone else.

Though I did, at one point, hold the title of second–best high school 7
player in the state of New Jersey, I was a mediocre oboist. My discipline was
lacking, my enthusiasm virtually nil, and my comprehension of rhythm (in
keeping with a lifelong math phobia) held me back considerably. But being
without an aptitude for music was, in my family, tantamount to being a
Kennedy who knows nothing of politics. Aptitude was something, perhaps
even the only thing, I possessed. As indifferent to the oboe as I was—and I
once began an orchestra rehearsal without noticing that I had neglected to
screw the bell, which is the entire bottom portion, onto the rest of my instrument—I managed to be good enough to play in the New Jersey All
State High School Orchestra as well as a local adult symphony. I even

gained acceptance into a music conservatory. These aren't staggering accomplishments unless you consider the fact that I rarely practiced. If I had
practiced with any amount of regularity, I could have been, as my parents
would have liked me to be, one of those kids who was schlepped to Juilliard on Saturdays. If I had practiced slightly more than that, I could have
gone to Juilliard for college. If I had practiced a lot I could have ended up
in the New York Philharmonic. This is not an exaggeration, merely a moot
point. I didn't practice. I haven't picked up the oboe since my junior year in
college, where, incidentally, I sat first chair in the orchestra even though I
did not practice once the entire time.

I never practiced and yet I always practiced. My memory is always of   8
being unprepared, yet I was forced to sit in the chair for so many hours
that I suspect something else must have been at work, a lack of consciousness about it, an inability to practice on my own. "Practice" was
probably among the top five words spoken in our family, the other four
probably being the names of our family members. Today, almost ten
years since I've practiced, the word has lost the resonance of our usage. I
now think of practice in terms of law or medicine. There is a television
show called *The Practice,* and it seems odd to me that I never associate the
word sprawled across the screen with the word that wove relentlessly
throughout our family discourse. For my entire childhood and adolescence, practicing was an ongoing condition. It was both a given and a
punishment. When we were bad, we practiced. When we were idle, we
practiced. Before dinner and TV and friends coming over and bedtime
and a thousand other things that beckoned with the possibility of taking
place without all that harrowing noise, we practiced. "You have practicing and homework," my mother said every day. In that order. My father
said the same thing without the homework part.

Much of the reason I could never quite get with the oboe–playing pro-   9
gram was that I developed, at a very young age, a deep contempt for the
Music Is My Bag world. Instead of religion, my family had music, and it was
the church against which I rebelled. I had clergy for parents. My father:
professional composer and arranger, keyboard player and trombonist,
brother of a high school band director in Illinois. My mother: pianist and
music educator of the high school production of *Carousel* genre. My own
brother a reluctant Christ figure. A typically restless second child in youth
(he quit piano lessons but later discovered he could play entirely by ear),
my brother recently completed the final mix of a demo CD of songs he
wrote and performed — mid-eighties pop, late Doobie Brothers groove. His
Los Angeles house is littered with Billy Joel and Bruce Hornsby sheet music,
back issues of *Stereo Review,* the liner notes to the digital remastering of John
Williams's score for *Star Wars.* Music is the Bag.

I compose songs in my sleep. I can't do it awake. I'll dream of songwrit-   10
ers singing onstage. I'll hear them perform new songs, songs I've never

heard, songs I therefore must have written. In childhood I never put one thought toward composing a song. It would have been like composing air, creating more of something of which there was already quite enough. Wind players like flutists and saxophonists need as much air as they can get. Oboists are always trying to get rid of air. They calibrate what they need to get the reed to vibrate, end up using even less, and dispense with the rest out the corners of their mouths. It's all about exhaling. On an eighth rest, they're as likely to blow air out as they are to steal a breath. There's always too much air for oboists, too much of everything, too many bars when they're not playing and too many bars where there's hardly anyone playing but them, too many percussion players dropping triangles on the floor, too many violinists playing "Eleanor Rigby" before the rehearsal starts. Orchestras have only two oboists, first chair and second chair, pilot and copilot, though the "co" in this case is, like all "co's," a misnomer. The second oboist is the perpetual backup system, the one on call, the one who jumps in and saves the other when his reed dries up in the middle of a solo, when he misses his cue, when he freezes in panic before trying to hit a high D. I've been first oboist and I've been second oboist and, let me tell you, first is better, but not by much. It's still the oboe. Unlike the gregarious violinist or the congenial cellist, the oboist is a lone wolf. To play the oboe in an orchestra is to complete an obstacle course of solos and duets with the first flutist who, if she is hard-core Music Is My Bag, will refer to herself as a "flautist." Oboe solos dot the great symphonies like land mines, the pizzicati that precede them are drumrolls, the conductor's pointing finger an arrow for the whole audience to see: Here comes the oboe, two bars until the oboe, now, *now*. It's got to be nailed, one flubbed arpeggio, one flat half note, one misplaced pinky in the middle of a run of sixteenth notes, and everyone will hear, *everyone*.

My parents' presence at a high school orchestra concert turned what should have been a routine event into something akin to the finals of the Olympic women's figure skating long program. Even from the blinding, floodlit stage I could practically see them in the audience, clucking at every error, grimacing at anything even slightly out of tune. Afterwards, when the other parents — musically illiterate chumps — were patting their kids on the head and loading the tuba into the station wagon, I would receive my critique. "You were hesitating in the second movement of the Haydn Variations." "You over-anticipated in the berceuse section of the Stravinsky." "Your tone was excellent in the first movement but then your chops ran out." My brother, who was forced for a number of years to play the French horn, was reduced to a screaming fight with our father in the school parking lot, the kind of fight only possible between fathers and sons. He'd bumbled too many notes, played out of tune, committed some treasonous infraction against the family reputation. My father gave him the business on the way out to the car, eliciting the alto curses of a fourteen–year–old, pages of music everywhere, an instrument case slammed on the pavement.

This sort of rebellion was not my style. I cried instead. I cried in the sev- 12 enth grade when the letter telling me I'd been accepted to the North Jersey regional orchestra arrived three days late. I cried in the tenth grade, when I ended up in the All State Band instead of the orchestra. I cried when I thought I'd given a poor recital (never mind that the audience thought I was brilliant—all morons), cried before lessons (under–prepared), cried after lessons (sentenced to a week of reviewing the loathsome F–sharp étude). Mostly I cried during practice drills supervised by my father. These were torture sessions wherein some innocent tooting would send my father racing downstairs from his attic study, screaming "Count, count, you're not *counting!* Jesus Christ!" Out would come a pencil—if not an actual conductor's baton—hitting the music stand, forcing me to repeat the tricky fingerings again and again, speeding up the tempo so I'd be sure to hit each note when we took it back down to real time. These sessions would last for hours, my mouth muscles shaking from atrophy, tears welling up from fatigue and exasperation. If we had a copy of the piano part, my mother would play the accompaniment, and together my parents would bark commands. "Articulate the eighth notes more. More staccato on the tonguing. Don't tap your foot, tap your toe inside your shoe." The postman heard a lot of this. The neighbors heard all of it. After practicing we'd eat dinner, but not before that song—"There's a smile on our face, and it seems to say all the wonderful things . . . " "Good practice session today," my mother would say, dishing out the casserole, WQXR's *Symphony Hall* playing over the kitchen speakers. "Yup, sounding pretty good," my father would say. "How about one more go at it before bed?"

My mother called my oboe a "horn." This infuriated me. "Do you 13 have your horn?" she'd ask every single morning. "Do you need your horn for school today?" She maintained that this terminology was technically correct, that among musicians, a "horn" was anything into which air was blown. My oboe was a $4,000 instrument, high–grade black grenadilla with sterling silver keys. It was no horn. But such semantics are a staple of Music Is My Bag, the overfamiliar stance that reveals a desperate need for subcultural affiliation, the musical equivalent of people in the magazine business who refer to publications like *Glamour* and *Forbes* as "books." As is indicated by the use of "horn," there's a subtly macho quality to Music Is My Bag. The persistent insecurity of musicians, especially classical musicians, fosters a kind of jargon that would be better confined to the military or major league baseball. Cellists talk about rock stops and rosin as though they were comparing canteen belts or brands of glove grease. They have their in–jokes and aphorisms, "The rock stops here," "Eliminate Violins In Our Schools."

I grew up surrounded by phrases like "rattle off that solo," "nail that 14 lick," and "build up your chops." Like acid–washed jeans, "chops" is a word that should only be invoked by rock and roll guitarists but is more often uttered with the flailing, badly timed anti–authority of the high school clarinet player. Like the violinist who plays "Eleanor Rigby" before rehearsal, the clarinet player's relationship to rock and roll maintains its distance. Rock and roll is about sex. It is something unloved by parents and therefore unloved by Music Is My Bag people, who make a vocation of pleasing their parents, of studying trig and volunteering at the hospital and making a run for the student government even though they're well aware they have no chance of winning. Rock and roll is careless and unstudied. It might possibly involve drinking. It most certainly involves dancing. It flies in the face of the central identity of Music Is My Baggers, who chose as their role models those painfully introverted characters from young adult novels—"the klutz," "the bookworm," "the late bloomer." When given a classroom assignment to write about someone who inspires her, Music Is My Bag will write about her grandfather or perhaps Jean–Pierre Rampal.* If the bad–attitude kid in the back row writes about AC/DC's Angus Young, Music Is My Bag will believe in her heart that this student should receive a failing grade. Rock and roll is not, as her parents would say when the junior high drama club puts on a production of *Grease*, "appropriate for this age group." Even in the throes of adolescence, Music Is My Bag will deny adolescence. Even at age sixteen, she will hold her ears when the rock and roll gets loud, saying it ruins her sense of overtones, saying she has sensitive ears. Like a retiree, she will classify the whole genre as nothing but a bunch of noise, though it is likely she is a fan of Yes.

During the years that I was a member of the New Jersey All State Or-   15
chestra I would carpool to rehearsals with the four or so other kids from my town who made All State every year. This involved spending as much as two hours each way in station wagons driven by people's parents and, inevitably, the issue would arise of what music would be played in the car. Among the most talented musicians in school was a freshman who, in addition to being hired by the Boston Symphony Orchestra at age twenty-two, possessed, as a fifteen–year–old, a ripe enthusiasm for the singer Amy Grant. This was back in the mid–1980s when Amy Grant's hits were still relegated to the Christian charts. Our flute-playing carpool–mate loved Amy Grant. Next to Prokofiev and the Hindemith Flute Sonata, Amy Grant occupied the number–one spot in this girl's studious, late-blooming heart. Since her mother, like many parents of Baggers, was devoted solely to her daughter's musical and academic career, she did most of the driving to those boony spots—Upper Chatham High School, Monmouth Regional, Long Branch Middle School. Mile after New Jersey Turnpike mile, we were

---

* **Jean–Pierre Rampal** (1922–2000): the first flutist in history to attract international attention. He began his career in his hometown of Marseilles, France; at the end of his career, he was a firmly established international virtuoso.

serenaded by the wholesome synthesizers of songs like "Saved by Love" and "Wait for the Healing," only to spill out of the car and take no small relief in the sound of twenty–five of New Jersey's best student violinists playing "Eleanor Rigby" before the six–hour rehearsal.

To participate in a six–hour rehearsal of the New Jersey All State 16 Band or Orchestra is to enter a world so permeated by Music Is My Bagdom that it becomes possible to confuse the subculture with an entire species, as if Baggers, like lobsters or ferns, require special conditions in order to thrive. Their ecosystem is the auditorium and the adjacent band room, any space that makes use of risers. To eat lunch and dinner in these venues is to see the accessories of Bagdom tumble from purses, knapsacks, and totes; here more than anyplace are the real McCoys, actual Music Is My Bag *bags*, canvas satchels filled with stereo Walkmen and A.P. math homework and Trapper Keeper notebooks featuring the piano–playing Schroeder from the *Peanuts* comic strip. The dinner break is when I would embark on oboe maintenance, putting the reed in water, swabbing the instrument dry, removing the wads of wax that, during my orthodontic years, I placed over my front teeth to keep the inside of my mouth from bleeding. Just as I had hated the entropy of recess back in my grade–school years, I loathed the dinner breaks at All State rehearsals. To maximize rehearsal time, the wind section often ate separately from the strings, which left me alone with the band types. They'd wolf down their sandwiches and commence with their jam session, a cacophonous white noise of scales, finger exercises, and memorized excerpts from their hometown marching band numbers. During these dinner breaks I'd generally hang with the other oboist. For some reason, this was almost always a tall girl who wore sneakers with corduroy pants and a turtleneck with nothing over it. This is fairly typical Music Is My Bag garb, though oboists have a particular spin on it, a spin characterized more than anything by lack of spin. Given the absence in most classical musicians of a style gene, this is probably a good thing. Oboists don't accessorize. They don't wear buttons on their jackets that say "Oboe Power" or "Who Are You Going to Tune To?"

There's high–end Bagdom and low–end Bagdom, with a lot of room in 17 between. Despite my parents' paramilitary practice regimes, I have to give them credit for being fairly high–end Baggers. There were no piano–key scarves in our house, no "World's Greatest Trombonist" figurines, no plastic tumblers left over from my father's days as director of the Stanford University Marching Band. Such accessories are the mandate of the lowest tier of Music Is My Bag, a stratum whose mascot is P.D.Q. Bach,* whose theme

---

* **P.D.Q. Bach:** Peter Schickele is a famed composer, musician, author, and satirist— but he is probably best known as the man who discovered the "lost works" of fabled genius P.D.Q. Bach, as Schickele publishes many musical compositions under that pseudonym.

song is "Piano Man," and whose regional representative is the kid in high school who plays not only the trumpet but the piano, saxophone, flute, string bass, accordion, and wood block. This kid, considered a wunderkind by his parents and the rest of the band community, plays none of these instruments well, but the fact that he knows so many different sets of fingerings, the fact that he has the potential to earn some college money by performing as a one-man band at the annual state teacher's conference, makes him a hometown hero. He may not be a football player. He may not even gain access to the Ivy League. But in the realm of Music Is My Bag, the kid who plays every instrument, particularly when he can play Billy Joel songs on every instrument, is the Alpha Male.

The flip side of the one-man-band kid are those Music Is My Baggers 18 who are not musicians at all. These are the kids who twirl flags or rifles in the marching band, kids who blast music in their rooms and play not air guitar but air keyboards, their hands fluttering out in front of them, the hand positions not nearly as important as the attendant head motions. This is the essence of Bagdom. It is to take greater pleasure in the reverb than the melody, to love the lunch break more than the rehearsal, the rehearsal more than the performance, the clarinet case more than the clarinet. It is to think nothing of sending away for the deluxe packet of limited-edition memorabilia that is being sold for the low, low price of one's entire personality. It is to let the trinkets do the talking.

I was twenty-one when I stopped playing the oboe. I wish I could 19 come up with a big, dramatic reason why. I wish I could say that I sustained some kind of injury that prevented me from playing (it's hard to imagine what kind of injury could sideline an oboist—a lip strain? Carpal tunnel?) or that I was forced to sell my oboe in order to help a family member in crisis or, better yet, that I suffered a violent attack in which my oboe was used as a weapon against me before being stolen and melted down for artillery. But the truth, I'm ashamed to say, has more to do with what in college I considered to be an exceptionally long walk from my dormitory to the music building, and the fact that I was wrapped up in a lot of stuff that, from my perspective at the time, precluded the nailing of Rachmaninoff licks. Without the prodding of my parents or the structure of a state-run music education program, my oboe career had to run on self-motivation alone—not an abundant resource—and when my senior year started I neither registered for private lessons nor signed up for the orchestra, dodging countless calls from the director imploring me to reassume my chair.

Since then, I haven't set foot in a rehearsal room, put together a fold- 20 ing music stand, fussed with a reed, marked up music, practiced scales, tuned an orchestra or performed any of the countless activities that had dominated my existence up until that point. There are moments every now and then when I'll hear the oboe-dominated tenth movement of the Bach *Mass in B Minor* or the berceuse section of Stravinsky's *Firebird* and long to find a workable reed and pick up the instrument again. But then I imagine how terrible I'll sound after eight dormant years and put the whole idea out of my mind before I start to feel sad about it. I can still smell the musty odor of the inside of my oboe case, the old–ladyish whiff of the velvet lining and the tubes of cork grease and the damp fabric of the key pads. Unlike the computer on which I now work, my oboe had the sense of being an ancient thing. Brittle and creaky, it was vulnerable when handled by strangers. It needed to be packed up tight, dried out in just the right places, kept away from the heat and cold and from anyone too stupid to confuse it with a clarinet.

What I really miss about the oboe is having my hands on it. I could   21 come at that instrument from any direction or any angle and know every indentation on every key, every spot that leaked air, every nick on every square inch of wood. When enough years go by, the corporeal qualities of an instrument become as familiar to its player as, I imagine, those of a long–standing lover. Knowing precisely how the weight of the oboe was distributed between my right thumb and left wrist, knowing, above all, that the weight would feel the same way every time, every day, for every year that I played, was a feeling akin to having ten years of knowledge about the curve of someone's back. Since I stopped playing the oboe, I haven't had the privilege of that kind of familiarity. That's not an exaggeration, merely a moot point.

Reading Closely

1. What might Daum's purpose be in writing about growing up with music? In your opinion, what is particularly fresh or provocative about her approach to this topic?

2. Daum writes at length about the Music Is My Bag culture. But she also writes about other "Bag" cultures. **Working with two or three class–mates,** describe these other cultures, listing the details of each of them that Daum provides and adding ones of your own. How do these Bag cultures differ? What do they have in common?

3. Condense Daum's essay into one paragraph. **Working with a class–mate,** trade paragraphs to compare what each of you thought was the most important information in the essay. Then condense your partner's paragraph into one sentence. Ask your partner if he or she agrees with your one-sentence condensation; if not, make any necessary adjust–ments. Be prepared to read your one-sentence condensations to the rest of the class.

Considering Larger Issues

1. "Music Is My Bag" is filled with descriptive details. Mark the descriptive passage that most affected you. Then write for five minutes about the reasons this passage affected you.

2. Look at the visual of the junior high orchestra. Is music the bag of all of these children or only some of them? What does the visual tell you about children's willingness to participate in a "bag" culture?

3. **COMBINING METHODS.** How does Daum *define* the phrase "Music Is My Bag"? According to her, what constitutes the idea of "bagness," and why do people become part of a "Bag" culture? Prepare to discuss your definitions with the rest of the class.

Thinking about Language

1. Using the context of the essay and your dictionary, define any of the following terms that are unfamiliar to you. Be prepared to share your answers with the rest of the class.

seminal (1)	perennial (4)	bars (10)
propensity (1)	benign (5)	gregarious (10)
tacit (2)	narcissistic (6)	congenial (10)
euphoria (2)	embouchure (6)	genre (14)
akin to (3)	mediocre (7)	boony (15)
harmonizing (3)	schlepped (7)	venues (16)

2. What specific descriptive language does Daum use to characterize the Music Is My Bag culture?

3. Which words or phrases could apply only to music culture and no other?

4. Which passages in this essay seem to be developed with objective details and denotative language? Which ones are developed with subjective details and connotative language? Why do you think Daum uses objective and subjective language in the way that she does?

Writing Your Own Descriptions

1. Draft a three- to four-page essay in which you describe in rich detail the Bag culture to which you (or maybe someone in your family) belong. Be sure to include descriptive details about how and why you joined that particular Bag. If you left that Bag, provide details for that change as well. Your overall purpose will be to inform. If possible, try to appeal to all five senses in your description. Refer to "Checking Over Descriptive Writing" on p. 61 as you draft and revise.

2. Daum writes about her frustrations as a Music Is My Bag young person. What evidence in her essay can you locate that accounts for her frustrations? for her satisfaction? What other reasons might account for her different reactions? Write a three- to four-page essay about a growing–up frustration of your own, perhaps one involving obeying, trying to obey, or disobeying your parents' rules. Describe your frustration, using both objective and subjective details. If a short narrative—or two—will help bring your description to life, don't hesitate to include it. **Consider working with another classmate** as you draft and revise, referring to "Checking Over Descriptive Writing" on p. 61.

ANNIE DILLARD
The Deer at Providencia

● Pittsburgh native Annie Dillard (b. 1945) has written poetry, essays, fiction, criticism, and a memoir, including the Pulitzer Prize–winning *Pilgrim at Tinker Creek* (1975), *Living by Fiction* (1982), *Teaching a Stone to Talk* (1982), and *An American Childhood* (1987). "The Deer at Providencia," taken from *Teaching a Stone to Talk*, exemplifies some of Dillard's best writing: it is an artfully informative description of a part of the natural world. As you read the essay, consider not only how Dillard uses description to dominate her informative piece but also how — and to what effect — she employs narration and comparison and contrast to convey her ideas about different kinds of suffering and responses to suffering.

> **Preview** Before you read the entire essay, just read the first paragraph and then write for five minutes about how it seems to prepare you for what will follow.

There were four of us North Americans in the jungle, in the Ecuadorian 1 jungle on the banks of the Napo River in the Amazon watershed. The other three North Americans were metropolitan men. We stayed in tents in one riverside village, and visited others. At the village called Providencia we saw a sight which moved us, and which shocked the men.

The first thing we saw when we climbed the riverbank to the village of 2 Providencia was the deer. It was roped to a tree on the grass clearing near the thatch shelter where we would eat lunch.

The deer was small, about the size of a whitetail fawn, but appar- 3 ently full-grown. It had a rope around its neck and three feet caught in the rope. Someone said that the dogs had caught it that morning and the villagers were going to cook and eat it that night.

This clearing lay at the edge of the little thatched hut village. We 4 could see the villagers going about their business, scattering feed corn for hens about their houses, and wandering down paths to the river to bathe. The village headman was our host; he stood beside us as we watched the deer struggle. Several village boys were interested in the deer; they formed part of the circle we made around it in the clearing. So also did four businessmen from Quito who were attempting to guide us around the jungle. Few of the very different people standing in this circle had a common language. We watched the deer, and no one said much.

The deer lay on its side at the rope's very end, so the rope lacked slack to 5 let it rest its head in the dust. It was "pretty," delicate of bone like all deer, and thin-skinned for the tropics. Its skin looked virtually hairless, in fact, and almost translucent, like a membrane. Its neck was no thicker than

my wrist; it was rubbed open on the rope, and gashed. Trying to paw it–
self free of the rope, the deer had scratched its own neck with its hooves.
The raw underside of its neck showed red stripes and some bruises
bleeding inside the muscles. Now three of its feet were hooked in the
rope under its jaw. It could not stand, of course, on one leg, so it could
not move to slacken the rope and ease the pull on its throat and enable
it to rest its head.

Repeatedly the deer paused, motionless, its eyes veiled, with only its   6
rib cage in motion, and its breaths the only sound. Then, after I would
think, "It has given up; now it will die," it would heave. The rope
twanged; the tree leaves clattered; the deer's free foot beat the ground.
We stepped back and held our breaths. It thrashed, kicking, but only one
leg moved; the other three legs tightened inside the rope's loop. Its hip
jerked; its spine shook. Its eyes rolled; its tongue, thick with spittle,
pushed in and out. Then it would rest again. We watched this for fifteen
minutes.

Once three young native boys charged in, released its trapped legs,   7
and jumped back to the circle of people. But instantly the deer scratched
up its neck with its hooves and snared its forelegs in the rope again. It
was easy to imagine a third and then a fourth leg soon stuck, like Brer
Rabbit and the Tar Baby.

We watched the deer from the circle, and then we drifted on to lunch.   8
Our palm–roofed shelter stood on a grassy promontory from which we
could see the deer tied to the tree, pigs and hens walking under village
houses, and black–and–white cattle standing in the river. There was even
a breeze.

Lunch, which was the second and better lunch we had that day, was hot   9
and fried. There was a big fish called *doncella*, a kind of catfish, dipped
whole in corn flour and beaten egg, then deep fried. With our fingers we
pulled soft fragments of it from its sides to our plates, and ate; it was delicate fish–flesh, fresh and mild. Someone found the roe, and I ate of that
too — it was fat and stronger, like egg yolk, naturally enough, and warm.

There was also a stew of meat in shreds with rice and pale brown   10
gravy. I had asked what kind of deer it was tied to the tree; Pepe had
answered in Spanish, "*Gama.*" Now they told us this was *gama* too, stewed.
I suspect the word means merely game or venison. At any rate, I heard
that the village dogs had cornered another deer just yesterday, and it
was this deer which we were now eating in full sight of the whole article.
It was good. I was surprised at its tenderness. But it is a fact that high
levels of lactic acid, which builds up in muscle tissues during exertion,
tenderizes.

After the fish and meat we ate bananas fried in chunks and served   11
on a tray; they were sweet and full of flavor. I felt terrific. My shirt was

wet and cool from swimming; I had had a night's sleep, two decent walks, three meals, and a swim—everything tasted good. From time to time each one of us, separately, would look beyond our shaded roof to the sunny spot where the deer was still convulsing in the dust. Our meal completed, we walked around the deer and back to the boats.

That night I learned that while we were watching the deer, the others   12
were watching me.

　　We four North Americans grew close in the jungle in a way that was   13
not the usual artificial intimacy of travelers. We liked each other. We stayed up all that night talking, murmuring, as though we rocked on hammocks slung above time. The others were from big cities: New York, Washington, Boston. They all said that I had no expression on my face when I was watching the deer—or at any rate, not the expression they expected.

　　They had looked to see how I, the only woman, and the youngest,   14
was taking the sight of the deer's struggles. I looked detached, apparently, or hard, or calm, or focused, still. I don't know. I was thinking. I remember feeling very old and energetic. I could say like Thoreau that I have traveled widely in Roanoke, Virginia. I have thought a great deal about carnivorousness; I eat meat. These things are not issues; they are mysteries.

Gentlemen of the city, what surprises you? That there is suffering here, or   15
that I know it?

　　We lay in the tent and talked. "If it had been my wife," one man said   16
with special vigor, amazed, "she wouldn't have cared *what* was going on; she would have dropped *everything* right at that moment and gone in the village from here to there to there, she would not have *stopped* until that animal was out of its suffering one way or another. She couldn't *bear* to see a creature in agony like that."

　　I nodded.   17

Now I am home. When I wake I comb my hair before the mirror above   18
my dresser. Every morning for the past two years I have seen in that mirror, beside my sleep-softened face, the blackened face of a burnt man. It is a wire-service photograph clipped from a newspaper and taped to my mirror. The caption reads: "Alan McDonald in Miami hospital bed." All you can see in the photograph is a smudged triangle of face from his eyelids to his lower lip; the rest is bandages. You cannot see the expression in his eyes; the bandages shade them.

　　The story, headed MAN BURNED FOR SECOND TIME, begins: 19

　　　"Why does God hate me?" Alan McDonald asked from his hospital bed.

"When the gunpowder went off, I couldn't believe it," he said. "I just couldn't believe it. I said, 'No, God couldn't do this to me again.' "

He was in a burn ward in Miami, in serious condition. I do not even know if he lived. I wrote him a letter at the time, cringing.

He had been burned before, thirteen years previously, by flaming 20 gasoline. For years he had been having his body restored and his face re-made in dozens of operations. He had been a boy, and then a burnt boy. He had already been stunned by what could happen, by how life could veer.

Once I read that people who survive bad burns tend to go crazy; 21 they have a very high suicide rate. Medicine cannot ease their pain; drugs just leak away, soaking the sheets, because there is no skin to hold them in. The people just lie there and weep. Later they kill themselves. They had not known, before they were burned, that the world included such suffering, that life could permit them personally such pain.

This time a bowl of gunpowder had exploded on McDonald.   22

"I didn't realize what had happened at first," he recounted. "And then I heard that sound from 13 years ago. I was burning. I rolled to put the fire out and I thought, 'Oh God, not again.'

"If my friend hadn't been there, I would have jumped into a canal with a rock around my neck."

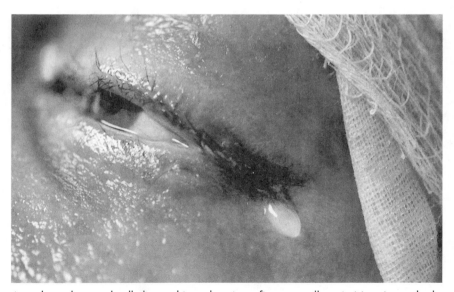

A student who was badly burned in a dormitory fire at a college in New Jersey looks out at the world through his bandages. This photograph was awarded a Pulitzer Prize.

His wife concludes the piece, "Man, it just isn't fair."

I read the whole clipping again every morning. This is the Big Time here,   23
every minute of it. Will someone please explain to Alan McDonald in his
dignity, to the deer at Providencia in his dignity, what is going on? And
mail me the carbon.

When we walked by the deer at Providencia for the last time, I said to Pepe,   24
with a pitying glance at the deer, *"Pobrecito"* — "poor little thing." But I was
trying out Spanish. I knew at the time it was a ridiculous thing to say.

Reading Closely

1. Dillard describes her fine jungle meal of fish, roe, deer, and fried bananas, even as she reminds her readers of the suffering deer. What impression do these intermixed details of taste and suffering convey to
   you?
2. Why does Dillard mention the men's reactions to her reaction to the
   deer? What is the point of these comparisons? How does the essay benefit from them? Prepare two sentences to report to the rest of the class.
3. Specifically, how does the visual of the burn victim enhance Dillard's
   essay? What passages become more vivid when compared to the visual?

Considering Larger Issues

1. Who might be the audience for this essay? In other words, what kind of
   person likes to read essays about travel and nature? In what ways does
   Dillard appeal to that audience in her essay?
2. **Working with two or three classmates,** discuss why Dillard writes
   about a captured deer and a burn victim. What is her purpose in discussing
   these two figures one after the other? Condense your conversation into two
   sentences, and report on your discussion to the rest of the class.
3. COMBINING METHODS. Underline the descriptive passages in the essay,
   bracket the *narrative* passages, and star any passages that set up a *comparison and contrast.* You may be able to work paragraph by paragraph. Prepare to discuss your findings with the rest of the class.
4. COMBINING METHODS. What purposes do the *narrative* and *comparison-and-
   contrast* passages help to fulfill? How is the larger informative purpose of
   the essay enhanced by these short narratives and comparisons?

Thinking about Language

1. Using the context of the essay and your dictionary, define any of the following terms that are unfamiliar to you. Be prepared to share your answers with the rest of the class.

metropolitan (1)   membrane (5)   lactic acid (10)
thatch (2)   promontory (8)   carnivorousness (14)
translucent (5)   roe (9)   *pobrecito* (24)

2. What specific descriptive language does Dillard use to evoke the sense of suffering? Which suffering seems more painful to you as a reader: that of the soon–to–be–butchered deer or of the burn victim? Why?

3. Which passages in this essay seem to be developed with objective details and denotative language? Which ones are developed with subjective details and connotative language? Why do you think Dillard uses objective and subjective language in the way that she does?

Writing Your Own Descriptions

1. Draft a three- to four–page essay in which you describe in rich detail one of your favorite meals, punctuating that description with a narration of how your meal came into being (how it met its death, was harvested, was prepared by another person, or was selected/purchased). You may want to describe the meal in one draft and then narrate its origins in another draft before you begin weaving the two parts of the essay together. The overall purpose is to demonstrate how much or how little thought we give to the ways our meals get to our plates. Be sure to appeal to the five senses throughout. Also, refer to "Checking Over Descriptive Writing" on p. 61.

2. Dillard writes about her apparently detached reaction to the suffering deer and her stronger, almost unaccountable reaction to Alan McDonald's suffering. What evidence in the text can you find that accounts for her different reactions? What else might account for them? Write a three- to four–page essay about an experience of your own that is comparable to Dillard's in either watching the deer or reading about McDonald. Describe your experience using both objective and subjective details. Use narration as necessary to tell your story, and compare how you felt at the time with how you currently feel about that situation. Have your feelings evolved, or have they remained unchanged? As you draft and revise, refer to "Checking Over Descriptive Writing" on p. 61.

JULIA ALVAREZ

Snow

Born in New York City, Julia Alvarez (b. 1950) was taken back to her parents' native Dominican Republic before she was one month old. There the family lived under the dictatorship of General Rafael Trujillo until they were forced to flee to the United States for good. At age 13 Alvarez was sent to a private boarding school for girls, where she repeatedly failed her English classes — at the same time that she was falling in love with the power of language and beginning to write seriously. After high school she attended Connecticut College, winning the school's poetry prize, and then transferred to Middlebury College, where she earned a B.A. Since earning her master of fine arts degree at Syracuse University in 1975, Alvarez has taught schoolchildren in Kentucky, bilingual students in Delaware, and senior citizens in North Carolina. She has also taught English at Phillips Andover Academy, the University of Vermont, and the University of Illinois. At present she is the writer-in-residence in the English department at her alma mater, Middlebury College.

Alvarez has published two collections of poetry, *Homecoming* (1984) and *The Other Side* (1995), and an essay collection, *Something to Declare* (1998), but she's best known for her novels, *How the Garcia Girls Lost Their Accents* (1991), *In the Name of the Butterflies* (1994), *Yo!* (1997), *In the Name of Salomé* (2000), and *A Cafecito Story* (2001). "Snow" is excerpted from *How the Garcia Girls Lost Their Accents.*

Preview   Can you think back to a grade school experience when you needed special attention from the teacher? Did you get the attention you needed? How did you feel about receiving — or not receiving — the attention?

Our first year in New York we rented a small apartment with a Catholic 1
school nearby, taught by the Sisters of Charity, hefty women in long
black gowns and bonnets that made them look peculiar, like dolls in
mourning. I liked them a lot, especially my grandmotherly fourth grade
teacher, Sister Zoe. I had a lovely name, she said, and she had me teach
the whole class how to pronounce it. *Yo-lan-da.* As the only immigrant in
my class, I was put in a special seat in the first row by the window, apart
from the other children so that Sister Zoe could tutor me without disturbing them. Slowly, she enunciated the new words I was to repeat:
laundromat, cornflakes, subway, snow.

Soon I picked up enough English to understand holocaust was in the 2
air. Sister Zoe explained to a wide-eyed classroom what was happening
in Cuba. Russian missiles were being assembled, trained supposedly on
New York City. President Kennedy, looking worried too, was on the television at home, explaining we might have to go to war against the Communists. At school, we had air-raid drills: an ominous bell would go off
and we'd file into the hall, fall to the floor, cover our heads with our
coats, and imagine our hair falling out, the bones in our arms going soft.

At home, Mami and my sisters and I said a rosary for world peace. I heard new vocabulary: *nuclear bomb, radioactive fallout, bomb shelter.* Sister Zoe explained how it would happen. She drew a picture of a mushroom on the blackboard and dotted a flurry of chalkmarks for the dusty fallout that would kill us all.

The months grew cold, November, December. It was dark when I got   3 up in the morning, frosty when I followed my breath to school. One morning as I sat at my desk daydreaming out the window, I saw dots in the air like the ones Sister Zoe had drawn—random at first, then lots and lots. I shrieked, "Bomb! Bomb!" Sister Zoe jerked around, her full black skirt ballooning as she hurried to my side. A few girls began to cry.

But then Sister Zoe's shocked look faded. "Why, Yolanda dear, that's   4 snow!" She laughed. "Snow."

"Snow," I repeated. I looked out the window warily. All my life I had   5 heard about the white crystals that fell out of American skies in the winter. From my desk I watched the fine powder dust the sidewalk and parked cars below. Each flake was different, Sister Zoe said, like a person, irreplaceable and beautiful.

Reading Closely

1. Besides the English words, what other details does Alvarez include that indicate how distinctive U.S. culture is or was at the time of the story?

2. Take a few minutes to list all the new things that Yolanda must learn at school. Then write for a few minutes about how she might relate these new things to the knowledge she brought with her from the Dominican Republic and the Catholic Church.

3. The title of this story is "Snow." But is that what the story is actually about? Write one paragraph summarizing the story. **Trade paragraphs with a classmate,** and annotate your partner's paragraph with information from the story that you've gleaned but your partner hasn't. Then work together to prepare a brief, unified report for the rest of the class or for a small group.

4. What is Alvarez's purpose in this essay?

Considering Larger Issues

1. Does Alvarez's story have a one-sentence thesis? If so, what is it? If her thesis is implied, write out what it might be.

2. Who is Alvarez's audience for this story? How might it fit within a novel entitled *How the Garcia Girls Lost Their Accents?*

3. What is the dominant impression of this story? Mark the specific descriptive details that enhance or fulfill this dominant impression. Which words, phrases, or events in the story seem to be dated at around 1962?

How does this dating enhance or detract from the dominant impression Alvarez wants to make? Be prepared to share your answers with the rest of the class.

4. **COMBINING METHODS.** How does Alvarez use *narration* to enhance her description? Which passages are more concerned with telling a story than with describing?

Thinking about Language

1. Define the following terms. You may refer to their context in the essay or your dictionary. Be prepared to share your answers with the rest of the class.

hefty (1)	holocaust (2)	fallout (2)
immigrant (1)	ominous (2)	irreplaceable (5)
enunciated (1)	rosary (2)	

2. The very last sentence is a simile, a comparison: "Each flake was different, . . . like a person, irreplaceable and beautiful." What is the effect of this simile at the end of the story? Do you think it makes the ending effective? Or does it cheapen the story?

Writing Your Own Descriptions

1. Think about one of your former teachers who was exceptionally effective with a student who was, in one way or another (physical, mental, emotional, cultural), different from the rest of the class. The difference may or may not have been obvious; the student may or may not have been you. Using "Snow" as a model and writing from the student's point of view, draft a two- to three-page description of how the teacher treated the student and how the student responded.

   As you begin drafting this essay, consider the various ways you might choose to arrange the information. List descriptive details, keeping in mind the dominant impression that all the details suggest. What aspects of the dominant impression can you develop? Can you arrange those aspects from least to most important? What is the chronology of the details? Which variation on a spatial arrangement would best serve your purpose? Write out a thesis statement. As you draft, be sure to refer to the guidelines for checking over descriptive writing on p. 61.

2. **Working with a classmate,** trade your drafts describing a teacher. Write out the dominant impression of your classmate's essay, underlining words or phrases that bring the impression into sharp focus. Number the descriptive details in the order your classmate has placed them, and decide if rearranging them would strengthen the overall effect. Then write out what the purpose of the essay seems to be, discussing how the arrangement of details and the effectiveness of the thesis statement help fulfill that purpose. After the two of you have worked together, revise your own essay, referring to the guidelines for checking over descriptive writing on p. 61.

BARRIE JEAN BORICH

What Kind of King

Barrie Jean Borich (b. 1959) has been awarded many literary prizes for her prose and poetry, which have been published in the books *Restoring the Color of Roses* (1993) and *My Lesbian Husband: Landscapes of a Marriage* (1999) as well as in literary journals such as *The Ruminator Review, The Gettysburg Review, 13th Moon, The Greenfield Review, Sinister Wisdom,* and *Sing Heavenly Muse!* Borich currently teaches creative writing and related courses at Hamline University. She lives with her partner, Linnea Stenson, in Minneapolis. "What Kind of King" first appeared in a 1999 issue of *The Gettysburg Review.*

Preview   Do you have a strong childhood memory of a couple who were different from the couples you knew best?

We are standing in J.C. Penney's men's department when I realize what   1
sort of king I have married. She is holding up ties, one with fluorescent triangles and intersecting lines, a pop art geometry assignment, the other a delicate Victorian print with inlaid roses that shimmer under the too-white department store lights.

"I'm leaning toward this one," Linnea says, lifting up the geometry   2
lesson. The harsh lights above her head highlight the gray in her hair. We are surrounded here by the base elements needed to conjure up what is commonly called a man — hangers hung with navy blue, forest green, and magnet gray suits and the caramel brown and unadorned black leather of men's accessories under glass. Paracelsus, who inspired those Renaissance alchemists who wanted to cure the world with the medicine of transformation, declared that *to conjure* meant "to observe anything rightly, to learn and understand what it is." Linnea conjures herself be-tween the neat department store racks, and I am suddenly aware that for some time now she has been buying all of her clothes in the men's de-partment, even her classic black wing tips. Even her white tube socks with the red or green stripe along the top. Even the silk boxers she sleeps in, or wears under her clothes on special occasions. Even her everyday underwear, the bright red, green, and blue bikini briefs that come in a clear plastic tube, tagged with a color photograph of a hard-jawed man of northern European descent, thick, blond hair on his chest, a long, muscled swimmer's body.

I wonder what I am to understand about our bodies when I observe   3
the two of us. I look at myself, my heavy eyeliner and mauve lipstick, a silk scarf tied around my throat that matches the leopard print of my gloves. Under my shirt I wear a satin underwire bra. I look at Linnea, noticing that the only items she buys outside of the men's department are her plain cot-ton and lycra sports bras, the kind designed to hold the breasts still and out

of the way. They are more comfortable than the Ace bandages women passing as men once used to bind their breasts, but with similar effect, the aim
to draw attention away from the possibility of a bust line, never to lift and
separate. In the days before gay liberation, women could be arrested,
charged with transvestism, for wearing fewer than three articles of
women's clothing. On any day of the week, Linnea does not pass that test.
Friends ask me why it matters what any of us wear. Our clothes, they say,
are just the facile presentation of our surfaces. The real person is within,
contained in the intangible soul. I want to agree, and then I find myself
daydreaming about a leopard print dress of silk georgette I saw in a mail-
order catalog, or I watch Linnea, a woman with a Ph.D. in literature, her face
pursed in concentration as she tries to choose between two silk neckties
stretched across her outstretched palms, and I feel certain there is something more than a surface at stake.

Here at J.C. Penney's, among the racks and cabinets of what is called   4
men's clothing, I can imagine Linnea in another time and place. She has
an unremarkable singing voice, but is a fine dancer. She has been known
to pull off a terrific lip synch and, unlike me, who has always had a hard
time talking to strangers and who has never been able to swallow just
one of anything intoxicating, Linnea is a model social drinker and can
strike up a conversation with almost anybody. She would be great working in any kind of watering hole. She could have easily been one of the
butches who worked as drag king impresarios in the mob–run show bars
in New York, the Village, in the 1940s. She would be elegant on stage in a
fine tailored tux, her hair cut short just as it is now, but slicked back
smooth with Brylcream or Rose's Butch Wax. She would change her
name for the stage to Lenny, or maybe Johnny, after her Italian grandfather from Hell's Kitchen, a gentle man tattooed from head to ankle. In
the Village drag shows, Johnny/Linnea would be the king with the ap-
proachable face, handsome in her command of the gentlemanly arts, the
mystery date all the ladies dream of, their faces lit amber in the boozy
candlelight, Johnny/Linnea waltzing out before the bare–bulbed foot-
lights, just as airborne as Kelly* or Astaire,* escorting Dietrich* in a sea-
blue sheath, dipping a reluctant Bette Davis* or twirling a taffeta–clad
Ginger Rogers* under her arm.

---

* **Gene Kelly** (1912–1996): Hollywood's most masculine song–and–dance man, best
known for his work in *Singin' in the Rain.*

* **Fred Astaire** (1899–1987): a sophisticated and debonair dancer and actor, most
famous for his dancing partnership with wholesome yet glamorous ***Ginger Rogers**
(1911–1995).

* **Marlene Dietrich** (1901–1992): German–born star of U.S. stage and screen, whose
stunning beauty had bisexual appeal.

* **Bette Davis** (1908–1989): a leading lady of Hollywood, known for her portrayal of
strong and complex characters — and for her memorable eyes.

Marlene Dietrich.

But what is it I see when I conjure up the image of Linnea on a drag   5
king stage? The old European fairy tales say the kings are the ones above
all the rest, the rulers of countries and people, but there are kings of
property and also those who possess a kingdom of self-knowledge, the
low-rent regents of self-rule who have always known who they are. A
drag king is no one's boss, an illusionary monarch, a magician with the
alchemist's amber light in her eyes. Some kinds of kings are easy to see—
the military leaders, the oil barons, the presidents, prime ministers, and
prom kings. There's the King of Pop, the King of Rock, the Elvis imper-
sonators swinging their hips in their beaded white jumpsuits. There's the
cartoon king selling fast-food burgers, King Kong scaling the Empire
State Building again, the terrified lion wailing all the way to Oz, "If I were
the king of the forrrrrrrest." There's the King of the Road, the King of
Kings, the King's English. There's Linnea and my king-sized King Koil
mattress. There's that merry old soul King Cole. There's King Midas, the
King of the Hill, the King of Swing, and the Customer is King. I wonder
what, if anything, this catalog of kings has in common with Linnea in her
two-toned wing tips and creased trousers. Does she share some qualities

with the kingly crested birds, the kingfisher, the ruby crowned kinglet? Is she the chessboard king? The laminated paper King of Hearts, ruler of the subconscious? The King of Pentacles, protector against evil spirits, a reliable husband but also a patriarch? What I see is the everyday checkerboard king, the player who has made it, panting, all the way to the other side of the board and now can move in whatever direction she chooses. So she does. She is a woman who wears men's clothes, except they aren't men's clothes to her, just her clothes, the clothes she likes.

At J.C. Penney's she hands me the geometry lesson tie. I move in, squint 6
to focus, then hold it back at arm's length again. "No," I tell her. "It's too awful. It hurts my eyes."

I hand it back to Linnea, who falls away from me in a long sigh. "So 7
you really hate it?"

Behind the glass counter a thin-boned woman clerk watches our ex- 8
change, a steady smile on her orangy lips. This Penney's is in a suburban shopping mall. I can't tell if she knows what kind of king her customer is, won't know unless she says the words, *thank you sir* or *thank you ma'am*. I have yet to meet a lesbian who doesn't recognize Linnea as one of her own kind, but straight people often address her as a man, and when we walk through the gay cruising zones of Minneapolis, Chicago, San Francisco, I watch the eyes of gay men fall from her face to her crotch and back up to her eyes, with just a fast glance toward me to wonder, I can only suppose, if I am his sister, his fag hag, or his wife of convenience. What people see depends on the context, on what they want to see, on what they are afraid to see.

I think of an old friend of mine, a woman proud to show off her un- 9
shaved legs, "untraditional beauty," she called it, wearing short striped skirts with big Doc Marten boots. She put up with every kind of heckling for years, but it was a department store clerk who finally did her in. One day, walking through a downtown Minneapolis store (with so many gay male employees some departments might be mistaken for an exclusive men's club) my friend passed by a young woman working behind the polished glass cosmetic case. The woman had thin tweaked eyebrows, pores smothered under foundation cream, and a twitch, some violent itch to spit at a queer. She leaned over the glistening glass and actually shouted: "Look. A transvestite!"

My friend's breasts were not bound. She was a woman wearing 10
many more than three pieces of women's clothing, despite her way of walking, in the long gait she learned in the military—unisex boots, yes, but also Hanes Her Way panties, a crop top bra, a black-and-white flared miniskirt, a black scoop-necked top from the junior women's department, slouch socks from women's hosiery, red sunglasses from the women's wall of the optical shop. Her furry legs, her soldier stride, her British made punk-boy boots—do three male props make her a

masquerading woman? Would she be arrested? My friend stopped dead and said simply, "I'm a lesbian," then continued on her way. When she got home she called the store to complain. But the skin around her eyes was too pale when she told me the story. She believed in being visible, in being out of the closet even under bleach bright department store lights, but this was too much exposure, a bad sunburn. Sometimes you have to cover up. The next day she shaved.

In fairy tales it is common for a king to come upon his bride in dis-   11 guise, masquerading as a beggar, a frog, a swan. The night I started falling for Linnea, I was the house manager for a lesbian theater, and she was a volunteer usher. We were still in our mid–twenties, and it was Saturday night. She was wearing a gray tuxedo with full tails and black velvet trim. I was wearing a little Jackie O suit—narrow skirt, bolero length jacket—made from a black knit fabric with a sunspot design sewn in with glittering amber thread. We had run into each other before—at parties, at the grocery store. We had never been unattached at the same time until now, but I had been watching her, been having fleeting daydreams of leaning into her embrace. I had warned friends not to date her first. When we talked I felt jolted into a full habitation of my body, surrounded by a bell of amber sunset, my skin glowing the color of that resin gem said to cure all ailments of the flesh.

That night in the theater there was an elemental pull between us. I   12 couldn't keep myself from touching her elbow, her shoulder, her collar. When she offered to help me set up the box office, I accepted, but it was slow going. We kept stopping and staring, watching each other's faces, a flimsy aluminum card table or a battered steel cash box floating like a Ouija board between us, until we both just laughed. I laughed because it was ridiculous—we had work to do, I had to find something to cover the table, had to sell tickets, had to ignore her. She laughed, she told me later, because she thought I was so pretty in my Jackie O suit.

This night was the last in a series of shows I had been working on   13 for over two years, with all of my closest friends, a group of lesbian actors, writers, and techies who had stumbled together through so much bad gossip, so many misbegotten love affairs, we needed to hire a professional mediator before we could finish what we had begun. My plan was to creep up to the front to watch this last show up close, but when we stood at the back of the auditorium as the house lights dimmed, Linnea let one arm fall over my shoulders and whispered, "This is it." She meant the show, the end of something, but I heard more. *This is it*: the next part of my life was beginning. In that moment of total darkness before the stage lights came up, I leaned back into her, that golden brown bell descending again, my muscles falling limp as she held me up. Had she had the nerve to keep her arm flung across my shoulders, I would have stayed by her side, eyes closed, magnetized, ignoring the show until the house lights came back up again. But she pulled her arm away, and I was

muscle and bone again, still hovering near but too shy to touch, wondering when we would really get together.

The next time I saw her was at an actual masquerade. Linnea was Patsy   14
Cline, the crowd favorite of the women's lip-synch show at Sappho's
Lounge, Tuesday nights when a downtown gay drag stage was trans-
formed into a lesbian dance bar. That night's performance also featured a
Janis Joplin in a floppy felt hat, limp blond hair, patched jeans, and a tie-
dyed T-shirt, who dropped hard to her knees at the climax of "Take it.
Take another little piece of my heart." There was a short, square, fair-
skinned woman in a plain black tux and sand-colored crew cut, Whitney
Houston's polar opposite, who leaned into the words of "The Greatest
Love of All" so earnestly she nearly knocked the unattached mike off the
four-foot-tall stage. Two other women wore vintage black dresses and
bright bleached hair—one a big girl, over six feet, the other short and
thin-waisted—and performed a number in which Doris Day sang a duet
with herself. Another woman squinted without her glasses and wore a
flouncy white Ginger Rogers gown as she spun around the stage like a
folk dancer to the tune of "Fernando's Hideaway." The sheer hem of her
dress fluttered like a flock of magician's doves.

   I didn't see Linnea until she stepped between the glittering tinsel   15
curtain strings. She wore a ruffled red dress that cinched tight around the
waist then belled out to her knees, a plain brown wig that had been set
in curlers and ratted, three-inch heels, and lipstick a brighter red than
the dress. She was perfect, a Patsy Cline concentrate, a refracted and am-
plified twin, in the same way any gender illusionist is so much more
than the real Judy Garland or Diana Ross or Barbra Streisand could ever
be. I had never seen anything like it before, a woman impersonating a
drag queen. When Patsy/Linnea twisted her hips while mouthing "I Fall
to Pieces" through red lips, into an unwired mike, all the girls in the audience screamed, and I fell a little further into fascination.

   But when I approached her after the show to gush over her perform-   16
ance, I was confused to find nothing between us but dead air. Soon,
however, I began to understand: she couldn't recognize me from inside
her disguise. "I *was* Patsy Cline," she told me later. "Linnea wasn't there,
couldn't be there, inside those clothes." Surrounded by the red bar fog
and the hot thump from the DJ's speakers, she smiled at me politely with
red lips that seemed to throb too in the pulsing light. A backstage star
nodding generously to a subject fan. I was dizzy with deprivation, the
molecules of my body pulling, scattering, spinning, but unacknowledged,
uncaught. In the old European stories, the king rescues the soiled queen-
to-be, curled up like a feral cat in front of a cold hearth, or redeems the
selfish princess who only reluctantly shares her dinner with the croaking
frog, her unrecognized lover. But I couldn't wait for Linnea to recognize
me. I needed to make a move; I had to conjure my king.

I knew I was going to see Linnea at a party soon after, so I planned 17
my wardrobe carefully. I chose an old pair of jeans, dyed green, the
knees worn through, my sex-catching clothes. Ass-snug and knee-
revealing, the pants had belonged to a woman I went out with only a
few times. I borrowed them one night after she and I were soaked in a
thunderstorm during a long walk around a dark city lake. She was pretty
enough to have been a high school prom queen. I had never been involved with such a girlie-girl before then; all my former lovers tended to
live a few degrees closer to the guy side of the scale. Walking with her
was a bit like wandering in a mirror — not that we looked so much alike.
She was shorter, had smoother features, fuller breasts, no ethnic nose, no
south Chicago accent. The similarity was from a deeper place, as if we
were broadcasting from the same pole. This woman and I went for lots of
long walks, and I began to feel like an image from those soft-focus greeting cards you see in the drug store, two women in Victorian sheaths and
heavy streams of hair, riding a bicycle together through the too-green
countryside, bare skin touching, one nipple almost showing, one
woman's hair falling over the other's shoulder as she leans forward to
whisper. I was attracted to the sameness, the echo, and she seemed to
like me too, so for a little while I thought we might be able to tune each
other in. But then she stopped returning my calls. I was not heart-
broken, but a little miffed, so I kept her pants.

These were the jeans I wore to the party, along with the sunspot 18
jacket of my Jackie O suit. Linnea wore tight jeans, cowboy boots, a wide
belt. All night we circled each other in our friend's kitchen, my body
shifting inside my clothes like the shapes we used to make in grade
school science class with metal filings and a little red magnet. Later we
heard friends had laid bets. Would I take her to my two-room apartment
with the whistling radiators? Would we do it right in front of the house
on the hard bench seat of Linnea's pickup? But she was too much the
gentleman for that. She promised to call. We each left alone.

During the week before our first date, I was a planet without an 19
orbit. I wandered through shopping malls, looking for a costume to
impress her, but found nothing. As the week dripped by, I found myself sweating when others shivered, was bundled up in wool shawls
and fake fur coats while others complained the heat was turned up too
high.

Years later Linnea took me to see the famous magician Harry Black- 20
stone Jr. He stood on an empty stage in a white tie and black tails and
levitated a burning light bulb over the astonished, upturned faces of the
crowd. Audience volunteers offered proof there were no wires, while
Blackstone circled the stage, keeping the bulb ever above their heads, an
incandescent vision. Anyone watching Linnea and me during our first
kiss would have seen something similar, a suspended moment, amber lit
and hovering. I wore black Capri pants and a little cashmere sweater

from the 1950s. Linnea wore jeans and cowboy boots and a man's dress shirt, just pressed. We stood close next to a steaming radiator, on the bright white stage of my bare–walled apartment. My body floated before her, quivering in its own glow. The slightest furl of her fingers pulled me closer.

A decade has passed since that first kiss, and last week a woman 21 we both know said to me, "I've noticed over all this time that you and Linnea have shifted the way you look, to opposite poles." Have we? I wear lipstick more often these days. I used to think it was too much trouble. The sunspot skirt doesn't fit, but I still wear the jacket. Linnea owns more suits, more ties, but she is older too. She takes dressing up more seriously. She doesn't do lip–synch shows anymore, though we named our amber–haired dog Patsy Cline. Linnea used to wear women's underpants (she refuses to call them panties), but switched because she likes how men's underwear feels against her skin. It is the same with men's shirts, men's pants. Linnea also abandoned her thin ribbed white cotton man's undershirts for sports bras because of gravity's demands on her upper body, and I recently bought a Wonderbra, the movie–star cleavage push–up kind, to wear with a velveteen dress I rented for a gay wedding. We have both put on some weight, so our undergarment needs have shifted. That is the main change.

When Linnea first started dating me, some women warned her not 22 to. "She seems strange," they told her. "Look how she dresses." I did always wear a few more than three items of women's clothing in the years most lesbians honored androgyny, and they may have been referring to my denim miniskirt, my black eyeliner, or my Jackie O suit. Linnea just smiled. She knew from chemistry which base elements yearn for each other. These days lesbians speak with another kind of certainty, separating our genders from our genitals, lining up beneath a myriad of headings: *butch* or *femme; femmy-butch* or *butchy-femme; femme top* or *butch bottom; femme-to-femme* or *butch-on-butch; transgender* or plain old *lesbian feminist*. And there are scientists now that tell us the old simple division of the world into easy categories, man or woman, boy or girl, is not precise enough to describe what may be five or more discernible sexes. But I don't trust science to be expressive enough to catalog the variations in a magnetic field that pull some to their opposite, others to their mirror, others to a mosaic of variations between the two. The clothes available for us to wear may be to some a utilitarian surface, something to cover and protect the skin, to others another industry designed to profit from our confusion about our bodies, but to me, to Linnea, they are the choices we feel compelled to choose, our connection to some hum in the distance of existence to which we feel drawn as strongly as we are pulled to each other.

But on this day, at J.C. Penney's, we masquerade as regular shoppers. 23 What I haven't told her yet is that I love her men's clothes because of how they make me feel, Queen Moon to her Sun King. I don't think it is commonly known that you don't have to be heterosexual to conjure such a feeling. "Buy the rose tie," I tell her. "You'll see."

"So you really hate the other one," she says, glancing back at it over 24 her shoulder.

"This one is so nice," I say. I hold it against her chest, my knuckles 25 grazing her breasts, and I feel that old amber levitation, the pull of positive and negative poles, even on this cluttered stage, beneath this too-bright and unfocused light. Over Linnea's shoulder I see the clerk watching us, biting her orange lips, her head cocked the way our dog Patsy's head tilts when she doesn't understand what we are trying to tell her. I am not sure what she observes in us. I would kiss Linnea right here, but getting kicked out of Penney's might ruin the feeling.

In Sanskrit the word for magnetized rock, the lodestone, is *chumbaka*, 26 "the kisser." In Chinese it is *t' su chi*, "loving stone." The central image of the alchemists was marriage, the union of opposites. They weren't talking about women who broadcast from different poles, but then they were men among men and not talking about women at all. The lodestone is also a conjuring rock. We see ourselves rightly. We learn and understand what we are, king and queen of our own desire. At Penney's, Linnea turns from me, but the kissing current keeps on flowing. She steps away for a moment, but only to buy this rose-stitched tie.

Reading Closely

1. Besides the clothing information, what details in this essay reveal the relationship between the narrator and Linnea?

2. Take a few minutes to list all the things that male and female clothes buyers and clothes wearers have in common. Then write for a few minutes about the distinct ways in which members of the two genders deal with clothing differently. What details does Borich include that indicate how clothing for "what is commonly called a man" and "what is commonly called a woman" is alike and different? What are the similarities and differences between Linnea and the narrator? between Linnea and all the other cross-dressers in this essay? What might be Borich's purpose in giving her readers this information?

3. What is this essay really about? In other words, what is Borich's purpose? Write one paragraph summarizing the entire essay. Then **trade paragraphs with a classmate,** and annotate your partner's paragraph with information from the piece that you've gleaned but your partner hasn't. Finally, work together to prepare a brief, unified report for the rest of the class or for a small group.

4. How does the visual of Marlene Dietrich enhance the overall essay? What specific details enhance specific passages of the essay?

Considering Larger Issues

1. Does Borich have a one-sentence thesis? If so, write it out. If her thesis is implied, write out what it might be.

2. Who is Borich's audience? Who might have been her intended audience when she wrote this essay? Who is her audience now?

3. Consider how well the vocabulary Borich uses and the incidents she describes reflect the needs and interests of her intended audience and of her current audience. **Working with one or two classmates,** list all the vocabulary and incidents that you feel are especially appropriate to either audience. Prepare a group response to share with the rest of the class.

4. COMBINING METHODS. Which passages in the essay seem to be more concerned with *narrating*, with telling a story, than with providing descriptive details? Mark those passages. Prepare to share your findings with the rest of the class.

5. COMBINING METHODS. Which passages in Borich's essay seem to be concerned with explaining the normality, the everydayness, of a lesbian relationship? How does the author *compare and contrast* a lesbian relationship with a heterosexual one?

Thinking about Language

1. Does any of Borich's language or vocabulary make you uncomfortable? Does any of it seem outdated? inappropriate? offensive? Write out any words and phrases that bother you, note which paragraph they're in, and then define any of them that are unfamiliar to you, using the context or a dictionary. Prepare to share your findings with the rest of the class, including the reason you listed each of the terms.

2. Using the context or a dictionary, define the following words: impresarios (4), patriarch (5), feral (16), utilitarian (22).

3. Underline all the comparisons (metaphors and similes) Borich employs to energize her essay, beginning with "what sort of king I have married" and "the geometry lesson" and continuing with "boozy candlelight" and "just as airborne as Kelly or Astaire." What effect do such comparisons have on the tone of the essay?

4. **Working with one or two classmates,** determine the dominant impression Borich is creating in this essay. Identify the specific descriptive language, and map out the organizational pattern that contributes to this impression. Prepare to share your group's findings with the rest of the class.

Writing Your Own Descriptions

1. In preparation for writing a two- to three-page essay describing one of your relatives who is different from you in several significant ways — age, education, sex, and so on — list all the ways the two of you are alike, the

things you have in common. Then list the ways you are definitely different from each other. List phrases replete with physical, emotional, intellectual, professional, academic, aesthetic, and/or athletic details.

Look over the details in the lists you wrote about your relative. What dominant impression do those details suggest? Is this the impression you want your readers to have? If so, start drafting your essay; if not, go back and add details to or delete them from the lists.

As you begin drafting the essay, consider the various ways you might choose to arrange the information. What aspects of the dominant impression can you develop? Can you arrange those aspects from least to most important? Is there a chronology of details? Would some variation on a spatial arrangement best serve your purpose? Write out a thesis statement. As you draft and revise, be sure to refer to the guidelines for checking over descriptive writing on p. 61.

2. **Working with a classmate,** trade your drafts describing a relative. Each of you should write out the dominant impression that the other's essay creates, underlining particular words or phrases that bring the impression into focus. Number the descriptive details in the order your classmate has used them, and decide if rearranging them would strengthen the overall effect. Discuss the effectiveness of the thesis as well. After you've worked together, revise your essay, referring to the guidelines for checking over descriptive writing on p. 61.

3. Draft a three- to four-page essay in which you describe someone whom you've gotten to know fairly well, either in person or online. The essay will be more interesting if you write about your first impression of this person (based on his or her looks, clothing, speech, writing style, and so on) and then recount what you've since learned about him or her. Although your essay will be mostly descriptive, it will also have elements of comparison and contrast, analysis of causes and consequences, definition, and narration. As you draft and revise, be sure to refer to the guidelines for checking over descriptive writing on p. 61.

E. B. WHITE

Once More to the Lake

In 1963, President John F. Kennedy presented E(lwyn) B(rooks) White (1899–1985) the Presidential Medal of Freedom to honor this quintessential American essayist, renowned for the wit, simplicity, and excellence of his writing. White published regularly and widely in magazines and books, contributing essays, editorials, and sketches to the *New Yorker* for some fifty years and to *Harper's* for five. Although he will be forever linked with William Strunk for their classic writing guide *The Elements of Style*, first published in 1959, as well as with fellow humorist James Thurber for their book *Is Sex Necessary? Or Why You Feel the Way You Do* (1928), White is perhaps best known for his classic children's books, *Stuart Little* (1945), *Charlotte's Web* (1952), and *The Trumpet of the Swan* (1970). The following selection was originally published in *Harper's* in 1941.

> **Preview** If you're familiar with White's children's books (or the movies by the same names), write for a few minutes about what you liked most about these works and what features or lessons have stayed with you as an adult.

August 1941

One summer, along about 1904, my father rented a camp on a lake in Maine and took us all there for the month of August. We all got ringworm from some kittens and had to rub Pond's Extract on our arms and legs night and morning, and my father rolled over in a canoe with all his clothes on; but outside of that the vacation was a success and from then on none of us ever thought there was any place in the world like that lake in Maine. We returned summer after summer—always on August 1 for one month. I have since become a salt-water man, but sometimes in summer there are days when the restlessness of the tides and the fearful cold of the sea water and the incessant wind that blows across the afternoon and into the evening make me wish for the placidity of a lake in the woods. A few weeks ago this feeling got so strong I bought myself a couple of bass hooks and a spinner and returned to the lake where we used to go, for a week's fishing and to revisit old haunts.

I took along my son, who had never had any fresh water up his nose and who had seen lily pads only from train windows. On the journey over to the lake I began to wonder what it would be like. I wondered how time would have marred this unique, this holy spot—the coves and streams, the hills that the sun set behind, the camps and the paths behind the camps. I was sure that the tarred road would have found it out, and I wondered in what other ways it would be desolated. It is strange how much you can remember about places like that once you allow your mind to return into the grooves that lead back. You remember one thing, and that suddenly reminds you of another thing. I guess I remembered clearest of all the early mornings, when the lake was cool and motion- less, remembered how the bedroom smelled of the lumber it was made of and of the wet woods whose scent entered through the screen. The partitions in the camp were thin and did not extend clear to the top of the rooms, and as I was always the first up I would dress softly so as not to wake the others, and sneak out into the sweet outdoors and start out in the canoe, keeping close along the shore in the long shadows of the pines. I remembered being very careful never to rub my paddle against the gunwale for fear of disturbing the stillness of the cathedral.

The lake had never been what you would call a wild lake. There were cottages sprinkled around the shores, and it was in farming country although the shores of the lake were quite heavily wooded. Some of the cottages were owned by nearby farmers, and you would live at the shore and eat your meals at the farmhouse. That's what our family did. But al- though it wasn't wild, it was a fairly large and undisturbed lake and there were places in it that, to a child at least, seemed infinitely remote and primeval.

I was right about the tar; it led to within half a mile of the shore. But when I got back there, with my boy, and we settled into a camp near a farmhouse and into the kind of summertime I had known, I could tell that it was going to be pretty much the same as it had been before—I knew it, lying in bed the first morning, smelling the bedroom and hear- ing the boy sneak quietly out and go off along the shore in a boat. I began to sustain the illusion that he was I, and therefore, by simple transposition, that I was my father. This sensation persisted, kept crop- ping up all the time we were there. It was not an entirely new feeling, but in this setting it grew much stronger. I seemed to be living a dual ex- istence. I would be in the middle of some simple act, I would be picking up a bait box or laying down a table fork, or I would be saying some- thing, and suddenly it would be not I but my father who was saying the words or making the gesture. It gave me a creepy sensation.

We went fishing the first morning. I felt the same damp moss cover- ing the worms in the bait can, and saw the dragonfly alight on the tip of my rod as it hovered a few inches from the surface of the water. It was the arrival of this fly that convinced me beyond any doubt that every- thing was as it always had been, that the years were a mirage and that there had been no years. The small waves were the same, chucking the rowboat under the chin as we fished at anchor, and the boat was the same boat, the same color green and the ribs broken in the same places, and under the floorboards the same fresh-water leavings and débris— the dead hellgrammite, the wisps of moss, the rusty discarded fishhook, the dried blood from yesterday's catch. We stared silently at the tips of our rods, at the dragonflies that came and went. I lowered the tip of mine into the water, tentatively, pensively dislodging the fly, which darted two feet away, poised, darted two feet back, and came to rest again a little farther up the rod. There had been no years between the ducking of this dragonfly and the other one—the one that was part of memory. I looked at the boy, who was silently watching his fly, and it was my hands that held his rod, my eyes watching. I felt dizzy and didn't know which rod I was at the end of.

We caught two bass, hauling them in briskly as though they were 6 mackerel, pulling them over the side of the boat in a businesslike man- ner without any landing net, and stunning them with a blow on the back of the head. When we got back for a swim before lunch, the lake was ex- actly where we had left it, the same number of inches from the dock, and there was only the merest suggestion of a breeze. This seemed an utterly enchanted sea, this lake you could leave to its own devices for a few hours and come back to, and find it had not stirred, this constant and trustworthy body of water. In the shallows, the dark, water–soaked sticks and twigs, smooth and old, were undulating in clusters on the bottom against the clean ribbed sand, and the track of the mussel was plain. A school of minnows swam by, each minnow with its small individual shadow, doubling the attendance, so clear and sharp in the sunlight. Some of the other campers were in swimming, along the shore, one of them with a cake of soap, and the water felt thin and clear and unsub- stantial. Over the years there had been this person with the cake of soap, this cultist, and here he was. There had been no years.

Up to the farmhouse to dinner through the teeming, dusty field, the 7 road under our sneakers was only a two–track road. The middle track was missing, the one with the marks of the hooves and the splotches of dried, flaky manure. There had always been three tracks to choose from in choosing which track to walk in; now the choice was narrowed down to two. For a moment I missed terribly the middle alternative. But the way led past the tennis court, and something about the way it lay there in the sun reassured me; the tape had loosened along the backline, the alleys were green with plantains and other weeds, and the net (installed in June and removed in September) sagged in the dry noon, and the whole place steamed with midday heat and hunger and emptiness. There was a choice of pie for dessert, and one was blueberry and one was apple, and the waitresses were the same country girls, there having been no passage of time, only the illusion of it as in a dropped curtain—the waitresses were still fifteen; their hair had been washed, that was the only difference—they had been to the movies and seen the pretty girls with the clean hair.

Summertime, oh summertime, pattern of life indelible, the fade- 8 proof lake, the woods unshatterable, the pasture with the sweetfern and the juniper forever and ever, summer without end; this was the back- ground, and the life along the shore was the design, their tiny docks with the flagpole and the American flag floating against the white clouds in the blue sky, the little paths over the roots of the trees leading from camp to camp and the paths leading back to the outhouses and the can of lime for sprinkling, and at the souvenir counters at the store the miniature birch-bark canoes and the postcards that showed things looking a little better than they looked. This was the American family at play, escaping the city heat, wondering whether the newcomers in the camp at the head of the cove were "common" or "nice," wondering whether it was true that the people who drove up for Sunday dinner at the farmhouse were turned away because there wasn't enough chicken.

It seemed to me, as I kept remembering all this, that those times and those summers had been infinitely precious and worth saving. There had been jollity and peace and goodness. The arriving (at the beginning of August) had been so big a business in itself, at the railway station the farm wagon drawn up, the first smell of the pine-laden air, the first glimpse of the smiling farmer, and the great importance of the trunks and your father's enormous authority in such matters, and the feel of the wagon under you for the long ten-mile haul, and at the top of the last long hill catching the first view of the lake after eleven months of not seeing this cherished body of water. The shouts and cries of the other campers when they saw you, and the trunks to be unpacked, to give up their rich burden. (Arriving was less exciting nowadays, when you sneaked up in your car and parked it under a tree near the camp and took out the bags and in five minutes it was all over, no fuss, no loud wonderful fuss about trunks.) 9

Peace and goodness and jollity. The only thing that was wrong now, really, was the sound of the place, an unfamiliar nervous sound of the outboard motors. This was the note that jarred, the one thing that would sometimes break the illusion and set the years moving. In those other summertimes all the motors were inboard; and when they were at a little distance, the noise they made was a sedative, an ingredient of summer sleep. They were one-cylinder and two-cylinder engines, and some were make-and-break and some were jump-spark, but they all made a sleepy sound across the lake. The one-lungers throbbed and fluttered, and the twin-cylinder ones purred and purred, and that was a quiet sound, too. But now the campers all had outboards. In the daytime, in the hot mornings, these motors made a petulant, irritable sound; at night, in the still evening when the afterglow lit the water, they whined about one's ears like mosquitoes. My boy loved our rented outboard, and his great desire was to achieve single-handed mastery over it, and authority, and he soon learned the trick of choking it a little (but not too much), and the adjustment of the needle valve. Watching him I would remember the things you could do with the old one-cylinder engine with the heavy flywheel, how you could have it eating out of your hand if you got really close to it spiritually. Motorboats in those days didn't have clutches, and you would make a landing by shutting off the motor at the proper time and 10 coasting in with a dead rudder. But there was a way of reversing them, if you learned the trick, by cutting the switch and putting it on again exactly on the final dying revolution of the flywheel, so that it would kick back against the compression and begin reversing. Approaching a dock in a strong following breeze, it was difficult to slow up sufficiently by the ordinary coasting method, and if a boy felt he had complete mastery over his motor, he was tempted to keep it running beyond its time and then reverse it a few feet from the dock. It took a cool nerve, because if you threw the switch a twentieth of a second too soon you would catch the flywheel when it still had speed enough to go up past center, and the boat would leap ahead, charging bull-fashion at the dock.

We had a good week at camp. The bass were biting well and the sun 11 shown endlessly, day after day. We would be tired at night and lie down in the accumulated heat of the little bedrooms after the long hot day and the breeze would stir almost imperceptibly outside and the smell of the swamp drift in through the rusty screens. Sleep would come easily and in the morning the red squirrel would be on the roof, tapping out his gay routine. I kept remembering everything, lying in bed in the mornings — the small steamboat that had a long rounded stern like the lip of a Ubangi, and how quietly she ran on the moonlight sails, when the older boys played their mandolins and the girls sang and we ate doughnuts dipped in sugar, and how sweet the music was on the water in the shining night, and what it had felt like to think about girls then. After breakfast we would go up to the store and the things were in the same place — the minnows in a bottle, the plugs and spinners disarranged and pawed over by the youngsters from the boys' camp, the Fig Newtons and the Beeman's gum. Outside, the road was tarred and cars stood in front of the store. Inside, all was just as it had always been, except there was more Coca-Cola and not so much Moxie and root beer and birch beer and sarsaparilla. We would walk out with the bottle of pop apiece and sometimes the pop would backfire up our noses and hurt. We explored the streams, quietly, where the turtles slid off the sunny logs and dug their way into the soft bottom; and we lay on the town wharf and fed worms to the tame bass. Everywhere we went I had trouble making out which I was, the one walking at my side, the one walking in my pants.

One afternoon while we were there at that lake a thunderstorm 12 came up. It was like the revival of an old melodrama that I had seen long ago with childish awe. The second-act climax of the drama of the electrical disturbance over a lake in America had not changed in any important respect. This was the big scene, still the big scene. The whole thing was so familiar, the first feeling of oppression and heat and a general air around camp of not wanting to go very far away. In mid-afternoon (it was all the same) a curious darkening of the sky, and a lull in everything that had made life tick; and then the way the boats suddenly swung the other way at their moorings with the coming of a breeze out of the new quarter, and the premonitory rumble. Then the kettle drum, then the snare, then the bass drum and cymbals, then crackling light against the dark, and the gods grinning and licking their chops in the hills. Afterward the calm, the rain steadily rustling in the calm lake, the return of light and hope and spirits, and the campers running out in joy and relief to go swimming in the rain, their bright cries perpetuating the deathless joke about how they were getting simply drenched, and the children screaming with delight at the new sensation of bathing in the rain, and the joke about getting drenched linking the generations in a strong indestructible chain. And the comedian who waded in carrying an umbrella.

When the others went swimming, my son said he was going in, too. 13 He pulled his dripping trunks from the line where they had hung all through the shower and wrung them out. Languidly, and with no thought of going in, I watched him, his hard little body, skinny and bare, saw him wince slightly as he pulled up around his vitals the small, soggy, icy garment. As he buckled the swollen belt, suddenly my groin felt the chill of death.

Reading Closely

1. **Working with several other classmates,** break into groups, one for each of the senses: sight, smell, hearing, touch, taste. With one sense as your guide, work as a team to record all the words and phrases in "Once More to the Lake" that help bring that sense to life. Compare your findings. Which group has been the most successful in locating descriptive details? Which sense seems to contribute the most toward creating the overall impression of this essay?

2. Look over the list that your group compiled. Which words or phrases most helped you enjoy or appreciate this essay? What feelings did White's language elicit from you?

3. Descriptive essays may fulfill several purposes. What textual evidence supports White's main purpose—to entertain his readers? Does White also use description to inform or argue a point? Mark any phrases or passages that fulfill one of these other purposes.

Considering Larger Issues

1. In one paragraph, indicate whether you identify with the father or with the son—and why.

2. What is the dominant impression of White's essay? **Work with two or three classmates** to discuss the dominant impression. As you focus on that impression, write out a list of the strategies White employs to reinforce it. Then prepare one sentence that conveys the dominant impression to the rest of the class. Find the sentence that serves as White's

thesis statement. Compare the thesis with the sentence you wrote with your group.

3. **COMBINING METHODS.** Draw a line down the center of a sheet of paper. On the left side, write down all the scenes and memories that concern White's childhood trips to the lake, and on the right side of the paper, write down the scenes having to do with White's adult trip to the lake. Whenever you can make a side–by–side *comparison and contrast*, do so. What is the overall effect of including comparison and contrast within this description?

4. What information does this essay provide about socioeconomic class in the United States? What characters in the essay represent different classes? Where does the young White fit in? How about the adult White and his son? How do they compare with the other characters? What is the adult White's attitude toward the other characters in the essay? What do your answers to these questions suggest about White's intended audience?

Thinking about Language

1. Use the context of the essay and your dictionary to define any of the following terms that you do not know. Be prepared to share your answers with the rest of the class.

salt–water man (1)	cultist (6)	melodrama (12)
placidity (1)	teeming (7)	lull (12)
desolated (2)	indelible (8)	moorings (12)
primeval (3)	infinitely (9)	premonitory (12)
transposition (4)	jollity (9)	
undulating (6)	mandolins (11)	

2. **Working with a classmate,** consider the descriptive language White employs to translate the lake into a place of worship. Locate specific words and phrases that denote and connote religion, prayer, a church, and the like. Then compare your findings with those of a classmate. Prepare to share your responses with the rest of the class.

Writing Your Own Descriptions

1. No doubt you have—or at least have had in the past—a familiar place to which you repeatedly return. Draft a three- to four-page essay in which you describe your earliest memories of that place (including your sensory memories)—perhaps a grandparent's home, a yearly vacation or work destination, or just a place where you gather with friends. **Ask one of your classmates to read your draft** and help you see if there are passages in it where your present experiences are coloring your early memories. You can use those passages to your advantage, to bring a deeper perspective to your memories as well as to that place. Refer to the guidelines for checking over descriptive writing on p. 61.

2. Consider a place that you often visit in terms of how it represents the passage of time. Focusing on your sense of your own mortality were you to return to that special place, draft a three- to four-page descriptive essay with a strong dominant impression. **Then consider trading drafts with a classmate.** Ask your classmate to mark passages where your description is solely descriptive as well as passages where elements of narration or comparison and contrast aid their development. Remember that the guidelines for checking over descriptive writing are on p. 61.

Plum Delicious

This quarter-page ad, which appeared in *Gourmet* magazine, uses a visual as well as text for the purpose of persuading the reader to buy an exotic kind of fruit. Words are an important part of the ad, but, as you can see, the image itself (which was in color in the magazine) says just as much as the words do.

> **Preview** As you look over the ad, concentrate on the descriptive detail that first caught your attention and then on the detail that held your attention the longest.

· · · · · · ➤

Reading Closely

1. What part of the Eden Pride plumcot ad drew your eye immediately? What did you notice only after looking at the ad for a while? Did you read the text before or after looking at the picture?
2. What descriptive details in this ad appeal to each of your five senses? How do the visual and the text work together to make the advertisement complete? How do they work together to fulfill the purpose of the ad?

Considering Larger Issues

1. Given the particular product being advertised and that the ad appeared in *Gourmet* magazine, what audience does the ad target? How would you profile the audience in terms of age, sex, occupations, hobbies, or interests? **With another classmate,** decide which words and phrases are intended to appeal to this audience. Prepare to share your answer with the rest of the class.
2. What is the overarching message of the ad?
3. **COMBINING METHODS.** How does the ad use other rhetorical methods of development besides description? Consider *process analysis* and *cause-and-consequence analysis,* in particular.

Thinking about Language

1. What does the headline for the ad actually say? What does it imply?
2. How do the ad writers make it seem as if the plumcots are worth the high cost of $50 for four pounds? What particular words and phrases do they use to create this effect?
3. Does the text of the ad use objective or subjective language, denotative or connotative words? How else might you describe phrases like "Eden Pride plumcot," "slightly downy," "alluring perfume," "gushes"? What

GOOD LIVING

When the
apricot met
the plum

Plum Delicious

With its slightly downy, yellow-orange skin and alluring perfume, the Eden Pride plumcot calls to mind a giant apricot. But bite into the translucent golden flesh, and it gushes an intensely plumlike juice. An experimental natural hybrid—half apricot, half plum—bred by Floyd Zaiger, the man who breeds the increasingly common Pluot, a plum-apricot cross in which plum characteristics prevail, Eden Prides are easily the most flavorful fruit of their kind. Their season is brief, however, and because the trees produce so few fruits, only one farmer, Steve Brenkwitz, of Tracy, California, is daring (or foolhardy) enough to grow them. How does he manage? Ask, and the genial farmer's eyes narrow. "If I told you," he says, "I'd have to kill you." *In the last week of May and the first week of June, Brenkwitz will overnight four pounds of plumcots for $50 (888-882-7742; edengarden.com).* —David Karp details do they provide or imply? What is their appeal? What overall impression do they help create? **Working with one or two classmates,** compare and refine your answers to these questions. Then prepare one set of answers to share with the rest of the class.

Writing Your Own Descriptions

1. Locate an online ad that persuaded you to buy (or seriously consider buying) the product. Write a phrase or a sentence that expresses the dominant impression of the ad. What connotative and denotative language and visual effects in the ad support that dominant impression?

    Draft a two- to three-page essay in which you describe the ad, using objective rather than subjective language as much as possible. State the dominant impression, and then discuss the different ways that the details, such as descriptions or images of people, clothing, or location, convey that impression. Include a copy of the ad with your essay, and underline the thesis statement. If it is implied, write it in the margin or at the beginning and label it.

2. Locate a newspaper or magazine ad that annoys or offends you (for example, because it is racist, sexist, crude, pretentious, or dishonest), one that gets your attention but turns you off. What is the purpose of the ad? Who is the targeted audience? What is the dominant impression? What connotations, specific details, and objective or subjective descriptions help fulfill the purpose, reach out for a specific audience, and create the dominant impression?

    Draft a two- to three-page essay in which you describe this ad using subjective language with negative connotations. Your purpose will be to describe the dominant impression and then move on to discuss the various ways that the descriptive details and connotations convey the ad's overall impression or effect. Include a copy of the ad with your essay.

✳ Additional Suggestions for Writing

1. Drawing on the readings in this chapter, draft a three- to four-page essay that describes the experience of being an outsider. Of course, as you convey the idea of outsider status with various descriptive details, you will also be defining it accordingly. You might review the classified ad at the beginning of the chapter, Borich's essay about the lives of a lesbian couple, White's account of his return with his son to a remembered vacation spot, Rember's description of doors that close, or Alvarez's literacy narrative. In what ways do each of these readings describe, imply, and define "outsiderness" on some level? and to what purpose? Remember that the guidelines for checking over descriptive writing can be found on p. 61.

2. Describe a typical meal with someone (or a group of people) you eat with frequently, using subjective and objective details, denotative and connotative language, and metaphors and similes that evoke all five senses and various sensibilities. Where do you eat? What do you eat? How do you behave while you eat? As you draft and revise, refer to the guidelines for checking over descriptive writing on p. 61.

3. Draft a three- to four-page essay in which you describe a first meeting with one particular person. What was your initial visual impression? What details do you need to include to convey that visual impression? Which details are subjective and which are objective? What is your dominant impression of that first meeting? What actions took place that might help you convey that dominant impression?

    First, develop your description of the meeting by coming up with details and examples. Then arrange the information you have generated so that each paragraph leads naturally into the next one. Make sure that you begin paragraphs with transitional sentences that remind readers of information from the previous paragraph and introduce new information to be covered in the next paragraph. Is your thesis explicit or implied? Write it out.

chapter **3**

···•

NARRATION

6 March 2004

Jimi Hendrix patchwork velvet jacket

The pre-eminent instrumentalist of his age, Jimi Hendrix changed the face of music with the ferocious electricity and expressiveness of his playing. (Gift of James Alan Hendrix).

Rock and Roll Hall of Fame and Museum, Cleveland

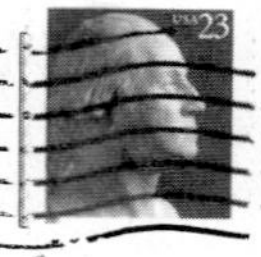

Dear Cheryl,

I'm having a good trip, but it would be better if you were along.

Had a good meeting in Indianapolis with the writing center directors in the CIC. Wisconsin, Michigan State, and Minnesota are doing things that are especially inspiring. But speaking of inspiration, I'm now at the Rock and Roll Hall of Fame, after having had a wonderful brunch this morning with Jay and Jill in Dayton. (They served Durian fruit imported from the Philippines – wow! Don't worry: I'm not bringing any home.) It's bliss here at the RRHF to sit in the front row of the Jimi Hendrix theater and then go gaze at one of his guitars on display. I saw Joan Jett's red Epiphone! The broken bass Paul Simonon is smashing on the cover of <u>London Calling</u>! Ani DiFranco's guitar! Bootsy Collins' 1975 Fender Precision! Frank Beard's fur-covered drum kit and the Eliminator coupe! David Byrne's Big Suit! The only way this could get any better is if I find a jacket like the one on this card to wear to CCCC.

I'll be home soon. Love, Jon

Cheryl Glenn
193 Sandy Ridge Road
State College, PA 16803

Become a member of the House That Rock Built.
For membership information call 800.349.ROCK.

*P*ostcards are an everyday kind of communication, casually sent and received. Yet despite their informality, most postcards are written and read with expectations of

- *a beginning that sets a scene:* "Dear Cheryl, I'm having a good trip, but it would be better if you were along."
- *a setting:* the Rock and Roll Hall of Fame and Museum, Cleveland, Ohio.
- *a middle that tells a story:* "Had a good meeting in Indianapolis with the writing center directors of the CIC. Wisconsin, Michigan State, and Minnesota are doing things that are especially inspiring. But speaking of inspiration, I'm now at the Rock and Roll Hall of Fame, after having had a wonderful brunch with Jay and Jill in Dayton. (They served durian, fruit imported from the Philippines — wow! Don't worry: I'm not bringing any home.) It's bliss here at the RRHF to sit in the front row of the Jimi Hendrix theater and then go gaze at one of his guitars on display. I saw Joan Jett's Epiphone! The broken bass Paul Simonon is smashing on the cover of *London Calling!* Ani DiFranco's guitar! Bootsy Collins' 1975 Fender Precision! Frank Beard's fur-covered drum kit and the Eliminator Coupe! David Byrne's big suit!"
- *an ending that brings the story to a close:* "The only way this could get any better is if I find a jacket like the one on this card to wear to CCCC. I'll be home soon. Love, Jon."
- *characters:* Jay, Jill, Jon.
- *description:* especially inspiring presentations, fruit imported from the Philippines, "fur-covered drum kit."

Even if you don't know Jon and Cheryl or Jay and Jill, even if you've never been to Cleveland, let alone the Rock and Roll Hall of Fame and Museum, the message on the postcard probably makes sense to you because it is an example of **narration** — it tells a story — and you understand how narration works. We use the components of narration — chronological order, characters, dialogue, setting, and description — as we gossip over lunch, explain the reasons we're late for a meeting, and talk about our vacation plans.

> **Looking at Your Own Literacy**   What kinds of postcards have you received or sent? What were the occasions for sending those postcards? What kinds of narratives did they contain? Besides postcard narratives, what other kinds of narratives do you often tell — or write? Write for a few minutes about the kinds of stories they are, why and how you deliver them, and who your audience is.

What Is Narration?

Because human beings are natural storytellers, narration is the most common method of communication. In fact, we use it and hear it so often that we don't think about it as narration. But newspapers, television comedies and dramas, news programs, movies, comic strips, lab reports, histories, (auto)biographies, diaries, and letters all depend on the conventions of narration to tell what happened, is happening, or will happen—and to whom. And as you already know from sending and receiving postcards and e-mails, entertaining your friends with jokes, seeing movies, and reading novels, an effective narrative is often much more than a simple report or forecast of events. By creating or retelling a sequence of occurrences, a speaker, writer, or filmmaker can use narration to argue a point, create a mood, or provide an example.

Because we need narration in order to make sense of the world, we often use it as the primary way of organizing a piece of writing or an oral presentation. At other times we tuck in a short narrative, or **anecdote,** to make a point within another kind of writing or speech. For instance, when an announcer on the Weather Channel is describing the icy weather that is expected in a certain area and encouraging people to stay home, she might relate a short narrative about a bad traffic accident caused by icy road conditions. The drivers involved in the accident, however, will no doubt tell their stories at greater length in a police or insurance report, with details about the series of events, setting, and characters.

In your academic writing as well, narration can be either a dominant or a subordinate structure. For example, if your instructor asks you to write an essay recounting a "transformative experience," you might decide to write about the important lesson in responsible drinking you learned from the near-fatal accident of a fraternity brother. In this case, you would give specific details about how the accident happened, how it affected you, and what resolutions you made in response to it. On the other hand, suppose you are writing an argument about the need for college students to develop a sense of responsibility. If one of your points is about responsible drinking, you could tell the story about the fraternity brother to support your argument, boiling it down to a mini-narrative on how a drinker's accident affected you. In short, narration can frame your entire essay or work on a smaller scale within a description, as shown in the newspaper weather forecast on p. 135.

Thinking about Narration

1. Look over the written text in the five-day forecast for central Pennsylvania. How is the information arranged? How does each day's forecast connect with the previous day's forecast? How is the local summary narrated differently from the main forecast?
2. What narrative do the pictures of the five-day forecast tell? How is that visual narrative the same as or different from the verbal narrative?

FIVE-DAY FORECAST

TODAY	TONIGHT	SUNDAY

Accumulating snow, mixing with rain late.	Windy and cold with more flurries.	Windy and cold with clouds and flurries.
36	20	28 / 18

MONDAY	TUESDAY	WEDNESDAY

Mostly sunny, but chilly.	Increasing clouds with periods of snow.	A mix of clouds and sun.
36 / 20	40 / 30	42 / 28

LOCAL SUMMARY

Snow this morning will accumulate 1-3 inches by afternoon, at which time it may change over to rain or drizzle. Heavier snow is likely in northern Pennsylvania. Snow will end tonight, and it will become very windy and cold. The wind will persist on Sunday with plenty of clouds and some flurries possible.

Why Use Narration?

When you use narration, you usually have one or more of four basic purposes: to report information, to support an argument, to provide an example, or to set a mood.

Every day, you communicate primarily by relating a sequence of incidents. Sharing stories is an important way to establish and maintain friendships, whether you're telling another parent about potty training your child or describing to your roommate the thrills of your recent white-water rafting trip. In fact, many people who live alone say they would like to have someone to whom they can recount the events of their day. On a more practical level, explaining to a mechanic what's wrong with your car or rescheduling a class in the registrar's office also requires that you report a series of incidents to explain what you want or need.

Not all narratives reporting information are delivered orally; many appear in newspaper articles, history books, scientific reports, and other printed and electronic forms. For instance, when John Hersey wrote about the terrible effects of the atomic bomb on the survivors of the Hiroshima bombing, he used a narrative to report the information:

> In August, 1946, a year after the bombing of Hiroshima, Hatsuyo Nakamura was weak and destitute. Her husband, a tailor, had been taken to the Army and had been killed at Singapore on the day of the city's capture, February 15, 1942. She lost her mother, a brother, and a sister to the atomic bomb. Her son and two daughters — ten, eight, and five years old — were buried in rubble when the blast of the bomb flung her house down. In a frenzy, she dug them out alive. A month after the bombing, she came down with radiation sickness; she lost most of her hair and lay in bed for weeks with a high fever in the house of her sister-in-law in the suburb of Kabe, worrying all the time about how to support her children. She was too poor to go to a doctor. Gradually, the worst of the symptoms abated, but she remained feeble; the slightest exertion wore her out.   — JOHN HERSEY, *HIROSHIMA*

Hersey's short opening recounts the series of events that Hatsuyo Nakamura experienced in the aftermath of the Hiroshima bombing — but it also sets the mood for the rest of the essay.

Try Your Hand   Everyone has experienced a disaster of one kind or another or knows of someone who has. A disaster doesn't have to be as horrific as the bombing of Hiroshima; it might involve the experience of working with a particular boss or taking a family vacation, or it might relate to a bad car purchase or a family tragedy. Take a few minutes to recount in writing the series of events of a disaster with which you are familiar. Try to narrate the disaster as objectively and unemotionally as possible, without using the narrative to argue a point or establish a mood.

A narrative can also provide powerful, convincing support for an argument. In a letter reprinted in the newspaper column "Dear Abby," one writer narrates a series of events that support her main point: people should pay attention to any symptoms of emotional distress in those who are close to them.

> Dear Abby,
>   Two months ago my youngest sister called me — collect again — sobbing that she felt alone and frightened in the world. She asked if we could meet for tea or if I could visit her. As a mother of twins and self-employed, I reminded her that having tea in a cafe is a luxury I cannot afford.

Last month she called me again. She wanted to spend Saturday night with us and make a pancake breakfast "for old times' sake." She told me she missed me and felt blue. (Abby, Saturday nights are reserved for my husband.)

Two weeks ago, my sister invited me to a matinee — her treat. She tearfully informed me that she was not sleeping well (she was being treated for depression and chronic fatigue syndrome). I told her, "Working people don't go to matinees, but when you get your life together, you'll know what 'chronic-living-life-fatigue' is."

My little sister will never call again. She took her life last week.

My sister had some of the best medical help available, and I know she was ultimately responsible for her own life. But I also know that I'll never again brush her hair out of her sleepy blue eyes or trade my blouse for her mauve lipstick, or tell her that she's not fat — she's beautiful.

Most of all, I will never forgive myself for not realizing how suicidal my sister was. Perhaps this letter will prevent others from making the mistakes I made.   — *Lesson Learned in the Worst of Ways*

This narrative could also support a broader argument: one person's illness, whether physical or mental, hurts more than just the patient. Narratives like this one appear in advice columns every day, with people using them to support a claim, a complaint, an assertion.

Try Your Hand   Think of a lesson you've learned or an opinion you've developed as the result of a personal experience. Recall first the most memorable experiences of your life, remembering how you responded to them. Then choose and focus on a particular experience that led you to form one strong opinion. In a page or so, narrate your experience in a way that supports your opinion.

A narrative can also provide examples to support or illustrate a generalization. In an essay by Amy Tan describing a visit to her Chinese American home by some non–Chinese friends, Tan provides a series of anecdotes that illustrate the generalization "Dinner threw me deeper into despair":

My relatives licked the ends of their chopsticks and reached across the table, dipping them into the dozen or so plates of food. Robert and his family waited patiently for platters to be passed to them. My relatives murmured with pleasure when my mother brought out the whole steamed fish. Robert grimaced. Then my father poked his chopsticks just below the fish eye and plucked out the soft meat. "Amy, your favorite," he said, offering me the tender fish cheek. I wanted to disappear.

At the end of the meal my father leaned back and belched loudly, thanking my mother for her fine cooking. "It's a polite Chinese custom to show you are satisfied," explained my father to our astonished guests.

Robert was looking down at his plate with a reddened face. The minister managed to muster up a quiet burp. I was stunned into silence for the rest of the night.   — Amy Tan, "Fish Cheeks"

Try Your Hand   Every family has thrown one (or more) of its members into a state of despair, or at least embarrassment, at some point. You may remember an event much like the one Tan relates when your family embarrassed you in front of people you didn't know well. Quickly write about one time when your family did just that. Or, if you prefer, write a different generalization about your family—perhaps of how they made you proud of them—and recount an example that supports your generalization.

Finally, a writer can use narrative writing simply to convey a mood or impression. For example, restaurant reviewers often take their readers through each step of their dining experience, from entering the restaurant to drinking an after-dinner coffee. Relating the experience in narrative form helps re-create the mood of the restaurant as wild and wacky, somber and formal, downhome and plentiful in its portions, or swanky and worth the expense. Or narration can evoke a more serious mood. In the following excerpt Graham Spanier, a U.S. citizen and the child of immigrants, relates a chance meeting with two German tourists in Richmond, Virginia, to create a mood tinged with sadness and regret:

I asked if they knew of a small town named Bunde, thinking quietly to myself about this horrid little place where my father's Uncle Willie had been hanged in a storefront window and set afire. Why yes — they lived there! Incredible, I thought, to meet someone from the small town where my family lived for generations.

"My family is from Bunde," I said. "Is there by any chance a cigar factory that is still there?"

"Yes," he exclaimed with amazement, "it is our factory."

I'm not a terribly emotional person, but I experienced in the span of a few moments more emotions than I knew were possible to feel in so short a time. I was stunned by the coincidence, incredibly excited by the opportunity to be able to find answers to a hundred questions that clamored in my mind. I also experienced horror thinking that I was inches away from the person who inherited from his grandfather the very house and business that Hitler had taken from my grandfather.

I suffered a silent rage as I contrasted the affluence of this young couple . . . with the poverty my father inherited. . . . My father died an unhappy man, never seeming to transcend the reality of his lot, always aspiring to the affluence he might have had but never did. . . .

"My grandfather built that factory," I said with a mixture of revelation and tact. "His name was Gustav Spanier. He left there in 1941."

"I know the name. Yes, I know that he was the founder." . . .

I knew he sensed the awkwardness of the moment when I asked if I might have his name and address. He was noticeably reluctant and said that he had no business card. I forced that one issue because I wanted to know. I got his name and address and gave him mine. The factory was known by his family's name: Andre.

My parting comments allowed for the possibility that I might someday visit, and their words were most encouraging. I know I will never hear from these people again. I must now struggle with the question of whether they will hear again from me.   —GRAHAM SPANIER, "Coincidence and Injustice"

Spanier's narrative creates an unsettling mood of sadness and uncertainty, as the grandchildren of a victim and a beneficiary of Adolf Hitler's murderous regime are brought together by fate and forced to face the unfairness of their losses and gains. Spanier's parting comments might cause his readers to reflect on the fates of their own families and the extent to which such fates are deserved or undeserved.

Try Your Hand   Your life as a college student may be markedly different from that of your parents or grandparents when they were your age. Reflect on the fate of your family, choosing one parent or grandparent in particular, and write a short narrative that shows how much further you've been able to move in life (financially, academically, or geographically) than that person, how your life represents a decline from his or hers, or maybe just how different from that person you feel. Try to make every part of your narrative sustain the mood (of ambition, admiration, frustration, good fortune, hard work, missed opportunities) you want to create.

Narration can also be used to give directions for a process or to analyze a process that has already occurred. Chapter 7, Process Analysis, demonstrates a number of process-writing techniques, including those that incorporate narrative elements of chronology, characters, description, dialogue, and setting. And as you'll see as you work through the other chapters in the book, narration can be used with other methods as well—as part of an argument or writing that uses exemplification, and especially as part of a cause-and-consequence analysis.

How Do You Read a Narrative?

Knowing how to read narratives carefully and critically is the first step to learning how to write your own. When you take the time to read narratives in this way, you become more sensitive to the features that make them successful. Strong narratives are shaped by a sequence of events, events that usually involve people who speak. Therefore, any effective narrative needs to make the sequence of events clear and the characters and their dialogue interesting. More specifically, though, you need to read a narrative with an eye to how well it fulfills its purpose (or multiple purposes): to report information, support an argument, provide an example, or set a mood. Remember, too, that how effective a narrative is may also depend to a large extent on who the intended readers are. As you read, then, you'll always want to keep in mind questions like the following: If the narrative is intended mainly just to report information, is the information clear? Or is the sequence of events confusing, or the amount of information too sketchy or too detailed to hold readers' interest? Will the intended readers feel that this narrative supports the writer's argument, or will many of them see it as weak or biased? Does the writer's language set the mood that he or she seems to intend? If so, how? If not, why not?

Look back at the Dear Abby letter (p. 136). As you read the opening paragraph, see how it introduces the two main characters ("my youngest sister" and "me") and launches a sequence of events with "Two months ago." Notice that each of the next two paragraphs also begins with an expression of time that makes it easy to follow the progression of events in the narrative: "Last month" and "Two weeks ago." All three of these paragraphs are also structured the same way: The first sentence tells about the younger sister's call, the next sentence or two say how the younger sister wanted to get together, and the last sentence tells how the writer refused. With this parallel structure, the writer establishes a clear pattern of events that reveals the relationship between the sisters—the younger one depressed, lonely, frightened, apparently not working, and reaching out for contact, the older one a busy self-employed wife and mother who not only refuses the contact but admonishes her sister for seeking it. Then, abruptly, there is a much shorter paragraph with just two short sentences that bring the story to a tragic climax: "My little sister will never call again. She took her life last week." The rest of the narrative consists of the writer's reflections in the aftermath of this tragic sequence of events and a direct statement of her purpose and intended audience: "Perhaps this letter will prevent others from making the mistakes I made." While setting a mood of sadness and remorse, this narrative makes a powerful argument that repeated pleas for emotional support should not be dismissed, even by those who think they're just too busy.

Most narratives you'll need to write won't be as dramatic or tragic as this one, and the events won't usually lend themselves to the kind of repeated paragraph structure that makes this narrative so compelling. Nor will you usually want or need to state your purpose and address your audience so directly. But even if you're writing a story that's intended to be funny or just informative, using clear time signals and shaping the narrative around a clear climax or turning point will help your readers follow the sequence of events and engage their interest. Notice also that the writer includes a couple of brief pieces of dialogue, one from each of the sisters, to help give the flavor of their relationship.

When reading any narrative, you'll also want to pay careful attention not only to what the characters say and do but also to what is unspoken and undone. What the author leaves out, in terms of actions and words, can be every bit as important as what is included. For instance, what role, if any, did their parents play in the sisters' lives? Had the sisters had this kind of relationship ever since childhood? When you consider both what is included and what is excluded, you'll get a clearer sense of the author's viewpoint. You'll begin to shape an opinion on what impression the author wants to make and whether that impression is balanced or deliberately slanted. As far as we know, the older sister's admonishments grew out of a frustration with (or maybe jealousy of) her younger sister's seemingly carefree life, so readers wonder about the source of the younger sister's chronic fatigue syndrome—as well as the reason it and the depression aren't mentioned until a parenthetical reference in the third paragraph. And although the writer acknowledges that she wasn't ultimately responsible for her sister's suicide, she seems to be portraying herself in the worst possible light. Is her remorse distorting her memory? Thinking about issues like these—how much your audience wants or needs to know, how much you want to reveal about yourself or other characters, and which details of the events will best serve your purpose—will help you as you consider what to include and what to leave out in your own narratives.

How Do You Write a Narrative?

Narratives can be the most absorbing and satisfying kind of writing to experience, whether they are read or watched on a screen, and writing them can be just as engaging. The key to writing an effective narrative can be expressed in one word: *choose.* When you are thinking about the incidents in a narrative, you'll no doubt come up with more ideas than you can use in the final draft. So, as you decide on the story you want to tell—and why—you'll need to choose the most important details, characters, and dialogue and make certain that the setting and organizational pattern work to your best advantage. Whether you are writing a paragraph- or essay–length narrative, these suggestions will help you.

Determining Your Purpose

The first step is to decide what your purpose is—not only whether you are trying to argue a point or create a mood, for example, but exactly what the point or mood is. Do you want your narrative to be the central focus of the piece of writing? If so, are you trying to explain how

you came to know racism, sexism, or some other aspect of American culture? or how you realized that your parents were not perfect? or how
your young son learned to keep trying despite initial failures? Alterna-
tively, will the sequence of incidents support another type of writing? If,
for example, your overall purpose is to support a thesis that your
school's campus needs more parking facilities, you might weave in a
short narrative that recounts a time when a classmate arrived on campus
at 7:00 A.M. to find a parking spot before her 8:00 A.M. class and could not
find even one empty space in the lot for her parking permit category. To
make your argument effective, you would not rely just on this anecdote
but would need to supply some statistical evidence as well.

African American writer bell hooks, for instance, opens one of her
books with an incident, a short narrative, that illustrates how racism
works and how strongly she feels about it:

> I am writing this essay sitting beside an anonymous white male that I
> long to murder. We have just been involved in an incident on an air-
> plane where K, my friend and traveling companion, has been called to
> the front of the plane and publicly attacked by white female stew-
> ardesses who accuse her of trying to occupy a seat in first class that is
> not assigned to her. Although she had been assigned the seat, she was
> not given the appropriate boarding pass. When she tries to explain they
> ignore her. They keep explaining to her in loud voices as though she is a
> child, as though she is a foreigner who does not speak airline English,
> that she must take another seat. They do not want to know that the airline
> has made a mistake. They want only to ensure that the white male who
> has the appropriate boarding card will have a seat in first class. Realiz-
> ing our powerlessness to alter the moment we take our seats. K moves to
> coach. And I take my seat next to the anonymous white man who quickly
> apologizes to K as she moves her bag from the seat he has comfortably
> settled in. I stare him down with rage, tell him that I do not want to hear
> his liberal apologies, his repeated insistence that "it was not his fault." I
> am shouting at him that it is not a question of blame, that the mistake
> was understandable, but that the way K was treated was completely un-
> acceptable, that it reflected both racism and sexism.
>
> — BELL HOOKS, *Killing Rage: Ending Racism*

This short narrative pulls readers into a key experience hooks had at the
same time that it pulls us into her text. Thus she provides an effective
opening for a book on the prevalence of racism and the reasons it must
be ended.

Considering Your Audience

Closely tied to the purpose of your narrative is the audience for it. In
fact, your audience is often the most important consideration in many of
the decisions you make about your writing. Are you narrating the day's

events for your private journal, writing an autobiographical sketch that some of your classmates will read, or recounting for your instructor a story about people neither of you know? Recognizing who the members of your audience are will help you calibrate the length of your narrative, decide on the amount of background detail you will provide or personal information you will disclose, and choose an effective organizational pattern.

If you're writing about the day's events in your private journal, you might include "insider information," emotional or personal details that will help you remember the events when you reread your entry at a later date. However, if you're writing for public consumption, you may need to include the kind of background information that you usually take for granted and you may decide to do without details that you are uncom-fortable revealing.

For example, consider the previous example from Amy Tan's "Fish Cheeks" (p. 137). Tan, who grew up at the intersection of Chinese and American cultures, describes an embarrassing cross–cultural experience that was undoubtedly one of many she experienced while growing up; but it is one that she shaped especially for the mostly non–Chinese, teenage readers of *Seventeen* magazine. Had she been writing for readers who were Chinese immigrants, Tan might not have needed to explain the details of Chinese table etiquette. For such readers she probably would have chosen and arranged the details in a very different way, perhaps mentioning her family members' burps and ways of serving themselves only in passing as a way of emphasizing the strange behavior of the non–Chinese visitors.

Establishing a Point of View

Like all good narrative writers, Tan establishes a steady point of view. The consistent use of first–person pronouns (*I*, *me*, *my*) and past–tense verbs all contribute to the viewpoint of an adult woman who is looking back on herself as an adolescent girl. When you write a narrative, you, too, will need a steady point of view. You might ask yourself the follow-ing questions: "Who is telling my story? Is the telling consistent?"

Try Your Hand   Rewrite the passage from "Fish Cheeks" from another character's point of view. How might the narrative read if Mr. Tan had written it? if Robert had? if the minister had?

Using Dialogue

Most narratives include characters, and those characters often speak. Your initial draft might include an overly detailed (maybe even artificial) conversation. But as you compose and revise, you'll come to see the importance of keeping only necessary dialogue and nonverbal communication. In "Fish Cheeks," you can see that Amy Tan uses two short sentences of dialogue: "Amy, your favorite" and "It's a polite Chinese custom to show you are satisfied." Her characters respond to these lines as well as to the action in the narrative—with murmurs, a grimace, a reddened face, embarrassment, and a burp—but no one else speaks. No other dialogue is necessary.

Whatever dialogue seems necessary to your narrative, make sure that it is accurate or, if you are relying on your memory or imagination, that it sounds authentic. Say the dialogue out loud to yourself to make sure that it sounds genuine.

● Organizing a Narrative

As with other types of writing, effective narratives have a purposeful pattern of organization. The organizational structure you choose for a narrative is directly related to your purpose and to the effect you want the story to create. Do you want to tell about a significant experience? a humorous one? Are you using your narrative to argue a thesis or to develop a mood? Regardless of the purpose, you should decide on an organizational pattern that will fulfill the purpose and help you make your point.

Virtually all narration follows some kind of **chronological organizational pattern,** telling about events essentially in the order they happened and often building to a **climax** (the highest point or turning point) that makes your point, "proves" your thesis, or establishes the mood you want to create. Within this basic framework, though, many variations are possible. Sometimes writers open a narrative by making an assertion and backing it up with a narrative example. Author Richard Wright does just that; he supports his assertion with a story that relates events from the beginning straight through to the end:

> My first lesson in how to live as a Negro came when I was quite small. We were living in Arkansas. Our house stood behind the railroad tracks. Its skimpy yard was paved with black cinders. Nothing green ever grew in that yard. The only touch of green we could see was far away, beyond the tracks, over where the white folks lived. But cinders were good enough for me and I never missed the green growing things. And anyhow cinders were fine weapons. You could always have a nice hot war with huge black cinders. All you had to do was crouch behind the brick pillars of a house with your hands full of gritty ammunition. And the first woolly black head you saw pop out from behind another row of pillars was your target. You tried your very best to knock it off. It was great fun.
> I never fully realized the appalling disadvantages of a cinder environment till one day the gang to which I belonged found itself engaged in a war with the white boys who lived beyond the tracks. As usual we laid

down our cinder barrage, thinking that this would wipe the white boys out. But they replied with a steady bombardment of broken bottles. We doubled our cinder barrage, but they hid behind trees, hedges, and the sloping embankments of their lawns. Having no such fortifications, we retreated to the brick pillars of our homes. During the retreat a broken milk bottle caught me behind the ear, opening a deep gash which bled profusely. The sight of blood pouring over my face completely demoralized our ranks. My fellow-combatants left me standing paralyzed in the center of the yard, and scurried for their homes. A kind neighbor saw me and rushed me to a doctor, who took three stitches in my neck. . . .

. . . From that time on, the charm of my cinder yard was gone. The green trees, the trimmed hedges, the cropped lawns grew very meaningful, became a symbol. Even today when I think of white folks, the hard, sharp outlines of white houses surrounded by trees, lawns, and hedges are present somewhere in the background of my mind. Through the years they grew into an overreaching symbol of fear.

—RICHARD WRIGHT, "The Ethics of Living Jim Crow"

Notice that Wright concludes with a restatement of his initial assertion. Ending with a restatement or not stating the assertion until the end are two common patterns in narration.

In other cases, instead of using a strictly chronological order, you might want to open or interrupt your narrative with a **flashback,** a glimpse of the past that illuminates the present. In *Cloister Walk,* a memoir and meditation on her spiritual retreat, laywoman Kathleen Norris uses a flashback to introduce the narrative about her temporary commitment to religious life. A long-ago Easter morning provides her an opening for discussing other Easters she has known, as well as the one she's currently spending at the monastery:

We each have a purse and matching hat. White gloves, socks with lace cuffs. Crinolines under stiff cotton skirts that make us feel important. Patent leather Mary Janes. My two sisters and I pose for a photograph before leaving for church. We stand by the station wagon. "Robin's egg blue," my mother had called it. I like to think of the car as an egg, my family hatching through the doors. For my youngest sister, it is her first purse. It distracts her. She swings it back and forth, hitting us on the knees. *Quit it,* we say. *Shush. Stand still for the picture.*

—KATHLEEN NORRIS, "Saved by a Rockette: Easters I Have Known"

At another place in her narrative Norris uses **flashforward,** a technique that takes readers to future events. On the Feast Day of St. Benedict, Norris's thoughts—and words—carry her and her readers a few moments into the future:

The heady talk has been stimulating, too much so. It is good to be sitting in silence, in the great abbey church, waiting for the feast-day Mass to begin. I seat myself in the choir with the other women as the monks gather in the baptistry. Soon they will sing an ancient chant, claiming their heritage as

"Reading" and Using Visuals in a Narrative

Many narratives use visuals. If you consider the "before" and "after" photographs in ads for any hair-growth, muscle-building, or weight-loss product, you'll see how just two pictures can tell a story. Greeting cards often carry drawings or cartoons that narrate how two people met, why they fell in love, why they miss each other, and so on. All these kinds of images can enhance your written narratives as well. Bar graphs or line graphs can also support a narrative by tracing the history of the projected future of statistical trends. Even if a visual doesn't help to explain your information or support your argument, it can help create a mood.

Evolution.

If you want to use visuals in writing an academic assignment, it is a good idea to check with your instructor beforehand. You also need to consider whether to include labels or captions (if the visuals do not already include them) and whether to refer to the visuals in your written text or let them stand on their own.

As with words, you want to choose visuals for your narratives carefully so that they help you achieve your purpose and appeal to your readers rather than distracting, boring, or confusing them. To succeed in these goals, you need to learn how to "read" visuals critically in the same way you do written narratives. For example, this series of drawings entitled "Evolution" (above) accompanied an advertisement for the Alexander Technique, a unique form of physical re-education widely used in music and drama schools to improve

Benedictines. Soon they will emerge from the cave and process down the aisle, two by two, in a cloud of incense. We will celebrate, which is something Benedictines do exceedingly well. And I will be strengthened by another joyful liturgy, something to remember when my mind wanders or sinks in the slough of despond. Something to come back to.

—KATHLEEN NORRIS, "July 11 Benedict's Cave"

the way a person uses his or her body. Proponents of the Alexander Technique argue that humans start out in life with naturally good posture, but that the way we study, read, work on a computer, and play sports damages our posture, so that we simply forget the best ways to stand, sit, and walk. The Alexander Technique is designed to reteach us these skills.

The visual tells this story as it fulfills its purposes of providing information (how and why posture declines) and making an argument (the Alexander Technique will improve posture). The narrative spans millions of years, as you can see, from the earliest *Pliopithecus* and *Ramapithecus* to the upright Cro–Magnon (a spear–carrying hunter with good posture) to the modern man, whose posture is damaged first by agricultural work, then by industrial work, and finally by bending over a computer. The silent characters in this visual narrative of human evolution convey the effects of tools on posture — in chronological order.

Notice how this visual implies that with each advance in technology or "civilization" beyond the hunting stage, humans have regressed further back toward the condition of chimpanzees, an unflattering comparison that presumably might encourage some readers to raise their eyes from the magazine (or the computer screen) and take a critical look at their own posture. The balanced structure of the series of drawings, gradually rising to a high point in the middle and then descending again, also creates a visually pleasing shape that draws the viewer's eye. (The shape of the chimpanzee at the beginning is even balanced by the shape of the computer–user at the end.) But the visual itself does not argue that the Alexander Technique will improve posture, and there's always the possibility that some readers who don't believe in evolution might even be put off by it. Whenever you look at a visual that seems intended as a narrative — and especially if you're thinking of using it as part of a written narrative — carefully consider its details, the overall effect the details create, and how well this effect achieves a particular purpose for the intended audience.

Whether you start at the beginning or use flashback or flashforward, make sure that your organizational pattern contributes to the purpose of your narrative (to report information, support an argument, provide an example, or set a mood).

As you lead readers through your narrative, you can help them by using **transitions,** words or phrases that guide readers clearly from one incident to the next. Words such as *first, then, afterward, when, second, finally,* and *before* and phrases such as *the next day, in the years to follow,* and *in time* all help your readers move through the story without becoming confused. In a biographical sketch of Britney Spears, *Rolling Stone* writer Chris Mundy recounts Spears's career–building years in chronological order, using careful transitions:

> "I don't think people realize how hard it was on my family to have me do this," says Spears. "It wasn't overnight."
>
> Some of the strains were financial. . . . And <u>then</u> there were the strains created by distance. <u>When she was nine years old</u>, Spears and her mother, who was pregnant, moved to New York so Spears could attend the Professional Performing Arts School. <u>Eventually</u>, with the arrival of Spears's baby sister, the three female Spears lived in Manhattan <u>while</u> the males resided in Louisiana.
>
> . . . In New York, Spears landed an off-Broadway play and a few commercials, and she won as a contestant on *Star Search*. <u>A year after that</u>, she moved to Orlando <u>for two years</u> to be a member of the new *Mickey Mouse Club*. <u>After a brief stint</u> back in Kentwood [Louisiana], she was shipped back to New York to audition for Jive Records. <u>This time</u>, Spears left Louisiana for good.   —CHRIS MUNDY, "The Girl Can't Help It"

The transitional words and phrases make it easy for readers to follow what Spears did — and when.

As you tell your story, choose the appropriate verb tense along with transitions to help readers understand where you are in the narrative and where you're going. In the preceding example about Spears, Mundy primarily uses the simple past tense (*was, moved, lived, resided, landed, won, moved, was shipped,* and *left*) to indicate actions that happened in the past. Compare Mundy's use of the simple past tense with bell hooks's use of a wide variety of verb forms in her narrative (see p. 142). For example, she uses three different present–tense forms to describe a series of events: present progressive tense (*am writing*) to indicate what she is doing at that moment; simple present tense (*long, accuse*) to describe a current event; and present perfect tense (*have been involved, has been called*) to call attention to something that began in the past but is ongoing.

Understanding and Using Narration

Analyzing Narratives

1. Reread the Dear Abby letter on p. 136. **Working with two or three classmates,** jot down the incidents that support the writer's thesis. Discuss whether the same story could support any other thesis, and prepare a brief presentation for the rest of the class.

2. How effective is the chronological ordering of events in the letter on p. 136? Would another order be more effective? Why or why not?

3. Reread the passage from Spanier's "Coincidence and Injustice" on p. 138. What injustice does the author imply? Does his story illustrate more than one injustice?

4. **Working with two or three classmates,** consider why Spanier's narrative is effective, particularly in light of all we now know about the Holocaust. What events does Spanier leave unmentioned? How does his selection of certain events and his silence about others help create a mood?

5. Return to your draft about the lesson you learned as a result of a memorable personal experience (p. 137). Number the events in your narrative; underline the characters and description; mark any dialogue. Then consider the purpose of the assignment, and decide whether these narrative elements in your draft help fulfill that purpose.

Planning and Writing Narratives

1. Reread the excerpt from Richard Wright's "The Ethics of Living Jim Crow" on p. 144 to remind yourself about how a chronological pattern of organization can work. Then write out, in order, a list of everything that has happened in your composition class so far today. Who spoke? Who read? Who wrote? How much did each person do? to what overall effect? How might the information you've gathered be shaped into a narrative? **Trade your information with a classmate,** and discuss the ways each of your lists might become a narrative.

2. Complete and respond to this sentence: "The first day of college is ___." (You could choose to focus on the first day of orientation, of registration for classes, or of classes themselves.) You might write about the first day being scary, exhausting, or confusing—or exciting, surprising, or exhilarating. Choose *one* descriptive term to set the mood, and begin writing down ideas, incidents, characters, snippets of dialogue—whatever you remember from your first day that might be useful in a narrative essay. **Share your list with two or three classmates,** noting any ideas they give you that might work successfully in your essay. Working as a group, revise the thesis (controlling idea) for each group member's essay.

3. Look over your notes for the previous question, and delete any details, characters, or dialogue that won't help develop the thesis statement by creating a particular mood. Referring to these notes and the following guidelines for checking over narrative writing, draft a two- to three-page narrative essay that supports your thesis statement about the first day of school.

4. How do you identify yourself? When you think about who you are, do you think of your age, sex, ethnicity, race, or class? your religion, occupation, or hometown? something else? Choose one of these aspects of yourself that you remember becoming conscious of at a specific time. Draft a two- to three-page narrative essay about this point in your life and the ways you've lived since that confirm or enhance this identity.

Revise your draft, using the following guidelines for checking over narrative writing.

5. Draft a three- to four-page retrospective account of your college life. From your imagined point of view on graduation day, describe your college years in the way you hope they turn out and will be regarded by others. If you prefer, write in the third person. What will have been the purpose of your education? What will have been your most important struggles and successes? Who will be the major characters? As you write, remember to consult the following guidelines for checking over narrative writing.

✓ Checking Over Narrative Writing

1. What is the main purpose of your narrative? Are you aiming just to record an informative sequence of incidents; or is your purpose to support a thesis, provide an example, or create a mood? How well have you achieved that purpose?

2. What is the thesis of your narrative? Is it stated or implied? Does anything in the narrative distract from or contradict the thesis?

3. Who is the audience for this narrative? What limitations or responsibilities do the audience members place on you? Have you provided any background information they need? more than they need? Have you revealed personal information you would prefer to keep to yourself?

4. What order are you using for the incidents in your narrative? Are you using chronological order? Number the incidents in your narrative *in the order they occurred.* Now use letters to indicate the order in which you have written about these incidents. Have you used flashback or flashforward? If so, is the technique effective? Might your readers be confused by it?

5. Have you used verb tenses correctly? Underline all the verbs and verb phrases. Do you use the present tense for incidents that are happening now? past or present perfect tense for incidents that happened in the past? and past perfect tense to indicate incidents that occurred before other events in the past?

6. Draw a circle around all the transitional words and phrases. Now read through your narrative. Are there other places where transitions would help your readers follow it more easily?

7. Do you use dialogue in your narrative? If so, does it help achieve your overall purpose?

8. If you're using visuals, do they help fulfill your overall purpose? Do you need to add labels, captions, or references in the written text?

READINGS

MALCOLM X
Prison Studies

Born Malcolm Little in Omaha, Nebraska, Malcolm X (1925–1965) is best known as a black militant leader who articulated concepts of race pride and black nationalism. As a child he and his family faced racism on a daily basis, including having their house burned down by the Ku Klux Klan; his father's murder and his mother's confinement in a mental institution further disrupted his childhood. In 1946, Malcolm was imprisoned on burglary charges, and it was there — in prison — that his life changed for the better. He learned to read fluently and converted to the Nation of Islam, a faith that professes the superiority of black people. Eventually, after a visit to Africa, he separated himself from the Nation of Islam and abandoned his antiwhite stance, but shortly thereafter, on February 21, 1965, he was assassinated. Three members of the Nation of Islam were convicted of the crime, although controversy over the verdict continues. The following essay is from *The Autobiography of Malcolm X* (1964), which Malcolm wrote in collaboration with Alex Haley.

> **Preview** Write for several minutes about what studies a person might undertake in a prison.

Thesis Statement

Many who today hear me somewhere in person, or on television, or those   1
who read something I've said, will think I went to school far beyond the
eighth grade. This impression is due entirely to my prison studies.

It had really begun back in the Charlestown Prison, when Bimbi first   2
made me feel envy of his stock of knowledge. Bimbi had always taken
charge of any conversation he was in, and I had tried to emulate him.
But every book I picked up had few sentences which didn't contain anywhere from one to nearly all of the words that might as well have been
in Chinese. When I just skipped those words, of course, I really ended up
with little idea of what the book said. So I had come to the Norfolk
Prison Colony still going through only book-reading motions. Pretty

soon, I would have quit even these motions, unless I had received the motivation that I did.

I saw that the best thing I could do was get hold of a dictionary—to study, to learn some words. I was lucky enough to reason also that I should try to improve my penmanship. It was sad. I couldn't even write in a straight line. It was both ideas together that moved me to request a dictionary along with some tablets and pencils from the Norfolk Prison Colony school. 3

I spent two days just riffling uncertainly though the dictionary's pages. I'd never realized so many words existed! I didn't know which words I needed to learn. Finally, to start some kind of action, I began copying. 4

In my slow, painstaking, ragged handwriting, I copied into my tablet everything printed on that first page, down to the punctuation marks. 5

I believe it took me a day. Then, aloud, I read back, to myself, everything I'd written on the tablet. Over and over, aloud to myself, I read my own handwriting. 6

I woke up the next morning, thinking about those words—immensely proud to realize that not only had I written so much at one 7

Malcolm X during a Nation of Islam rally in New York City in 1963.

time, but I'd written words that I never knew were in the world. More-over, with a little effort, I also could remember what many of these words meant. I reviewed the words whose meanings I didn't remember. Funny thing, from the dictionary first page right now, that "aardvark" springs to my mind. The dictionary had a picture of it, a long–tailed, long–eared, burrowing African mammal, which lives off termites caught by sticking out its tongue as an anteater does for ants.

I was so fascinated that I went on—I copied the dictionary's next 8 page. And the same experience came when I studied that. With every succeeding page, I also learned of people and places and events from history. Actually the dictionary is like a miniature encyclopedia. Finally the dictionary's A section had filled a whole tablet—and I went on into the B's. That was the way I started copying what eventually became the entire dictionary. It went a lot faster after so much practice helped me to pick up handwriting speed. Between what I wrote in my tablet, and writ-ing letters, during the rest of my time in prison I would guess I wrote a million words.

I suppose it was inevitable that as my word–base broadened, I could 9 for the first time pick up a book and read and now begin to understand what the book was saying. Anyone who has read a great deal can imag-ine the new world that opened. Let me tell you something: from then until I left the prison, in every free moment I had, if I was not reading in the library, I was reading on my bunk. You couldn't have gotten me out of books with a wedge. Between Mr. Muhammad's teachings, my correspondence, my visitors—usually Ella and Reginald—and my reading of books, months passed without my even thinking about being imprisoned. In fact, up to then, I never had been so truly free in my life.

As you can imagine, especially in a prison where there was heavy 10 emphasis on rehabilitation, an inmate was smiled upon if he demon-strated an unusually intense interest in books. There was a sizable num-ber of well–read inmates, especially the popular debaters. Some were said by many to be practically walking encyclopedias. They were almost celebrities. No university would ask any student to devour literature as I did when this new world opened to me, of being able to read and *under-stand.*

I read more in my room than in the library itself. An inmate who 11 was known to read a lot could check out more than the permitted maxi-mum number of books. I preferred reading in the total isolation of my own room.

When I had progressed to really serious reading, every night at 12 about ten P.M. I would be outraged with the "lights out." It always seemed to catch me right in the middle of something engrossing.

Fortunately, right outside my door was a corridor light that cast a 13 glow into my room. The glow was enough to read by, once my eyes adjusted to it. So when "lights out" came, I would sit on the floor where I could continue reading in that glow.

At one–hour intervals the night guards paced past every room. Each 14 time I heard the approaching footsteps, I jumped into bed and feigned sleep. And as soon as the guard passed, I got back out of bed onto the floor area of that light–glow, where I would read for another fifty–eight minutes — until the guard approached again. That went on until three or four every morning. Three or four hours of sleep a night was enough for me. Often in the years in the streets I had slept less than that.

I have often reflected upon the new vistas that reading opened to 15 me. I knew right there in prison that reading had changed forever the course of my life. As I see it today, the ability to read awoke inside me some long dormant craving to be mentally alive. I certainly wasn't seeking any degree, the way a college confers a status symbol upon its students. My homemade education gave me, with every additional book that I read, a little bit more sensitivity to the deafness, dumbness, and blindness that was afflicting the black race in America. Not long ago, an English writer telephoned me from London, asking questions. One was, "What's your alma mater?" I told him, "Books." You will never catch me with a free fifteen minutes in which I'm not studying something I feel might be able to help the black man.

Every time I catch a plane, I have with me a book that I want to 16 read — and that's a lot of books these days. If I weren't out here every day battling the white man, I could spend the rest of my life reading, just satisfying my curiosity — because you can hardly mention anything I'm not curious about. I don't think anybody ever got more out of going to prison than I did. In fact, prison enabled me to study far more intensively than I would have if my life had gone differently and I had attended some college. I imagine that one of the biggest troubles with colleges is there are too many distractions, too much panty–raiding, fraternities, and boola–boola and all of that. Where else but in prison could I have attacked my ignorance by being able to study intensely sometimes as much as fifteen hours a day?

Reading Closely

1. **With three or four classmates,** discuss what you learned about life in prison and the opportunities for reading there that you didn't know before you read this narrative. What surprised you the most? What pleased you the most? Prepare a group response to share with the rest of the class.

2. What is this narrative about? In no more than two paragraphs, retell Malcolm X's narrative. Then condense your paragraphs to one, leaving in only the crucial information.

3. What specific details does the visual offer? How do those details enhance the essay?

Considering Larger Issues

1. Early on, Malcolm X tells his readers that his skill at using language gives a mistaken impression of his formal education. Who is his audience for this remark? For whom does this narrative seem to be written? What might be his purpose in referring to the gap between his use of language and his formal education?

2. What is the overall purpose of this narrative? How is that purpose related to the audience?

3. Who are the characters in this narrative? How are they portrayed, and to what effect? How does their dialogue support Malcolm X's overall purpose?

4. What is the thesis of this narrative? Write it out in one sentence. Now, **work with three or four classmates** to share your sentences and come to a group decision on the thesis. Write out your group's decision as well as the incidents and descriptions that help to support or illustrate that thesis. Be prepared to share your ideas with the rest of the class.

5. COMBINING METHODS. Malcolm X's story about prison life is a powerful literacy narrative. But it's also an analysis of *causes and consequences*. Mark the passages that analyze causes and consequences, and explain how these passages help fulfill the overall purpose of the narrative. Be prepared to share your ideas with the rest of the class.

Thinking about Language

1. Define the following words or phrases, either by using the essay context or by turning to your dictionary. Be prepared to share your answers with the rest of the class.

emulate (2)	rehabilitation (10)	feigned (14)
riffling (4)	engrossing (12)	dormant (15)
burrowing (7)	corridor (13)	

2. How many paragraphs does Malcolm X use in this essay? How many sentences are in each paragraph? How many words are in each paragraph? in each sentence? What are the averages? Paragraph length and sentence length are two ways an author establishes his or her own style. What do these averages tell you about Malcolm X's writing style? What is the effect on the reader?

Writing Your Own Narratives

1. Malcolm X's quest for greater literacy is one that all college students embark upon, if not to the same degree. Think about what you hope to gain from your undergraduate education. Make notes about the series of steps that lies ahead of you. What would you sacrifice, or what might you be sacrificing, for this education? In an essay of three to four pages, write a narrative that recounts your gains as well as any losses (such as

losing touch with certain friends or family) as you became an educated American. Refer to "Checking Over Narrative Writing" on p. 150.

2. Draft a three- to four-page narrative that traces the educational progress — or lack thereof — of one of your parents. Determine a specific purpose for your narrative early on. Then develop a thesis statement that grows out of that purpose, making sure that each incident in the narrative supports the thesis. Consider what your parent gained — and lost — in the process. You may want to invent some dialogue and include a visual or two as a way to make your essay come alive. Be sure to refer to the guidelines for checking over narrative writing on p. 150.

DAVID SEDARIS
Me Talk Pretty One Day

David Sedaris (b. 1957) taught writing at the Art Institute of Chicago for two years before making a splash on the national scene as a radio commentator, essayist, playwright, and humorist. A regular commentator on National Public Radio's *Morning Edition* and a contributor to the *New Yorker* and *Esquire* magazines, Sedaris has also written nearly ten plays with his sister Amy, including *Incident, One Woman Shoe, The Little Frieda Mysteries, Stump the Host,* and *Stitches.* He has also published several collections of essays, including *Barrel Fever* (1994), *Naked* (1997), *Holidays on Ice* (1997), and *Me Talk Pretty One Day* (2000), from which the following essay is taken. In 2001, Sedaris received the Thurber Prize for American Humor and was named *Time* Magazine's Humorist of the Year. Sedaris currently lives in Paris.

> **Preview**   Have you ever tried to learn a foreign language? If so, what influence did your teachers — or a particular teacher — have on your success or failure? Take a few minutes to write about your learning experience.

At the age of forty-one, I am returning to school and have to think of   1
myself as what my French textbook calls "a true debutant." After paying my tuition, I was issued a student ID, which allows me a discounted entry fee at movie theaters, puppet shows, and Festyland, a far-flung amusement park that advertises with billboards picturing a cartoon stegosaurus sitting in a canoe and eating what appears to be a ham sandwich.

I've moved to Paris with hopes of learning the language. My school   2
is an easy ten-minute walk from my apartment, and on the first day of class I arrived early, watching as the returning students greeted one another in the school lobby. Vacations were recounted, and questions were raised concerning mutual friends with names like Kang and Vlatnya. Regardless of their nationalities, everyone spoke in what sounded to me like excellent French. Some accents were better than others, but the students exhibited an ease and confidence I found intimidating. As an added discomfort, they were all young, attractive, and well dressed, causing me to feel not unlike Pa Kettle* trapped backstage after a fashion show.

The first day of class was nerve-racking because I knew I'd be ex   3
pected to perform. That's the way they do it here — it's everybody into the language pool, sink or swim. The teacher marched in, deeply tanned from a recent vacation, and proceeded to rattle off a series of administrative announcements. I've spent quite a few summers in Normandy, and I

---

* **Pa Kettle:** a country-bumpkin character in many movies of the 1950s.

took a monthlong French class before leaving New York. I'm not completely in the dark, yet I understood only half of what this woman was
saying.

"If you have not *meimslsxp* or *lgpdmurct* by this time, then you should   4
not be in this room. Has everyone *apzkiubjxow?* Everyone? Good, we shall
begin." She spread out her lesson plan and sighed, saying, "All right, then,
who knows the alphabet?"

It was startling because (a) I hadn't been asked that question in a   5
while and (b) I realized, while laughing, that I myself did *not* know the
alphabet. They're the same letters, but in France they're pronounced differently. I know the shape of the alphabet but had no idea what it actually sounded like.

"Ahh." The teacher went to the board and sketched the letter *a*. "Do   6
we have anyone in the room whose first name commences with an *ahh?*"

Two Polish Annas raised their hands, and the teacher instructed   7
them to present themselves by stating their names, nationalities, occupations, and a brief list of things they liked and disliked in this world. The
first Anna hailed from an industrial town outside of Warsaw and had
front teeth the size of tombstones. She worked as a seamstress, enjoyed
quiet times with friends, and hated the mosquito.

"Oh, really," the teacher said. "How very interesting. I thought that   8
everyone loved the mosquito, but here, in front of all the world, you
claim to detest him. How is it that we've been blessed with someone as
unique and original as you? Tell us, please."

The seamstress did not understand what was being said but knew   9
that this was an occasion for shame. Her rabbity mouth huffed for
breath, and she stared down at her lap as though the appropriate come-
back were stitched somewhere alongside the zipper of her slacks.

The second Anna learned from the first and claimed to love sunshine   10
and detest lies. It sounded like a translation of one of those Playmate of
the Month data sheets, the answers always written in the same loopy
handwriting: "Turn-ons: Mom's famous five-alarm chili! Turnoffs: insecurity and guys who come on too strong!!!!"

The two Polish Annas surely had clear notions of what they loved   11
and hated, but like the rest of us, they were limited in terms of vocabulary, and this made them appear less than sophisticated. The teacher
forged on, and we learned that Carlos, the Argentine bandonion player,
loved wine, music, and, in his words, "making sex with the womens of
the world." Next came a beautiful young Yugoslav who identified herself
as an optimist, saying that she loved everything that life had to offer.

The teacher licked her lips, revealing a hint of the saucebox we   12
would later come to know. She crouched low for her attack, placed her
hands on the young woman's desk, and leaned close, saying, "Oh yeah?
And do you love your little war?"

While the optimist struggled to defend herself, I scrambled to think   13
of an answer to what had obviously become a trick question. How often

is one asked what he loves in this world? More to the point, how often is one asked and then publicly ridiculed for his answer? I recalled my mother, flushed with wine, pounding the tabletop late one night, saying, "Love? I love a good steak cooked rare. I love my cat, and I love . . ." My sisters and I leaned forward, waiting to hear our names. "Tums," our mother said. "I love Tums."

The teacher killed some time accusing the Yugoslavian girl of master- 14 minding a program of genocide, and I jotted frantic notes in the margins of my pad. While I can honestly say that I love leafing through medical textbooks devoted to severe dermatological conditions, the hobby is be- yond the reach of my French vocabulary, and acting it out would only have invited controversy.

When called upon, I delivered an effortless list of things that I detest: 15 blood sausage, intestinal pâtés, brain pudding. I'd learned these words the hard way. Having given it some thought, I then declared my love for IBM typewriters, the French word for *bruise*, and my electric floor waxer. It was a short list, but still I managed to mispronounce *IBM* and assign the wrong gender to both the floor waxer and the typewriter. The teacher's reaction led me to believe that these mistakes were capital crimes in the country of France.

"Were you always this *palicmkrexis?*" she asked. "Even a *fiuscrzsa ticiwel-* 16 *mun* knows that a typewriter is feminine."

I absorbed as much of her abuse as I could understand, thinking— 17 but not saying—that I find it ridiculous to assign a gender to an inani- mate object incapable of disrobing and making an occasional fool of it- self. Why refer to crack pipe or Good Sir Dishrag when these things could never live up to all that their sex implied?

The teacher proceeded to belittle everyone from German Eva, who 18 hated laziness, to Japanese Yukari, who loved paintbrushes and soap. Italian, Thai, Dutch, Korean, and Chinese—we all left class foolishly be- lieving that the worst was over. She'd shaken us up a little, but surely that was just an act designed to weed out the deadweight. We didn't know it then, but the coming months would teach us what it was like to spend time in the presence of a wild animal, something completely un- predictable. Her temperament was not based on a series of good and bad days but, rather, good and bad moments. We soon learned to dodge chalk and protect our heads and stomachs whenever she approached us with a question. She hadn't yet punched anyone, but it seemed wise to protect ourselves against the inevitable.

Though we were forbidden to speak anything but French, the teacher 19 would occasionally use us to practice any of her five fluent languages.

"I hate you," she said to me one afternoon. Her English was flawless. 20 "I really, really hate you." Call me sensitive, but I couldn't help but take it personally.

After being singled out as a lazy *kfdtinvfm*, I took to spending four 21 hours a night on my homework, putting in even more time whenever we were assigned an essay. I suppose I could have gotten by with less, but I was determined to create some sort of identity for myself: David the hard worker, David the cut–up. We'd have one of those "complete this sentence" exercises, and I'd fool with the thing for hours, invariably settling on something like "A quick run around the lake? I'd love to! Just give me a moment while I strap on my wooden leg." The teacher, through word and action, conveyed the message that if this was my idea of an identity, she wanted nothing to do with it.

My fear and discomfort crept beyond the borders of the classroom 22 and accompanied me out onto the wide boulevards. Stopping for a coffee, asking directions, depositing money in my bank account: these things were out of the question, as they involved having to speak. Before beginning school, there'd been no shutting me up, but now I was convinced that everything I said was wrong. When the phone rang, I ignored it. If someone asked me a question, I pretended to be deaf. I knew my fear was getting the best of me when I started wondering why they don't sell cuts of meat in vending machines.

My only comfort was the knowledge that I was not alone. Huddled 23 in the hallways and making the most of our pathetic French, my fellow students and I engaged in the sort of conversation commonly overheard in refugee camps.

"Sometime me cry alone at night."   24

"That be common for I, also, but be more strong, you. Much work 25 and someday you talk pretty. People start love you soon. Maybe tomorrow, okay."

Unlike the French class I had taken in New York, here there was no 26 sense of competition. When the teacher poked a shy Korean in the eyelid with a freshly sharpened pencil, we took no comfort in the fact that, unlike Hyeyoon Cho, we all knew the irregular past tense of the verb *to defeat*. In all fairness, the teacher hadn't meant to stab the girl, but neither did she spend much time apologizing, saying only, "Well, you should have been *vkkdyo* more *kdeynfulh.*"

Over time it became impossible to believe that any of us would ever 27 improve. Fall arrived and it rained every day, meaning we would now be scolded for the water dripping from our coats and umbrellas. It was mid-October when the teacher singled me out, saying, "Every day spent with you is like having a cesarean section." And it struck me that, for the first time since arriving in France, I could understand every word that someone was saying.

Understanding doesn't mean that you can suddenly speak the lan– 28 guage. Far from it. It's a small step, nothing more, yet its rewards are intoxicating and deceptive. The teacher continued her diatribe and I settled back, bathing in the subtle beauty of each new curse and insult.

"You exhaust me with your foolishness and reward my efforts with 29 nothing but pain, do you understand me?"

The world opened up, and it was with great joy that I responded, "I 30 know the thing that you speak exact now. Talk me more, you, plus, please, plus."

Reading Closely

1. "The teacher marched in, deeply tanned from a recent vacation, and proceeded to rattle off a series of administrative announcements." The preceding sentence resonates with the teacher's power in this narrative. Locate other passages in Sedaris's narration where he refers to the teacher's power. How many times does he refer to it?

2. What are the stages Sedaris goes through to learn French? Which stages seem to be positive ones? negative ones? What other stages does he describe?

3. What are the benefits of Sedaris's decision to learn French? to endure language school? What are the unpleasant consequences of his decision? What would you like — or not like — about the literacy experience he has chosen?

4. What is Sedaris's purpose in writing this essay? What specific events, characters, dialogue, and settings help support your answer?

Considering Larger Issues

1. What is the setting for this narration, and what significance does it have for Sedaris's overall purpose? What is his purpose?

2. Think about the audience for Sedaris's wickedly funny writing. What kinds of people would enjoy his writing and his subject? Locate the details and incidents that he uses to interest such an audience. Be prepared to share your response with the rest of the class.

3. What is the thesis of Sedaris's narration? Write it out in one sentence. How do mentions of his teacher, his classmates, and himself help support and develop his thesis? Prepare a brief report for the rest of the class.

4. Besides the teacher, who are the other characters in this essay? What do they say? How does Sedaris use these characters and their dialogue to support his main point and carry out his purpose for writing the essay?

5. **COMBINING METHODS.** How does Sedaris *compare* his literacy in English with his literacy in French? What is the overall effect of these comparisons?

6. Write for a few minutes about the power a teacher has, drawing from your own experiences with teachers. **Working with two or three students,** read your responses aloud and compare them. Then prepare a group response to share with the rest of the class.

Thinking about Language

1. Throughout his essay, Sedaris demonstrates the limits of any vocabulary, especially of his French vocabulary. Choose two of the following terms from Sedaris's English vocabulary and define them, either from the context of the essay or from your dictionary. Be prepared to share your answers with the rest of the class.

debutant (1)	genocide (14)	temperament (18)
saucebox (12)	dermatological (14)	diatribe (28)
masterminding (14)	deadweight (18)	

2. Underline all the words in this essay that you cannot define. Then circle the words you need to define in order to understand a passage. **Work with two or three classmates** to define the words you have circled, determining their meaning either from context or by using your dictionary.

3. Locate all the terms and phrases in the essay that signify transition. How often does Sedaris use transitions? Does he ever imply the passage of time or a change in location? If so, identify the places where he does so. How does his use of transitional words or phrases move his essay forward?

4. Jot down the descriptive words and phrases Sedaris uses to distinguish one classmate from another. Translate Sedaris's description into your own words, describing each classmate in a way that individualizes him or her.

Writing Your Own Narratives

1. Sedaris's goal is to speak French fluently. What career, health, family, academic, or athletic goal have you set for yourself? What specific steps have you taken to reach that goal? Which steps have been easy or just as you expected? Which steps have been surprisingly difficult or different from what you expected? What have you learned on the way to achieving your goal?

   After responding to these questions, draft a three- to four-page narrative essay about the process of striving for or reaching your specific goal. What is the purpose of your narrative? What thesis do you want your narrative to support? Order the steps carefully, and consider including important characters besides yourself and revealing dialogue as well as key details about the setting. Your final draft should include only the steps, characters, dialogue, and other details that help make your point. Refer to "Checking Over Narrative Writing" on p. 150.

2. Freewrite for a few minutes about a time when you trusted someone because of that person's status or position. The authority figure might have been a teacher, doctor, nurse, dentist, member of the clergy, coach, firefighter, police officer, salesclerk, or car mechanic. What was good — or bad — about your experience with this person? What did you learn from

it? Use your freewriting as the basis for a three- to four-page narrative about this experience with trust and authority. As you draft and revise, refer to the guidelines for checking over narrative writing on p. 150.

3. Consider the importance of psychology in the practice of teaching. **Working alone or with a classmate,** write down all the reasons you can think of for the importance of enthusiasm, empathy, and kindliness in teachers' relations with their students. Are these sensibilities less important than, more important than, or just as important as technical skill and knowledge? Decide on a thesis statement and provide some examples that support it, either from personal experience or from the experiences of other students you know. Then write a three- to four-page essay in which you support your thesis by weaving in these short narratives, referring to "Checking Over Narrative Writing" on p. 150.

JACEY BLOUCH
Dance to Liven Up Your Life

● Jacey Blouch, a native of Lebanon, Pennsylvania, wrote the following essay as a sophomore majoring in integrative arts at Penn State University. Following graduation, she plans to attend graduate school to earn a degree in interior design. In her essay, Blouch uses narrative to describe the impact that dance has had on her life—physically, intellectually, socially, and emotionally.

> **Preview**   What do you think of Blouch's basic argument—that dance enhances her life in many ways? Have any of your extracurricular activities had a similar effect on your life?

Waiting silently backstage, we watch the lights begin to dim. The stage crew gives the "go" signal, as we quietly tiptoe out onto the stage and take our places. We all stand still with our heads down. A cold breeze from the auditorium wraps around our bodies as the curtain opens. In the few seconds before the music starts, our minds go blank. A sense of panic begins to make our hearts beat faster. Suddenly our bodies take over and we all begin to dance.

I decided to take private dance lessons when I was four years old. For the first six years, I practiced tap, ballet, and tumbling once a week. The classes were held in a small one-room schoolhouse with floor-to-ceiling mirrors on every wall. Some might envision dance rooms with posters of European castles, theater actors, or rock-and-roll stars. That was not the case in this room. The light pink walls were mostly bare, with a few ballet posters pinned up sporadically around the perimeter. There were few distractions for students, and therefore, we all learned how to pay close attention to our instructors. It was as if we were all together in our own little world. It did not matter what our surroundings were, because our imaginations took flight. I imagined that I was a ballerina in the famous ballets in New York City. When selecting a leotard to wear to class, I always chose one that I thought a special dancer would wear.

My mother usually drove me and my best friend to class. We listened to the upbeat tunes on the radio, and my mother talked in her serene, calming voice. Sometimes I became nervous, thinking I might not perform well that day. Other times I anticipated putting on my dancing shoes and twirling around before class started. Perhaps I was too young to realize that dance class was not just about the physical movement of the body but also the unlimited things I could learn. Little did I know that the names of certain dance moves would stick in my mind. I remember them still and know exactly what they mean: pirouettes, piques, and port de bras. Dancing gave me a head start even before I reached kindergarten: reading over my ballet terms before class helped me feel comfortable learning and taking tests later at school. I had already formed good study habits, which I applied to my academic subjects.

As I grew older, I enrolled in more progressive dance classes such as 4 jazz, funk, and later gymnastics. Lessons were filled with difficult techniques. We practiced what seemed like a million repetitions of the same steps. Every class offered different combinations of moves to popular music selections. I can remember working hard on leaps across the floor, while simultaneously working to perfect my pointed toes and soar in the air as high as I could. I felt like I was gaining more skill and knowledge than the average athlete so that in gym class, where only the basics were covered, I knew the intricate maneuvers for each style of dance and the physical limits of the body.

From dance I learned that stretching is an important part of any 5 workout because it allows muscles to relax and absorb oxygen before any activity takes place. In stretches that sometimes tested my abilities, my teacher taught me to spread my toes apart "like a duck" and squeeze them to the floor for balance. I never realized how my body could become so focused in a single moment. Learning different combinations of moves and general techniques helps the body's sense of balance and hand–eye coordination. If a dancer was struggling to keep her balance, our instructor advised her to think of "pushing your belly button to the floor." It was an exercise to mentally find the center of gravity by imagining that a string was pulling her belly button to the ground. It was an odd instruction, but surprisingly it worked. During street–fair performances, where stages were often uneven, I once encountered a sloping floor as I landed from a leap. I slid and almost crashed right into a large speaker on the front of the stage. I quickly stood up straight and envisioned my belly button being pulled down perpendicular to the stage. It might seem like a lot to think about while dancing, but it worked. In time, this strategy feels very natural.

Most audiences view dancers only as physical beings. What people 6 do not realize is that dancing affects a person emotionally and mentally as well. At times when I could not execute a move correctly, I became extremely frustrated. However, I learned that as I persevered at these difficult tasks, I began to master them. As I excelled, I gained confidence in myself and this confidence extended to other areas of my life. Before I entered dance, I wasn't involved in many other activities. Typically, I was too nervous to participate within a group of peers. I did not want to disappoint anyone on my team. Fortunately, I made many friends in my dance classes who had the same feelings, and together we overcame our fears. Two sisters from my class, Renatta and Paula, had a habit of diving right into new moves, whether or not they could do them correctly. After watching these girls, I also attempted the new moves, even though I knew I would sometimes mess them up. When others in the class forgot their footwork or lost the rhythm of the music, they worked hard to improve their skills. We all worked hard to help the class work better as a group.

My most memorable experiences were the frequent recitals, parades, and annual street–fair performances. These events gave us the opportunity to show our relatives and friends how we strived to perfect our talents all year long. Dancing along the streets in the freezing cold or on a stage in the sweltering heat was not something I particularly enjoyed. But after our performances, I felt accomplished and proud. During the recital preparation, our instructor explained the content and history of the music and themes associated with the dancing styles. I learned the history of modern dance from participating in a stage performance entitled *Vaudeville to Video*, with my dance number representing the early '90s rap music. Another favorite was the stage show *Dance around the World*. I learned about different ethnic and cultural backgrounds from people all over the world.

My last year of dance instruction was during my freshman year in high school. To my surprise and happiness, I was selected to be on the varsity cheerleading squad for my school's football and basketball teams. I decided then to retire from the dance studio and focus entirely on cheerleading. Taking dance classes for eleven years helped me excel particularly at the band dances. My memorization skills grew sharp from the long, complex competition routines we performed as a cheering squad year after year. Dancing also prepared me for social dances in school and at parties. Once, at a friend's birthday party, I stood along the wall debating with myself about dancing on the dance floor. When I did, I was proud to bust out a few moves in front of my friends. Without my dancing background, I would not have been able to keep the rhythm, show off my flexibility, and have a great time.

I am very thankful for the opportunity to dance. I loved participating in such a diversified and challenging activity. It has helped me entertain others, gain confidence, expand my skills, and become a well–rounded person. Even though I do not perform much at this point in my life, the rush of dancing is one I will never forget.

Reading Closely

1. How does Blouch connect her description of learning to dance with the values of learning to dance?

2. Blouch recalls her experience as "not just about the physical movement of the body." What information given at the beginning of her essay might lead you to believe that dancing is only physical? How does she demonstrate the nonphysical features of dancing?

3. What do you learn about the writer herself as you read her essay? What is your dominant impression of her? What words or phrases contribute to this dominant impression? **Working with another classmate,** compare your ideas.

Considering Larger Issues

1. What is the overall purpose of Blouch's essay? What sequence of events does she use to support this purpose? Jot down these events in chronological order.

2. Who might be the audience for this essay? What information helps you determine that audience? What might the audience members already know about dancing? What might they want to know more about? How are purpose and audience connected in this essay?

3. What is the thesis of Blouch's essay? Is it stated or implied? Write it out.

4. How does Blouch organize her essay? Try outlining or mapping it out in a cluster. How else might she have organized it? to what effect? **Working with one or two classmates,** discuss your findings and prepare a group response to share with the rest of the class.

5. **COMBINING METHODS.** How does Blouch employ *cause-and-consequence analysis* in her narrative? What passages are particularly effective in terms of analyzing causes and consequences? Prepare to share your response with the rest of the class.

Thinking about Language

1. Use the context of the essay and your dictionary to define the following terms. Be prepared to share your answers with the rest of the class.

tumbling (2)	pirouettes (3)	execute (6)
sporadically (2)	intricate (4)	vaudeville (7)
serene (3)	perpendicular (5)	

2. Reread Blouch's essay, and mark all the words and phrases that emphasize her development as a dancer. How do these words and phrases help further her overall purpose?

3. How does Blouch use transitional words and phrases to help readers understand the time element of her essay? Underline all the transitions. Does she use transitions to signify anything other than time? How?

4. Blouch's essay includes a good number of descriptive details. Mark the ones that you think are most helpful in enabling you to appreciate her dancing lessons and skills. Be prepared to share your findings with the rest of the class.

Writing Your Own Narratives

1. Blouch's essay is about learning to take seriously what seems at first to be merely a hobby. Think back to your first impression of a so-called hobby, one that you initially thought was silly or superficial but that you eventually came to appreciate as valuable or substantial. Try to remember the events that happened during your first encounter—and later as you began to change your mind. Describe these events in sequence and

your perceptions of these events in as much detail as possible. Draft without stopping to edit—not yet, anyway. Read over your narrative to see if you have written with a purpose that can be shaped into a thesis statement. As you revise your draft into a two- to three–page narrative, remember to rely on the guidelines for checking over narrative writing on p. 150.

2. Using Blouch's essay as a model, think about dancing as an alternative kind of literacy that she developed. Then consider if you've developed an alternative kind of literacy that has affected you socially, physically, and/or intellectually. Draft a three- to four–page narrative in which you introduce this form of literacy to your audience, explain how you learned it, and provide examples of its effects. Like Blouch, you'll be mixing the methods of rhetorical development in order to write a successful essay. Be sure to check the guidelines for narrative writing on p. 150.

JEFF DRAYER
Bedside Terror

After publishing *The Cost-Effective Use of Leeches and Other Musings of a Medical School Survivor* (1998), Jeff Drayer (b. 1971) has continued to write essays about his life as a physician. "Bedside Terror," which appeared on the online periodical <www.salon.com> in June 2000, recounts his inexperience as an intern. "Bedside Terror" reveals how much information and how many procedures interns still need to learn — for the sake of the patients, other medical personnel, and the interns' own professional and personal growth. As you read the essay, consider whether you've ever been knowingly treated by an intern — and what difference that made. Also consider how Drayer uses narration to convey suspense and worry.

Preview Have you or anyone close to you ever had a terrifying experience in a hospital? What was the cause of the terror? How was the situation handled?

This summer thousands of med school graduates will be unleashed on unsuspecting patients, and I know why the public should be scared. 1

June 5, 2000, I tore down the last flight of stairs and burst into the hallway. A crowd of people turned as I rushed, white coat flapping behind me like a superhero's cape, into their midst. They parted readily, forming a narrow trail for me to pass into the room, wherein raged a small tornado of activity. At the eye lay an enormous, pale, heaving man. 2

"He's in V-tach, Doctor," a nearby nurse informed me breathlessly. "Oxygen sats down in the 80s." From nowhere an EKG appeared in my hand. I held it up and frowned thoughtfully. And as I stared at the series of lines and curves that held volumes of critical information about this dying man's cardiac function, one throbbing thought pulsed its way to the very front of my brain: I have no idea what the hell I'm doing. 3

Only 10 minutes before I had been sound asleep, dreaming that dream in which I live in a far-off land where people can have all the bowel movements they want and I don't have to report them to my resident. Suddenly, there was this terrible, insane beeping, the kind that didn't stop no matter how many times I hit my alarm clock or tried to check my laundry. 4

It had been my beeper, of course. And when I groggily answered it, only to get some woman asking for the intern on call, I became irate. After all, didn't she know I was just a med student? 5

But then, as I looked around at the sterile beige call room and the hard plastic hospital bed beneath me, I came to a realization. That graduation ceremony a month before. That Oath. Maybe I was the intern on call. Shit. 6

169

The Association of American Medical Colleges estimates that 18,391   7
people like me—fresh from medical school—will be unleashed on the
patients of this country on July 1. We will infiltrate local hospitals, clinics
and medical centers near you. Despite the four years we spent memorizing textbooks and not sleeping, many will feel, like I did on that day,
completely ill-prepared to be a doctor.

Contrary to popular belief, there are no actual classes in med school   8
on how to perform medical interventions. Sure, we sat for hours on
end learning all the atoms in the pyridine ring and their fascinating
relation to the pentose shunt. But spinal taps, Pap smears, staunching
the uncontrollable bleeding caused by a zealous nurse-practitioner—
these we simply had to pick up along the way. And if, through bad luck,
poor timing or sheer lack of interest, we did not witness a particular
procedure, such as draining an abscess, well, there was nothing you
could do.

BEDSIDE TERROR

So there I stood, with 300 pounds of cirrhotic liver slowly degenerat-   9
ing from decades of alcohol abuse and emphysematous lungs worn
down by thousand of packs of cigarettes, quivering violently next to me.

I closed my eyes and tried to remember that graph from physiology class four years before, the one about cardiac output or something. It felt so nice to have my eyes closed.

"You want a liter of fluids?" a tall nurse asked, the way my mom used 10 to "ask" me if I wanted some broccoli as she heaped it onto my plate. Startled, I nodded mutely, and turned to see a blond nurse hauling in paddles, glass vials and other vaguely familiar things.

"Should I put some gel on his chest?" she asked. It didn't sound like 11 it could hurt and she seemed so excited about it, so I nodded again. A large nurse began to draw some blood, and after several moments asked if I'd like her to draw some blood. I nodded once more.

Suddenly, two paddles appeared in my hand, just as I'd seen so 12 many times on television, and once in that class we had to take a few weeks before. Did I want to put them on the patient's chest, the blond nurse asked, in order to assess his cardiac rhythm? Another nod as the cold steel contacted the cooling flesh.

"Still V–tach," someone announced. I squinted at the monitor and 13 tried to remember whether ventricular tachycardia was a squiggly pattern or a sawtooth pattern.

"Everyone stand back and let the doctor shock him!" the tall nurse 14 yelled. I looked around—it was just me and the patient, alone in the middle of a circle of people, like the losers in some children's game. The tall nurse looked me in the eye: "You're all clear."

I sure didn't feel all clear, though. In fact, I felt pretty confused. After 15 all, there I was, the lone M.D. responsible for this patient's deteriorating medical condition. True, there were two residents elsewhere in the hospital with a year or two more experience than I, but their job was simply to answer any questions I had, and I didn't particularly think that a 10–minute telephone conversation was in order at the moment.

Besides, I had enough knowledge floating around in the part of my 16 head that used to contain baseball statistics to pass the national boards. I should be able to handle this, shouldn't I?

People have always told me that there was more to medicine than 17 just pure knowledge, but I had never believed them, until this very minute. They had said that the difference between being a medical student and an intern was the ability to take what little knowledge you had gained and put it all together. Was this true? Closing my eyes, I took a deep breath.

I opened them again to see the paddles still clutched in my hands. 18 Put it all together, I thought. Ventricular tachycardia—the part of the heart that pumped the blood to the rest of body was spasming uncontrollably, such that very little blood got pushed anywhere. How do you stop that? I could not remember.

"Doctor? You're clear." Clear? Clear. I looked down at the paddles— 19 there was only one button on each. With nothing else to do, I pushed, unleashing a terrible "ker–CHUNK!" I looked back at the monitor, as the sawteeth gave way to a spiky pattern. Spiky, I knew, was good.

"Pressure's back to 100 over 60," someone announced, dialing a 20 phone. "You want me to call intensive care?" I nodded, happy to know that this patient would soon be in a place where he wasn't my responsibility and could have all the arrhythmias he wanted. A smiling nurse handed me the chart and suggested I sign the orders. "Great work, doctor," she said, her eyes like saucers. I hadn't done a single thing, or even said a word. I nodded one last time.

Throughout medical school, there are two rules that are constantly 21 being pounded into each student's moist, softened brain. The first is that it's OK to admit that you don't know something. This is based on the idea that nobody knows everything, and if you don't know the answer, it's much better to admit to it rather than go off half–cocked and possibly screw something up like an idiot.

The second rule is that no matter what, under no circumstances 22 should you ever ever admit that you don't know something. The idea behind this is that we're doctors, damn it, and we need to act — after all this training, we have to know something and it's better to take your best guess and go with it (full–cocked) instead of just standing around doing nothing like an idiot.

It was the first rule that found a special place in my heart; in fact, I 23 perfected it. Because if you don't know something as a student, you have a built–in excuse: You're still learning. But somehow, there's this idea that once you make the jump to doctor, you have all the answers. Heck, that had always been my impression, based mostly on the events portrayed on "St. Elsewhere." I just figured all this knowledge and the ability to use it would occur magically with no explanation, much in the way the liver, I'm told, controls how well your blood clots.

But as it turned out, I was no different the day after graduation than 24 I was the day before. It's true, I had a brand new diploma and could legally be sued for a whole new set of reasons. But when I found myself leafing through my textbook of internal medicine, I realized that even though I was officially a doctor, I still hadn't heard of half the diseases. My heart then began to race and I broke out in a sweat, which I knew were the symptoms of something, though I couldn't quite put my finger on it. All I knew was that after four years and $142,863, I felt hopelessly, frighteningly unprepared.

After all, medical school had given us what it could, but what it 25 could not teach us was what it's like to have to care for a patient with no backup. It never told us how it feels to be the last line of defense between a dying man and death.

Yet as I stood watching the patient's bed being wheeled toward the 26 intensive care unit, I realized that I had indeed learned something in medical school. And though it didn't seem like much at the time, it was, perhaps, the most valuable lesson I would ever get. Until you know everything there is to know, it's OK to listen to others who are more experienced, and learn from them. Maybe some doctors would pretend to know it all, but I could keep the humility of the med student alive.

Reading Closely

1. The author relates a series of incidents involving "an enormous, pale, heaving man" (paragraphs 2–3, 9–14, 18–20). What do you learn from this series of incidents?

2. **Working with two or three classmates,** compare your responses to "Bedside Terror." What did you learn from this essay that you didn't know before? What information made you want to know more? Share your findings with the rest of the class.

3. What information do you get from the visual that you don't get from the essay? What information or emotions are enhanced when you consider the visual and the essay together? How do the visual and verbal language fulfill the author's purpose?

Considering Larger Issues

1. Decide on the main purpose of Drayer's narrative: to report events, create a mood, or argue a point. Prepare a brief response to share with the rest of the class.

2. Determine the point Drayer is making. How do the incidents in his essay work to support his point? Prepare a brief response to share with the rest of the class.

3. This essay appeared on the Web at <www.salon.com> under the heading "Health." Who are the readers of salon.com? Describe them in terms of age, sex, income, interests, and any other characteristics you can think of. How might the readers of salon.com change if you consider only readers of the "Health" section in particular?

4. **COMBINING METHODS.** Mark the passages that use *descriptive* details, make *comparisons*, or *analyze consequences*. What is the effect of each of these passages? Prepare to share your findings with the rest of the class.

Thinking about Language

1. "Bedside Terror" is a play on the common phrase "bedside manner," which is used to describe how well doctors relate to their patients. What is the effect of replacing the word *manner* with *terror*?

2. The title of the essay helps create a mood of fear. Locate all the words and phrases in "Bedside Terror" that suggest fear. Write them out.

3. Locate all the words and phrases throughout the essay that suggest rushing. Write them out.

4. **Working with two classmates,** compare the language that suggests fear and the language that suggests rushing. Discuss why both kinds of words are necessary to the success of this narrative, and report your conclusions to the class.

Writing Your Own Narratives

1. Look through books, manuals, and magazines until you locate a narrative that simply reports events in an unemotional or even bland way. **Working with two or three classmates,** discuss whether any of you could actually reproduce those events by reading that narrative account. As a group, draft a narrative that recounts those events, but enhance it with invented descriptive details so that you can also establish a mood. Prepare to share your group's results with the rest of the class.

   Use your group's narrative as the basis for a two- to three-page individual narrative essay that reports events at the same time that it establishes a mood. As you draft and revise, refer to the guidelines for checking over narrative writing on p. 150.

2. One point that Drayer's essay makes is that book knowledge does not always translate into practical knowledge. Sometimes, a person needs to practice alongside someone more experienced in order to learn. Draft a two- to three-page narrative essay that supports this thesis. Remember that the guidelines for checking over narrative writing are on p. 150.

MAYA ANGELOU

Finishing School

Born Marguerita Johnson in 1928 in St. Louis, Maya Angelou spent much of her time while growing up with her Arkansas grandmother. Early on, Angelou made a career as a singer and actress, then as a film director, a civil rights leader, and a journalist. Author of over a dozen best-selling books, from *I Know Why the Caged Bird Sings* (1969) to *A Song Flung Up to Heaven* (2002), she is also an acclaimed poet, educator, dancer, editor, and public speaker. In 1993, she became the second poet in U.S. history to recite an original work ("On the Pulse of the Morning") for a presidential inauguration. Angelou teaches at Wake Forest University, where she has been the Reynolds Professor of American Studies since 1981. "Finishing School" is excerpted from *I Know Why the Caged Bird Sings.*

Preview   What reasons can you give for why a bird might continue to sing in captivity?

Recently a white woman from Texas, who would quickly describe herself   1
as a liberal, asked me about my hometown. When I told her that in Stamps my grandmother had owned the only Negro general merchandise store since the turn of the century, she exclaimed, "Why, you were a debutante." Ridiculous and even ludicrous. But Negro girls in small Southern towns, whether poverty-stricken or just munching along on a few of life's necessities, were given as extensive and irrelevant preparations for adulthood as rich white girls shown in magazines. Admittedly the training was not the same. While white girls learned to waltz and sit gracefully with a tea cup balanced on their knees, we were lagging behind, learning the mid–Victorian values with very little money to indulge them. . . .

We were required to embroider and I had trunkfuls of colorful dish–   2
towels, pillowcases, runners and handkerchiefs to my credit. I mastered the art of crocheting and tatting, and there was a lifetime's supply of dainty doilies that would never be used in sacheted dresser drawers. It went without saying that all girls could iron and wash, but the finer touches around the home, like setting a table with real silver, baking roasts and cooking vegetables without meat, had to be learned elsewhere. Usually at the source of those habits. During my tenth year, a white woman's kitchen became my finishing school.

Mrs. Viola Cullinan was a plump woman who lived in a three–   3
bedroom house somewhere behind the post office. She was singularly unattractive until she smiled, and then the lines around her eyes and mouth which made her look perpetually dirty disappeared, and her face looked like the mask of an impish elf. She usually rested her smile until

late afternoon when her women friends dropped in and Miss Glory, the cook, served them cold drinks on the closed-in porch.

The exactness of her house was inhuman. This glass went here and   4
only here. That cup had its place and it was an act of impudent rebellion to place it anywhere else. At twelve o'clock the table was set. At 12:15 Mrs. Cullinan sat down to dinner (whether her husband had arrived or not). At 12:16 Miss Glory brought out the food.

It took me a week to learn the difference between a salad plate, a   5
bread plate and a dessert plate.

Mrs. Cullinan kept up the tradition of her wealthy parents. She was   6
from Virginia. Miss Glory, who was a descendant of slaves that had worked for the Cullinans, told me her history. She had married beneath her (according to Miss Glory). Her husband's family hadn't had their money very long and what they had "didn't 'mount to much."

As ugly as she was, I thought privately, she was lucky to get a husband   7
above or beneath her station. But Miss Glory wouldn't let me say a thing against her mistress. She was very patient with me, however, over the housework. She explained the dishware, silverware and servants' bells. The large round bowl in which soup was served wasn't a soup bowl, it was a tureen. There were goblets, sherbet glasses, ice-cream glasses, wine glasses, green glass coffee cups with matching saucers, and water glasses. I had a glass to drink from, and it sat with Miss Glory's on a separate shelf from the others. Soup spoons, gravy boat, butter knives, salad forks and carving platter were additions to my vocabulary and in fact almost represented a new language. I was fascinated with the novelty, with the fluttering Mrs. Cullinan and her Alice-in-Wonderland house.

Her husband remains, in my memory, undefined. I lumped him with   8
all the other white men that I had ever seen and tried not to see.

On our way home one evening, Miss Glory told me that Mrs. Culli-   9
nan couldn't have children. She said that she was too delicate-boned. It was hard to imagine bones at all under those layers of fat. Miss Glory went on to say that the doctor had taken out all her lady organs. I reasoned that a pig's organs included the lungs, heart, and liver, so if Mrs. Cullinan was walking around without those essentials, it explained why she drank alcohol out of unmarked bottles. She was keeping herself embalmed.

When I spoke to Bailey about it, he agreed that I was right, but he   10
also informed me that Mr. Cullinan had two daughters by a colored lady and that I knew them very well. He added that the girls were the spitting image of their father. I was unable to remember what he looked like, although I had just left him a few hours before, but I thought of the Coleman girls. They were very light-skinned and certainly didn't look very much like their mother (no one ever mentioned Mr. Coleman).

My pity for Mrs. Cullinan preceded me the next morning like the   11
Cheshire cat's smile. Those girls, who could have been her daughters,

were beautiful. They didn't have to straighten their hair. Even when they were caught in the rain, their braids still hung down straight like tamed snakes. Their mouths were pouty little cupid's bows. Mrs. Cullinan didn't know what she missed. Or maybe she did. Poor Mrs. Cullinan.

For weeks after, I arrived early, left late and tried very hard to make 12 up for her barrenness. If she had her own children, she wouldn't have had to ask me to run a thousand errands from her back door to the back door of her friends. Poor old Mrs. Cullinan.

Then one evening Miss Glory told me to serve the ladies on the 13 porch. After I set the tray down and turned toward the kitchen, one of the women asked, "What's your name, girl?" It was the speckled-faced one. Mrs. Cullinan said, "She doesn't talk much. Her name's Margaret."

"Is she dumb?"   14

"No. As I understand it, she can talk when she wants to but she's 15 usually quiet as a little mouse. Aren't you, Margaret?"

I smiled at her. Poor thing. No organs and couldn't even pronounce 16 my name correctly.

"She's a sweet little thing, though."   17

"Well, that may be, but the name's too long. I'd never bother myself. 18 I'd call her Mary if I was you."

Bea Arthur (left) and Esther Rolle played a contentious mistress and maid in the 1970s sitcom *Maude*.

I fumed into the kitchen. That horrible woman would never have the   19
chance to call me Mary because if I was starving I'd never work for her. . . .

That evening I decided to write a poem on being white, fat, old and   20
without children. It was going to be a tragic ballad. I would have to
watch her carefully to capture the essence of her loneliness and pain.

The very next day, she called me by the wrong name. Miss Glory and   21
I were washing up the lunch dishes when Mrs. Cullinan came to the
doorway. "Mary?"

Miss Glory asked, "Who?"   22

Mrs. Cullinan, sagging a little, knew and I knew. "I want Mary to go   23
down to Mrs. Randall's and take her some soup. She's not been feeling
well for a few days."

Miss Glory's face was a wonder to see. "You mean Margaret, ma'am.   24
Her name's Margaret."

"That's too long. She's Mary from now on. Heat that soup from last   25
night and put it in the china tureen and, Mary, I want you to carry it
carefully."

Every person I knew had a hellish horror of being "called out of his   26
name." It was a dangerous practice to call a Negro anything that could be
loosely construed as insulting because of the centuries of their having
been called niggers, jigs, dinges, blackbirds, crows, boots and spooks.

Miss Glory had a fleeting second of feeling sorry for me. Then as she   27
handed me the hot tureen she said, "Don't mind, don't pay that no mind.
Sticks and stones may break your bones, but words. . . . You know, I been
working for her for twenty years."

She held the back door open for me. "Twenty years. I wasn't much   28
older than you. My name used to be Hallelujah. That's what Ma named
me, but my mistress give me 'Glory,' and it stuck. I likes it better too."

I was in the little path that ran behind the houses when Miss Glory   29
shouted, "It's shorter too."

For a few seconds it was a tossup over whether I would laugh (imag-   30
ine being named Hallelujah) or cry (imagine letting some white woman
rename you for her convenience). My anger saved me from either out-
burst. I had to quit the job, but the problem was going to be how to do
it. Momma wouldn't allow me to quit for just any reason.

"She's a peach. That woman is a real peach." Mrs. Randall's maid was   31
talking as she took the soup from me, and I wondered what her name
used to be and what she answered to now.

For a week I looked into Mrs. Cullinan's face as she called me Mary.   32
She ignored my coming late and leaving early. Miss Glory was a little annoyed because I had begun to leave egg yolk on the dishes and wasn't
putting much heart in polishing the silver. I hoped that she would complain to our boss, but she didn't.

Then Bailey solved my dilemma. He had me describe the contents of   33
the cupboard and the particular plates she liked best. Her favorite piece

was a casserole shaped like a fish and the green glass coffee cups. I kept his instructions in mind, so on the next day when Miss Glory was hanging out clothes and I had again been told to serve the old biddies on the porch, I dropped the empty serving tray. When I heard Mrs. Cullinan scream, "Mary!" I picked up the casserole and two of the green glass cups in readiness. As she rounded the kitchen door I let them fall on the tiled floor.

I could never absolutely describe to Bailey what happened next, be- 34 cause each time I got to the part where she fell on the floor and screwed up her ugly face to cry, we burst out laughing. She actually wobbled around on the floor and picked up shards of the cups and cried, "Oh, Momma. Oh, dear Gawd. It's Momma's china from Virginia. Oh, Momma, I sorry."

Miss Glory came running in from the yard and the women from the 35 porch crowded around. Miss Glory was almost as broken up as her mistress. "You mean to say she broke our Virginia dishes? What we gone do?"

Mrs. Cullinan cried louder. "That clumsy nigger. Clumsy little black 36 nigger."

Old speckled-face leaned down and asked, "Who did it, Viola? Was it 37 Mary? Who did it?"

Everything was happening so fast, I can't remember whether her ac- 38 tion preceded her words, but I know that Mrs. Cullinan said, "Her name's Margaret, goddamn it, her name's Margaret." And she threw a wedge of broken plate at me. It could have been the hysteria which put her aim off, but the flying crockery caught Miss Glory right over her ear and she started screaming.

I left the front door wide open so all the neighbors could hear. 39

Mrs. Cullinan was right about one thing. My name wasn't Mary. 40

Reading Closely

1. What were Angelou's duties at the Cullinan home?
2. Why was Mrs. Cullinan so exacting about housekeeping?
3. What passages in the narrative help you trace the changes Mrs. Cullinan goes through in her treatment of and attitude toward Margaret?
4. What specific information can you glean from the visual in terms of setting, characters, and dialogue? How effectively does this visual enhance Angelou's narrative?

Considering Larger Issues

1. What is the overall purpose of this narrative? How do the title, the characters, the setting, and the sequence of events work together to fulfill that purpose?

2. **Working with another classmate or two,** analyze Angelou's use of dialogue in this narrative. Which passages are most effective in helping her fulfill her purpose? Which ones most illuminate the contrast between Angelou's home life and working life? to what effect?

3. COMBINING METHODS.   Angelou uses *description* and *comparison and contrast* to enhance her narrative. Mark the relevant passages and explain their power to improve the narrative.

Thinking about Language

1. Using a dictionary or the context of the selection, define the following terms, preparing to share your answers with the rest of the class.

liberal (1)	impish (3)	ballad (20)
debutante (1)	impudent (4)	construed (26)
ludicrous (1)	embalmed (9)	fleeting (27)
tatting (2)	Cheshire cat (11)	a peach (31)
sacheted (2)	pouty (11)	dilemma (33)
perpetually (3)	barrenness (12)	

2. What can you say about the differences between a soup bowl and a tureen, or among a goblet, sherbet glass, ice–cream glass, wineglass, and water glass. What about the differences between a soup spoon and a tablespoon, or a butter knife and a carving knife? What does this knowledge — or lack thereof — say, if anything, about you? What did it say about Angelou?

3. What does the title, "Finishing School," mean for this narrative? What specific passages help you understand how Angelou is using that term? What specific vocabulary is necessary for passing "courses" in this school? Be prepared to share your answers with the rest of the class.

Writing Your Own Narratives

1. Like Angelou, we've all experienced a time in our life when someone treated us unfairly, as though we were "lower" than that person. Draft a three– to four–page essay in which you narrate your story of unfair treatment, making sure to include a title, a setting, a cast of characters, and a sequence of events. As you draft, decide on a specific audience (which could even be the person who treated you unfairly) and a specific purpose (which might be to report the information, make an argument, or set a mood). Refer to the guidelines for checking over narrative writing on p. 150.

2. You may have an experience with name–calling to relate, one that's painful for you to remember, whether you were the one doing the name–calling or the victim of it. Draft a three– to four–page essay in which you narrate your name–calling story, making sure to include characters, descriptive details, and a sequence of events. You should have a specific audience in mind as well as an overall purpose. Refer to the guidelines for checking over narrative writing on p. 150.

STEVE EARLE

A Death in Texas

Steve Earle (b. 1955) is a former heroin addict who spent time in a Tennessee prison on drug charges. But he is best known for his writing and singing of country music, which won him the country Artist of the Year designation in *Rolling Stone's* Critics' Poll after his debut in 1986. He has also earned eight Grammy nominations. Outside of his music career, Earle has worked as an activist against the death penalty with a variety of groups, including Amnesty International; he has also campaigned for welfare rights and the elimination of land mines. His album *Transcendental Blues* (2000) features "Over Yonder (Jonathan's Song)," a tribute to Jonathan Nobles, the subject of the following essay, which appeared in *Tikkun* magazine in 2001. Earle has also published a book of short stories, *Doghouse Roses* (2001) and was the subject of the documentary film *Just an American Boy* (2003).

> **Preview**   As you read "A Death in Texas," notice how Earle uses a narrative to argue against that death.

"Hey, man."   Jonathan Wayne Nobles grins at me through inch-thick   1
wire-reinforced glass, hunching over to speak in a deep, resonant voice through the steel grate below. A feeble "What's up?" is the best I can manage. The visiting area in Ellis One Unit is crowded with other folks who have traveled, in some cases thousands of miles, to visit relatives and correspondents on Texas' Death Row. They sit at intervals in wooden chairs surrounding a cinder block and steel cage that dominates the center of the room. There are cages within the cage as well, reserved for inmates under disciplinary action and "death watch" status. Falling into the latter category, Jon must squeeze his considerable bulk into one of these phone-booth-sized enclosures.

It's an awkward moment for both of us. In the 10 years we have cor-   2
responded, we have never met face to face. The occasion is auspicious. Jon and I will spend eight hours a day together for the next three days and another three days next week. Then the state of Texas will transport Jon, chained hand and foot, 11 miles to the Walls unit in downtown Huntsville. There he will be pumped full of chemicals that will collapse his lungs and stop his heart forever. This is not a worst-case scenario. It is a certainty. Jonathan Nobles has precisely 10 days to live. And I, at Jon's request, will attend the execution as one of his witnesses.

Over the next few days a routine develops. I arrive at Ellis at 8:30 in   3
the morning. We usually spend the first two hours talking about music, politics, religion — subjects that we have covered thoroughly enough in letters over the years to know that we have widely divergent views and tastes. We fill the long awkward silences that seem inevitable in prison

181

Death-row inmate Jonathan Nobles on October 18, 1987.

visiting areas with trips to the vending machines for soft drinks, candy, and potato chips. I pass Jon's goodies to the guard on duty through a small opening in the steel mesh.

Inevitably, we move on to life behind bars, drugs, and recovery— topics where we share considerably more common ground. We are both recovering addicts who got clean only when we were locked up. Jon began reading about recovery and attending 12–step meetings in prison years ago. I can remember a time, back when I was still using drugs, when the recovery–speak that filled his letters made me extremely un-comfortable. Now it is a language that we share—sort of a spiritual shorthand that cuts through the testosterone and affords us a conven-ient, if uncomfortable, segue to the business at hand.

There are arrangements to be made. If Jon's body were to go un-claimed, as is the case with half of the men executed in Texas, he would be buried in the prison cemetery on the outskirts of Huntsville. Called "Peck-erwood Hill" by the locals, it is a lonely space filled with concrete crosses, adorned only with the interred inmates' prison numbers. Those executed by the state are easily identifiable by the "X" preceding their number. There are no names on the stones. Jon doesn't want to wind up there.

Instead, he wants to be buried in Oxford, England—a place he's never seen. One of his pen pals, a British woman named Pam Thomas, has de-scribed it to him in her letters. He likes the picture Pam paints of the spring-time there, when the bluebells are in bloom. Jon says that Pam is working on permission from a landowner there. I have Plan B on the back burner. A Dominican community in Galway, Ireland, has offered Jon a final resting place. At some point in the proceedings, it dawns on me that I have spent the past hour helping a living, breathing man plan his own burial.

One thing Jon and I don't talk about much is the movement to abol-ish the death penalty. In fact, Jon is suspicious of abolitionists. We were "introduced" by a pen pal of his and an acquaintance of mine. She had heard that I sometimes corresponded with inmates and asked if she could give Jon my address. I said sure. Within a month, I received my first letter. It was a page and a half long in a beautiful flowing script. It contained a lot of the usual tough rhetoric and dark humor I had learned to expect in letters from inmates. After several readings, I real-ized that the jailhouse small talk was merely a medium, a vehicle for one pertinent piece of information—that Jonathan Wayne Nobles was guilty of the crimes he was charged with.

In 1986 Jon was convicted (almost entirely on the strength of his own confession) of stabbing Kelley Farquhar and Mitzi Johnson–Nalley to death. He also admitted stabbing Ron Ross, Nalley's boyfriend, who lost an eye in the attack. Jon never took the stand during his trial. He sat im-passively as the guilty verdict was read and, according to newspaper ac-counts, only flinched slightly when District Judge Bob Jones sentenced him to death.

When Jon arrived at Ellis he quickly alienated all of the guards and   9
most of the inmates. He once broke away from guards while returning to
his cell from the exercise yard and climbed the exposed pipes and bars in
the cell block, kicking down television sets suspended outside on the bottom tier. On another occasion he cut himself with a razor blade, knowing
that the guards would have to open his cell to prevent him from bleeding
to death. He just wanted to hit one officer before he passed out.

But somehow, somewhere along the line, in what is arguably the most   10
inhumane environment in the "civilized" world, Jonathan Nobles began to
change. He became interested in Catholicism and began to attend Mass. He
befriended the Catholic clergy who ministered in the prison system, including members of the Dominican Order of Preachers. He eventually became a lay member of the order and ministered to his fellow inmates, even
standing as godfather at inmate Cliff Boggess' baptism. He later helped of-
ficiate at the Mass that was celebrated the night before Boggess' execution.
I watched this transformation in the letters that I received.

The Jonathan Nobles who sits on the other side of the glass from me   11
in September 1998 is a different man from the one the state of Texas sentenced to die almost 12 years ago. The greatest evidence of this fact is the
way Jon is treated by everyone he encounters. A prison clerk, displaying
genuine regret, interrupts our visit. She needs Jon to sign some papers.
Jon does so and then informs me that the documents allow me to pick
up his personal property and distribute it to a list of people detailed in a
note the clerk will hand me on my way out. Inmate James Beathard, on
his way down the line to visit with a family member, stops to talk and
Jon introduces us. The guard patiently waits until the exchange is over
before escorting him to his assigned cubicle. Socialization during inmate
transfer is a clear violation of policy, but a lot of the rules have relaxed
for Jon. He says it's like the last week of the school year. I believe it's
more likely that he has earned the genuine respect of everyone here.

I excuse myself to go to the bathroom. The truth is, I simply need a   12
break. On the way back I run into Father Stephen Walsh, a Franciscan
friar from Boston who travels regularly to minister to the Catholic inmates at Ellis. He will serve as Jonathan's spiritual adviser, waiting with
Jon in the holding cell over at the Walls until he's escorted into the death
chamber itself. There, he will administer the last rites.

Every visit ends the same way. A guard gives us a five-minute warn-   13
ing, and Jon hurriedly dictates a list of "things to do" that I must commit
to memory, since visitors are not allowed to bring writing instruments
and paper into the unit. Then Jon presses his palm against the glass and I
mirror his with mine. Jon says, "I love you. I'll see you tomorrow."

Over the past few days the other witnesses have arrived in Huntsville.   14
I had dinner with Dona Hucka, Jon's aunt. She is the only blood relative
to make the trip and she has driven all night to be here. Pam Thomas is

in from England. Both are already on the unit when I arrive. We take turns leaning close to the glass while a prison employee takes Polaroid snapshots of each of us with Jon. The prison provides this service for the fee of eight dollars each.

It's 10 o'clock in the morning. There isn't much time left. At 12:30 we   15 will be asked to leave the unit and Jon will be transported to the Walls. In the death chamber, we will be able to hear Jon over a speaker in the witness room, but this is our last opportunity to speak to him. Jon divides the remaining time between us more or less equally. I go first. Jon looks tired; the stress is showing for the first time. He leans down and motions me closer. I realize he's assessing my condition as well. "You all right, man?" I tell him that I'm okay. Jon is not convinced.

"I'm worried about you. You don't have to be Superman or nothin'.   16 This is insane shit that's goin' on here today. You don't have to be strong for the women if that's what you're thinkin'. They're big girls. You need to take care of yourself."

"I know, Jon. I'm all right. I went to a meeting last night and my   17 manager's here now. I've also got a couple of friends up from Houston who have done this before."

"Witnessed?"   18

"Yeah." That seemed to make him feel better. "Okay, but if you need   19 to cry, it's all right. Go ahead and cry."

"When this is all over, I'll cry."   20

"Promise?"   21

"I promise."   22

Jon shifts gears suddenly. Back to business. He looks both ways to   23 make sure the guard isn't watching. "Take this." With much effort he pushes a tiny slip of tightly rolled paper, the diameter of a toothpick, through the impossibly tight mesh. Somehow he pulls it off. "That's my daughter's phone number in California. My sister read it to me over the phone last night. They're going to strip search me and I can't take anything to the Walls and I'm afraid I'll forget it. Give it to Father Walsh. Then I'll have it when I make my last phone calls."

I poke the paper in the watch pocket of my Levi's. There are a few   24 other requests. He wants me to call his foster mother and his sister after the execution, and send flowers to two women who worked for the prison who were kind to him over the years. I promise that I won't forget. "All right, bro. Take care of yourself and your kids. Tell Dona to come back." Hands against the glass one last time.

"I love you, Jonathan."   25

"I love you too, bro."   26

Noon   I head back into Huntsville. My manager, Dan Gillis, arrived last   27 night and not a moment too soon. Suddenly, driving has become difficult. The world has taken on a kind of surrealistic patina. I need someone to drive for the rest of the day. Also waiting at the hotel are two friends from the abolition movement, Karen Sebung and Ward Larkin. Both have witnessed executions, and they have made the trip to assist in any way they can. We talk over arrangements for the transportation and cremation of Jon's body, which, as it turns out, Dan has already taken care of. I make a couple of phone calls and check my messages. Then I shower, shave, and put on a pair of black jeans, a blue short–sleeve shirt, and a black linen sport coat.

4:00   We leave the hotel. Dan drives us to Hospitality House, a guest 28 residence operated by the Baptist Church for the families of inmates. Dona and Pam, as well as Pam's friend Caroline, are staying there. The two other witnesses, Bishop Carmody of the East Texas diocese and the Reverend Richard Lopez of the Texas Department of Corrections, are already there when we arrive. We are assembled here for an orientation session to be conducted by the Reverend Jim Brazzil, the chaplain at the Walls unit. He and the warden will be the only two people inside the chamber with Jon when he dies. He goes through the execution process step–by–step so that we will know what to expect and, though it's obvious he speaks with authority, I'm not listening. I can't concentrate, so I just nod a lot. It doesn't matter. No matter how well or poorly the witnesses are prepared, they are going to kill Jon anyway.

5:05   Reverend Brazzil answers his cell phone. It's Father Walsh, who's 29 over at the Walls with Jon and wants the phone number, the one that Jon passed me through the . . . oh my God. I can't find it. I was sure that I transferred the slip from my other jeans into my wallet when I changed clothes, but it's simply not there. Dan runs to the motel and checks my room, but it's hopeless. Reverend Brazzil relays the bad news to Father Walsh. I feel awful.

5:30   We arrive at the visitors' center across the street from the Walls 30 unit. Karen Sebung accompanies me as far as the waiting area, where we witnesses are searched, then Dona and Pam are escorted to another room by a female officer. When they return, a large man enters the room and introduces himself as an officer of the prison's internal affairs division. If we should feel faint, he says, medical attention is available. He also warns us that anyone who in any way attempts to disrupt the "process," as he calls it, will be removed from the witness area immediately. Nothing about my body is working right. My feet and hands are cold and the side of my neck is numb.

5:55   The corrections officer returns. "Follow me, please." We walk across 31 the street and through the front door of the old Gothic prison administration building. We turn left as soon as we enter and find ourselves in the waiting area of the governor's office, where we are asked to wait once again. There are two reporters there. The other three members of the press pool, along with the victims' family members, have already been escorted to the witness area, which is divided by a cinder block wall. The two sets of witnesses will never come in contact with each other.

6:00   We're led through a visiting area similar to the one at Ellis, then 32 out into the bright evening sun for a moment and turn left down a short sidewalk. Another left and we enter a small brick building built into the side of the perimeter wall. We enter the tiny room in single file. Father Walsh appears from somewhere inside the death chamber to join us. The reporters enter last, and the door is locked behind us. I can hear the reporters scratching on their notepads with their pencils. There is only room for three of us—Dona, me, and Pam—in the front row. Dona grabs my left hand and squeezes it hard. She already has tears in her eyes.

Jon is strapped to a hospital gurney with heavy leather restraints 33 across his chest, hips, thighs, ankles, and wrists.

His arms are wrapped in Ace bandages and extended at his sides on 34 boards. At either wrist, clear plastic tubes protrude from the wrappings, snaking back under the gurney and disappearing through a plastic tube set in a bright blue cinder block wall. I think I see movement behind the one-way glass mirror on the opposite wall—the executioner getting into position. Jon is smiling at us, his great neck twisted uncomfortably sideways. A microphone suspended from the ceiling hangs a few inches above his head. The speaker above our heads crackles to life and Jon speaks, craning his head around to see the victims' witnesses in the room next door.

"I know some of you won't believe me, but I am truly sorry for what 35 I have done. I wish that I could undo what happened back then and bring back your loved ones, but I can't." Jon begins to sob as he addresses Mitzi Nalley's mother. "I'm sorry. I'm so sorry. I wish I could bring her back to you. And Ron . . . I took so much from you. I'm sorry. I know you probably don't want my love, but you have it."

Turning to me, he seems to regain his composure somewhat. He 36 even manages to smile again. "Steve, I can't believe that I had to go through all this to see you in a suit coat. Hey man, don't worry about the phone number, bro. You've done so much. I love you. Dona, thank you for being here. I know it was hard for you. I love you. Pam, thank you for coming from so far away. Thanks for all you have done. I love you. Bishop Carmody, thank you so much. Reverend Lopez and you, Father Walsh, I love you all. I have something I want to say. It comes from I Corinthians. It goes . . ." and Jon recites the lengthy piece of scripture that he agonized over for weeks, afraid he would forget when the time came. He remembers every word.

When he finishes reciting he takes a deep breath and says, "Father, 37 into thy hands I commend my spirit." The warden, recognizing the prearranged signal he and Jon had agreed on, nods toward the unseen executioner and Jon begins to sing.

"Silent night / Holy night . . ."   38

He gets as far as "mother and child" and suddenly the air explodes 39 from his lungs with a loud barking noise, deep and incongruous, like a child with whooping cough—"HUH!!!" His head pitches forward with such force that his heavy, prison–issue glasses fly off his face, bouncing from his chest and falling to the green tile floor below.

And then he doesn't move at all. I watch his eyes fix and glaze over, 40 my heart pounding in my chest and Dona squeezing my hand. Dead men look . . . well, dead. Vacant. No longer human. But there is a protocol to be satisfied. The warden checks his watch several times during the longest five minutes of my life. When the time is up, he walks across the room and knocks on the door. The doctor enters, his stethoscope ear–pieces already in place. He listens first at Jon's neck, then at his chest, then at his side. He shines a small flashlight into Jon's eyes for an instant and then, glancing up at the clock on his way out, intones, "6:18."

We are ushered out the same way we came, but I don't think any of 41 us are the same people who crossed the street to the prison that day. I know I'm not. I can't help but wonder what happens to the people who work at the Walls, who see this horrific thing happen as often as four times a week. What do they see when they turn out the lights? I can't imagine.

I do know that Jonathan Nobles changed profoundly while he was in 42 prison. I know that the lives of people he came in contact with changed as well, including mine. Our criminal justice system isn't known for re–habilitation. I'm not sure that, as a society, we are even interested in that concept anymore. The problem is that most people who go to prison get out one day and walk among us. Given as many people as we lock up, we better learn to rehabilitate someone. I believe Jon might have been able to teach us how. Now we'll never know.

Reading Closely

1. What did you learn about the death penalty from this essay that you didn't know before?

2. List all the observations Earle makes that seem true to you and those that seem false.

3. What feelings about crime, prison, prisoners, and the death penalty does Earle's essay provoke in you? What specific passages do you find the most moving—either positively or negatively?

4. How does the picture of Jonathan Nobles affect your response to this essay?

Considering Larger Issues

1. Overall, what do you think is the purpose of Earle's narrative essay: to report information, to support an argument, to provide an example, or to establish a mood? Mark the passages in the essay that support your answer.

2. **Working with a classmate,** discuss the audience for this essay. Because Earle's essay appeared in *Tikkun* magazine, you could say that his audience includes all *Tikkun* readers. (To find out more about this magazine, go to <www.tikkun.org>). As you reread the piece, whom do you think he's talking to? explaining to? With your partner, discuss the issue of multiple audiences.

3. COMBINING METHODS.   What comparisons does Earle make between Nobles and Mitzi Johnson–Nalley and between Nobles and Ron Ross? What is the effect of these comparisons?

Thinking about Language

1. Using the context of the essay or your dictionary, define the following terms, preparing to share your answers with the rest of the class.

auspicious (2)	interred (5)	Gothic (31)
worst–case scenario (2)	spiritual adviser (12)	gurney (33)
divergent (3)	assessing (15)	protrude (34)
testosterone (4)	surrealistic (27)	protocol (40)
segue (4)	patina (27)	

2. What specific words, phrases, or passages establish Earle's tone in this essay? What is the distinctive attitude he presents toward his subject?

Writing Your Own Narratives

1. Draft a three- to four–page essay in which you narrate the treatment of Jonathan Nobles from the point of view of Mitzi Johnson–Nalley's mother or of Ron Ross. In what ways has Nobles been treated better than Johnson–Nalley or Ross? In what ways might Nobles's religious conversion be convenient for him? Your narrative should highlight what you see as either the fairness or the unfairness of his punishment. Be sure to refer to the guidelines for checking over narrative writing on p. 150.

2. Narrate a story about the students you know best, showcasing their attitudes or abilities. Imagine an audience critical of today's college students, judging them as having inappropriate attitudes about or aptitudes for succeeding in college or later in life. Before you begin writing your narrative, you might want to do some research on the dropout rate at your college each year, keeping in mind that most colleges lose over half of their incoming freshmen before graduation. Be sure to follow the guidelines for checking over narrative writing on p. 150.

GARY SOTO
Black Hair

● Gary Soto (b. 1952) was born and raised in Fresno, California. In addition to numerous books of poems, including *The Elements of San Joaquin* (1977), *Black Hair* (1985), and *Home Course in Religion: New Poems* (1991), he has published three collections of essays, mostly focusing on his memories of growing up as a Mexican American: *Living Up the Street* (1985), *Small Faces* (1986), and *A Summer Life* (1990). A recipient of many literary awards, as well as fellowships from the Guggenheim Foundation, the National Endowment for the Arts, and the California Arts Council, Soto continues to write for adults and young people. In "Black Hair," a narrative piece excerpted from *Living Up the Street*, Soto mixes the rhetorical methods.

> **Preview** What physical attribute do you and other members of your family share? Is it immediately noticeable?

There are two kinds of work: One uses the mind and the other uses muscle. As a kid I found out about the latter. I'm thinking of the summer of 1969 when I was a seventeen-year-old runaway who ended up in Glendale, California, working for Valley Tire Factory. To answer an ad in the newspaper I walked miles in the afternoon sun, my stomach slowly knotting on a doughnut that was breakfast, my teeth like bright candles gone yellow. 1

I walked in the door sweating and feeling ugly because my hair was still stiff from a swim at the Santa Monica beach the day before. Jules, the accountant and part owner, looked droopily through his bifocals at my application and then at me. He tipped his cigar in the ashtray, asked my age as if he didn't believe I was seventeen, but finally, after a moment of silence, said, "Come back tomorrow. Eight-thirty." 2

I thanked him, left the office, and went around to the chain-link fence to watch the workers heave tires into a bin; others carted uneven stacks of tires on hand trucks. Their faces were black from tire dust, and when they talked — or cussed — their mouths showed a bright pink. 3

From there I walked up a commercial street, past a cleaners, a motorcycle shop, and a gas station where I washed my face and hands; before leaving I took a bottle that hung on the side of the Coke machine, filled it with water, and stopped it with a scrap of paper and a rubber band. 4

The next morning I arrived early at work. The assistant foreman, a potbellied Hungarian, showed me a time card and how to punch in. He showed me the Coke machine and the locker room with its slimy shower, and also pointed out the places where I shouldn't go: the ovens where the tires were recapped and the customer service area, which had a slashed couch, a coffee table with greasy magazines, and an ashtray. He 5

190

introduced me to Tully, a fat man with one ear who worked the buffers that resurfaced the whitewalls. I was handed an apron and a face mask and shown how to use the buffer: lift the tire and center it, inflate it with a foot pedal, press the buffer against the white band until cleaned, and then deflate and blow off the tire with an air hose.

With a paintbrush he stirred a can of industrial preserver. "Then slap 6 this blue stuff on." While he was talking a coworker came up quietly behind him and goosed him with the air hose. Tully jumped as if he had been struck by a bullet and then turned around cussing and cupping his genitals in his hands as the other worker walked away calling out foul names. When Tully turned to me, smiling his gray teeth, I lifted my mouth into a smile because I wanted to get along. He has to be on my side, I thought. He's the one who'll tell the foreman how I'm doing.

I worked carefully that day, setting the tires on the machine as if they 7 were babies, because it was easy to catch a finger in the rim that expanded to inflate the tire. At the day's end we swept up the tire dust and emptied the trash into bins.

At five the workers scattered for their cars and motorcycles while I 8 crossed the street to wash at a burger stand. My hair was stiff with dust and my mouth showed pink against the backdrop of my dirty face. I ordered a hotdog and walked slowly in the direction of the abandoned house where I had stayed the night before. I lay under the trees and within minutes was asleep. When I woke my shoulders were sore, and my eyes burned when I squeezed the lids together.

From the backyard I walked dully through a residential street, and as   9
evening came on, the TV glare in the living rooms and the headlights of
passing cars showed against the blue drift of dusk. I saw two children
coming up the street with snow cones, their tongues darting at the
packed ice. I saw a boy with a peach and wanted to stop him but felt
embarrassed by my hunger. I walked for an hour, only to return and discover the house lit brightly. Behind the fence I heard voices and saw a
flashlight poking at the garage door. A man on the back steps mumbled
something about the refrigerator to the one with the flashlight.

I waited for them to leave but had the feeling they wouldn't because   10
there was a commotion of furniture being moved. Tired, even more desperate, I started walking again with a great urge to kick things and tear
the day from my life. I felt weak and my mind kept drifting because of
hunger. I crossed the street to a gas station where I sipped at the water
fountain and searched the Coke machine for change. I started walking
again, first up a commercial street, then into a residential area where I
lay down on someone's lawn and replayed a scene at home — my mother
crying at the kitchen table, my stepfather yelling with food in his mouth.
They're cruel, I thought, and warned myself that I should never forgive
them. How could they do this to me?

When I got up from the lawn it was late. I searched out a place to   11
sleep and found an unlocked car that seemed safe. In the backseat, with
my shoes off, I fell asleep but woke up startled about four in the morning when the owner, a nurse on her way to work, opened the door. She
got in and was about to start the engine when I raised my head to explain my presence. She screamed so loudly when I said "I'm sorry" that I
sprinted from the car with my shoes in hand. Her screams faded, then
stopped altogether, as I ran down the block, hid behind a trash bin, and
waited for a police siren to sound. Nothing. I crossed the street to a
church where I slept stiffly on cardboard in the balcony.

I woke up feeling tired and greasy. It was early and a few streetlights   12
were still lit, the east growing pink with dawn. I washed myself from a
garden hose and returned to the church to break into what looked like a
kitchen. Paper cups, plastic spoons, a coffee pot littered on a table. I
found a box of Nabisco crackers and ate until I was full.

At work I spent the morning at the buffer, but was then told to help   13
Iggy, an old Mexican who was responsible for choosing tires that could
be recapped without the risk of exploding at high speeds. Every morning
a truck would deliver used tires, and after I unloaded them Iggy would
step among the tires to inspect them for punctures and rips on the side-
walls.

With yellow chalk he marked circles and Xs to indicate damage and   14
called out "junk." Tires that could be recapped got a "goody" from Iggy,
and I placed them on my hand truck. When I had a stack of eight I

kicked the truck at an angle and balanced off to another work area, where Iggy again inspected the tires, scratching Xs and calling out "junk."

Iggy worked only until three in the afternoon, at which time he went 15 to the locker room to wash and shave and to dress in a two-piece suit. When he came out he glowed with a bracelet, watch, rings, and a shiny fountain pen in his breast pocket. His shoes sounded against the asphalt. He was the image of a banker stepping into sunlight with millions on his mind. He said a few low words to workers with whom he was friendly and none to people like me.

I was seventeen, stupid because I couldn't figure out the difference 16 between an F78 14 and a 750 14 at sight. Iggy shook his head when I brought him the wrong tires, especially since I had expressed interest in being his understudy. "Mexican, how can you be so stupid?" he would yell at me, slapping a tire from my hands. But within weeks I learned a lot about tires, from sizes and makes to how they are molded in iron forms to how Valley stole from other companies. Now and then we received a truckload of tires, most of them new or nearly new, and they were taken to our warehouse in the back, where the serial numbers were ground off with a sander. On those days the foreman handed out Cokes and joked with us as we worked to get the numbers off.

Most of the workers were Mexican or black, though a few redneck 17 whites worked there. The base pay was a dollar sixty-five but the average was three dollars. Of the black workers, I knew Sugar Daddy the best. His body carried 250 pounds and armfuls of scars, and he had a long knife that made me jump when he brought it out from his boot without warning. At one time he had been a singer and had cut a record in 1967 called *Love's Chance*, which broke into the R & B charts. But nothing came of it. No big contract, no club dates, no tours. He made very little from record sales, only enough for an operation to pull a steering wheel from his gut when, drunk and mad at a lady friend, he slammed his Mustang into a row of parked cars.

"Touch it," he smiled at me one afternoon as he raised his shirt, his 18 black belly kinked with hair. Scared, I traced the scar that ran from his chest to the left of his belly button, and I was repelled but hid my disgust.

Among the Mexicans I had few friends because I was different, a 19 *pocho** who spoke bad Spanish. At lunch they sat in tires and laughed over burritos, looking up at me to laugh even harder. I also sat in tires while nursing a Coke and felt dirty and sticky because I was still living on the street and had not had a real bath in over a week. Nevertheless, when the border patrol came to round up the nationals, I ran with them

* ***pocho:*** Mexican slang meaning "outsider."

as they scrambled for the fence or hid among the tires behind the warehouse. The foreman, who thought I was an undocumented worker, yelled
at me to run, to get away. I did just that. At the time it seemed fun because there was no risk, only a good-hearted feeling of hide-and-seek,
and besides, it meant an hour away from work on company time. When
the police left we came back, and some of the nationals made up stories
of how they were almost caught—how they outraced the police. Some of
the stories were so convoluted and unconvincing that everyone laughed
and shouted *"mentiras,"** especially when one described how he overpow-
ered a policeman, took his gun away, and sold the patrol car. We laughed
and he laughed, happy to be there to make up such a story.

    If work was difficult, so were the nights. I still had not gathered 20
enough money to rent a room, so I spent the nights sleeping in parked
cars or in the church balcony. After a week I found a newspaper ad for a
room for rent, phoned, and was given directions. Finished with work, I
walked the five miles down Mission Road looking back into the traffic
with my thumb out. No rides. After eight hours of handling tires I was
frightening to drivers, I suppose, since they seldom looked at me; if they
did, it was a quick glance. For the next six weeks I would try to hitchhike,
but the only person to stop was a Mexican woman who gave me two
dollars to take the bus. I told her it was too much and that no bus ran
from Mission Road to where I lived, but she insisted that I keep the
money and trotted back to her idling car. It must have hurt her to see me
day after day walking in the heat and looking very much the dirty Mexican to the many minds that didn't know what it meant to work at hard
labor. That woman knew. Her eyes met mine as she opened the car door,
and there was a tenderness that was surprisingly true—one for which
you wait for years but when it comes it doesn't help. Nothing changes.
You continue on in rags, with the sun still above you.

    I rented a room from a middle-aged couple whose lives were a 21
mess. She was a schoolteacher and he was a fireman. A perfect setup, I
thought. But during my stay there they would argue for hours in their
bedroom.

    When I rang at the front door both Mr. and Mrs. Van Deusen an- 22
swered and didn't bother to disguise their shock at how awful I looked.
But they let me in all the same. Mrs. Van Deusen showed me around the
house, from the kitchen and bathroom to the living room with its grand
piano. On her fingers she counted out the house rules as she walked me
to my room. It was a girl's room with lace curtains, scenic wallpaper of a
Victorian couple enjoying a stroll, a canopied bed, and stuffed animals in
a corner. Leaving, she turned and asked if she could do laundry for me.
Feeling shy and hurt, I told her no; perhaps the next day. She left and I

---

* **mentiras:** Spanish: "lies."

undressed to take a bath, exhausted as I sat on the edge of the bed probing my aches and my bruised places. With a towel around my waist I
hurried down the hallway to the bathroom where Mrs. Van Deusen had
set out an additional towel with a tube of shampoo. I ran water into the
tub and sat on the closed toilet, watching the steam curl toward the ceiling. When I lowered myself into the tub I felt my body sting. I soaped a
washcloth and scrubbed my arms until they lightened, even glowed
pink, but I still looked unwashed around my neck and face no matter
how hard I rubbed. Back in the room I sat in bed reading a magazine,
happy and thinking of no better luxury than a girl's sheets, especially
after nearly two weeks of sleeping on cardboard at the church.

I was too tired to sleep, so I sat at the window watching the neigh-   23
bors move about in pajamas, and, curious about the room, looked
through the bureau drawers to search out personal things — snapshots, a
messy diary, and high-school yearbook. I looked up the Van Deusens'
daughter, Barbara, and studied her face as if I recognized her from my
own school — a face that said "promise," "college," "nice clothes in the
closet." She was a skater and a member of the German Club; her greatest
ambition was to sing at the Hollywood Bowl.

After a while I got into bed, and as I drifted toward sleep I thought   24
about her. In my mind I played a love scene again and again and altered
it slightly each time. She comes home from college and at first is indifferent to my presence in her home, but finally I overwhelm her with deep
pity when I come home hurt from work, with blood on my shirt. Then
there was another version: Home from college she is immediately taken
with me, in spite of my work-darkened face, and invites me into the
family car for a milkshake across town. Later, back at the house, we sit in
the living room talking about school until we're so close I'm holding her
hand. The truth of the matter was that Barbara did come home for a
week but was bitter toward her parents for taking in boarders (two others besides me). During that time she spoke to me only twice: Once,
while searching the refrigerator, she asked if we had any mustard; the
other time she asked if I had seen her car keys.

But it was a place to stay. Work had become more and more difficult.   25
I worked not only with Iggy but also with the assistant foreman, who
was in charge of unloading trucks. After they backed in I hopped on top
to pass the tires down, bouncing them on the tailgate to give them an
extra spring so they would be less difficult to handle on the other end.
Each truck was weighted down with more than two hundred tires, each
averaging twenty pounds, so that by the time the truck was emptied and
swept clean I glistened with sweat and my T-shirt stuck to my body. I
blew snot threaded with tire dust onto the asphalt, indifferent to the customers who watched from the waiting room.

The days were dull. I did what there was to do from morning until   26
the bell sounded at five; I tugged, pulled, and cussed at tires until I was

listless and my mind drifted and caught on small things, from cold sodas
to shoes to stupid talk about what we would do with a million dollars. I
remember unloading a truck with Hamp, a black man.

"What's better than a sharp lady?" he asked me as I stood sweaty on 27
a pile of junked tires. "Water. With ice," I said.

He laughed with his mouth open wide. With his fingers he pinched 28
the sweat from his chin and flicked at me. "You be too young, boy. A
woman can make you a god."

As a kid I had chopped cotton and picked grapes, so I knew work. I 29
knew the fatigue and the boredom and the feeling that there was a good
possibility that you might have to do such work for years, if not for a
lifetime. In fact, as a kid I had imagined a dark fate: to marry Mexican
poor, work Mexican hours, and in the end die a Mexican death, broke
and in despair.

But this job at Valley Tire Company confirmed that there was some- 30
thing worse than fieldwork, and I was doing it. We were all doing it, from
the foreman to the newcomers like me, and what I felt heaving tires for
eight hours a day was felt by everyone—black, Mexican, redneck. We all
despised those hours but didn't know what else to do. The workers were
unskilled, some undocumented and fearful of deportation, and all struck
with uncertainty at what to do with their lives. Although everyone
bitched about work, no one left. Some had worked there for twelve
years; some had sons working there. Few quit; no one was ever fired. It
amazed me that no one gave up when the border patrol jumped from
their vans, batons in hand, because I couldn't imagine any work that
could be worse—or any life. What was out there, in the world, that made
men run for the fence in fear?

Iggy was the only worker who seemed sure of himself. After five 31
hours of "junking," he brushed himself off, cleaned up in the washroom,
and came out gleaming with an elegance that humbled the rest of us.
Few would look him straight in the eye or talk to him in our usual stupid
way because he was so much better. He carried himself as a man should—
with Old World "dignity"—while the rest of us muffed our jobs and
talked dully about dull things as we worked. From where he worked in
his open shed he would now and then watch us with his hands on his
hips. He would shake his head and click his tongue in disgust.

The rest of us lived dismally. I often wondered what the others' 32
homes were like; I couldn't imagine that they were much better than our
workplace. No one indicated that his outside life was interesting or intriguing. We all looked defeated and contemptible in our filth at the
day's end. I imagined the average welcome at home: Rafael, a Mexican
national who had worked at Valley for five years, returned to a beaten
house full of kids dressed in mismatched clothes and playing kick the
can. As for Sugar Daddy, he returned home to a stuffy room where he
would read and reread old magazines. He ate potato chips, drank beer,

and watched TV. There was no grace in dipping socks into a washbasin where later he would wash his cup and plate.

There was no grace at work. It was all ridicule. The assistant foreman 33 drank Cokes in front of the newcomers as they laced tires in the afternoon sun. Knowing that I had a long walk home, Rudy, the college student, passed me waving and yelling "Hello" as I started down Mission Road on the way home to eat out of cans. Even our plump secretary got into the act by wearing short skirts and flaunting her milky legs. If there was love, it was ugly. I'm thinking of Tully and an older man whose name I can no longer recall fondling one another in the washroom. I had come in cradling a smashed finger to find them pressed together in the shower, their pants undone and partly pulled down. When they saw me they smiled with their pink mouths but didn't bother to push away.

How we arrived at such a place is a mystery to me. Why anyone 34 would stay for years is an even deeper concern. You showed up, but from where? What broken life? What ugly past? The foreman showed you the Coke machine, the washroom, and the yard where you'd work. When you picked up a tire, you were amazed at the black it could give off.

Reading Closely

1. What information does Soto casually relate about his physical appearance throughout the narrative? What effect does his appearance have on how he feels about himself? about how others regard and treat him?

2. Soto is now an English professor. Which details in his narrative reveal the promise of the man this seventeen–year–old boy will become? Be prepared to share your answer with the rest of the class.

3. What setting has Soto created for his narrative?

4. What is the significance of physical labor for Soto? What does he say is its significance for the Chicano community? Take a few minutes to write a paragraph in response.

5. Look closely at the photograph on p. 191. What characteristics do the men in it share? How does the photograph enhance (or fail to enhance) Soto's narrative essay?

Considering Larger Issues

1. Reread the first four paragraphs of the essay. How do they establish a mood for the narrative? Read the last four paragraphs. What effect do they have on you as a reader? Is establishing a mood the only purpose of this essay?

2. **Work with one or two classmates** to determine which specific passages report information, support an argument, provide an example, or

establish a mood. Prepare a group response to share with the rest of the class.

3. **COMBINING METHODS.**   How does Soto support the *comparison* he makes in the opening sentence: "There are two kinds of work: One uses the mind and the other uses muscle"? Mark the passages that support this comparison, including those that illustrate the *consequences* of each kind of work. What effect does Soto's comparison have on his narrative?

Thinking about Language

1. Make a list of the words, phrases, and references to places in the essay that you do not understand or that confuse you. Then, **working with two or three classmates,** compare your lists and try to answer one another's questions.

2. What specific words and phrases does Soto use to reveal the pervasiveness of racism?

3. Mark the places where Soto includes dialogue. What do these passages contribute to his essay?

4. **Working with two or three classmates,** discuss how Soto narrates his first day on the job. What characters, events, dialogue, and other details does he include that develop the notion of physical work? Make a list of all the words, phrases, and incidents that support that idea. Prepare to report to the rest of the class.

Writing Your Own Narratives

1. Write a three- to four-page essay about an incident you've witnessed or experienced that illustrates an aspect of race, ethnicity, religion, or gender in our society. What was the context of the incident? What led up to it? What was the climax? What were its consequences? Refer to "Checking Over Narrative Writing" (p. 150) as you draft and revise.

2. Draft a three- to four-page narrative that illustrates your sense of belonging to a racial, ethnic, religious, political, or social group, or to a group of men or women. At what moment did you feel a sense of belonging? Try to make that moment come alive for your readers by selecting and using dialogue, characters, a particular setting, and a thoughtfully organized series of events. As you draft and revise, refer to the guidelines for checking over narrative writing on p. 150.

3. Using Soto's essay as a model, draft a three- to four-page essay in which you narrate an experience from your own life that demonstrates relations between a group you belong to and another group (religious, cultural, racial, educational, and so on). How does your experience compare and contrast with Soto's when he took his first job? You can illustrate the amount of change—or stability—in relations between groups. As you draft and revise, refer to "Checking Over Narrative Writing" on p. 150.

Tales of Woe and Wonder

The following narrative appeared in 2003 in *Golf Monthly*, one of Britain's lead-ing golf publications. Using both verbal and visual language, the narrative tells the stories of ups and downs in four professional golfers' careers. As you read the narrative, consider its overall purpose.

> **Preview** How do the title and subtitle work together to prepare you to read?

. . . . . . ➤

Reading Closely

1. All narratives have characters. Who are the characters in this narrative? What do you know about them?
2. What visual details draw you into the narrative? Which ones report in-formation, argue a point, provide an example, or set a mood?
3. Which verbal details draw you into the narrative? Which ones report in-formation, argue a point, provide an example, or set a mood?

Considering Larger Issues

1. What is the narrative's overall purpose? How do each of the following components contribute to that purpose: the headline, the bold print, the column of photos, and the graphs?
2. **Working with one or two classmates,** trace the four narratives in this piece, noting any transitional words, phrases, or markers.
3. COMBINING METHODS. **Continue working with your classmate(s),** and identify the visual and verbal elements of other rhetorical methods: *comparison and contrast, description, exemplification, cause-and-consequence analysis,* and *argumentation*. Be prepared to share your findings with the rest of the class.
4. This visual narrative appeared in a British magazine. Who would be the target audience? What might be this audience's special characteristics? How might they differ from the characteristics of a U.S. audience?

Thinking about Language

1. Using the context or a dictionary—or asking someone who knows the vocabulary of golf—define the following terms. Be prepared to share your answers with the rest of the class.

Tales of woe and wonder

Club changes don't always produce immediate success. Here's a selection of top player's experiences

<<Payne Stewart
SWAPPED THEN CHOPPED

THE CHANGE Stewart switched from forged blades to cast cavity-backs at the end of 1993.
WHAT HAPPENED NEXT He had his worst ever season in 1994, dropping from sixth to 123rd.
THE OUTCOME With help from his sponsors, and a gradual adjustment, he won again early in 1995, climbed back to 12th on the Money List, and never again dropped out of the top 40.

1

STEWART'S NIGHTMARE SEASON

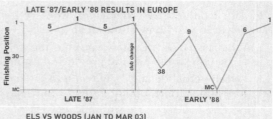

<<Ian Woosnam
DIP IN FORM

THE CHANGE Woosie had carried all before him in 1987 but then opted for a financially lucrative switch to relative Japanese unknown, Maruman.
WHAT HAPPENED NEXT His form dipped in early 1988 both at home and in the States.
THE OUTCOME The short-lived "slump" ended with a win in May, and was finally banished by a fine-tuning club-fitting session in Japan.

2

LATE '87/EARLY '88 RESULTS IN EUROPE

<<Ernie Els
MOVED THEN GROOVED

THE CHANGE Els won six times in 2002, but his contract was up and Titleist won the bidding.
WHAT HAPPENED NEXT He won the Mercedes Championship by eight shots first time out.
THE OUTCOME He went on to nearly win his first six stroke play tournaments with his new clubs, reducing Tiger's World Ranking point lead by 1.6 before the end of March.

3

ELS VS WOODS (JAN TO MAR 03)

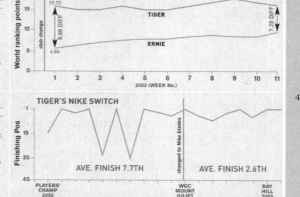

<<Tiger Woods
STILL NO.1, ONLY BETTER

THE CHANGE Tiger finally switched to Nike irons for the WGC event at Mount Juliet in September.
WHAT HAPPENED NEXT He shot rounds of 65, 65, 67, 66 for a 25-under-par winning total.
THE OUTCOME In eight events since putting Nike blades in the bag, Tiger has won four and finished no worse that seventh, recording a mind-boggling average result of 2.6th.

4

TIGER'S NIKE SWITCH

200

forged blades (1)   finishing position (2)   world ranking point
cast cavity–backs (1)   contract (3)   lead (3)
money list position (1) bidding (3)   irons (4)
lucrative (2)   stroke play (3)   under par (4)

Writing Your Own Narratives

1. Watch a golf match or another kind of sports event—then watch the postgame show. Take notes while you listen to the analysis and watch clips of the event. What seems to be the purpose of the postgame show? How do the words and visuals fulfill that purpose? What roles do the analysts play? Draft a two- to three-page essay in which you narrate chronologically the postgame show. Yours will be an informational narrative because you'll be recounting the show, but you'll also be describing how it fulfilled its purpose. Refer to the guidelines for checking over narrative writing on p. 150.

2. Compose a three- to four-page narrative in which you use both words and images to inform a reader about your progress (or lack of progress) in college so far. As you plan your narrative, consider who will be the characters, what those characters will say, and what the setting will be. Also consider what kind of "progress" you'll focus on and during what particular time. As you draft and revise, refer to the guidelines for checking over narrative writing on p. 150.

✳ Additional Suggestions for Writing

1. Draft a three- to four-page narrative essay in which you argue a thesis that relates education to identity. As you argue, you may find that you're also explaining a process and maybe even creating a mood. Consider modeling your essay on one of the narratives in this chapter, imitating the writer's strategies for making and supporting his or her points. Refer to the guidelines for checking over narrative writing (p. 150) as you draft and revise.

2. Several essays in this chapter explore issues of class. What makes someone a member of the upper class, middle class, or lower class: money, education, social status, occupation, or race? What are the effects of these distinctions? How do you behave, how have you behaved, and how would you like to behave in response to class distinctions? Drawing on your responses to these questions, draft a three- to four-page narrative essay in which you explore issues of class that you have experienced. You may find yourself using comparison and contrast or cause and consequence as you write. Remember that the guidelines for checking over narrative writing can be found on p. 150.

3. Draft a three- to four-page narrative essay on the subject of online courses. If you have ever taken (or are now taking) an online, computer-mediated, or distance-learning course, use that course as the basis for your narrative essay. Freewrite for ten minutes about your experience, jotting down ideas on paper as they come to mind. From those ideas, try to determine a purpose for your essay, and from that purpose, a tentative thesis. Depending on your audience, your narration might also draw on *cause-and-consequence analysis, process analysis, comparison and contrast,* and *argumentation.*

The acclaimed
New York Times
bestseller

STEPHEN KING

A MEMOIR OF THE CRAFT

On Writing

chapter 4

EXEMPLIFICATION

explain
Clarify
Support

analyze
argue
add interest

Why we use

"A one-of-a-

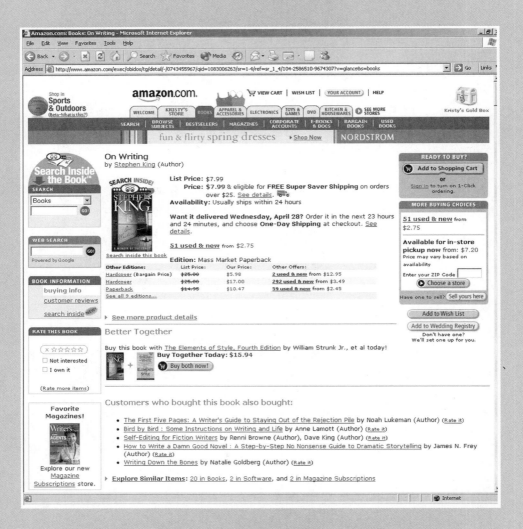

Amazon.com: Books: On Writing - Microsoft Internet Explorer

File   Edit   View   Favorites   Tools   Help

Back   •   Search   Favorites   Media

Address   http://www.amazon.com/exec/obidos/tg/detail/-/0743455967/qid=1083006263/sr=1-4/ref=sr_1_4/104-2586510-9674307?v=glance&s=books   Go   Links

amazon.com.   VIEW CART | WISH LIST | YOUR ACCOUNT | HELP

Shop in **Sports & Outdoors** (Beta- What is this?)

WELCOME | KRISTY'S STORE | BOOKS | APPAREL & ACCESSORIES | ELECTRONICS | TOYS & GAMES | DVD | KITCHEN & HOUSEWARES | SEE MORE STORES

Kristy's Gold Box

SEARCH | BROWSE SUBJECTS | BESTSELLERS | MAGAZINES | CORPORATE ACCOUNTS | E-BOOKS & DOCS | BARGAIN BOOKS | USED BOOKS

fun & flirty spring dresses   ▸ Shop Now   NORDSTROM

Search Inside the Book™

SEARCH

Books
GO!

WEB SEARCH
GO!
Powered by Google

BOOK INFORMATION
buying info
customer reviews
search inside

RATE THIS BOOK
x ☆☆☆☆☆
☐ Not interested
☐ I own it
(Rate more items)

Favorite Magazines!
Writer's AGENTS
Explore our new Magazine Subscriptions store.

On Writing
by Stephen King (Author)

SEARCH INSIDE!
STEPHEN KING
A MEMOIR OF THE CRAFT

Search inside this book

List Price: $7.99
Price: $7.99 & eligible for **FREE Super Saver Shipping** on orders over $25. See details.
Availability: Usually ships within 24 hours

Want it delivered Wednesday, April 28? Order it in the next 23 hours and 24 minutes, and choose **One-Day Shipping** at checkout. See details.

51 used & new from $2.75

Edition: Mass Market Paperback

Other Editions:	List Price:	Our Price:	Other Offers:
Hardcover (Bargain Price)	$25.00	$5.98	2 used & new from $12.95
Hardcover	$25.00	$17.00	292 used & new from $3.49
Paperback	$14.95	$10.47	59 used & new from $2.45

See all 9 editions...

▸ See more product details

Better Together

Buy this book with The Elements of Style, Fourth Edition by William Strunk Jr., et al today!
Buy Together Today: $15.94
Buy both now!

READY TO BUY?
Add to Shopping Cart
or
Sign in to turn on 1-Click ordering.

MORE BUYING CHOICES

51 used & new from $2.75

Available for in-store pickup now from: $7.20
Price may vary based on availability

Enter your ZIP Code
Choose a store

Have one to sell? Sell yours here

Add to Wish List

Add to Wedding Registry
Don't have one?
We'll set one up for you.

Customers who bought this book also bought:

- The First Five Pages: A Writer's Guide to Staying Out of the Rejection Pile by Noah Lukeman (Author) (Rate it)
- Bird by Bird : Some Instructions on Writing and Life by Anne Lamott (Author) (Rate it)
- Self-Editing for Fiction Writers by Renni Browne (Author), Dave King (Author) (Rate it)
- How to Write a Damn Good Novel : A Step-by-Step No Nonsense Guide to Dramatic Storytelling by James N. Frey (Author) (Rate it)
- Writing Down the Bones by Natalie Goldberg (Author) (Rate it)

▸ **Explore Similar Items:** 20 in Books, 2 in Software, and 2 in Magazine Subscriptions

Internet

*W*hen Amazon.com customers call up a particular book, they see a description of it as well as a list of other books that buyers of that book also tend to purchase. Customers who bought Stephen King's *On Writing* also bought other works about writing: Noah Lukeman's *The First Five Pages*, Anne Lamott's *Bird by Bird*, Rennie Browne and Dave King's *Self-Editing for Fiction Writers*, the twenty–fifth anniversary edition of William K. Zinsser's *On Writing Well*, and James N. Frey's *How to Write a Damn Good Novel*. The folks at Amazon.com make generalizations about their read-ers—for example, that people who want to read a certain book also want to read books related to it in some way—and provide examples to support their generalization. They hope to persuade readers to "buy into" it, and apparently many do. In this case **exemplification**—providing examples—is not only a way to make sense; it is also a way to make money.

> **Looking at Your Own Literacy**   When you read a book, do you want to read other books that are related to it in some way? Are those books related in terms of author, subject, historical period? Take a few min-utes to write about your reading habits, making a generalization and then providing an example or two.

What Is Exemplification?

Every day, we make generalizations about people, places, or things, generalizations based on what we've read, seen, or experienced. We might assert that Italian food is fattening, that college athletes don't graduate, that English majors easily find jobs. We might say that Holly-wood marriages are shaky, that Michael Moore's films are biased, that the Lakers are always strong (yet troubled), that if you want to read *On Writing*, you'll also want to read *On Writing Well*. All these generalizations may be true, but unless we back them up with concrete examples—sto-ries, facts, statistics, ideas—chances are our listeners or readers won't immediately believe us, won't understand us, or won't be interested in our point. We need examples of the caloric components of specific Italian foods, graduation statistics, Moore's story lines, and the Lakers' power. Specific examples make all sorts of conversation and writing come alive—and ring true.

In writing, exemplification can be the dominant rhetorical method of development for an entire essay or a supporting method within a work developed with any other method, from narration to argument. For in-stance, when I write a strong letter of recommendation for a student, I always provide examples of the student's strengths. For a student who wanted an internship at the Museum of Contemporary Photography in

Chicago, I opened one paragraph with a generalization that she had planned her career seriously and then I backed up my generalization with examples:

> Just a glance at her résumé will show you how seriously she's planned for her career in art. Even as she worked as a bookstore cashier in order to finance her undergraduate studies at Penn State, she found the time and opportunity to work as a curator's assistant at Penn State's own Palmer Museum of Art, one of those jewels one sometimes finds on a college campus. During the summer between her junior and senior years of college, she lived with her grandparents in Cincinnati, Ohio, and worked as an intern at the Cincinnati Art Museum. After graduating Phi Beta Kappa in art history, Jennifer spent the summer in Paris, perfecting her French and studying in the museums. In late summer, she took off for Greenwich, Connecticut, where she worked as a nanny for the school year. While her young charges were in school, Jennifer worked three days a week as assistant to the curator at the Bruce Museum of Arts and Sciences. Jennifer is a young woman who knows what she's after, what she's doing, and how she'll do it. She is impressive.

Thinking about Exemplification

1. Look over the Web page from Amazon.com (p. 204) that features *On Writing*. What specific information does the page provide for you? What is your response to this page? Are you convinced that *On Writing* might be a good book for writers? Why or why not?

2. **Working with a classmate,** list all the points that online reviewers make in their discussion of *On Writing* on the following pages. Do they provide ample reasons for you to consider buying the book? Write a generalization about King's book, about whether it is a good book for beginning college writers, and, specifically, why or why not. Then follow your generalization with examples from the reviews that support it. Share your group response with the rest of the class.

Why Use Exemplification?

Human beings tend to generalize, but listeners or readers want and need examples before they will pay much attention to any generalization or believe the person who's making it. Therefore, we use exemplification every day to illustrate or support the generalizations we make. More specifically, exemplification helps us achieve four specific purposes: to explain and clarify, to analyze, to argue, or to add interest.

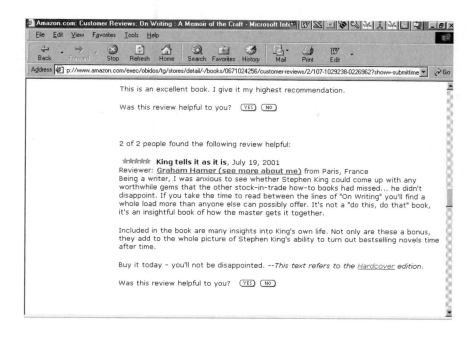

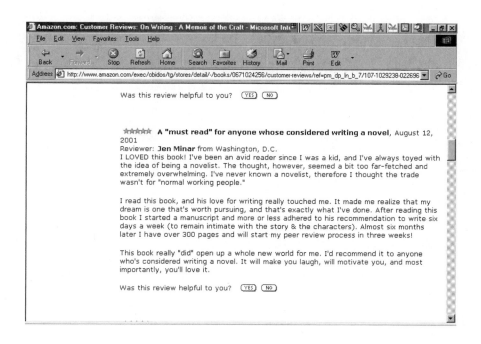

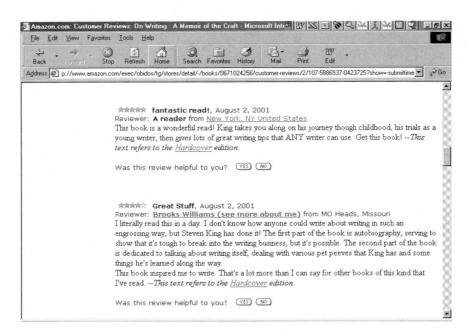

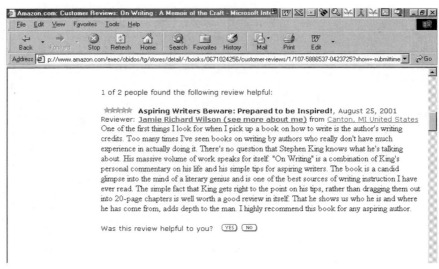

Examples help explain and clarify by expanding a generalization. In *On Writing*, King comes up with a number of generalizations about writers: at one point, for instance, he asserts:

> There are no bad dogs, according to the title of a popular training manual, but don't tell that to the parent of a child mauled by a pit bull or a rottweiler; he or she is apt to bust your beak for you. And no matter how much I want to encourage the man or woman trying for the first time to write seriously, I can't lie and say there are no bad writers. Sorry, but there are *lots* of bad writers. Some are on-staff at your local newspaper, usually reviewing little-theater productions or pontificating about the local sports teams. Some have scribbled their way to homes in the Caribbean, leaving a trail of pulsing adverbs, wooden characters, and vile passive-voice constructions behind them. Others hold forth at open-mike poetry slams, wearing black turtlenecks and wrinkled khaki pants; they spout doggerel about "my angry lesbian breasts" and "the tilted alley where I cried my mother's name."
> —STEPHEN KING, *On Writing*

King offers a number of examples of bad writers, all in support of his generalization that there are lots of them.

Try Your Hand   Write a generalization about a group or class of people. You might start out writing about your own family: "The Glenns like to . . ."; or you might write about a group different from one to which you belong: fraternity brothers, working mothers, college graduates, computer "nerds," rich people, poor people, and so on. After you've made your generalization, back it up with three specific examples.

We also use exemplification when we want to analyze, either for ourselves or for an audience. In a column that appears every Sunday in *Parade* magazine, Marilyn vos Savant, who is listed in the "Guinness Book of World Records" Hall of Fame for "Highest IQ," answers questions and analyzes processes, causes, or consequences for the folks who write in to her. The following exchange between vos Savant and Donald Anderson illustrates the use of examples in process analysis, for Anderson explicitly asks vos Savant to analyze and explain the process of sex determination:

> You wrote that an embryo, regardless of the genetic sex determined at conception, will become feminized unless "key masculinizing influences occur. Every embryo — male (XY) *and* female (XX) — contains structures capable of developing into either male or female sex organs. Only if certain activity occurs properly can any XY embryo head in the direction of becoming all male. If it does not occur, all embryos head in the direction of becoming females, almost by default."
>
> I'm very surprised. I thought the sex determined at conception was definitive. What "activity" must occur to make an XY embryo stay masculine?
> —DONALD ANDERSON
> Des Plaines, Ill.

It surprised plenty of other readers too. There are *many* activities required at highly specific times for normal sexual differentiation, regardless of the genetic sex.

For example, all embryos have sexually indeterminate gonads, which
develop into either testicles or ovaries. A "testis-organizing" activity
helps the Y chromosome turn them into testes. Later, the testes must
secrete an inhibiting substance to make certain ducts atrophy (otherwise,
they become female fallopian tubes). They also must secrete testosterone
to stimulate the development of other ducts instead (which will become
the male *vas deferens*).

The biological organism is sensitive and complex indeed, and so are
the causes of all sorts of sexual variance.   — MARILYN VON SAVANT

Until he had read vos Savant's discussion of the potential for every embryo to develop into an individual of either sex, Anderson thought he'd
understood embryonic sexual development. So he asks vos Savant to explain the process more fully. She does, providing a clear example at
every step: first, "all embryos have sexually indeterminate gonads." Second, "a 'testis-organizing' activity helps the Y chromosome turn [those
gonads] into testes." Vos Savant goes on to provide examples for each of
the remaining steps in the process.

> **Try Your Hand**   Processes are easier to understand when examples ac-
> company each step. Think of a process you have mastered. Write out
> the name of the process and the basic steps you follow when you per-
> form it. Then go back and provide an example—an anecdote, fact, or
> other illustration—for each step, a specific example that brings that
> step alive.

In writing as in conversation, we also use examples when trying to
convince someone to consider our point of view; assertions alone are
usually not enough to bring the listener or reader to our way of thinking. In the following excerpt, which also appeared in *Parade* magazine,
14-year-old Heather Dambly uses examples to argue that her parents
should let her go to parties:

Why are parents so overprotective? Last night I asked if I could go to a
party. My mom said "no" and gave her ridiculous reason that boys and
things she wouldn't want me to get involved in would be there. First of
all, it really was just a small party with no drugs or anything of the sort.
Second, I am in high school, so of course there will be boys! Finally, the
drugs are my choice. Keeping me home from a party will not keep me
from doing drugs. I could get them anywhere — in school, at football
games, or from friends. I do not use drugs. But making me have no social life will not keep me away from them. I think my parents should let
me go to parties and stop being so overprotective.

Clearly, Dambly is responding, point by point, to her parents' objections, and she is offering concrete examples (size of the party, inevitability of boys being there, pervasiveness of drugs) to support her main point and convince readers — not to mention her own parents.

> **Try Your Hand**   Think about something you want to do but have been told not to do, or about something you don't want to do but know you should. Write a sentence describing the forbidden activity or obligation. Then make a list of the reasons you do or do not want to do it.

Sometimes, examples do nothing more — or less — than add interest. For instance, the award–winning author Tim O'Brien provides long lists of examples to illustrate the many belongings carried by U.S. soldiers fighting in the Vietnam War:

The things they carried were largely determined by necessity. Among the necessities or near necessities were P-38 can openers, pocket knives, heat tabs, wrist watches, dog tags, mosquito repellent, chewing gum, candy, cigarettes, salt tablets, packets of Kool-Aid, lighters, matches, sewing kits, Military Payment Certificates, C rations, and two or three canteens of water. Together, these items weighed between fifteen and twenty pounds, depending upon a man's habits or rate of metabolism. Henry Dobbins, who was a big man, carried extra rations; he was especially fond of canned peaches in heavy syrup over pound cake. Dave Jensen, who practiced field hygiene, carried a toothbrush, dental floss, and several hotel-size bars of soap he'd stolen on R&R in Sydney, Australia. Ted Lavender, who was scared, carried tranquilizers until he was shot in the head outside the village of Than Khe in mid-April. By necessity, and because it was SOP [standard operating procedure], they all carried steel helmets that weighed five pounds including the liner and camouflage cover. They carried the standard fatigue jackets and trousers. Very few carried underwear. On their feet they carried jungle boots — 2.1 pounds — and Dave Jensen carried three pairs of socks and a can of Dr. Scholl's foot powder as a precaution against trench foot. Until he was shot, Ted Lavender carried six or seven ounces of premium dope, which for him was a necessity. Mitchell Sanders, the RTO [radio telephone operator] carried condoms. Norman Bowker carried a diary. Rat Kiley carried comic books. Kiowa, a devout Baptist, carried an illustrated New Testament that had been presented to him by his father, who taught Sunday school in Oklahoma City, Oklahoma. As a hedge against bad times, however, Kiowa also carried his grandmother's distrust of the white man, his grandfather's old hunting hatchet. Necessity dictated. Because the land was mined and booby-trapped, it was SOP for each man to carry a steel-centered, nylon-covered flak jacket, Simonov carbines and black-market Uzis and .38 caliber Smith & Wesson handguns and 66 mm LAWs and shotguns and silencers and blackjacks and bayonets and C-4 plastic explosives. Lee Strunk carried a slingshot; a weapon of last resort, he called it. Mitchell Sanders carried brass knuckles. Kiowa carried his grandfather's feathered hatchet. Every third or fourth man carried a Claymore antipersonnel mine — 3.5 pounds with its firing device. They all carried at least one M-18 colored smoke grenade — twenty-four ounces. Some carried CS or teargas grenades. Some carried white-phosphorus grenades. They carried all they could bear, and then some, including a silent awe for the terrible power of the things they carried.   — TIM O'BRIEN, *The Things They Carried*

O'Brien's list of the things the soldiers carried exemplifies the burdens of war, adding interest — and building tension — until the final and deadliest examples. In this excerpt from his novel, O'Brien matter-of-factly recounts the "things"; yet the danger and fearsomeness of the Vietnam War are implicit in every item, in every mention of weaponry and firearms.

Try Your Hand   Think back to your last big move. Maybe it was just a few weeks ago, when you moved onto campus. Maybe it was years ago, when you and your family moved across the country. Think about the logistics of the move, and then write a list of all the things you carried (either by hand, in huge boxes, or in a van). If you have never moved or don't remember moving, make a list of all the things you took on a vacation or an outing, such as a picnic.

How Do You Read Exemplification?

Examples that are concrete, real, or striking make for the strongest, most effective support of any generalization, no matter what their purpose or intended audience. In order to use exemplification effectively in your writing, you'll need to learn how to read essays using exemplification by other writers with a critical eye. By concentrating on several key features of essays that use exemplification successfully, you'll be able to evaluate the ones you read and plan out the ones you write.

First of all, read carefully to establish what generalization the author is making — as well as why and to whom. What belief, understanding, or feeling does the author want you to take away from the examples? Take another look at the preceding excerpt from Tim O'Brien's *The Things They Carried*. A prize-winning novelist, O'Brien is undoubtedly using exemplification here to add interest to his story, which is aimed at readers of fiction. In this case, he might be writing more specifically for readers interested in fiction about war; many of his readers are no doubt Vietnam War buffs or even veterans, who read both fiction and nonfiction about that war. Therefore, as O'Brien develops his generalization and the examples to support it, he works to fulfill his overall purpose (adding interest) with his audience in mind.

O'Brien's generalization is clear: "The things they carried were largely determined by necessity." Once you've extracted the generalization from the reading, assess it to determine whether it sounds clear or plausible—or if it seems confusing, too sweeping, or biased in some way. O'Brien's generalization seems to be clear and plausible: it doesn't seem to be a controversial assertion, and he qualifies or limits it with "largely." However, when you know or suspect that the generalization *does* argue a point (as in the excerpt from Heather Dambly on p. 210), you'll want to keep that bias in mind as you read through the examples and judge how effective they are in achieving that purpose.

"[C]an openers, pocket knives, heat tabs, wrist watches, dog tags, mosquito repellent, . . ."—O'Brien's first examples do indeed sound like a list of necessities. By the time he finishes this part of the list, he mentions that "these items weighed between fifteen and twenty pounds," a statement that both supports the "necessary" quality of the things the soldiers carried and adds interest to the passage. But then O'Brien moves into examples of individual soldiers, each of whom carries things that are personal necessities. These examples pack more emotion—they add more interest—than the initial ones of can openers and pocket knives because they personalize the men who fought in Vietnam. Finally, O'Brien moves into examples of the weapons they carried, including both high-tech, standard-issue ones and low-tech personalized ones. By arranging his examples in this way, by saving the most essential and most serious things they carried for the end, the writer achieves the maximum emotional impact. Notice how he ends with a generalization that extends the meaning of his original one—that the burdens the soldiers had to carry were almost unbearable not only physically but emotionally as well. When in your reading you encounter examples that stir your emotions—or just your curiosity—try to understand how and why the writer uses those examples.

How Do You Write Using Exemplification?

Coming up with a generalization and examples to support it may sound like an easy task—and it can be. But like any other kind of writing, exemplification makes demands on the writer. Because it can be used for any subject and purpose, you'll want to begin by carefully determining your subject and your purpose: What generalization do you want to exemplify—and why? You'll also need to consider your audience, develop appropriate examples, and arrange those examples effectively.

Considering Your Subject

Did you come up with your subject, or was it assigned to you? For example, has your sociology professor asked you to identify and cite evidence of patterns of alcohol consumption on your campus? Has your music professor asked you to provide examples as part of a historical analysis of patriotic songs and lyrics? Has your cultural anthropology instructor asked you to write about examples of racism and sexism that you've experienced or observed? If you are writing about an assigned topic, you probably already have a generalization ("Alcohol consumption on this campus is a major safety issue"), but you may need to narrow it or revise it in some other way, depending on the assignment ("Although students are drinking less beer and wine, consumption of other, more potent alcoholic beverages has increased sharply in recent years"). If writing about this subject is your own idea, then you will need to focus on a generalization about the subject that you can back up or illustrate with examples.

Considering Your Purpose

Whether writing an essay or passage using exemplification was your idea or your instructor's, you should determine the purpose of your examples before you begin developing them. Why do you want to exemplify this particular generalization? In the cartoon on p. 215, for example, Cathy has a long list of examples—or, in her case, excuses. In Cathy's case, the generalization is implied but very clear: she does not want to go out sometime—not anytime, in fact. Her purpose is to explain to her audience—the mustached man (who in the original color version of the comic strip is wearing gold slacks, a green striped jacket, a pink shirt, and a red–and–white polka dot tie)—why she is unable to accept his invitation. Her possible examples are "I'm engaged"; "I'm seriously involved"; "I'm busy all month"; and "I'm too distraught over a recent break-up. I wouldn't be good company." Cathy's problem is deciding which (if any) of these examples will achieve her persuasive purpose. In fact, in any writing activity it's your overall purpose that determines your choice of examples, whether they are intended to explain or clarify, analyze, argue, or add interest. Your purpose also shapes your thesis statement.

Considering Your Audience

Cathy's broader audience—fans of the comic strip—don't believe her excuses for a moment, nor will they see them as a series of related examples. Besides, Cathy's fans have watched her try to get out of a date many times before. But to her intended audience—the guy in the gold slacks—one of her examples just might ring true, which is why she alludes to his probable responses after each excuse. Whoever the members of your audience are, you'll need to try to imagine their reactions—just as Cathy does—to be sure that your examples are appropriate for them and will convince them of your generalization, help them understand it, or make them interested in it. Your audience and your purpose always go hand-in-hand.

© 1998, Cathy Guisewite, by permission of Universal Press Syndicate.

Considering Specific Examples

Once you have a generalization about your subject, you'll need to make a list of as many examples as you can think of. **Anecdotes** (brief stories), facts, statistics, and ideas can all serve as examples that support or illustrate a generalization. In the following excerpt, Jonathan Kozol uses an anecdote to support his generalization about homeless people as untouchables:

> While we talk we watch an old man nearby who is standing flat and motionless against the wall, surrounded by two dozen bright red shopping bags from Macy's. Every so often, someone stops to put a coin into his hand. I notice the care with which the people drop their coins, in order that their hands do not touch his. When I pass that spot some hours later he will still be there. I'll do the same. I'll look at this hand — the fingers worn and swollen and the nails curled in like claws — and I will drop a quarter and extract my hand and move off quickly.
>
> —JONATHAN KOZOL, "Untouchables"

Eva Payne uses facts to support the generalization that she is "handy":

> I trained my hands to take shorthand at 120 words per minute and type 70 words per minute. My hands can make the best pie crust you have ever tasted. I can raise green beans and make raspberry jelly with my hands.   —EVA PAYNE, "Handy"

Michelle Stacey uses statistics to back up her generalization about Americans' habit of overeating:

> But this is not a bagel as nature or the U.S. government intended, which would be a moderate two to three ounces and 150 to 250 calories; instead, this is a behemoth, puffed up to five or six ounces and probably 400 calories, accounting for almost half of the six to eleven daily bread servings recommended by the USDA's Food Guide Pyramid.
>
> —MICHELLE STACEY, "All You Can Eat"

Finally, Brent Staples uses hypothetical scenarios to illustrate his generalization that public suspicions of black men as dangerous actually place *him*, a black man, in danger:

> . . . I soon gathered that being perceived as dangerous is a hazard in itself. I only needed to turn a corner into a dicey situation, or crowd some frightened, armed person in a foyer somewhere, or make an errant move after being pulled over by a policeman. Where fear and weapons meet — and they often do in urban America — there is always the possibility of death.   —BRENT STAPLES, "Just Walk on By"

As you list various kinds of examples, you'll see that some of them are only loosely related to your generalization. In fact, you may find that your list of examples calls for a narrower or slightly different generalization. Also keep in mind that your audience and purpose will influence which kinds of examples (anecdotes, facts, statistics) are most appropriate. Whichever kind(s) and however many you list, choose only those that are directly **relevant** to your generalization, those that support or illustrate at least one aspect of it. Examples that are used to make an argument must also be **representative** of the whole group covered by the generalization. For instance, if you're writing about current alcohol consumption on your campus, you won't want to include an anecdote from 1995, which would not be relevant, or to concentrate only on fraternity houses, which might not be representative. If you do, you should revise your generalization to reflect your focus.

There are no hard-and-fast rules for how many examples to provide, but keep in mind that you usually need a range of examples for any one generalization, especially one making an argument. In other words, draft more examples than you need, and, as you revise, choose only those that will help prove your generalization to the most skeptical member of your audience, explain it to the most confused, or interest the most bored.

Arranging All the Parts

If exemplification is the framework for your entire essay, then each paragraph will need to be related to your thesis, to the generalization you are trying to illustrate or prove. For instance, if you are responding to your professor's assignment about alcohol consumption, your entire essay should support whatever generalization about drinking alcohol you come up with. If you generalize that alcohol abuse on your campus is increasing, you'll need specific examples (probably including anecdotes, statistics, and facts) of such problems as binge drinking, drinking contests, underage drinking, alcohol-related traffic accidents, on-campus accidents (falling off balconies, passing out in public or in dorm rooms), alcohol-related academic difficulties, inappropriate sexual activity caused by alcohol, and so on.

The more examples you include, the more important it is to arrange them in some kind of purposeful order so that the reader doesn't lose sight of the connection between them — the generalization. For instance, you may want to arrange them chronologically (along a time line), the way vos Savant does on p. 209. You may want to arrange them emphatically, starting with the least serious kinds of alcohol abuse and placing the most serious at the end. (Notice how Dambly uses emphatic organization on p. 210.) Or you may want to group them into examples dealing with beer and wine and those dealing with hard liquor, if this distinction seems important in understanding patterns of alcohol abuse. You may want to begin with anecdotes and move on to statistics and facts, reverse this order, or alternate between types of examples to avoid monotony. Regardless of the method you select for organizing your examples, you'll need to use transitional words and phrases (*for instance; likewise; an even more serious episode of binge drinking* . . .) to guide readers smoothly from one to the next.

"Reading" and Using Visuals in Exemplification

As you use exemplification in writing, you may find that words are not enough. To support your generalization or explain your verbal examples, you may need to use a visual or a group of visuals. Women's monthly fashion magazines, for instance, usually carry an article that features descriptions of the latest look, whether it's low-slung pants, round–toe pumps, chandelier earrings, or even pony-tails. But in order to teach readers how to carry out this new look, the magazine must include a series of photographs of the actual articles or of models displaying the actual look. For instance, in the following display from *Latina* magazine, fashion editor Victoria Sánchez–Lincoln provides a wide range of examples that support her generalization that blue is the season's "color of cool."

To choose and use visuals effectively for exemplification, you can benefit from studying how other writers have used visuals. Given that the purpose of exemplification in the *Latina* visual is simply to add interest (and not to provide an exhaustive list of examples or to argue that red is also a "cool color"), the editor successfully does just that. For an audience made up of young women, she provides an array of clothing and accessories oriented toward them, including one item labeled as a "Great buy: $10." Notice that the visual examples provide a pleasing mixture of stripes, solids, and prints, of curves and straight lines. For this audience of young women, many of whom are still unsure of their own fashion instincts, Sánchez–Lincoln also provides a list of written examples of how to incorporate the new blue fashions into a wardrobe, suggesting that navy blue can serve as a neutral color the same way black does, that pairing turquoise with blue can create a pleasant surprise, and that lighter–colored jeans would look best with the halter top.

Cities heavily involved with the tourist industry use visuals in a similar way. Every tourist bureau circulates a photographic extravaganza, both in print brochures and in animated Web sites, that exemplifies all the reasons tourists should visit its city—for the fancy restaurants, musical entertainment, zoos, theme parks, skiing, scuba diving, botanical gardens, and so on. Remember that bar graphs, line graphs, or pie charts can support or serve as statistical examples. Even if a visual isn't needed to explain your information or support your argument, it can add interest.

If you want to use visuals in writing for an academic assignment, it is a good idea to check with your instructor beforehand. You also need to consider whether to include labels or captions (if the visuals do not already include them) and whether to refer to the visuals in your written text or let them stand on their own.

You've got rhythm...

And we've got blues. Check out our soulful picks in the color of cool

Fashion pages edited by Victoria Sánchez-Lincoln

Cascade Blues
necklace ($16)
and Fiesta
earrings ($8:
800/MERVYNS
for both items)

DKNY Jeans
halter ($34:
select Macy's
stores)

Express shorts ($35:
expressfashion.com
or 877/415–4551)

Great
buy: $10

Wet Seal sunglasses
($10: wetseal.com)

Guess Footwear
sandals ($98:
800/39–GUESS
or guess.com)

Putu by J. MacLear
bag at D.P.
Accessories ($42:
203/847–7103)

How to wear it

■ Add another neutral to your
wardrobe: Navy can be as basic
as black; it goes with everything
and is never boring.

■ Teeny blue hot pants a bit
too extreme? Find just-as-
bold tropical prints on beach
skirts or cabana pants, perfect
for covering up after a day
at *la piaya*. *Latina's* golden
rule: Let them hang low on
your sexy hips!

■ Be surprising. Go exotic and
bright by pairing your blue pick
with turquoise.

■ Sure, you can wear jeans
with this sexy halter (which
enhances your bust with its
horizontal stripes). Just pick
lighter-wash denim jeans for
the strongest impact.

Sisley top ($34:
800/535–4491)

LATINA JULY 2001   41

If you need to use exemplification within an essay that uses a different primary pattern (comparison and contrast, or description, for example), you'll still need to organize the examples effectively — chronologically, emphatically, or in some other way — within your paragraph or passage. You'll also need to decide where your generalization should go in relation to the examples. It will usually come first, but sometimes — especially in an introductory paragraph or passage — you may want to use one or more examples to lead up to it. And after a series of examples or even just one long example, it's a good idea to remind your readers of your generalization and, if possible, extend the point you're making with it. This is what Gretel Ehrlich does in the following passage, where she is writing about a particular kind of man, the cowboy:

> The iconic myth surrounding him is built on American notions of heroism: the index of a man's value as measured in physical courage. Such ideas have perverted manliness into a self-absorbed race for cheap thrills. In a rancher's world, courage has less to do with facing danger than with acting spontaneously — usually on behalf of an animal or another rider. If a cow is stuck in a boghole he throws a loop around her neck, takes his dally (a half hitch around the saddle horn), and pulls her out with horsepower. If a calf is born sick, he may take her home, warm her in front of the kitchen fire, and massage her legs until dawn. One friend, whose favorite horse was trying to swim a lake with hobbles on, dove under water and cut her legs loose with a knife, then swam her to shore, his arm around her neck lifeguard-style, and saved her from drowning. Because these incidents are usually linked to someone or something outside himself, the westerner's courage is selfless, a form of compassion.
> — GRETEL EHRLICH, "About Men"

In this passage Ehrlich makes a generalization about the courage of cowboys, focusing on the idea of acting spontaneously. She then uses three examples, each more dramatic than the previous one, to bring it to life. She concludes by restating the idea she introduced almost as an afterthought in the original generalization: a cowboy's courage usually benefits not himself, but others.

Understanding and Using Exemplification

Analyzing Exemplification

1. Stephen King writes about various kinds of writers (p. 208). List all the kinds he describes. What examples can you add to his lists? How do these examples (yours as well as King's) support King's purpose for writing?

2. In the excerpts on pp. 208–12, the writers use vocabulary that evokes their subject matter. For instance, Stephen King talks about "poetry

slams" and "doggerel," and Tim O'Brien writes about "R&R" and "SOP." Reread each excerpt, and underline the subject–specific terminology that each writer uses.

3. **Working with a classmate,** compare the words you have both under-lined in response to the previous question. Using your dictionary or the context, define any words you don't know. Then turn back to the ex-cerpts to find other words that you do not know, and work together to define those terms.

Planning and Writing Essays Using Exemplification

1. Writing for no more than five minutes, give examples that illustrate the reasons Heather Dambly's parents should be careful about their daugh-ter's partying (see p. 210). Include examples from your own experience and observations. Then add examples from other people's experiences that you have heard, witnessed, or read about. **Working with one or two classmates,** discuss and combine your lists of examples.

2. Turn to p. 211 and copy—word for word—the excerpt from Tim O'Brien's essay on "the things they carried." (When you copy by hand, the words, phrases, and rhythms stay in your mind longer than if you were to type them.) Now write a passage of approximately the same length, copying his style as closely as possible, about the things you and your friends carry in college.

3. Using your responses from question 1, draft a two- to three–page essay in which you agree with either Dambly or her parents on the subject of whether 14–year–olds should be allowed to go to unchaperoned parties. Because your purpose is to convince the reader to accept your general-ization, you should provide ample supporting examples, many of which should be statistics or facts. You will probably need to conduct library or Internet research in order to come up with such examples, and you may also want to conduct interviews to gather anecdotes that support or dif-fer from your own experiences. Refer to the following guidelines for checking over the use of exemplification.

4. Respond to Stephen King's generalization that there are "lots of bad writers" by drafting your own generalization about the prevalence of bad movies, Web sites, parents, teachers, or another group of people or things. Write a three- to four–page essay in which you invite the reader to consider your point of view. As you draft and revise, refer to the fol-lowing guidelines for checking over the use of exemplification.

✓ Checking Over the Use of Exemplification

1. What is the generalization that you need to illustrate or support?

2. What is the purpose of your examples? to explain or clarify the general-ization? to analyze it? to argue for it? to add interest? Do all your ex-amples help to fulfill this purpose?

3. Who is your audience? Are all your examples appropriate for that audience?

4. List all your examples. Are there enough of them? Are there too many? Are they all relevant to the generalization? If your generalization makes an argument, are the examples representative? Does your generalization need to be narrowed?

5. How are your examples arranged? Will the arrangement be effective in holding your readers' attention? Have you used transitional words and phrases to guide readers from one example to the next? Do readers need to be reminded of your generalization in your conclusion or at any point along the way?

6. If you're using visuals, do they help fulfill your overall purpose? Do you need to add labels, captions, or references in the written text?

READINGS

GRETEL EHRLICH
About Men

Gretel Ehrlich (b. 1946) grew up in California and studied at Bennington College, the UCLA Film School, and the New School for Social Research. She began writing full-time in 1979. She has written eloquently about the American West, publishing poetry, essays, short stories, and novels that have earned her awards from the National Endowment for the Arts, the Guggenheim Foundation, the Whiting Foundation, and the Wyoming Council for the Arts. Among her many books are the best-selling novel *Heart Mountain* (1988) and an essay collection, *The Solace of Open Spaces* (1985), from which the following work is taken.

> **Preview** You read an excerpt from this essay earlier in the chapter (p. 220). On the basis of that reading, what kind of generalization and examples might you expect from Ehrlich in this longer piece?

When I'm in New York but feeling lonely for Wyoming I look for the   1
Marlboro ads in the subway. What I'm aching to see is horseflesh, the
glint of a spur, a line of distant mountains, brimming creeks, and a reminder of the ranchers and cowboys I've ridden with for the last eight
years. But the men I see in those posters with their stern, humorless
looks remind me of no one I know here. In our hellbent earnestness to
romanticize the cowboy we've ironically disesteemed his true character.
If he's "strong and silent" it's because there's probably no one to talk to.
If he "rides away into the sunset" it's because he's been on horseback
since four in the morning moving cattle and he's trying, fifteen hours
later, to get home to his family. If he's "a rugged individualist" he's also
part of a team: ranch work is teamwork and even the glorified open-
range cowboys of the 1880s rode up and down the Chisholm Trail in the
company of twenty or thirty other riders. Instead of the macho, trigger-
happy man our culture has perversely wanted him to be, the cowboy is
more apt to be convivial, quirky, and softhearted. To be "tough" on a

ranch has nothing to do with conquests and displays of power. More often than not, circumstances—like the colt he's riding or an unexpected blizzard—are overpowering him. It's not toughness but "toughing it out" that counts. In other words, this macho, cultural artifact the cowboy has become is simply a man who possesses resilience, patience, and an instinct for survival. "Cowboys are just like a pile of rocks—everything happens to them. They get climbed on, kicked, rained and snowed on, scuffed up by wind. Their job is 'just to take it,'" one old–timer told me.

A cowboy is someone who loves his work. Since the hours are   2
long—ten to fifteen hours a day—and the pay is $30 he has to. What's required of him is an odd mixture of physical vigor and maternalism. His part of the beef–raising industry is to birth and nurture calves and take care of their mothers. For the most part his work is done on horseback and in a lifetime he sees and comes to know more animals than people. The iconic myth surrounding him is built on American notions of hero-ism: the index of a man's value as measured in physical courage. Such ideas have perverted manliness into a self-absorbed race for cheap thrills. In a rancher's world, courage has less to do with facing danger than with acting spontaneously—usually on behalf of an animal or an-other rider. If a cow is stuck in a boghole he throws a loop around her neck, takes his dally (a half hitch around the saddle horn), and pulls her out with horsepower. If a calf is born sick, he may take her home, warm her in front of the kitchen fire, and massage her legs until dawn. One friend, whose favorite horse was trying to swim a lake with hobbles on, dove under water and cut her legs loose with a knife, then swam her to shore, his arm around her neck lifeguard–style, and saved her from drowning. Because these incidents are usually linked to someone or something outside himself, the westerner's courage is selfless, a form of compassion.

The physical punishment that goes with cowboying is greatly un-   3
derplayed. Once fear is dispensed with, the threshold of pain rises to meet the demands of the job. When Jane Fonda asked Robert Redford (in the film *Electric Horseman*) if he was sick as he struggled to his feet one morning, he replied, "No, just bent." For once the movies had it right. The cowboys I was sitting with laughed in agreement. Cowboys are rarely complainers; they show their stoicism by laughing at them-selves.

If a rancher or cowboy has been thought of as a "man's man"—   4
laconic, hard–drinking, inscrutable—there's almost no place in which the balancing act between male and female, manliness and femininity, can be more natural. If he's gruff, handsome, and physically fit on the outside, he's androgynous at the core. Ranchers are midwives, hunters, nurturers, providers, and conservationists all at once. What we've inter-

preted as toughness—weathered skin, calloused hands, a squint in the eye and a growl in the voice—only masks the tenderness inside. "Now don't go telling me these lambs are cute," one rancher warned me the first day I walked into the football–field–sized lambing sheds. The next thing I knew he was holding a black lamb. "Ain't this little rat good-lookin'?"

So many of the men who came to the West were Southerners—men 5 looking for work and a new life after the Civil War—that chivalrousness and strict codes of honor were soon thought of as western traits. There were very few women in Wyoming during territorial days, so when they did arrive (some as mail–order brides from places like Philadelphia) there was a standoffishness between the sexes and a formality that persists now. Ranchers still tip their hats and say, "Howdy, ma'am" instead of shaking hands with me.

Even young cowboys are often evasive with women. It's not that 6 they're Jekyll and Hyde creatures—gentle with animals and rough on women—but rather, that they don't know how to bring their tenderness into the house and lack the vocabulary to express the complexity of what they feel. Dancing wildly all night becomes a metaphor for the ex-plosive emotions pent up inside, and when these are, on occasion, re-leased, they're so battery–charged and potent that one caress of the face or one "I love you" will peal for a long while.

The geographical vastness and the social isolation here make emo- 7 tional evolution seem impossible. Those contradictions of the heart between respectability, logic, and convention on the one hand, and im-pulse, passion, and intuition on the other, played out wordlessly against the paradisical beauty of the West, give cowboys a wide–eyed but drawn look. Their lips pucker up, not with kisses but with immutability. They may want to break out, staying up all night with a lover just to talk, but they don't know how and can't imagine what the consequences will be. Those rare occasions when they do bare themselves result in confusion. "I feel as if I'd sprained my heart," one friend told me a month after such a meeting.

My friend Ted Hoagland wrote, "No one is as fragile as a woman but 8 no one is as fragile as a man." For all the women here who use "fragile-ness" to avoid work or as a sexual ploy, there are men who try to hide theirs, all the while clinging to an adolescent dependency on women to cook their meals, wash their clothes, and keep the ranch house warm in winter. But there is true vulnerability in evidence here. Because these men work with animals, not machines or numbers, because they live outside in landscapes of torrential beauty, because they are confined to a place and a routine embellished with awesome variables, because calves die in the arms that pulled others into life, because they go to the moun-tains as if on a pilgrimage to find out what makes a herd of elk tick, their strength is also a softness, their toughness, a rare delicacy.

Reading Closely

1. What is this essay about? In one paragraph, summarize the entire essay.

2. What did you learn about cowboys from this essay? What did you already know? What surprised you the most? What do you want to know more about? Write out your responses.

3. What special part does the opening paragraph play in the overall essay? Write out your answer. Then, **working with two or three classmates,** compare answers. If there is a big difference among your answers, share them with the rest of the class.

4. What is the purpose of Ehrlich's essay? How does the visual support that purpose? What specific passages or details support that purpose?

Considering Larger Issues

1. Who is Ehrlich's audience for this essay? Imagine the primary audience for it—the actual readers she wrote it for in the first place. (If you think about her purpose for writing this essay, you'll have an easier time determining her audience.) What broader audience is reading her essay now? Share your responses with the rest of the class.

2. What generalizations does Ehrlich make about men who are westerners? List and number them. What examples does she provide for each generalization? **Working with two or three classmates,** compare the generalizations and examples you have found.

3. COMBINING METHODS. **Working with two or three classmates,** mark or list all the rhetorical methods Erhlich employs to support her generalizations: the *narratives, descriptions, comparisons and contrasts, cause-and-consequence analyses, process analyses, arguments.* You may want to divide up this activity, preparing a short report to share with the rest of the class.

Thinking about Language

1. Using the context of the essay or your dictionary, define the following terms. Be prepared to share your answers with the rest of the class.

convivial (1)	stoicism (3)	chivalrousness (5)
cultural artifact (1)	laconic (4)	peal (6)
maternalism (2)	inscrutable (4)	immutability (7)
iconic (2)	androgynous (4)	pilgrimage (8)

2. Ehrlich uses stereotypes to develop her essay. Without looking back at the essay, write a brief definition of each of the following phrases: "strong and silent"; "rides away into the sunset"; "rugged individualist"; and "toughing it out." **Working with a classmate,** compare your definitions. Where do they overlap? diverge?

3. How do the phrases listed in the previous question play on people's preconceived ideas of men, cowboys, and westerners? How do these particular word choices contribute to Ehrlich's essay?

4. Can the phrases listed in question 2 be applied to groups of people other than cowboys? If so, under what circumstances?

Writing Your Own Essays Using Exemplification

1. Using Ehrlich's essay as a model, prepare to write a three- to four-page essay about men, women, children, boyfriends, or some other group of your choice. First determine the generalization you want to make about this group. Then list all the examples that will support your generalization. As you freewrite and begin drafting your essay, write out the specific purpose you want to fulfill.

2. Look over the examples you've gathered for the previous question. Do they all fit under the umbrella of your generalization? Is each one relevant to the generalization? Can you classify the examples in different categories? If so, how? What is the dominant trait for each category? You may find that you can use classification to organize your exemplification essay. (For more on classification, see Chapter 5.) Using classification, or another method of organization that works with your generalization and examples, draft your essay. Remember to refer to "Checking Over the Use of Exemplification" on p. 221.

3. Think of another kind of work that is romanticized in ways that distort the characteristics of the actual men and women who do the work: firefighter, police officer, teacher, nurse, doctor, attorney, flight attendant, computer-support person, writer, and so on. Draft a three- to four-page essay in which you explore this line of work. Like Ehrlich, begin your essay by discussing popular misconceptions about this particular group of people, and then move on to different features of the generalization that you want to "prove." As you draft and revise, refer to "Checking Over the Use of Exemplification" on p. 221.

BRENT STAPLES

Just Walk on By: A Black Man Ponders His Power to Alter Public Space

Brent Staples (b. 1951) received a Ph.D. in psychology from the University of Chicago in 1982 and has drawn on his background in that field throughout his career as a leading print journalist. He's best known for his essays on culture and politics, which have appeared in the *Chicago Sun-Times*, the *Chicago Reader*, the *New York Times*, and *Down Beat, Harper's*, and *Ms.* magazines. A member of the editorial board of the *New York Times* since 1990, Staples has also published a memoir, *Parallel Time: Growing Up in Black and White*, which appeared in 1994. The following essay first appeared in *Harper's* in 1986, and a slightly different version appeared in *Parallel Time*.

> **Preview** What does it mean to "alter public space"? As you read Staples's essay, consider the ways that a particular kind of person — for example, a white woman, a gay man, a devout Christian, a person with a disability, a homeless person — can change the emotional climate of a particular place.

My first victim was a woman — white, well dressed, probably in her late twenties. I came upon her late one evening on a deserted street in Hyde Park, a relatively affluent neighborhood in an otherwise mean, impoverished section of Chicago. As I swung onto the avenue behind her, there seemed to be a discreet, uninflammatory distance between us. Not so. She cast back a worried glance. To her, the youngish black man — a broad six feet two inches with a beard and billowing hair, both hands shoved into the pockets of a bulky military jacket — seemed menacingly close. After a few more quick glimpses, she picked up her pace and was soon running in earnest. Within seconds she disappeared into a cross street. 1

That was more than a decade ago. I was twenty–two years old, a graduate student newly arrived at the University of Chicago. It was in the echo of that terrified woman's footfalls that I first began to know the unwieldy inheritance I'd come into — the ability to alter public space in ugly ways. It was clear that she thought herself the quarry of a mugger, a rapist, or worse. Suffering a bout of insomnia, however, I was stalking sleep, not defenseless wayfarers. As a softy who is scarcely able to take a knife to a raw chicken — let alone hold one to a person's throat — I was surprised, embarrassed, and dismayed all at once. Her flight made me feel like an accomplice in tyranny. It also made it clear that I was indistinguishable from the muggers who occasionally seeped into the 2 area from the surrounding ghetto. That first encounter, and those that followed, signified that a vast, unnerving gulf lay between nighttime pedestrians — particularly women — and me. And I soon gathered that being perceived as dangerous is a hazard in itself. I only needed to turn a corner into a dicey situation, or crowd some frightened, armed person in a foyer somewhere, or make an errant move after being pulled over by a policeman. Where fear and weapons meet — and they often do in urban America — there is always the possibility of death.

In that first year, my first away from my hometown, I was to become   3 thoroughly familiar with the language of fear. At dark, shadowy intersections, I could cross in front of a car stopped at a traffic light and elicit the *thunk, thunk, thunk, thunk* of the driver — black, white, male, or female — hammering down the door locks. On less traveled streets after dark, I grew accustomed to but never comfortable with people crossing to the other side of the street rather than pass me. Then there were the standard unpleasantries with policemen, doormen, bouncers, cab-drivers, and others whose business it is to screen out troublesome individuals *before* there is any nastiness.

I moved to New York nearly two years ago and I have remained an   4 avid night walker. In central Manhattan, the near-constant crowd cover minimizes tense one-on-one street encounters. Elsewhere — in SoHo, for example, where sidewalks are narrow and tightly spaced buildings shut out the sky — things can get very taut indeed.

After dark, on the warrenlike streets of Brooklyn where I live, I often   5 see women who fear the worst from me. They seem to have set their faces on neutral, and with their purse straps strung across their chests bandolier-style, they forge ahead as though bracing themselves against being tackled. I understand, of course, that the danger they perceive is not a hallucination. Women are particularly vulnerable to street violence, and young black males are drastically overrepresented among the perpetrators of that violence. Yet these truths are no solace against the kind of alienation that comes of being ever the suspect, a fearsome entity with whom pedestrians avoid making eye contact.

It is not altogether clear to me how I reached the ripe old age of   6 twenty-two without being conscious of the lethality nighttime pedestrians attributed to me. Perhaps it was because in Chester, Pennsylvania, the small, angry industrial town where I came of age in the 1960s, I was scarcely noticeable against a backdrop of gang warfare, street knifings, and murders. I grew up one of the good boys, had perhaps a half-dozen fistfights. In retrospect, my shyness of combat has clear sources.

As a boy, I saw countless tough guys locked away; I have since   7 buried several, too. They were babies, really — a teenage cousin, a brother of twenty-two, a childhood friend in his mid-twenties — all gone down in episodes of bravado played out in the streets. I came to doubt the virtues of intimidation early on. I chose, perhaps unconsciously, to remain a shadow—timid, but a survivor.

The fearsomeness mistakenly attributed to me in public places often 8 has a perilous flavor. The most frightening of these confusions occurred in the late 1970s and early 1980s, when I worked as a journalist in Chicago. One day, rushing into the office of a magazine I was writing for with a deadline story in hand, I was mistaken for a burglar. The office manager called security and, with an ad hoc posse, pursued me through the labyrinthine halls, nearly to my editor's door. I had no way of proving who I was. I could only move briskly toward the company of someone who knew me.

Another time I was on assignment for a local paper and killing time 9 before an interview. I entered a jewelry store on the city's affluent Near North Side. The proprietor excused herself and returned with an enormous red Doberman pinscher straining at the end of a leash. She stood, the dog extended toward me, silent to my questions, her eyes bulging nearly out of her head. I took a cursory look around, nodded, and bade her good night.

Relatively speaking, however, I never fared as badly as another black 10 male journalist. He went to nearby Waukegan, Illinois, a couple of summers ago to work on a story about a murderer who was born there. Mistaking the reporter for the killer, police officers hauled him from his car at gunpoint and but for his press credentials would probably have tried to book him. Such episodes are not uncommon. Black men trade tales like this all the time.

Over the years, I learned to smother the rage I felt at so often being 11 taken for a criminal. Not to do so would surely have led to madness. I now take precautions to make myself less threatening. I move about with care, particularly late in the evening. I give a wide berth to nervous people on subway platforms during the wee hours, particularly when I have exchanged business clothes for jeans. If I happen to be entering a building behind some people who appear skittish, I may walk by, letting them clear the lobby before I return, so as not to seem to be following them. I have been calm and extremely congenial on those rare occasions when I've been pulled over by the police.

And on late-evening constitutionals I employ what has proved 12 to be an excellent tension-reducing measure: I whistle melodies from Beethoven and Vivaldi and the more popular classical composers. Even steely New Yorkers hunching toward nighttime destinations seem to relax, and occasionally they even join in the tune. Virtually everybody seems to sense that a mugger wouldn't be warbling bright, sunny selections from Vivaldi's *Four Seasons*. It is my equivalent of the cowbell that hikers wear when they know they are in bear country.

Reading Closely

1. How does Staples's essay make you feel? Does it remind you of any experiences you have had? If so, how?

2. What is Staples's purpose in writing this essay? What has he learned as a
   result of the experience he describes? And how does what he's learned
   connect with his overall purpose for writing?

3. Rewrite the opening paragraphs from the white woman's point of view.
   What details are you including? What feelings are you experiencing?
   What are you seeing, thinking, or planning?

Considering Larger Issues

1. As he explains the feelings of a black man in public places, what point is
   Staples making? How does he exemplify this point? Make a brief list of
   his anecdotes, examples, and facts. Does he prove his point? **Working
   with three or four classmates,** prepare a group response for the rest
   of the class.

2. COMBINING METHODS. Mark all the passages in this essay that are *narratives,*
   descriptions, or *cause-and-consequence analyses.* How does Staples use each of
   these methods to support his main point? How does each method work
   differently yet effectively?

3. This essay was originally published in *Harper's* magazine, a monthly periodical that includes readings on politics, culture, literature, and the arts.
   Characterize a typical member of Staples's intended audience. What information in the essay itself supports your description?
       Since its original publication, the essay has appeared in a large number of anthologies for college writing courses. Describe a typical member
   of this second audience. Are Staples's examples equally effective for both
   audiences? Why or why not?

Thinking about Language

1. Relying on the context of the essay or your dictionary, define the following words, preparing to share your answers with the rest of the class.

uninflammatory (1)	taut (4)	ad hoc (8)
wayfarers (2)	bandolier–style (5)	labyrinthine (8)
tyranny (2)	lethality (6)	berth (11)
dicey (2)	bravado (7)	constitutionals (12)

2. List all the words and phrases that Staples uses to create an atmosphere
   of danger, vulnerability, and risk. **Working with two or three classmates,** compare your answers. Prepare a group response to share with
   the rest of the class.

Writing Your Own Essays Using Exemplification

1. Using Staples's essay as a model, draft a paragraph of at least six sentences that focuses on your own experiences in public space. Perhaps you feel unsafe walking or exercising in secluded — or even populated — areas, day or night, because of your size, sex, looks, race, or some other characteristic. Or you may not worry at all about yourself in public; you may feel stronger and safer than others. Or perhaps you worry that your presence is threatening.

   From those six sentences, compose a generalization about your presence in public space, and then support it with specific examples, including facts, anecdotes, statistics, or ideas. You may need to conduct library or Web research in order to locate enough examples. As you expand your list into a three- to four-page essay, be sure to refer to the guidelines for checking over the use of exemplification on p. 221.

2. Think about a specific person you know. Make a generalization about that person's public presence — for example, as vulnerable, unapproachable, confident, inviting, threatening — and draft a three- to four-page essay in which you develop that generalization with examples. **Consider working with one or two classmates.** Be sure to refer to the guidelines for checking over the use of exemplification (p. 221) as you draft and revise.

3. Using Staples's essay as a model, draft a paragraph of at least six sentences that focuses on your experience presenting yourself in cyberspace. You may want to focus on your experience in a MUD, MOO, or chat room; with a blog, listserv, or newsgroup; or even just with e-mail and instant messaging. How do you try to present yourself to your online readers? Is it deliberately different from the presence you create (or try to create) in "real time"? How do readers react to your online presence, and how do their reactions compare with those of people you interact with in real time? Include at least two specific examples in your paragraph. After you've written it, make a generalization about your online presence, connecting it with an overall purpose.

EVA PAYNE

Handy

Eva Payne (b. 1948) returned to college after the last of her three children enrolled in kindergarten. Like many returning students, Payne worried that she'd
forgotten too much, that younger students would work circles around her,
that she was taking a huge risk. These worries proved to be unfounded. As an
English major, she graduated from Oregon State University with honors. The
following essay was part of her application for membership in the Oregon
State chapter of Mortar Board, a national undergraduate honorary society.

> **Preview** As you read her brief essay, consider what Payne's purpose
> might be for using exemplification.

January 30, 1998

I grew up as the little sister of two smart siblings. My older sister was 1
valedictorian of her graduating class and won a full scholarship to Eastern Michigan State College. My brother was an electronic whiz kid, a
ham radio operator by the time he was twelve. I was the one that the
high school counselor told, "Plan a career where you will work with your
hands; you aren't college material."

I believed him and worked for twenty years to become good with 2
my hands. I trained my hands to take shorthand at 120 words per
minute and type at 70 words per minute. My hands can make the best
pie crust you have ever tasted. I can raise green beans and make raspberry jelly with my hands. I learned to drive a fire truck, operate a
pumper, and drag a two-inch line into a burning building. I've cleared
airways and felt ribs splinter beneath my hands while giving CPR.
My hands have given comfort to desperate people in the back of
ambulances. I learned to tie bowline knots and rappel down the sides of
buildings, make croissants, train a dog, make children laugh, and sew
dresses — all with my hands.

Then my husband encouraged me to go to college. I thought of lots 3
of excuses to stay home — home where I did things so well and seldom
failed. He convinced me to try, saying I could always withdraw if it
looked like I was in over my head. I registered as a home economics
major; it sounded like something I could do with my hands. I had always
worked with my hands, as a dishwasher, a carhop, a truck driver, a wait-
ress, a cook, a secretary, a bookkeeper, a firefighter, a wife, and as a
mother. I know that I am a handy person. I discovered at Oregon State
that the advice my high school counselor gave me twenty-five years ago
was only half of the story. I am "college material," and my life has been
enormously enriched by my discovery that I am mentally as well as
manually dexterous.

Reading Closely

1. What examples does Payne provide to prove that she's handy? Can these examples be classified in any way? How?

2. From the evidence in the reading, how can you account for Payne's success in college? What did she do between high school and college that might have helped her? Does your life compare with hers in any way? Do you know anyone whose life story is similar to Payne's? Write out your responses.

3. What is Payne's purpose in writing this essay? What examples help her fulfill that purpose?

4. Look closely at the visual. What do you imagine this woman can do? What details support your answer?

Considering Larger Issues

1. **Working with two or three classmates,** answer the following questions. Other than the members of the Mortar Board selection committee, who else might be Payne's audience for this essay? How does she appeal to her audience? What details in her essay appeal to you? Prepare your group's responses for the rest of the class.

2. Have you ever been told that you weren't the right type, or the right "material," for something or that you were better suited for something else? In what ways did you succeed—or fail—because of, or in spite of, what others said about you?

3. COMBINING METHODS. Payne sets up a *comparison and contrast* between being manually and mentally dexterous—but her examples are all of manual dexterity. How does her comparison and contrast help develop her overall *generalization*? Would her essay have been strengthened or weakened by including examples of her mental dexterity? Or does the essay itself provide a sufficient example?

Thinking about Language

1. Payne uses a number of lists. Underline each of them. What is the overall effect of these lists?

2. How do Payne's lists reflect her topic?

Writing Your Own Essays Using Exemplification

1. Make a list of generalizations that fit you. Choose one, and then use a prewriting technique (see the Introduction, pp. 20–24) to come up with a list of examples that support this generalization. Draft a three- to four-page autobiographical essay with a one-word title in which you generalize about yourself—and prove your generalization. The guidelines for checking over the use of exemplification can be found on p. 221.

2. Using your response to question 2 under "Considering Larger Issues" as a starting point, draft a three- to four-page essay using exemplification in which you show how someone's observation about you turned out to be wrong—or right. You may want to choose a pivotal experience in your life that proved the point, but in any case be sure to include several examples that show that the observation was correct—or that disprove it decisively. **Consider working with two or three classmates,** referring to the guidelines for checking over the use of exemplification (p. 221) as you draft and revise.

MICHELLE STACEY
All You Can Eat

Writers use exemplification not only to back up generalizations but also to develop and crystallize them, as in the following essay. Michelle Stacey (b. 1959) opens "All You Can Eat" with a very broad generalization, "The capacity of the human mind for self-deception is, it appears, bottomless," and then goes on to apply this generalization to the portions of food Americans eat in restaurants. Stacey, who has been an editor at *Mademoiselle*, *Savvy*, and *Outside* magazines and has also written for the *New Yorker*, is the author of *Consumed: Why Americans Love, Hate, and Fear Food* (1995) and *The Fasting Girl: A True Victorian Medical Mystery* (2002). The following essay originally appeared in 1998 as a column in *Elle*.

> **Preview** Have you ever thought about the amount of food Americans eat? about the size of restaurant portions?

The capacity of the human mind for self-deception is, it appears, bottom- 1
less. I plow into the vast, raisin-dotted pillowiness of my New York-style, bakery-made morning bagel and think: Bagel and coffee for breakfast, no butter, no cream cheese, pretty virtuous, *n'est-ce pas?* But this is not a bagel as nature or the U.S. government intended, which would be a moderate two to three ounces and 150 to 250 calories; instead, this is a behemoth, puffed up to five or six ounces and probably 400 calories, accounting for almost half of the six to eleven daily bread servings recommended by the USDA's Food Guide Pyramid. If I continue my see-no-evil approach, I can easily rack up innumerable quantities of fat and calories in a day of restaurant meals: steaming heaps of pasta, usually eight ounces instead of the USDA's suggested two; gargantuan chicken breasts that look as if they were cut from a three-foot-tall hen; baked potatoes that take up half the plate. Americans are on a portion pig-out, a swing to the far side of last decade's dainty nouvelle cuisine. "I don't care," proclaims a fast-food customer in a recent TV commercial, "just SuperSize me."

The problem goes beyond a simple ratcheting-up that leaves the 2
door open for studied ignorance ("But I only ate *one!*"). American food has strayed so far from its original standards that our eyes, and instincts, can hardly be trusted anymore. Even nutrition experts can no longer guess what's in a portion. Further complicating things are the standards put out by the government — "airline portions," according to one expert. "Portion size is reaching a crisis," says Lisa Young, nutritionist and adjunct faculty member at New York University, who is writing her doctoral dissertation on the subject. "The problem is that there's a huge discrepancy between oversize restaurant portions and tiny government portions. So while three cups of pasta, the usual restaurant size, is too much, the half cup on the USDA chart isn't a realistic serving either."

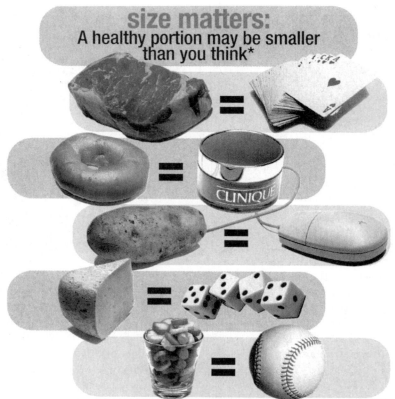

size matters:
A healthy portion may be smaller
than you think*

*Information for this chart comes from the American Dietetic Association; for the bagel, ELLE substituted a jar of face powder for a hockey puck.

Young, who notes that "portion sizes have gotten a lot larger in the last decade, and so have people," conducted a test of 200 dietitians and nutritionists at a 1996 convention of the American Dietetic Association. She asked them to guess the fat and calorie content of various popular dishes, including Caesar salad with grilled chicken and a tuna-salad sandwich. All participants underestimated by about 20 percent. The average estimate for a hamburger and onion rings was 863 calories and 44 grams of fat; the reality was 1,550 calories and 101 grams of fat. Similarly, a study several years ago found that a group of severely overweight people trying to lose weight—people "fairly well-educated in terms of nutrition," according to the study's head researcher—were actually eating twice as many calories per day as they thought they were. Such wishful thinking may account for the fact that official dietary-intake surveys in the last few years, based on daily food diaries, showed people eating barely enough calories to maintain body weight, while actual weights have been increasing dramatically.

The inability to estimate a total calorie count may have been beside   4 the point in the days before the car–and–computer culture, but in this stationary age, calorie–creep has put a lot of people over the edge. It's terribly tempting to let restaurant chefs or even grocery stores be one's authority on how much to eat, but mostly they're authorities on pleasing people. Listen to them for a while and your eye gets retrained; pretty soon you'll think a ten–ounce steak is average (a USDA "serving" of meat is two to three ounces, about the size of a deck of cards).

There's a route to be charted between restaurant–gargantuan and   5 USDA–ascetic, says Young. First, fight the food–as–bargain impulse: It is not a mortal sin to leave food on your plate, even though you paid for it. Next, plan in advance: If you're going out to dinner, try to imagine what you'll want, and adjust the rest of your day accordingly. "It's absurd to go to an Italian restaurant and order the broiled filet of sole, dry," Young says. "You want pasta. So eat less bread earlier in the day and more protein. Then, for dinner, consider getting an appetizer portion of pasta — that's usually a cup and a half. By USDA standards that's three portions of bread, but I think that's a reasonable amount of food, along with a salad."

So, if you want to splurge, go ahead — just don't kid yourself that a   6 stack of pancakes that stretches across a twelve–inch plate is magically the same as the four–inch pancakes described in the average calorie chart. The clean–plate club closed its doors a long time ago.

Reading Closely

1. Stacey warns readers about portion control. Which of her examples surprised you the most? How did the visual affect you?

2. Stacey advises her readers to control their own portions. List the specific steps she provides for portion control. What is her purpose in writing this essay?

3. List the points that Stacey makes. Under each point, jot down the examples or details she includes to help make that point. **Working with two or three classmates,** compare your findings. Prepare a group response to share with the rest of the class.

Considering Larger Issues

1. Who is the audience for this essay? In what ways does Stacey tailor the information to that audience? Write out your answers.

2. Unlike Brent Staples, who uses personal anecdotes, or Jonathan Kozol, who uses narratives about others, Stacey uses "objective" types of

examples—facts and statistics from research studies and expert opinions—to support her generalization. What effect do these examples have on her essay?

3. Compare the information provided by the visual with that provided by the essay. What point does the visual make? How do the items on the right side of the equal signs in the visual relate to the interests of the intended audience? (For instance, consider the Clinique jar as a replacement for a hockey puck.)

4. Now that you've considered the generalization and specific examples in Stacey's essay, think about your own eating habits. Begin by listing all the foods you've eaten so far today. What would Stacey think about this amount of food? Would she think it's too much, too little, or just right? Write out your response.

5. What foods do you eat for their nutritional value? What foods do you eat because they're convenient? because you like the taste? What foods do you wish you ate more of? less of? Make a list in response to each of these questions. Then look over your lists and try to come up with a generalization about yourself as an eater.

6. **COMBINING METHODS.** Although Stacey's essay is predominantly one of exemplification, several paragraphs analyze *causes and consequences*. Mark those paragraphs, and be prepared to discuss their contribution to the essay.

Thinking about Language

1. Using the context of the essay or your dictionary, define the following terms. Be prepared to share your answers with the rest of the class.

   behemoth (1)   nouvelle cuisine (1)   USDA–ascetic (5)
   gargantuan (1)   discrepancy (2)

2. What phrases does Stacey use to reinforce the ideas of "bigness," "hugeness," and "too much'"? Do any of these phrases strike you as inappropriate or exaggerated? Which ones?

Writing Your Own Essays Using Exemplification

1. Using the information you gleaned from inventorying your own eating habits for question 5 under "Considering Larger Issues," improve your generalization about yourself as an eater and then back up that generalization with specific examples. With your closest friend as your audience and maintaining or attaining a sensible weight as your purpose, draft a three- to four-page essay in which you analyze your eating habits, using many examples. Refer to the guidelines for checking over the use of exemplification on p. 221.

2. When did you begin to think about patterns in your personal behavior: eating, driving, drinking, smoking, partying, gossiping, instant

messaging, online gaming, and so on? Think back to a time when you were unaware of the consequences of a particular kind of behavior: you did what you wanted, when you wanted to, and didn't give it much thought. Then consider the ways you have become more self-conscious about that behavior. Draft a three- to four-page essay that is written from either your carefree or your self-conscious point of view, generalizing about your behavior. As you draft and revise, refer to the guidelines for checking over the use of exemplification on p. 221.

DIANE RAVITCH

The Language Police: How Pressure Groups Restrict What Students Learn

Research professor of education at New York University, Diane Ravitch (b. 1938) has achieved an impressive career as a writer, teacher, and political adviser and has established her reputation as a leading historian of education. Among her twenty books and over 300 articles are *The Great School Wars: New York City, 1805–1973* (1974); *The Revisionists Revised* (1978); *The Troubled Crusade: American Education, 1945–1980* (1983); *The Schools We Deserve* (1985); *What Do Our 17-Year-Olds Know?* (1995); *Left Back: A Century of Failed School Reforms* (2000); and *The Language Police: How Pressure Groups Restrict What Students Learn* (2003), from which the following excerpt is taken.

Preview What does the term "language police" mean to you? How might the "language police" monitor your reading, writing, or speaking?

The greatest dangers to liberty lurk in insidious encroachment by men of zeal, well-meaning but without understanding.   – Justice Louis D. Brandeis

I decided to write this book as a way of solving a mystery. After many 1 years of studying the history of education and writing about the politics of education, I discovered some things that shocked me. Almost by accident, I stumbled upon an elaborate, well-established protocol of beneficent censorship, quietly endorsed and broadly implemented by textbook publishers, testing agencies, states, and the federal government. I did not learn about this state of affairs in one fell swoop, but one step at a time. Like others who are involved in education, be they parents or teachers or administrators or journalists or scholars, I had always assumed that textbooks were based on careful research and designed to help children learn something valuable. I thought that tests were designed to assess whether they had learned it. What I did not realize was that educational materials are now governed by an intricate set of rules to screen out language and topics that might be considered controversial or offensive. Some of this censorship is trivial, some is ludicrous, and some is breathtaking in its power to dumb down what children learn in school.

Initially these practices began with the intention of identifying and 2 excluding any conscious or implicit statements of bias against African Americans, other racial or ethnic minorities, and females, whether in tests or textbooks, especially any statements that demeaned members of these groups. These efforts were entirely reasonable and justified. However, what began with admirable intentions has evolved into a surprisingly broad and increasingly bizarre policy of censorship that has gone far beyond its original scope and now excises from tests and textbooks words, images, passages, and ideas that no reasonable person would consider biased in the usual meaning of that term.

The story that I now tell began in 1997, when Bill Clinton delivered 3 his State of the Union address. On that occasion, Clinton declared his support for national tests, and said that the states should test fourth-grade children in reading and eighth-grade children in mathematics, to make sure that they could meet national standards of proficiency. Soon after the president gave that speech, the U.S. Department of Education contracted with test publishers to develop voluntary national tests [VNTs] of reading and mathematics for those grades. The goal was to provide individual test scores to parents of specific children, to their teachers, and to their schools.

Congress never approved the VNT. The tests were controversial from the 4 start. Many Republicans feared that any national test commissioned by the government was the first step on a slippery slope toward federal control of education. Many Democrats objected to the emphasis on testing as opposed to new general-purpose funding. By the time Clinton left office in January 2001, his VNT proposal was dead, even though it consistently ranked high in public-opinion polls. For nearly three years, however, NAGB* and the test publishers who won the federal contract worked faithfully to bring the idea to fruition, keeping a watchful eye on Congress to see whether it would eventually be authorized. It never was.

During the time that the VNT was a live possibility, the first priority 5 was to create test questions. As a new member of the board, I was assigned to a committee that reviewed reading passages for the fourth-grade test. The committee included experienced teachers and a state superintendent of education. All of us read the passages submitted by the test contractor, a major publisher that had won a multimillion-dollar contract from the Department of Education. The committee approved passages that seemed appropriate for fourth-grade students and rejected passages that seemed dull, obscure, or incoherent. Our goal was to find short reading passages of about one to three pages, both fiction and nonfiction, written in language that was clear, vivid, and engaging, as well as test questions that gauged children's comprehension of what they had read.

Our committee evaluated many passages for fourth-grade students. 6 The passages had been previously published in children's magazines or anthologies; before they reached us, they had been thoroughly vetted by the original publisher's in-house experts. We too read them with care. As stewards of the VNT, we knew that we had to exercise extreme caution,

---

* **NAGB:** National Assessment Governing Board, a nonpartisan federal agency that has supervised national educational testing since 1990.

since parents, teachers, and the media in every part of the United States would complain if anything inaccurate or untoward were to slip through unnoticed.

Most of the stories were unobjectionable; none was great literature,   7 but for the most part, they were fairly engaging stories about children, animals, science, or history. Nearly two years later, I was surprised to learn that the passages approved by our committee had subsequently been evaluated yet again by the test contractor's "bias and sensitivity review" panel. This panel, it turned out, recommended the elimination of several stories that we had approved. I learned that it was standard operating procedure in the educational testing industry to submit all passages and test questions to a bias and sensitivity review. Typically those who serve on these review panels are not drawn from academic fields such as English or history. Usually they have a professional background in bilingual education, diversity training, English as a second language, special education, guidance, or the education of Native Americans or other special populations. Such panels are hired by publishers, as well as by state education agencies, to screen every test and every textbook for potential bias. In the case of the voluntary national tests, the panel that scrutinized the items found biases that none of us—neither test experts nor members of NAGB—had perceived.

There are always other test passages to use, so the acceptance or rejection   8 of these particular passages is hardly a cause for alarm. What is alarming, however, is the absurd reasoning that was invoked to justify the elimination of these readings. Consider that the test contractor, Riverside Publishing, is responsible for one of the most esteemed tests in the nation, the Iowa Test of Basic Skills; consider that it assembled a reputable and experienced group of people to conduct the bias and sensitivity review. The judgments expressed by this panel were not idiosyncratic; they represented state-of-the-art thinking in the practice of bias review. The reviewers acted in compliance with what are considered industry standards. The process of analyzing text that I will describe is now being applied routinely to other tests and textbooks used in American schools. The bias and sensitivity reviewers work with assumptions that have the inevitable effect of stripping away everything that is potentially thought-provoking and colorful from the texts that children encounter. These assumptions narrow what children are exposed to, at least on tests and in textbooks. Parents, teachers, and the public need to be aware of these assumptions and the reasoning process behind them, because they are reducing the curriculum in the schools to bland pabulum.

So what did the bias and sensitivity reviewers recommend? The only   9 way to explain their strained interpretations is to give actual examples. I cannot reproduce the stories, because some of them may yet appear one day as test passages. But I will paraphrase the story sufficiently so that the reader may judge whether the charge of bias is persuasive. The examples, I believe, will demonstrate that the concept of bias has become detached from its original meaning and has been redefined into assumptions that defy common sense.

THE HISTORY AND USES OF PEANUTS

Two of the stories that the bias reviewers rejected were short informational passages about peanuts. One passage described peanuts as legumes, in the same family as peas and beans, and lauded them as nutritious. The bias panel recommended the elimination of this selection because it asserted that peanuts are a healthy snack. It was wrong to describe peanuts as nutritious, said the panel, because some people may have a severe allergic reaction to them. At first glance, this judgment would seem to lie outside the scope of a bias and sensitivity review. The reviewers apparently assumed that a fourth-grade student who was allergic to peanuts might get distracted if he or she encountered a test question that did not acknowledge the dangers of peanuts. The NAGB reading committee recommended keeping the passage and adding an acknowledgment that some people are allergic to peanuts.

The second passage was a brief history of peanuts. It said that peanuts were first cultivated by South American Indians, especially the Incas. After Spanish explorers conquered the Incas, and Portuguese explorers defeated many Brazilian tribes, it said, the peanut was shipped to Europe for cultivation. Later, in the United States, African slaves planted and developed peanut crops. The famed scientist George Washington Carver discovered hundreds of uses for the peanut. This was not the world's most exciting story, but the NAGB reading committee concluded that it contained some interesting historical information as well as praise for an African American scientist, all of which were pluses. However, the bias and sensitivity panelists opposed the passage for two reasons: first, it used the term *African slave,* and second, it stated that Spanish and Portuguese explorers defeated native tribes. To the NAGB reading committee, these were puzzling judgments. Why was it wrong to use the term *African slave?* (Apparently the correct usage now is *enslaved African.*) Nor did we understand why the panel wanted to kill the passage for saying that some Brazilian tribes had been defeated by European explorers. The bias reviewers did not challenge the historical accuracy of this statement, but they did not want it to appear. They must have concluded that these facts would hurt someone's feelings. Whose feelings would be wounded? Children of Spanish descent? Children of Portuguese descent? Children descended from Brazilian tribes? Perhaps the word *tribe* was offensive. None of this was clear. What was clear, however, was that the passage did not express anything that a reasonable person would consider biased toward any group.

WOMEN AND PATCHWORK QUILTING

The bias and sensitivity reviewers rejected a passage about patch- 12
work quilting by women on the western frontier in the mid–nineteenth
century. The passage explained that mothers in that time taught their
daughters to sew, and together they made quilts for the girl's dowry
when she married. Quilting was an economic necessity because it saved
money, and there were no factory–made quilts available until the end of
the nineteenth century. The passage briefly explained how quilts were
assembled and described them as works of art. The information in the
passage was historically accurate, but the bias and sensitivity panel (as
well as the "content expert panel") objected to the passage because it
contained stereotypes of females as "soft" and "submissive." Actually, the
passage did nothing of the sort. It was a description of why quilting was
important to women on the frontier and how it was done. Nothing in the
passage excluded the possibility that mothers and daughters were riding
the range, plowing the fields, and herding cattle during the day. The reviewers objected to the portrayal of women as people who stitch and
sew, and who were concerned about preparing for marriage. Historical
accuracy was no defense for this representation of women and girls,
which they deemed stereotypical.

THE BLIND MOUNTAIN CLIMBER

One of the stranger recommendations of the bias and sensitivity 13
panel involved a true story about a heroic young blind man who hiked
to the top of Mount McKinley, the highest peak in North America. The
story described the dangers of hiking up an icy mountain trail, especially
for a blind person. The panel voted 12–11 to eliminate this inspiring
story. First, the majority maintained that the story contained "regional
bias," because it was about hiking and mountain climbing, which favors
students who live in regions where those activities are common. Second,
they rejected the passage because it suggested that people who are blind
are somehow at a disadvantage compared to people who have normal
sight, that they are "worse off" and have a more difficult time facing dangers than those who are not blind.

"Regional bias," in this instance, means that children should not be 14
expected to read or comprehend stories set in unfamiliar terrain. A story
that happened in a desert would be "biased" against children who have
never lived in a desert, and a story set in a tropical climate would be biased against those who have never lived in a tropical climate. Consider
the impoverishment of imagination that flows from such assumptions:
No reading passage on a test may have a specific geographical setting;
every event must occur in a generic locale. Under these assumptions, no
child should be expected to understand a story set in a locale other than

the one that he or she currently lives in or in a locale that has no distinguishing characteristics.

Even more peculiar is the assumption by the panel's majority that it 15 is demeaning to applaud a blind person for overcoming daunting obstacles, like climbing a steep, icy mountain trail. It is not unreasonable, I believe, to consider blindness to be a handicap for a person facing physical danger. By definition, people who are blind cannot see as much or as well as people who have sight. Is it not more difficult to cope with dangerous situations when one cannot see? Yet, perversely, the bias and sensitivity panel concluded that this story celebrating a blind athlete's achievements and his heroism was biased against people who are blind. Blindness, apparently, should be treated as just another personal attribute, like the color of one's hair, or one's height. In the new meaning of bias, it is considered biased to acknowledge that lack of sight is a disability.

GENDER BIAS IN A FABLE OF AESOP

The bias and sensitivity reviewers did find a reading selection that 16 had the earmarks of gender bias. It was Aesop's familiar fable "The Fox and the Crow." In the story, Master Fox spies Mistress Crow sitting on a tree branch with a piece of cheese in her beak. He flatters her, tells her that she has a beautiful voice, and when she opens her beak to sing, the cheese falls to the cunning fox. The panel, of course, spied gender bias at work since the crow—a female—is vain and foolish, while the fox—a male—is intelligent and clever. The crow represented the stereotypical depiction of women as overly concerned about their appearance and easily deceived by flattering men. The fact that this gender relationship had been part of the Aesop story for generations was irrelevant. The NAGB reading committee did not want to lose the Aesop fable, because it was all too rare to find any instances of classic literature on national tests of reading. So, to ameliorate the concerns of the bias committee, we proposed to switch the gender of the fox and the crow, either to make them both the same gender, or to make Mistress Fox the flatterer of Master Crow. Aesop might be startled to find a woman flattering a man or a guy flattering another guy or a woman flattering another woman, but at least we were able to hang on to a classic fable.

A STORY CONDEMNED BY ASSOCIATION

Another passage suggested for deletion by the bias reviewers was an 17 animal fable taken from an anthology edited by William J. Bennett, the former secretary of education, author, and political commentator known for his conservative views. The fable, attributed to Native Americans, told about animals emerging from the darkness to "find" sunlight. Several members of the panel suggested that Bennett's name alone would be sufficient to distress many teachers and parents. They did not suggest that fourth–grade children taking the tests would be distressed, since Bennett's name would be unknown to them. The panel also rejected the fable because it implied that "darkness" and "blackness" were synony-mous with fumbling around or not being able to see. The members saw this linkage as bias, presumably suggesting racial bias. Only one of the bias experts on the review panel argued that it was censorship to delete this passage simply because of the political views of its anthologist. However, even this member agreed with the other panel members that the fable should be removed because of its unfortunate references to darkness. So far as the panel was concerned, to show a preference for light over darkness was a manifestation of bias.

DELETING MOUNT RUSHMORE

Perhaps the most startling analysis by the bias reviewers concerned a [18] short biography of Gutzon Borglum, who designed the monument at Mount Rushmore. This monument, consisting of gigantic heads of Presi-dents George Washington, Thomas Jefferson, Abraham Lincoln, and Theodore Roosevelt, is located in the Black Hills of South Dakota. It is one of the most famous, most widely reproduced images in the United States. Millions of tourists have traveled to South Dakota to see it. Whether one likes it or hates it, it is there. For most people, the monu-ment has positive connotations, suggesting a sense of history and patri-otism.

The bias panel recommended that the biography of Borglum be [19] dropped because Mount Rushmore is offensive to Native Americans. The panel maintained that the monument "is an abomination to the Black Hills because many Lakota people consider the Black Hills to be a sacred place to pray." This is surely a dilemma. The Borglum sculpture on Mount Rushmore exists; it is an acclaimed national monument. Yet American children should not be allowed to read about it or its sculptor on a test because this might offend Lakota Indians, who wish that the sculpture were not there. The desire to rewrite history is one that contin-ually plagues bias reviewers, as we shall see.

CLASS DISTINCTIONS IN THE ANCIENT WORLD

The bias panel did not like a story about growing up in ancient [20] Egypt. The story contrasted how people's ways of living varied in accor-dance with their wealth and status. Some lived in palaces, others were noblemen, others were farmers or city workers. The size and grandeur of one's house, said the story, depended on family wealth. To the naked eye, the story was descriptive, not judgmental. But the bias and sensitivity reviewers preferred to eliminate it, claiming that references to wealth and class distinctions had an "elitist" tone. The fact that these class distinctions were historically accurate was irrelevant to the reviewers. In the world that they wanted children to read about, class distinctions did not exist, not now and not in the past, either.

AN ENVIRONMENTALLY SOUND DWELLING

One of the most charming informational stories that our committee 21 reviewed was about a rotting stump in the forest that provided shelter and food to a succession of insects, birds, plants, and animals. The story probably would have passed muster with flying colors in light of its environmentalist emphasis on nature's ways of recycling except that it made the fatal mistake of comparing the rotting stump to an apartment house for the many different creatures of the forest. The twenty members of the bias committee voted unanimously to reject this passage because, in their view, it contained a negative, demeaning stereotype of apartments and people who live in them. If this passage were included on a test, the panel claimed, poor inner–city children would be upset: "Youngsters who have grown up in a housing project may be distracted by similarities to their own living conditions. An emotional response may be triggered."

This was a strained reading of the story. First, it is untrue that only 22 those who are poor live in apartment houses. There are luxury high–rise apartment houses, as well as apartment buildings occupied by middle-income people. Second, the story tried to show the environmental beauty of the rotting tree stump, to describe the stump as a gracious and inviting home, as well as a restaurant, to all sorts of creatures. The story did not portray either the tree stump or the insects and forest animals in a negative light. Yet the bias committee imagined that poor children who had grown up in a housing project would see themselves as insects living in a rotting tree stump if they read this passage. Following the logic of the bias reviewers, every story had to be read literally, with no allowances for simile, metaphor, or allusion.

THE SILLY OLD LADY

The bias panel rejected a passage about a silly old woman who keeps 23 piling more and more gadgets on her bicycle until it is so overloaded that it tumbles over. The language was clever, the illustrations were amusing, and the story was higher in literary quality than the other fourth–grade reading passages proposed for the test. But the bias panel rejected it. They felt that it contained a negative stereotype of an eccentric old woman who constantly changed her mind; apparently women, and especially women of a certain age, must be depicted only in a positive light. Why would it upset or distract fourth–grade children to see an older woman acting eccentrically or changing her mind? The bias panel thought that children would get the wrong idea about older women if they read such a story. They might conclude that all women of a certain age behaved in this way.

THE ARROGANT KING

This story, a folktale from Asia, was about a king who had a marvelous 24 elephant. The king is jealous because his subjects admire the elephant more than they admire him. He tells the elephant trainer to command the animal to do more and more difficult tricks, until the elephant ascends into the air with the trainer and flies away to a better kingdom. In the original story, the wise king in the next kingdom eventually reduces the worthless king to ashes, but that "violent" conclusion was deleted by an earlier bias review. The bias panel rejected the passage because the king was portrayed as mean and jealous. The panelists did not like this negative characterization, even though the king was indeed mean and jealous. Furthermore, the king used harsh language; he yelled, he roared, he screamed, and he shouted at the elephant's trainer. Of course, if the king had been a mild and friendly fellow, the story would not have made any sense at all, but the bias panel did not approve of such behavior. The panelists also objected because the trainer had called the king "a worthless fool" when he flew away with the beautiful elephant. But the trainer was right: the king was a worthless fool. I could not imagine what any of these complaints had to do with bias and sensitivity. Was the passage biased against arrogant and jealous kings? Were they afraid that children would be upset to read about a king who yelled and screamed at an underling?

THE EVEN EXCHANGE

This story came from a children's book by an African American author. 25 It was about an African American girl who wanted to learn how to jump rope like the other girls in her neighborhood. She meets a neighbor who is an expert at jumping rope, but who is attending summer school because she is not very good at math. The new girl is good at math, so the two agree to teach each other what they do best. The bias reviewers did not like this story at all. They found that it had serious bias problems because it showed an African American girl who was weak in math and was attending summer school. The fact that this character thought of herself as not very good at math was also deeply offensive and stereotypical, the bias reviewers believed. Even though the author was African American and her book was intended to bolster the self–esteem of black girls, that did not carry any weight with the bias panel. African American children could be portrayed only in a positive light. Anything that showed weakness suggested negative stereotyping. In this case, one African American girl was good at math, and the other was not. So far as I could tell, the story showed human variability, not negative racial stereotyping, with each girl displaying different weaknesses and different strengths.

THE SELFISH RICH BAKER

This tale was about a rich baker who got angry when a poor traveler 26 sniffed his wares. The baker goes to court to demand that the poor fellow pay him for the smells he had "stolen." The judge, however, rules in favor of the poor man and fines the rich baker for his meanness. The bias committee unanimously opposed the passage on grounds of socioeconomic bias. The panelists claimed that the story set up an antagonism between the rich baker and the poor traveler. It presumed the poor traveler to be guilty of doing something wrong because of his poverty. Of course, the story did no such thing. The rich baker was rebuked and fined for his arrogance and hostility, begrudging the poor traveler even a whiff of his baked goods. He was judged harshly for his lack of charity and his greed. I could not understand how reviewers could regard this passage as biased against the poor traveler unless they failed to grasp the point of the story.

THE FRIENDLY DOLPHIN

This passage was about dolphins and what wonderful creatures they 27 are. It told the story of a legendary dolphin that guided ships through a dangerous channel. Perhaps in anticipation of a bias review, the story left out the part of the legend in which a passenger on one ship shoots the faithful dolphin, which survives but never guides that particular ship again. Fourth graders would probably enjoy reading about dolphins, particularly ones that befriend humans. No matter; the bias reviewers unanimously rejected the story for having a regional bias in favor of those who live by the sea. Once again, the concept of regional bias presumes that any story that takes place in a singular location—the sea, the mountains, the desert, a forest, the jungle—is inherently inaccessible to those who don't live in the same location.

NO MORE OWLS

The passage about owls was like a children's encyclopedia entry. It 28 described how their keen eyesight and hearing enabled them to hunt at night for rodents. When I saw that this passage was rejected, I imagined that it was because of the violence associated with hunting (although that's how owls survive). I was wrong. The passage was rejected because a Native American member of the bias committee said that owls are taboo for the Navajos. Consequently the entire committee agreed that the passage should be dropped. The test publisher added a notation that the owl is associated with death in some other cultures and should not be mentioned anymore, neither in texts nor in illustrations.

Here is a classic problem presented by today's bias and sensitivity 29 review process. If any cultural group attributes negative connotations to anything, or considers it taboo or offensive, then that topic will not be referred to, represented, described, or illustrated on tests. But owls exist. They are real birds. They are not creatures of the imagination. Nevertheless, to avoid giving offense, the tests will pretend that owls don't exist. Owls are to be deleted and never again mentioned to the highly vulnerable and sensitive.

Reading Closely

1. What is Ravitch's purpose in writing *The Language Police?* How do you know?

2. Which two examples did you find the most surprising? the least surprising? Why?

3. **Working with a classmate,** discuss your response to Ravitch's findings. Can you think of any taboo subjects that Ravitch downplays or omits altogether? Be prepared to present your response and findings to the rest of the class.

Considering Larger Issues

1. Who might be the audience for Ravitch's book? In other words, who is likely to read a book called *The Language Police?* Can you visualize and name a person who would read her book? How might that audience respond to it? How does that audience's response compare with your response?

2. If you have an opportunity, ask one of your parents or an older friend about the textbook materials he or she encountered in school. What subjects were covered? Which ones were neglected? What topics were ignored altogether? How does this older person think educational materials have changed?

3. **Working with another classmate or two,** discuss what your small group makes of Ravitch's report that many words and ideas have become taboo. How do these assertions compare with your own educational experiences? Be prepared to share your answers with the rest of the class.

4. **COMBINING METHODS.**   Mark the passages where Ravitch uses other rhetorical methods of development to help fulfill her overall purpose. For each of these passages, note how the rhetorical method used works to the writer's advantage. Compare your findings with those of the rest

of the class. At the end of your class discussion, count how many other methods of development Ravitch uses.

Thinking about Language

1. Using the context of the essay or your dictionary, define each of the following terms. Be prepared to share your answers with the rest of the class.

protocol (1)	submissive (12)	plagues (19)
proficiency (3)	stereotypical (12)	accordance (20)
obscure (5)	demeaning (15)	eccentric (23)
vetted (6)	perversely (15)	arrogant (24)
untoward (6)	earmarks (16)	bolster (25)
pabulum (8)	cunning (16)	legendary (27)
paraphrase (9)	ameliorate (16)	taboo (29)
legumes (10)	fumbling (17)	vulnerable (29)

2. Look over the preceding list of vocabulary words. What do they tell you about Ravitch's sense of audience?

3. **Working with another classmate,** make a two-column list of objective and subjective words and phrases used in this selection. How does each of these categories of words help the writer fulfill her purpose? Compare your findings with those of the rest of the class.

Writing Your Own Essays Using Exemplification

1. Think back on your education so far. If possible, make a chronological list of the most memorable topics you've studied and learned about in school. Then review your list, marking topics that seemed controversial (at the time), exciting, or even dangerous. Freewrite for five minutes about those subjects. Finally, draft a two- to three-page essay using exemplification in which you assert a generalization about the importance of learning those subjects. Be sure to include your opinions about censorship and appropriateness. Remember to consult the guidelines for checking over the use of exemplification on p. 221.

2. Draft a three- to four-page essay in which you review the textbook or syllabus for one of your courses. Using Ravitch's argument as the basis of your essay (see <www.languagepolice.com> for additional information), evaluate the textbook or syllabus in terms of the following: included information, purposefully excluded information, censorship, and appropriateness. You may want to interview your instructor as well as conduct online research as ways to explore the range of materials that *could* have been included in the textbook or syllabus. After you've completed your research and your careful study of the textbook or syllabus, **consider meeting with two or three classmates** who are working on this topic to discuss your findings and your writing. As you draft and revise, refer to the guidelines for checking over the use of exemplification on p. 221.

JONATHAN KOZOL

The Human Cost of an Illiterate Society

Jonathan Kozol (b. 1936) is a social critic whose writings on the American educational system, child-care programs, homelessness, and poverty have raised Americans' consciousness about the nation's social failings. Among Kozol's many publications are *Death at an Early Age: The Destruction of the Hearts and Minds of Negro Children in the Boston Public Schools* (1967); *Illiterate America* (1985); *Rachel and Her Children: Homeless Families in America* (1988); *Savage Inequalities: Children in America's Schools* (1991); *Amazing Grace: The Lives of Children and the Conscience of a Nation* (1996); *Ordinary Resurrections: Children in the Years of Hope* (2000); and *A Fierce Injustice: Apartheid Schooling in America* (2004). For the beauty and power of his writing, Kozol has won the National Book Award twice. "The Human Cost of an Illiterate Society" is excerpted from *Illiterate America* and demonstrates a successful mixing of the rhetorical methods.

> **Preview**   Think about the title of this essay. How do you define literacy? illiteracy? Do you know of anyone who is illiterate, according to your definition?

PRECAUTIONS. READ BEFORE USING.
Poison: Contains sodium hydroxide (caustic soda-lye).
Corrosive: Causes severe eye and skin damage, may cause blindness.
Harmful or fatal if swallowed.
If swallowed, give large quantities of milk or water.
Do not induce vomiting.
Important: Keep water out of can at all times to prevent contents from violently erupting . . .   —WARNING ON A CAN OF DRĀNO

We are speaking here no longer of the dangers faced by passengers on 1
Eastern Airlines or the dollar costs incurred by U.S. corporations and tax-payers. We are speaking now of human suffering and of the ethical dilemmas that are faced by a society that looks upon such suffering with qualified concern but does not take those actions which its wealth and ingenuity would seemingly demand.

Questions of literacy, in Socrates' belief, must at length be judged as 2
matters of morality. Socrates could not have had in mind the moral compromise peculiar to a nation like our own. Some of our Founding Fathers did, however, have this question in their minds. One of the wisest of those Founding Fathers (one who may not have been most compassionate but surely was more prescient than some of his peers) recognized the special dangers that illiteracy would pose to basic equity in the political construction that he helped to shape.

"A people who mean to be their own governors," James Madison 3
wrote, "must arm themselves with the power knowledge gives. A popular

government without popular information or the means of acquiring it, is but a prologue to a farce or a tragedy, or perhaps both."

Tragedy looms larger than farce in the United States today. Illiterate 4 citizens seldom vote. Those who do are forced to cast a vote of questionable worth. They cannot make informed decisions based on serious print information. Sometimes they can be alerted to their interests by aggressive voter education. More frequently, they vote for a face, a smile, or a style, not for a mind or character or body of beliefs.

The number of illiterate adults exceeds by 16 million the entire vote cast 5 for the winner in the 1980 presidential contest. If even one third of all illiterates could vote, and read enough and do sufficient math to vote in their self-interest, Ronald Reagan would not likely have been chosen president. There is, of course, no way to know for sure. We do know this: Democracy is a mendacious term when used by those who are prepared to countenance the forced exclusion of one third of our electorate. So long as 60 million people are denied significant participation, the government is neither of, nor for, nor by, the people. It is a government, at best, of those two thirds whose wealth, skin color, or parental privilege allows them opportunity to profit from the provocation and instruction of the written word.

The undermining of democracy in the United States is one "expense" 6 that sensitive Americans can easily deplore because it represents a contradiction that endangers citizens of all political positions. The human price is not so obvious at first.

Since I first immersed myself within this work I have often had 7 the following dream: I find that I am in a railroad station or a large department store within a city that is utterly unknown to me and where I cannot understand the printed words. None of the signs or symbols is familiar. Everything looks strange: like mirror writing of some kind. Gradually I understand that I am in the Soviet Union. All the letters on the walls around me are Cyrillic. I look for my pocket dictionary but I find that it has been mislaid. Where have I left it? Then I recall that I forgot to bring it with me when I packed my bags in Boston. I struggle to remember the name of my hotel. I try to ask somebody for directions. One person stops and looks at me in a peculiar way. I lose the nerve to ask. At last I reach into my wallet for an ID card. The card is missing. Have I lost it? Then I remember that my card was confiscated for some reason, many years before. Around this point, I wake up in a panic.

This panic is not so different from the misery that millions of adult 8 illiterates experience each day within the course of their routine existence in the U.S.A.

Illiterates cannot read the menu in a restaurant. 9

They cannot read the cost of items on the menu in the *window* of the 10 restaurant before they enter.

Illiterates cannot read the letters that their children bring home from 11 their teachers. They cannot study school department circulars that tell them of the courses that their children must be taking if they hope to pass the SAT exams. They cannot help with homework. They cannot write a letter to the teacher. They are afraid to visit in the classroom. They do not want to humiliate their child or themselves.

Illiterates cannot read instructions on a bottle of prescription medi- 12 cine. They cannot find out when a medicine is past the year of safe consumption; nor can they read of allergenic risks, warnings to diabetics, or the potential sedative effect of certain kinds of nonprescription pills. They cannot observe preventive health care admonitions. They cannot read about "the seven warning signs of cancer" or the indications of blood–sugar fluctuations or the risks of eating certain foods that aggravate the likelihood of cardiac arrest.

Illiterates live, in more than literal ways, an uninsured existence. 13 They cannot understand the written details on a health insurance form. They cannot read the waivers that they sign preceding surgical procedures. Several women I have known in Boston have entered a slum hospital with the intention of obtaining a tubal ligation and have emerged a few days later after having been subjected to a hysterectomy. Unaware of their rights, incognizant of jargon, intimidated by the unfamiliar air of fear and atmosphere of ether that so many of us find oppressive in the confines even of the most attractive and expensive medical facilities, they have signed their names to documents they could not read and which nobody, in the hectic situation that prevails so often in those overcrowded hospitals that serve the urban poor, had even bothered to explain.

Childbirth might seem to be the last inalienable right of any female 14 citizen within a civilized society. Illiterate mothers, as we shall see, already have been cheated of the power to protect their progeny against the likelihood of demolition in deficient public schools and, as a result, against the verbal servitude within which they themselves exist. Surgical denial of the right to bear that child in the first place represents an ultimate denial, an unspeakable metaphor, a final darkness that denies even the twilight gleamings of our own humanity. What greater violation of our biological, our biblical, our spiritual humanity could possibly exist than that which takes place nightly, perhaps hourly these days, within such overburdened and benighted institutions as the Boston City Hospital? Illiteracy has many costs; few are so irreversible as this.

Even the roof above one's head, the gas or other fuel for heating that 15 protects the residents of northern city slums against the threat of illness in the winter months become uncertain guarantees. Illiterates cannot read the lease that they must sign to live in an apartment which, too often, they cannot afford. They cannot manage check accounts and therefore seldom pay for anything by mail. Hours and entire days of difficult travel (and the cost of bus or other public transit) must be added to the real cost of whatever they consume. Loss of interest on the check accounts they do not have, and could not manage if they did, must be regarded as another of the excess costs paid by the citizen who is excluded from the common instruments of commerce in a numerate society.

"I couldn't understand the bills," a woman in Washington, D.C., re- 16 ports, "and then I couldn't write the checks to pay them. We signed things we didn't know what they were."

Illiterates cannot read the notices that they receive from welfare of- 17 fices or from the IRS. They must depend on word–of–mouth instruction from the welfare worker—or from other persons whom they have good reason to mistrust. They do not know what rights they have, what deadlines and requirements they face, what options they might choose to exercise. They are half–citizens. Their rights exist in print but not in fact.

Illiterates cannot look up numbers in a telephone directory. Even if 18 they can find the names of friends, few possess the sorting skills to make use of the yellow pages; categories are bewildering and trade names are beyond decoding capabilities for millions of nonreaders. Even the emergency numbers listed on the first page of the phone book—"Ambulance," "Police," and "Fire"—are too frequently beyond the recognition of nonreaders.

Many illiterates cannot read the admonition on a pack of cigarettes. 19 Neither the Surgeon General's warning nor its reproduction on the package can alert them to the risks. Although most people learn by word of mouth that smoking is related to a number of grave physical disorders, they do not get the chance to read the detailed stories which can document this danger with the vividness that turns concern into determination to resist. They can see the handsome cowboy or the slim Virginia lady lighting up a filter cigarette; they cannot heed the words that tell them that this product is (not "may be") dangerous to their health. Sixty million men and women are condemned to be the unalerted, high–risk candidates for cancer.

Illiterates do not buy "no–name" products in the supermarkets. They 20 must depend on photographs or the familiar logos that are printed on the packages of brand–name groceries. The poorest people, therefore, are denied the benefits of the least costly products.

Illiterates depend almost entirely upon label recognition. Many la- 21 bels, however, are not easy to distinguish. Dozens of different kinds of Campbell's soup appear identical to the nonreader. The purchaser who cannot read and does not dare to ask for help, out of the fear of being stigmatized (a fear which is unfortunately realistic), frequently comes home with something which she never wanted and her family never tasted.

Illiterates cannot read instructions on a pack of frozen food. Packages 22 sometimes provide an illustration to explain the cooking preparations; but illustrations are of little help to someone who must "boil water, drop the food—*within* its plastic wrapper—in the boiling water, wait for it to simmer, instantly remove."

Even when labels are seemingly clear, they may be easily mistaken. A 23 woman in Detroit brought home a gallon of Crisco for her children's dinner. She thought that she had bought the chicken that was pictured on the label. She had enough Crisco now to last a year—but no more money to go back and buy the food for dinner.

Recipes provided on the packages of certain staples sometimes tempt 24 a semiliterate person to prepare a meal her children have not tasted. The longing to vary the uniform and often starchy content of low-budget meals provided to the family that relies on food stamps commonly leads to ruinous results. Scarce funds have been wasted and the food must be thrown out. The same applies to distribution of food-surplus produce in emergency conditions. Government inducements to poor people to "explore the ways" by which to make a tasty meal from tasteless noodles, surplus cheese, and powdered milk are useless to nonreaders. Intended as benevolent advice, such recommendations mock reality and foster deeper feelings of resentment and of inability to cope. (Those, on the other hand, who cautiously refrain from "innovative" recipes in preparation of their children's meals must suffer the opprobrium of "laziness," "lack of imagination . . .")

Illiterates cannot travel freely. When they attempt to do so, they en- 25 counter risks that few of us can dream of. They cannot read traffic signs and, while they often learn to recognize and to decipher symbols, they cannot manage street names which they haven't seen before. The same is true for bus and subway stops. While ingenuity can sometimes help a man or woman to discern directions from familiar landmarks, buildings, cemeteries, churches, and the like, most illiterates are virtually immobilized. They seldom wander past the streets and neighborhoods they know. Geographical paralysis becomes a bitter metaphor for their entire existence. They are immobilized in almost every sense we can imagine. They can't move up. They can't move out. They cannot see beyond. Illiterates may take an oral test for drivers' permits in most sections of America. It is a questionable concession. Where will they go? How will they get there? How will they get home? Could it be that some of us might like it better if they stayed where they belong?

Travel is only one of many instances of circumscribed existence. 26 Choice, in almost all of its facets, is diminished in the life of an illiterate adult. Even the printed TV schedule, which provides most people with the luxury of preselection, does not belong within the arsenal of options in illiterate existence. One consequence is that the viewer watches only what appears at moments when he happens to have time to turn the switch. Another consequence, a lot more common, is that the TV set remains in operation night and day. Whatever the program offered at the hour when he walks into the room will be the nutriment that he accepts and swallows. Thus, to passivity, is added frequency — indeed, almost un-interrupted continuity. Freedom to select is no more possible here than in the choice of home or surgery or food.

"You don't choose," said one illiterate woman. "You take your wishes 27 from somebody else." Whether in perusal of a menu, selection of high-ways, purchase of groceries, or determination of affordable enjoyment, illiterate Americans must trust somebody else: a friend, a relative, a stranger on the street, a grocery clerk, a TV copywriter.

"All of our mail we get, it's hard for her to read. Settin' down and 28 writing a letter, she can't do it. Like if we get a bill . . . we take it over to my sister–in–law . . . My sister–in–law reads it."

Billing agencies harass poor people for the payment of the bills for 29 purchases that might have taken place six months before. Utility compa-nies offer an agreement for a staggered payment schedule on a bill past due. "You have to trust them," one man said. Precisely for this reason, you end up by trusting no one and suspecting everyone of possible deceit. A submerged sense of distrust becomes the corollary to a constant need to trust. "They are cheating me . . . I have been tricked . . . I do not know . . ."

Not knowing: This is a familiar theme. Not knowing the right word for 30 the right thing at the right time is one form of subjugation. Not knowing the world that lies concealed behind those words is a more terrifying feeling. The longitude and latitude of one's existence are beyond all easy apprehension. Even the hard, cold stars within the firmament above one's head begin to mock the possibilities for self–location. Where am I? Where did I come from? Where will I go?

"I've lost a lot of jobs," one man explains. "Today, even if you're a 31 janitor, there's still reading and writing . . . They leave a note saying, 'Go to room so–and–so . . .' You can't do it. You can't read it. You don't know."

"The hardest thing about it is that I've been places where I didn't 32 know where I was. You don't know where you are . . . You're lost."

"Like I said: I have two kids. What do I do if one of my kids starts 33 choking? I go running to the phone . . . I can't look up the hospital phone number. That's if we're at home. Out on the street, I can't read the sign. I get to a pay phone. 'Okay, tell us where you are. We'll send an ambu-lance.' I look at the street sign. Right there, I can't tell you what it says. I'd have to spell it out, letter for letter. By that time, one of my kids would be dead . . . These are the kinds of fears you go with, every single day . . ."

"Reading directions, I suffer with. I work with chemicals . . . That's 34 scary to begin with . . ."

"You sit down. They throw the menu in front of you. Where do you 35 go from there? Nine times out of ten you say, 'Go ahead. Pick out some-thing for the both of us.' I've eaten some weird things, let me tell you!"

Menus. Chemicals. A child choking while his mother searches for a 36 word she does not know to find assistance that will come too late. An-other mother speaks about the inability to help her kids to read: "I can't read to them. Of course that's leaving them out of something they should have. Oh, it matters. You *believe* it matters! I ordered all these books. The kids belong to a book club. Donny wanted me to read a book to him. I told Donny: 'I can't read.' He said: 'Mommy, you sit down. I'll read it to you.' I tried it one day, reading from the pictures. Donny looked at me. He said, 'Mommy, that's not right.' He's only five. He knew I couldn't read . . .''

A landlord tells a woman that her lease allows him to evict her if 37 her baby cries and causes inconvenience to her neighbors. The consequence of challenging his words conveys a danger which appears, unlikely as it seems, even more alarming than the danger of eviction. Once she admits that she can't read, in the desire to maneuver for the time in which to call a friend, she will have defined herself in terms of an explicit impotence that she cannot endure. Capitulation in this case is preferable to self–humiliation. Resisting the definition of oneself in terms of what one cannot do, what others take for granted, represents a need so great that other imperatives (even one so urgent as the need to keep one's home in winter's cold) evaporate and fall away in face of fear. Even the loss of home and shelter, in this case, is not so terrifying as the loss of self.

"I come out of school. I was sixteen. They had their meetings. The di– 38 rectors meet. They said that I was wasting their school paper. I was wasting pencils . . ."

Another illiterate, looking back, believes she was not worthy of her 39 teacher's time. She believes that it was wrong of her to take up space within her school. She believes that it was right to leave in order that somebody more deserving could receive her place.

Children choke. Their mother chokes another way: on more than 40 chicken bones.

People eat what others order, know what others tell them, struggle 41 not to see themselves as they believe the world perceives them. A man in California speaks about his own loss of identity, of self–location, definition:

"I stood at the bottom of the ramp. My car had broke down on the 42 freeway. There was a phone. I asked for the police. They was nice. They said to tell them where I was. I looked up at the signs. There was one that I had seen before. I read it to them: ONE WAY STREET. They thought it was a joke. I told them I couldn't read. There was other signs above the ramp. They told me to try. I looked around for somebody to help. All the cars was going by real fast. I couldn't make them understand that I was lost. The cop was nice. He told me: 'Try once more.' I did my best. I couldn't read. I only knew the sign above my head. The cop was trying to be nice. He knew that I was trapped. 'I can't send out a car to you if you can't tell me where you are.' I felt afraid. I nearly cried. I'm forty–eight years old. I only said: 'I'm on a one–way street . . .' "

Perhaps we might slow down a moment here and look at the 43
realities described above. This is the nation that we live in. This is a society that most of us did not create but which our President and other
leaders have been willing to sustain by virtue of malign neglect. Do we
possess the character and courage to address a problem which so many
nations, poorer than our own, have found it natural to correct?

The answers to these questions represent a reasonable test of our be- 44
lief in the democracy to which we have been asked in public school to
swear allegiance.

Reading Closely

1. What generalization is Kozol implying about illiteracy? What generalization is he implying about people who are literate? Write out statements
   of each of these generalizations and of Kozol's purpose in making them.

2. Which of Kozol's examples support his generalization about people who
   are illiterate?

3. Which of Kozol's examples support his generalization about people who
   are literate?

4. How does Kozol define illiteracy? What examples does he provide to
   support his definition?

5. **Working with a classmate,** compare your answers to questions 2
   through 4.

Considering Larger Issues

1. What is Kozol's purpose in writing this essay? What strategies does he
   use to involve his audience? Which strategy is most effective?

2. COMBINING METHODS. Briefly list and number all the anecdotes Kozol uses
   as examples. How many does he use? What do these *narratives* contribute
   to the essay? How does this technique affect the overall style of the
   essay?

3. COMBINING METHODS. Kozol uses *cause-and-consequence analysis* to help make
   his points. Mark all these passages. What does he portray as the consequences of illiteracy? What effect does this list of consequences have on
   you as a reader? as a college student? as a citizen? Be prepared to share
   your answers with the rest of the class.

4. Take a few minutes to write about the first time you realized that some
   people in your country are illiterate. What were your feelings when you
   came into contact with them—or heard about them? What kind(s) of
   people were they? Why were they illiterate? What could you do about
   their illiteracy? **Discuss your written response with two or three
   classmates.**

Thinking about Language

1. Define the following terms, using the essay context or your dictionary. Be prepared to share your answers with the rest of the class.

morality (2)	circulars (11)	ruinous (24)
looms (4)	admonitions (12)	circumscribed (26)
mendacious (5)	tubal ligation (13)	perusal (27)
provocation (5)	jargon (13)	capitulation (37)
Cyrillic (7)	inalienable (14)	

2. How many of Kozol's examples are obviously taken from the poor? How many are taken from other socioeconomic groups? What—if any—differences can you detect between being (1) poor and illiterate, and (2) middle class (or higher) and illiterate? How might the situations be the same?

    What words or phrases does Kozol use that help you determine the differences and the similarities between the two situations? Write down your responses, and be prepared to share them with the rest of the class.

Writing Your Own Essays Using Exemplification

1. Reread your response to question 4 under "Considering Larger Issues." Have your feelings about illiterates or illiteracy changed after reading Kozol's essay? If so, how? What generalization might you make about illiteracy on the basis of your own experience and observations and the examples in the essay?

    Draft a three- to four-page essay on illiterates or on another group that can't or doesn't participate fully in public life. Open with a generalization about this group, and present examples that support your generalization. You may want to do some online research about the group or to find or create some visuals to illustrate your essay. Remember that "Checking Over the Use of Exemplification" can be found on p. 221.

2. In paragraph 2, Kozol writes about Socrates' belief that questions of literacy must be judged as matters of morality. In what ways are literacy and morality linked? What sorts of judgments about people in terms of their literacy does our culture make? Craft a two- to three-page essay in which you explore the relationship between literacy and morality. Make a generalization, and then support it with a series of examples. Refer to "Checking Over the Use of Exemplification" on p. 221.

3. How might you describe what it means to have computer literacy? Which members of your family have it? Who doesn't? What difference does this make in their lives, if any? How important do you think it is to have computer literacy today? Draft a three- to four-page essay in which you assert a generalization about computer literacy and provide a series of examples to support your assertion. As you prepare your essay, be sure to keep your overall purpose in mind. Refer to the guidelines for checking over the use of exemplification on p. 221.

TED ALLEN
The Laws of Fashion

Best known for his role as the food and wine authority on the television series *Queer Eye for the Straight Guy*, Chicago native Ted Allen is a contributing editor at *Esquire* magazine, where his "Things a Man Should Know" column regularly appears. This selection includes three parts of one of his columns, a forty-seven-item list called "The Laws of Fashion" that appeared in the March 2003 issue, with illustrations by Tim Bower.

> **Preview**   What one law of fashion do you always follow? What law of fashion does a parent or friend always follow — and try to get you to follow?

· · · · · · ➤

Reading Closely

1. **Working with a classmate,** identify the generalizations and examples in item 1. Which examples seem to illustrate which generalizations? Be prepared to share your answers with the rest of the class.

2. How many examples does Allen provide for the generalizations in items 11 and 32? Do you think that number sufficiently illustrates the generalizations? Why or why not?

3. How do Tim Bower's visuals enhance Allen's generalizations and examples?

Considering Larger Issues

1. Do you agree with Allen's generalization about the way men dress? Why or why not?

2. Who is Allen's primary audience? How can you tell? How does Allen work to reach that audience? Who might be the secondary audience for his column? What specific information might interest this audience?

3. Assuming that these excerpts are representative, how would you describe the tone of Allen's column? What words and phrases does he use to establish that tone in item 1? How does he maintain it in the later items?

4. Now that you've read excerpts from Allen's "The Laws of Fashion" and considered his generalizations and examples, what do you think about your own sense of fashion or style? Is there someone whose style you admire and try to emulate?

5. **COMBINING METHODS.** Besides exemplification, what other rhetorical methods does the writer use? **Working with another classmate or**

1. Know Yourself. *Then* Get Dressed.

Sounds simple. It isn't. It is the rare man who really understands what looks best on a person of his station—and what does not. Rarer still is the man who keeps pace with the changes in his circumstances. Like his circumference, for example. Most men, as they thicken, will suffer for months with painfully constricting waistbands before either Sweatin' to the Oldies or copping to a larger size. Then there are those too silly to understand that they're too young to smoke a pipe. (FYI, no charge: Every man alive is too young to smoke a pipe.) All one can do to master rule number one is this: Look in the mirror. Think. Repeat as necessary.

11. Your collar should complement your face.

Round face? Point collar. Narrow face? Spread collar. Cris Collinsworth? With a neck like that, the highest–sitting collar money can buy.

32. The right suit amplifies your physical strengths and diminishes your shortcomings.

A large man should wear solids, especially dark ones, and avoid large, loud patterns. A short man elongates his silhouette with a suit, partic–ularly a striped suit, eschewing the sport–coat–and–pants look be–cause it chops in half what little verticality he has. And ye of the ample booty: Go with ventless jackets or those with a rear vent rather than side–vented models, which will flap above your prodigious glutes like a signal flag.

two, mark these other methods of development and note how each one contributes to Allen's overall purpose.

Thinking about Language

1. Using the context or your dictionary, define any of the following terms that are unfamiliar to you: Be prepared to share your answers with the rest of the class.

station (1)	amplifies (32)	verticality (32)
circumference (1)	diminishes (32)	prodigious (32)
constricting (1)	silhouette (32)	glutes (32)
complement (11)	eschewing (32)	

2. What specific terms does Allen use to describe physical characteristics? Are the terms positive, negative, or neutral?

3. In items 1 and 32, Allen uses mostly complete sentences, whereas in item 11 he uses mostly very short phrases. Why might he have done so? What effect do the two different styles create?

Writing Your Own Essays Using Exemplification

1. Using this excerpt from Allen's column as a model, draft your own set of laws about a subject you know well or are interested in researching. (It might even be the laws of fashion for a group other than Allen's audience, such as full-time college students.) Using words and visuals, consider your overall purpose, your generalization, and the number of examples you can provide. Your work will not result in a traditional essay, but it can still be representative of the effective use of exemplification. As you draft and revise, refer to the guidelines for checking over the use of exemplification on p. 221.

2. Using your response to the preview questions (p. 263) and to item 4 under "Considering Larger Issues" (p. 263), draft a two- to three-page essay in which you analyze your own sense of style. Think back to how it developed, who your models have been, why you're satisfied or dissatisfied with it, and whether or how you'd like it to evolve and improve. Assert a generalization; then support that generalization with a series of vivid examples. You may want to refer to the advice you've gleaned—or the models (either positive or negative) you've identified with—from television programs such as *Queer Eye for the Straight Guy* and *What Not to Wear*, from fashion magazines, from friends and relatives, or from online sources. Your essay using exemplification might include both visuals as well as other methods of development (narration, comparison and contrast, process analysis, and cause-and-consequence analysis). As you draft and revise, refer to the guidelines for checking over the use of exemplification on p. 221.

✱ Additional Suggestions for Writing

1. Write a generalization about someone you know well who has a public persona. List all the examples you can think of that clarify or explain your generalization. **Working with a classmate,** review your generalization and your list, discussing any changes you may want to make to either one. Then draft a two- to three-page essay in which you develop your generalization and begin to link it to your subject's public persona, making connections between the private person whom you know well and the public person whom everyone else sees. Remember that "Checking Over the Use of Exemplification" can be found on p. 221.

2. **Working with a classmate,** discuss the importance of reading and writing in Kozol's essay. Then discuss the importance of these basic skills in your own lives. Has the importance of these two skills changed for you over the years? Do you expect them to be more or less important in the future? What will be the effect of their importance to you? Draft a three- to four-page essay using exemplification that makes a generalization about the importance of reading and writing in your life. As you draft and revise, refer to the guidelines for checking over the use of exemplification (p. 221).

3. Pretend that you are responding to a sociology professor's assignment about alcohol consumption (p. 213) or another activity that is potentially unhealthy or dangerous. Make a list of such activities that you have participated in, witnessed, or heard about. After you make your list, **work with a classmate** to compare and merge lists. Then draft a three- to four-page essay in which you generalize about one of those activities and provide examples — including anecdotes, facts, or statistics — that support your generalization. You may want to conduct library or Internet research, interview people who currently or formerly participated in the activity, or relate personal anecdotes. As you draft, revise, and assess examples, be sure to refer to the guidelines for checking over the use of exemplification on p. 221.

chapter **5**

.... •

CLASSIFICATION
AND DIVISION

Brother's PIZZA 238·PENN

FREE DELIVERY

DELIVERY HOURS:
11AM   to MID. - Mon thru Thurs.
11AM   to 2AM - Fri & Sat.
NOON to 10PM - Sunday

* Minimum $5.00 delivery order

PIZZA - New York Style - THIN CRUST

Large (16 inches)...$4.90
Sicilian (PAN PIZZA - 12 Slices).........................$8.70
Each Topping..$1.50
Half-Topping $0.80
TOPPINGS: Pepperoni • Ham • Sausage •
Ground Beef • Bacon • Onions • Black Olives •
Green Peppers • Mushrooms

STROMBOLIS

Sm.-9" - $3.20   Md.-14" - $6.00   Lg.-18" - $8.00
#1. Ham, Cheese & Pepperoni
#2. Meatballs & Mozzarella
#3. Spinach, Mushrooms & Mozzarella
#4. Ricotta + 2 stuffings
#5. Hot Sausage, Mozzarella, Green Peppers & Onions
#6. Steak, Green Peppers & Onions

* Always with sauce on the side
* X-tra Sauce   Small $.40   Large $1.00
* X-tra Stuffings each $.30 $1.00 $1.00

SUBS

Wedges (Hoagies done on a pizza shell) $3.50
12 inches bread $3.00
With melted cheese $3.50
Italian • Ham & Cheese • Turkey • Provolone • Tuna • Chicken
• Fish
All subs have mayo, lettuce, tomatoes, onions, black olives
& hot-banana peppers. Please, if you do not like
something, let us know.

GRINDERS

With special sauce & melted cheese $3.50
Meatballs, Chicken • Veal • Eggplant Parmigiana

DRINKS

Pepsi, Diet-Pepsi, 7-UP, Mt. Dew,
Root Beer, Iced Tea ....$0.80 (16 oz.)

CHEESE STEAKS

Whole - 12" $3.50
Half - 7" $2.50
Philly - Grilled meat, onions, green pepper, mushrooms, sauce &
melted cheese on top
California - Grilled meat, onions, green pepper, mushrooms,
melted cheese, lettuce, tomatoes & Italian dressing

SALADS

Served with bread and butter

	Sm.	Lg.
Tossed Salad - Lettuce, Tomatoes, Onions, Green Peppers, Hot		
Peppers & Black Olives.	$1.80	$1.80
Antipasto Salad - Lettuce, Tomatoes, Onions, Green Peppers,		
Mozzarella Cheese, Salami, Mushrooms, Ham & Turkey.		
	$2.70	$3.40
Chef's Salad - Lettuce, Tomatoes, Onions, Green Peppers,		
Mozzarella Cheese, Salami, Mushrooms, Ham, Turkey & Egg.		
	$2.90	$3.60
Tuna Salad - Lettuce, Tomatoes, Tuna & Egg.		
	$2.50	$3.20

Dressings: Italian (House), Lite Italian, French, Thousand
Island, Blue Cheese, Ranch, Fat Free French, Fat Free Ranch

* X-tra Dressing $.30

SIDE ORDERS

French Fries $1.25
Cheese Fries $1.55
Mozzarella sticks w/sauce $2.50
Garlic Bread Sticks w/sauce $2.50
Garlic Bread Sticks w/melted cheese & sauce $3.50
Breaded Mushrooms $1.55
Buffalo Wings (1 dozen) w/blue cheese $3.20
25 Wings w/blue cheese $5.00
Onion Rings $1.30
Jalapeño Poppers...$2.00

hen college students head for their favorite pizza place, they usually grab a menu, even if they already know what they want to order. When they arrive at Brother's Pizza in State College, Pennsylvania, they see that "New York style pizza" and "Sicilian style pizza" are listed under "Pizza." Pepperoni, ham, sausage, ground beef, bacon, onions, black olives, green peppers, and mushrooms are listed under "Toppings." And French fries, cheese fries, mozzarella sticks, garlic bread sticks, breaded mushrooms, and so on are listed under "Side Orders." In fact, all the restaurant's offerings are classified into the categories of "Pizza," "Toppings," "Strombolis," "Subs," "Grinders," "Drinks," "Cheese Steaks," "Salads," and "Side Orders." Whoever designed the menu uses classification and a closely related method, division, to help customers make sense of what Brother's Pizza has to offer.

We use classification and division every day, without giving these methods much thought. We figure out what we want to eat, see, do, or buy based on what we learn from how things are classified or divided. When we go to a restaurant, we choose what we want to eat and drink from specific categories on the menu. When we want to go to the movies, we look at the movie listings in the local paper, expecting to see, at a glance, a classification of which movies are playing, where, and when. And when we want to buy something in a store, we look for it in a specific department or aisle, because we know the store is divided up by categories of merchandise. As a writer, you too will have occasion to use classification and division for various purposes.

> **Looking at Your Own Literacy** Think back to a time when you were classified — and labeled — on the basis of your reading, writing, or speaking ability. Take a few minutes to reflect on your place in the classification and division and write about how you felt and what you learned about being labeled.

What Are Classification and Division?

Classification and division are different ways of thinking and talking about information, but they are a kind of mirror image of each other, and they usually work in tandem. **Classification** is the process of sorting specific things into more general categories; **division** is the process of breaking a general whole into more specific parts — which are often categories. We encounter classification and division when, for example, we're looking for a doctor in the Yellow Pages. Knowing that the Yellow Pages as a whole are divided into specific products or services, we look under the heading "Physician" and find that this service as a whole is subdivided into smaller parts based on specialties, from "Allergy &

Clinical Immunology" to "Dermatology" and "General Practice." And specific doctors are classified into a list under each specialty. Likewise, we
expect grocery stores to use classification and division to help us locate
the product we want: typically all the products in the store are classified
by type—produce, meat, dairy, and so on—and all products within each
type are classified into subtypes. For instance, the meats are classified
into chicken, pork, beef, and lamb; cured, fresh, and frozen. And the store
is divided into sections and subsections for each type and subtype.

The ways in which listings in the Yellow Pages and products in a
store are classified and divided demonstrate one of the purposes of classification and division: to inform or teach. But these methods can also be
used to please or entertain and to argue. In the most general sense, they
offer a way to put an array of items into groups and then to label each
group—or to define and label groups and then put items into each one.

We routinely make sense of our world by sorting incidents, people,
places, steps, and topics into categories and then labeling the categories.
Each time you put away your groceries, you classify them. You put frozen
foods into the freezer, items that need to be kept cold into the refrigerator, and products that can be kept at room temperature, such as cereals
or flour, into the pantry or cupboards. Whenever you sort items according to their similarities and differences—whether you're separating your
clothes from your roommate's at the Laundromat, deciding which of
your many friends to invite to your small party, or filling out your schedule according to required courses for your particular major and courses
that are general requirements—you are using classification.

Division is slightly different. Instead of sorting a number of items
into categories, you're dividing one item into its parts (and often analyzing the connections among the parts). Instead of looking at something
from the bottom up, you're looking from the top down. Think back to
your groceries—let's say you bring in several bags of items that need to
be put away. And let's say that instead of thinking of the situation in
terms of the groceries—taking each item out of the bag and deciding
where to put it (how to classify it)—you instead think in terms of your
kitchen and its physical parts: the refrigerator, the freezer, and the pantry
or cupboards. You move to each part in turn, taking the items that go in
that part out of the shopping bags and putting those items away before
moving on to the next part. By mentally dividing up the kitchen, you've
divided up all the groceries.

In fact, when most of us put away groceries, we use classification and
division simultaneously. Maybe we put the shopping bags down in front
of whatever part of the kitchen is closest to the door—say, the pantry—
and look into the bags for items that belong in that part (division). Before
we finish putting those away we notice the ice cream starting to melt,
and we rush to get it into the freezer (classification). While we're there,
we look in the bags for other items that belong in that part (division),

and so on. Whether as physical processes or writing strategies, classifying and dividing usually go hand in hand.

When classification and division constitute the dominant pattern in a whole essay, each section of the essay is about a category or a main part. If you were writing an essay about your summer job preparing food in a fast-food restaurant, for instance, you might open by dividing the menu (or classifying the items on it) into sandwiches, meal deals, drinks, and desserts. Then you might move into a discussion of your work as a sandwich-maker, discussing hamburgers, cheeseburgers, fish sandwiches, super-fattening and double hamburgers, and kiddy burgers. You could move from one classification of food to the next, describing each of the items that you prepared, until you've fleshed out an entire essay.

You can also use classification and division in a supporting passage or paragraph. For instance, if you're writing a narrative about buying a used car or an analysis of the process, you might mention two classes of used cars: smart choices and big risks. In a certain paragraph, you might list some smart choices in a sentence or two and give the reasons why you think so. In the same paragraph or in another one, you might do the same for the big risks. Such information would bring your essay alive and make it more interesting to your readers, maybe even entertaining or persuading them at the same time.

The annual auto issue of *Consumer Reports* contains all sorts of information that is presented using classification and division. The visual on pp. 274–75 appeared in the April 2004 issue as part of the section on used cars.

Thinking about Classification and Division

1. Read over the classification from *Consumer Reports*. What is the overall purpose of this classification? How easy is it to read and understand?

2. Do you own or have you driven one of the cars listed in the *Consumer Reports* guide? If so, which one? Write a quick response to *Consumer Reports* based on your experience with this car. If you don't have experience with any of these cars, then classify a car or another kind of product you do know about as either reliable or to be avoided, and explain why.

Why Classify and Divide?

When we use classification and division, we often do so simply with an informative purpose, whether we are classifying or dividing the contents of a store, a kitchen, or popular music charts. For example, in the

2004 CARS

USED CARS
The best & worst

Overall, cars are getting more reliable every year (see "Reliability Trends," on page 16). But buying any used vehicle entails some risk.

The lists on these pages give you a rundown of the models that were the most trouble-free and troublesome in CR's latest subscriber survey. The survey drew about 675,000 responses from owners who reported on any serious problems they'd had with their cars, minivans, SUVs, and pickups in the previous year. For the detailed reliability ratings on which these lists are based, see pages 82–93.

Reliable used cars shows all the models that were above average in reliability.

CR Good Bets are the best of the reliable used cars. They have performed well in our road tests and have been consistently better than average in overall reliability.

Used cars to avoid includes all the models, by year, that were below average in reliability.

Repeat offenders are vehicles that are especially risky buys. They have exhibited several years of poor overall reliability.

> The lists on these pages are compiled from overall reliability data covering 1996 through 2003 models. CR Good Bets and Repeat Offenders include only models for which we have sufficient data for at least three model years. Models that were new in 2002 or 2003 do not appear. Problems with the engine, cooling system, transmission, and drive system are weighted more heavily than other problems. 2WD, 4WD, and AWD stand for two-, four-, and all-wheel drive, respectively.

Reliable used cars

CR GOOD BETS

These models represent the best of both worlds: They have performed well in CONSUMER REPORTS tests over the years and have had much-better-than-average reliability for multiple years. They are listed alphabetically.

Acura Integra
Acura MDX
Acura RL
Acura TL
Buick Regal
Chrysler
  PT Cruiser
Ford Escort
Geo/Chevrolet
  Prizm
Honda Accord
Honda Civic
Honda CR-V
Honda Odyssey
Honda Prelude
Honda S2000
Infiniti G20
Infiniti I30, I35
Infiniti QX4
Isuzu Oasis
Lexus ES300

Lexus GS300/GS400,
  GS430
Lexus LS400,
  LS430
Lexus RX300
Lincoln Town Car
  (except 2003)
Mazda 626
Mazda Millenia
Mazda MPV
Mazda MX-5 Miata
Mazda Protegé
Mercury Tracer
Nissan Altima
Nissan Maxima
Nissan Pathfinder
Subaru Forester
Subaru Impreza
Subaru Legacy
Subaru Outback

Toyota 4Runner
Toyota Avalon
Toyota Camry
Toyota Camry
  Solara
Toyota Celica
Toyota Corolla
Toyota Echo
Toyota Highlander
Toyota Land
  Cruiser
Toyota RAV4
Toyota Sequoia
Toyota Sienna
Toyota Tacoma
Toyota Tundra

1999 Honda CR-V

2000 Buick Regal

These models showed better-than-average reliability in our latest survey; they are listed alphabetically by price range and model year. All prices are rounded to the nearest $1,000. The price ranges are what you'd pay for a typically equipped vehicle with average mileage.

LESS THAN $6,000
Buick Century '97-98
Chevrolet Prizm '98-00
Ford Escort '97-01, F-150 (2WD) '96, Ranger (2WD) '96-97
Geo Prizm '96-97, Tracker '96-97
Honda Civic '96
Mazda 626 '98, B-Series (2WD) '96-98, Protegé '96-99
Mercury Tracer '97-99
Nissan Altima '96-97, Pickup '96-97, Sentra '96-99
Saturn S-Series '96, '98-99
Subaru Impreza '96-97
Suzuki Sidekick '96-97
Toyota Corolla '96-98, Tercel '96-97

$6,000-$8,000
Acura Integra '96
Chevrolet Prizm '01
Ford Crown Victoria '97-98, Escort '02, F-150 (2WD) '97, Mustang '98, Ranger (2WD) '98-99
Honda Accord '96-97, Civic '97-99
Infiniti G20 '96
Mazda 626 '99, B-Series (2WD) '99, Millenia '96, MX-5 Miata '96-97, Protegé '00
Mercury Grand Marquis '97-98
Nissan Altima '98-99, Frontier '98, Maxima '96, Sentra '00
Saturn S-Series '01
Subaru Impreza '98, Legacy/Outback '96-98

Toyota Camry '96-97, Corolla '99-00, Echo '00-01, RAV4 '96-97, Tacoma '96-97

$8,000-$10,000
Acura CL '97-98, Integra '97-98, TL '96
Buick Century '00-01, Regal '99
Chevrolet Prizm '02
Ford Crown Victoria '99-00, F-150 (2WD) '98-99, F-150 (4WD) '97, Mustang '99, Ranger (2WD) '00
Honda Accord '98, Civic '00, CR-V '97-98, Odyssey '96, Prelude '96
Hyundai Elantra '02
Infiniti I30 '96-98
Isuzu Oasis '96-98
Lincoln Continental '98, Town Car '96-97
Mazda 626 '00, B-Series (2WD) '00, Millenia '97-98, Protegé '01
Mercury Grand Marquis '99
Mitsubishi Eclipse '00
Nissan Altima '00, Frontier '99, Maxima '97-98, Pathfinder '96-97, Sentra '01
Saturn S-Series '02
Subaru Forester '98, Impreza '99
Toyota Avalon '96-98, Camry '98, Celica '96-98, Corolla '01-02, Echo '02, Previa '96, RAV4 '98-99, T100 '96-97, Tacoma '98

$10,000-$12,000
Acura Integra '99, TL '97-98

PHOTO AT TOP BY TRACEY KROLL

following excerpt, Roberto Suro classifies Latino gathering places called *cantinas*, drawing on the experiences of Houston police sergeant Art Valdez, who patrols Magnolia, Houston's Latino district:

> Valdez can do a typology of Magnolia's cantinas as precisely as if he were categorizing butterflies by genus and species, except that it is a human caste system he describes. At one end, there are the raucous dance halls, some of them big Quonset huts, where younger men, mostly

Buick Regal '00
Chrysler PT Cruiser '01
Ford F-150 (2WD) '00, F-150 (4WD) '98, Mustang '00
Honda Accord '99, Civic '01, CR-V '99, Odyssey '97-98, Prelude '97-98
Infiniti G20 '99, Q45 '96, QX4 '97-98
Lexus ES300 '96
Lincoln Continental '99, Town Car '98
Mazda 626 '01-02, Millenia '99, MPV '00, MX-5 Miata '99, Protegé '02
Mercedes-Benz C-Class '96-97
Mercury Grand Marquis '00
Nissan Altima '01, Frontier '00, Maxima '99, Pathfinder '98
Subaru Impreza '00, Legacy/Outback '99
Toyota 4Runner '96-97, Camry '99-00, Camry Solara '99, RAV4 '00, Sienna '98, T100 '98, Tacoma '99

$12,000-$14,000
Acura CL '99, Integra '00, RL '96-97
BMW 3 Series '97, Z3 '97
Buick Century '02-03, Regal '01-02
Chevrolet Impala '02, Silverado 1500 (2WD) '00
Chrysler PT Cruiser '02
GMC Sierra 1500 (2WD) '00
Honda Accord '00, Civic '02, CR-V '00, Prelude '99
Hyundai Elantra '03
Infiniti G20 '00, I30 '99, Q45 '97
Lexus ES300 '97-98
Lincoln Continental '00, Town Car '99
Mazda Millenia '00, MPV '01, MX-5 Miata '00, Protegé '03
Mitsubishi Eclipse '01
Nissan Maxima '00, Pathfinder '99, Xterra '00
Subaru Forester '00, Impreza '01, Legacy/Outback '00
Toyota 4Runner '98, Avalon '99, Camry '01, Celica '99-00, Corolla '03, Sienna '99, Tacoma '00

$14,000-$16,000
Acura Integra '01, RL '98, TL '99
BMW Z3 '98
Buick LeSabre '02
Chevrolet Silverado 1500 (2WD) '01
Ford F-150 (2WD) '01, F-150 (4WD) '00
GMC Sierra 1500 (2WD) '01
Honda Accord '01, Civic '03, CR-V '01, Prelude '00
Infiniti G20 '01, Q45 '98, QX4 '99
Lexus ES300 '99, GS300/GS400 '96, LS400 '96, SC400 '96
Mazda Millenia '01, MX-5 Miata '01-02
Nissan Maxima '01, Pathfinder '00, Xterra '01
Subaru Forester '01, Impreza '02, Legacy '01, Outback '01
Toyota 4Runner '99, Camry Solara '00, Celica '01, Land Cruiser '96, Prius '01, RAV4 '01, Sienna '00, Tacoma '01, Tundra '00

$16,000-$18,000
Acura RL '99, TL '00
BMW Z3 '99
Buick Regal '03
Chevrolet Impala '03
Ford F-150 (2WD) '02
Honda Accord '02, Prelude '01
Hyundai Santa Fe '02
Infiniti G20 '02, I30 '00
Lexus SC400 '97
Lincoln Town Car '00

Mazda Millenia '02, MPV '02, MX-5 Miata '03
Pontiac Vibe '03
Toyota 4Runner '00, Avalon '00, Camry '02, Camry Solara '01, Celica '02, Land Cruiser '97, Prius '02, RAV4 '02, Sienna '01, Tacoma '02, Tundra '01

$18,000-$20,000
Acura CL '01, RSX '02-03, TL '01
BMW 3 Series '99
Buick LeSabre '03
Ford F-150 (2WD) '03
Honda CR-V '02, Element '03, Odyssey '00
Infiniti I30 '01, Q45 '99, QX4 '00
Lexus ES300 '00, GS300/GS400 '98, LS400 '97-98, RX300 '99
Lincoln Town Car '01
Mazda6 '03
Nissan Altima '03, Frontier '03, Maxima '02, Pathfinder '01
Toyota Avalon '01, Camry Solara '02, Prius '03, Sienna '02

$20,000-$22,000
Acura CL '02, RL '00
BMW Z3 '00
Honda Accord '03, Odyssey '01, S2000 '00
Hyundai Santa Fe '03
Lexus GS300/GS400 '99
Nissan Maxima '03, Pathfinder '02, Xterra '03
Subaru Forester '03
Toyota Camry '03, Camry Solara '03, Celica '03, Highlander '01, Land Cruiser '98, RAV4 '03, Tacoma '03, Tundra '02

$22,000-$26,000
Acura RL '01
BMW 5 Series '99, Z3 '01
Ford F-150 (4WD) '03
Honda CR-V '03, Odyssey '02, S2000 '02
Infiniti I35 '02, QX4 '01-02
Lexus ES300 '01, GS300/GS400 '00, IS300 '01-02, LS400 '99, RX300 '00
Lincoln Town Car '02
Nissan Pathfinder '03
Toyota 4Runner '01-02, Avalon '02, Highlander '02, Land Cruiser '99, Sienna '03, Tundra '03

$26,000-$30,000
Acura RL '02
BMW 3 Series '02, 5 Series '00
Honda Odyssey '03, Pilot '03, S2000 '03
Infiniti G35 '03, I35 '03, Q45 '01
Lexus ES300 '02, IS300 '03, LS400 '00, LX470 '99, RX300 '01
Nissan 350Z '03, Murano '03
Porsche Boxster '00
Saab 9-5 '03
Toyota Avalon '03, Highlander '03, Land Cruiser '00

$30,000 AND UP
Acura MDX '01-03
BMW 5 Series '01-03
Infiniti FX '03, Q45 '02
Lexus ES300 '03, GS300/GS400 '01, GS300/GS430 '02-03, LS400 '01, LS430 '02-03, LX470 '00-03, RX300 '02-03, SC430 '02
Toyota Land Cruiser '01-02, Sequoia '01-02

Used cars to avoid

These models showed below-average reliability in our latest survey. They are listed alphabetically by make, model, and year.

Audi A4 (4-cyl.) '97-98, '01-02; A4 (V6) '96-98, '02; A6 (V6) '98-00, '02-03; A6 (V6 Turbo) '00-01; TT '01-02
BMW 7 Series '97-99, '02-03; X5 '00-02
Buick Park Avenue '97-98, '01; Roadmaster '96; Skylark '96-97
Cadillac Catera '97-01; CTS '03; DeVille '96-98, '00-01, '03; Escalade '02-03; Seville '96-98, '00-03
Chevrolet Astro '96-03; Blazer '96-03; C1500 '97-98; Camaro '97-99, '01; Caprice '96; Cavalier '96; Corsica, Beretta '96; Corvette '98, '00-03; Express 1500 '96-03; K1500 '96-98; Malibu '97-01; S-10 '96-03; Silverado 1500 (4WD) '99-00, '02-03; Suburban '96-00, '03; Tahoe '96-99, '03; TrailBlazer '02-03; Venture '97-00; Venture (4WD) '02
Chrysler 300M '99, '03; Cirrus '96; Concorde '96-99; New Yorker, LHS '96, '99; Sebring Convertible '96-97, '01; Town & Country '96-97, '99-02; Voyager (4-cyl.) '02; Voyager '01, '03
Dodge Caravan '96-01, '03; Caravan (4-cyl.) '02; Dakota (2WD) '97-98; Dakota (4WD) '96, '98-01; Durango '98-00; Grand Caravan '96-97, '99-02; Intrepid '96-99; Neon '96-00; Ram 1500 '96-99, '01-02; Ram 1500 (2WD) '00; Ram Van/Wagon 1500 '96, '98-00; Stratus '96; Stratus (4-cyl.) '97-99
Ford Contour (4-cyl.) '97-98; Contour (V6) '96, '98, '00; Crown Victoria '03; Econoline Wagon, Van 150 '96, '01-03; Escape '01; Excursion '01; Expedition '03; Explorer '00, '02; Explorer (4WD) '98-99, '01; Explorer Sport Trac '03; Focus '00-01; Mustang '03; Ranger (4WD) '00-02; Taurus Wagon '02; Windstar '96-01
GMC Envoy '02-03; Jimmy '96-01; S-15 Sonoma '96-03; Safari '96-01; Savana Van 1500 '96-03; Sierra 1500 (2WD) '97-98; Sierra 1500 (4WD) '96-00, '02-03; Suburban '96-99; Yukon '96-99, '03; Yukon XL '00, '03
Honda Passport '98-99

Hummer H2 '03
Hyundai Santa Fe '01; Sonata '01; XG350 '02
Isuzu Rodeo '98-99
Jaguar S-Type '00-03; XJ8 '99-00; X-Type '02-03
Jeep Grand Cherokee '96-03
Kia Sedona '02
Land Rover Discovery '00-01; Freelander '02
Lincoln Navigator '03; Town Car '03
Mazda B-Series (4WD) '00-02; Tribute '01
Mercedes-Benz C-Class '01-03; CLK '02; E-Class '03; E-Class (AWD) '00-01; M-Class '98-02; S-Class '00, '02; SLK '03
Mercury Cougar '99-01; Grand Marquis '03; Mountaineer '00, '02; Mountaineer (4WD) '98-99, '01; Mystique (4-cyl.) '97-98; Mystique (V6) '96, '98, '00; Sable Wagon '02
Mini Cooper '02-03
Mitsubishi Eclipse '00; Galant '96, '02
Nissan Sentra '03
Oldsmobile 88 '97-98; Alero '99-01; Aurora '96, '01; Bravada '97-03; Cutlass '97-99; Cutlass Ciera '96; Silhouette '97-00; Silhouette (AWD) '02
Plymouth Breeze '96-99; Grand Voyager '96-97, '99-00; Neon '96-00; Voyager '96-00
Pontiac Aztek '01, '03; Bonneville '97-98, '00-03; Firebird '97, '99-01; Grand Am '96-97, '99-01; Grand Prix '97-98; Montana '00; Montana (AWD) '02; Sunfire '96; TransSport, Montana '97-99
Saturn L-Series (V6) '00-02; SW '00; Vue '02-03
Subaru Baja '03; Legacy Outback (6-cyl.) '03
Toyota 4Runner (V6) '03
Volkswagen Golf '96-03; Jetta '96-03; New Beetle '98-03; Passat '98-00; Passat (4-cyl.) '02; Passat (V6) '96-97
Volvo S90/V90 '97-98; S40/V40 '00; S80 '99-00; V70/Cross Country '98-01; XC90 '03

REPEAT OFFENDERS

Be especially careful when considering these models. They have shown several years of much-worse-than-average overall reliability. They are listed alphabetically.

Audi A6
BMW 7 Series
Cadillac Seville
Chevrolet Astro
Chevrolet Blazer
Chevrolet S-10 (4WD)
Chrysler Town & Country (AWD)
Dodge Grand Caravan (AWD)
Dodge Neon
GMC Jimmy

GMC Safari
GMC Sonoma (4WD)
Jaguar S-Type
Jeep Grand Cherokee
Mercedes-Benz M-Class
Oldsmobile Bravada
Oldsmobile Cutlass
Plymouth Neon
Volkswagen Golf
Volkswagen Jetta
Volkswagen New Beetle

Mexican and mostly illegals, are drawn by the abundant bar girls, most of them now young Salvadorans, who will dance and perhaps do more, depending on the money. When there are fights, they are usually over women.

Then there are the simple bars frequented by older men who remain tied to home, whatever their immigration status. They mostly drink without women and listen to little *conjuntos,* which are minstrel groups with a few guitars and maybe an accordion that play old songs. And now there are the new places that play salsa and other sounds with tropical rhythms rarely heard when the barrio was populated predominately by mountain and desert people.

At the other end of the spectrum are the fancy places with neon lights outside and bouncers in slick suits where Mexican-Americans go. The music is eclectic, some rock, a lot of country and western, but mostly *tejano,* a kind of country-rock combination that originated in south Texas and is sung in Spanish. The customers are English-speaking young people in their twenties and thirties out on dates. Most have come back to the old neighborhood from new suburban barrios. Valdez does not bother with them.   — ROBERTO SURO, "Houston: Cantina Patrol"

In these brief paragraphs, Suro informs his readers about the various kinds of cantinas in Houston and the kind of Latino or Latina who frequents each kind. When he discusses "the fancy places," he divides that category further, according to the kind of music that is played there.

Try Your Hand Undoubtedly, you socialize somewhere: restaurants, dorm lounges, church functions, clubs, coffee shops, bookstores, gyms. Using Suro's categories, or categories like his, try to classify the kinds of places you frequent. If you can divide one of those categories further, do so. If you notice that another classmate is writing about the same kinds of places, compare your reponses and prepare to report to the rest of the class.

Classification and division are also used to entertain, to give pleasure to readers. In his best-selling book, stand-up comedian and television star Jerry Seinfeld divides human existence into two parts:

You can divide your whole life into two basic categories.
You're either staying in or going out.
Everything else is irrelevant detail.

The urge to go out and then return is very strong. Just
look at what happens to people when they don't want to
stay home and they have to. They become despondent. Or
if someone's locked out of their house and can't
get in when they want? They go nuts.
We must go out. We must go back.

When you're out, everything's a little out of control and
exciting. Something could happen. You might see
something. You might find out something. You might even
be a part of something. We've got to go out there.

When you're back in your house you're like the conductor
of an orchestra. You know where everything is and how to
work it. You move confidently from one part of your
house to another. You know exactly where you're going

and what will happen when you get there.
You're the maestro of a symphony with nothing on
but socks and underwear.
And it's because we know it so well that
we've got to get out.   —Jerry Seinfeld, *SeinLanguage*

Perhaps you are able to imagine Seinfeld's delivery of this division: we're either "staying in or going out." By classifying where we want to be into only two categories, he figures he's got us covered: in or out. For support, Seinfeld includes examples of what we do when we are in or out. According to Seinfeld, wherever we are, we wish we were in the other category instead.

Try Your Hand   Let's imagine that you can classify your existence in terms of staying in and going out. Draw a line down the center of a sheet of paper, and then write "staying in" at the top of one side and "going out" at the top of the other. Make a list of all the things you do when you stay in and another list of all the things you do when you go out. How might you cluster your activities on either and both sides of the line? Do you detect any patterns? Does any information come as a surprise?

Classification and division can also be used to argue a point or convince a reader to consider a particular opinion. For example, by classifying crimes by type—including vehicle thefts, larcenies, break-ins, robberies, rapes, and murders—and then dividing an area into neighborhoods, a writer might reveal that certain neighborhoods have more crime of a certain type. The information that such a classification and division reveals can then be used to persuade readers that one neighborhood should initiate a neighborhood watch program, another should have regular police patrols, and yet another should be avoided altogether, if possible.

In fact, the act of classifying and dividing can itself make an argument. In the United States, there's a tradition of classifying all the residents into various racial categories—whether for police reports, job or college applications, or marriage and driver's licenses. For example, in 2000 the U.S. Census Bureau used the following racial classifications:

RACE
    One race
      White
      Black or African American
      American Indian and Alaska Native
      Asian
        Asian Indian

        Chinese
        Filipino
        Japanese
        Korean
        Vietnamese
        Other Asian
    Native Hawaiian and Other Pacific Islander
        Native Hawaiian
        Guamanian or Chamorro
        Samoan
        Other Pacific Islander
    Some other race
Two or more races

Race alone or in combination with one or more other races
White
Black or African American
American Indian and Alaska Native
Asian
Native Hawaiian and Other Pacific Islander
Some other race

HISPANIC OR LATINO AND RACE
    Total Population
Hispanic or Latino (of any race)
    Mexican
    Puerto Rican
    Cuban
    Other Hispanic or Latino
Not Hispanic or Latino
    White alone

                —U.S. DEPARTMENT OF COMMERCE, *Profiles of General*
                    Demographic Characteristics: 2000 Census of Popula-
                    tion and Housing, Technical Documentation

    However, as we all know, racial classifications are even more compli-cated than the preceding form indicates; they are complicated by ethnic-ity, culture, geography, and loyalty. In an attempt to convince her readers to think beyond tidy racial classifications, Inez Peterson writes about the difficulties of answering a woman who asked "what part Indian" she is. The woman who asked "should know better than to ask such an ignorant question," writes Peterson, whose response follows:

    What I do know is that if we divide ourselves, we are doing the work of the dominant culture; there is no need for them to keep us down, for we do it to ourselves. What is true too: if I had no need of this generosity of spirit, to include all of us, the mixed-bloods, the traditions, the urbans, the full-bloods, I might be just as exclusive as my author-colleague.
    I do not enjoy the privileged status of only one race, nor can I claim a traditional upbringing. My grandmother died believing it best not to pass

on her Salish tongue. My white father abandoned his children and their mother, leaving nothing but his blood in my veins and a twisted belief in the ongoing nature of absented love. I do not know my own traditions.

However, if I do not allow myself the right to dance intertribals, or sit in on non-Quinault sweat house ceremonies, or participate in rituals not specific to the Northwest, is not this the expected acquiescence of assimilation? Because my untaught mother taught me no tradition whatsoever, am I to refuse when a loving older Kiowa woman wants to teach me about fringing shawls? If I should exclude myself from belonging on the basis of my nontraditional upbringing and of the color of my skin, it would bring about unbearable loneliness.

. . . And so when she asked me, "What part Indian are you?"

I said, "I think it is my heart. "   —INEZ PETERSON, "What Part Moon?"

Writing movingly and convincingly, Peterson helps readers see the insignificance of percentages (What part _____ are you?) and of those categorizations so prevalent on standard applications and forms. To choose to identify herself as an Indian seems, finally, more important to Peterson than to have the "right" skin or hair color, or the traditions or skills of an Indian. She needs neither the blessing of an Indian person nor the permission of a white person to classify herself as Indian, which she has done. Nevertheless, although she purposefully refuses to divide herself into parts, racial classifications still linger in her essay, in her own mind as well as the minds of others. She does not argue that "Indianness" does not exist, that it is not a category. Instead, she argues that it resides not in "blood" or rituals but in the heart.

Try Your Hand   Which racial category—or categories—do you mark when you're filling out an application? How might you subdivide your particular category or categories, given your heritage? Which identification feels most appropriate to you or "fits you the best"? Why?

How Do You Read Classification and Division?

It's usually easy to spot an essay or a passage that consists of classification or division—either a collection of people, ideas, or things are being put into categories, or one idea or thing is being broken into distinct parts. But noticing the organizational pattern is only one aspect of reading a classification and division *critically*, which is a key skill you need to develop in order to write one yourself. Reading critically means looking closely to analyze how successful the classification or division is, not only in general but also in terms of its specific purpose and intended audience. For example, do the categories or parts make sense, or do they seem to overlap or leave out some important part of the subject? Are they clear, entertaining, or persuasive, or do they seem confusing, dull, or unconvincing to potential readers? As you learn to read classifications and divisions in these ways, chances are you'll also be getting better at writing them as well.

To get an idea of what a critical reading involves, look back at Roberto Suro's classification of Houston's cantinas on p. 274. How does the author organize the subject—and, more important, why? Suro classifies all the cantinas in town in order to inform—specifically, to explain how different social classes, nationalities, and genders of native and immigrant Spanish speakers can be found at specific kinds of cantinas. An author's purpose won't always be presented in a clear thesis statement, but Suro's essay opens with an explicit one that states his explanatory purpose: "Valdez can do a typology of Magnolia's cantinas as precisely as if he were categorizing butterflies by genus and species, except that it is a human caste system he describes." Although the title of this particular essay, "Houston: Cantina Patrol," provides little hint about its content, the titles and introductions of other essays might help orient you to the writers' principles of organization and purpose.

Notice that the key feature of each of Suro's cantina categories is the patrons, whom he groups by nationality, age, and gender. As he develops these categories, he enriches the description of each one with details of the cantinas' appearance and atmosphere as well as additional details about the patrons, such as their immigration status and the music they enjoy. In general, each of his categories seems clearly defined and clearly distinguished from the others, except that in the second paragraph it's not entirely clear whether "the new places that play salsa and other sounds with tropical rhythms" make up a different category than "the simple bars frequented by older men" or just a newer subcategory. Notice also that Suro defines two of the Spanish words he uses, *conjuntos* and *tejano*, while leaving *barrio* and *salsa* undefined. What does this difference suggest? He seems to be writing for readers who have some general familiarity with Latino culture but not a detailed knowledge of Latino musical styles.

Finally, as you read a classification or division critically, you'll want to think not only about the information the author supplies but also about what has been left unsaid. What information might Suro have omitted from his classification? For example, are there cantinas with a predominantly gay or lesbian clientele? Are cantinas (or specific kinds of cantinas) located in residential neighborhoods, commercial areas, or elsewhere? And would including that information enhance or detract from his essay? Could Houston's cantinas be classified differently—geographically, for instance? And if they were, would that new organizational pattern better fulfill the author's purpose or be easier for readers to follow? Asking questions like these will help you think about all the factors that go into an effective classification or division and understand better how to write one.

How Do You Write Using Classification and Division?

Keep the following guidelines in mind as you begin writing using classification or division or a combination of the two. As you generate ideas, draft, and revise, you'll want to make sure that you have established and carried out a clear purpose, are making choices appropriate for your particular audience, and are following a consistent principle of classification or division, so that your categories or parts don't overlap or leave anything out. Following these guidelines will help you decide on the most effective way to organize the categories or parts and the appropriate amount of detail to devote to each one. You'll also want to make sure that you conclude by extending the point you're making through classification or division and that you consider whether visuals such as charts, graphs, photographs, or drawings might enhance it.

● Determining Your Purpose

First, you'll need to determine why you are imposing your organizational pattern on this group of items. Your first–year writing instructor might ask you to classify the different types of students at your school in a humorous way (that is, to entertain). Your history professor might ask you to organize the various causes of World War I into categories as part of an assignment to decide which causes were most important (to argue). Or your social psychology professor might have you divide the pressures college students face into different kinds in order to train you to analyze human behavior (to inform). If you can determine *why* you are classifying and dividing students, causes, or pressures, then you'll have the basis for your audience analysis, your thesis statement, your method of arranging categories or parts, your choice of details, and your conclusions.

Do you want to teach and explain? If you're the announcer for the popular Westminster Kennel Club Dog Show, for instance, you'll no doubt need to explain to your viewing audience the reasons dogs are classified in certain ways. You may also want to give the history of a particular breed or tell something about previous winners in a particular category. These classifications help the viewing audience understand and enjoy the show better; the information also helps them make their own choice of a winning dog. Here is part of what the announcer for the 1998 Westminster show said:

> *Hound Dogs*
> Hounds were traditionally bred to help hunters track and course game. There are two divisions of this group: the sight hounds that hunt by sight and are speedy coursers with incredible flash and style, and the

scent hounds that hunt by smell alone. Hounds are generally soft, pleasant animals and many of them are top rated companions.

Sporting Dogs
   Originally bred to help man find and retrieve game, the dogs in the
sporting group have innate instincts in the water and in the woods. Point-
ers and Setters mark the game, Spaniels flush quarry so the hunter can
shoot, and the Retrievers recover the game after it has been shot. All of
these dogs are known for their keen sense of smell and soft mouths.

Toy Dogs
   Toy dogs are true companion animals. Their only task is to please
people and keep them company. Many of these breeds were long favored by royalty and were the very symbol of high style and taste. Despite their small size, many of them are first rate watchdogs, quick to announce the approach of strangers.

Clearly, what the announcer said to viewers was either an education in
or a reminder of the various classes of dogs, including information about
specific breeds, personality types, and work potential.

   If you want to please or entertain, and you are a famous writer, you
might find yourself classifying readers' questions to you, the way best–
selling author Stephen King did in an article published in the *New York
Times Book Review*. King classifies his readers' questions into three categories — (1) the "one–of–a–kind" questions, (2) the "old standards," and
(3) the "real weirdies" — and supplies examples for each. For instance, he
offers the following example of one–of–a–kind questions:

> There was . . . the young woman who wrote to me from a penal institu-
> tion in Minnesota. She informed me that she was a kleptomaniac. She
> further informed me that I was her favorite writer, and she had stolen
> every one of my books she could get her hands on. "But after I stole *Dif-*
> *ferent Seasons* from the library and read it, I felt moved to send it back,"
> she wrote. "Do you think this means you wrote this one the best?" After due
> consideration, I decided that reform on the part of the reader has nothing
> to do with artistic merit. I came close to writing back to find out if she had
> stolen *Misery* yet but decided I ought to just keep my mouth shut.
> — STEPHEN KING, "'Ever Et Raw Meat?' and Other Weird Questions"

(If you've read the book or seen the movie *Misery*, you'll know that it's a
scary tale about an author's "biggest fan," who kidnaps him and holds
him captive.) King goes on to supply examples of "old standards," which
he describes as the "questions that come up without fail in every dull interview the writer has ever given or will ever give":

> Where do you get your ideas? (I get mine in Utica.)
> How do you get an agent? (Sell your soul to the Devil.)
> Do you have to know somebody to get published? (Yes; in fact, it helps
>   to grovel, toady and be willing to perform twisted acts of sexual de-
>   pravity at a moment's notice, and in public if necessary.)

How do you start a novel? (I usually start by writing the number 1 in the
  upper right-hand corner of a clean sheet of paper.)
How do you write best sellers? (Same way you get an agent.)
How do you sell your book to the movies? (Tell them they don't want it.)
What time of day do you write? (It doesn't matter; if I don't keep busy
  enough, the time inevitably comes.)
Do you ever run out of ideas? (Does a bear defecate in the woods?)
Who is your favorite writer? (Anyone who writes stories I would have
  written had I thought of them first.)

When King gets to the third category, "the one that fascinates [him]
most," he is at his most playful:

> Here I am, bopping down the street, on my morning walk, when some
> guy pulls over in his pickup truck or just happens to walk by and says,
> "Hi, Steve! Writing any good books lately?" I have an answer for this;
> I've developed it over the years out of pure necessity. I say, "I'm taking
> some time off." I say that even if I'm working like mad, thundering down
> homestretch on a book. The reason *why* I say this is because no other an-
> swer seems to fit. Believe me, I know. In the course of the trial and error that
> has finally resulted in "I'm taking some time off," I have discarded about
> 500 other answers.
>   Having an answer for "You writing any good books lately?" is a good
> thing, but I'd be lying if I said it solves the problem of *what the question
> means.* It is this inability on my part to make sense of this odd query, which
> reminds me of that zen riddle — "Why is a mouse when it runs?" — that
> leaves me feeling mentally shaken and impotent. You see, it isn't just
> *one* question; it is a *bundle* of questions, cunningly wrapped up in one
> package.

King isn't setting out to educate or persuade us; we read his classifications for pure pleasure, laughing to ourselves that this world-famous author gets bugged by the language games his readers set up for him.

If you want to use classification and division in order to argue a
point, you'll want to treat the categories or parts in ways that encourage
people to adopt your point of view or change their behavior. Sociolinguist Deborah Tannen writes about seven "conversation traps" that men
and women get themselves into with the opposite sex: apologies, criticism, thank-yous, fighting, praise, complaints, and jokes. This essay was
first published in *Redbook,* a magazine for women in their twenties and
thirties. In the section on fighting, Tannen writes:

> Many men expect the discussion of ideas to be a ritual fight — explored
> through verbal opposition. They state their ideas in the strongest possible
> terms, thinking that if there are weaknesses someone will point them out,
> and by trying to argue against those objections, they will see how well
> their ideas hold up.
>   Those who expect their own ideas to be challenged will respond to
> another's ideas by trying to poke holes and find weak links — as a way

of *helping.* The logic is that when you are challenged you will rise to the occasion: Adrenaline makes your mind sharper; you get ideas and insights you would not have thought of without the spur of battle.

But many women take this approach as a personal attack. Worse, they find it impossible to do their best work in such a contentious environment. If you're not used to ritual fighting, you begin to hear criticism of your ideas as soon as they are formed. Rather than making you think more clearly, it makes you doubt what you know. When you state your ideas, you hedge in order to fend off potential attacks. Ironically, this is more likely to *invite* attack because it makes you look weak.

Although you may never enjoy verbal sparring, some women find it helpful to learn how to do it. An engineer who was the only woman among four men in a small company found that as soon as she learned to argue she was accepted and taken seriously. A doctor attending a hospital staff meeting made a similar discovery. She was becoming more and more angry with a male colleague who'd loudly disagreed with a point she'd made. Her better judgment told her to hold her tongue, to avoid making an enemy of this powerful senior colleague. But finally she couldn't hold it in any longer, and she rose to her feet and delivered an impassioned attack on his position. She sat down in a panic, certain she had permanently damaged her relationship with him. To her amazement, he came up to her afterward and said, "That was a great rebuttal. I'm really impressed. Let's go out for a beer after work and hash out our approaches to this problem. "   – DEBORAH TANNEN, "BUT WHAT DO YOU MEAN?"

Tannen offers the women in her audience advice on how to argue like men. She does not offer advice on how men can notice, be sensitive to, or adapt to the linguistic habits of women speakers. Her essay attempts to persuade or move women to adopt more forceful, less "nice" office language and to reinforce women who are already using these sociolinguistic strategies.

When you've determined your purpose (to inform or teach, to entertain, or to argue), you've come close to determining the **thesis statement** (the controlling idea) for your classification or division. In order to develop your thesis statement, you need to answer this question: what is my point, exactly, in devising this classification or division?

Considering Your Audience

As in every other kind of writing, you must consider your audience when using classification and division. Had Deborah Tannen submitted her essay on office language to *Esquire*, a magazine for men, chances are she'd have used the same categories but talked about them differently. As she pointed out differences between the ways men and women use and respond to language, she might have focused on the disappointments and frustrations men experience in talking with women. She probably would have demonstrated to her male readers the specific language habits they should change as well as ways to make those changes in order to have more productive conversations with their female colleagues.

When you're writing an essay based on classification and division, or using classification and division within an essay, be sure to consider your audience carefully. Decide who your readers are and how best to pitch your writing to those readers. For instance, if you're writing a column for the student newspaper that just sets out to inform readers about various kinds of restaurants on or near campus, you might decide to classify them on the basis of price. If your column is about where to go for a special occasion, however, you'll want to reenvision your readers as celebrants; therefore, you might want to make your classification more persuasive in purpose, describing upscale restaurants and clubs and their individual atmospheres and specialties. Audience analysis is closely related to purpose: as you consider *how* to achieve your purpose, you'll need to consider the effect these strategies will have on your readers.

Defining the Categories or Parts

To be successful, a classification or division must follow a **ruling principle** for the categories or parts—a uniform way of grouping the information. For example, the principle ruling the list of physicians in the Yellow Pages is their medical specialty. Under this principle, the list is *consistent*—every category is a medical specialty. It is *exclusive*—the listings don't overlap, and no physician is listed in more than one. And it is *complete*—every physician is listed.

When you set up categories and parts, you'll want to make sure to meet these three qualifications. For example, if you were writing the newspaper column about restaurants, you wouldn't want to mix categories such as "full meals under $10" and "full meals $10–20" with ones such as "Italian" and "informal." This classification is not consistent or exclusive; because the ruling principle is price for the first two categories, type of food for the third, and atmosphere for the fourth, a single restaurant could fall into two or even three categories. Any of these principles might work perfectly well for your column, but they can't be combined.

Or say that you were writing a paper for a political science class and making an argument based on a survey of students at your school about their political affiliation. If your survey covered only Republicans and Democrats, your classification would be incomplete and your argument would be weakened because some students are probably independents and supporters of the Green, Libertarian, or other smaller parties—not to mention those who have no interest in politics at all.

As this example suggests, we often tend to classify or divide things into only two opposing groups—black or white, male or female, conservative or liberal. Sometimes this is useful, but be careful not to oversimplify a classification or division by creating too few categories or parts.

● **Arranging All the Parts**

Of course, you need to keep all these considerations in mind as you draft an essay or passage using classification or division, but your purpose and your thesis statement, in particular, will actually determine the organizational pattern. You might find a good reason to move (1) chronologically; (2) logically, based on the way one category or part relates to the next; or (3) emphatically, starting with the least important category or part and ending with the most important—which could be the largest, the most complex, the most entertaining, or the most persuasive.

In a classification and division that extends over several paragraphs or a whole essay, you'll want to introduce each of the categories or parts with a **topic sentence** that not only reflects your thesis statement but also previews the ways you will develop that category or part. As you move from one category or part to the next, use **transitional words** or phrases that take the reader along with you: "How to give and take criticism is *another* conversation trap"; "*When you're back in your house* you're like the conductor of an orchestra."

The Stephen King excerpt (p. 282) about readers' questions is organized emphatically. King explains why in his introductory paragraph, which itself contains a two-part division:

> It seems to me that, in the minds of readers, writers actually exist to serve two purposes, and the more important may not be the writing of books and stories. The primary function of writers, it seems, is to answer readers' questions. These fall into three categories. The third is the one that fascinates me most, but I'll identify the other two first.

King makes clear the reason for his organizational pattern: he is saving his favorite question category for last.

The following example from a student essay is organized logically:

> There are four types of people when it comes to paying back credit cards. They are "store-in-drawers," "cash advancers," "minimum monthers," and "over-indulgers." The "store-in-drawers" keep their card or cards in a safe drawer somewhere and use them only in extreme emergencies. For example, they might use one in order to rent a car in the event that theirs is unusable. The "cash advancers" use their cards as an easier way to make purchases. Basically, what they do is use the bank's money to make purchases and then pay the bill in full when they receive it. . . . The "minimum monthers" use their cards . . . and pay back the minimum balance that the credit card company asks for. The remainder of their bill, which goes unpaid, is subject to interest. The "over-indulgers" use their credit cards for everything. These people get into major financial troubles.

The four categories of credit card users are organized in a logical sequence that is easy to follow, from those who use cards least to those
who use them most.

● **Providing Details**

The details and examples that you use in explaining each category or
part help keep your classification or division appropriately balanced,
consistent, and complete. For instance, if you're writing a newspaper column on various kinds of student eateries—on-campus, off-campus, and
private residential—you might want to include details from all types of
eating places on campus: the dormitories, the rathskeller, the fraternity
and sorority houses, the café run by the school of restaurant management, and so on. All the details also bring your categories to life.

The amount and kinds of details you need to provide depend on
your subject, your audience, and your purpose. For instance, you may
need to give more explanation or examples for categories or parts that
are larger, more complex, more important to your purpose, or less familiar to your readers. In any case, it's a good idea to vary the discussion of
different categories or parts just to avoid monotony, especially if there
are more than two or three of them.

Look at the King examples again (p. 282). He classifies readers' questions into three categories—the one-of-a-kind questions, the old standards, and the real weirdies—and provides detailed examples of each: an
anecdote about the first category, a list of the items in the second, and a
description of his feelings about the third. The names of his categories
are interesting, but it is the different kinds of detail with which he develops each category that bring his classification and division to life.

● **Considering Your Conclusion**

Why are you classifying or dividing this subject? What did your classification or division reveal to you? What do you want your readers to
know, understand, enjoy, or do as a result of reading it? As you consider
how to conclude your essay or passage using classification or division,
you'll need to ask yourself these questions. Don't merely restate the thesis. You can make your conclusion purposeful and effective by carrying
the thesis further and making an additional point.

Stephen King's conclusion to his essay about readers' questions
(p. 282) carries forward the tone of the essay yet also makes a point:

> Do I mind these questions? Yes . . . and no. Anyone minds questions that
> have no real answers and thus expose the fellow being questioned to be
> not a real doctor but a sort of witch doctor. But no one—at least no one

"Reading" and Using Visuals in Classification and Division

This chapter uses a number of visuals, from the Brother's Pizza menu (p. 270) and the *Consumer Reports* used car guide (pp. 274–75) to the following "Style Yourself a Star" layout from *Latina* magazine. Each of these visuals is a model of classification or division, yet they look different, have different purposes, and make different points. You also

Latina fashion

Style yourself a star

We put out a casting call to real mujeres who wanted to become their music idols. Here's how you can follow in their almost famous footsteps

Shakira chic

Carla Prudencio, 25, *model, co-owner of a body-jewelry company,* boliviana
Starry inspiration: "Shakira is a free spirit. So many things—her dual culture and love of rock—influence her. You see it in her style."
Latina style: We paired a fitted suede vest with embellished jeans and a coin belt. Carla was overcome with an impulse to belly-dance.
Get inspired: Wherever, whenever, but not to work. Wear this take on Shakira's rockera look to the club or the mall—never to *la oficina.*
Passport vest, $29. Parasuco jeans, $95. Coin belt, $20. Fantaseyes cuff (on her right wrist), $18. Arden B. cuff, $18. See Shopping Guide for details.

Esta modelo y empresaria boliviana de 25 años decidió vestirse como Shakira. "Es un espíritu libre y la influyen sus dos culturas. Se ve en su estilo", dice. Latina la vistió con jeans, chaleco de gamuza y cinturón de monedas.

Selena style

Paulina Marin, 21, *retail manager,* ecuatoriana
Starry inspiration: "Selena's best accessory was her confidence. She did her own thing, the way I like to do, and it was fabulous."
Latina style: Paulina pulls off her own fabulous interpretation in true Selena spirit—in a ruffled top, jeans, and the singer's favorite accent, a newsboy hat.
Get inspired: Ruffles too frilly? Try a simple button-down white shirt—knotted strategically to show a little tummy.
Parasuco top, $50. Frankie B. jeans, $115. XOXO mules, $74. H&M hoops, $4; hm.com. Mervyn's cap, $16. See Shopping Guide for details.

La administradora de ventas ecuatoriana se inspiró en el look de Selena. "El mejor accesorio de Selena era su confianza en sí misma," dice. La vestimos con una blusa de volantes fruncidos, jeans y una gorra de ala.

J. Lo cool

Mareesa Hernandez, 26, *publishing assistant,* puertorriqueña
Starry inspiration: "They say the clothes make a woman, but Jennifer Lopez makes the clothes. She's not afraid to show off her curves, and her style is so unpredictable."
Latina style: Mareesa says she "identifies with J. Lo's whole urban-sexy thing"—so we put her in a *curva*-hugging jumpsuit with cargo detailing. Sunglasses are a must!
Get inspired: If a one-piece doesn't suit you, try a cropped jacket and hip-hugging jeans.
Frankie B. jumpsuit, $187. Aviator glasses by Gloria Vanderbilt, $20. Viltraux earrings, $135. Avon necklace, $15. See Shopping Guide for details.

La asistente editorial puertorriqueña de 26 años se inspiró en J. Lo. "Ella no teme mostrar sus curvas y sus estilos son impredecibles," dice. La vestimos en un jumper de cintura baja y, claro, un par de espejuelos oscuros.

can use various kinds of visuals to enhance your own classifications and divisions, but to understand how to do so most effectively, you need to learn how to "read" visuals closely and critically the same way you do written classifications and divisions. Learning to do this kind of analysis will help you understand what kinds of visuals and what details and arrangements of them are most effective (and which ones are not effective) in achieving your purpose, appealing to your audience, and supporting the points you're making in your written text.

In every issue of *Latina* magazine, readers can study the feature entitled "Latina Fashion," which offers a classification of different looks that they may want to copy or adopt. For this issue, three "real *mujeres* [women]" were invited to demonstrate how to achieve three types of looks based on three famous Latina singers. The primary purpose of this classification is to explain, but it also entertains readers and makes an argument ("Style yourself") that they should try out one of the looks.

In this classification, the visuals are actually more important than the accompanying words, for the "real women" who want to look like Shakira, Selena, or J. Lo need visual information. In fact, notice that the pictures of the three "real women" are much larger than the ones of the three stars, reinforcing the message in large type at the top of the feature that readers can transform themselves into their idols. Notice also how the feature seems to be aimed mostly at English-speaking readers, with most of the text in English, but that it also appeals to Spanish speakers by mixing in some Spanish words with the English text and then by translating some of the text into Spanish at the bottom. Finally, different fonts and type sizes are used to set off the main heading; the introduction; the headings of the three "looks"; and the information about the three "real *mujeres*," the brands and prices of the clothing and accessories, and the Spanish translations.

As you prepare your own classifications and divisions, consider using visuals of some kind, reviewing the ones throughout this book in order to determine which kind might work best for your writing project. As you can see, visuals can emphasize or clarify points you want the reader to understand or agree with, or they can make your classification or division more entertaining. If you want to use visuals in writing for an academic assignment, it is a good idea to check with your instructor beforehand. You also need to consider whether to include labels or captions (if the visuals do not already include them) and whether to refer to the visuals in your written text or to let them stand on their own.

with a modicum of simple human kindness — resents questions from people who honestly want answers. And now and then someone will ask a really interesting question, like, Do you write in the nude? The answer — not generated by computer — is: I don't think I ever have, but if it works, I'm willing to try it.

In his conclusion, King manages to take seriously readers' questions that are genuinely serious. He also takes the opportunity to display his wit.

Understanding and Using Classification and Division

Analyzing Classification and Division

1. What did you learn from Roberto Suro's explanation of cantinas on p. 274 that you didn't already know? What did you learn about your own ability to translate place such as "cantinas" into words and categories?

2. **Working with another student,** write out the ruling principle and the consistent and exclusive categories that Suro uses. Discuss how his classification helps you both to understand and to appreciate Magnolia's nightlife. Be prepared to share your answers with the rest of your class.

3. **Working with one or two classmates,** discuss how Inez Peterson handles classification in the excerpt on p. 278. What is her ruling principle? What are her consistent and exclusive categories? Share your small group's responses with the rest of the class.

4. **Working with another student,** devise a brief, coauthored response to the Peterson excerpt on identity. What do the two of you think of Peterson's ideas? What issues did you think about as you read the excerpt? Have they ever occurred to you before? If so, when? Why do they seem important? How are your responses alike and different? Prepare a joint response to share with the rest of the class.

Planning and Writing Essays Using Classification and Division

1. Reread the Jerry Seinfeld excerpt on p. 276. He divides life into two categories or parts: staying in or going out. Imagine a third category of life, and make a list of activities and emotions that could help develop that third category.

2. Concentrate on the Deborah Tannen excerpt (p. 283). Circle all the references to women, and underline the references to men. Now rewrite the passage from a man's point of view, imagining how he feels in each situation and how the woman's behavior affects him. Use this rewriting as the basis for a two- to three-page essay that restates Tannen's classification and division from another point of view. Refer to the following guidelines for checking over the use of classification and division.

3. Look around the room at your classmates. In how many ways could you organize them? List at least three ruling principles you could use. What ultimate purpose would each principle serve? Choose one ruling

principle, and apply it by coming up with a list of categories. Are your categories complete? Are they exclusive? Using your findings, draft a three- to four-page classification essay, referring to "Checking Over the Use of Classification and Division."

4. How would you classify the dozen or so restaurants closest to your campus? What might be the purpose of such a classification? What other ruling principles can you think of to classify the same group of restaurants? Choose one ruling principle to develop into a three- to four-page essay. How does the ruling principle relate to your purpose? Be sure to refer to "Checking Over the Use of Classification and Division."

5. Using your notes from question 1, draft a three- to four-page essay in which you divide life into three categories or parts and develop each of them. Keep the following questions in mind as you draft: What is your purpose? your thesis statement? your ruling principle? your organizational pattern? What information does your conclusion provide beyond that provided in your introduction? As you draft and revise, refer to the following guidelines for checking over the use of classification and division.

✓ Checking Over the Use of Classification and Division

1. Why are you writing about this group of items, or this one item? What is your purpose? Does your thesis statement reflect that purpose?

2. Who is your audience? Have you taken your audience into consideration in defining parts or categories and providing details about them?

3. What is your ruling principle? Are your categories or parts consistent and exclusive, or is there overlap among them? Are they complete, or are there items or pieces that they don't cover? If you have only two categories or parts, are you oversimplifying?

4. How have you organized the categories or parts? Is the arrangement effective? Have you used topic sentences and transitional words or phrases to help the reader follow your points and move from one category or part to the next?

5. What details and examples have you provided for each category or part? Underline them. Do any categories or parts need more explanation? Do any have too much?

6. What does your classification or division show the reader? What is the point of your conclusion? Underline your conclusion. Does it merely restate the thesis, or does it make an additional point in an effective way?

7. Have you used any visuals as part of your classification or division? If so, do they help make your points more effectively? Do you need to add labels, captions, or references to the visuals in the text? If you have not used any visuals, should you?

READINGS

WILLIAM ZINSSER

College Pressures

William Zinsser (b. 1922) has taught at Yale University, worked at the *New York Herald Tribune,* contributed regularly to the *New Yorker, Life,* and other leading magazines, and written or edited over a dozen books on topics ranging from drama and music to sightseeing and writing. His *On Writing Well* (1980) is widely considered to be required reading for nonfiction writers. Among his recent books are *American Places: A Writer's Pilgrimage to 15 of This Country's Most Visited and Cherished Sites* (1992); *Inventing the Truth: The Art and Craft of Memoir* (1995); and *Writing about Your Life: A Journey into the Past* (2004). Besides teaching and writing, Zinsser has served as executive editor of the Book-of-the-Month Club.

In the following essay, which was first published in 1979 in *Country Journal* magazine, Zinsser classifies the pressures faced by college students, most of which he sees as stemming from students' need to succeed financially. He suggests that it is this need to prepare themselves for lives of financial security that keeps students from enjoying their youth, their current opportunities, and the pleasure of learning for learning's sake. As you read the following essay, keep track of how — and why — Zinsser classifies and divides college pressures.

> **Preview** Write for three minutes or so about the pressures you feel as a college student.

Dear Carlos: I desperately need a dean's excuse for my chem midterm which will begin in about 1 hour. All I can say is that I totally blew it this week. I've fallen incredibly, inconceivably behind.

Carlos: Help! I'm anxious to hear from you. I'll be in my room and won't leave it until I hear from you. Tomorrow is the last day for . . .

Carlos: I left town because I started bugging out again. I stayed up all night to finish a take home make-up exam and am typing it to hand in on the 10th. It was due on the 5th. P.S. I'm going to the dentist. Pain is pretty bad.

Carlos: Probably by Friday I'll be able to get back to my studies. Right now I'm going to take a long walk. This whole thing has taken a lot out of me.

Carlos: I'm really up the proverbial creek. The problem is I really *bombed* the history final. Since I need that course for my major . . .

Carlos: Here follows a tale of woe. I went home this weekend, had to help my Mom, & caught a fever so didn't have much time to study. My professor . . .

Carlos: Aargh! Nothing original but everything's piling up at once. To be brief, my job interview . . .

Hey Carlos, good news! I've got mononucleosis.

Who are these wretched supplicants, scribbling notes so laden with anxiety, seeking such miracles of postponement and balm? They are men and women who belong to Branford College, one of the twelve residential colleges at Yale University, and the messages are just a few of the hundreds that they left for their dean, Carlos Hortas—often slipped under his door at 4 A.M.—last year.

But students like the ones who wrote those notes can also be found on campuses from coast to coast—especially in New England and at many other private colleges across the country that have high academic standards and highly motivated students. Nobody could doubt that the notes are real. In their urgency and their gallows humor they are authentic voices of a generation that is panicky to succeed.

My own connection with the message writers is that I am master of Branford College. I live in its Gothic quadrangle and know the students well. (We have 485 of them.) I am privy to their hopes and fears—and also to their stereo music and their piercing cries in the dead of night ("Does anybody *ca-a-are?*"). If they went to Carlos to ask how to get through tomorrow, they come to me to ask how to get through the rest of their lives.

Mainly I try to remind them that the road ahead is a long one and that it will have more unexpected turns than they think. There will be plenty of time to change jobs, change careers, change whole attitudes and approaches. They don't want to hear such liberating news. They want a map—right now—that they can follow unswervingly to career security, financial security, Social Security, and, presumably, a prepaid grave.

What I wish for all students is some release from the clammy grip of the future. I wish them a chance to savor each segment of their education as an experience in itself and not as a grim preparation for the next step. I wish them the right to experiment, to trip and fall, to learn that defeat is as instructive as victory and is not the end of the world.

My wish, of course, is naive. One of the few rights that America does not proclaim is the right to fail. Achievement is the national god, venerated in our media—the million-dollar athlete, the wealthy executive—and glorified in our praise of possessions. In the presence of such a potent state religion, the young are growing up old.

I see four kinds of pressure working on college students today: economic pressure, parental pressure, peer pressure, and self-induced pressure. It is easy to look around for villains — to blame the colleges for charging too much money, the professors for assigning too much work, the parents for pushing their children too far, the students for driving themselves too hard. But there are no villains, only victims.

"In the late 1960s," one dean told me, "the typical question that I got   8
from students was 'Why is there so much suffering in the world?' or 'How can I make a contribution?' Today it's 'Do you think it would look better for getting into law school if I did a double major in history and political science, or just majored in one of them?'" Many other deans confirmed this pattern. One said: "They're trying to find an edge — the intangible something that will look better on paper if two students are about equal."

Note the emphasis on looking better. The transcript has become a sa-   9
cred document, the passport to security. How one appears on paper is more important than how one appears in person. *A* is for Admirable and *B* is for Borderline, even though, in Yale's official system of grading, *A* means "excellent" and *B* means "very good." Today, looking very good is no longer good enough, especially for students who hope to go on to law school or medical school. They know that entrance into the better schools will be an entrance into the better law firms and better medical practices where they will make a lot of money. They also know that the odds are harsh. Yale Law School, for instance, matriculates 170 students from an applicant pool of 3,700; Harvard enrolls 550 from a pool of 7,000.

It's all very well for those of us who write letters of recommendation   10
for our students to stress the qualities of humanity that will make them good lawyers or doctors. And it's nice to think that admission officers are really reading our letters and looking for the extra dimension of commitment or concern. Still, it would be hard for a student not to visualize these officers shuffling so many transcripts studded with *A*s that they regard a *B* as positively shameful.

The pressure is almost as heavy on students who just want to gradu-   11
ate and get a job. Long gone are the days of the "gentleman's C," when students journeyed through college with a certain relaxation, sampling a wide variety of courses — music, art, philosophy, classics, anthropology, poetry, religion — that would send them out as liberally educated men and women. If I were an employer I would rather employ graduates who have this range and curiosity than those who narrowly pursued safe subjects and high grades. I know countless students whose inquiring minds exhilarate me. I like to hear the play of their ideas. I don't know if they're getting *A*s or *C*s, and I don't care. I also like them as people. The country needs them, and they will find satisfying jobs. I tell them to relax. They can't.

Nor can I blame them. They live in a brutal economy. Tuition, room,   12
and board at most private colleges now comes to at least $7,000, not

counting books and fees.* This might seem to suggest that the colleges are getting rich. But they are equally battered by inflation. Tuition covers only 60 percent of what it costs to educate a student, and ordinarily the remainder comes from what colleges receive in endowments, grants, and gifts. Now the remainder keeps being swallowed by cruel costs—higher every year—of just opening the doors. Heating oil is up. Insurance is up. Postage is up. Health-premium costs are up. Everything is up. Deficits are up. We are witnessing in America the creation of a brotherhood of paupers—colleges, parents, and students, joined by the common bond of debt.

Today it is not unusual for a student, even if he works part time at 13 college and full time during the summer, to accrue $5,000 in loans after four years—loans that he must start to repay within one year after graduation. Exhorted at commencement to go forth into the world, he is already behind as he goes forth. How could he not feel under pressure throughout college to prepare for this day of reckoning? I have used "he" incidentally, only for brevity. Women at Yale are under no less pressure to justify their expensive education to themselves, their parents, and society. In fact, they are probably under more pressure. For although they leave college superbly equipped to bring fresh leadership to traditionally male jobs, society hasn't yet caught up with this fact.

Along with economic pressure goes parental pressure. Inevitably, the 14 two are deeply intertwined.

I see many students taking pre-medical courses with joyless tenacity. 15 They go off to their labs as if they were going to the dentist. It saddens me because I know them in other corners of their life as cheerful people.

"Do you want to go to medical school?" I ask them.   16

"I guess so," they say, without conviction, or "Not really."   17

"Then why are you going?"   18

"Well, my parents want me to be a doctor. They're paying all this 19 money and . . ."

Poor students, poor parents. They are caught in one of the oldest 20 webs of love and duty and guilt. The parents mean well; they are trying to steer their sons and daughters toward a secure future. But the sons and daughters want to major in history or classics or philosophy—subjects with no "practical" value. Where's the payoff on the humanities? It's not easy to persuade such loving parents that the humanities do indeed pay off. The intellectual faculties developed by studying subjects like history and classics—an ability to synthesize and relate, to weigh cause and effect, to see events in perspective—are just the faculties that make creative leaders in business or almost any general field. Still, many fathers would rather put their money on courses that point toward a specific

---

* *Note:* Zinsser's essay was published in 1979; the figures quoted for tuition and other expenses would be much higher today.

profession—courses that are pre-law, pre-medical, pre-business, or, as I sometimes heard it put, "pre-rich."

But the pressure on students is severe. They are truly torn. One part 21 of them feels obliged to fulfill their parents' expectations; after all, their parents are older and presumably wiser. Another part tells them that the expectations that are right for their parents are not right for them.

I know a student who wants to be an artist. She is very obviously an 22 artist and will be a good one—she has already had several modest exhibits. Meanwhile she is growing as a well-rounded person and taking humanistic subjects that will enrich the inner resources out of which her art will grow. But her father is strongly opposed. He thinks that an artist is a "dumb" thing to be. The student vacillates and tries to please everybody. She keeps up with her art somewhat furtively and takes some of the "dumb" courses her father wants her to take—at least they are dumb courses for her. She is a free spirit on a campus of tense students—no small achievement in itself—and she deserves to follow her muse.

Peer pressure and self-induced pressure are also intertwined, and 23 they begin almost at the beginning of freshman year.

"I had a freshman student I'll call Linda," one dean told me, "who 24 came in and said she was under terrible pressure because her roommate, Barbara, was much brighter and studied all the time. I couldn't tell her

". . . and give me good abstract-reasoning ability, interpersonal skills, cultural perspective, linguistic comprehension, and a high sociodynamic potential."

that Barbara had come in two hours earlier to say the same thing about Linda."

The story is almost funny—except that it's not. It's symptomatic of 25 all the pressures put together. When every student thinks every other student is working harder and doing better, the only solution is to study harder still. I see students going off to the library every night after dinner and coming back when it closes at midnight. I wish they could sometimes forget about their peers and go to a movie. I hear the clacking of typewriters in the hours before dawn. I see the tension in their eyes when exams are approaching and papers are due: "Will I get everything done?"

Probably they won't. They will get sick. They will get "blocked." They 26 will sleep. They will oversleep. They will bug out. Hey Carlos, help!

Part of the problem is that they do more than they are expected to 27 do. A professor will assign five-page papers. Several students will start writing ten-page papers to impress him. Then more students will write ten-page papers, and a few will raise the ante to fifteen. Pity the poor student who is still just doing the assignment.

"Once you have twenty or thirty percent of the student population 28 deliberating overexerting," one dean points out, "it's bad for everybody. When a teacher gets more and more effort from his class, the student who is doing normal work can be perceived as not doing well. The tactic works, psychologically."

Why can't the professor just cut back and not accept longer papers? 29 He can, and he probably will. But by then the term will be half over and the damage done. Grade fever is highly contagious and not easily reversed. Besides, the professor's main concern is with his course. He knows his students only in relation to the course and doesn't know that they are also overexerting in their other courses. Nor is it really his business. He didn't sign up for dealing with the student as a whole person and with all the emotional baggage the student brought along from home. That's what deans, masters, chaplains, and psychiatrists are for.

To some extent this is nothing new: a certain number of professors 30 have always been self-contained islands of scholarship and shyness, more comfortable with books than with people. But the new pauperism has widened the gap still further, for professors who actually like to spend time with students don't have as much time to spend. They also are overexerting. If they are young, they are busy trying to publish in order not to perish, hanging by their fingernails onto a shrinking profession. If they are old and tenured, they are buried under the duties of administering departments—as departmental chairmen or members of committees—that have been thinned out by the budgetary axe.

Ultimately it will be the students' own business to break the circles 31 in which they are trapped. They are too young to be prisoners of their parents' dreams and their classmates' fears. They must be jolted into believing in themselves as unique men and women who have the power to shape their own future.

"Violence is being done to the undergraduate experience," says Car- 32 los Hortas. "College should be open–ended: at the end it should open many, many roads. Instead, students are choosing their goal in advance, and their choices narrow as they go along. It's almost as if they think that the country has been codified in the type of jobs that exist — that they've got to fit into certain slots. Therefore, fit into the best–paying slot.

"They ought to take chances. Not taking chances will lead to a life of 33 colorless mediocrity. They'll be comfortable. But something in the spirit will be missing."

I have painted too drab a portrait of today's students, making them 34 seem a solemn lot. That is only half of their story; if they were so dreary I wouldn't so thoroughly enjoy their company. The other half is that they are easy to like. They are quick to laugh and to offer friendship. They are not introverts. They are usually kind and are more considerate of one another than any student generation I have known.

Nor are they so obsessed with their studies that they avoid sports 35 and extracurricular activities. On the contrary, they juggle their crowded hours to play on a variety of teams, perform with musical and dramatic groups, and write for campus publications. But this in turn is one more cause of anxiety. There are too many choices. Academically, they have 1,300 courses to select from; outside class they have to decide how much spare time they can spare and how to spend it.

This means that they engage in fewer extracurricular pursuits than 36 their predecessors did. If they want to row on the crew and play in the symphony they will eliminate one; in the '60s they would have done both. They also tend to choose activities that are self–limiting. Drama, for instance, is flourishing in all twelve of Yale's residential colleges as it never has before. Students hurl themselves into these productions — as actors, directors, carpenters, and technicians — with a dedication to create the best possible play, knowing that the day will come when the run will end and they can get back to their studies.

They also can't afford to be the willing slave of organizations like the 37 *Yale Daily News.* Last spring at the one–hundredth anniversary banquet of that paper — whose past chairmen include such once and future kings as Potter Stewart, Kingman Brewster, and William F. Buckley, Jr.* — much was made of the fact that the editorial staff used to be small and totally committed and that "newsies" routinely worked fifty hours a week. In effect they belonged to a club; Newsies is how they defined themselves at

---

* *Note:* Stewart is a former U.S. Supreme Court Justice; Brewster is a former president of Yale; and Buckley is a conservative editor and columnist.

Yale. Today's student will write one or two articles a week, when he can, and he defines himself as a student. I've never heard the word Newsie except at the banquet.

If I have described the modern undergraduate primarily as a driven 38 creature who is largely ignoring the blithe spirit inside who keeps trying to come out and play, it's because that's where the crunch is, not only at Yale but throughout American education. It's why I think we should all be worried about the values that are nurturing a generation so fearful of risk and so goal–obsessed at such an early age.

I tell students that there is no one "right" way to get ahead—that 39 each of them is a different person, starting from a different point and bound for a different destination. I tell them that change is a tonic and that all the slots are not codified nor the frontiers closed. One of my ways of telling them is to invite men and women who have achieved success outside the academic world to come and talk informally with my students during the year. They are heads of companies or ad agencies, editors of magazines, politicians, public officials, television magnates, labor leaders, business executives, Broadway producers, artists, writers, economists, photographers, scientists, historians—a mixed bag of achievers.

I ask them to say a few words about how they got started. The stu- 40 dents assume that they started in their present profession and knew all along that it was what they wanted to do. Luckily for me, most of them got into their field by a circuitous route, to their surprise, after many detours. The students are startled. They can hardly conceive of a career that was not pre-planned. They can hardly imagine allowing the hand of God or chance to nudge them down some unforeseen trail.

Reading Closely

1. How does Zinsser convince you that he knows what he's talking about? In other words, what qualifies him to write about student pressures? Mark all the passages that you think support Zinsser's qualifications and knowledge.

2. Does Zinsser's classification of college pressures seem applicable? List all the college pressures that have remained constant since Zinsser wrote his essay. Then make a list of any that are outdated. Finally, make a list of the pressures you now face that Zinsser couldn't have easily predicted. **Working with one or two classmates,** compare your answers. Prepare to report to the rest of the class on your group's ruling principle, categories, and detailed description of each category.

3. How does the cartoon on p. 296 complement Zinsser's classification of college pressures? How does it suggest differences from Zinsser's classification?

Considering Larger Issues

1. What is Zinsser's purpose in writing "College Pressures"? Who are the members of his audience? How are his purpose and audience connected? Write out your answers.

2. Identify Zinsser's thesis statement and his topic sentences. How does each of the topic sentences support or extend the thesis statement?

3. Zinsser writes from his own point of view, that of a faculty member. **Working with a classmate,** rewrite one of the paragraphs from a student's point of view. Be prepared to share your paragraph with your classmates.

4. **COMBINING METHODS.** How does Zinsser use *narration, description,* and *cause-and-consequence analysis* to support his argument? Mark the passages that use each of these methods of development. How does each passage contribute to the overall argument?

Thinking about Language

1. Use the context of the essay or your dictionary to define the following words. Be prepared to share your answers with the rest of the class.

supplicants (1)	synthesize (20)	codified (32)
gallows (2)	vacillates (22)	introverts (34)
privy (3)	muse (22)	blithe (38)
venerated (6)	symptomatic (25)	magnates (39)
exhorted (13)	pauperism (30)	circuitous (40)

2. What words and phrases does Zinsser use to move readers from one category to the next? Write them down.

Writing Your Own Essays Using Classification and Division

1. Referring to your answer for question 2 under "Reading Closely," respond to Zinsser's essay by writing for a few minutes about the various pressures you feel at college, including pressures that Zinsser does and does not mention. **Working with one or two classmates,** compare your responses. Where do they diverge? Read aloud some of your responses to see which ones the entire class shares and which ones are unique to one person. What categories would your class construct for "college pressures"?

   Use this information as the basis for a three- to four-page essay on pressures at your college. As you draft and revise, refer to the guidelines for checking over the use of classification and division on p. 291.

2. Zinsser writes about the intertwined economic, self-imposed, and parental pressures that students feel. What pressures do you feel—such as social, sexual, dietary, or religious—that don't necessarily have to do with your being a student? Draft a three- to four-page essay in which you classify and divide these other pressures and discuss the ways they intertwine. Refer to the guidelines for checking over the use of classification and division on p. 291.

CAROLYN FOSTER SEGAL

The Dog Ate My Disk, and Other Tales of Woe

● Carolyn Foster Segal is an English professor at Cedar Crest College in Allen-
town, Pennsylvania, where she specializes in American literature, poetry, creative writing, computer-enhanced English, and women's film. Her print publications include poems in *Buffalo Spree Magazine; Phoebe: A Journal of Feminist
Scholarship, Theory, and Aesthetics;* and *The Bucks County Writer.* The following essay
first appeared in the *Chronicle of Higher Education,* a newspaper for college faculty
and administrators, in 2000.

Preview What does the title tell you this essay is about? Do you have
any school-related excuses that are equivalent to a dog eating a disk?

Taped to the door of my office is a cartoon that features a cat explaining   1
to his feline teacher, "The dog ate my homework." It is intended as a gently humorous reminder to my students that I will not accept excuses for
late work, and it, like the lengthy warning on my syllabus, has had absolutely no effect. With a show of energy and creativity that would be
admirable if applied to the (missing) assignments in question, my students persist, week after week, semester after semester, year after year, in
offering excuses about why their work is not ready. Those reasons fall
into several broad categories: the family, the best friend, the evils of
dorm life, the evils of technology, and the totally bizarre.

The Family. The death of the grandfather/grandmother is, of   2
course, the grandmother of all excuses. What heartless teacher would
dare to question a student's grief or veracity? What heartless student
would lie, wishing death on a revered family member, just to avoid a
deadline? Creative students may win extra extensions (and days off) with
a little careful planning and fuller plot development, as in the sequence
of "My grandfather/grandmother is sick"; "Now my grandfather/grand-
mother is in the hospital"; and finally, "We could all see it coming—my
grandfather/grandmother is dead."

Another favorite excuse is "the family emergency," which (always)   3
goes like this: "There was an emergency at home, and I had to help my
family." It's a lovely sentiment, one that conjures up images of Louisa
May Alcott's little women rushing off with baskets of food and copies of
Pilgrim's Progress, but I do not understand why anyone would turn to my
most irresponsible students in times of trouble.

The Best Friend. This heartwarming concern for others extends   4
beyond the family to friends, as in, "My best friend was up all night and I
had to (a) stay up with her in the dorm, (b) drive her to the hospital, or

(c) drive to her college because (1) her boyfriend broke up with her, (2) she was throwing up blood [no one catches a cold anymore; everyone throws up blood], or (3) her grandfather/grandmother died."

At one private university where I worked as an adjunct, I heard an   5
interesting spin that incorporated the motifs of both best friend and dead relative: "My best friend's mother killed herself." One has to admire the cleverness here: A mysterious woman in the prime of her life has al-legedly committed suicide, and no professor can prove otherwise! And I admit I was moved, until finally I had to point out to my students that it was amazing how the simple act of my assigning a topic for a paper seemed to drive large numbers of otherwise happy and healthy middle-aged women to their deaths. I was careful to make that point during an off week, during which no deaths were reported.

The Evils of Dorm Life.   These stories are usually fairly pre-   6
dictable; almost always feature the evil roommate or hallmate, with my student in the role of the innocent victim; and can be summed up as fol-lows: My roommate, who is a horrible person, likes to party, and I, who am a good person, cannot concentrate on my work when he or she is partying. Variations include stories about the two people next door who were running around and crying loudly last night because (a) one of them had boyfriend/girlfriend problems; (b) one of them was throwing up blood; or (c) someone, somewhere, died. A friend of mine in graduate school had a student who claimed that his roommate attacked him with

"I loved those complex, uninhibited, sometimes erotic, tales with their ample dose of mystery and mayhem. Now they just say 'faulty disk' when they turn in a late paper."

From CABLE ON ACADEME by Carole Cable © 1994. By permission of the University of Texas Press.

a hammer. That, in fact, was a true story; it came out in court when the bad roommate was tried for killing his grandfather.

The Evils of Technology.   The computer age has revolutionized   7 the student story, inspiring almost as many new excuses as it has In-ternet businesses. Here are just a few electronically enhanced ex-planations:

- The computer wouldn't let me save my work.
- The printer wouldn't print.
- The printer wouldn't print this disk.
- The printer wouldn't give me time to proofread.
- The printer made a black line run through all my words, and I know you can't read this, but do you still want it, or wait, here, take my disk. File name? I don't know what you mean.
- I swear I attached it.
- It's my roommate's computer, and she usually helps me, but she had to go to the hospital because she was throwing up blood.
- I did write to the newsgroup, but all my messages came back to me.
- I just found out that all my other newsgroup messages came up under a diferent name. I just want you to know that its really me who wrote all those messages, you can tel which ones our mine because I didnt use the spelcheck! But it was yours truely :) Anyway, just in case you missed those messages or dont belief its my writting, I'll repeat what I sad: I thought the last movie we watched in clas was borring.

The Totally Bizarre.   I call the first story "The Pennsylvania Chain   8 Saw Episode." A commuter student called to explain why she had missed my morning class. She had gotten up early so that she would be wide awake for class. Having a bit of extra time, she walked outside to see her neighbor, who was cutting some wood. She called out to him, and he waved back to her with the saw. Wouldn't you know it, the safety catch wasn't on or was broken, and the blade flew right out of the saw and across his lawn and over her fence and across her yard and severed a tendon in her right hand. So she was calling me from the hospital, where she was waiting for surgery. Luckily, she reassured me, she had remem-bered to bring her paper and a stamped envelope (in a plastic bag, to avoid bloodstains) along with her in the ambulance, and a nurse was mailing everything to me even as we spoke.

That wasn't her first absence. In fact, this student had missed most of   9 the class meetings, and I had already recommended that she withdraw from the course. Now I suggested again that it might be best if she dropped the class. I didn't harp on the absences (what if even some of this story were true?). I did mention that she would need time to recuperate and that mak-ing up so much missed work might be difficult. "Oh, no," she said, "I can't

drop this course. I had been planning to go on to medical school and become a surgeon, but since I won't be able to operate because of my accident, I'll have to major in English, and this course is more important than
ever to me." She did come to the next class, wearing — as evidence of her recent trauma — a bedraggled Ace bandage on her left hand.

You may be thinking that nothing could top that excuse, but in fact I 10
have one more story, provided by the same student, who sent me a letter
to explain why her final assignment would be late. While recuperating
from her surgery, she had begun corresponding on the Internet with a
man who lived in Germany. After a one–week, whirlwind Web romance,
they had agreed to meet in Rome, to rendezvous (her phrase) at the
papal Easter Mass. Regrettably, the time of her flight made it impossible
for her to attend class, but she trusted that I — just this once — would accept late work if the pope wrote a note.

Reading Closely

1. What categories does Segal provide for students' excuses? Do these categories seem believable? What about the examples within each category?
2. After reading this essay, how do you think Segal handles late work in her
   own courses?
3. How do you think the teachers in the cartoon on p. 302 might handle
   late work in their courses? What details support your answer?

Considering Larger Issues

1. Who is the audience for this essay? What is Segal's purpose? How do her
   audience and purpose intersect?
2. What is Segal's tone in this essay? How is it related to her audience and
   purpose — and, more important, how is her tone appropriate to the topic?
3. Would Segal need to change the tone if she were writing to students taking her course? Why or why not? Explain. Rewrite one paragraph as
   though it were directed at students.
4. **COMBINING METHODS.** How does Segal use *definition, comparison and contrast,*
   and *cause-and-consequence analysis* to develop her argument? Mark the specific passages that use methods other than classification and division.
   Working with a classmate, compare your responses and prepare to
   report your findings to the rest of the class.

Thinking about Language

1. Use the context of the essay or your dictionary to define the following
   terms. Be prepared to share your answers with the rest of the class.

feline (1)	adjunct (5)	harp (9)
veracity (2)	motifs (5)	papal (10)

2. Refer to question 2 under "Considering Larger Issues." What specific words or phrases reflect Segal's tone? How would you rewrite any of those phrases to convey a more sympathetic tone?

Writing Your Own Essays Using Classification and Division

1. **Working with two or three classmates,** discuss the excuses you've each given teachers for late homework, absences, or other problems. Work together to group your excuses into categories, remembering to organize according to a ruling principle. Using your notes from this group activity, draft individual two- to three-page essays in which you recount the categories of and reasons for your excuses. Your audience will be other students, and your purpose will be to entertain. As you draft and revise, refer to the guidelines for checking over the use of classification and division on p. 291.

2. Reread Segal's essay, annotating her points as you read. Use your annotations as the basis for a three- to four-page classification-and-division essay about student excuses that speaks to teachers from a student's point of view. Your essay might focus on the ways teachers are unfeeling, unforgiving, or gullible—or sympathetic, tolerant, or fair and impartial in enforcing uniform deadlines for all students. Yours can be a positive, a neutral, or a defensive response to Segal. Refer to the guidelines for checking over the use of classification and division (p. 291) as you draft and revise.

JESSICA MOYER

My Circle of Friends

Jessica Moyer (b. 1976) was an English major at Penn State University when she wrote the following essay. A native Pennsylvanian, Moyer has worked part-time as a server in a popular restaurant during breaks from school as well as in a campus cafeteria. She has also volunteered at a women's shelter. She hopes to become either an English teacher or a counselor.

Preview As you read Moyer's essay, compare your circle of friends with hers. Is there any overlap? divergence?

As I sit here and think about the friends that I have had or do have in my life, I am amazed at the eclectic opportunities and diversities that each of my friendships has offered me, whether they were developed in high school, at college, or through work. I am a complex person with many different and sometimes seemingly contradictory personality traits, yet my personality as a whole can be divided into three very distinct but general categories: the academic side, the work side, and the social side. I seem to have one specific friend for each side of my personality, as well as a best friend who is in a category all her own. 1

At this point, my academic side makes up a huge part of my life. I attend college full-time and plan to continue my education when I graduate next December. Since I do take my academic side so seriously, the friends that I classify as my school friends must also have high academic standards for themselves. Tania, a friend from my writing class, will probably proofread this essay when I have finished writing it. As Tania and I are both English majors, we can sit for hours and discuss each other's fiction or poetry. I call Tania when I need to go to the library and want a study buddy. She has helped me with library research strategies as well as ideas for stories. We try to take the same classes so that we can help each other with notes and assignments. Tania and I have much in common when it comes to school and writing, but since Tania is a relatively new friend of mine, I am not really sure if she meshes with any other aspects of my personality. 2

As Tania helps me with academics, my co-worker Jeff really keeps my job fun. During summers and holidays, I go home to a waitressing job that provides the majority of my income. My co-workers and I socialize and get along while at work, but we do not spend time together outside the job. Since most of the people I work with are not in college and have the job year round, full-time, essentially the only thing that we have in common is our job. Our relationship consists of complaints about stingy tips and competitions to see who can sell the most shrimp popper appetizers in a four-hour period. When I run into Jeff outside of 3 work, I find that our conversation always ends up back at the restaurant. Jeff and I have completely different life goals and experiences, and we both recognize our friendship as work–related. Without Jeff to joke around with at work, I would not have the positive work environment that I do. On the other hand, Jeff is not the person I call when I want to study or socialize outside of work.

Unlike my work and academic sides, my social life can be broken   4 down further into different categories, each with a different set of friends exclusive to that category. The social "me" encompasses every activity I take part in outside of work and school, including partying, as well as athletics. As with those who represent the other aspects of my personality, the friends included in my social realm generally do not intermix with one another, unless they have common interests. Sometimes, however, they do intrude into other aspects of my life. For example, I find myself a bit tired today as a result of a 4 A.M. phone call from my friend Delmar in New York City. Although I love Delmar, he just does not understand that middle–of–the–night phone calls are not conducive to a productive academic Tuesday for me. Delmar, a guitarist in a punk rock band in New York City, definitely classifies as a "party" friend. Partying with Delmar can mean anything from dancing in clubs to just hanging out listening to music. I call Del when I want to get away to New York for a weekend break from school. Since his band schedule is so different from my school one, and I am so busy during the week, weekends are really the only time we can spend together.

Every weeknight finds me kickboxing, jogging, or lifting weights   5 since athletics is a very important part of my social activities. I definitely would not call Delmar if I wanted a friend to join me at the gym, but I would call my friend Zac, who is training for a marathon next month and devotes much of his free time to exercise. As a nutrition major and weightlifting expert, he offers me advice and knowledge that has been priceless to me in developing my own exercise regimen. On the flip side, Zac does not like to party, so he falls into my fitness category only. Do not get me wrong—Zac does like to have fun, but since his idea of fun (a pickup basketball game) and Del's idea of fun (all–night dancing) clash, I keep these two friends separate. I, on the other hand, enjoy pickup basketball games as well as all–night dancing, so I get along with both of them, just at different times.

In describing the classifications of my school, work, and social   6 friends, I have left my most complete and complex friend as the last and most important category. As my best friend, Becca not only shares my academic goals, but also relates with me on a social level. I met Becca my freshman year because she lived right across the hall from me in the dorm. The more we talked and got to know each other, the more we realized that we had much in common. We could go for a job together during the day and then get ready together for a party that night. We have different majors, but we both think that academics are important. My best friend encompasses so many of my own personality traits that she defies all my attempts to classify her.

As I speak of the different people whom I consider my friends, I realize   7 that they really have almost nothing in common with one another. If I threw a party and invited all my friends from the different aspects of my life, my work friends would huddle together, as would my academic friends and my social friends (with the exception of Zac, who probably would not show up). I find it necessary to classify my friends according to the different aspects of my life because they each have such distinct personalities. Except for Becca, I relate to each of them only in a very few ways.

I feel guilty sticking each one into a category, but it is important to   8 remember that these categories are not permanent barriers among my friends but only ways to organize my own mind. I think that having many diverse friendships is as important for my individual growth as having one friend who complements my total personality.

Reading Closely

1. What is the ruling principle of this essay? What are the categories of classification that Moyer uses?

2. How does Moyer use examples to explain each of her categories? What are the advantages and disadvantages of using one extended example for each category rather than several briefer ones?

3. What picture do you get of Moyer from her essay? What information does she include about herself that makes her like many other college students? What information makes her different from many others? How does her classification reveal the kind of person she is? **Working with two or three classmates,** compare your responses. Prepare a group response for the rest of the class.

4. What is Moyer's purpose in writing this essay?

Considering Larger Issues

1. How does Moyer's classification expand the meaning of the word *friends?* Do you agree with her approach? That is, do you think she has tried to apply the word to relationships that you wouldn't define as friendships?

2. Have you ever tried to classify your friends? If so, what were your purpose and your ruling principle? If not, can you think of a purpose and a ruling principle you might use to do so?

3. **COMBINING METHODS.** Mark the passages in which Moyer uses *narration* to make her point. Where does she use *comparison and contrast?* What about *cause-and-consequence analysis?* How do each of these methods contribute to her overall classification and division?

Thinking about Language

1. What words and phrases does Moyer use that give this essay a casual tone? Make a list, and then **compare lists with two or three class-mates.**

2. What might be Moyer's purpose for using a casual tone? What is the overall effect of this tone? What other tone might she have taken? to what effect? What words or phrases could she use to replace the ones that create a casual tone?

Writing Your Own Essays Using Classification and Division

1. Draft a three- to four-page essay in which you classify your friendships by using a ruling principle different from the one Moyer uses. You may want to classify your male friends and your female friends, your musical friends and your athletic friends. Or you might try classifying your friendships according to the different stages of your life (for example, childhood friends, teenage friends, and so on). Remember that "Checking Over the Use of Classification and Division" can be found on p. 291.

2. How do you imagine your circle of friends classifies you? Where might you fit within the categories of friendship each of them may devise? Draft a three- to four-page essay in which you classify yourself in this way, writing either from your own point of view or from the point of view of one or more of your friends. As you draft and revise, refer to the guidelines for checking over the use of classification and division on p. 291.

3. How are friends classified and divided on popular television shows such as *Will and Grace, That '70s Show,* and *Friends*? Draft a three- to four-page essay in which you classify television friends. As you draft and revise, refer to the guidelines for checking over the use of classification and division on p. 291.

LAURA SESSIONS STEPP

Alpha Girl: In Middle School, Learning to Handle the ABCs of Power

Pulitzer Prize–winning writer Laura Sessions Stepp (b. 1951) has been writing and speaking about children and families for over a decade. She has played a key role in the White House Conference on Raising Responsible Teenagers; the U.S. Surgeon General's Heathy People 2000 panel on adolescence; the Board on Children, Youth, and Families, at the National Academy of Sciences; and the Casey Journalism Center on Children and Families at the University of Maryland. Specializing in adolescence topics for the "Style" section of the *Washington Post,* where "Alpha Girl" was originally published in 2002, Stepp published the book *Our Last Best Shot: Guiding Our Children through Early Adolescence* in 2000.

> **Preview**   Think back to middle school. What might an "alpha girl" be?

The seventh-grade alpha female slides a size-zero body into her designated spot in the school cafeteria, her perfect blond hair swinging across her shoulders like a 1960s Breck girl's. A half-dozen ladies-in-waiting assume seats around her as she leans over to whisper something to her favorite of the moment.

Whitney Bullock, seated at a another seventh-grade table several rows away, takes it all in with a grimace.

"Do you see how she cups her hand around her mouth so when she talks?" Whitney asks, mimicking the hand gesture she knows well. "That means she's talking about someone, saying something that probably is not very nice."

Whitney, of the broad shoulders and wiry black hair, has been snubbed more than once by this girl. If you're a woman reading this, you can feel her pain.

If you're a man, you probably don't have a clue.

With all the debate among professionals over girls as victims, very few people talk about this: In middle school, girls have the only power that counts at that moment, social power. These alphas — named after the first letter in the Greek alphabet — are the brightest stars in their constellation, defining life as the young teen knows it. They decide that American Eagle shirts are what you wear with jeans, Dasani water is what you drink at lunch, Jen is persona non grata at their lunchroom table and Brittany must ask Adam to Courtney's party.

They hang over guys at school and telephone guys at home at night, becoming increasingly direct as they get older. Girl or guy, you don't dare get in their way because they can slice you up with a word or a look.

Kids both rely on and resent them, and primatologist Jane Goodall would spot them in a minute.

Although alpha females can be found among many species in many 8 habitats, Goodall was one of the first scientists to identify them among chimpanzees in Tanzania. She shocked gender theorists in the 1960s with the finding that some female chimps kill the young of other females in an effort to maintain their dominant position in the troops.

Since then, primate experts have discovered females among other 9 ape types who lead by cooperation rather than intimidation — the bonobos, for example. In any middle school cafeteria today you'll see examples of this type also, and there's some reason to believe these girls are on the rise. But let's stick with alphas for the moment.

Alphas have been around forever, assuming their thrones based on 10 beauty, dress, family or sheer force of personality. Back when girls didn't or couldn't compete with boys in the classroom and on the playing field, pubescent alpha females learned at their mother's knee a roundabout route to power that they then passed on to their daughters. Hollywood captured them on-screen in movies such as *Heathers* in 1989 and 1997's *Romy and Michele's High School Reunion*.

What we most remember is their power to exclude.   11

Lauren Kepple, a freshman at American University, knew a girl 12 named Stephanie in fifth grade. "I had just been moved into a class for gifted kids and was assigned a locker next to Stephanie's," she recalls. "She said something that made me feel I was not good enough."

Alphas, she says, "zero in on your biggest failing. If you have weight 13 issues, they'll go right to your weight."

Lauren's friend Meredith McGloin, another AU student, says, "I've 14 never seen guys be so cruel." Her reaction to the alpha girls in middle school? "To go off in my corner and read books. I was going to shut them out before they shut me out."

Goritza Ninova, 16, recently moved to Northern Virginia from Bul- 15 garia and knows all about alphas. Sipping cappuccino at the Pentagon City Mall, dressed in a zipped-up cardigan, jeans and chunky black shoes from her native country, she describes the alphas there, starting at age 11 or so.

"They wear tight jeans, tight, low-cut shirts and lots of makeup. 16 When they walk by a guy, they move their butts just so. They think they can get anything or anyone they want." There's a Bulgarian word for them, she says: *tarikatka*. In Bulgaria, a tarikatka went after Goritza's boyfriend. "She was so self-confident. I was scared," Goritza recalls. Fortunately, "she scared my boyfriend as well."

Girls flout the wishes of an alpha at their peril. Tegan Hendrickson, a 17 senior at Thomas S. Wootton High School in Rockville, fell out of favor with Jenny in seventh grade. Before she knew it, Jenny's friends started a whisper campaign that Tegan, who liked to wear black clothes, was a Satanist.

"People would come up to me and tell me to go to hell, then laugh," 18
she remembers. "I'd say, 'Been there. Done that. Want a reference?' It was pretty cruel."

THE WANNA BETAS

Tegan is a beta, and no one knows an alpha like a beta, the second 19
Greek letter, the second–brightest star. Betas usually make better grades than alphas. They run faster in track and play a sweet violin. Parents tell them they're wonderful just the way they are, even if they don't think they're as pretty as the alphas. Teachers tell them their personalities are changing, that the label that applies to them right now may not apply next year or the year after that.

All they want to be in middle school, however, is an alpha. Whitney 20
Bullock is an example.

This is Whitney's first year at E. H. Marsteller, a Manassas school of 21
1,000 students in grades six through eight. Arriving a year after everyone else was difficult, especially during lunchtime, the main event each day.

"I'd head over to one table and see one of the popular girls and 22
think, 'Oh, I better not sit there. I might say something stupid.' Then I'd head toward another and the same thing would happen."

Finally, at her brother's school's football game, she found a classmate 23
she thought would be a friend.

She and the girl were the only kids from Marsteller. They shared a 24
slice of pizza. At school the following Monday, Whitney approached her girl in a hall between classes with a big smile.

"Hi!" she said. The girl, standing with some other girls, mumbled a 25
greeting and turned back to her friends. Whitney got the message and slid away.

Undeterred, she sought out the girl at the next several Saturday 26
games, and again, the girl couldn't have been more friendly. They continued to share food on the bleachers, and Whitney met the girl's family. On school days, however, she got the cold shoulder, occasionally accompanied by a glare.

"She made made me feel really self-conscious about who I am," 27
Whitney says.

Alphas have a way of doing that, their smugness often mistaken for 28
self–esteem. Recently in music class, another popular girl asked if she could cheat off Whitney's paper during a test. Whitney, stalling, asked her why she wanted to.

"Because I'm really good at it," the girl replied. 29

"It took me a while to say no," Whitney says. "The thought kept run- 30
ning through my head that if I say yes, she'll like me and maybe I'll be

popular." Whitney turned her down, and later a friend heard the girl
bragging that she had cheated off Whitney's paper anyway.

Whitney admits she's done some things to try to fit in with the al- 31
phas. She has cussed like they do (not in front of her teachers, of course;
a beta would never do that). When alphas say something about someone, she acts as if she knows what they're talking about even though she
doesn't have a clue. At home she has a closet full of shirts that, until recently, she didn't wear because she was afraid the alphas wouldn't like
them.

But after her experience on the football bleachers, she took out a 32
couple of those shirts to wear. The more she watched the alphas, the
more it seemed they didn't care about the things she did, and she realized that she cared about things like her reputation and her grades.

She tells herself that she learned from the girl who shunned her. 33
"Now I'm careful whom I'm friends with. I won't change myself just so
someone will like me."

Who is that self? The beta thinks about that question a lot. On 34
some mornings before school, Whitney stands in front of a mirror
and, following the advice of a teen magazine, tries to come up with five
things she likes about herself. When telling this story, she can think of
three.

"I have power inside," she says, "but it's hard for me to see it as 35
clearly in myself as I see it in other girls."

Just wait a few years, Tegan Hendrickson would tell Whitney from 36
her vantage point of five more years. Tegan is president of Wootton's film
club, which nominated her for the Miss Wootton contest this month, a
spoof on Miss America designed to raise money. She didn't make it to
the finals—betas rarely do—and was a bit put out, but not overly so.
She has come to terms with the fact that she is different from a lot of the
girls at Wootton.

She loves Latin and history and musicals. She uses big words when 37
she speaks, her conversation pouring forth as rapidly as white water. She
wears her hair short and dyed red.

It's not that alphas don't bother her. This year several of them moved 38
into her area, drama, acting superior to the crew and to those in each
cast who don't play starring roles.

"This one girl acts like she's always right and can do no wrong. She 39
bosses us around when we're working, then avoids us out of class. It's really irksome," she says. "They get this whole attitude thing when they
don't get their way."

Betas such as Tegan know something the alphas don't, something 40
the betas learn from *their* mothers. Alphas can flame out eventually.
The cheerleader may marry the quarterback, but five years later she either dumps him or gets dumped and goes to work as a night-shift

cashier at Swill–Mart. Meanwhile, the lesser stars learn to fly airplanes and practice law.

A BETTER LETTER

Along the way, betas may evolve into the third type of girl, a girl 41 who rules based not on what she appears to be but on what she does. This girl isn't easily labeled because her role is changing as women's roles change. We'll call her a gamma, the third letter of the Greek alpha–bet, known in science as being one of three or more closely related chemical substances. The designation seems appropriate because produc–tive and task–oriented relationship–building is one thing that distin–guishes gammas from alphas.

"They're someone everyone says is a friend," says AU student Lauren 42 Kepple.

Older women remember this type, though there weren't as many 43 gammas in earlier generations as there are now. Gammas used to be the student council vice president and co–editor of the yearbook. Nowadays, they are elected president and vice president, assisted by other gammas who crank out the election posters. They have influence onstage and off, and, thanks to the new world order that followed Title IX, they know they don't have to manipulate and posture to acquire it.

They've watched their sisters graduate from Princeton, their moms go 44 to work and television's Buffy slay vampires. They've seen Mia Hamm kick a soccer ball and Reese Witherspoon graduate from Harvard in the popular movie *Legally Blonde*, befriending everyone along the way.

They are careful listeners, easy to talk to and laugh with, and Jessi 45 Reedy, one of Whitney Bullock's classmates at Marsteller, is practicing to be one. "I jump from group to group," she says. "At lunch, I'll just grab a couple of kids to sit with. If I see someone sitting by herself, I'll usually go up to her."

It's not that gammas don't like being center stage. Jessi admits she 46 loved the notice she received for wearing a watch to school that she had gotten from a package of Lucky Charms cereal. "I'm expected to do things like that," she says, having an alpha moment.

Yet gammas characteristically talk about activities they're doing for 47 others, not for themselves. Alpha power "is all about me," says Abbey Race, student government president at Marsteller. "Leadership is about representing something or someone else."

Gammas start coming into their own in high school, and one of the 48 first things they learn is that it's not easy to cultivate leadership and stay agreeable.

Donna Lin, a gamma senior athlete at Rockville's Wootton, says that 49 back in first grade, she was the kid in her neighborhood who would say,

"Let's go outside and play," and everyone did. Now she has to choose her words carefully. In volleyball at Wootton, a sport at which she shines, "if someone was playing badly, I don't think I'd say, 'You suck.' I'd probably say something like, 'It looks like you're tired, but I know you can do this.'"

They love details, these gammas, and plan circles around anyone 50 else, including the boys. Exhibit A is Wootton's senior planning commit- tee. It's made up of 27 students chosen by their teachers: four boys and 23 girls.

Senior Brian Footer, who isn't on the committee, suspects he knows 51 why it is so overwhelmingly female.

"These girls are goal–oriented and headstrong," he says. "Guys are lazy, 52 I guess, or they don't care, or they're not thinking about that stuff yet."

Mix alphas and gammas together, as school organizations like Woot– 53 ton's senior committee inevitably do, and it sometimes can be hard to tell the difference between the two. These girls are still, after all, trying on different selves like they would new clothes.

At one point in a meeting just days before the Miss Wootton contest, 54 three girls on the committee had their hands up, two girls were talking at one time and senior class President Joyce Fu, a slightly built, soft–spoken girl, stood silently at the lectern. Committee members have been known to yell at one another, even make one another cry.

The burden on the gamma can be heavy. Another gamma, Kristin 55 Smart, president of Wootton's student council, sympathizes with Joyce. "Some girls just don't know when to stop," she says. At student council meetings, "I sometimes feel like a kindergarten teacher having to separate the children."

Wootton Principal Rebecca Newman has no tolerance for such be– 56 havior at the 2,000–student school. "You're the role models for this school," she tells student leaders. "You better do it right, because if you don't, I'm in your face."

You wouldn't know it now by looking at Newman, an outspoken, 57 power–suited lead dog, but she started life as a beta. Adopted by loving but extremely poor parents, she says she spent most of her kindergarten year under her teacher's desk, hiding from the rest of the kids.

Maybe that's why she has a special place in her heart for gammas 58 who are cultivating their own brand of power. She has worked hard to move them beyond personality, hiring faculty members who encourage them to take science and play sports. Girls now make up half of Woot– ton's science classes and half of the athletes, she says with pride. Last year, the largely female senior leadership produced an outdoor rock fes- tival that raised $25,000 so that a dying boy could visit Australia.

Yet too many Wootton girls still don't understand that lasting power 59 comes from paying attention to issues of substance, she says. In other words, there are too many alphas.

For those girls, she says, "it's still who you're dating, or who said 60 something cutting to whom. We've got to move beyond that, get them to see there is so much more."

Reading Closely

1. How does Stepp classify middle school girls? What qualities does she include for each class of girls?
2. What specific examples does Stepp include for each class of girls?
3. Which of Stepp's categories do you think the girls in the photograph on p. 313 fit into? Why do you think so?

Considering Larger Issues

1. Are there male equivalents to the alpha girls? beta girls? gamma girls? What might they be — and what might their qualities be?
2. **Together with two or three classmates,** discuss how you think young girls develop into alpha girls, beta girls, or gamma girls.
3. What might parents do to help their daughters develop into (or prevent them from developing into) one of these categories? Be specific, and be prepared to share your response with the rest of the class.
4. What is Stepp's purpose in making this classification? Is she just trying to describe certain behavior? Or is she making an argument — and if so, what is it?
5. Whom does Stepp seem to think of as her readers? How much does she assume they know about teenage girls? How can you tell?
6. COMBINING METHODS. How does Stepp use *narration* as part of her classification and division of middle school girls? Mark the passages where she does so, and explain how they contribute to her analysis.

Thinking about Language

1. Using the context of the essay or your dictionary, define the following terms. Be prepared to share your answers with the rest of the class.

   size–zero (1)   pubescent (10)   smugness (28)
   grimace (2)   cappuccino (15)   lasting power
   persona non grata (6)   flout (17)   (59)
   primatologist (7)   undeterred (26)
   gender theorists (8)   sought out (26)

2. Stepp uses "alpha," "beta," and "gamma" as categories. How appropriate do you find these terms, based on animal behavior, for groups of teenage girls? Can you think of another name to describe each category? Be prepared to share your answers with the rest of the class.

Writing Your Own Essays Using Classification and Division

1. Stepp refers to Jane Goodall's work with primates, comparing some aggressive chimps with alpha girls and bonobos with cooperative, or gamma, girls. In an essay of three to four pages, classify teenage girl or boy behavior according to another set of animal equivalents. You might do some research to find visuals that illustrate your categories. **Ask a classmate to respond to your draft,** and be sure to refer to the guidelines for checking over the use of classification and division on p. 291.

2. Stepp's article suggests that many middle school girls "grow out of" certain behaviors and change categories as they grow older. Draft a three- to four-page essay in which you distinguish middle school students from both high school and college students by the different attitudes or behavioral patterns of the three groups. Be sure to include some examples of individuals you've known (including yourself, if you choose) who have changed noticeably since middle school. Or if you think most individuals don't change significantly as they mature, choose an individual and divide up his or her life into various parts—such as school, family, friendships, romantic relationships—to show how his or her basic personality or approach to life remains constant from one part to the next. Refer to the guidelines for checking over the use of classification and division on p. 291.

STEPHANIE ERICSSON
The Ways We Lie

San Francisco native Stephanie Ericsson (b. 1953) has published widely — and for many years. But she is probably best known for her four autobiographical books, the first two of which focus on her recovery from addiction — *Shamefaced: The Road to Recovery* and *Women of AA: Recovering Together* (both in 1985) — and the last two on her eventual recovery from her husband's sudden death — *Companion through the Darkness: Inner Dialogues on Grief* (1993) and *Companion into the Dawn: Inner Dialogues on Loving* (1994).

"The Ways We Lie" first appeared in 1992 in *Utne Reader*, a magazine that covers a wide range of social, political, and lifestyle topics. Ericsson's essay was the cover story for an issue focused on the political ramifications of questions surrounding the honesty of public figures (such as President Bill Clinton, then newly elected, and Anita Hill, who had recently accused Supreme Court nominee Clarence Thomas of sexual harassment). It was reprinted in *Companion into the Dawn.*

Preview   Do you ever lie? When? What kinds of lies do you tell?

The bank called today and I told them my deposit was in the mail, even 1
though I hadn't written a check yet. It'd been a rough day. The baby I'm pregnant with decided to do aerobics on my lungs for two hours, our three–year–old daughter painted the living–room couch with lipstick, the IRS put me on hold for an hour, and I was late to a business meeting because I was tired.

I told my client that traffic had been bad. When my partner came 2
home, his haggard face told me his day hadn't gone any better than mine, so when he asked, "How was your day?" I said, "Oh, fine," knowing that one more straw might break his back. A friend called and wanted to take me to lunch. I said I was busy. Four lies in the course of a day, none of which I felt the least bit guilty about.

We lie. We all do. We exaggerate, we minimize, we avoid confronta- 3
tion, we spare people's feelings, we conveniently forget, we keep secrets, we justify lying to the big–guy institutions. Like most people, I indulge in small falsehoods and still think of myself as an honest person. Sure I lie, but it doesn't hurt anything. Or does it?

I once tried going a whole week without telling a lie, and it was par- 4
alyzing. I discovered that telling the truth all the time is nearly impossible. It means living with some serious consequences: The bank charges me $60 in overdraft fees, my partner keels over when I tell him about my travails, my client fires me for telling her I didn't feel like being on time, and my friend takes it personally when I say I'm not hungry. There must be some merit to lying.

319

But if I justify lying, what makes me any different from slick politi-   5
cians or the corporate robbers who raided the S&L industry? Saying it's
okay to lie one way and not another is hedging. I cannot seem to escape
the voice deep inside me that tells me: When someone lies, someone
loses.

What far-reaching consequences will I, or others, pay as a result of   6
my lie? Will someone's trust be destroyed? Will someone else pay *my*
penance because I ducked out? We must consider the *meaning of our actions.* Deception, lies, capital crimes, and misdemeanors all carry meanings. *Webster's* definition of *lie* is specific:

> 1: a false statement or action especially made with the intent to de-
> ceive;
>
> 2: anything that gives or is meant to give a false impression.

A definition like this implies that there are many, many ways to tell a   7
lie. Here are just a few.

THE WHITE LIE

A man who won't lie to a woman has very little consideration for her
feelings.   — BERGEN EVANS

The white lie assumes that the truth will cause more damage than a   8
simple, harmless untruth. Telling a friend he looks great when he looks
like hell can be based on a decision that the friend needs a compliment
more than a frank opinion. But, in effect, it is the liar deciding what is
best for the lied to. Ultimately, it is a vote of no confidence. It is an act of
subtle arrogance for anyone to decide what is best for someone else.

Yet not all circumstances are quite so cut-and-dried. Take, for in-   9
stance, the sergeant in Vietnam who knew one of his men was killed in
action but listed him as missing so that the man's family would receive
indefinite compensation instead of the lump-sum pittance the military
gives widows and children. His intent was honorable. Yet for twenty
years this family kept their hopes alive, unable to move on to a new life.

FAÇADES

Et tu, Brute?   — CAESAR

We all put up façades to one degree or another. When I put on a suit   10
to go to see a client, I feel as though I am putting on another face, obeying the expectation that serious businesspeople wear suits rather than
sweatpants. But I'm a writer. Normally, I get up, get the kid off to school,
and sit at my computer in my pajamas until four in the afternoon. When
I answer the phone, the caller thinks I'm wearing a suit (though the UPS
man knows better).

But façades can be destructive because they are used to seduce oth- 11
ers into an illusion. For instance, I recently realized that a former friend
was a liar. He presented himself with all the right looks and the right
words and offered lots of new consciousness theories, fabulous books to
read, and fascinating insights. Then I did some business with him, and
the time came for him to pay me. He turned out to be all talk and no
walk. I heard a plethora of reasonable excuses, including in-depth descriptions of the big break around the corner. In six months of work, I
saw less than a hundred bucks. When I confronted him, he raised both
eyebrows and tried to convince me that I'd heard him wrong, that he'd
made no commitment to me. A simple investigation into his past revealed a crowded graveyard of disenchanted former friends.

IGNORING THE PLAIN FACTS

Well, you must understand that Father Porter is only human.
— A MASSACHUSETTS PRIEST

In the '60s, the Catholic Church in Massachusetts began hearing 12
complaints that Father James Porter was sexually molesting children.
Rather than relieving him of his duties, the ecclesiastical authorities simply moved him from one parish to another between 1960 and 1967, actually providing him with a fresh supply of unsuspecting families and
innocent children to abuse. After treatment in 1967 for pedophilia, he
went back to work, this time in Minnesota. The new diocese was aware
of Father Porter's obsession with children, but they needed priests and
recklessly believed treatment had cured him. More children were abused
until he was relieved of his duties a year later. By his own admission,
Porter may have abused as many as a hundred children.

Ignoring the facts may not in and of itself be a form of lying, but 13
consider the context of this situation. If a lie is *a false action done with the intent to deceive*, then the Catholic Church's conscious covering for Porter created irreparable consequences. The church became a co-perpetrator with
Porter.

DEFLECTING

When you have no basis for an argument, abuse the plaintiff.   — CICERO

I've discovered that I can keep anyone from seeing the true me by 14
being selectively blatant. I set a precedent of being up-front about intimate issues, but I never bring up the things I truly want to hide; I just let
people assume I'm revealing everything. It's an effective way of hiding.

Any good liar knows that the way to perpetuate an untruth is to de- 15
flect attention from it. When Clarence Thomas exploded with accusations

that the Senate hearings were a "high–tech lynching," he simply switched the focus from a highly charged subject to a radioactive subject. Rather than defending himself, he took the offensive and accused the country of racism. It was a brilliant maneuver. Racism is now politically incorrect in official circles—unlike sexual harassment, which still rewards those who can get away with it.

Some of the most skilled deflectors are passive–aggressive people 16
who, when accused of inappropriate behavior, refuse to respond to the accusations. This you–don't–exist stance infuriates the accuser, who, understandably, screams something obscene out of frustration. The trap is sprung and the act of deflection successful, because now the passive–aggressive person can indignantly say, "Who can talk to someone as unreasonable as you?" The real issue is forgotten and the sins of the original victim become the focus. Feeling guilty of name–calling, the victim is fully tamed and crawls into a hole, ashamed. I have watched this fighting technique work thousands of times in disputes between men and women, and what I've learned is that the real culprit is not necessarily the one who swears the loudest.

OMISSION

The cruelest lies are often told in silence.   – R. L. STEVENSON

Omission involves telling most of the truth minus one or two key facts 17
whose absence changes the story completely. You break a pair of glasses that are guaranteed under normal use and get a new pair, without mentioning that the first pair broke during a rowdy game of basketball. Who hasn't tried something like that? But what about omission of information that could make a difference in how a person lives his or her life?

For instance, one day I found out that rabbinical legends tell of an– 18
other woman in the Garden of Eden before Eve. I was stunned. The omission of the Sumerian goddess Lilith from Genesis—as well as her demonization by ancient misogynists as an embodiment of female evil— felt like spiritual robbery. I felt like I'd just found out my mother was really my stepmother. To take seriously the tradition that Adam was created out of the same mud as his equal counterpart, Lilith, redefines all of Judeo–Christian history.

Some renegade Catholic feminists introduced me to a view of Lilith 19
that had been suppressed during the many centuries when this strong goddess was seen only as a spirit of evil. Lilith was a proud goddess who defied Adam's need to control her, attempted negotiations, and when this failed, said adios and left the Garden of Eden.

This omission of Lilith from the Bible was a patriarchal strategy to 20
keep women weak. Omitting the strong–woman archetype of Lilith from Western religions and starting the story with Eve the Rib has helped keep

Christian and Jewish women believing they were the lesser sex for thousands of years.

STEREOTYPES AND CLICHÉS

Where opinion does not exist, the status quo becomes stereotyped and all
originality is discouraged.   —BERTRAND RUSSELL

Stereotype and cliché serve a purpose as a form of shorthand. Our 21
need for vast amounts of information in nanoseconds has made the
stereotype vital to modern communication. Unfortunately, it often shuts
down original thinking, giving those hungry for the truth a candy bar of
misinformation instead of a balanced meal. The stereotype explains a situation with just enough truth to seem unquestionable.

All the "isms"—racism, sexism, ageism, et al.—are founded on and 22
fueled by the stereotype and the cliché, which are lies of exaggeration,
omission, and ignorance. They are always dangerous. They take a single
tree and make it a landscape. They destroy curiosity. They close minds
and separate people. The single mother on welfare is assumed to be
cheating. Any black male could tell you how much of his identity is
obliterated daily by stereotypes. Fat people, ugly people, beautiful
people, old people, large-breasted women, short men, the mentally ill,
and the homeless all could tell you how much more they are like us than
we want to think. I once admitted to a group of people that I had a
mouth like a truck driver. Much to my surprise, a man stood up and said,
"I'm a truck driver, and I never cuss." Needless to say, I was humbled.

GROUPTHINK

Who is more foolish, the child afraid of the dark, or the man afraid of the
light?   —MAURICE FREEHILL

Irving Janis, in *Victims of Group Think*, defines this sort of lie as a psy- 23
chological phenomenon within decision-making groups in which loyalty
to the group has become more important than any other value, with the
result that dissent and the appraisal of alternatives are suppressed. If
you've ever worked on a committee or in a corporation, you've encountered groupthink. It requires a combination of other forms of lying—ignoring facts, selective memory, omission, and denial, to name a few.

The textbook example of groupthink came on December 7, 1941. 24
From as early as the fall of 1941, the warnings came in, one after another,
that Japan was preparing for a massive military operation. The navy
command in Hawaii assumed Pearl Harbor was invulnerable—the
Japanese weren't stupid enough to attack the United States' most important base. On the other hand, racist stereotypes said the Japanese weren't
smart enough to invent a torpedo effective in less than 60 feet of water

(the fleet was docked in 30 feet); after all, U.S. technology hadn't been able to do it.

On Friday, December 5, normal weekend leave was granted to all the 25 commanders at Pearl Harbor, even though the Japanese consulate in Hawaii was busy burning papers. Within the tight, good–ole–boy cohesiveness of the U.S. command in Hawaii, the myth of invulnerability stayed well entrenched. No one in the group considered the alternatives. The rest is history.

OUT–AND–OUT LIES

The only form of lying that is beyond reproach is lying for its own sake.
— OSCAR WILDE

Of all the ways to lie, I like this one the best, probably because I get 26 tired of trying to figure out the real meanings behind things. At least I can trust the bald–faced lie. I once asked my five–year–old nephew, "Who broke the fence?" (I had seen him do it.) He answered, "The murderers." Who could argue?

At least when this sort of lie is told it can be easily confronted. As the 27 person who is lied to, I know where I stand. The bald–faced lie doesn't toy with my perceptions — it argues with them. It doesn't try to refashion reality, it tries to refute it. *Read my lips. . . .* No sleight of hand. No guessing. If this were the only form of lying, there would be no such things as floating anxiety or the adult–children–of–alcoholics movement.

DISMISSAL

Pay no attention to that man behind the curtain! I am the Great Oz!
— THE WIZARD OF OZ

Dismissal is perhaps the slipperiest of all lies. Dismissing feelings, 28 perceptions, or even the raw facts of a situation ranks as a kind of lie that can do as much damage to a person as any other kind of lie.

The roots of many mental disorders can be traced back to the dis– 29 missal of reality. Imagine that a person is told from the time she is a tot that her perceptions are inaccurate. *"Mommy, I'm scared."* "No you're not, darling." *"I don't like that man next door, he makes me feel icky."* "Johnny, that's a terrible thing to say, of course you like him. You go over there right now and be nice to him."

I've often mused over the idea that madness is actually a sane reac– 30 tion to an insane world. Psychologist R. D. Laing supports this hypothesis in *Sanity, Madness and the Family,* an account of his investigation into the families of schizophrenics. The common thread that ran through all of the families he studied was a deliberate, staunch dismissal of the patient's perceptions from a very early age. Each of the patients started out

with an accurate grasp of reality, which, through meticulous and me-
thodical dismissal, was demolished until the only reality the patient
could trust was catatonia.

Dismissal runs the gamut. Mild dismissal can be quite handy for for- 31
giving the foibles of others in our day-to-day lives. Toddlers who have
just learned to manipulate their parents' attention sometimes are dismissed out of necessity. Absolute attention from the parents would require so much energy that no one would get to eat dinner. But we must
be careful and attentive about how far we take our "necessary" dis-
missals. Dismissal is a dangerous tool, because it's nothing less than a lie.

DELUSION

We lie loudest when we lie to ourselves.   – Eric HOFFER

I could write the book on this one. Delusion, a cousin of dismissal, is 32
the tendency to see excuses as facts. It's a powerful lying tool because it
filters out information that contradicts what we want to believe. Alcoholics who believe that the problems in their lives are legitimate reasons
for drinking rather than results of the drinking offer the classic example
of deluded thinking. Delusion uses the mind's ability to see things in
myriad ways to support what it wants to be the truth.

But delusion is also a survival mechanism we all use. If we were to 33
fully contemplate the consequences of our stockpiles of nuclear weapons
or global warming, we could hardly function on a day-to-day level. We
don't want to incorporate that much reality into our lives because to do
so would be paralyzing.

Delusion acts as an adhesive to keep the status quo intact. It shame- 34
lessly employs dismissal, omission, and amnesia, among other sorts of
lies. Its most cunning defense is that it cannot see itself.

• • •

The liar's punishment [. . .] is that he cannot believe anyone else.
                                        – GEORGE BERNARD SHAW

These are only a few of the ways we lie. Or are lied to. As I said ear- 35
lier, it's not easy to entirely eliminate lies from our lives. No matter how
pious we may try to be, we will still embellish, hedge, and omit to lubri-
cate the daily machinery of living. But there is a world of difference between telling functional lies and living a lie. Martin Buber once said, "The
lie is the spirit committing treason against itself." Our acceptance of lies
becomes a cultural cancer that eventually shrouds and reorders reality
until moral garbage becomes as invisible to us as water is to a fish.

How much do we tolerate before we become sick and tired of being 36
sick and tired? When will we stand up and declare our *right* to trust?
When do we stop accepting that the real truth is in the fine print? Whose

lips do we read this year when we vote for president? When will we stop being so reticent about making judgments? When do we stop turning over our personal power and responsibility to liars?

Maybe if I don't tell the bank the check's in the mail I'll be less toler- 37 ant of the lies told me every day. A country song I once heard said it all for me: "You've got to stand for something or you'll fall for anything."

Reading Closely

1. Without looking back at the essay, list as many of Ericsson's ways of lying as you can remember. Which one "stung" you? Why?

2. Why does Ericsson believe that lies are necessary? Which kinds of lies do you believe are so?

3. Which kinds of lies do you tell the most? Which do you most detest hearing? Why? Be prepared to share your answers with the rest of the class.

Considering Larger Issues

1. **With a classmate or two,** discuss questions of honesty currently circulating in the news. Which athletes, actors, politicians, or others are being questioned about lying? What is your opinion of their truth–telling?

2. As you consider all the ways we lie, what do you think of the author? Does she seem to be honest—or a liar? After all, she writes, "Like most people, I indulge in small falsehoods and still think of myself as an honest person." What do you think?

3. What evidence in the text helps you determine whether Ericsson is a dedicated liar or a dedicated writer investigating lying? Be prepared to share your answer with the rest of the class.

4. What is Ericsson's purpose in writing this essay, and what audience is she writing it for? Is she primarily trying to explore her own feelings? discourage her readers from telling lies? rouse them to action against liars and "acceptance of lies" in public life? Point to the evidence in the essay that supports your answers.

5. COMBINING METHODS. Mark the places where Ericsson uses *exemplification* to support her classification and division of "The Ways We Lie." Do you think she gives enough examples for each type of lying? Are all of the examples effective? Why or why not?

Thinking about Language

1. Using a dictionary or the context of the essay, define the following terms. Be prepared to share your answers with the rest of the class.

haggard (2)	penance (6)	façades (10)
travails (4)	pittance (9)	plethora (11)

ecclesiastical (12)   omission (17)   dissent (23)
irreparable (13)   misogynists (18)   gamut (31)
blatant (14)   renegade (19)
culprit (16)   stereotype (21)

2. What differences can you discern among the following words: *deception, lies, capital crimes,* and *misdemeanors*?

Writing Your Own Essays Using Classification and Division

1. What are the merits of lying? Using Ericsson's essay as a model of classification and division, draft a three- to four-page essay in which you categorize the advantages to social interaction of lying. Or if you prefer, categorize the merits of telling the truth. Remember to consult the guidelines for checking over the use of classification and division on p. 291.

2. Considering your response to item 1 under "Considering Larger Issues," draft a three- to four-page essay about kinds of lying, dishonesty, or cheating that are currently appearing in the media. Whether you decide to use real public figures, characters in television shows or movies, or both, remember to include a ruling principle, consistent and exclusive categories, and vivid details and examples. Do some online research, if necessary, to find details and examples, and illustrate your essay with at least two visuals. Refer to the guidelines for checking over the use of classification and division on p. 291.

AMY TAN
Mother Tongue

Amy Tan (b. 1952) is a California native who grew up surrounded by strong influences of both Chinese and American culture. She attended high school in Switzerland and went to eight different colleges before earning a master's degree in linguistics from San Jose State University. Before her literary career took off, Tan held a variety of jobs, ranging from tending bar and counseling the developmentally disabled to working as a corporate communications specialist. Realizing she was becoming a workaholic, she began writing stories about the intersection of her parents' traditional life in China with her own life as an Americanized Chinese American woman. When her first novel, *The Joy Luck Club* (1989), won both the *Los Angeles Times* Book Award and the National Book Award, she was able to devote herself full-time to writing. Since *The Joy Luck Club*, she has published *The Kitchen God's Wife* (1991); *The Moon Lady* (1992); *The Chinese Siamese Cat* (1994); *One Hundred Secret Senses* (1995); *The Bonesetter's Daughter* (2000); and a collection of essays called *The Opposite of Fate: A Book of Musings* (2003).

"Mother Tongue," which first appeared in the literary journal *Threepenny Review* (1990), is dedicated to her mother and illustrates Tan's linguistic expertise and training. It also exemplifies a successful mixed-method essay.

> **Preview** What is your "mother tongue"? What language—or what kind of language—do you speak at home, with close family members? How is that language different from the one you speak at school?

I am not a scholar of English or literature. I cannot give you much more than personal opinions on the English language and its variations in this country or others.

I am a writer. And by that definition, I am someone who has always loved language. I am fascinated by language in daily life. I spend a great deal of my time thinking about the power of language—the way it can evoke an emotion, a visual image, a complex idea, or a simple truth. Language is the tool of my trade. And I use them all—all the Englishes I grew up with.

Recently, I was made keenly aware of the different Englishes I do use. I was giving a talk to a large group of people, the same talk I had already given to half a dozen other groups. The nature of the talk was about my writing, my life, and my book, *The Joy Luck Club*. The talk was going along well enough, until I remembered one major difference that made the whole talk sound wrong. My mother was in the room. And it was perhaps the first time she had heard me give a lengthy speech, using the kind of English I have never used with her. I was saying things like, "The intersection of memory upon imagination" and "There is an aspect of my fiction that relates to thus–and–thus"—a speech filled with carefully wrought grammatical phrases, burdened, it suddenly seemed to me, with nominalized forms, past perfect tenses, conditional phrases, all the forms of standard English that I had learned in school and through books, the forms of English I did not use at home with my mother.

Just last week, I was walking down the street with my mother, and I again found myself conscious of the English I was using, the English I do use with her. We were talking about the price of new and used furniture and I heard myself saying this: "Not waste money that way." My husband was with us as well, and he didn't notice any switch in my English. And then I realized why. It's because over the twenty years we've been to-gether I've often used that same kind of English with him, and some-times he even uses it with me. It has become our language of intimacy, a different sort of English that relates to family talk, the language I grew up with.

So you'll have some idea of what this family talk I heard sounds like, I'll quote what my mother said during a recent conversation which I videotaped and then transcribed. During this conversation, my mother was talking about a political gangster in Shanghai who had the same last name as her family's, Du, and how the gangster in his early years wanted to be adopted by her family, which was rich by comparison. Later, the gangster became more powerful, far richer than my mother's family, and one day showed up at my mother's wedding to pay his respects. Here's what she said in part:

"Du Yusong having business like fruit stand. Like off the street kind. He is Du like Du Zong—but not Tsung-ming Island people. The local people call putong, the river east side, he belong to that side local people. That man want to ask Du Zong father take him in like become own family. Du Zong father wasn't look down on him, but didn't take se-riously, until that man big like become a mafia. Now important person, very hard to inviting him. Chinese way, came only to show respect, don't stay for dinner. Respect for making big celebration, he shows up. Mean give lots of respect. Chinese custom. Chinese social life that way. If too important won't have to stay too long. He come to my wedding. I didn't see, I heard it. I gone to boy's side, they have YMCA dinner. Chinese age I was nineteen."

You should know that my mother's expressive command of English belies how much she actually understands. She reads the *Forbes* report, listens to *Wall Street Week*, converses daily with her stockbroker, reads all of Shirley MacLaine's books with ease—all kinds of things I can't begin to understand. Yet some of my friends tell me they understand 50 per-cent of what my mother says. Some say they understand 80 to 90 per-cent. Some say they understand none of it, as if she were speaking pure Chinese. But to me, my mother's English is perfectly clear, perfectly natural. It's my mother tongue. Her language, as I hear it, is vivid, direct, full of observation and imagery. That was the language that helped shape the way I saw things, expressed things, made sense of the world.

Lately, I've been giving more thought to the kind of English my mother   8
speaks. Like others, I have described it to people as "broken" or "fractured" English. But I wince when I say that. It has always bothered me that I can think of no way to describe it other than "broken," as if it were damaged and needed to be fixed, as if it lacked a certain wholeness and soundness. I've heard other terms used, "limited English," for example. But they seem just as bad, as if everything is limited, including people's perceptions of the limited English speaker.

I know this for a fact, because when I was growing up, my mother's   9
"limited" English limited *my* perception of her. I was ashamed of her English. I believed that her English reflected the quality of what she had to say. That is, because she expressed them imperfectly her thoughts were imperfect. And I had plenty of empirical evidence to support me: the fact that people in department stores, at banks, and at restaurants did not take her seriously, did not give her good service, pretended not to understand her, or even acted as if they did not hear her.

My mother has long realized the limitations of her English as well.   10
When I was fifteen, she used to have me call people on the phone to pretend I was she. In this guise, I was forced to ask for information or even to complain and yell at people who had been rude to her. One time it was a call to her stockbroker in New York. She had cashed out her small portfolio and it just happened we were going to go to New York the next week, our very first trip outside California. I had to get on the phone and say in an adolescent voice that was not very convincing, "This is Mrs. Tan."

And my mother was standing in the back whispering loudly, "Why   11
he don't send me check, already two weeks late. So mad he lie to me, losing me money."

And then I said in perfect English, "Yes, I'm getting rather concerned.   12
You had agreed to send the check two weeks ago, but it hasn't arrived."

Then she began to talk more loudly. "What he want, I come to New   13
York tell him front of his boss, you cheating me?" And I was trying to calm her down, make her be quiet, while telling the stockbroker, "I can't tolerate any more excuses. If I don't receive the check immediately, I am going to have to speak to your manager when I'm in New York next week." And sure enough, the following week there we were in front of this astonished stockbroker, and I was sitting there red-faced and quiet, and my mother, the real Mrs. Tan, was shouting at his boss in her impeccable broken English.

We used a similar routine just five days ago, for a situation that was   14
far less humorous. My mother had gone to the hospital for an appoint-

ment, to find out about a benign brain tumor a CAT scan had revealed a month ago. She said she had spoken very good English, her best English, no mistakes. Still, she said, the hospital did not apologize when they said they had lost the CAT scan and she had come for nothing. She said they did not seem to have any sympathy when she told them she was anxious to know the exact diagnosis, since her husband and son had both died of brain tumors. She said they would not give her any more information until the next time and she would have to make another appointment for that. So she said she would not leave until the doctor called her daughter. She wouldn't budge. And when the doctor finally called her daughter, me, who spoke in perfect English — lo and behold — we had assurances the CAT scan would be found, promises that a conference call on Monday would be held, and apologies for any suffering my mother had gone through for a most regrettable mistake.

I think my mother's English almost had an effect on limiting my 15 possibilities in life as well. Sociologists and linguists probably will tell you that a person's developing language skills are more influenced by peers. But I do think that the language spoken in the family, especially in immigrant families which are more insular, plays a large role in shaping the language of the child. And I believe that it affected my results on achievement tests, IQ tests, and the SAT. While my English skills were never judged as poor, compared to math, English could not be considered my strong suit. In grade school I did moderately well, getting perhaps B's, sometimes B–pluses, in English and scoring perhaps in the sixtieth or seventieth percentile on achievement tests. But those scores were not good enough to override the opinion that my true abilities lay in math and science, because in those areas I achieved A's and scored in the ninetieth percentile or higher.

This was understandable. Math is precise; there is only one correct 16 answer. Whereas, for me at least, the answers on English tests were always a judgment call, a matter of opinion and personal experience. Those tests were constructed around items like fill–in–the–blank sentence completion, such as, "Even though Tom was _____, Mary thought he was _____." And the correct answer always seemed to be the most bland combinations of thoughts, for example "Even though Tom was shy, Mary thought he was charming," with the grammatical structure "even though" limiting the correct answer to some sort of semantic opposites, so you wouldn't get answers like, "Even though Tom was foolish, Mary thought he was ridiculous." Well, according to my mother, there were very few limitations as to what Tom could have been and what Mary might have thought of him. So I never did well on tests like that.

The same was true with word analogies, pairs of words in which you 17 were supposed to find some sort of logical, semantic relationship — for example, "*Sunset* is to *nightfall* as _____ is to _____." And here you would be presented with a list of four possible pairs, one of which showed the same kind of relationship: *red* is to *spotlight, bus* is to *arrival, chills* is to *fever, yawn* is to *boring.* Well, I could never think that way. I knew what the tests were asking, but I could not block out of my mind the images already created by the first pair, *"sunset* is to *nightfall"* — and I would see a burst of colors against a darkening sky, the moon rising, the lowering of a curtain of stars. And all the other pairs of words — red, bus, spotlight, boring — just threw up a mass of confusing images, making it impossible for me to sort out something as logical as saying: "A sunset precedes nightfall" is the same as "a chill precedes a fever." The only way I would have gotten that answer right would have been to imagine an associative situation, for example, my being disobedient and staying out past sunset, catching a chill at night, which turns into feverish pneumonia as punishment, which indeed did happen to me.

I have been thinking about all this lately, about my mother's English, 18 about achievement tests. Because lately I've been asked as a writer, why there are not more Asian Americans represented in American literature. Why are there few Asian Americans enrolled in creative writing pro- grams? Why do so many Chinese students go into engineering? Well, these are broad sociological questions I can't begin to answer. But I have noticed in surveys — in fact, just last week — that Asian students, as a whole, always do significantly better on math achievement tests than in English. And this makes me think that there are other Asian–American students whose English spoken in the home might also be described as "broken" or "limited." And perhaps they also have teachers who are steering them away from writing and into math and science, which is what happened to me.

Fortunately, I happen to be rebellious in nature and enjoy the chal- 19 lenge of disproving assumptions made about me. I became an English major my first year in college, after being enrolled as pre–med. I started writing nonfiction as a freelancer the week after I was told by my former boss that writing was my worst skill and I should hone my talents to- ward account management.

But it wasn't until 1985 that I finally began to write fiction. And at first 20 I wrote using what I thought to be wittily crafted sentences, sentences that would finally prove I had mastery over the English language. Here's an ex- ample from the first draft of a story that later made its way into *The Joy Luck Club,* but without this line: "That was my mental quandary in its nascent state." A terrible line, which I can barely pronounce.

Fortunately, for reasons I won't get into today, I later decided I 21 should envision a reader for the stories I would write. And the reader I decided upon was my mother, because these were stories about mothers. So with this reader in mind — and in fact she did read my early drafts — I began to write stories using all the Englishes I grew up with: the English I spoke to my mother, which for lack of a better term might be described as "simple"; the English she used with me, which for lack of a better term might be described as "broken"; my translation of her Chinese, which could certainly be described as "watered down"; and what I imagined to be her translation of her Chinese if she could speak in perfect English, her internal language, and for that I sought to preserve the essence, but neither an English nor a Chinese structure. I wanted to capture what language ability tests can never reveal: her intent, her passion, her imagery, the rhythms of her speech and the nature of her thoughts.

Apart from what any critic had to say about my writing, I knew I 22 had succeeded where it counted when my mother finished reading my book and gave me her verdict: "So easy to read."

Reading Closely

1. What is your immediate response to this essay's title? Respond to Tan's enumeration of the different Englishes she and many other people use, particularly with family members, and list them. Did any of these Englishes surprise, offend, or puzzle you? How many of them do you use?

2. Compare your responses to question 1 **with those of two or three classmates.** Where do you and your classmates agree and disagree with one another? Prepare a group response for the rest of the class.

Considering Larger Issues

1. Who is the audience for Tan's essay? What is her purpose in writing this essay? How do audience and purpose intersect for Tan?

2. What connections does Tan make between speaking and writing? Why does she emphasize the importance of knowing which English you're using?

3. Referring to your list of the different Englishes (question 1, under "Reading Closely"), discuss the real differences and similarities of these Englishes. How does Tan's narrative voice soften the process of learning and using these different Englishes, particularly in terms of their intimate or businesslike quality? In other words, what sorts of narratives and examples does she provide for the reasons she and her mother speak a range of Englishes? What examples does she provide for the consequences of using each English?

4. Tan uses herself and her mother as examples throughout this essay. Despite her reliance on two characters, how might Tan be speaking to the politics of language use in the United States? What do you know about the politics of who's saying what—and how—in U.S. culture? Write for five minutes in response to these questions.

5. COMBINING METHODS. Besides classification and division, what other methods of writing and thinking does Tan use to develop this essay?

Break into small groups of two or three classmates, with each group looking over the essay for places where Tan uses *description, definition, narration, comparison and contrast, process analysis, cause-and-consequence analysis,* or *argumentation.* Report your group's finding to the rest of the class.

Thinking about Language

1. Use the context of the essay or your dictionary to define the following terms. Be prepared to share your answers with the rest of the class.

keenly (3)	expressive (7)	portfolio (10)
nominalized (3)	wince (8)	impeccable (13)
conditional phrases (3)	empirical (9)	benign (14)
transcribed (5)	guise (10)	insular (15)

2. What is the overall effect of the final paragraph: "Apart from what any critic had to say about my writing, I knew I had succeeded where it counted when my mother finished reading my book and gave me her verdict: 'So easy to read'"? What is Tan explicitly saying? What is she implying? To what overall effect? Why does she make this single sentence a separate paragraph?

3. How would you describe Tan's tone? How does her tone relate to her audience and purpose?

Writing Your Own Essays Using Classification and Division

1. Think of a way to classify your use of language. What categories do you come up with? What examples can you provide for each category? Draft a three- to four-page essay in which you recount your language use. Make sure that your thesis statement reflects your purpose. The guidelines for checking over the use of classification and division can be found on p. 291.

2. Listen for a few days to how your friends or family members (a group of twelve or so people) use one or more languages or dialects. Then draft a three- to four-page essay in which you analyze the language use of this group, classifying the members into categories based on a ruling principle related to their language choices, such as vocabulary, style, and appropriateness. As you draft and revise, **consider working with a classmate;** and refer to "Checking Over the Use of Classification and Division" on p. 291.

TIMOTHY NOAH

Laura Bush: Bitch or Victim?

Timothy Noah (b. 1958), a contributing editor at the *Washington Monthly*, regularly writes for the "Chatterbox" column in the online magazine *Slate* <slate .msn.com>. He has also worked as assistant managing editor at *U.S. News and World Report* and as a reporter in the Washington bureau of the *Wall Street Journal*. "Laura Bush: Bitch or Victim?" originally appeared in *Slate* on May 9, 2001, a few months after George W. Bush was inaugurated as president.

Preview If you were to give Laura Bush a one-word label, what would it be?

The May 9 *Wall Street Journal* reports that President Bush is scrambling to find $30 million for the "Save America's Treasures" program, which subsidizes local historic preservation. Dubya had initially proposed terminating the program, which had been embraced by Hillary Clinton when she was first lady. But now Hillary's successor has embraced the program, too, and so Bush is trying to persuade Congress to let it live. This appears to be the first documented instance in which Laura Bush has influenced federal policy-making. It is therefore the first bit of evidence for the news media to weigh as it considers whether Laura Bush is a bitch or a victim.

In putting the choice so starkly, Chatterbox intends no disrespect toward Mrs. Bush, who seems from a distance to be a nice and reasonably well-adjusted person. Rather, Chatterbox is recognizing the press's unattractive tendency to caricature and pigeonhole first ladies. We start with the fact that fulfilling the hoary role of unpaid hostess/mother figure to a modern nation is inherently stressful. Judith Shulevitz, Margaret Talbot, and Mrs. Chatterbox have all described vividly the ways in which the office of first lady has become a torture chamber. All three writers recommend that the anachronistic tradition of making the president's wife "first lady," as opposed to letting her enjoy a separate and private existence, be done away with. (Actually, Shulevitz recommends that the government provide the first ladies tranquilizers free of charge, but she's being Swiftian.) Within the wider press corps, too, there's a similar consensus that the first lady tradition doesn't jibe with contemporary life. Most reporters aren't permitted to say so, however, because that would be "editorializing." But neither are they permitted to show deference to the first ladies themselves because that would be buying into an antifeminist value system. So what they do is pummel, behind a transparently insincere veil of deference, whoever happens to be first lady at the time. (British tabloids do something similar with the royals, though in that case the veil is now threadbare, and the inevitable collapse of the

A dinner celebrating the 200th anniversary of the White House was attended by five of the six living first ladies: (left to right) Barbara Bush, Lady Bird Johnson, Hillary Clinton, Betty Ford, and Rosalynn Carter. At the time, a few days after the 2000 election, Laura Bush (bottom) was unsure whether she would be joining their ranks.

archaic institution seems closer at hand.) The accepted method to beat up first ladies is to categorize them as bitches or victims.

First ladies who respond to the stress by becoming ever so slightly more cranky or assertive than would otherwise be the case get tagged *bitches*. (The term itself, and similarly harsh ones like "harpy" and "Lady Macbeth," are taboo, but the concepts are not. The same goes for "victim.") Thus Nancy Reagan and, to a lesser extent, Rosalynn Carter. When reporters used to call Rosalynn a "steel magnolia," that was code for "bitch." First ladies who have (Hillary Clinton) or develop (Eleanor Roosevelt) ambitious social-policy agendas of their own also wind up in the bitch column. As the accompanying historical chart shows, during the past quarter century there has been a marked trend away from victims and toward bitches. Chatterbox sees this as mild progress, though best of all would be for the whole demeaning process to disappear.

BITCH	VICTIM
Eleanor Roosevelt	
cheech	Bess Truman
	Mamie Eisenhower
	Jackie Kennedy
	Lady Bird Johnson
	Pat Nixon
	Betty Ford
Rosalynn Carter	
Nancy Reagan	
	Barbara Bush
Hillary Clinton	
Laura Bush?	Laura Bush?

Victims had a long run starting in the late 1940s. Indeed, even Eleanor   4
Roosevelt, a championship bitch, started out a victim crippled by low self-
esteem and jealous rage toward her husband's lover, Lucy Mercer. (This is
all retrospective pigeonholing, since little of this was widely known during
her lifetime.) There followed the shy Bess Truman (probably the happiest of
the victims), the alcoholic Mamie Eisenhower, and the whispery and vulnerable Jackie Kennedy, whose husband victimized her by committing serial adultery and, ultimately, getting assassinated. When Jackie married the
aging Greek shipping magnate Aristotle Onassis for the money and security he could give her, she morphed into a bitch. After Onassis' death,
though, the twice-widowed Jackie O. once again took her first husband's
name and re-established herself as a victim, albeit an unusually glamorous
one. Lady Bird was a victim by virtue of the simple fact that she married the
most overbearing man to occupy the White House during the 20th century
(with the exception of Teddy Roosevelt). Pat Nixon was the greatest victim
of the post-war era, and probably the greatest victim since Mary Todd Lincoln, marking perhaps the only similarity between America's worst and
greatest presidents. Pat despised being a politician's wife; Dick promised
he'd give it up; and then he made her first lady, subjecting her to national
disgrace in the bargain. Betty Ford was initially viewed as a jolly bitch, assertive and modern in a 1970s sort of way, and only later emerged as an ad-
dict/victim. Barbara Bush was, and remains, beloved as a warm and
motherly victim who watched her hair turn prematurely white and suffered depression in silence (too risky for a politician's wife to seek treatment). Though there's a significant minority that maintains that Barbara is
really an under-the-radar "rhymes with rich" (which is how she once described Geraldine Ferraro).

Laura Bush's power play on historic preservation tilts her toward the   5
bitch column, but only very slightly because tradition dictates that first
ladies are *supposed* to promote girly causes like literacy and beautification.
Indeed, if they don't, they risk being labeled as bitches! As a former
librarian, Laura is likely to be viewed by the public more as bespectacled

victim than bitch (though this stereotype doesn't have much allure for Chatterbox, who in his time has encountered more than a few tyrannical librarians). Suffering through Dubya's extended adolescence, which officially ended on his 40th birthday, and unofficially continues unabated, would seem to qualify Laura as victim, as does her endurance of whatever degree of substance abuse the president engaged in during that period. On the other hand, Laura's rumored insistence that the drinking Dubya straighten up and fly right or else she'd leave him makes her look like a fierce mama bear, which, however admirable, may translate for some into "bitch." On yet another hand, unless Chatterbox has somehow missed them, no anecdotes have thus far emerged about the first lady throwing any kind of hissy fit—a crucial prerequisite to winning the badge of "bitch." At the same time, "the first lady is a bitch" stories are much easier for journalists to write than "the first lady is a victim" stories because the latter usually require a tearful sit–down interview with the victim herself. So expect at least a scattering of bitch stories about Laura Bush, even if history's final judgment is that she's really a victim.

Reading Closely

1. What is this essay about, really? Translate the essay into one, easy–to–read paragraph.
2. How does Noah define the two major categories he uses? What examples does he provide for each category?
3. **Working with a classmate,** mark all the passages with which you strongly agree or disagree. Prepare to report to the rest of the class, contributing to a discussion about categories.

Considering Larger Issues

1. What is Noah's purpose in writing this essay? Who is his audience? How do audience and purpose intersect in this essay?
2. How does Noah compare and contrast his two basic terms, *bitch* and *victim?* What are the consequences of using just two basic categories? What are the consequences of using only these two categories? Are there two other terms that Noah could have used for the same ideas? How might a different choice of terms have affected his essay?
3. COMBINING METHODS. In what ways does this classification and division *argue* a point? What is the specific point and the support for that point?

Thinking about Language

1. Use your dictionary or the context of the essay to define the following terms. Be prepared to share your answers with the rest of the class.

subsidizes (1)   anachronistic (2)   harpy (3)
starkly (2)   jibe (2)   retrospective (4)
caricature (2)   deference (2)   morphed (4)
pigeonhole (2)   pummel (2)   unabated (5)
hoary (2)   archaic (2)   prerequisite (5)

2. How do you define *bitch* and *victim*? Do Noah's definitions resemble or differ from your own?

3. What kinds of code language, whether mentioned by Noah or not, have the media used to communicate the concepts of *bitch* and *victim* in regard to first ladies? For whom other than first ladies do they use such terms?

4. What is the overall tone of this essay? What specific terms (other than *bitch* and *victim*) or passages contribute to this tone?

5. Noah contrasts "making the president's wife 'first lady'" with "letting her enjoy a separate and private existence," and he defines *first lady* as "unpaid hostess/mother figure to a modern nation" (paragraph 2). What are the implications of using the term *first lady* for the president's wife? How does it affect the way Americans view the women who hold that role? What do the photographs on p. 336 suggest about the ways first ladies are viewed by the public or portrayed in the media?

Writing Your Own Essays Using Classification and Division

1. Consider one group of public figures (like first ladies) that you know something about: sports figures, television hosts, business leaders, actors, politicians, teachers, members of the clergy, and so on. If you were to classify them into two basic categories, what would those categories be? In an essay of three to four pages, classify this group of public figures, using your classification to argue a point. Refer to the guidelines for checking over the use of classification and division on p. 291.

2. Rewrite Noah's essay on first ladies for a different audience. Decide on an audience, a purpose, a thesis statement, and the specific words or phrases you need to change in order to reach your audience. **Consider working with a classmate** as you draft a two- to three-page essay, using classification and division, that categorizes first ladies. As you draft and revise your individual essays, refer to the guidelines for checking over the use of classification and division on p. 291.

GEORGE SAUNDERS

My Amendment

Before enrolling in a writing program at Syracuse University, Chicago native George Saunders (b. 1958) earned a degree in geophysical engineering and worked not only in that field but also as a knuckle-puller in a slaughterhouse, a convenience store clerk, a doorman at a Beverly Hills condominium, and a roofer in Chicago. Now he teaches creative writing at Syracuse and continues to publish frequently. His book-length writings include two short story collections, *CivilWarLand in Bad Decline* (1996) and *Pastoralia* (2000), and a children's book, *The Very Persistent Gappers of Frip* (2000). Saunders's prize-winning short fiction has been published in many magazines, including the *New Yorker*, where "My Amendment" first appeared in 2004.

> **Preview**   President George W. Bush has endorsed a constitutional amendment banning gay marriage. What do you think of such a ban? Is there something else you'd like to ban — or create — through a constitutional amendment?

As an obscure, middle-aged, heterosexual short-story writer, I am often   1
asked, George, do you have any feelings about Same-Sex Marriage?

To which I answer, Actually, yes, I do.   2

Like any sane person, I am against Same-Sex Marriage, and in favor   3
of a constitutional amendment to ban it.

To tell the truth, I feel that, in the interest of moral rigor, it is neces-   4
sary for us to go a step further, which is why I would like to propose a
supplementary constitutional amendment.

In the town where I live, I have frequently observed a phenomenon I   5
have come to think of as Samish-Sex Marriage. Take, for example, K, a
male friend of mine, of slight build, with a ponytail. K is married to S, a
tall, stocky female with extremely short hair, almost a crewcut. Often,
while watching K play with his own ponytail as S towers over him, I
have wondered, Isn't it odd that this somewhat effeminate man should
be married to this somewhat masculine woman? Is K not, on some level,
imperfectly expressing a slight latent desire to be married to a man? And
is not S, on some level, imperfectly expressing a slight latent desire to be
married to a woman?

Then I ask myself, Is this truly what God had in mind?   6

Take the case of L, a female friend with a deep, booming voice. I have   7
often found myself looking askance at her husband, H. Though H is basically pretty masculine, having neither a ponytail nor a tight feminine
derrière like K, still I wonder: H, when you are having marital relations
with L, and she calls out your name in that deep, booming, nearly male
voice, and you continue having marital relations with her (i.e., you are

not "turned off"), does this not imply that you, H, are, in fact, still "turned on"? And doesn't this indicate that, on some level, you, H, have a slight latent desire to make love to a man?

Or consider the case of T, a male friend with an extremely small 8 penis. (We attend the same gym.) He is married to O, an average–looking woman who knows how to fix cars. I wonder about O. How does she know so much about cars? Is she not, by tolerating this non–car–fixing, short–penised friend of mine, indicating that, on some level, she wouldn't mind being married to a woman, and is therefore, perhaps, a tiny bit functionally gay?

And what about T? Doesn't the fact that T can stand there in the shower 9 room at our gym, confidently towelling off his tiny unit, while O is at home changing their sparkplugs with alacrity, indicate that it is only a short stroll down a slippery slope before he is completely happy being the "girl" in their relationship, from which it is only a small fey hop down the same slope before T is happily married to another man, perhaps my car me-chanic, a handsome Portuguese fellow I shall refer to as J?

Because my feeling is, when God made man and woman He had some- 10 thing very specific in mind. It goes without saying that He did not want men marrying men, or women marrying women, but also what He did not want, in my view, was feminine men marrying masculine women.

Which is why I developed my Manly Scale of Absolute Gender. 11

Using my Scale, which assigns numerical values according to a set of 12 masculine and feminine characteristics, it is now easy to determine how Manly a man is and how Fem a woman is, and therefore how close to a Samish–Sex Marriage a given marriage is.

Here's how it works. Say we determine that a man is an 8 on the 13 Manly Scale, with 10 being the most Manly of all and 0 basically a Neuter. And say we determine that his fiancée is a –6 on the Manly Scale, with a –10 being the most Fem of all. Calculating the difference between the man's rating and the woman's rating—the Gender Differential—we see that this proposed union is not, in fact, a Samish–Sex Marriage, which I have defined as "any marriage for which the Gender Differential is less than or equal to 10 points."

Friends whom I have identified as being in Samish–Sex Marriages 14 often ask me, George, given that we have scored poorly, what exactly would you have us do about it?

Well, one solution I have proposed is divorce—divorce followed by 15 remarriage to a more suitable partner. K, for example, could marry a voluptuous high–voiced NFL cheerleader, who would more than offset his tight feminine derrière, while his ex–wife, S, might choose to become involved with a lumberjack with very large arms, thereby neutralizing her thick calves and faint mustache.

Another, and of course preferable, solution would be to repair the 16 existing marriage, converting it from a Samish–Sex Marriage to a healthy

Normal Marriage, by having the feminine man become more masculine and/or the masculine woman become more feminine.

Often, when I propose this, my friends become surly. How dare I, 17 they ask. What business is it of mine? Do I think it is easy to change in such a profound way?

To which I say, It is not easy to change, but it is possible. 18

I know, because I have done it. 19

When young, I had a tendency to speak too quickly, while gesturing 20 too much with my hands. Also, my opinions were unfirm. I was constantly contradicting myself in that fast voice, while gesturing like a girl. Also, I cried often. Things seemed so sad. I had long blond hair, and liked it. My hair was layered and fell down across my shoulders, and, I admit it, I would sometimes slow down when passing a shopwindow to look at it, to look at my hair! I had a strange constant feeling of being happy to be alive. This feeling of infinite possibility sometimes caused me to laugh when alone, or even, on occasion, to literally skip down the street, before pausing in front of a shopwindow and giving my beautiful hair a cavalier toss.

To tell the truth, I do not think I would have scored very high on my 21 Manly Scale, if the Scale had been invented at that time, by me. I suspect I would have scored so Fem on the test that I would have been prohibited from marrying my wife, P, the love of my life. And I think, somewhere in my heart, I knew that.

I knew I was too Fem. 22

So what did I do about it? Did I complain? Did I whine? Did I expect 23 activist judges to step in on my behalf, manipulating the system to accommodate my peculiarity?

No, I did not. 24

What I did was I changed. I undertook what I like to think of as a 25 classic American project of self-improvement. I made videos of myself talking, and studied these, and in time succeeded in training myself to speak more slowly, while almost never moving my hands. Now, if you ever meet me, you will observe that I always speak in an extremely slow and manly and almost painfully deliberate way, with my hands either driven deep into my pockets or held stock–still at the ends of my arms, which are bent slightly at the elbows, as if I were ready to respond to the slightest provocation by punching you in the face. As for my opinions, they are very firm. I rarely change them. When I feel like skipping, I absolutely do not skip. As for my long beautiful hair — well, I am lucky, in that I am rapidly going bald. Every month, when I recalculate my ranking on the Manly Scale, I find myself becoming more and more Manly, as my hair gets thinner and my girth increases, thickening my once lithe, almost girlish physique, thus insuring the continuing morality and legality of my marriage to P.

My point is simply this: If I was able to effect these tremendous posi- 26
tive changes in my life, to avoid finding myself in the moral/legal quagmire of a Samish–Sex Marriage, why can't K, S, L, H, T, and O do the same?

I implore any of my readers who find themselves in a Samish–Sex Mar- 27
riage: Change. If you are a feminine man, become more manly. If you are a masculine woman, become more feminine. If you are a woman and are thick–necked or lumbering, or have ever had the slightest feeling of attraction to a man who is somewhat pale and fey, deny these feelings and, in a spirit of self–correction, try to become more thin–necked and light–footed, while, if you find it helpful, watching videos of naked masculine men, to sort of retrain yourself in the proper mode of attraction. If you are a man and, upon seeing a thick–waisted, athletic young woman walking with a quasi–mannish gait through your local grocery, you imagine yourself in a passionate embrace with her, in your car, a car that is parked just outside, and which is suddenly, in your imagination, full of the smell of her fresh young breath — well, stop thinking that! Are you a man or not?

I, for one, am sick and tired of this creeping national tendency to let 28
certain types of people take advantage of our national good nature by marrying individuals who are essentially of their own gender. If this trend continues, before long our towns and cities will be full of people like K, S, L, H, T, and O, people "asserting their rights" by dating, falling in love with, marrying, and spending the rest of their lives with whomever they please.

I, for one, am not about to stand by and let that happen. 29

Because then what will we have? A nation ruled by the anarchy of 30
unconstrained desire. A nation of willful human hearts, each lurching this way and that and reaching out for whatever it spontaneously desires, trying desperately to find some comforting temporary shred of warmth in a mostly cold world, totally unconcerned about the external form in which that other, long–desired heart is embodied.

That is not the kind of world in which I wish to live. 31

I, for one, intend to become ever more firmly male, enjoying my 32
golden years, while watching P become ever more female, each of us vigilant for any hint of ambiguity in the other.

And as our children grow, should they begin to show the slightest 33
hint of some lingering residue of the opposite gender, P and I will lovingly pull them aside and list all the particulars by which we were able
to identify their unintentional deficiency.

Then, together, we will devise a suitable correction.   34

And, in this way, the race will go on.   35

Reading Closely

1. What kinds of information does the author provide to enhance his role
   as an expert on gay marriage, constitutional amendments, and marriage
   in general? Mark all the passages that highlight his expertise.
2. Mark all the information in the essay that surprises you. In the margins,
   write the reasons you are surprised.
3. What is Saunders classifying in this essay? What is his ruling principle?
   Are his categories exclusive and exhaustive?

Considering Larger Issues

1. Take a few minutes to write out what you see as Saunders's thesis. What
   is his purpose in writing this essay? How does his thesis reflect his purpose?
2. Who do you think Saunders intends as his audience for this essay? How
   do you know? How does his attention to audience support his purpose?
3. **Working with a classmate,** discuss the author's sense of humor. Saunders is known to appreciate irony and satire (ways of making fun of
   something while pretending to be serious). How far along were you before you realized that Saunders was being satirical? What specific passages can be read ironically? How do the drawings on p. 342 contribute
   to the humor—and to Saunders's thesis? Be prepared to share your answers with the rest of the class.
4. COMBINING METHODS. In what specific passages does Saunders use *narration* to develop his overall purpose? What about *exemplification* and *cause-
   and-consequence analysis*—how does he use these rhetorical methods to develop his classification and division?
5. The introduction to this chapter discusses how the act of classifying and
   dividing can itself make an argument. How does Saunders's essay make
   the same point?

Thinking about Language

1. **Working with two or three classmates,** divide up the following
   terms and define them, using a dictionary or the context of the essay. Report your findings to the rest of your group.

obscure (1)	voluptuous (15)	anarchy (30)
moral rigor (4)	surly (17)	unconstrained
phenomenon (5)	cavalier (20)	(30)
latent (5)	provocation (25)	spontaneously
askance (7)	girth (25)	(30)
derrière (7)	lithe (25)	vigilant (32)
functionally (8)	quagmire (26)	ambiguity (32)
alacrity (9)	implore (27)	lingering residue
fey (9)	gait (27)	(33)

2. Divide a sheet of paper into three columns with the headings *feminine*, *masculine*, and *human*. Now make lists of all the positive features that can be attributed to people in each of these categories. Be prepared to share your answers with the rest of the class.

Writing Your Own Essays Using Classification and Division

1. Draft a three- to four-page essay in which you classify your own past, current, and hoped-for personal relationships. If you don't want to reveal personal information about yourself, feel free to use irony and satire the way Saunders does, but do devise categories that fit your own experiences and plans. As you draft and revise, refer to the guidelines for checking over the use of classification and division on p. 291.

2. Draft a three- to four-page essay in which you classify the kinds of student-teacher relationships you've observed, maybe including ones you've experienced as well. You'll need to devise a ruling principle as well as categories that fit your observations. If you can extend your classification and division to include the causes and consequences within each classification, you'll probably enrich your overall essay. Remember to use the guidelines for checking over the use of classification and division on p. 291.

NATURE

Contents

One of the most popular scientific magazines in the English-speaking world, *Nature* has maintained its reputation as a first-rate educational tool by combining interesting yet scholarly reports of research, museums, recent books, and other scientific news with artful and inviting photography. Since the establishment of the Nature Publishing Group in 1869, *Nature* has evolved with the times, simultaneously reflecting contemporary scientific advances and explorations while teaching its readers. The URL at the top of the page <www.nature.com/nature> demonstrates the publishing group's commitment to new media as well as new science, for the Web site provides access to scientific papers even before they are published in print.

> **Preview** Do you often look at the table of contents before reading a magazine? Why, or why not? If so, how helpful do you usually find it to be?

. . . . . . ➤

Reading Closely

1. On first glance, what do you learn from this page?
2. What information is being classified and divided? What is the purpose of this classification and division?

Considering Larger Issues

1. What is the ruling principle of this classification and division? What kinds of information do you find in each category?
2. **Working with one or two classmates,** discuss the organization and appearance of this page. Do you think the organization is as effective as possible? Would you move any information to another category? What about the physical arrangement—would a different layout of the categories work better? How effective do you find the different type sizes and fonts? the illustrations? Be prepared to share your group's findings with the rest of the class.
3. COMBINING METHODS. This table-of-contents page includes classification and division, to be sure. But what other rhetorical methods do you see?

Thinking about Language

1. **Working with one or two classmates,** define each of the categories.
2. Translate the information in one of the categories into a paragraph. How does the overall effect of your paragraph compare to that of the magazine's presentation?

nature contents

13 November 2003 Volume 426 issue no. 6963 www.nature.com/nature

cover lines

The Macmillan Building,
4 Crinan St,
London N1 9XW, UK
Tel 44 (0) 20 7833 4000
e-mail: nature@nature.com
▶ http//www.nature.com/
nature

The Guide to Authors is available in full on:
▶ http//www.nature.com/
nature/submit/gta
and in shortened form, in this issue, page 204.

nature publishing group

editorials

news

news features

correspondence

books and arts

concepts

news and views

Nature® (ISSN 0028-0836) is published weekly on Thursday, except the last week in December, by Nature Publishing Group (The Macmillan Building, 4 Crinan Street, London N1 9XW). Registered as a newspaper at the British Post Office. Annual subscription for the Americas US$775 (institutions/corporate), US$159 (individual making personal payment). Canada residents please add 7% GST (No. 140911595). North and South American orders to: *Nature*, Subscription Dept, PO Box 5055, Brentwood, TN 37024-5055, USA. Other orders to *Nature*, Brunel Road, Basingstoke, Hants RG21 2XS, UK. Periodicals postage paid at New York, NY 10010-1707, and additional mailing offices. Authorization to photocopy material for internal or personal use, or internal or personal use of specific clients, is granted by *Nature* to libraries and others registered with the Copyright Clearance Center (CCC) Transactional Reporting Service, provided the relevant copyright fee is paid direct to CCC, 222 Rosewood Drive, Danvers, MA 01923, USA. identification code for *Nature*: 0028-0836/03. US Postmaster send address changes to: Nature, PO Box 5055, Brentwood, TN 37024-5055; CPC PUB AGREEMENT #40032744. Published in Japan by Nature Japan K.K., MG Ichigaya Bldg, 5F, 19-1 Haraikatamachi,Shinjuku-ku, Tokyo 162-0841, Japan. © 2003 Nature Publishing Group.

Writing Your Own Essays Using Classification and Division

1. In the introduction to this chapter, you saw how classification and division can help you organize a group of things so that they make sense to you. By using classification and division, you can make connections and discover relationships. Think of your relatives: How might you classify them? What would your ruling principle be (other than relative status, such as aunt, uncle, sister, and so on)? What people make up each category? What would you name each category? Develop a three- to four-page essay that classifies your relatives in either an informative or an entertaining way. **Consider asking a classmate** to comment on your essay as you draft and revise it for submission. Respond to your classmate's draft as well, using the guidelines for checking over the use of classification and division on p. 291.

2. In chapter 9 on definition, you are asked to define terms you regularly use: *education, love, family, responsibility, security, satisfaction, loyalty, childhood, failure, success, happiness.* Choose one of these terms, write down all the words and phrases that come to mind when you hear it, and devise categories for all the ideas and situations you come up with. Then draft a three- to four-page classification essay about your word. Be sure to decide on a purpose for your classification: to inform, to entertain, or to argue a point. As you draft and revise, refer to "Checking Over the Use of Classification and Division" on p. 291.

3. To enhance the overall effect of the essay you wrote for question 1 *or* 2, create a visual layout (perhaps like the one shown here from *Nature*) that reflects the same information.

✱ Additional Suggestions for Writing

1. Make a list of all the television talk shows you can think of. **Ask your roommate or a classmate** to help you add to your list. How might you classify and divide these shows so that your categories are exhaustive and exclusive?

    Work with two classmates to expand your list, focus on a purpose for your classification and division, and decide on examples for each category. Then draft a three- to four-page essay that classifies and divides television talk shows. Revise your draft, using comments from your classmates and referring to "Checking Over the Use of Classification and Division" (p. 291) before preparing your final essay.

2. In her original *Redbook* article, Deborah Tannen (p. 283) discusses seven specific "conversation traps": apologies, criticism, thank-yous, fighting, praise, complaints, and jokes. Choose one of these categories of conversation and subdivide it into several smaller categories, according to the sex of the participants (all women, all men, one woman and one man, one woman and several men, one man and several women, and so on), their status in relation to one another, or the social situation or context. Because so many different combinations are possible, you need not make your classification a complete one, but do provide examples of conversation — and conversation traps — within each subcategory. You may want to include several troubling, rewarding, or informative experiences that you've participated in or observed. Draft a three- to four-page essay, and revise it using comments and suggestions **from one or two classmates** as well as the guidelines for checking over the use of classification and division (p. 291).

chapter **6**

....●

COMPARISON
AND CONTRAST

THE MAN ON THE LEFT
IS 75 TIMES MORE LIKELY TO BE STOPPED BY THE POLICE WHILE DRIVING THAN
THE MAN ON THE RIGHT.

It happens every day on America's highways. Police stop drivers based on their skin color rather than for the way they are driving. For example, in Florida 80% of those stopped and searched were black and Hispanic, while they constituted only 5% of all drivers. These humiliating and illegal searches are violations of the Constitution and must be fought. Help us defend your rights. Support the ACLU.

american civil liberties union
125 Broad Street, 18th Floor, NY, NY 10004 www.aclu.org

Courtesy of DeVito/Verdi, New York.

*B*lack men are seventy-five times more likely to be stopped by the police while driving than white men, even if the black man is Martin Luther King Jr. and the white man is Charles Manson, a mass murderer. According to the ad on the opposite page, in Florida 80 percent of those stopped and searched were black and Hispanic. Figures like these have resonated all across the United States, resulting in a new term: *racial profiling*. Racial profiling statistics have provided state governments and law enforcement officials specific reasons for reevaluating their guidelines on who is treated as suspicious.

Who is *not* treated as suspicious (that is, who is *not* stopped and searched) makes up the necessary second part of the comparison and contrast. If in Florida 80 percent of those stopped and searched are black and Hispanic, then the other 20 percent must belong to other racial and ethnic groups, including non-Hispanic whites, Asians, and American Indians. If in Florida 5 percent of all drivers are black or Hispanic, then 95 percent of all drivers must belong to other racial and ethnic groups. Numbers like these, presented in comparison and contrast, help us make sense of our world, find answers for things we don't understand, and fit new events or concepts (such as racial profiling) into the framework of what we already know.

Looking at Your Own Literacy In your experiences driving, riding, walking, or just being in school, what have you learned about profiling? Write for a few minutes about how your appearance might make you appear suspicious—or not. What has been the effect of your appearance as compared with that of one of your friends?

What Are Comparison and Contrast?

When you hear "compare and contrast," you may think of an artificial exercise used only in academic settings, but comparison and contrast are actually among the most important methods we use to make sense of the world. We use **comparison** when considering how two or more things are alike, to see what they have in common (for example, both black and white men drive in Florida). We use **contrast,** on the other hand, to show how two or more things are different (for example, black men are much more likely to be stopped by the police than white men).

Every day we call on comparison and contrast to evaluate information and find the answers we need. We notice a sign in the grocery store that says, "National brand $4.00, OUR brand $3.00"; we try on several pairs of athletic shoes before making a purchase because we want to buy the best pair; and we trace two possible routes on a map in order to determine the best way out of a city. In each of these situations we first establish a **basis for comparison,** the shared feature of the two or more things we are comparing (for example, the convenience of the route, the versatility of the shoes, and so on), what they have in common. Then we decide on the **points of the comparison,** the features that we will compare or contrast (Which route has less traffic? Which route flows into the beltway? Which route is longer?).

We can also use comparison and contrast as the overall organizational pattern for a piece of writing or as a supporting passage within another organizational pattern, such as classification and division, definition, or exemplification. We use comparison and contrast to help us understand or explain one relationship, situation, object, or personality in terms of another. In fact, one particular kind of comparison, called **analogy,** draws a likeness between one thing and something entirely different, usually something more familiar or less abstract. Here's an example of an analogy written by a student:

> Writing a paper is like spring cleaning. The first phase of cleaning is like researching: you have to look through lots of material, deciding what to keep and what to throw away. The goal is to keep only what is useful. Once you've gotten rid of all the junk, you'll need to organize whatever you have left. Organization is the key to a clean house, as well as a well-written paper. Once everything is in its place, it's time to buff and polish — clean up your prose, fix your spelling, tidy sloppy sentences.

The ad on p. 355 for Lipton tea is based on comparison and contrast.

Thinking about Comparison and Contrast

1. How are coffee and tea alike? How are they different? What is Lipton's purpose in presenting this comparison and contrast?
2. What difference between tea and coffee is Lipton pointing out in this advertisement? Why is Lipton emphasizing this particular difference?
3. How do the visual and the text work together in this ad?

Why Use Comparison and Contrast?

Comparison and contrast are fundamental ways of thinking about any situation. They help us make sense of the world — the way an analysis of racial profiling does — by revealing information. Although you often employ this combined method in both speaking and writing, rarely do you start by setting out to compare and contrast. Instead, your topic, purpose, and audience will naturally lead you to use comparison and contrast. Whenever you are being asked or asking others to consider the merits, advantages and disadvantages, or similarities and differences of

A CUP OF TEA HAS ____% LESS CAFFEINE THAN A CUP OF COFFEE.

(HINT)

Would you have guessed tea has less than half the caffeine of coffee? An 8 oz. cup of coffee contains 100 mg. of caffeine. An 8 oz. cup of tea, on the other hand, has 40 mg. — that's 60% less. The gentle lift of tea, hot or iced, will relax and revive you. And now that you know the facts about tea's caffeine content, you can enjoy it more often. For the latest news about the benefits of tea, call the Lipton Tea and Health Information Center toll free at **1-888-LIPTON-T** (1-888-547-8668).

Caffeine levels can vary based on several factors including brewing method and time. 300 mg. a day is generally defined as moderate caffeine consumption. © 1998 Lipton

two or more things — tea and coffee, for instance — you're being called on
to compare and contrast. And you'll want to establish your purpose from
the very beginning. In writing, the main purposes for which the method
of comparison and contrast is used include explaining, evaluating choices,
persuading, and entertaining.

In order to explain his complicated feelings about ownership of land,
David Mas Masumoto compares and contrasts himself with his childhood friend Jessie Alvarado, whose family worked the farmland that Masumoto's family owned:

> In 1966, while in the sixth grade at Del Rey Elementary School, I sat
> next to Jessie Alvarado. We had what, I later learned, was a symbiotic
> relationship. We'd cheat on tests together — he'd open a book so I could
> read the needed information, and then he copied my response. I pro-
> vided the answers, he took the risks.
>
> But that was before they told me he was Mexican and I was Japanese.
> Our cultures were different they said; he ate tortillas and I ate rice at home.
> We each had "our own thing" and belonged in different worlds despite
> both living in this small farm community just south of Fresno, California.
>
> That was before they told me that my family was the farmers, and his
> family was the farm workers. We owned the land; he came to work for
> us. Nature rewarded us differently. While we talked about profits,
> Jessie's family spoke of hard-earned wages. We worked in all four sea-
> sons in our fields; he came to labor seasonally. My family would pass the
> land to the next generation. His family's dream was for the next genera-
> tion to get out of the fields. We were supposed to be on opposite sides,
> even though we both sweated and itched the same each summer as we
> picked peaches in one-hundred-degree heat.
>
> That was before they told me he was poor and I was rich. It made me
> feel guilty yet confused as a kid growing up.
>
> – DAVID MAS MASUMOTO, "Belonging on the Land"

Masumoto establishes his basis for comparison when he mentions his
"symbiotic relationship" with Jessie Alvarado. Just as these two sixth
graders had one, so did their fathers: one owned the land, the other
worked it. Then Masumoto acknowledges what the boys had in common: they cheated together, both lived near Fresno, and both picked
peaches each summer. Their differences were their cultural backgrounds
(Mexican and Japanese), what they ate at home, and — most important —
how their families earned a living. His purpose is to explore his discomfort with the discrepancies between their lives.

Try Your Hand Think back to a friendship you established early in
life, only to discover that you two were "supposed" to be different.
Using comparison or contrast, explain in two sentences your relationship with your friend. Share your written thoughts with a classmate to
see if your comparison or contrast is clear.

Often we use comparison and contrast to help ourselves or others make choices. For instance, imagine that you're in Santa Fe, New Mexico, for a vacation during the last part of June and the first part of July and have budgeted $50 to see a dance performance. Therefore, you've already established a basis for comparison. You see the ad on p. 358 and note that you have a choice: you can see the Martha Graham Dance Company or the Maria Benitez Teatro Flamenco. Hmmm. The prices are similar; there is just a $5 difference. So your decision might depend on whether you want to see modern dance or traditional dance—or whether you want to go to a performance near the beginning of your stay or near the end. Using one or both of these points of comparison, you make your choice.

Try Your Hand   Think of the last time you used comparison and contrast to make a choice — maybe about which movie to see, which person to go out with, or which shirt to buy. In a single paragraph, write about your decision. What was the basis for comparison? What were the points of comparison or contrast? What was your final decision?

Insurance agents can be among the most persuasive comparers and contrasters. When trying to sell you a policy, good agents often ask if they can compare coverage and then contrast rates and deductibles with your current policy. They are trying to underbid your current carrier—or at least compete with it. They want to persuade you to do business with their company.

But people use comparison and contrast to persuade their audience to do other things besides buy a product or become aware of racial profiling (as in the ACLU ad that opens this chapter). In the following excerpt, William F. Shugart II uses comparison and contrast in an attempt to persuade his readers to support the creation of four-year degree programs in football and basketball:

Many colleges and universities grant bachelor's degrees in vocational subjects. Art, drama, and music are a few examples, but there are others. Undergraduates who major in these areas are typically required to spend only about one of their four years in basic English, math, history and science courses; the remainder of their time is spent in the studio, the theater or the practice hall honing the creative talents they will later sell as professionals.

Although a college education is no more necessary for success in the art world than it is in the world of sports, no similar option is available for students whose talents lie on the athletic field or in the gym. Majoring in physical education is a possibility, of course, but while PE is hardly a rigorous demanding discipline, undergraduates pursuing a degree in that major normally must spend many more hours in the classroom than

THE MARTHA GRAHAM DANCE COMPANY

Extraordinary Modern Dance
Distinctive Style!
- New York Times

Only New Mexico Appearance
July 4, 5, 6
Tickets $40.00
Order your tickets today!

MARIA BENITEZ TEATRO FLAMENCO

IN OBSESION OSCURA
(DARK OBSESSION)

A full evening of fiery
traditional Flamenco!

June 25, 26, 27, 28 & 29
Tickets $35.00

Santa Fe Stages 3rd Summer Festival
June 3 - August 3, 1997

Dance   Theatre   Music   Drama

At the Greer Garson Theatre Center on St. Michaels Drive

Call the Santa Fe Stages Box Office for tickets
and information on our 1997 season
including 8 other outstanding productions:

505-982-6683

Santa Fe Stages
The International Theatre Festival

their counterparts who are preparing for careers on the stage. While the music major is receiving academic credit for practice sessions and recitals, the PE major is studying and taking exams in kinesiology, exercise physiology and nutrition. Why should academic credit be given for practicing the violin, but not for practicing a three-point shot?

—William F. Shugart II, "Why Not a Football Degree?"

In this case, Shugart focuses on the similarities between college sports and college arts: both take special talent, dedication, and practice. Both are vocational subjects, yet college arts provide students opportunities for a degree that college sports do not.

Try Your Hand   Think of a time when you compared and contrasted your college plans or degree program with that of another person. When did you do this? With whom did you compare yourself? What was the basis for comparison? What were the points of comparison? Write for ten minutes about what you learned or decided by comparing and contrasting yourself with the other person.

Finally, comparison and contrast can be used to entertain. We don't have to make a decision or change our mind; we get to enjoy. In the following excerpt, sports commentator Bob Costas compares two of the most famous sports icons:

There are significant differences between Muhammed Ali and Michael Jordan, but perhaps the most significant similarity is right there on the surface: physical beauty. Grace, style, magnetism—they were wonders to behold. Beyond any objective measures of excellence and achievement, that is a good part of why they moved us. Why quibble with the obvious?   — Bob Costas, "Ali and Jordan"

In the following excerpt about the Democratic and Republican national conventions, Jacob Weisberg uses both comparison and contrast to poke fun at both conventions—and at the parties they represent:

Political conventions are largely exercises in reciprocal theft. Democrats attempted to replicate the impeccably choreographed 1980 Republican convention in Detroit for many years. They finally got it right in 1992 in New York. Republicans tried to copy the Democrats' glitzy compassion-fest of 1992 and finally got it right in 2000 in Philadelphia.

In Los Angeles, Democrats are busy plagiarizing, with slight modification, much of what worked for the Republicans two weeks ago. Republicans had a blind mountain climber. Today, Democrats had a legless long-distance runner (I'm waiting for a mute politician). Republicans had "ordinary people" speaking from the podium; Democrats have officials performing live "interviews" with ordinary people, which is not an improvement. . . .

Yet there are still differences between a Republican convention and a Democratic convention, differences that speak to the persistent temperamental disparity between the two parties.

For one thing, Republican conventions are perfectly ordered, with a crisp, businesslike feel. Every speech is vetted and released to the press ahead of the event. All the placards in the hall are officially designated. Spontaneity does not break out. Speakers stand alone on a vast, bald stage.

A Democratic convention, by contrast, is incorrigibly chaotic. Delegates shout out comments and wave homemade placards. Moments of spontaneity occur despite the attempt to keep to a script. The podium is busy, with lots of people milling around and schmoozing.
    —JACOB WEISBERG, "The Difference between the Two Conventions"

Weisberg is obviously having fun with his comparison and contrast: he makes the two parties sound like plagiarizing college writers in their sameness (featuring speakers with physical disabilities; paying attention to "ordinary people") and like rival fraternities in their differences, one upright and "businesslike" ("perfectly ordered"; using "officially designated" placards), and the other fun-loving and casual ("incorrigibly chaotic"; "milling around and schmoozing").

How Do You Read Comparison and Contrast?

As with any other kind of writing, the first step in learning how to write an effective comparison–and–contrast essay is knowing how to read one critically. Once you've established that you're reading this type of writing, make a habit of examining it closely to see how the writer sets up the comparison or contrast and how successful it is—both in general terms and for the author's specific purpose and audience. Are the things being compared or contrasted clear, or are they vague or confusing? Does the writer help you see similarities or differences you hadn't recognized, or does he or she strain to find or exaggerate ones that hardly exist? Whether the purpose of the comparison and contrast is to explain, evaluate a choice, entertain, or argue a point, how well does the writing do so for the intended readers (whose identity you may have to figure out)?

Look back at the passage by David Mas Masumoto on p. 356, and consider first the title, "Belonging on the Land." It alerts you that the passage deals somehow with a feeling of connection to some land, although it doesn't suggest what will be compared or contrasted. Whether you can glean information from the title or not, keep reading, paying special attention to the effect of the introduction:

In 1966, while in the sixth grade at Del Rey Elementary School, I sat next to Jessie Alvarado. We had what, I later learned, was a symbiotic relationship.

Here, the title and introduction work together to prepare you for the purpose of the comparison and contrast, which seems to be explanatory, maybe even entertaining. At the beginning of the next paragraph, however, the author suddenly shifts to his main point. The thesis at the end of this paragraph, "We each had 'our own thing' and belonged in different worlds," will sustain the rest of the passage, informing the reader of the differences between the two boys.

Notice how Masumoto organizes the contrasts between his two subjects. They appear one after another in three paragraphs, each beginning with the phrase "that was before they told me," and are often stated in short, blunt ways: "he was Mexican and I was Japanese," "We owned the land; he came to work for us." But the effect isn't monotonous because Masumoto uses different sentence structures and lengths and twice acknowledges similarities: "despite both living in this small farm community," "even though we both sweated and itched the same." Also notice that he starts with the least significant contrasts (ethnicity, diet), gradually develops the economic differences between the two families, and leads up to the most important contrast of all, where Masumoto states his personal feelings: "he was poor and I was rich. It made me feel guilty yet confused. . . ."

As you evaluate the comparisons and contrasts authors make, you'll also want to consider what others could have been made—but weren't. In this case, you might wonder what Jessie felt about the boys' relationship—whether he too was confused or harbored any feelings of resentment, or if he might have taken advantage of his relationship with David. Think about what else is left unsaid as well: for instance, sometimes the writer's intended audience is obvious, but in this excerpt Masumoto gives us few clues about whom he sees as his audience: people interested in issues of social or economic class differences? children who don't yet recognize such differences? landowners? farmworkers? What is *not* on the page (or the screen) can be every bit as important as what is there.

How Do You Write Using Comparison and Contrast?

Besides the rhetorical elements that we're considering in every chapter—purpose, audience, thesis—writing that compares and contrasts has unique elements: the basis and points of comparison. These provide the framework for two characteristic organizational patterns.

Determining Your Purpose

The first question you should ask yourself is, "Why am I making this comparison and contrast?" Did your history instructor assign you to compare and contrast two books on the war against Iraq and to recommend one over the other (to evaluate a choice)? Are you applying for a grant to study abroad for a semester and being asked to sketch out the advantages and disadvantages of doing so (to argue)? Does an exam for an art course ask you to explain the similarities and differences between the Cubist and Expressionist painters (to explain)? Whether you're writing for school, for your job, or in some other context, you'll use comparison and contrast in order to explain something, to evaluate a choice, to argue a point, or just to entertain. Sometimes these purposes overlap, but you'll always have one dominant purpose that you need to keep in mind.

Considering Your Audience

After establishing your purpose, your second question should be, "For whom am I writing this comparison and contrast?" Are you writing for your teacher? yourself? your parents? a friend? a boss? Are you writing to your girlfriend to try to convince her the two of you should be friends first (but lovers second) instead of being "just friends"? Are you writing to your parents to explain the differences between placing your children in school-sponsored as opposed to church-sponsored day care? Are you e-mailing your adviser to explore the pros and cons of majoring in dance, your first love, as opposed to the more practical physical therapy?

Audience and purpose work hand-in-hand to affect other aspects of your comparison and contrast: the basis and points of comparison, how much emphasis you give one point over another, the order in which points are presented. If you are trying to decide where to place your children in day care, you will no doubt weigh such points of comparison as cost, distance from home and work, staff, equipment, and atmosphere. Although cost might be your most immediate concern, your spouse might be more concerned with staff and equipment and your employer with how distance affects your work schedule. Your parents might be more interested in the religious or educational atmosphere (and be more willing to help you out financially, depending on which option you choose). You will want to gauge the elements of your comparison and contrast to fit your audience; therefore, it's vital to have a sense of that audience as you draft and revise.

Considering the Basis and Points of Comparison

What features or elements of your subject have you chosen to compare? If you're comparing your own academic success with that of a high school classmate who made the same grades, who works about the same number of hours, and who like you has a small child to care for, then you are comparing two "like" things. But if you are comparing your success with that of a genius who isn't a parent and has never had to hold a job, then you're "comparing apples and oranges"—a phrase we use when two very different things are being compared without any rational basis.

Points of comparison grow out of your initial basis for comparison. If you are comparing the advantages and disadvantages of attending a two–year as opposed to a four–year college, your basis is that both kinds of school provide higher education, and you may want to establish such points of comparison as cost, course offerings, faculty, and distance from home. But those points are obvious. You will sometimes need to move beyond the obvious; for instance, what the lifetime potential payoffs for a degree from each kind of college are, or whether you would be more likely to go on for a bachelor's degree if you started at one or the other. If you're applying to college or transferring from one kind to the other, or if you're applying for scholarship support, you may find yourself developing these points in your letter of application or your statement of purpose. In every comparison and contrast, you'll want to identify several appropriate and well–supported points of comparison so that your thesis is adequately supported and your conclusion is indisputable.

Considering Your Thesis Statement

Your purpose and your basis for comparison will come together in your thesis statement. An effective thesis statement answers the question, "What do I want this comparison and contrast to do?" If you're comparing two literary characters or two sports figures, for instance, why are you doing so? Do you want to explain something to readers? to evaluate a choice for them? to argue a point to them? to entertain them? Your thesis should also indicate whether you will concentrate on similarities, differences, or both. Finally, a strong thesis statement makes a point about your subjects, so that your comparison is more than just an empty exercise.

Not all thesis statements are just one sentence long. For instance, when Anthony Lane entertains his readers by comparing older Hollywood actors with younger ones, he uses a three–sentence–long thesis statement to focus on his main point:

> One thing for sure: Paramount has picked the right time to release a movie that showcases the skills of an older generation. Put *Twilight* next to the list of Oscar nominations for Best Actor, which includes Jack Nicholson, Peter Fonda, Robert Duvall, and Dustin Hoffman, and the whole thing starts to look like a campaign, or, at any rate, a cri de coeur, from Hollywood: <u>Where have all the smoothies gone? What is lacking in the lusty youth of America? Instead of young Nicholsons and Hackmans, what we get nowadays is an almost indistinguishable roster of boys with big chins: Chris O'Donnell, Matthew McConaughey, Matt Damon.</u> Matt Damon! Cary Grant would have tipped him five bucks for being a good bellhop. The biggest laugh I have had in the past couple

of years came from a *Vanity Fair* cover story that hailed McConaughey as
the next Paul Newman. As *Twilight* demonstrates, there isn't much wrong
with the current one. I would love to think that in forty years' time, in the re-
make of *Twilight*, Matt and Chris will sit at a table and deal cards, or enjoy
a craggy conversation about prostates and old peckers. But don't count
on it.   — ANTHONY LANE, "Golden Oldies"

Lane's thesis statement conveys the argumentative purpose of his entertaining essay: to demonstrate that the old Hollywood is still the best
Hollywood because the older actors (the "smoothies") have spent time
earning a respect that goes well beyond their looks, unlike the "roster of
boys with big chins."

Arranging and Developing the Comparison

Writing that compares and contrasts has traditionally been organized
in two ways: (1) the writer makes a point-by-point case for subject A and
then does the same for subject B (and subject C if necessary, and so on),
emphasizing each subject, or (2) the writer compares and contrasts each
point of subject A with the corresponding point of subject B and then
moves on to the next point, with the emphasis on the points of comparison themselves rather than the subjects.

If you're writing a short, simple comparison and contrast, with only a
few points of comparison, then the first organizational pattern might be
the best one for your purpose. You'll want to open with an introduction
including a thesis statement and move quickly to your first subject. Even
a thesis statement as simple as "Living in Corvallis, Oregon, is every bit
as desirable as living in State College, Pennsylvania" can work if you are
responding to folks who wonder how you could possibly enjoy living in
two drastically different locations. You could talk about the geography of
Corvallis, the size of the town and suburbs, the university, and the
weather, then talk about these same points for State College, following
the same order. Therefore, taking them one at a time, you could prove
that these two cities are both desirable places in which to live.

If you're developing a longer, more complicated comparison and
contrast, however, the second organizational pattern will probably be a
better choice, because the first requires readers to hold all the points of
the first subject in their minds while waiting to read about those of the
second subject. You could use a similar thesis statement but then discuss
each of the points of comparison one at a time in relation to both subjects. For instance, you could write, "Even though Corvallis, Oregon, and
State College, Pennsylvania, are on opposite sides of the United States,
they offer uncannily similar ways of life." Then, using the points of comparison as the main ideas of your topic sentences, you would introduce
each point in turn, discussing both cities in each paragraph and using

transitional words or phrases to move between one subject and the other and from one point to the next.

You'll want to support all your points with an adequate but not necessarily equal amount of detail. Relevant details will bring your comparison and contrast to life and make it purposeful—clear, convincing, or entertaining. But providing exactly the same amount or kinds of detail in the same order for each point or each subject can make your writing sound mechanical and monotonous. So try to introduce some variation, such as giving more detail for points that are more important, complex, or unexpected. In addition, unless you're deliberately exaggerating for humorous effect, your claims of similarity or difference shouldn't sound forced or overstated, especially if you're making an analogy. Don't be afraid to acknowledge that your subjects are alike in some ways and different in others.

Reaching a Conclusion

Whatever organizational pattern you choose, you should end with a concluding paragraph (or two) that moves beyond the mere restatement of the thesis to answer this important question: So what? In "Golden Oldies," Anthony Lane brings home his comparison of older and younger actors with a scene from *Twilight*: can any of us truly imagine the likes of a mature Matt Damon and Chris O'Donnell enjoying "a craggy conversation about prostates and old peckers"?

Understanding and Using Comparison and Contrast

Analyzing Comparison and Contrast

1. After you read the chapter-opening ACLU advertisement about racial profiling, how did you feel? What did you think of that you hadn't considered before?

2. Who is the intended audience of the ACLU ad? What evidence from the text or visual can you provide to support your answer?

3. According to the excerpt by David Masumoto (p. 356), what are the terms by which young friends are often compared and contrasted? **Working with another classmate,** enumerate the ways. Prepare to report your findings to the rest of the class.

Planning and Writing Essays Using Comparison and Contrast

1. Look again at the excerpt from Anthony Lane's comparison and contrast of the "smoothies" with the "boys with big chins" (p. 363). Write a paragraph or two comparing and contrasting two generations of athletes, musicians, writers, teachers, spouses, parents, or workers, copying the structure of Lane's piece as closely as you can.

"Reading" and Using Visuals in Comparison and Contrast

You can diagram your comparison and contrast in order to make sure you have covered all the points of comparison in the case of all your subjects, or vice versa. The following illustration shows how you might diagram the essay about life in Corvallis, Oregon, and State College, Pennsylvania:

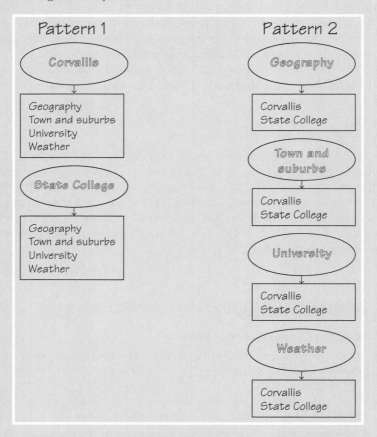

In addition, writers often use visuals in presenting a comparison or contrast to readers. Visuals such as bar graphs, line graphs, pie charts, ads like the one on p. 355, and "before and after" photos quickly reveal how two or more subjects size up in comparison with each other. Whether you want to indicate Republican and Democratic voting preferences according to age or state, the daily ranges in temperature of two cities, or unemployment rates across a period of months or years, visuals can help explain your information and make your point.

In order to choose or compose visuals that will work effectively, though, you need to analyze the information that a visual contains or the point that it makes as well as how it conveys that information or point. You need not only to be able to "read" a visual, but also to read it critically, to judge how well or poorly it achieves its purpose. Consider the following set of tables that display quantitative information. These tables originally appeared in *Becoming Gentlemen: Women, Law School, and Institutional Change*, a book that investigates the differences between the law school experiences of men and women.

Table 1   Mean Statistics for Incoming Students

	College GPA			Rank in College			LSAT		
	N	Mean	σ	N	Mean	σ	N	Mean	σ
Men	542	3.49	.31	544	78.44	20.35	544	40.98	4.16
Women	408	3.52	.28	409	80.13	18.45	413	40.87	4.09
		p = .143			p = .188			p = .677	

Table 2   Mean Law School GPAs

	First-Year GPA (GPA1)			Second-Year GPA (GPA2)			Third-Year GPA (GPA3)		
	N	Mean	σ	N	Mean	σ	N	Mean	σ
Men	532	0.932	.524	397	1.005	.456	382	1.047	.425
Women	397	0.771	.475	303	0.853	.429	294	0.923	.416
		p = .000			p = .000			p = .000	

The tables are reprinted with permission from Lani Guinier, Michelle Fine, and Jane Balin, *Becoming Gentlemen* (Boston: Beacon Press, 1997).

What do these tables show, and how well do they show it? Each table is clearly labeled and divided into three parts: undergraduate grade–point average (GPA), class rank, and Law School Application Test (LSAT) score for Table 1, and GPA for each of the three years of law school in Table 2. Each part is subdivided into three columns, headed *N*, *Mean*, and σ, and two rows, labeled *Men* and *Women*, followed by "*p =*" and a number. Notice how presenting the information in these visually parallel ways makes it easier for readers to follow.

Imagine, for example, if some of the parts started with the N column, some with the *Mean* column, and some with the σ column, or if some of them listed men first and others women first. Arranging each part in the same way makes it much easier to see the patterns within and the significance of the statistical information.

As you can tell, though, these tables are written with a specific kind of audience in mind: people who are accustomed to reading this kind of statistical information and are familiar with the terms and abbreviations used. You may already be familiar with these terms if you've studied statistics. But if not, N refers to the number of subjects (men or women) in each group, and *mean* refers to the mathematical average of the GPAs, class ranks, or LSAT scores of all the subjects in the group. The numbers under the σ symbol are the standard deviation, a measure of how close all the individual numbers are to the mean. Finally, p refers to the probability or likelihood of these GPAs, ranks, or scores occurring by chance; the lower p is, the more statistically reliable the information.

Table 1, then, shows that both men and women enter law school with differences in credentials so slight as to be insignificant. Men enter law school with a college GPA (on a 4.0 scale) of 3.49, plus or minus 0.31 (3.18–3.80), and women enter with a slightly higher college GPA of 3.52, plus or minus 0.28 (3.24–3.80). The probability of these GPAs occurring by chance is 0.143 (or 14 in 100 times). Whereas men enter with an average undergraduate class rank of 78.44 (plus or minus 20.35), women's average class rank is only slightly lower at 80.13 (plus or minus 18.45), with a probability of 0.188 (or 18 in 100). Men's LSAT scores average 40.98 (plus or minus 4.16 out of a possible 48), and women's average scores are almost the same at 40.87 (plus or minus 4.09), although in this case the probability is a high 0.677 (or 68 in 100).

Table 2 displays a comparison of men's and women's law school performance over the next three years. If you carry over the information you gathered in Table 1, you can see that despite their equivalent qualifications upon entering law school, women lag behind men in their GPA beginning from year one, when men's average GPA is 0.932 (plus or minus 0.524, on a 1.2 scale) and women's average GPA is 0.771 (plus or minus 0.475, on a 1.2 scale). During the second and third years, both groups improve their cumulative GPAs; women close the gap slightly, but they continue to lag behind. In the second year, men average 1.005 as compared with the women's 0.853; in the third year, men average 1.047 as compared with the women's 0.923. The probability of these GPAs occurring by chance are less than one in a thousand (0.000). Now, unless you're familiar with law school GPAs, you won't know that they're based on a 1.2 scale (as opposed to the 4.0 scale with which you're probably familiar). But it's not essential that you know this information because you can still see the persistent statistical differences between male and female students as both groups work their way through three years of law school.

If you're one of those readers who skims over these kinds of visual or statistical displays, you may want to slow down and read for as much information as you can interpret given your background knowledge because visual displays, especially those conveyed in tables, can carry every bit as much information as words. Although the key information is not highlighted in any special way in these tables, it's available to the average interested reader. In *Becoming Gentlemen*, the authors apparently considered that their intended readers—who might include law school students, professors, and administrators as well as feminists and others—were familiar enough with the conventions of statistics to understand terminology like *mean* and *p* and to find the key information, the mean differences between men and women, "buried" in the middle columns of each part of the tables. Or maybe these tables were explained and discussed in the main text of the book. If you're creating your own tables to show comparisons and contrasts, though, consider whether highlighting the key information in some way—such as by using boldface or italic type—might help your readers grasp its significance more quickly and easily.

Any reader who understands that the "mean" column contains the key information, however, will have no trouble understanding the basic premise conveyed in these tables: men and women enter law school with the same credentials, yet they leave on a much different footing, with men faring significantly better than women. The information conveyed in the tables doesn't reveal exactly what those differences are or what causes them, but it's presented in a clear, convincing format, one that the authors can use as evidence for their argument that men and women experience law school in different ways.

2. Often we engage in comparison and contrast to make a decision. For example, how did you come to attend this school? Make a list of the colleges where you were accepted; then list the features you considered as you compared them, such as location, cost, financial assistance, academic programs, physical appearance, student population. Draft a two- to three-page essay in which you explain your decision to attend this college. If you didn't choose among several colleges, then explain how you came to choose one of the courses you're taking this term instead of one or more others that you considered. As you work, refer to the following guidelines for checking over the use of comparison and contrast.

3. **Working with a classmate,** plan a comparison-and-contrast essay about the two of you. What might be the basis for your comparison? What points would you compare or contrast? Most important, what would be a realistic purpose for comparing and contrasting yourselves? After you have answered these questions, draft a two- to three-page essay relying on the input of your classmate and the following guidelines for checking over the use of comparison and contrast.

✓ Checking Over the Use of Comparison and Contrast

1. What is the purpose of your comparison and contrast? Is it to explain, to evaluate a choice, to persuade, to entertain? Do you achieve that purpose?

2. Who is the audience? Have you taken the audience into consideration in developing the comparison and contrast?

3. What is the thesis statement? Underline it. Does it make a strong point?

4. What is the basis for comparison? Do the subjects you are comparing have at least one point in common?

5. What are the points of comparison? Have you considered points that go beyond the obvious?

6. How have you organized the comparison and contrast—according to pattern 1 or pattern 2 (see p. 366)? Is the organization easy to follow? If not, would the other pattern make it easier to follow?

7. Is there appropriate supporting detail for each subject and point? Is there too much information on one subject or point and not enough on others? Or is the supporting detail so similar as to be monotonous?

8. How do you move readers from one subject and one point of comparison to the next? Underline the transitional words or phrases that you have used. Are there other places where transitions are needed?

9. If you are using visuals, do they clearly convey the points you want them to make? Do you need to add labels, captions, or references in the written text?

10. What's the point of your comparison and contrast? Does the conclusion go beyond your thesis to answer the question "So what?"

READINGS

DEBORAH TANNEN
Cross Talk

Linguist Deborah Tannen (b. 1945) came to national attention in 1990 with the publication of *You Just Don't Understand* and consolidated her reputation as an expert in the ways people communicate — or fail to communicate — with *Talking from 9 to 5* (1993), *Gender and Discourse* (1994), *The Argument Culture* (1998), and *I Only Say This Because I Love You* (2002). But long before she became famous among the general public, this professor of linguistics at Georgetown University had established herself as a brilliant and prolific academic scholar by carefully exploring the connections between language and the situations in which it is used. Tannen's specialty is sociolinguistics, the study of the intersection between society and language (between class and language, gender and language, ethnicity and language, race and language, geographic location and language). The following essay, "Cross Talk," is excerpted from *You Just Don't Understand.*

> **Preview**   As you read, consider if—and if so, where—Tannen inserts her own opinion as she compares and contrasts.

A woman who owns a bookstore needed to have a talk with the store man– 1
ager. She had told him to help the bookkeeper with billing, he had agreed, and now, days later, he still hadn't done it. Thinking how much she disliked this part of her work, she sat down with the manager to clear things up. They traced the problem to a breakdown in communication.

She had said, "Sarah needs help with the bills. What do you think 2
about helping her out?" He had responded, "OK," by which he meant, "OK, I'll think about whether or not I want to help her." During the next day, he thought about it and concluded that he'd rather not.

This wasn't just an ordinary communication breakdown that could 3
happen between any two people. It was a particular sort of breakdown that tends to occur between women and men.

Most women avoid giving orders. More comfortable with decision- 4
making by consensus, they tend to phrase requests as questions, to give
others the feeling they have some say in the matter and are not being
bossed around. But this doesn't mean they aren't making their wishes
clear. Most women would have understood the bookstore owner's question, "What do you think about helping her out?" as assigning a task in a
considerate way.

The manager, however, took the owner's words literally. She had 5
asked him what he thought; she hadn't told him to *do* anything. So he
felt within his rights when he took her at her word, thought about it and
decided not to help Sarah.

Women in positions of authority are likely to regard such responses 6
as insubordination: "He knows I am in charge, and he knows what I
want; if he doesn't do it, he is resisting my authority."

There may be a kernel of truth in this view — most men are inclined to 7
resist authority if they can because being in a subordinate position makes
them intensely uncomfortable. But indirect requests that are transparent to
women may be genuinely opaque to men. They assume that people in authority will give orders if they really want something done.

These differences in management styles are one of many manifesta- 8
tions of gender differences in how we talk to one another. Women use
language to create connection and rapport; men use it to negotiate their
status in a hierarchical order. It isn't that women are unaware of status or
that men don't build rapport, but that *the genders tend to focus on different
goals.*

THE SOURCE OF GENDER DIFFERENCES

These differences stem from the way boys and girls learn to use lan- 9
guage while growing up. Girls tend to play indoors, either in small
groups or with one other girl. The center of a girl's social life is her best
friend, with whom she spends a great deal of time sitting, talking and exchanging secrets. It is the telling of secrets that makes them best friends.
Boys tend to play outdoors, in larger groups, usually in competitive
games. It's doing things together that makes them friends.

Anthropologist Marjorie Harness Goodwin compared boys and girls 10
at play in a black innercity neighborhood in Philadelphia. Her findings,
which have been supported by researchers in other settings, show that
the boys' groups are hierarchical: high-status boys give orders, and low-
status boys have to follow them, so they end up being told what to do.
Girls' groups tend to be egalitarian: girls who appeared "better" than others or gave orders were not countenanced and in some cases were ostra-
cized.

So while boys are learning to fear being "put down" and pushed 11
around, girls are learning to fear being "locked out." Whereas high-status

boys establish and reinforce their authority by giving orders and resisting doing what others want, girls tend to make suggestions, which are
likely to be taken up by the group.

CROSS-GENDER COMMUNICATION IN THE WORKPLACE

The implications of these different conversational habits and con- 12
cerns in terms of office interactions are staggering. Men are inclined to
continue to jockey for position, trying to resist following orders as much
as possible within the constraints of their jobs.

Women, on the other hand, are inclined to do what they sense their 13
bosses want, whether or not they are ordered to. By the same token,
women in positions of authority are inclined to phrase their requests as
suggestions and to assume they will be respected because of their authority. These assumptions are likely to hold up as long as both parties are
women, but they may well break down in cross-gender communication.

When a woman is in the position of authority, such as the bookstore 14
owner, she may find her requests are systematically misunderstood by
men. And when a woman is working for a male boss, she may find that
her boss gives bald commands that seem unnecessarily imperious because most women would prefer to be asked rather than ordered. One
woman who worked at an all-male radio station commented that the
way the men she worked for told her what to do made her feel as if she
should salute and say, "Yes, boss."

Many men complain that a woman who is indirect in making re- 15
quests is manipulative: she's trying to get them to do what she wants
without telling them to do it. Another common accusation is that she is
insecure: she doesn't know what she wants. But if a woman gives direct
orders, the same men might complain that she is aggressive, unfeminine
or worse.

Women are in a double bind: *If we talk like women, we are not respected. If* 16
we talk like men, we are not liked.

We have to walk a fine line, finding ways to be more direct without 17
appearing bossy. The bookstore owner may never be comfortable by directly saying, "Help Sarah with the billing today," but she might find some
compromise such as, "Sarah needs help with the billing. I'd appreciate it if
you would make some time to help her out in the next day or two."
This request is clear, while still reflecting women's preferences for giving reasons and options.

What if you're the subordinate and your boss is a man who's offend- 18
ing you daily by giving you orders? If you know him well enough, one
potential solution is "metacommunication" — that is, talk about communication. Point out the differences between women and men, and discuss
how you could accommodate to each other's styles. (You may want to
give him a copy of this article or my book.)

© 1998. Reprinted by permission of United Features Syndicate.

But if you don't have the kind of relationship that makes metacom-   19
munication possible, you could casually, even jokingly, suggest he give
orders another way. Or just try to remind yourself it's a crosscultural difference and try not to take his curtness personally.

HOW TO HANDLE A MEETING

There are other aspects of women's styles that can work against us in a   20
work setting. Because women are most comfortable using language to create rapport with someone they feel close to, and men are used to talking in
a group where they have to prove themselves and display what they know,
a formal meeting can be a natural for men and a hard nut to crack for
women. Many women find it difficult to speak up at meetings; if they do,
they may find their comments ignored, perhaps later to be resuscitated by
a man who gets credit for the idea. Part of this is simply due to the expectation that men will have more important things to contribute.

But the way women and men tend to present themselves can aggra-   21
vate this inequity. At meetings, men are more likely to speak often, at
length and in a declamatory manner. They may state their opinions as
fact and leave it to others to challenge them.

Women, on the other hand, are often worried about appearing to   22
talk too much—a fear that is justified by research showing that when
they talk equally, women are perceived as talking more than men. As a
result, many women are hesitant to speak at a meeting and inclined to
be succinct and tentative when they do.

DEVELOPING OPTIONS

Working on changing your presentational style is one option; an- 23
other is to make your opinions known in private conversation with the
key people before a meeting. And if you are the key person, it would be
wise to talk personally to the women on your staff rather than assuming
all participants have had a chance to express themselves at the meeting.

Many women's reticence about displaying their knowledge at a 24
meeting is related to their reluctance to boast. They find it more humble
to keep quiet about their accomplishments and wait for someone else to
notice them. But most men learn early on to display their accomplishments and skills. And women often find that no one bothers to ferret out
their achievements if they don't put them on display. Again, a woman
risks criticism if she talks about her achievements, but this may be a risk
she needs to take, to make sure she gets credit for her work.

I would never want to be heard as telling women to adopt men's 25
styles across the board. For one thing, there are many situations in which
women's styles are more successful. For example, the inclination to make
decisions by consensus can be a boon to a woman in a managerial position. Many people, men as well as women, would rather feel they have
influence in decision–making than be given orders.

Moreover, recommending that women adopt men's styles would be 26
offensive, as well as impractical, because women are judged by the
norms for women's behavior, and doing the same thing as men has a
very different, often negative, effect.

A STARTING POINT

Simply knowing about gender differences in conversational style 27
provides a starting point for improving relations with the women and
men who are above and below you in a hierarchy.

The key is *flexibility*; a way of talking that works beautifully with one 28
person may be a disaster with another. If one way of talking isn't working, try another, rather than trying harder to do more of the same.

Once you know what the parameters are, you can become an ob- 29
server of your own interactions, and a style–switcher when you choose.

Reading Closely

1. What's this selection about? In one paragraph, summarize the entire passage.
2. What reasons does Tannen give or imply for the source of differences
   between the ways men and women use language?

3. **Working with a classmate,** list all the common purposes men and women have for using language. Then, using information from the read-ing, list the ways Tannen says men use language and then list the ways she says women use language. Do you think that what Tannen writes is true? Can you think of any exceptions to her generalizations? Report your responses to the class.

4. Which of Tannen's generalizations about gender differences in language does the Dilbert cartoon strip on p. 374 demonstrate — or disprove?

Considering Larger Issues

1. Who is Tannen's audience for this essay? What evidence from the essay supports your answer? Write out your answers.

2. What is the purpose of Tannen's essay? **Working with a classmate,** compare responses and, together, determine the purpose.

3. Assuming that Tannen's scholarly opinions about the ways men and women use language are correct, what are some aspects about your own use of language that you might like to change? List some ways that you currently use language. Then, alongside each point, write the way you'd like to change it. What might be the consequences of your change?

4. Think about another person in your life who uses language in ways that you wish would change. What does this person do? Does the person's use of language seem to be affected by his or her gender? How might it change for the better? What would be the result?

5. COMBINING METHODS. In what ways does Tannen use comparison and contrast to fulfill the overall purpose of her essay? Mark the passages in which she uses *description, narration,* and *exemplification* to support that overall purpose.

Thinking about Language

1. Using the context of the selection or your dictionary, define each of the following terms. Be prepared to share your answers with the rest of the class.

insubordination (6)	ostracized (10)	inequity (21)
transparent (7)	systematically (14)	declamatory (21)
opaque (7)	bald (14)	succinct (22)
manifestations (8)	imperious (14)	ferret out (24)
rapport (8, 20)	double bind (16)	reticence (24)
hierarchical (10)	metacommunication	boon (25)
egalitarian (10)	(18)	parameters (29)
countenanced (10)	resuscitated (20)	

2. What specific language (specialized words, terms, phrases) does Tannen use that convinces her readers of her professionalism and expertise? List and define these words, terms, and phrases, and compare your list and definitions with those of your classmates.

3. To reach readers beyond the academic world, Tannen had to modify her writing style from that of a professor. Reviewing the preceding excerpt, who do you think she writes like, if not a professor? What does this example of her writing sound like? **Working with one or two class-mates,** write out the words, phrases, and sentences that support your answers to these questions.

Writing Your Own Essays Using Comparison and Contrast

1. Using your responses to questions 3 and 4 under "Considering Larger Issues," draft a three- to four-page essay in which you compare your use of language with the way it is used by a member of the opposite sex or by someone from another generation or culture. Map out the points of comparison, and tell your side of the language story. Your essay will be especially pointed if you offer suggestions for improving communication in your conclusion. Refer to the guidelines on p. 370, "Checking Over the Use of Comparison and Contrast."

2. Draft a three- to four-page self-portrait based mostly on your use of language. In what ways, if any, is your use of language affected by whether you are a man or woman? How do the specific ways you use language help or hinder you? Compare and contrast your current language use with how you would like to use language to your advantage. As you draft and revise, refer to the guidelines for checking over the use of comparison and contrast on p. 370.

SUZANNE BRITT

Neat People vs. Sloppy People

North Carolina native Suzanne Britt teaches part-time at Meredith College in Raleigh, North Carolina, and has published essays and columns in *Authors Ink*, the *Cleveland Plain Dealer*, the *Charlotte Observer*, and a range of other magazines and newspapers. Her books include a history of Meredith College, two writing textbooks, and two collections of essays, *Skinny People Are Dull and Crunchy Like Carrots* (1982) and *Show and Tell* (1983), where the following essay first appeared.

> **Preview** If people can be divided into the two basic categories that Britt focuses on, in which category do you belong: neat or sloppy? What specific evidence can you supply for your answer?

I've finally figured out the difference between neat people and sloppy people. The distinction is, as always, moral. Neat people are lazier and meaner than sloppy people.

Sloppy people, you see, are not really sloppy. Their sloppiness is merely the unfortunate consequence of their extreme moral rectitude. Sloppy people carry in their mind's eye a heavenly vision, a precise plan, that is so stupendous, so perfect, it can't be achieved in this world or the next.

Sloppy people live in Never–Never Land. Someday is their métier.   3
Someday they are planning to alphabetize all their books and set up
home catalogs. Someday they will go through their wardrobes and mark
certain items for tentative mending and certain items for passing on to
relatives of similar shape and size. Someday sloppy people will make
family scrapbooks into which they will put newspaper clippings, postcards, locks of hair, and the dried corsage from their senior prom. Someday they will file everything on the surface of their desks, including the
cash receipts from coffee purchases at the snack shop. Someday they will
sit down and read all the back issues of *The New Yorker*.

For all these noble reasons and more, sloppy people never get neat.   4
They aim too high and wide. They save everything, planning someday to
file, order, and straighten out the world. But while these ambitious plans
take clearer and clearer shape in their heads, the books spill from the
shelves onto the floor, the clothes pile up in the hamper and closet, the
family mementos accumulate in every drawer, the surface of the desk is
buried under mounds of paper, and the unread magazines threaten to
reach the ceiling.

Sloppy people can't bear to part with anything. They give loving at-   5
tention to every detail. When sloppy people say they're going to tackle
the surface of a desk, they really mean it. Not a paper will go unturned;

not a rubber band will go unboxed. Four hours or two weeks into the excavation, the desk looks exactly the same, primarily because the sloppy person is meticulously creating new piles of papers with new headings and scrupulously stopping to read all the old book catalogs before he throws them away. A neat person would just bulldoze the desk.

Neat people are bums and clods at heart. They have cavalier atti- 6 tudes towards possessions, including family heirlooms. Everything is just another dust-catcher to them. If anything collects dust, it's got to go and that's that. Neat people will toy with the idea of throwing the children out of the house just to cut down on the clutter.

Neat people don't care about process. They like results. What they 7 want to do is get the whole thing over with so they can sit down and watch the rasslin' on TV. Neat people operate on two unvarying prin- ciples: Never handle any item twice, and throw everything away.

The only thing messy in a neat person's house is the trash can. The 8 minute something comes to a neat person's hand, he will look at it, try to decide if it has immediate use and, finding none, throw it in the trash.

Neat people are especially vicious with mail. They never go through 9 their mail unless they are standing directly over a trash can. If the trash can is beside the mailbox, even better. All ads, catalogs, pleas for charitable con- tributions, church bulletins, and money-saving coupons go straight into the trash can without being opened. All letters from home, postcards from Europe, bills, and paychecks are opened, immediately responded to, then dropped in the trash can. Neat people keep their receipts only for tax pur- poses. That's it. No sentimental salvaging of birthday cards or the last letter a dying relative ever wrote. Into the trash it goes.

Neat people place neatness above everything, even economics. They 10 are incredibly wasteful. Neat people throw away several toys every time they walk through the den. I knew a neat person once who threw away a perfectly good dish drainer because it had mold on it. The drainer was too much trouble to wash. And neat people sell their furniture when they move. They will sell a La-Z-Boy recliner while you are reclining in it.

Neat people are no good to borrow from. Neat people buy every- 11 thing in expensive little single portions. They get their flour and sugar in two-pound bags. They wouldn't consider clipping a coupon, saving a leftover, reusing plastic nondairy whipped cream containers, or rinsing off tin foil and draping it over the unmoldy dish drainer. You can never borrow a neat person's newspaper to see what's playing at the movies. Neat people have the paper all wadded up and in the trash by 7:05 A.M.

Neat people cut a clean swath through the organic as well as the in- 12 organic world. People, animals, and things are all one to them. They are so insensitive. After they've finished with the pantry, the medicine cabi- net, and the attic, they will throw out the red geranium (too many leaves), sell the dog (too many fleas), and send the children off to board- ing school (too many scuff-marks on the hardwood floors).

Reading Closely

1. Britt divides people into two general categories: neat and sloppy. But she also connects each of these categories with other personal attributes. What are they? Are the connections believable? What support can you give for your answers? Be prepared to share your answers with the rest of the class.

2. In her opening paragraph, Britt writes, "The distinction is, as always, moral." How exactly does she develop the morality issues in her comparison and contrast?

3. What is the basis for comparison that Britt employs? What specific points of comparison does she use?

Considering Larger Issues

1. Britt uses opposites as a way to categorize people. **Working with another classmate or two,** develop a third category of people to which you can compare and contrast both neat and sloppy people. Name the category and the specific behavorial and "moral" characteristics of that group. Be prepared to share your group response with the rest of the class.

2. What do you see as the purpose for Britt's essay? as her intended audience? How are the two related?

3. Are there any similarities between neat and sloppy people that Britt has left unmentioned?

4. Where on the spectrum between serious and humorous do you rank Britt's essay? What specific passages support your answer? Be prepared to share your response with the rest of the class.

5. COMBINING METHODS. Mark the places where Britt uses *cause-and-effect analysis*. How do these passages enhance her essay?

6. What comparisons and contrasts can you draw between the two photographs on pp. 378–79? Do you think they support Britt's analysis of the moral differences between neat people and sloppy people? Or do they call it into question?

Thinking about Language

1. Using a dictionary or the context of the essay, define the following terms:

moral rectitude (2)	meticulously (5)	salvaging (9)
stupendous (2)	scrupulously (5)	swath (12)
métier (3)	cavalier (6)	organic (12)
excavation (5)	unvarying (7)	inorganic (12)

2. In paragraph 4, Britt uses three fairly short sentences followed by a very long one. What effect does this sequence create, and how does it relate to the point she's making in this paragraph?

Writing Your Own Essays Using Comparison and Contrast

1. Using Britt's essay as a model, draft a three- to four-page essay in which you divide people into two groups who exhibit opposite characteristics: fast and slow, honest and dishonest, hardworking and lazy, extroverted and introverted, or some other set of easy opposites. If you consider Britt's essay to be serious, then write a serious essay. If you consider it to be humorous, then try humor. Be sure to refer to the guidelines for checking over the use of comparison and contrast on p. 370.

2. Movies, television shows, and sports events all feature people who are compared and contrasted: *Lord of the Rings'* Legolas Greenleaf and Tree-beard, Gandolf and Sauron; *Seinfeld's* Jerry and Kramer; *Everybody Loves Raymond's* Ray and Robert; Shaquille O'Neal and Yao Ming; Lebron James and Carmelo Anthony. Choose two people or types of people who share a basis for comparison, and draft an essay of three to four pages comparing and contrasting them for a specific purpose. Be sure to refer to the guidelines for checking over the use of comparison and contrast on p. 370.

BOB COSTAS
Ali and Jordan

● Bob Costas (b. 1952), an award-winning sports announcer, anchored NBC's Summer Olympics coverage in Barcelona (1992) and Atlanta (1996), and has earned a reputation as a newscaster, news anchor, and investigative reporter. He frequently appears on *Dateline NBC, Today, On the Record,* and *InterNight.* In addition to his television journalism, Costas writes for print media. "Ali and Jordan" appeared in a special issue of *Rolling Stone* devoted to icons in 2003.

> **Preview**   What do you already know about Muhammad Ali and Michael Jordan? What points of comparison would you provide for them?

There are significant differences between Muhammad Ali and Michael Jordan, but perhaps the most significant similarity is right there on the surface: physical beauty. Grace, style, magnetism—they were wonders to behold. Beyond any objective measures of excellence and achievement, that is a good part of why they moved us. Why quibble with the obvious? If the outcome of each of Ali's fights had been the same, his every audacious utterance and action unchanged, but he looked like Sonny Liston, we've got a whole different story here.

Now grant to Jordan a world of talent and heart but a less abundant dose of dynamism. Maybe we've got Roy Orbison instead of Elvis. Here is where Ali and MJ are most connected to the marquee athlete of this generation, Tiger Woods. For all his transcendent skill and unbending will, Woods is also the most telegenic performer in sports, his star quality and presence so palpable they mesmerize not just viewers but opponents. If you must draw distinctions even among kings, Jordan may have been a better basketball player than Ali was a boxer, and Woods may soon demonstrate an even greater mastery of his game. This is the stuff of sports debate. Pick your man, make your case. But beyond the arena, there is no argument. Ali is the undisputed champ. In all of American sports, only Jackie Robinson matches or exceeds Ali's social impact. By the time Ali came along, most of America felt pretty comfortable with what Robinson had done. But Ali put the challenge back in. He wasn't asking for inclusion or acceptance, he was demanding to be respected on his terms only. Otherwise, screw you.

Ali represented a sea change in the kind of athlete America would be forced to tolerate and would ultimately learn to embrace. He brought together the two moral and cultural issues that defined his generation: race and Vietnam. While Arthur Ashe (the most admirable sports figure I've known) had a much more sophisticated grasp of issues, and many others, including Jim Brown, Curt Flood and Billie Jean King, made principled stands, symbolically Ali pulled it all together: black pride, liberation and

individuality, rejecting mainstream notions of acceptable behavior, especially by black athletes and entertainers. Ali brought Sixties politics to
sports. And he paid a price for it, giving up three prime years in the ring
when, after his refusal to accept induction into the military, reactionary
boxing commissioners stripped him of his title and sent him into athletic
exile. For all Ali knew, he'd never fight again, never see another big
purse. He risked it all for what be believed. Ultimately this earned him
the respect of even those who initially reviled him.

Muhammad Ali represented the passion, rage and high–spiritedness   4
of his time, and in the process he helped change the sporting culture
with his appealing brashness. Of course, there are unintended conse-

quences here. Almost all the trash talkers who followed him, the Warren Sapps, Jeremy Shockeys, et al., lack his appealing freshness and wit. But you can't blame Ali for that. I mean, England Dan and John Ford Coley aren't Bob Dylan's fault.

And neither is it Michael Jordan's fault that he came to prominence 5 when the issues were less vividly drawn, the moral high ground less clear. The whole context was different. Robinson and Ali had made their points and ultimately prevailed. There were no comparable dragons for Jordan to slay. Still, while Jordan was daring in competition, he was cautious to a fault away from it. Jordan grew up in North Carolina. The choice between Harvey Gantt and race–baiting Jesse Helms in a Senate race there seemed pretty clear. Still, Jordan begged off, famously (or infamously) remarking, "Republicans buy sneakers, too." And how about the company that makes those sneakers and enriches Jordan? Couldn't MJ have held Nike to account both on its overseas labor practices and on the whole idea of marketing sneakers to kids at prices exceeding the rent on their mothers' apartments? Couldn't Jordan's voice of reason make a difference?

Still, Jordan has been generous to charities, and if he does nothing 6 else, he has stood for something important: excellence. Not talent—that's a gift—but the constant, honest pursuit of excellence. That's an expression of character, and a welcome one at that, as is the dignity, even elegance that Jordan, and Woods, bring to a sports landscape blighted by the boorish and the inane. Even if they choose not to be as outspoken as athletes of earlier eras, surely Jordan and Woods realize that their nearly universal popularity is evidence of a changed world, a world that the likes of Jackie Robinson and Muhammad Ali fought to create.

Reading Closely

1. What did you learn about Muhammad Ali and Michael Jordan from this essay that you didn't know before you read it? What does Costas believe the biggest difference between them is?

2. Costas writes about the different qualities of Ali, Jordan, and Tiger Woods. List them. What positive qualities does Costas suggest they all share? Which ones does he see as unique to one of the men? What negative qualities does he see in each of them? Prepare to share your responses with the rest of the class.

3. How does the visual on p. 384 enhance the text—or does it? Provide specific examples for your answer.

4. What other comparisons involving sports and music figures does Costas make besides the one between Ali and Jordan? Who are these other figures, and how do they measure up to the likes of Ali and Jordan?

Considering Larger Issues

1. What is Costas's purpose in comparing Ali and Jordan? What specific passages help him achieve this purpose?

2. What is Costas's thesis statement? How does it reflect his purpose?

3. Issues of physical beauty and personality seem central to this essay. What other characteristics of Ali and Jordan might the author have compared? What characteristics of sports figures are most often analyzed and compared? Why do you think Costas focuses on the characteristics he does?

4. What differences does historical context make to a celebrity? In other words, why must Ali be considered in relation to the 1960s? What about Jordan and Woods — how are they explained in terms of the twenty-first century? What does Costas expect his readers to know beforehand as they read his essay? **Discuss these questions with three or four classmates,** and prepare to report your answers to the rest of the class.

5. COMBINING METHODS. Costas's comparison-and-contrast essay depends on other methods of development to help support his overall purpose. Mark passages where he uses *description, narration,* and *cause-and-consequence analysis* to support his comparison and contrast.

Thinking about Language

1. Are there any terms in this essay whose meanings you are unsure of? If so, write them down. Then define each word on your lists as well as the ones listed below, either from the essay context or by consulting your dictionary. Be prepared to share your answers with the rest of the class.

magnetism (1)	sea change (3)	race-baiting (5)
audacious (1)	mainstream (3)	boorish (6)
dynamism (2)	reactionary (3)	inane (6)
mesmerize (2)	prominence (5)	

2. **Working with one or two classmates,** discuss the tone or attitude Costas takes toward his subjects. What words or phrases help establish his tone? What is its overall effect? Given the readership of *Rolling Stone,* how does Costas match his tone to his audience? Be prepared to share your findings with the rest of the class.

Writing Your Own Essays Using Comparison and Contrast

1. Consider your academic (or athletic) achievements in relation to those of your parents or another relative from a generation other than your own. What points of comparison can you establish? what points of contrast? What role does the generational difference make in terms of political and social backdrops, financial advantages or disadvantages, home life, or individual opportunity? Draft an essay of three to four pages in which

you explore this relationship, making sure that you have an overall purpose and an intended audience. Do some research, if necessary, to learn about conditions in the earlier (or later) generation. Refer to "Checking Over the Use of Comparison and Contrast" (p. 370).

2. Consider your academic achievements so far: maybe you're an established honor student, or maybe you've barely mustered the courage to take your first college course. However you feel about your current academic status, compare and contrast your current self–assessment with the student you were years ago. In what ways have you improved, declined, or stayed the same? What are some of your old habits or skills that you want to recall — or get rid of? In what ways do these differences and similarities support or impede your academic progress? As you draft and revise your three- to four-page essay, refer to the guidelines for checking over the use of comparison and contrast on p. 370.

3. How might you compare and contrast two people in the same line of work but from markedly different generations? You might consider leading actors (Ben Affleck and Clint Eastwood), film directors (Demi Moore and Steven Spielberg), television personalities (Katie Couric and Kelly Ripa), or politicians (Barack Obama and Jesse Jackson) — but whomever you choose, think of them as representatives of a particular generation. Draft an essay of three to four pages that compares these two people. Be sure to consult the guidelines for checking over the use of comparison and contrast on p. 370.

ROBIN HATFIELD
Smoothing Rough Edges

A native Pennsylvanian, Robin Hatfield (b. 1978) was a college undergraduate when she wrote the following essay. Hatfield majored in English education at Penn State University and is currently teaching at Tyrone (PA) High School. In the essay, she addresses a very common situation: sibling rivalry, often a child's first experience in comparison and contrast.

> **Preview**   What do you know, firsthand or secondhand, about sibling rivalry? As you read Hatfield's essay, think about which supporting details are unique to her and her brother and which ones might be universal.

Although a difference of three years between siblings is not drastic, those   1
years still manage to influence the realities and perceptions of childhood experiences. At least they did for my brother David and me. I was always striving to grow up faster and close the gap between our experiences. Since I was one of the few girls living in a nearly all–boy neighborhood, I tried to toughen up and gain his attention by persistently tagging along. If Dave walked, I ran to catch up with him. If he rode away on his bike, I sprung on mine to follow. If he and his friends climbed trees to ambush the other warring tribe of neighborhood boys, I climbed after them. I competed with and followed Dave in everything, especially athletics, but I always took a little longer to find where I fit in, always trailed a little behind his precocious dedication. In my mind, those three years signified an impassable division—my younger age made it impossible for me to understand and join my brother's life. But starting in high school, changes in both our lives wore down the rough edges of my competitiveness, just as water rushing over rocks erodes their jagged edges into smooth, polished stone. I was no longer competing against my brother because our attitudes and experiences had been refined into incredible likeness.

Dave was quick to commit to what he loved. When he entered sev-   2
enth grade as a tall, skinny adolescent, a history teacher encouraged him to join the wrestling team and begin a weight lifting program. The training and practices, disciplines and rewards, challenges and the sport of wrestling itself provided an outlet for Dave's energy. After one year, he was hooked. As wrestling camps, extra practices, and seven–mile runs became habit, Dave's developing muscles provided balance for his slim 6′1″ frame. From fourth to ninth grade, I faithfully attended his matches with my parents to watch him grapple with and conquer not only his opponents but also his chronic asthma, even if it caused him to collapse after a match. From the bleachers, I witnessed him wrestle and win on the same day that he had surgery on his ear. I sat beside him at the

dinner table when he denied himself second helpings, and waited for him as he ran extra laps after a grueling practice so he could "make weight" for an upcoming match. Dave was a machine that ran on dedication, and wrestling was his life.

David's dedication to wrestling served as a model for me, but unlike 3 him, I couldn't find my niche and adhere to one activity. Wrestling was an integral part of my brother's being, while I only managed to jump frustratingly from activity to activity. From fifth to eighth grade, I dabbled in volleyball and softball, toyed with soccer and gymnastics, and amused myself with dancing and cheerleading. I was decent at each activity, but I wasn't satisfied. I couldn't cling to one of my diversions the way my brother clung to wrestling, and I felt that I was missing something. I thought that Dave had things figured out. He was "the wrestler," and I was just "Robin," or occasionally "Dave's sister." I needed to make a name for myself and escape from his shadow.

Establishing a separate identity didn't come automatically. When I 4 entered high school as a freshman, David was the strong and handsome senior captain of the wrestling team. I still faithfully attended his matches, but the picture of my invincible brother started to deteriorate before my eyes. I watched as he was hospitalized for several extreme asthma attacks. His usually quick motions slowed as his strength declined, and matches were often interrupted with his petitions to the referee to take a whiff of his inhaler. The newspapers daily lowered him in the state rankings, then finally dropped him completely. No amount of discipline could overcome his trials, and at his last match, when the referee lifted his opponent's hand in victory, my brother's head and shoulders sagged. His dream of being the state champion had been snatched from his reach.

All the while, I was still searching to find where I belonged. I had 5 played soccer during the fall of my freshman year and decided to keep in shape by competing in track during the spring. Track was the first sport that completely caught my interest. Pushing my legs and lungs to work harder not only trimmed seconds from my time, but also gave me focus. I thrived on the anxious feeling when I crouched in the blocks before I exploded at the sound of the gun. The track even *smelled* good. Every one of my senses told me that track was *my* sport, that I finally had something to commit to. Finally I could relate to my brother's experiences, and he could relate to mine. The gap between our ages was closing.

Even though I was no longer competing with my brother, I was be- 6 coming more like him by accepting new challenges. My coaches needed another girl to run the 100- and 300-yard hurdles, and although I was an unlikely candidate at only 5'2", they asked me to try. I agreed, and became one of the few people to make track a full-contact sport. It seemed that I tackled the hurdles more frequently than I cleared them, but my coaches, and my brother, appreciated my aggressiveness. I put as much effort into running as my brother put into wrestling. After practice I would run extra miles to build endurance or practice hurdle techniques.

Through this, Dave and I switched roles. He supported me at my meets—cheered me on when I won, and understood how I felt when I fell behind wheezing and coughing from my own asthma. He bragged to his friends when his "firecracker sister" hit a hurdle so hard that it broke, but he also brought me bags of ice to soothe the bruises and convinced my parents that I could handle the physical beating of hurdles. He laughed when he looked at my bloody knee and ankle and suggested that I wear a long dress to the prom. The love and attention he gave me was what I had been chasing after since childhood.

Over my high school years, Dave went off to college and heard accounts of my races, read the newspaper clippings about me that my parents had mailed to him, and called me after my big meets. When I was the team captain during my junior year, Dave heard about my going to the hospital for asthma problems. He listened to my dad tell him that I wasn't looking too good or moving too fast on the track anymore. On the phone I confessed that the last two hurdles wore me out, and he understood—the last two minutes of wrestling matches were what had always defeated him, too. During my last race, running with a stress-fractured foot, I finished one place short of qualifying for the state championships. Dave understood, and his soothing words over the phone comforted me. Following my brother had come full circle. We had ended up at the same place, although it took me a while longer to commit myself to get there.

Looking back, I see that my brother's and my experiences throughout childhood were very distinct. He led and I followed. He was immediately committed to athletics while I had to search and test, but we ended up very similar in our dedication, successes, and failures. The gaps between our experiences had decreased as we aged. I no longer compete with Dave; I trust that I no longer need to. We've both grown up, and the rough edges have been smoothed.

Reading Closely

1. As you read Hatfield's essay, did a comparison with one of your own siblings or other relatives come to mind? What passages in Hatfield's essay reminded you of your own family comparison?

2. What part does the following passage play in this essay: "I watched as he was hospitalized for several extreme asthma attacks. His usually quick motions slowed as his strength declined, and matches were often interrupted with his petitions to the referee to take a whiff of his inhaler" (paragraph 4)? How might you account for the fact that Hatfield introduces her own asthma only in passing and so late in the essay?

3. What picture do you have of Dave? of Robin? **Working with a class-mate,** devise descriptions of these two siblings, and share your portraits with the class.

Considering Larger Issues

1. Hatfield organizes her essay by first talking about her brother and then talking about herself, repeating this pattern, and finally talking about both of them together. Consider this organizational pattern in light of the two basic patterns discussed in this chapter (p. 364). In what ways is her divergence from those traditional patterns successful—or not?

2. How does the conclusion of Hatfield's essay relate to the introduction? What is her thesis statement? How does the conclusion go further than the thesis statement in helping you understand this sibling relationship?

3. Rewrite the opening paragraph from the young Dave's point of view. What is the overall effect of Robin's point of view? What changes are introduced by Dave's point of view?

4. Who is the audience for this essay? What is the purpose? How do audience and purpose come together? **Working with one or two class-mates,** compare your answers and prepare a group response for the rest of the class.

5. **COMBINING METHODS.** Besides the narrative passage mentioned in question 2 under "Reading Closely," what other methods does Hatfield use to develop and support her comparison and contrast? Where else does she use *narration*—and to what effect? Mark passages where she uses *exemplification* and *cause-and-consequence analysis*, commenting on their effect as well.

Thinking about Language

1. Using the context of the essay or your dictionary, define the following words. Be prepared to share your answers with the rest of the class.

precocious (1)   niche (3)   petitions (4)
"make weight" (2)   integral (3)

2. What words or phrases suggest the mutual love and respect that Hatfield and her brother share?

Writing Your Own Essays Using Comparison and Contrast

1. Because we often cannot avoid being compared and contrasted—or comparing and contrasting ourselves—with a sibling, comparison is often the source of sibling rivalry. Do you compete with any of your brothers, sisters, or other relatives? Using information from question 1 under "Reading Closely," draft a three- to four-page essay in which you compare and contrast yourself with one of your relatives. Make sure you

have a basis for comparison and points of comparison, following the guidelines in "Checking Over the Use of Comparison and Contrast" (p. 370). The most important question to answer as you begin this essay is, "Why am I comparing myself with this particular relative?"

2. Serena and Venus Williams; Ken Griffey and Ken Griffey Jr.; Brent, John, and Drew Barrymore; Jeff, Beau, and Lloyd Bridges; Michael and Janet Jackson; George H. W. and George W. Bush—these are just a few of the famous people from the same family. Choose one of these sets, or a set of your own, and plan a comparison-and-contrast essay about them. First of all, you'll want to decide why you want to compare the family members you've chosen. What might be the basis for comparison? the points of comparison? Following the guidelines that appear in "Checking Over the Use of Comparison and Contrast" (p. 370), draft a three- to four-page essay. **Consider working with a classmate** to revise each other's essays before submitting them to your instructor.

BRUCE CATTON

Grant and Lee: A Study in Contrasts

Bruce Catton (1899–1978) was a student at Oberlin College when he enlisted for military service in World War I; when he returned from the war, he chose not to complete his studies but to write. He worked in a wide range of capacities with the *Cleveland Plain Dealer* and other newspapers, served as a government speechwriter and information director, and pursued his life-long passion for the Civil War, becoming one of the foremost historians of that conflict. The author of eighteen books, Catton was awarded the Pulitzer Prize and the National Book Award for *A Stillness at Appomattox* (1953).

In the following essay, first published in 1956 in *The American Story*, Catton enriches our understanding of the complicated relationship between Civil War generals Ulysses S. Grant and Robert E. Lee. Despite their different backgrounds and loyalties, Catton makes clear, they shared important traits.

> **Preview**   As you read this comparison and contrast, consider the organizational method Catton employed and the reasons he chose this particular method of organization.

When Ulysses S. Grant and Robert E. Lee met in the parlor of a modest   1
house at Appomattox Court House, Virginia, on April 9, 1865, to work out the terms for the surrender of Lee's Army of Northern Virginia, a great chapter in American life came to a close, and a great new chapter began.

These men were bringing the Civil War to its virtual finish. To be   2
sure, other armies had yet to surrender, and for a few days the fugitive confederate government would struggle desperately and vainly, trying to find some way to go on living now that its chief support was gone. But in effect it was all over when Grant and Lee signed the papers. And the little room where they wrote out the terms was the scene of one of the poignant, dramatic contrasts in American history.

They were two strong men, these oddly different generals, and they   3
represented the strengths of two conflicting currents that, through them, had come into final collision.

Back of Robert E. Lee was the notion that the old aristocratic concept   4
might somehow survive and be dominant in American life.

Lee was tidewater Virginia, and in his background were family, cul-   5
ture, and tradition . . . the age of chivalry transplanted to a New World which was making its own legends and its own myths. He embodied a way of life that had come down through the age of knighthood and the English country squire. America was a land that was beginning all over again, dedicated to nothing much more complicated than the rather hazy belief that all men had equal rights, and should have an equal chance in the world. In such a land Lee stood for the feeling that it was somehow of advantage to human society to have a pronounced inequality in the

social structure. There should be a leisure class, backed by ownership of land; in turn, society itself should be keyed to the land as the chief source of wealth and influence. It would bring forth (according to this ideal) a class of men with a strong sense of obligation to the community; men who lived not to gain advantage for themselves, but to meet the solemn obligations which had been laid on them by the very fact that they were privileged. From them the country would get its leadership; to them it could look for the higher values — of thought, of conduct, of personal deportment — to give it strength and virtue.

Lee embodied the noblest elements of this aristocratic ideal. Through   6
him, the landed nobility justified itself. For four years, the Southern states had fought a desperate war to uphold the ideals for which Lee stood. In the end, it almost seemed as if the Confederacy fought for Lee; as if he himself was the Confederacy . . . the best thing that the way of life for which the Confederacy stood could ever have to offer. He had passed into legend before Appomattox. Thousands of tired, underfed, poorly clothed Confederate soldiers, long-since past the simple enthusiasm of the early days of the struggle, somehow considered Lee the symbol of everything for which they had been willing to die. But they could not quite put this feeling into words. If the Lost Cause, sanctified by so much

Grant and Lee at Appomattox.

heroism and so many deaths, had a living justification, its justification was General Lee.

Grant, the son of a tanner on the Western frontier, was everything Lee   7
was not. He had come up the hard way, and embodied nothing in particular except the eternal toughness and sinewy fiber of the men who grew up beyond the mountains. He was one of a body of men who owed reverence and obeisance to no one, who were self-reliant to a fault, who cared hardly anything for the past but who had a sharp eye for the future.

These frontier men were the precise opposites of the tidewater aris-   8
tocrats. Back of them, in the great surge that had taken people over the Alleghenies and into the opening Western country, there was a deep, implicit dissatisfaction with a past that had settled into grooves. They stood for democracy, not from any reasoned conclusion about the proper ordering of human society, but simply because they had grown up in the middle of democracy and knew how it worked. Their society might have privileges, but they would be privileges each man had won for himself. Forms and patterns meant nothing. No man was born to anything, except perhaps to a chance to show how far he could rise. Life was competition.

Yet along with this feeling had come a deep sense of belonging to a   9
national community. The Westerner who developed a farm, opened a shop, or set up in business as a trader could hope to prosper only as his own community prospered—and his community ran from the Atlantic to the Pacific and from Canada down to Mexico. If the land was settled, with towns and highways and accessible markets, he could better himself. He saw his fate in terms of the nation's own destiny. As its horizons expanded, so did his. He had, in other words, an acute dollars-and-cents stake in the continued growth and development of his country.

And that, perhaps, is where the contrast between Grant and Lee be-   10
comes most striking. The Virginia aristocrat, inevitably, saw himself in relation to his own region. He lived in a static society which could endure almost anything except change. Instinctively, his first loyalty would go to the locality in which that society existed. He would fight to the limit of endurance to defend it, because in defending it he was defending everything that gave his own life its deepest meaning.

The Westerner, on the other hand, would fight with an equal tenacity   11
for the broader concept of society. He fought so because everything he lived by was tried to growth, expansion, and a constantly widening horizon. What he lived by would survive or fall with the nation itself. He could not possibly stand by unmoved in the face of an attempt to destroy the Union. He would combat it with everything he had, because he could only see it as an effort to cut the ground out from under his feet.

So Grant and Lee were in complete contrast, representing two dia-   12
metrically opposed elements in American life. Grant was the modern

man emerging; beyond him, ready to come on the stage, was the great age of steel and machinery, of crowded cities and a restless, burgeoning vitality. Lee might have ridden down from the old age of chivalry, lance in hand, silken banner fluttering over his head. Each man was the perfect champion of his cause, drawing both his strengths and his weaknesses from the people he led.

Yet it was not all contrast, after all. Different as they were—in back- 13 ground, in personality, in underlying aspiration—these two great soldiers had much in common. Under everything else, they were marvelous fighters. Furthermore, their fighting qualities were really very much alike.

Each man had, to begin with, the great virtue of utter tenacity and fi- 14 delity. Grant fought his way down the Mississippi Valley in spite of acute personal discouragement and profound military handicaps. Lee hung on in the trenches at Petersburg after hope itself had died. In each man there was an indomitable quality . . . the born fighter's refusal to give up as long as he can still remain on his feet and lift his two fists.

Daring and resourcefulness they had, too; the ability to think faster 15 and move faster than the enemy. These were the qualities which gave Lee the dazzling campaigns of Second Manassas and Chancellorsville and won Vicksburg for Grant.

Lastly, and perhaps greatest of all, there was the ability, at the end, to 16 turn quickly from war to peace once the fighting was over. Out of the way these two men behaved at Appomattox came the possibility of a peace of reconciliation. It was a possibility not wholly realized, in the years to come, but which did, in the end, help the two sections to become one nation again . . . after a war whose bitterness might have seemed to make such a reunion wholly impossible. No part of either man's life became him more than the part he played in their brief meeting in the McLean house at Appomattox. Their behavior there put all succeeding generations of Americans in their debt. Two great Americans, Grant and Lee—very different, yet under everything very much alike. Their encounter at Appomattox was one of the great moments of American history.

Reading Closely

1. What did you learn about the Civil War from this essay that you didn't know before you read it? What does Catton believe the war was about? What was at stake?

2. Catton writes about the different qualities of Lee, the Southerner, and of Grant, the Westerner. List them. Do any of these qualities overlap? Do any of them balance each other? Are there any that are direct opposites? Prepare to share your responses with the rest of the class.

3. How does the visual enhance the text? Provide specific examples.

Considering Larger Issues

1. What is Catton's thesis statement? How does it relate to his purpose in comparing the two generals? Does he fulfill his purpose, in your opinion?

2. Although Catton is writing about a war between the North and South, he refers to these two generals as a *Westerner* and a *Southerner.* How do his definitions compare with your own, contemporary definitions of those terms? How do they overlap with or diverge from your definition of a *Northerner*? Do you feel like a Westerner, Southerner, or Northerner? Why? According to which definition? Write out your response, and then **exchange responses with a classmate.** Comment on each other's responses. Then return each other's responses and answer any questions your classmate has raised.

3. **COMBINING METHODS.** Catton's comparison–and–contrast essay depends on the definitions mentioned in the previous question to help support his overall purpose. But Catton uses other methods for making sense of these generals as well. Mark passages where he uses *description, narration,* and *cause-and-consequence analysis* to support his comparison and contrast.

Thinking about Language

1. Are there any terms in this essay whose meanings you are unsure of? If so, write them down. Then define each word on your list, as well as the ones listed below, either from the context of the essay or by consulting your dictionary.

poignant (2)	leisure class (5)	surge (8)
tidewater (5)	embodied (6)	tenacity (11)
chivalry (5)	obeisance (7)	indomitable (14)
transplanted (5)		

2. **Working with two or three classmates,** identify all the confident assertions that Catton makes about nineteenth–century beliefs, values, leaders, and battle. What is the effect of Catton's tone of certainty on your reading of his essay? Compose a group response, and share it with the rest of the class.

Writing Your Own Essays Using Comparison and Contrast

1. **Consider working with a classmate** to compare and contrast the characteristics of Civil War–era Southerners and contemporary cowboys, using Catton's essay and "About Men" by Gretel Ehrlich (p. 223) as your sources. How do both descriptions help explain the courtly behavior of cowboys? Draft a three- to four-page essay in which you use your comparison and contrast as a way to consider the consequences of Southerners moving west and becoming courtly cowboys. Be sure to refer to "Checking Over the Use of Comparison and Contrast" (p. 370).

2. The Westerners in Catton's essay also have much in common with the cowboys in Ehrlich's essay. Draft a short essay (two to three pages) in which you compare and contrast Catton's mid–nineteenth–century Westerners with Ehrlich's contemporary cowboys. Use "Checking Over the Use of Comparison and Contrast" (p. 370) to make sure you've met all the criteria of a successful essay using comparison and contrast, especially in terms of your thesis statement and conclusion.

3. Although people in every geographical region of the United States shop at the Gap, buy McDonald's hamburgers, and see blockbuster Hollywood movies, regional differences remain. How might you compare and contrast two people in the same line of work from markedly different regions? You might consider leading singers (Dolly Parton and Bruce Springsteen), athletes (Shaquille O'Neal and Kobe Bryant), business entrepreneurs (Bill Gates and Ted Turner), television personalities (Garrison Keillor and Jerry Seinfeld), politicians (George W. Bush and Nancy Pelosi) — whomever you choose, think of them as representatives of particular regions. Draft an essay of three to four pages that compares these two people. Be sure to consult the guidelines for checking over the use of comparison and contrast on p. 370.

DAVE BARRY

Guys vs. Men

Associated with the *Miami Herald* since 1983, Dave Barry (b. 1947) is one of the most widely syndicated columnists in the United States. He is best known for his humorous writings, but his commentary also earned him a 1988 Pulitzer Prize. Besides writing a daily newspaper column, Barry is lead guitarist for the Rock Bottom Remainders and has published a number of best-selling books, among them *Babies and Other Hazards of Sex: How to Make a Tiny Person in Only 9 Months, with Tools You Probably Have around the House* (1984), *Stay Fit and Healthy until You're Dead* (1985), *Dave Barry's Bad Habits: A 100% Fact-Free Book* (1993), *Dave Barry Is Not Taking This Sitting Down* (2000), and *Tricky Business* (2002). The following selection was first published as the introduction *to Dave Barry's Complete Guide to Guys* (1995).

> **Preview** Write for a few minutes about the differences you see between "guys" and "men."

This is a book about guys. It's *not* a book about men. There are already 1
way too many books about men, and most of them are *way* too serious.

Men itself is a serious word, not to mention *manhood* and *manly*. Such 2
words make being male sound like a very important activity, as opposed
to what it primarily consists of, namely, possessing a set of minor and
frequently unreliable organs.

But men tend to attach great significance to Manhood. This results in 3
certain characteristically masculine, by which I mean stupid, behavioral
patterns that can produce unfortunate results such as violent crime, war,
spitting, and ice hockey. These things have given males a bad name.[1] And
the "Men's Movement," which is supposed to bring out the more positive
aspects of Manliness, seems to be densely populated with loons and
goobers.

So I'm saying that there's another way to look at males: not as ag- 4
gressive macho dominators; not as sensitive, liberated, hugging drum-
mers; but as *guys*.

And what, exactly, do I mean by "guys"? I don't know. I haven't 5
thought that much about it. One of the major characteristics of guyhood
is that we guys don't spend a lot of time pondering our deep innermost
feelings. There is a serious question in my mind about whether guys actually *have* deep innermost feelings, unless you count, for example, loyalty to the Detroit Tigers, or fear of bridal showers.

But although I can't define exactly what it means to be a guy, I can 6
describe certain guy characteristics, such as:

---

[1] Specifically, "asshole."

GUYS LIKE NEAT STUFF

By "neat," I mean "mechanical and unnecessarily complex." I'll give   7
you an example. Right now I'm typing these words on an *extremely* powerful computer. It's the latest in a line of maybe ten computers I've
owned, each one more powerful than the last. My computer is chock full
of RAM and ROM and bytes and megahertzes and various other items
that enable a computer to kick data–processing butt. It is probably capable of supervising the entire U.S. air–defense apparatus while simultaneously processing the tax return of every resident of Ohio. I use it
mainly to write a newspaper column. This is an activity wherein I sit and
stare at the screen for maybe ten minutes, then, using only my forefin-
gers, slowly type something like:

Henry Kissinger* looks like a big wart.   8

I stare at this for another ten minutes, have an inspiration, then am–   9
plify the original thought as follows:

Henry Kissinger looks like a big fat wart.   10

Then I stare at that for another ten minutes, pondering whether I   11
should try to work in the concept of "hairy."

This is absurdly simple work for my computer. It sits there, humming   12
impatiently, bored to death, passing the time between keystrokes via
brain–teaser activities such as developing a Unified Field Theory of the
universe and translating the complete works of Shakespeare into rap.[2]

In other words, this computer is absurdly overqualified to work for   13
me, and yet soon, I guarantee, I will buy an *even more powerful* one. I won't
be able to stop myself. I'm a guy.

Probably the ultimate example of the fundamental guy drive to have   14
neat stuff is the Space Shuttle. Granted, the guys in charge of this program *claim* it has a Higher Scientific Purpose, namely to see how humans
function in space. But of course we have known for years how humans
function in space: They float around and say things like: "Looks real
good, Houston!"

No, the real reason for the existence of the Space Shuttle is that it is   15
one humongous and spectacularly gizmo–intensive item of hardware.
Guys can tinker with it practically forever, and occasionally even get it to
work, and use it to place *other* complex mechanical items into orbit,
where they almost immediately break, which provides a great excuse to
send the Space Shuttle up *again*. It's Guy Heaven.

Other results of the guy need to have stuff are Star Wars, the recre-   16
ational boating industry, monorails, nuclear weapons, and wristwatches

---

* **Henry Kissinger** (b. 1923): foreign policy adviser to President Nixon and U.S.
secretary of state, 1973–77.

[2] To be or not? I got to *know*.
   Might kill myself by the end of the *show*.

that indicate the phase of the moon. I am not saying that women haven't been involved in the development or use of this stuff. I'm saying that, without guys, this stuff probably would not exist; just as, without women, virtually every piece of furniture in the world would still be in its original position. Guys do not have a basic need to rearrange furniture. Whereas a woman who could cheerfully use the same computer for fifty–three years will rearrange her furniture on almost a weekly basis, sometimes in the dead of night. She'll be sound asleep in bed, and suddenly, at 2 A.M., she'll be awakened by the urgent thought: *The blue-green sofa needs to go perpendicular to the wall instead of parallel, and it needs to go there* RIGHT NOW. So she'll get up and move it, which of course necessitates moving other furniture, and soon she has rearranged her entire living room, shifting great big heavy pieces that ordinarily would require several burly men to lift, because there are few forces in Nature more powerful than a woman who needs to rearrange furniture. Every so often a guy will wake up to discover that, because of his wife's overnight efforts, he now lives in an entirely different house.

(I realize that I'm making gender–based generalizations here, but my 17 feeling is that if God did not want us to make gender–based generalizations, She would not have given us genders.)

GUYS LIKE A REALLY POINTLESS CHALLENGE

Not long ago I was sitting in my office at the *Miami Herald's* Sunday 18 magazine, *Tropic*, reading my fan mail,[3] when I heard several of my guy coworkers in the hallway talking about how fast they could run the forty–yard dash. These are guys in their thirties and forties who work in journalism, where the most demanding physical requirement is the ability to digest vending–machine food. In other words, these guys have absolutely no need to run the forty–yard dash.

But one of them, Mike Wilson, was writing a story about a star high– 19 school football player who could run it in 4.38 seconds. Now if Mike had written a story about, say, a star high–school poet, none of my guy coworkers would have suddenly decided to find out how well they could write sonnets. But when Mike turned in his story, they became *deeply* concerned about how fast they could run the forty–yard dash. They were so concerned that the magazine editor, Tom Shroder, decided that they should get a stopwatch and go out to a nearby park and find out. Which they did, a bunch of guys taking off their shoes and running around barefoot in a public park on company time.

This is what I heard them talking about, out in the hall. I heard Tom, 20 who was thirty–eight years old, saying that his time in the forty had been

---

[3] Typical fan letter: "Who cuts your hair? Beavers?"

5.75 seconds. And I thought to myself: This is ridiculous. These are middle-aged guys, supposedly adults, and they're out there *bragging* about their performance in this stupid juvenile footrace. Finally I couldn't stand it anymore.

"Hey!" I shouted. *"I could beat 5.75 seconds."* 21

So we went out to the park and measured off forty yards, and the 22 guys told me that I had three chances to make my best time. On the first try my time was 5.78 seconds, just three-hundredths of a second slower than Tom's, even though, at forty-five, I was seven years older than he. So I just *knew* I'd beat him on the second attempt if I ran really, really hard, which I did for a solid ten yards, at which point my left hamstring muscle, which had not yet shifted into Spring Mode from Mail-Reading Mode, went, and I quote, "pop."

I had to be helped off the field. I was in considerable pain, and I was 23 obviously not going to be able to walk right for weeks. The other guys were very sympathetic, especially Tom, who took the time to call me at home, where I was sitting with an ice pack on my leg and twenty-three Advil in my bloodstream, so he could express his concern.

"Just remember," he said, *"you didn't beat my time."* 24

There are countless other examples of guys rising to meet pointless 25 challenges. Virtually all sports fall into this category, as well as a large part of U.S. foreign policy. ("I'll bet you can't capture Manuel Noriega!"* "Oh YEAH??")

GUYS DO NOT HAVE A RIGID AND WELL-DEFINED MORAL CODE

This is not the same as saying that guys are bad. Guys *are* capable of 26 doing bad things, but this generally happens when they try to be Men and start becoming manly and aggressive and stupid. When they're being just plain guys, they aren't so much actively *evil* as they are *lost.* Because guys have never really grasped the Basic Human Moral Code, which I believe was invented by women millions of years ago when all the guys were out engaging in some other activity, such as seeing who could burp the loudest. When they came back, there were certain rules that they were expected to follow unless they wanted to get into Big Trouble, and they have been trying to follow these rules ever since, with extremely irregular results. Because guys have never *internalized* these rules. Guys are similar to my small auxiliary backup dog, Zippy, a guy dog[4] who has been told numerous times that he is *not* supposed to (1) get

---

* **Manuel Noriega** (b. 1934): Panamanian dictator removed from power by armed U.S. intervention in 1989.

[4] I also have a female dog, Earnest, who *never* breaks the rules.

into the kitchen garbage or (2) poop on the floor. He knows that these are the rules, but he has never really understood *why*, and sometimes he gets to thinking: Sure, I am *ordinarily* not supposed to get into the garbage, but obviously this rule is not meant to apply when there are certain extenuating[5] circumstances, such as (1) somebody just threw away some perfectly good seven–week–old Kung Pao Chicken, and (2) I am home alone.

And so when the humans come home, the kitchen floor has been 27 transformed into Garbage–Fest USA, and Zippy, who usually comes rushing up, is off in a corner disguised in a wig and sunglasses, hoping to get into the Federal Bad Dog Relocation Program before the humans discover the scene of the crime.

When I yell at him, he frequently becomes so upset that he poops on 28 the floor.

Morally, most guys are just like Zippy, only taller and usually less hairy. 29 Guys are *aware* of the rules of moral behavior, but they have trouble keeping these rules in the forefronts of their minds at certain times, especially the present. This is especially true in the area of faithfulness to one's mate. I realize, of course, that there are countless examples of guys being faithful to their mates until they die, usually as a result of being eaten by their mates immediately following copulation. Guys outside of the spider community, however, do not have a terrific record of faithfulness.

I'm not saying guys are scum. I'm saying that many guys who con- 30 sider themselves to be committed to their marriages will stray if they are confronted with overwhelming temptation, defined as "virtually any temptation."

Okay, so maybe I *am* saying guys are scum. But they're not *mean-* 31 *spirited* scum. And few of them — even when they are out of town on business trips, far from their wives, and have a clear–cut opportunity — will poop on the floor.

GUYS ARE NOT GREAT AT COMMUNICATING THEIR INTIMATE FEELINGS, ASSUMING THEY HAVE ANY

This is an aspect of guyhood that is very frustrating to women. A guy 32 will be reading the newspaper, and the phone will ring; he'll answer it, listen for ten minutes, hang up, and resume reading. Finally his wife will say: "Who was that?"

And he'll say: "Phil Wonkerman's mom."   33
(Phil is an old friend they haven't heard from in seventeen years.)   34
And the wife will say, "Well?"   35
And the guy will say, "Well what?"   36

---

[5] I am taking some liberties here with Zippy's vocabulary. More likely, in his mind, he uses the term *mitigating*.

And the wife will say, "What did she *say?*"   37

And the guy will say, "She said Phil is fine," making it clear by his   38
tone of voice that, although he does not wish to be rude, he is trying to
read the newspaper, and he happens to be right in the middle of an important panel of "Calvin and Hobbes."

But the wife, ignoring this, will say, "That's *all* she said?"   39

And she will not let up. She will continue to ask district–attorney–style   40
questions, forcing the guy to recount the conversation until she's satisfied
that she has the entire story, which is that Phil just got out of prison after
serving a sentence for a murder he committed when he became a drug addict because of the guilt he felt when his wife died in a freak submarine accident while Phil was having an affair with a nun, but now he's all
straightened out and has a good job as a trapeze artist and is almost
through with the surgical part of his sex change and recently became happily engaged to marry a prominent member of the Grateful Dead, so in
other words he is fine, which is *exactly* what the guy told her in the first
place, but is that enough? No. She wants to hear *every single detail.*

Or let's say two couples get together after a long separation. The two   41
women will have a conversation, lasting several days, during which they
discuss virtually every significant event that has occurred in their lives
and the lives of those they care about, sharing their innermost thoughts,
analyzing and probing, inevitably coming to a deeper understanding of
each other, and a strengthening of a cherished friendship. Whereas the
guys will watch the play–offs.

This is not to say the guys won't share their feelings. Sometimes   42
they'll get quite emotional.

"That's not a FOUL??" they'll say.   43

Or: "YOU'RE TELLING ME THAT'S NOT A FOUL???"   44

I have a good friend, Gene, and one time, when he was going   45
through a major medical development in his life, we spent a weekend
together. During this time Gene and I talked a lot and enjoyed each
other's company immensely, but—this is true—the most intimate personal statement he made to me is that he has reached Level 24 of a video
game called "Arkanoid." He had even seen the Evil Presence, although he
refused to tell me what it looks like. We're very close, but there is a limit.

You may think that my friends and I are Neanderthals, and that a lot   46
of guys are different. This is true. A lot of guys don't use words at *all.*
They communicate entirely by nonverbal methods, such as sharing bait.

Are you starting to see what I mean by "guyness"? I'm basically talking   47
about the part of the male psyche that is less serious and/or aggressive
than the Manly Manhood part, but still essentially very male. My feeling
is that the world would be a much better[6] place if more males would

---

[6] As measured by total sales of [my] book.

Example Chart

Men	Guys
Vince Lombardi	Joe Namath
Oliver North	Gilligan
Hemingway	Gary Larson
Columbus	Whichever astronaut hit the first golf ball on the Moon
Superman	Bart Simpson
Doberman pinschers	Labrador retrievers
Abbott	Costello
Captain Ahab	Captain Kangaroo
Satan	Snidely Whiplash
The pope	Willard Scott
Germany	Italy
Geraldo	Katie Couric

stop trying so hard to be Men and instead settle for being Guys. Think of the historical problems that could have been avoided if more males had been able to keep their genderhood in its proper perspective, both in themselves and in others. ("Hey, Adolf, just because you happen to possess a set of minor and frequently unreliable organs, that is no reason to invade Poland.") And think how much happier women would be if, instead of endlessly fretting about what the males in their lives are thinking, they could relax, secure in the knowledge that the correct answer is: *very little.*

Yes, what we need, on the part of both genders, is more understand-   48
ing of guyness. And that is why I wrote this book. I intend to explore in detail every major facet of guyhood, including the historical facet, the sociological facet, the physiological facet, the psychosexual facet, and the facet of how come guys spit so much. Every statement of fact you will

Stimulus–Response Comparison Chart: Women vs. Men vs. Guys

Stimulus	Typical Woman Response	Typical Man Response	Typical Guy Response
An untamed river in the wilderness.	Contemplate its beauty.	Build a dam.	See who can pee the farthest off the dam.
A child who is sent home from school for being disruptive in class.	Talk to the child in an effort to determine the cause.	Threaten to send the child to a military academy.	Teach the child how to make armpit farts.
Human mortality	Religious faith	The pyramids	Bungee–jumping

read in this book is either based on actual laboratory tests, or else I made it up. But you can trust me. I'm a guy.

Reading Closely

1. Define *guy* and *man,* according to Barry. What details does Barry provide about how each of them lives his life?

2. How would you relate the characteristics of these two groups of males with U.S. culture? Discuss your responses **with several classmates,** determining whether you all read Barry's piece in similar or different ways. Share your group's findings with the rest of the class.

3. How does the information organized in either chart extend Barry's examples?

Considering Larger Issues

1. What is the purpose of this introduction? Who is Barry's audience? How does his audience affect his purpose, and how does his purpose influence the way he addresses his audience? Write out your answers, supplying evidence from the selection as support.

2. How exactly do the two charts near the end enhance the thesis? What is Barry's thesis?

3. Determine the organizational pattern, and make an outline of the selection that shows the pattern of organization. As you look over your outline and the selection, consider why Barry uses this particular organizational pattern. Be prepared to share your response with the rest of the class.

4. **COMBINING METHODS.** How does Barry use *cause-and-consequence analysis* to support his comparison and contrast? Mark the specific cause–and–consequence passages, and discuss their impact with your classmates.

Thinking about Language

1. Referring to the context or to your dictionary, define the following terms. Be prepared to share your answers with the rest of the class.

loons (3)	gender–based (17)	forefronts (29)
dominators (4)	hamstring (22)	recount (40)
megahertzes (7)	internalized (26)	Neanderthals (46)
burly (16)	extenuating (26)	nonverbal (46)

2. How might Barry define *maturity?* What are the various ways he illustrates this term — in the selection? Write out your answers, and prepare to share them with the rest of the class.

3. **Working with two or three classmates,** discuss the initial effect of the opening paragraph as well as its overall effect after you've read the

entire selection. What evidence from Barry's text supports your responses? How would you describe the style of Barry's opening? Share your responses with the rest of the class.

Writing Your Own Essays Using Comparison and Contrast

1. Attend or watch a sporting event **with a group of students** (or others) that includes both sexes. Pay careful attention to the way(s) various spectators respond, taking copious and very careful notes as you observe how others observe the game. Can you compare and contrast your findings in any meaningful way? Did the men react differently from the guys? Did the women respond differently from either or both of those two male groups? Draft a two- to three-page essay in which you compare and contrast the behavior of either the men and the guys or the males and the females. Be sure to follow the guidelines in "Checking Over the Use of Comparison and Contrast" (p. 370).

2. Can women be broken down into two groups comparable to "men" and "guys"? If so, draft a three- to four-page essay, modeled after Barry's, in which you compare and contrast these two groups of women. Make assertions about each group, and support your assertions with examples and details. Be sure to establish clear points of comparison. If your examples can be ironic and humorous, like Barry's, so much the better. As you draft and revise, be sure to follow the guidelines in "Checking Over the Use of Comparison and Contrast" (p. 370).

If Experience Is Equal, Who Gets Hired?

"CareerBuilders," a weekly feature in the State College, Pennsylvania, newspaper *Centre Daily Times*, explores aspects of finding and keeping jobs or enhancing one's employment opportunities. The following column, which appeared in "CareerBuilders" in February 2003, deals with the subjective — yet often controllable — issues that can make or break a job application.

Preview Consider the last time you interviewed for a job. What qualifications did you bring to the interview? What were you lacking, if anything?

Any time you apply for a job, you're one of numerous candidates, but once employers consider experience, training and fit — usually determined by your résumé — the list begins to narrow. Interviews are scheduled and the rest is up to you. 1

This week, we'll take a look at three people going for the same job, all with similar credentials. The difference is that each candidate takes a different approach to the job-search process. 2

We've laid out three scenarios and asked our CareerBuilder experts which candidate is the most likely to receive a job offer: 3

Candidate A: He responds to an ad in the newspaper and sends in a carefully crafted cover letter and résumé. Although he really wants the job, he fights the urge to call and ask if the company has received it. He does not want to appear "pushy." He is called in for the interview, in which he presents himself well when meeting with human resources, even if he comes across a bit nervous. Candidate A doesn't provide references — they never ask, so he doesn't offer. He doesn't have any questions about the job, but is extremely grateful for the interview. He responds to the interviewer with a hand-written thank-you note the next day. He does not call to check on status. 4

Candidate B: Candidate B knows a guy who knows a guy who works for the company. After sitting on an employee's desk for weeks, B's résumé eventually gets to the vice president of human resources, who then gives him a call for an interview. He doesn't bother to follow up with his friend's friend beforehand. He has an effective interview but he appears a bit too aggressive, asking questions about vacation time, bonuses and tuition reimbursement. He follows up the interview with a thank-you e-mail and calls the next day to check on status. 5

Candidate C: Candidate C's resume is in the company's database from a previous inquiry. When called for an interview, she forwards a revised résumé and a list of references. Because of traffic, Candidate C shows up for the interview 10 minutes late. Still, she proceeds to interview very well and 6 asks the potential employer a few questions about the job and the company. She sends a typed thank–you letter two days after the interview. She waits one week before calling to check on her application.

OUR EXPERTS RESPOND

"Candidate C has the leg up because she sent a revised résumé and the list of references, though the list isn't always important early in the process.   7

The fact she showed up 10 minutes late is unfortunate, but not a   8 deal–killer. She demonstrated having done her homework and a sincere interest in the company by asking questions about the job and the company. Sending the thank–you letter two days later was fine; no one is sitting around waiting for those anyway. Smart of her to wait a week before checking on the status. Most employers and recruiters are conducting multiple searches, so to think there will be a decision made the next day is naïve and can signal desperation. Not following up at all suggests a lack of interest, disorganization and/or passiveness, none of which are attractive traits to an employer."

– VIRGINIA CLARKE, consultant, Spencer Stuart, Chicago

"My choice is Candidate C. When invited for the interview, she ap-   9
propriately displayed initiative by sending an updated résumé and references. Despite the fact that she was late—I will assume she left home
allowing sufficient travel time and faced traffic, a variable she cannot
control—she interviewed very well, asked key questions and promptly
followed up with a thank-you letter. Hopefully, in her letter she expressed continued interest in the position. In short, she appears to have
been persistent and persuasive throughout the entire process.

Candidate A made several serious mistakes: He displayed no initia-   10
tive; he did not call to check on the status—both before and after the interview; he provided no references; and he asked no pertinent questions.
Candidate B leveraged himself well through networking with someone
he knew at the company, but he displayed two critical flaws. He did not
follow up to thank his friend's friend, perhaps to gain some additional
insight about the company. Although he interviewed well, he asked inappropriate questions for an initial interview, reflecting that he was more
interested in what the company offered him than what he could offer the
company."

    – DOUG MORRISON, CPRW, executive director, Career Power, Charlotte, N.C.

"Of the three candidates presented, I easily choose Candidate C for   11
the position. Candidate A's hesitancy in inquiring about the status of his
résumé, offering references and his nervousness interviewing showed a
lack of confidence. Candidate B's interview displayed a 'what are you
going to give me' attitude. Candidate B showed no interest in the company as a whole or the position and he was pushy. Candidate C showed
a proactive quality by having her information current and forwarding
her résumé without prompting.

She displayed confidence in herself by offering her references. Her   12
preparation showed by the questions she asked.

She displayed professionalism and courtesy by sending her thank-   13
you letter within a respectable time and giving the interviewer time to
organize results before placing her follow-up call. Although she was late,
she was well organized, professional, prepared, confident and interested
in the opportunity."

    – VICKI LAYDE, CPC, senior consultant, The Opportunities Group, Chicago

"While none of these candidates interviewed perfectly, I would favor   14
Candidate C. Candidate A appears too cautious, playing it safe and not
extending himself. He is inwardly eager, but how does the employer
know this? A survey performed by the National Association of Colleges
and Employers found that communication skills are at the top of an employer's wish list.

Candidate A does not ask questions—a big mistake. He does not ex-   15
press his personality and comes across nervous, which will unsettle the
interviewer.

Candidate B is too focused on the personal benefits of the position.   16
The employer does not learn much about him. He probably had the best
chance since he had an inside referral, but he doesn't capitalize on that.
His follow–up is unprofessional and pushy.

Candidate C makes a mistake in arriving late. A check of her refer–   17
ences can determine if this is a chronic problem. However, she is proactive, motivated, prepared and thinks strategically. Over the long term, she
may be more successful. It is critical to prepare for an interview by researching the company and asking questions. An interview should be a
two–way exchange. She follows up in a professional and timely manner."
— CAROLYN DOUGHERTY, CPC, president, IntelliSource, Inc., Philadelphia

Reading Closely

1. What are the strengths and weaknesses of each of the three candidates?
2. What is the basis for comparison? What are the points of comparison?
   What do all three candidates have in common?

Considering Larger Issues

1. What is the overall purpose of this article? Who is the intended audience? How do considerations of purpose and audience work together?
2. What is your evaluation of the three candidates? Do you agree that candidate C is the strongest? What advice would you give each of the three
   candidates if they were each offered a follow–up interview? if none of
   them received an offer but were preparing for an interview with another
   company? Be prepared to share your responses with the rest of the class.
3. **With two or three classmates,** discuss what the responses of the four
   "experts" reveal about employers or about people who advise employers
   about hiring. What points of comparison and contrast can you find between the experts? Report on your findings to the class.
4. COMBINING METHODS. Each expert's response uses *cause-and-consequence
   analysis* to explain his or her reaction to the applicants. Mark where each
   expert mentions the consequences of a specific action or inaction by one
   of the applicants.
5. The visual on p. 409 depicts the three job applicants as if they were con-
   testants in a game show. Do you find this way of looking at the situation
   amusing, or would a more serious illustration be more appropriate for
   this piece of writing? How, if at all, does the illustration enhance the text?

Thinking about Language

1. Using a dictionary or the context of the essay, define the following terms.
   Be prepared to share your answers with the rest of the class.

scenarios (3)   recruiters (8)   proactive (11)
crafted (4)   passiveness (8)   professionalism
human resources (4)   variable (9)   (13)
leg up (7)   pertinent (10)   strategically (17)
deal–killer (8)

2. Mark the words and phrases used to describe each of the candidates. What do each of these sets of adjectives connote? What words could replace them, making the connotation more positive or more negative? Be prepared to share your ideas with the rest of the class.

Writing Your Own Essays Using Comparison and Contrast

1. Draft a three- to four-page essay that compares two job–application experiences. You might compare the unsuccessful and successful interviews you've had, your bad experience with the good experience you're planning to have next time, or your experience and that of one of your friends with whom you share similar credentials. **Review your draft with a classmate,** and refer to the guidelines for checking over the use of comparison and contrast on p. 370.

2. In college, you are expected to devote most of your time to learning a great deal of new information and new skills. Once you dedicate yourself to doing so, you may find that you're leaving some of your past skills and interests behind. Draft a two- to three-page essay in which you compare and contrast your feelings about all the things you're learning and all the things you seem to be leaving behind. You don't need to spend the same amount of time discussing the past and the present; just be sure to clarify your attitudes toward each of these time periods. Establish a purpose, a pattern of organization, and a specific audience as you draft and revise. Also refer to the guidelines for checking over the use of comparison and contrast on p. 370.

ZORA NEALE HURSTON
How It Feels to Be Colored Me

Zora Neale Hurston (1891–1960) was one of the most productive writers, researchers, and anthropologists of the early twentieth century. Born in the all-black community of Eatonville, Florida (a community that shaped her outlook on life and writing), Hurston left home at an early age to work for a traveling theater company before finishing high school in Baltimore. She entered Howard University in 1920, supporting herself as a manicurist and writing for the university's literary magazine in her spare time. In 1925 she moved to New York City, where she participated in the African American literary and artistic movement known as the Harlem Renaissance. During her early years in New York, Hurston attended Barnard College (the undergraduate women's college of Columbia University) and studied with the renowned anthropologist Franz Boaz, who encouraged her to tap her Florida background to enrich her scholarly study of folklore and provide raw material for her prolific writings.

Despite her influence during the Harlem Renaissance, Hurston faded from public attention for many years afterwards. It wasn't until Alice Walker edited and republished some of her work in the 1970s that Hurston was "rediscovered." Her many books include *Jonah's Gourd Vine* (1934), *Mules and Men* (1935), *Their Eyes Were Watching God* (1937), *Dust Tracks on a Road* (1942), and *I Love Myself: when I Am Laughing . . . and Then Again when I Am Looking Mean and Impressive* (1979). Originally published in 1928, "How It Feels to Be Colored Me" was taken from *I Love Myself*, a collection of stories and essays.

Preview   What might Zora Neale Hurston mean by the title of this essay?

I am colored but I offer nothing in the way of extenuating circumstances 1
except the fact that I am the only Negro in the United States whose grandfather on the mother's side was *not* an Indian chief.

I remember the very day that I became colored. Up to my thirteenth 2
year I lived in the little Negro town of Eatonville, Florida. It is exclusively a colored town. The only white people I knew passed through the town going to or coming from Orlando. The native whites rode dusty horses, the Northern tourists chugged down the sandy village road in automobiles. The town knew the Southerners and never stopped cane chewing* when they passed. But the Northerners were something else again. They were peered at cautiously from behind curtains by the timid. The more venturesome would come out on the porch to watch them go past and got just as much pleasure out of the tourists as the tourists got out of the village.

The front porch might seem a daring place for the rest of the town, 3
but it was a gallery seat for me. My favorite place was atop the gate–post.

---

* **cane chewing:** chewing sugar–cane stalks.

Proscenium box for a born first–nighter. Not only did I enjoy the show, but I didn't mind the actors knowing that I liked it. I usually spoke to them in passing. I'd wave at them and when they returned my salute, I would say something like this: "Howdy–do–well–I–thank–you–where–you–goin'?" Usually automobile or the horse paused at this, and after a queer exchange of compliments, I would probably "go a piece of the way" with them, as we say in farthest Florida. If one of my family happened to come to the front in time to see me, of course negotiations would be rudely broken off. But even so, it is clear that I was the first "welcome–to–our–state" Floridian, and I hope the Miami Chamber of Commerce will please take notice.

During this period, white people differed from colored to me only in   4
that they rode through town and never lived there. They liked to hear me "speak pieces" and sing and wanted to see me dance the parse–me–la, and gave me generously of their small silver for doing these things, which seemed strange to me for I wanted to do them so much that I needed bribing to stop. Only they didn't know it. The colored people gave no dimes. They deplored any joyful tendencies in me, but I was their Zora nevertheless. I belonged to them, to the nearby hotels, to the country — everybody's Zora.

But changes came in the family when I was thirteen, and I was sent   5
to school in Jacksonville. I left Eatonville, the town of the oleanders, as Zora. When I disembarked from the river–boat at Jacksonville, she was no more. It seemed that I had suffered a sea change. I was not Zora of Orange County any more. I was now a little colored girl. I found it out in certain ways. In my heart as well as in the mirror, I became a fast brown — warranted not to rub nor run.

But I am not tragically colored. There is no great sorrow dammed up in   6
my soul, nor lurking behind my eyes. I do not mind at all. I do not belong to the sobbing school of Negrohood who hold that nature somehow has given them a lowdown dirty deal and whose feelings are all hurt about it. Even in the helter–skelter skirmish that is my life, I have seen that the world is to the strong* regardless of a little pigmentation more or less. No, I do not weep at the world — I am too busy sharpening my oyster knife.*

Someone is always at my elbow reminding me that I am the grand-   7
daughter of slaves. It fails to register depression with me. Slavery is sixty years in the past. The operation was successful and the patient is doing

* **the world is to the strong:** an allusion to the biblical passage (in Ecclesiastes 9:11) that reads "The race is not to the swift, nor the battle to the strong."

* **sharpening my oyster knife:** an allusion to the saying "The world is my oyster," which appears in Shakespeare's *The Merry Wives of Windsor.*

Zora Neale Hurston.

well, thank you. The terrible struggle* that made me an American out of a potential slave said "On the line!" The Reconstruction said "Get set!"; and the generation before said "Go!" I am off to a flying start and I must not halt in the stretch to look behind and weep. Slavery is the price I

---

* **the terrible struggle:** the Civil War.

paid for civilization, and the choice was not with me. It is a bully adventure and worth all that I have paid through my ancestors for it. No one
on earth ever had a greater chance for glory. The world to be won and
nothing to be lost. It is thrilling to think—to know that for any act of
mine, I shall get twice as much praise or twice as much blame. It is quite
exciting to hold the center of the national stage, with the spectators not
knowing whether to laugh or to weep.

The position of my white neighbor is much more difficult. No brown   8
specter pulls up a chair beside me when I sit down to eat. No dark ghost
thrusts its leg against mine in bed. The game of keeping what one has is
never so exciting as the game of getting.

I do not always feel colored. Even now I often achieve the uncon-   9
scious Zora of Eatonville before the Hegira. I feel most colored when I
am thrown against a sharp white background.

For instance at Barnard. "Beside the waters of the Hudson"* I feel my   10
race. Among the thousand white persons, I am a dark rock surged upon,
and overswept, but through it all, I remain myself. When covered by the
waters, I am; and the ebb but reveals me again.

Sometimes it is the other way around. A white person is set down in our   11
midst, but the contrast is just as sharp for me. For instance, when I sit in
the drafty basement that is The New World Cabaret with a white person,
my color comes. We enter chatting about any little nothing that we have
in common and are seated by the jazz waiters. In the abrupt way that jazz
orchestras have, this one plunges into a number. It loses no time in cir-
cumlocutions, but gets right down to business. It constricts the thorax and
splits the heart with its tempo and narcotic harmonies. This orchestra
grows rambunctious, rears on its hind legs and attacks the tonal veil
with primitive fury, rending it, clawing it until it breaks through to the
jungle beyond. I follow those heathen—follow them exultingly. I dance
wildly inside myself; I yell within, I whoop; I shake my assegai above
my head, I hurl it true to the mark *yeeeeooww!* I am in the jungle and living in the jungle way. My face is painted red and yellow and my body is
painted blue. My pulse is throbbing like a war drum. I want to slaughter
something—give pain, give death to what, I do not know. But the piece
ends. The men of the orchestra wipe their lips and rest their fingers. I
creep back slowly to the veneer we call civilization with the last tone
and find the white friend sitting motionless in his seat, smoking calmly.

"Good music they have here," he remarks, drumming the table with   12
his fingertips.

Music. The great blobs of purple and red emotion have not touched   13
him. He has only heard what I felt. He is far away and I see him but

---

* **"Beside the waters of the Hudson":** Barnard College is near the Hudson River
in New York City.

dimly across the ocean and the continent that have fallen between us. He is so pale with his whiteness then and I am *so* colored.

At certain times I have no race, I am *me*. When I set my hat at a certain 14
angle and saunter down Seventh Avenue, Harlem City, feeling as snooty as the lions in front of the Forty–Second Street Library,* for instance. So far as my feelings are concerned, Peggy Hopkins Joyce* on the Boule Mich* with her gorgeous raiment, stately carriage, knees knocking to-gether in a most aristocratic manner, has nothing on me. The cosmic Zora emerges. I belong to no race nor time. I am the eternal feminine with its string of beads.

I have no separate feeling about being an American citizen and col- 15
ored. I am merely a fragment of the Great Soul that surges within the boundaries. My country, right or wrong.

Sometimes, I feel discriminated against, but it does not make me 16
angry. It merely astonishes me. How *can* any deny themselves the pleas-ure of my company? It's beyond me.

But in the main, I feel like a brown bag of miscellany propped against 17
a wall. Against a wall in company with other bags, white, red and yellow. Pour out the contents, and there is discovered a jumble of small things priceless and worthless. A first–water diamond, an empty spool, bits of bro-ken glass, lengths of string, a key to a door long since crumbled away, a rusty knife–blade, old shoes saved for a road that never was and never will be, a nail bent under the weight of things too heavy for any nail, a dried flower or two still a little fragrant. In your hand is the brown bag. On the ground before you is the jumble it held — so much like the jumble in the bags, could they be emptied, that all might be dumped in a single heap and the bags refilled without altering the content of any greatly. A bit of colored glass more or less would not matter. Perhaps that is how the Great Stuffer of Bags filled them in the first place — who knows?

Reading Closely

1. Why do you think Hurston opens her essay by saying that she is "the only Negro in the United States whose grandfather on the mother's side was *not* an Indian chief"?

2. What specific details about Hurston's childhood does this essay reveal? How does Hurston use these experiences to explain her adult outlook on race?

---

* **the lions in front of the Forty–Second Street Library:** two statues of lions that stand in front of the main building of the New York (City) Public Library, on Fifth Avenue at Forty–second Street.

* **Peggy Hopkins Joyce:** a famous beauty who set fashions in the 1920s.

* **the Boule Mich:** the Boulevard Saint–Michel, a street in Paris.

3. Hurston makes several generalizations about how it feels to be "colored." What are they? What evidence does she provide to support her assertions? Are you convinced? **Work with a classmate** to write out collaborative responses to these questions.

4. What does the visual tell you about "how it feels to be colored" Zora Neale Hurston?

Considering Larger Issues

1. What is the purpose of this essay? Who is its audience? What evidence within the essay can you find for your answers? Write out your answers, and prepare to share them with the rest of the class.

2. This essay was originally published in 1928. How does that date help explain some of Hurston's opinions, especially ones that would be unacceptable or highly controversial today?

3. What is the basis for comparison that Hurston establishes? What are the points of comparison? What do you consider to be the major differences—if any—between black and white people in the United States today? How might you reshift Hurston's focus?

4. Respond to Hurston's sentence, "Slavery is the price I paid for civilization" (paragraph 7). What does this statement mean to you? **Working with three or four classmates,** discuss this statement as a conclusion. Report your group's response to the rest of the class.

5. COMBINING METHODS. Mark passages where Hurston uses *narration* to support her overall purpose. What is the effect of each of these passages?

Thinking about Language

1. By using the context of the essay or your dictionary, define each of the following terms. Be prepared to share your answers with the rest of the class.

extenuating (1)	helter–skelter (6)	rambunctious
chugged (2)	flying start (7)	(11)
proscenium (3)	bully (7)	assegai (11)
queer (3)	specter (8)	veneer (11)
deplored (4)	Hegira (9)	saunter (14)
oleanders (5)	surged upon (10)	raiment (14)
sea change (5)	circumlocutions	cosmic (14)
warranted (5)	(11)	

2. How many meanings does the term *colored* have in this essay? How many different words does Hurston use that could mean "colored"? Write out your answers.

Writing Your Own Essays Using Comparison and Contrast

1. Using your response to question 2 in "Thinking about Language" if possible, draft a three- to four-page essay in which you compare and con-

trast your sense of color, race, or history with that of someone else in your family—a cousin, perhaps, or one or both of your parents or grandparents. Keep in mind the ways the two of you treat this concept in the same way or differently as you develop your points of comparison, thesis statement, and support. Refer to "Checking Over the Use of Comparison and Contrast" on p. 370, and make sure you have a clear purpose for writing.

2. Consider Hurston's assertion that "slavery is sixty years in the past. The operation was successful and the patient is doing well" (paragraph 7). In terms of your own experience, knowledge, or observation, do you agree or disagree with Hurston's conclusion now that slavery is more than twice as far in the past? What are the points of comparison between your viewpoint and Hurston's regarding the relative weight of racism in the world—or in the United States? Write a three- to four-page comparison-and-contrast essay about these points of view. Do a little background research on early twentieth-century U.S. history as well as more recent history and writings to support and enrich your essay. As you draft, consider the kinds of information you hope to reveal as you compare and contrast. Refer to "Checking Over the Use of Comparison and Contrast" on p. 370.

3. Describe your sense of yourself as a person with or without a particular racial or ethnic identity, or with a mixed identity. Draft a three- to four-page comparison-and-contrast essay related to this idea, using "Checking Over the Use of Comparison and Contrast" on p. 370, and taking care to determine your purpose for writing. **Consider exchanging drafts with one or two classmates** and reviewing one another's work before each of you submits your final draft.

WILLIAM SHAKESPEARE

Sonnet 18

Perhaps the best-known wordsmith in the English language, William Shake-speare (1564–1616) left us with brilliantly drawn dramatic histories, comedies, tragedies, and romances, as well as with a peerless collection of sonnets. "Shall I compare thee to a summer's day," Sonnet 18, remains one of his most famous.

> **Preview**   As you read this poem, consider the various points of compari-son that Shakespeare employs.

Shall I compare thee to a summer's day?
Thou art more lovely and more temperate:
Rough winds do shake the darling buds of May,
And summer's lease hath all too short a date:
Sometimes too hot the eye of heaven shines,   5
And often is his gold complexion dimmed:
And every fair from fair sometimes declines,
By chance or nature's changing course untrimmed;
But thy eternal summer shall not fade,
Nor lose possession of that fair thou ow'st,   10
Nor shall death brag thou wander'st in his shade,
When in eternal lines to time thou grow'st:
So long as men can breathe, or eyes can see,
So long lives this, and this gives life to thee.

Reading Closely

1. What analogies does the speaking voice of this poem use to illustrate his admiration?

2. Copy out the sonnet, word by word. Then translate the poetry into con-temporary prose. What does the poem say? **Working with one or two classmates,** compare paragraphs. Discuss the differences and similari-ties among your paragraphs with the rest of the class.

Considering Larger Issues

1. What basis of comparison does Shakespeare use? What are the points of comparison in this poem?

2. What does the final line mean? What is its importance?

3. Who might be the audience for this poem? What is the poem's purpose? How does the audience affect the purpose, and vice versa? **Working**

with one or two classmates, compare your answers. Then prepare a group response to share with the rest of the class.

4. **COMBINING METHODS.** How does Shakespeare use *cause-and-consequence analysis* in his poem?

Thinking about Language

1. Define the following words and phrases, using the context of the poem and your dictionary. Be prepared to share your answers with the rest of the class.

temperate (2)	summer's lease (4)	ow'st (10)
darling (3)	untrimmed (8)	shade (11)

2. Think about some love songs with which you're familiar. They don't have to be current ones, just as long as you know some phrases, lines, or choruses by heart. Write out as much of each song as you can. Do the lyrics make comparisons? analogies? Are they effective?

Writing Your Own Essays Using Comparison and Contrast

1. Sometimes our words fall short of their mark. When we struggle to put our thoughts into words, we often resort to comparison or analogy. Draft a short essay (two pages) in which you demonstrate that comparison can make meaning come alive in ways that words used with literal meanings simply cannot. You may want to use song lyrics or poetry to help prove your points. Be sure to refer to the guidelines for checking over the use of comparison and contrast on p. 370.

2. Using information from question 2 under "Thinking about Language," draft an essay in which you demonstrate the persuasive power of a particular song that uses comparison and contrast. **Consider working with a classmate** to review each other's drafts and revisions, referring often to "Checking Over the Use of Comparison and Contrast" (p. 370).

ROZ CHAST

The Berlitz Guide
to Parent-Teacher Conferences

The quirky cartoons of Roz Chast (b. 1954) have been a regular feature of the *New Yorker* magazine since 1978. From the start, her work helped reshape the style of what are referred to as "gag" cartoons, in which people commiserate about the everyday details of their lives. Chast's cartoons, featuring neurotic characters drawn in childlike renditions, give little clue to her prestigious training at the Rhode Island School of Design. But for those fans who admire her steady hand and clear vision, she proves herself to be an artistic and comedic genius week after week. This cartoon appeared in the magazine in 1999.

Preview Do you know what typically goes on at a parent-teacher conference?

· · · · · · ➤

Reading Closely

1. On first glance, what do you learn from this cartoon?
2. Why is it entitled "The Berlitz Guide to Parent–Teacher Conferences"?

Considering Larger Issues

1. Judging from your own experience as a student, parent, or teacher in some setting other than school, how much truth is there in this comparison and contrast?
2. What are the points of comparison? Why are they being made?
3. In what ways, if any, do the drawings complement or otherwise enhance the words in the cartoon?
4. Does this cartoon seem intended for an audience of teachers, parents, students, or someone else? **Discuss this issue with three or four classmates,** and report your findings to the class.

Thinking about Language

1. Read the words and phrases in the left–hand column. If you could take the teacher's comments at face value, what do they mean? **Working with a classmate,** compare what the teacher really means by each comment to what a parent might take it to mean. Prepare to share your findings with the rest of the class.

2. What is the tone of this cartoon? Does it seem to be honest, lighthearted, mean–spirited — or something else? How does the language help create this tone?

Writing Your Own Essays Using Comparison and Contrast

1. If you have ever been the subject of a negative evaluation by a teacher, boss, or some other authority figure, draft a two- to three–page essay that compares or contrasts each criticism that was made of you with your own perceptions of how justified it was. The purpose of your short essay should not be to defend yourself but to explain the differences in perception between the authority figure and yourself. (You could even write about a positive evaluation if you feel you were praised excessively or for the wrong reasons.) As you draft, refer to the guidelines for checking over the use of comparison and contrast on p. 370.

2. If you cannot remember how you were described by teachers when you were younger, perhaps you can remember how you looked. Compare and contrast a middle school or early high school photograph of yourself with your college identification card or driver's license photograph. In what ways are you the same? different? to what extent? Draft a two-page essay that includes the photographs and compares your appearance, then and now. Be sure to refer to the guidelines for checking over the use of comparison and contrast on p. 370.

3. At some point, almost everyone has been in the teacher's position of having to find polite language for unpleasant truths. Think of such a situation in your own life, and try creating a cartoon in which you contrast what you said with what you meant. Include a background statement, if necessary, to explain the context, and find or create some visuals to enhance the effect of your written text. Or if you prefer, simply write an essay about your experience, referring to the guidelines for checking over the use of comparison and contrast on p. 370.

✱ Additional Suggestions for Writing

1. Often we engage in comparison and contrast to make a decision. For example, how did you decide on a college major, area of concentration, or degree program? If you haven't already decided, how are you deciding? Make a list of the possibilities you considered or are considering; then list the features of each one that are most and least desirable. Personal interest, aptitude, reputation of the faculty, career and earning potential—these are some of the features you may have considered or may want to consider. (You might have to research some of them.) Reduce your list of possibilities to the top two, and then draft a two-page comparison-and-contrast essay that reveals information as it explains your decision or helps focus on your future decision. Be sure to refer to "Checking Over the Use of Comparison and Contrast" (p. 370) as you draft.

2. In college you have to read and write—a lot. These skills usually develop together, yet some people like reading more than writing, or vice versa. Draft a two- to three-page essay in which you compare and contrast your feelings about reading and writing. You may want to consider both school-related and personal reading and writing, or you may choose to concentrate on one or the other. Regardless of your purpose and pattern of organization, be sure to explain your attitudes in terms of a comparison and contrast. As you work, refer to the guidelines for checking over the use of comparison and contrast on p. 370.

3. Choose two contemporary entertainers, sports personalities, or other figures who have had similar professional or public roles but handled them differently: Serena Williams and Jennifer Capriati; Tom Cruise and Will Smith; Ellen DeGeneres and Oprah Winfrey; Latrell Sprewell and Rasheed Wallace; Jim Carrey and Jack Black; Fiona Apple and Ani DiFranco; Cher and Tina Turner; Colin Powell and Condoleezza Rice; Hillary Rodham Clinton and Dianne Feinstein; or any other pairing that you come up with. What might be the basis for the differences in how the two figures conduct themselves in public settings or present themselves to the public? After you establish a basis for comparison, come up with points of comparison and contrast, and, finally, use your comparison and contrast to make a point. **Work closely with at least one classmate,** asking for help, good questions and ideas, and a review of your drafts. (See "Checking Over the Use of Comparison and Contrast," on p. 370.)

chapter 7

PROCESS ANALYSIS

Gabe —
   I went to Garth's house for dinner. There is pizza in the frige for you to eat.

               To heat up pizza: (try one or the other)

Garth's Way:	Our way:
-put pizza slices on plate to left. ⬅	-put pizza slices on metal tray to right. ➡
- put plastic wrap over it	- put on top rack of oven.
-heat in microwave on [Auto Cook] then [1]	- push ① upper oven ② 200 ③ start/enter
	- when oven beeps, take pizza out.
DO NOT put metal tray in microwave (will catch on fire 🔥).	NO PLASTIC WRAP OR IT WILL MELT IN OVEN.

- Have carrots with meal 🔥
- have MILK with meal
- DO NOT EAT IN TV ROOM !!!
   If your friends are here, call me at Garth's (234-9014) so I can come home + watch you OR go to their house after dinner + LEAVE A NOTE WHERE YOU ARE!!
- Clean up after yourself !!
               — Lydia

*E*very day people leave notes for others, explaining how to complete a process. In this case Lydia is writing to her younger brother, Gabe, giving him directions for two possible ways to heat up leftover pizza (as well as what to eat and drink with his pizza and how to behave). Like Gabe, we often know what we want to do, but we're not sure how to do it. We need an analysis of the process, and in Gabe's case Lydia has analyzed two alternative processes for achieving the same result. Whether he decides to try "Garth's way" by using the microwave or "our way" by using the regular oven, Gabe has all the information he needs to complete the process. Whether we're explaining how to heat up pizza or how to drive to someone's house, how our eyes perceive color or how a bill in Congress becomes a law, we are analyzing a process.

Looking at Your Own Literacy When was the last time you left an instructional note for someone — or when one was left for you? What was that note about? How detailed and clear were the instructions?

What Is Process Analysis?

A **process** is a series of actions that always leads to the same result, no matter how many times it's repeated. The purpose of **process analysis** is to explain the process by breaking it down into a fixed order of steps. Like narration, process analysis is chronological — it's organized according to time — but narration is concerned with a onetime event. A process analysis, on the other hand, is concerned with an event that is replicable, that can be duplicated. For instance, if you're changing a tire on your motorcycle, you'd be better off following clearly ordered, step-by-step instructions than listening to a friend tell a story about a time she changed the tire on her motorcycle. You need to know exactly what to do, in what order, how the steps in the process relate to one another, and how each step leads to the desired outcome. You need a process analysis, not a story.

Every day we analyze processes to understand the world around us. You already know the steps in a wide variety of processes such as setting the time on a watch, cleaning your contact lenses, logging on to your computer, videotaping a television program, or preparing a particular food. In fact, you often know the steps so well that you don't even think of them anymore; you just do them. But most of us are always interested in learning how to do something else, from how to study successfully or write competently to how to negotiate relations with coworkers and classmates and maintain friendships. In fact, process analysis has become such an important part of our lives that it is big business: books analyzing processes are always among the best-sellers. Consider the following popular titles: *God Is My Broker: A Monk-Tycoon Reveals the 7½ Laws of Spiritual and Financial Growth, 8 Weeks to Optimum Health: A Proven Program for Taking Full Advantage of Your Body's Natural Healing Power,* and *The Motley Fool Investment Guide: How the Fool Beats Wall Street's Wise Men and How You Can Too.* Interestingly, books about making money are always among the top sellers.

Although such books may or may not actually help you make money or stay healthy, process analysis can also be pleasurable and in-teresting for its own sake. Many people buy cookbooks just to read recipes they never make themselves; others buy weight-loss books, in-vestment magazines, or car-repair manuals to read about processes they are curious about but don't perform on a regular basis, if ever. But whenever we have to explain a process to someone else, we consciously break it into easy-to-follow steps, like those on the back of a box of Alka-Seltzer Plus Cold Liqui-Gels.

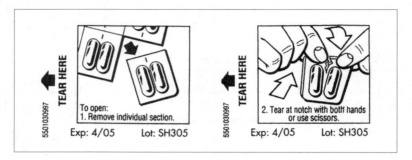

Thinking about Process Analysis

1. Look over the visual and textual instructions for removing the Alka-Seltzer Plus gelcaps from their package.
2. Why do the instructions include pictures?
3. What purpose do the words serve? Rewrite the instructions using words only.

Why Use Process Analysis?

A process analysis can have one—or both—of two explanatory pur-poses. A **directive process analysis** is often a set of step-by-step in-structions for a customer, patient, worker, or some other person to follow, like the instructions for removing gelcaps from their package. But a process analysis can be more than just a set of instructions: a writer can use it to explain the mysteries of how something happens or is done or to persuade an audience of the advantages or disadvantages of doing it, or of doing it one way as opposed to another. Writers of such

informative process analyses, which explain how something works or is done, don't necessarily expect or want readers to carry out the process themselves.

A directive process analysis is usually instructional, the kind of advice you might find in a weight-loss book, investment guide, or cookbook. You should usually be able to replicate the process, like the one presented in the accompanying recipe for Dr. Atkins's beef stew.

> **Try Your Hand**   Read through the beef stew recipe carefully, marking all the terms and phrases that are unclear to you. Work with two or three classmates to clarify the directions so that each of you can follow the recipe. Report your questions and solutions to the rest of the class.

Whether directive or informative, process analysis can provide instruction and pleasure as well as satisfy intellectual curiosity. For instance, most children want to know how Santa Claus, the Easter bunny, and the tooth fairy operate, and where babies come from. They may have no intention of doing anything with this information; they simply want to know the things that grown–ups know. So they turn to process analysis, gleaning information from older siblings, from friends, from books. In *The Facts of Life*, Jonathan Miller and David Pelham provide three–dimensional, movable illustrations that show the development of a baby from conception to birth. As they discuss chromosomes, DNA, fetuses, testes, yolk sacks, and uteruses, the authors provide a thorough, carefully ordered, step–by–step analysis of just how babies are made and then born:

> Compared with the simple job of making and delivering sperm, the female task is far more difficult and requires much more complicated apparatus. In addition to making the egg cells in the ovaries, the female has to provide a place in which the fertilized egg can be sheltered and nourished during the nine-month development period needed by the growing baby. Most of this development takes place in the uterus.
> —JONATHAN MILLER AND DAVID PELHAM, *The Facts of Life*

The preceding excerpt is informative, but Miller and Pelham's overall explanation (from loving an adult of the opposite sex to welcoming a new baby), annotated and illustrated with pop–up drawings, is both informative and directive.

> **Try Your Hand**   Write a brief process analysis, one that is both directive and informative. In a paragraph, tell readers how to prepare a nutritionally balanced breakfast, lunch, or supper. Your audience will be your classmates.

Informational process analysis is more versatile than directional process analysis: you can use it to share information, such as how to drop a class; you can use it to entertain readers with information on, say, dog training, skydiving, or race car driving; or you can use it to argue that a particular process is the most successful, quickest, safest, or best one to follow or advocate. Some best–selling books fit both the directive and informational categories of process analysis: the writer claims that if you "buy my book and follow my program," you'll be able to lose weight, win friends, become rich, or even understand people's behavior in New York City. For example, consider the following excerpts from international guidebooks to New York City:

JAPAN

From "Chikyu no Aruki-kata (How to Walk on Earth)," Vol. 38: New York 2000–2001 edition, published by Diamond Big Co.

At the movies   As the film starts, the audience gets absorbed immediately. Although you are not allowed to make noise in the cinema, some people shout and cry. Literally, it is breathless movie-watching. If you are watching an action film, there will be a storm of applause and cheers at victorious scenes. This noise isn't unpleasant but heightens excitement.

ENGLAND

From "Manhattan," by Vanessa Letts, published by Cadogan.

Eavesdropping   Keep your ears pricked at all times and you will be as entertained as much by what you hear as by what you see. Behind the gruff exteriors, Manhattanites are a wistful, open-hearted lot, and, perhaps because over 40 per cent are immigrants, they have a knack of muscling newcomers into instant conversations which can culminate in lifelong friendships.

ITALY

From "Guidebook for New York and Washington," published by Touring Club Italiano.

Style in motion   Walking is important to New Yorkers. Numerous office workers, at exactly 5 o'clock, will walk out of their buildings, quickly taking off their dress shoes and putting on sneakers for their long treks to the subway or buses. Like in the Woody Allen movies (a New Yorker to the extreme), people are constantly walking, not just for exercise, but to relieve stress and to socialize. "Will you come with me?" is a common question that usually ends up in a 20-, 30- or 50-block walk.

These excerpts provide both directions and information to their readers.

Try Your Hand   Guidebook writers like their readers to believe that they are learning the secrets of a place. Make a list of basic directions you would give a visitor to your hometown or current place of residence. Then take a few minutes to annotate that initial list, providing your readers with additional information for analysis. Share your lists with another classmate, comparing the directions and the additional information each of you supplied — and the reasons why you did.

How Do You Read a Process Analysis?

The heading for this section — "How Do You Read a Process Analysis?" — suggests that you're about to read just that: a process analysis of how to read a process analysis. Actually, this section is about learning to read a process analysis *critically*, not just understanding what one means but also judging its effectiveness — and you don't have to follow a specific series of steps to do so. But if you make a habit of reading a process analysis in this way—thinking about how well it explains the process and achieves other purposes the writer intends for a specific audience—you'll glean more information from it and will be better able to write your own process analyses with success.

If there's a title or heading, that's where you'll start, to see if it provides a clue to how the author wants you to read the process analysis. Take another look at the process analysis that opens this chapter (on p. 428). The heading, "Gabe," indicates that Gabe is being addressed by an author (Lydia), but it's not until you read the introduction and the thesis that Lydia's purpose is revealed: "I went to Garth's house for dinner. There is pizza in the fri[d]ge for you to eat. To heat up pizza: (try one [way] or the other)." As you know, there two basic types of process analysis, descriptive and informative, and Lydia makes clear that hers is an *informative* one. She wants Gabe to be able to do more than just understand the process of heating up pizza; she expects him to be able to replicate the process, to heat up his own pizza—as well as to do or not do certain other things.

Whether a process analysis is descriptive or informative, it can serve one of three overall purposes: to explain a process, to entertain readers with an explanation, or to argue the positive or negative attributes of a particular process. Although Lydia mentions a negative feature of each pizza–heating process for Gabe to avoid, she concentrates on fulfilling an explanatory purpose. As she does, she includes a number of necessary details that enhance her step–by–step explanation.

One key aspect of reading a process analysis critically is to evaluate how knowledgeable and experienced the author appears to be in terms of this process. Lydia seems to be both, as she explains two ways for Gabe to heat up his pizza: "Garth's way" and "our way." Apparently, she's set up the kitchen so that he can either "put pizza slices on plate to left ←" or "put pizza slices on metal tray to right →." And she's set up the explanation so that the two possible processes are shown side by side, with an underlined heading for each alternative, a line between them, and each step and sub-step clearly indicated with dashes or numbers. Because she's giving the steps in list form from top to bottom, Lydia doesn't need to indicate the relationship between them with words or phrases like "first," "next," or "after five minutes." When you're writing a process analysis in full sentences and paragraphs, however, it's usually a good idea to begin each step with some indication of how it relates to the previous one.

Notice also how Lydia draws special attention to key tasks in the process that Gabe should do—or things he should avoid—with capital letters, underlining, exclamation points, or combinations of these methods. For her audience—a small child—signals like these may well be a good idea, although it's worth noting that the more they're used, the less attention readers will pay to them. When you're writing for an adult audience, try to find other ways to emphasize the key points you want to make in your analysis. For example, you might start out the sentence about the most crucial step in the process with "Most important, be sure to . . ."

Finally, as you read a process analysis, think not just about what the writer says but what he or she doesn't say. For example, Lydia doesn't tell Gabe where to find the plastic wrap or the carrots, remind him to use a pot holder to take the metal tray out of the oven, or specify what cleaning up involves. Presumably, he's old enough and familiar enough with the kitchen that she feels he doesn't need these instructions (or maybe she just ran out of space on the page). By thinking about what the writer leaves out, you may be able to learn something about writing your own process analyses without confusing or boring readers with too much detail or puzzling them by omitting necessary information.

How Do You Write a Process Analysis?

Whether it's directive or informative, your process needs to be explanatory. Therefore, you'll want to select and order the details about the process with care, explaining the steps thoroughly and accurately so that they can be replicated or easily understood. From writing out directions for making egg salad to explaining how a fossil is formed, you'll also need to consider your audience and purpose, arrange the steps in the process carefully, and add transitions to make the order of the steps clear for your readers.

Considering the Process

What process are you concentrating on? Will you cover all of this process or only part of it? For instance, if your goal is to teach your brother how to make pizza, you'll have to consider how much of this process you (and he) can handle in the first lesson. In other words, where will you start? Where will you end? It's easier to write a process analysis if you limit the scope of the process you are explaining. If you decide to start by teaching your brother how to make a simple pizza, you'll probably begin with a ready–made crust or with a pizza mix. A later lesson, based on the earlier one, might begin with making pizza dough from scratch.

Considering Your Audience

No matter what kind of process analysis you are writing, you will always need to think carefully about the best way to present the process to your audience. What does your audience already know about the topic? What terms or phrases will you need to define or explain? If your brother is the audience and making a simple pizza is the process you are explaining, then you'll need to determine how much or how little he already knows about cooking. If he already knows how to mix dough,

then you can start with letting the dough rise. But he may not understand the necessity of punching down dough to release the air bubbles, a
detail that a more experienced baker would know. Considering how
much your audience knows, or doesn't know, will help you determine
how many steps you need to break down the process into and how
much detail to include in each step.

Considering your audience will also help you decide which **point of
view** to use: first-, second-, or third-person point of view. When the
process analysis is directive—when the audience may actually be carrying out the process—writers often use second-person point of view; in
other words, they speak directly to "you." In the note on p. 428, Lydia
writes directly to Gabe, explaining the process of heating up pizza and
always using or implying "you": "You, Gabe, should put pizza slices on
the plate to the left"; "You, Gabe, should not put the metal tray in the microwave." She is explaining a process, directing Gabe, and giving commands. When the process analysis is informational, writers often resort
to first-person ("I" or "we") or third-person ("he," "she," "it," "they") point of
view. In the excerpt from the Italian guidebook to New York City on p. 433,
for instance, the writer describes the walking process of New Yorkers in
the third person: "Numerous office workers, at exactly 5 o'clock, will walk
out of their buildings, quickly taking off their dress shoes and putting on
sneakers for their long treks to the subway or buses."

● **Considering Your Purpose**

The point of view you choose to use connects your topic and your
audience to your purpose—what you want the audience to do with the
explanation provided in your analysis. In many cases, your purpose will
be determined by a class assignment, a specific request for information,
or a request for a solution to a problem. Perhaps your brother-in-law
has asked you how to take the subway from the airport to downtown, or
your geology professor has asked you to explain how sediment turns
into rock. Maybe your daughter wants to know how to get chocolate
stains out of her white cotton blouse, or a coworker has asked how to
deal with a customer's complaint. In other cases, you yourself will decide
on your purpose for writing. You may write out the pizza-heating directions because you want your brother to be able to fix his own supper.
You may want to analyze the complex process of applying for off-
campus housing in order to argue that it should be simplified. You may
simply want your readers to be able to replicate the steps you've written
down for them; but especially if you are writing an informative process
analysis, you may also want the audience to appreciate the steps in the
process themselves for their beauty, their efficiency, the skill they require—
or to recognize how inefficient, unpleasant, or ridiculous the process is.

Whatever your purpose, it should help you to focus your **thesis statement,** which provides a general overview of the process and its significance. For example, in an article for the women's magazine *Latina*, author Mimi Valdez writes about the powerful benefits of boxing, "That's the great thing about a boxing workout: Just as you're almost spent doing one thing, you move on to another, which seems easier because it involves fresh moves and muscles." She develops this thesis as she describes the process of training to box:

> I figured the best way to learn to box was to train with a real fighter. So I called a boxing gym and requested a Latino trainer. . . . Jason explains the pace of the workout—train three minutes, rest for one—just like in rounds of boxing. We begin jumping rope to warm up. If you have pretty good endurance—if you don't collapse after two flights of stairs—rope skipping isn't hard to master. But by the last set, I'm so tired that my skills fly out the window, with me longing to escape with them. Then we switch gears, heading over to the mirror to shadowbox, to learn the proper stance for throwing punches. . . .
>
> Just as I get the maneuvers (or think I have), Jason moves me to the punching bags. He puts boxing gloves on me, and I try to translate what I learned about punching onto the jumpy little speed bag, but apparently it knows more about dodging punches than I do about throwing them. We switch to the big, hanging punching bag, which is attached with elastic to both the ceiling and floor. I'm trying to throw two left jabs and a right while circling the bag and keeping my form. Instead, I'm all over the place, not making a dent. And the bag stays where it is, still as a stone. "Don't worry about strength," Jason says. "The first day is all about form."   — MIMI VALDEZ, "Mimi Throws Her Punches"

Written to demonstrate the benefits of boxing to a female audience, Valdez's article contains a sidebar with a more specific purpose, telling readers how to find an instructor:

> If you prefer working one-on-one with a trainer, locate a boxing gym in the yellow pages. Make sure it has a strong female membership, so you'll feel comfortable there. Before you commit to join, ask if they have a fitness program you can try for a month, working out with an instructor three or four times a week. The cost will be anywhere from $100 to $200 monthly. Otherwise, check out your local fitness center to see if they have aerobic classes in boxing — it's fun to do it in a group. Often called Cardio Boxing, these aerobic classes build your heart and lung capacity as well as muscle strength, especially firming the arms, shoulders, and back. Whichever you choose, one-on-one or a class, don't forget: Always warm up and stretch before exercise, and cool down afterward.

As you can see, a writer can have two different purposes for writing about a process and can address two or more different audiences. In the preceding passages, Valdez seems merely to want to interest her female readers in her exercise regimen. But in the sidebar she's more specific about both her purpose and her audience: she wants to help those who are interested begin the exercise program for themselves. Both careful audience analysis and an awareness of purpose are crucial as you develop your process analysis.

● Considering Your Method of Organization

Like narration, a process analysis is presented as a chronological sequence of actions or steps. But unlike narration, a process analysis usually has a fixed order: the steps are always the same; the results are always the same. Therefore, when Valdez describes her boxing workout, she's describing the general sequence of actions (steps or groups of steps) in any boxing workout. She skips rope, practices maneuvers, shadowboxes, punches the speed bag and the big bag, goes one–on–one with Jason, and then does lunges and sit–ups, reminded by her boxing instructor that "boxers do complete workouts." The results of complete workouts are the same as well: when she leaves after an hour, she feels "great." But when she wakes up the next morning, she feels "pretty sore all over, but particularly sore in [her] arms and shoulders."

When readers already understand some steps of the process or don't need to know them at all, a process analysis may condense a long series of steps into just a few short steps. In the analysis on the opposite page, Shutterfly.com wants readers to know how easy it is to deliver 35mm-quality pictures from their digital cameras. As you read each step in the three–step process, you'll see that the writer assumes the reader has a digital camera and knows how to use it and how to upload pictures.

Process analysis visuals can move readers step–by–step, or they can include all the steps in one visual, like the Shutterfly ad on p. 439.

● Considering the Necessary Details

To successfully explain a process, writers need to include clear, pertinent details for each step. In her description of a boxing workout, Valdez includes a number of vivid, specific details:

> I'm all riled up and I concentrate. There is a proper formation for your body to be in before you can throw punches. For example, right-handers should have the right leg behind, left in front; right toes slightly pointed out; knees bent so that your weight is evenly balanced in the stance. I make a few left jabs (short, quick punches) at Jason's grin in the mirror. Noticing how my elbows fly up each time, he shows me how my fighting-mad punching is making me vulnerable. I should be keeping my chin down and my elbows in at my sides, throwing punches straight from there. If I don't, and instead I lift my elbows, it signals to the other boxer that my punch is coming.

"Reading" and Using Visuals in a Process Analysis

An effective process analysis often includes visuals. When we follow a directional process analysis, we like—and often need—to see that process in pictures. For that reason, home and car repair manuals, science books, and cookbooks use many visuals to explain a system or process from start to finish. Good cookbooks and specialized magazines are especially valuable for their photographs and drawings of individual processes (chopping, dicing, wallpapering, pitching, putting) and of finished products (casseroles, walls, gardens). And good doctors and pharmacists always try to ensure that you know how to take your medication. Although visuals more commonly accompany directional process analyses, they are also an important enhancement to many informational process analyses, making them more interesting, more easily understood, and more helpful.

To use visuals effectively in your own process analyses, you need to study ones used by other writers to see how clearly they convey information in visual form and, specifically, how well they do so for their particular purpose and audience. The accompanying visual, for example, is part of a folding pocket guide for installing sheetrock or drywall that features instructions in English, in Spanish, and in pictures. Perhaps the most interesting feature of this visual is how much information is omitted. This guide is intended for someone who already knows how to install drywall—not for someone who wants to learn how to do it. Drywall installation is a skilled job involving careful measuring, cutting, hanging, patching, sanding, and finishing. This series of pictures, then, serves only as a sketch of the key steps in the job, something the worker and supervisor can look at or point to for reference. Experienced drywall workers will bring much more knowledge and know-how to the installation than this visual provides. For instance, the third panel includes a picture of a "mud tray/bandeja para resanar" with no explanation of how it is involved in the process, but presumably workers familiar with drywall installation won't need an explanation.

Valdez wants her readers to understand exactly how the practice is done; she wants them to know that one misstep or mispunch can undo all her careful training. Including such vivid details also helps bring her process analysis to life, making it interesting to read.

● Providing Transitions

As you lead your readers through the steps of your process analysis, be sure to include transitional words or phrases that help them understand the progression. In the following account of bronze casting,

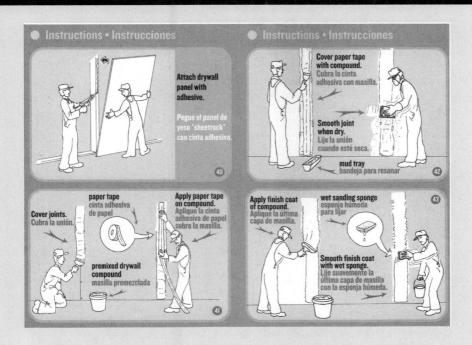

As you can see, the visual explanation can be a more efficient reference than a verbal one, particularly when there is a language barrier. Although a supervisor and a worker might not speak the same language, both of them can understand the pictures and will already understand the general process. Notice that some of the smaller items involved in drywall installation — such as the roll of paper tape and the wet sanding sponge — are also shown "blown up" to a larger size so that they can be identified more easily. Other panels of this pocket guide show pictures of other tools and supplies involved in drywall installation, along with their English and Spanish names.

Nancy Ellis moves her readers through a complicated yet well-explained process: the transformation of Estella Loretto's eight-foot-tall clay figure, *Morning Prayer*, into a bronze sculpture:

> Because Estella lived with this large clay woman in her studio for so many months as the artwork progressed, observing her from all angles and especially in the morning light, she knew instinctively when the sculpture was complete and ready for the mold-maker. For this critical part of the process, she chose Brett Chromer, a Santa Fe sculptor who has extensive experience making molds for other artists.

Chromer first decides where he will put the shims — ultimately, the seams — into the clay (*Morning Prayer* was cast in 17 separate sections). Next, layers of silicone rubber material are brushed over the original, creating a mold — a perfect imprint of the original that will be used for casting all other pieces in the edition. "Keys" are permanently affixed to the last coating of rubber, so the separated parts of the "mother mold" always can be accurately reassembled. After a final coat of plaster has set, the mold is broken open and the original artwork is removed, and the mold is ready for Shidoni [a foundry in Santa Fe].

At the foundry, wax is layered with a brush into the rubber mold, creating a perfect wax copy of the original. It is the wax reproduction that will be used to create another mold into which the molten bronze will be poured. Wax bars, called sprues, and a wax pour cup are attached to the work, along with sumps and gates, to create a system of channels to allow bronze to flow bottom to top.

The wax copy is now dipped in a colloidal silica slurry and coated with stucco, creating a second ceramic mold. This shell, when dry, is heated in a kiln to 1,600 degrees Fahrenheit, causing the wax to flush out and giving name to this process, lost wax.

Now, *Morning Prayer* is ready for the most visual and dramatic part of the process: pouring the molten bronze (Shidoni's mix is 95 percent copper, 1 percent manganese, and 4 percent silicone, heated to 2,000 degrees). The ceramic molds are heated and placed in a sand pit, where bronze from the furnace is ladled into them. When cool, the molds are broken off with hammers and pneumatic tools, and the bronze sculpture is sandblasted before being sent to the metal shop. Here *Morning Prayer*'s 17 sections are carefully welded back together and the seams "chased" with grinders. The fully assembled bronze sculpture is now given a final cleansing sandblast so that it will accept the patina.

Estella is deeply involved in the patination of *Morning Prayer,* during which hot chemicals are applied to its bronze surface, oxidizing and changing color. Her excitement is contagious as she supervises this final stage, with assistance from the Shidoni staff. "It's like a painting," she explains, working the sculpture's skin with finer and finer grades of steel pads. "I like a soft, warm, radiant look."

Completely engrossed in this hard, hot work, Estella is ready for the first coating of wax over the finished face of *Morning Prayer.* She stands back. "It's like having a baby," she says; "You can't rush any part of the process." Climbing back up on the ladder, she looks directly into the eyes of *Morning Prayer.*

Estella is obviously thrilled with this first edition of *Morning Prayer,* which is cast, like most of her monumental pieces, in an edition of seven. There were some difficult issues to be resolved — Estella re-sculpted her face at one point, seeking a more subtle, more serene smile — during the period of nearly a year that it took to bring *Morning Prayer* from original concept to completion.   —NANCY ELLIS, "The Art of Casting Bronze"

The transitional words and phrases ("first," "next," "after a final coat," "at the foundry," "now," "here") and the specific details ("17 separate sections"; "wax is layered with a brush into the rubber mold"; "wax bars . . . and a wax pour cup are attached to the work . . . to create a system of channels to allow bronze to flow bottom to top"; "heated in a kiln to 1,600 degrees"; "95 percent copper, 1 percent manganese, and 4 percent silicone") all work to help us follow Ellis's account of these steps.

Ellis's concluding sentences reconfirm her artistic appreciation of the process, an appreciation she wants her readers to share: "'You can tell how happy she is,' says Estella, her own eyes brimming with tears. 'She's so happy; it almost makes me cry.'" Ellis's process analysis is both directive and informational, a replicable process to be understood and appreciated.

Understanding and Using Process Analysis

Analyzing Process Analysis

1. **Working with two or three classmates,** reread the guidebook descriptions of New York and New Yorkers (p. 433). Using these descriptions as models, individually draft a paragraph that analyzes, step-by-step, one way you could explain your current place of residence and/or your neighbors. Share your drafts with one another, and suggest any steps that might strengthen each person's paragraph.

2. How might the excerpt from *The Facts of Life* (p. 432) represent a book that is both directive and informative? Write out your response.

Planning and Writing Essays Using Process Analysis

1. Think for a minute: What processes are you really good at? Which one could you teach to someone else? The process can be as simple as shifting gears in a car or making a pot of tea, as unexpected as preparing the perfect bath, or as adventurous as snowboarding without a hitch. Jot down a few ideas for process analysis papers, and then write about each possible topic for a few minutes. Which topic seems the most promising? Can you remember all the necessary steps, in order? Can you weave in the necessary details and explanations? Would a visual or two help readers understand the process better?

    Trade papers with a classmate, and help each other decide which idea might work best for each of you. Try to help each other come up with a thesis statement that reflects the basic purpose of the essay.

2. Look over the syllabus for this class. Jot down what you need to do in order to succeed in the class, based on both the requirements and expectations listed on the syllabus and your own sense of your strengths and weaknesses. Now try to break down the process of taking this course, numbering the steps. Next to each step, add the details and necessary information explaining that particular step. What might be the thesis statement of such an essay? Who, besides your instructor, might be your audience?

3. Share the ideas about succeeding in this particular class that you generated in response to the previous question. **Working with two or three**

classmates, write down all the steps that you agree upon. In a separate list, write down the steps that were unique to each of you. (You might show the lists to your instructor and ask him or her to complete or improve upon them.) In what ways are your thoughts about success the same? different? In what ways are the steps for success the same? different?

4. Look over your notes for question 1 in this section. What process have you decided you'd most like to develop into an essay? With your class-mates as your audience, draft a three- to four-page process analysis essay that develops your thesis statement. **Share your draft with one or two classmates** to get their responses before you revise it for sub-mission. Refer to the following guidelines for checking over the use of process analysis.

5. Go back to the notes you gathered on how best to succeed in this course for questions 2 and 3. Taking into consideration what your classmates advised, what your instructor may have advised, what the syllabus says, and what your own academic abilities and achievements are, draft a two-page process analysis essay that sets out a plan for success in your first-year writing course. Your instructor will be your audience, and your thesis statement will focus on your plans for achieving success in this course. Refer to the following guidelines for checking over the use of process analysis.

✓ Checking Over the Use of Process Analysis

1. What is the purpose of your process analysis? Is it directional or infor-mational? In one sentence, write out the specific purpose; in other words, what's in it for the reader?

2. What is your thesis? If you cannot locate a thesis statement, then write out the main idea of your essay.

3. Who are your readers? What do they already know about the process? How much background information do they need? Have you defined terms that they probably won't know? Should you add more details to your explanation? streamline your explanation? break the process down into more steps? condense it into fewer steps?

4. Have you ordered your process analysis chronologically? Is the sequence of steps clear and complete?

5. Underline all the transitional words or phrases. Do they lead readers clearly from one step or group of steps to the next?

6. What is the purpose of your conclusion? Do you want your readers to feel a sense of confidence that they can reproduce the process? Or do you want them to appreciate the details of the process?

7. Does your process analysis include visuals? How exactly do the visuals enhance the verbal part of the analysis? Do you need to add captions, la-bels, or references to the visuals in the text?

READINGS

KATHY ANTONIOTTI

Marshmallow Mayhem: Fun (and Sweet) Alternative to Toy Guns

Kathy Antoniotti has worked at the Akron (Ohio) *Beacon Journal* since 1989, first as a correspondent and later as a photo archivist. She began writing a crafts column in 1999 and later developed the syndicated "Kids Craft" column, which specializes in projects for children. One such project is the subject of the following reading, first published in her column in 2004.

> **Preview** When you think of marshmallows, what comes to mind? Share your answers with the rest of the class.

I have always believed that guns are not toys and children should not be encouraged to think they are. That was never a problem when my own daughters were children. They didn't ask to play with guns—toy guns or otherwise. At that time, Barbie didn't have one camouflage item in her wardrobe, so even tiny toy guns weren't needed to complete her ensemble. 1

Then they grew up and started bringing home their own children—wouldn't you figure—all of them are boys. In the beginning, we didn't allow their gender to influence our decisions when purchasing gifts. Two of them are learning how to cook on a Little Tikes stove and one has even made his favorite chocolate confections in an Easy Bake oven. Hey, even superheroes have to eat, right? But there's little doubt—they much prefer to play games where the good guys rid the world of evildoers, even if a smoking finger does the shooting. 2

But I hadn't anticipated the fun that began when Grandpa ambushed the boys with a contraption that fires lung-propelled miniature marshmallows. I guess I shouldn't have been surprised that 3 marshmallow blow guns would be such a hit in the newsroom, either. For a day, the newsroom floor was littered with multicolored marshmallows instead of rubber bands, the ammunition of choice. And you thought reporters were serious.

Still, there are some parents who don't approve of their children playing with guns of any sort, and that's OK. But if you love squirt guns, this marshmallow blaster is much less messy, and you can eat the ammunition after you take out the bad guys or your best buddy.   4

I found directions for this craft at www.ignitethefire.com/pipegun .html through an Internet search. I didn't find a lot of information, but I did find a discussion forum from folks who have been making and selling them at craft shows and a diagram to help build them. You will need an adult to cut the pipe, which comes in 10–foot sections. You can make four guns from each 10–foot section and buy the connectors, all for about $10. They can be sanded and painted, wrapped with colored duct tape, decorated with stickers, or left plain. You may need to gently tap the sections with a hammer to connect them. Use the picture for proper assembly.   5

Supplies you will need for each blow gun: 6

- One section of 1/2–inch PVC Schedule 40 pipe and pipe cutter
- Two 1/2–inch elbows
- Two 1/2–inch tees
- Two 1/2–inch end caps
- Two nickels
- Small hammer
- Miniature marshmallows

You will need to cut the pipe into the following lengths for each gun: 7

- One 8–inch piece
- One 7–inch piece
- Two 4–inch pieces
- One 3–inch piece
- Two 2–inch pieces

Assemble all the pieces. Connect the 8–inch and 7–inch section with a tee. Place a nickel inside the bottom of the tee to prevent air from going down into the handle, and attach a 4–inch piece beneath it for the handle. Place a cap on the end of the pipe.   8

Place a tee connection upside down on the back of the 7–inch piece and close off the opposite end of the tee with a nickel. Add a 2–inch piece of pipe at the back of the tee connector. Place the other 2–inch piece in the top of the tee.   9

Place elbows on the ends of each of the 2–inch pieces.   10

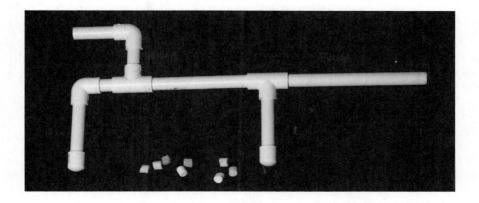

Connect a 4-inch piece of pipe to the back elbow for the back handle 11
and cap.

Connect the 3-inch piece of pipe to the top elbow for a mouthpiece.   12

Smooth any rough edges from the mouthpiece with sandpaper.   13

Additional instructions: Do not glue the pieces together. You may   14
need to separate them to remove stuck marshmallows. To get the best
distance, place your marshmallows in the mouth-piece rather than in the
barrel. Remember to fill your lungs with air before you place your
mouth on the trigger. Do not use any objects other than marshmallows
as ammunition.

Reading Closely

1. What is the Antoniotti's attitude toward the "marshmallow blaster"?
   What specific phrases or passages reveal her attitude?

2. How does the author specify the differences she sees between girls and
   boys? What do these differences have to do with toy weapons? Be prepared to share your answers with the rest of the class.

Considering Larger Issues

1. Place a sheet of paper over the visual. Now reread the essay and try to
   visualize what such a toy weapon might look like. Sketch what you envision, and then compare your sketch (representing your understanding
   of what you've read) with the actual visual. How should you change
   your sketch in order to comply with the verbal description? What specific details from the published visual help you better understand the
   verbal description? Be prepared to share your answers with the rest of
   the class.

2. What is Antoniotti's purpose in writing this essay? Who is her audience?
   How do issues of purpose and audience converge? Cite passages from
   the selection to support your answers.

3. **COMBINING METHODS.** Mark where Antoniotti uses *exemplification* and *comparison and contrast* in the introductory part of her essay, before the actual process analysis. **Working with two or three classmates,** discuss how effectively she uses these other methods and what they contribute (or don't contribute) to her process analysis essay.

Thinking about Language

1. Using a dictionary or the context of the essay, define the following terms and phrases. Be prepared to share your answers with the rest of the class.

ensemble (1)	forum (5)	tees (6)
confections (2)	PVC (6)	barrel (14)
contraption (3)	elbows (6)	

2. Underline all the words and phrases in the essay that have to do with war. Then circle all the words and phrases that have to do with play. Which kind of language does the author use more frequently? to what effect? What is the overall effect of merging the language of war and play in this short process analysis?

Writing Your Own Essays Using Process Analysis

1. Draft a three- to four-page essay in which you analyze a process for a specific audience. Yours will be a directional process analysis, one you expect the audience to be able to replicate. Choose a process that you're familiar with, one for which you know the terminology, the order of steps, and the pitfalls. Be sure to include information that can help your audience avoid problems in the process. If possible, enhance your process analysis by including visuals of the steps, the finished product, or both. Be sure to refer to the guidelines for checking over the use of process analysis on p. 444.

2. Think back to your childhood, to a game you liked to play or a craft you enjoyed. Draft a two- to three-page essay in which you provide step-by-step information about that process—not so your audience can replicate it but rather so they can appreciate your childhood pleasure. **Trade drafts with another classmate who is working on the same assignment,** and respond to each other's drafts according the guidelines for checking over the use of process analysis on p. 444.

RACHEL DILLON
Mission Possible

● When Rachel Dillon (b. 1980) wrote this essay, she was an undergraduate secondary education major at Penn State University, specializing in English and
communication. She is now teaching high school English in Pittsburgh. If
you've ever faced a research paper assignment, then you know the worry that
Dillon felt throughout the process.

> **Preview** If you've ever been assigned a research project, what was your
> first reaction? your second reaction? What steps did you go through to
> meet your deadline?

"Your mission, whether you choose to accept it or not, is to write a research   1
paper." To most college students, this mission seems impossible; it's a specialized kind of skill that they've never developed. Who knows how to
write a research paper? And even if they know how to write one, who'd
want to? The research paper assignment brings fear and loathing to nearly
every student, everywhere. No wonder so many students resist learning the
process of research writing, and with the ever-growing supply of research
papers on the Internet, seek out quick solutions for their problem:

> **Research Papers for Sale!** Visit here to download research papers for
> sale! **Writing Assistance!** The only service through which your writing
> project is personally directed by a former college instructor, Harvard grad-
> uate & PhD: "Quality is our top priority!" Confidential. Since 1975.

> **Need Help with Your Research Project?** An extensive database of
> research projects on all subjects at the click of your mouse. Low-priced and
> top-quality.

No matter how enticing these advertisements seem to be, they are clever
booby traps that will lead you away from the mission at hand, and ultimately to plagiarism and failure. In order to successfully accomplish this
mission, then, all special agents must develop the research and writing
skills necessary for the assignment. (After all, research writing is a crucial
stage in their college-level intellectual development.) So if you are willing to attempt this mission, be prepared to follow a detailed process as
you defy the odds and accomplish the mission of writing a research
paper. The impossible mission becomes possible when you follow my
process from beginning to end.

I was assigned my mission on the first day of my class, "Women's   2
Rhetorics and Feminist Pedagogies." It was right there, on the syllabus,
which said that 25% of my final grade would be based on a research
project. That didn't seem so bad except that the syllabus also said that I'd
have to develop my project over the course of the semester; I'd have to

submit various parts of my research early on. And the professor kept emphasizing that each of us had to find a way to "own" our topics. Until then, I had never made any connection between doing research and owning the topic. Among the various pages of the syllabus, I found long explanations of those early research–related assignments: research topic lists, annotated bibliographies, a research project overview, all due before the final project due date. With the task of finding and researching a topic and the additional burden of making it "my own," the research paper assignment was a mission that overwhelmed and frightened me. I knew that if I was to carry out this mission, I'd have to prepare, so I followed a process and prevailed.

The first step in overcoming my anxiety was choosing a topic that ful-   3
filled the requirements for the project, and also interested me. If I was to make this project mine, I had to really care about what I was writing about. So I began reading and researching women speakers and writers, especially those who were practicing feminism. Suddenly, I remembered Kathy Acker, whose work I'd come across when I was preparing a unit plan on Nathaniel Hawthorne's *The Scarlet Letter* for the high–school English class I was student-teaching. Author of such works as *Blood & Guts in High School* and *Don Quixote*, Acker wrote feminist responses to canonical male writers, to Nathaniel Hawthorne, in particular. Her writings were edgy and sexy, the kind of contemporary writing that I thought my high school students would enjoy and could use for access into Hawthorne's more old–fashioned writing and plot. The second step I took in my research project was reading additional works by Acker and as much scholarship on her writings as I could manage. Just as soon as I became familiar with her and her work, I began to list possible topics, angles I could take on her for my research paper. I was feeling confident.

The next step, though, was probably the most difficult for me, and it   4
might be for you, too: narrowing down the subject. I knew I couldn't read and write about every work ever written by Acker; likewise, it would be impossible for me to find every piece of commentary on her. In order to clearly define what the topic and thesis statement of my paper might be, I had to consider the goal of this project, which my teacher had provided in the syllabus: the paper must focus on a course–related issue. I looked back at the required readings for the course and thought about how Kathy Acker might best fit into "Women's Rhetorics and Feminist Pedagogies." I decided to focus on the specific ways Acker successfully resisted "classic" texts, in particular *The Scarlet Letter*, which I knew I would be expected to teach at the high school level very soon. Just as soon as I was able to narrow down my topic in a way that met the teacher's objectives, I was also able to narrow down my research and work. I began reading and researching only those of Acker's writings that spoke directly to *The Scarlet Letter*. I took notes and organized them according to their chronological relevance to the novel. Then, I began developing supporting ideas. After I was sure to have at least ten bibliographic

sources and a thesis statement with enough information to support it, I sat down to write my first draft.

Many special agents fumble the mission at this point because they do not understand the steps that drafting entails. Once the actual writing is under way, it is crucial to get peer feedback at an early stage. After I had a solid start on my draft, I met with other students in my English class, and we began to read each other's papers and discuss the direction our research projects were taking. We gave and received feedback, and then we each returned to our computers — that's where I began to revise my earlier draft according to the good advice I'd received. (It was hard for me to learn how to use my peers, but once we got into the habit of helping each other, we stayed together all term.) The success of the revision step (or steps) will vary based on the quality of the feedback received. If the feedback is high quality, the writer may have more work to do than if the feedback is weak. One writer might discover that she has far too much material and too broad a focus, while another may learn that he needs to supply even more supporting material, which means more reading and research on the topic. In any case, it will probably be necessary to reorganize the paper if the peer feedback is any good. To continue the revising process, I had to work alone for a while to be sure that the paper was organized in the most effective way (in my case, chronologically), with an introduction, thesis (controlling idea), and the supporting points following, ending with the conclusion.

After completing the second draft of my paper, I continued my revisions by discussing the draft with both the professor and teaching assistant (the graduate student also assigned to the course). Both offered feedback and tips — different in their focus and advice — that would help ensure the success of the mission. It was back to the computer for me, time to revise for a third draft. After I felt satisfied with this draft, I met again with the members of my peer group for some final feedback. This session was beneficial to me, as they found errors in spelling, punctuation, and sentence structure that I had missed. I'd been too focused on the substance of my research to think about the surface of my paper. After receiving their feedback, I headed back to my computer for the last time, to fix any typos or grammatical errors. And reading my paper one final time, I realized, with satisfaction, that the impossible was now possible. By following through the process of preparing, drafting, and revising, I was able to write an A research paper. Mission accomplished!

Reading Closely

1. What details does Dillon include that reveal information about her as a student, a future teacher, and/or a reader?
2. What are the steps of the process that Dillon is analyzing? Write them out.

Considering Larger Issues

1. What is Dillon's purpose for writing this essay? What textual evidence can you provide to support your answer?
2. Who is Dillon's audience? What specific information in the essay helps you determine her audience?
3. What is Dillon's thesis statement?
4. **COMBINING METHODS.** Dillon *analyzes causes and consequences* in parts of her essay. Mark the passages in which she uses this method, and then, **working with two or three classmates,** discuss why she does so. What overall effect does the cause–and–consequence analysis have? Prepare to share your responses with the rest of the class.

Thinking about Language

1. Use the context of the essay or your dictionary to define the following terms. Be prepared to share your answers with the rest of the class.

loathing (1)	pedagogies (2)	edgy (3)
rhetorics (2)	annotated (2)	commentary (4)
feminist (2)	canonical (3)	peer feedback (5)

2. List the technical terms or phrases relating to a research assignment that Dillon includes.

Writing Your Own Essays Using Process Analysis

1. What school–related process have you carried out successfully? It could be a school–only process, or one related to successful balancing of responsibilities at school and at home. What are the steps of this process? Which steps are unique to your experience and abilities, and which ones are replicable by others? Draft a three- to four–page essay in which you write about the successful use of the process. Make sure all the steps and details you include help develop your thesis statement about this process. If a visual would enhance your essay, include one. Refer to "Checking Over the Use of Process Analysis" (p. 444).
2. Refer back to the chapter–opening example: Lydia's instructions to Gabe for reheating pizza (p. 428). Writing from Gabe's point of view, draft a two–page essay in which you explain to your older sister how to do some household or everyday activity, one that a ninth–grade boy would know how to do. Refer to "Checking Over the Use of Process Analysis" (p. 444).

JESSICA MITFORD
The Embalming of Mr. Jones

Jessica Mitford (1917–1996) was born into a wealthy, aristocratic English family. Her early life was one of leisure and gentility, but she eventually rebelled against the atmosphere of sheltered ignorance in which she was brought up. She went to Spain to support the anti-fascists during the country's civil war in the 1930s and later immigrated to the United States, where she continued her activism in left-wing politics and also took up investigative journalism.

Mitford had a productive life as a writer. Besides newspaper articles, she wrote fiction, autobiography, and other nonfiction that explored topics ranging from her own upbringing to the U.S. funeral, obstetrics, and prison systems; her books include *Daughters and Rebels* (1960), *The American Way of Death* (1963), *Kind and Unusual Punishment* (1973), *A Fine Old Conflict* (1976), and *The American Way of Birth* (1992). The following self-contained excerpt is from *The American Way of Death*.

Preview   What is your experience with "the American way of death"?

Embalming is indeed a most extraordinary procedure, and one must   1
wonder at the docility of Americans who each year pay hundreds of millions of dollars for its perpetuation, blissfully ignorant of what it is all about, what is done, how it is done. Not one in ten thousand has any idea of what actually takes place. Books on the subject are extremely hard to come by. They are not to be found in most libraries or bookshops.

In an era when huge television audiences watch surgical operations   2
in the comfort of their living rooms, when, thanks to the animated cartoon, the geography of the digestive system has become familiar territory even to the nursery school set, in a land where the satisfaction of curiosity about almost all matters is a national pastime, the secrecy surrounding embalming can, surely, hardly be attributed to the inherent gruesomeness of the subject. Custom in this regard has within this century suffered a complete reversal. In the early days of American embalming, when it was performed in the home of the deceased, it was almost mandatory for some relative to stay by the embalmer's side and witness the procedure. Today, family members who might wish to be in attendance would certainly be dissuaded by the funeral director. All others, except apprentices, are excluded by law from the preparation room.

A close look at what does actually take place may explain in large   3
measure the undertaker's intractable reticence concerning a procedure that has become his major *raison d'être.** Is it possible he fears that public

---
* ***raison d'être:*** reason for being.

453

information about embalming might lead patrons to wonder if they really want this service? If the funeral men are loath to discuss the subject
outside the trade, the reader may, understandably, be equally loath to go
on reading at this point. For those who have the stomach for it, let us
part the formaldehyde curtain. . . .

The body is first laid out in the undertaker's morgue—or rather, Mr.   4
Jones is reposing in the preparation room—to be readied to bid the
world farewell.

The preparation room in any of the better funeral establishments   5
has the tiled and sterile look of a surgery, and indeed the embalmer-
restorative artist who does his chores there is beginning to adopt the
term "dermasurgeon" (appropriately corrupted by some mortician-
writers as "demisurgeon") to describe his calling. His equipment, consisting of scalpels, scissors, augers, forceps, clamps, needles, pumps, tubes,
bowls, and basin, is crudely imitative of the surgeon's as is his technique,
acquired in a nine- or twelve-month post–high-school course in an embalming school. He is supplied by an advanced chemical industry with a
bewildering array of fluids, sprays, pastes, oils, powders, creams, to fix or
soften tissue, shrink or distend it as needed, dry it here, restore the moisture there. There are cosmetics, waxes, and paints to fill and cover features, even plaster of Paris to replace entire limbs. There are ingenious
aids to prop and stabilize the cadaver: a Vari–Pose Head Rest, the
Edwards Arm and Hand Positioner, the Repose Block (to support the
shoulders during the embalming), and the Throop Foot Positioner, which
resembles an old–fashioned stocks.

Mr. John H. Eckels, president of the Eckels College of Mortuary Sci-   6
ence, thus describes the first part of the embalming procedure: "In the
hands of a skilled practitioner, this work may be done in a comparatively
short time and without mutilating the body other than by slight in-
cision—so slight that it scarcely would cause serious inconvenience if
made upon a living person. It is necessary to remove all the blood, and
doing this not only helps in the disinfecting, but removes the principal
cause of disfigurements due to discoloration."

Another textbook discusses the all–important time element: "The   7
earlier this is done, the better, for every hour that elapses between death
and embalming will add to the problems and complications encountered. . . ." Just how soon should one get going on the embalming? The
author tells us, "On the basis of such scanty information made available
to this profession through its rudimentary and haphazard system of
technical research, we must conclude that the best results are to be obtained if the subject is embalmed before life is completely extinct—that
is, before cellular death has occurred. In the average case, this would
mean within an hour after somatic death." For those who feel that there
is something a little rudimentary, not to say haphazard, about this advice, a comforting thought is offered by another writer. Speaking of fears

entertained in early days of premature burial, he points out, "One of the effects of embalming by chemical injection, however, has been to dispel fears of live burial." How true; once the blood is removed, chances of live burial are indeed remote.

To return to Mr. Jones, the blood is drained out through the veins 8 and replaced by embalming fluid pumped in through the arteries. As noted in *The Principles and Practices of Embalming*, "every operator has a favorite injection and drainage point—a fact which becomes a handicap only if he fails or refuses to forsake his favorites when conditions demand it." Typical favorites are the carotid artery, femoral artery, jugular vein, subclavian vein. There are various choices of embalming fluid. If Flextone is used, it will produce a "mild, flexible rigidity. The skin retains a velvety softness, the tissues are rubbery and pliable. Ideal for women and children." It may be blended with B. and G. Products Company's Lyf-Lyk tint, which is guaranteed to reproduce "nature's own skin texture . . . the velvety appearance of living tissue." Suntone comes in three separate tints: Suntan; Special Cosmetic Tint, a pink shade "especially indicated for young female subjects"; and Regular Cosmetic Tint, moderately pink.

About three to six gallons of a dyed and perfumed solution of 9 formaldehyde, glycerin, borax, phenol, alcohol, and water is soon circulating through Mr. Jones, whose mouth has been sewn together with a "needle directed upward between the upper lip and gum and brought out through the left nostril," with the corners raised slightly "for a more pleasant expression." If he should be buck-toothed, his teeth are cleaned with Bon Ami and coated with colorless nail polish. His eyes, meanwhile, are closed with flesh-tinted eye caps and eye cement.

The next step is to have at Mr. Jones with a thing called a trocar. This 10 is a long, hollow needle attached to a tube. It is jabbed into the abdomen, poked around the entrails and chest cavity, the contents of which are pumped out and replaced with "cavity fluid." This done, and the hole in the abdomen sewed up, Mr. Jones's face is heavily creamed (to protect the skin from burns which may be caused by leakage of the chemicals), and he is covered with a sheet and left unmolested for a while. But not for long—there is more, much more, in store for him. He has been embalmed, but not yet restored, and the best time to start restorative work is eight to ten hours after embalming, when the tissues have become firm and dry.

The object of all this attention to the corpse, it must be remembered, 11 is to make it presentable for viewing in an attitude of healthy repose. "Our customs require the presentation of our dead in the semblance of normality . . . unmarred by the ravages of illness, disease or mutilation," says Mr. J. Sheridan Mayer in his *Restorative Art*. This is rather a large order since few people die in the full bloom of health, unravaged by illness and unmarked by some disfigurement. The funeral industry is equal to the challenge: "In some cases the gruesome appearance of a mutilated or

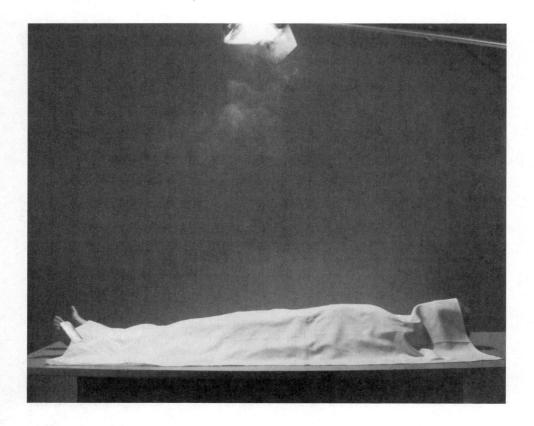

disease–ridden subject may be quite discouraging. The task of restoration may seem impossible and shake the confidence of the embalmer. This is the time for intestinal fortitude and determination. Once the formative work is begun and affected tissues are cleaned or removed, all doubts of success vanish. It is surprising and gratifying to discover the results - which may be obtained."

The embalmer, having allowed an appropriate interval to elapse, re-   12
turns to the attack, but now he brings into play the skill and equipment of sculptor and cosmetician. Is a hand missing? Casting one in plaster of Paris is a simple matter. "For replacement purposes, only a cast of the back of the hand is necessary; this is within the ability of the average operator and is quite adequate." If a lip or two, a nose or an ear should be missing, the embalmer has at hand a variety of restorative waxes with which to model replacements. Pores and skin texture are simulated by stippling with a little brush, and over this cosmetics are laid on. Head off? Decapitation cases are rather routinely handled. Ragged edges are trimmed, and head joined to torso with a series of splints, wires, and

sutures. It is a good idea to have a little something at the neck—a scarf or high collar—when time for viewing comes. Swollen mouth? Cut out tissue as needed from inside the lips. If too much is removed, the surface contour can easily be restored by padding with cotton. Swollen necks and cheeks are reduced by removing tissue through vertical incisions made down each side of the neck. "When the deceased is casketed, the pillow will hide the suture incisions . . . as an extra precaution against leakage, the suture may be painted with liquid sealer."

The opposite condition is more likely to be present itself—that of 13 emaciation. His hypodermic syringe now loaded with massage cream, the embalmer seeks out and fills the hollowed and sunken areas by injection. In this procedure the backs of the hands and fingers and the underchin area should not be neglected.

Positioning the lips is a problem that recurrently challenges the inge- 14 nuity of the embalmer. Closed too tightly, they tend to give a stern, even disapproving expression. Ideally, embalmers feel, the lips should give the impression of being ever so slightly parted, the upper lip protruding slightly for a more youthful appearance. This takes some engineering, however, as the lips tend to drift apart. Lip drift can sometimes be remedied by pushing one or two straight pins through the inner margin of the lower lip and then inserting them between the two front upper teeth. If Mr. Jones happens to have no teeth, the pins can just as easily be anchored in his Armstrong Face Former and Denture Replacer. Another method to maintain lip closure is to dislocate the lower jaw, which is then held in its new position by a wire run through holes which have been drilled through the upper jaws at the midline. As the French are fond of saying, *il faut souffrir pour être belle.**

If Mr. Jones has died of jaundice, the embalming fluid will very likely 15 turn him green. Does this deter the embalmer? Not if he has intestinal fortitude. Masking pastes and cosmetics are heavily laid on, burial garments and casket interiors are color–correlated with particular care, and Jones is displayed beneath rose–colored lights. Friends will say, "How *well* he looks." Death by carbon monoxide, on the other hand, can be rather a good thing from an embalmer's viewpoint: "One advantage is the fact that this type of discoloration is an exaggerated form of a natural pink coloration." This is nice because the healthy glow is already present and needs but little attention.

The patching and filling completed, Mr. Jones is now shaved, washed, 16 and dressed. Cream–based cosmetic, available in pink, flesh, suntan, brunette, and blonde, is applied to his hands and face, his hair is shampooed and combed (and, in the case of Mrs. Jones, set), his hands manicured. For the horny–handed son of toil special care must be taken;

---

* ***il faut souffrir pour être belle:*** it is necessary to suffer in order to be beautiful.

cream should be applied to remove ingrained grime, and the nails cleaned. "If he were not in the habit of having them manicured in life, trimming and shaping is advised for better appearance—never questioned by kin."

Jones is now ready for casketing (this is the present participle of the verb "to casket"). In this operation his right shoulder should be depressed slightly "to turn the body a bit to the right and soften the appearance of lying flat on the back." Positioning the hands is a matter of importance, and special rubber positioning blocks may be used. The hands should be cupped slightly for a more lifelike, relaxed appearance. Proper placement of the body requires a delicate sense of balance. It should lie as high as possible in the casket, yet not so high that the lid, when lowered, will hit the nose. On the other hand, we are cautioned, placing the body too low "creates the impression that the body is in a box." 17

Jones is next wheeled into the appointed slumber room where a few last touches may be added—his favorite pipe placed in his hand or, if he was a great reader, a book propped into position. (In the case of little Master Jones a Teddy bear may be clutched.) Here he will hold open house for a few days, visiting hours 10 A.M. to 9 P.M. 18

Reading Closely

1. What is your immediate response to Mitford's essay? Be prepared to share your response with rest of the class.
2. What did you learn about embalming that you didn't know before you read this process analysis?
3. What are the individual steps in the process that Mitford is analyzing? Is her analysis directional, informational, or both? **Work with three or four classmates** to come up with an answer and the reasons for it.
4. What stage in the embalming process does the visual depict?

Considering Larger Issues

1. Who is the audience for Mitford's essay? How does audience affect the kind of process analysis this is, and vice versa?
2. What details does Mitford use to help fulfill her purpose in writing? What exactly is her purpose?
3. What specific information does Mitford include or not include to create an informational process analysis? a directional process analysis? What kinds of information are necessary for each kind of process analysis?
4. **COMBINING METHODS.** In which passages does Mitford use *description? narration?* Mark those passages, and account for their importance to the overall essay.

Thinking about Language

1. Define the following words using the context of the essay or your dictionary. Be prepared to share your answers with the rest of the class.

docility (1)   intractable (3)   distend (5)
perpetuation (1)   reticence (3)   mutilating (6)
inherent (2)   loath (3)   rudimentary (7)
mandatory (2)   reposing (4)   trocar (10)
apprentices (2)   augers (5)

2. Reread the first two paragraphs. What effect did they have on you when you first read them? What is their overall effect on the essay? What do they reveal about the author's style (her distinctive tone and use of language)?

Writing Your Own Essays Using Process Analysis

1. If you have ever grieved for someone who died, or if you attended the funeral or memorial service, what steps did you go through—from learning about the death to recovering from your grief? Draft a three- to four-page directional and informative analysis of this process, using your classmates as your audience. Be sure to focus on one part of this process—breaking it down into steps or groups of steps—that your audience could replicate. Refer to "Checking Over the Use of Process Analysis" on p. 444.

2. Mitford's tone in this essay is ironic: Americans are "blissfully ignorant" of what goes on behind "the formaldehyde curtain." Using Mitford's essay and her tone as a model, draft a three- to four-page process analysis of something with which you're familiar but of which others are blissfully ignorant. Try to have some fun as you draft your essay, providing details that might surprise your readers and perhaps an amusing visual or two. **Consider working with one or two classmates** to make sure that you include enough detail to fulfill your purpose. Your process analysis should be informational. Refer to "Checking Over the Use of Process Analysis" (p. 444).

BERNICE WUETHRICH

Getting Stupid

Before joining the staff of Burness Communications in 2000, Bernice Wuethrich was an exhibition writer and editor for the Smithsonian Institution's National Museum of Natural History as well as a freelance science writer. Her essays have appeared in *New Scientist, Science, Science News,* and *Smithsonian Magazine;* she has also coauthored the book *Dying to Drink: Confronting Binge Drinking on College Campuses* (2000). The following article appeared in the March 2001 issue of *Discover.*

Preview   What kind of topic might "Getting Stupid" be about?

The most recent statistics from the U.S. Substance Abuse and Mental 1
Health Services Administration's National Household Survey on Drug
Abuse indicate that nearly 7 million youths between the ages of 12 and
20 binge–drink at least once a month. And despite the fact that many
colleges have cracked down on drinking, Henry Wechsler of the Harvard
School of Public Health says that two of every five college students still
binge–drink regularly. For a male that means downing five or more
drinks in a row; for a female it means consuming four drinks in one session at least once in a two–week period.

Few teens seem to worry much about what such drinking does to 2
their bodies. Cirrhosis of the liver is unlikely to catch up with them for
decades, and heart disease must seem as remote as retirement. But new
research suggests that young drinkers are courting danger. Because their
brains are still developing well into their twenties, teens who drink excessively may be destroying significant amounts of mental capacity in
ways that are more dramatic than in older drinkers.

Scientists have long known that excessive alcohol consumption 3
among adults over long periods of time can create brain damage, ranging from a mild loss of motor skills to psychosis and even the inability to
form memories. But less has been known about the impact alcohol has
on younger brains. Until recently, scientists assumed that a youthful
brain is more resilient than an adult brain and could escape many of the
worst ills of alcohol. But some researchers are now beginning to question
this assumption. Preliminary results from several studies indicate that the
younger the brain is, the more it may be at risk. "The adolescent brain is
a developing nervous system, and the things you do to it can change it,"
says Scott Swartzwelder, a neuropsychologist at Duke University and the
U.S. Department of Veterans Affairs.

Teen drinkers appear to be most susceptible to damage in the hip– 4
pocampus, a structure buried deep in the brain that is responsible for
many types of learning and memory, and the prefrontal cortex, located

behind the forehead, which is the brain's chief decision maker and voice of reason. Both areas, especially the prefrontal cortex, undergo dramatic change in the second decade of life.

Swartzwelder and his team have been studying how alcohol affects 5 the hippocampus, an evolutionary old part of the brain that is similar in rats and humans. Six years ago, when Swartzwelder published his first paper suggesting that alcohol disrupts the hippocampus more severely in adolescent rats than in adult rats, "people didn't believe it," he says. Since then, his research has shown that the adolescent brain is more easily damaged in the structures that regulate the acquisition and storage of memories.

Learning depends on communication between nerve cells, or neu- 6 rons, within the hippocampus. To communicate, a neuron fires an electrical signal down its axon, a single fiber extending away from the cell's center. In response, the axon releases chemical messengers, called neurotransmitters, which bind to receptors on the receiving branches of neighboring cells. Depending on the types of neurotransmitters released, the receiving cell may be jolted into action or settle more deeply into rest.

But the formation of memories requires more than the simple firing 7 or inhibition of nerve cells. There must be some physical change in the hippocampus neurons that represents the encoding of new information. Scientists believe that this change occurs in the synapses, the tiny gaps between neurons that neurotransmitters traverse. Repeated use of synapses seems to increase their ability to fire up connecting cells. Laboratory experiments on brain tissue can induce this process, called long-term potentiation. Researchers assume that something similar takes place in the intact living brain, although it is impossible to observe directly. Essentially, if the repetitive neural reverberations are strong enough, they burn in new patterns of synaptic circuitry to encode memory, just as the more often a child recites his ABCs, the better he knows them.

Swartzwelder's first clue that alcohol powerfully disrupts memory in 8 the adolescent brain came from studying rat hippocampi. He found that alcohol blocks long-term potentiation in adolescent brain tissue much more than in adult tissue. Next, Swartzwelder identified a likely explanation. Long-term potentiation—and thus memory formation—relies in large part on the action of a neurotransmitter known as glutamate, the brain's chemical kingpin of neural excitation. Glutamate strengthens a cell's electrical stimulation when it binds to a docking port called the NMDA receptor. If the receptor is blocked, so is long-term potentiation, and thus memory formation. Swartzwelder found that exposure to the equivalent of just two beers inhibits the NMDA receptors in the hippocampal cells of adolescent rats, while more than twice as much is required to produce the same effect in adult rats. These findings led him to suspect that alcohol consumption might have a dramatic impact on the ability of adolescents to learn. So he set up a series of behavioral tests.

First, Swartzwelder's team dosed adolescent and adult rats with alco-   9
hol and ran them through maze–learning tests. Compared with the adult
rats, the adolescents failed miserably. To see whether similar results held
true for humans, Swartzwelder recruited a group of volunteers aged 21 to
29 years old. He couldn't use younger subjects because of laws that for-
bid drinking before age 21. He chose to split the volunteers into two
groups: 21 to 24 years old and 25 to 29 years old. "While I wouldn't argue
that these younger folks are adolescents, even in their early twenties
their brains are still developing," Swartzwelder says. After three drinks,
with a blood–alcohol level slightly below the National Highway Traffic
Safety Administration's recommended limit—.08 percent—the younger
group's learning was impaired 25 percent more than the older group's.

Intrigued by these results, Swartzwelder's colleague Aaron White, a   10
biological psychologist at Duke, set out to discover how vulnerable the
adolescent brain is to long–term damage. He gave adolescent and adult
rats large doses of alcohol every other day for 20 days—the equivalent
of a 150–pound human chugging 24 drinks in a row. Twenty days after
the last binge, when the adolescent rats had reached adulthood, White
trained them in a maze–memory task roughly akin to that performed by
a human when remembering the location of his car in a parking garage.

Both the younger and older rats performed equally well when sober.   11
But when intoxicated, those who had binged as adolescents performed
much worse. "Binge alcohol exposure in adolescence appears to produce
long–lasting changes in brain function," White says. He suspects that

early damage caused by alcohol could surface whenever the brain is taxed. He also suspects that the NMDA receptor is involved, because just as alcohol in the system inhibits the receptor, the drug's withdrawal overstimulates it—which can kill the cell outright.

Students who drink heavily sometimes joke that they are killing a few   12 brain cells. New research suggests that this is not funny. Some of the evidence is anatomical: Michael De Bellis at the University of Pittsburgh Medical Center used magnetic resonance imaging to compare the hippocampi of subjects 14 to 21 years old who abused alcohol to the hippocampi of those who did not. He found that the longer and the more a young person had been drinking, the smaller his hippocampus. The average size difference between healthy teens and alcohol abusers was roughly 10 percent. That is a lot of brain cells.

De Bellis speculates that the shrinkage may be due to cell damage   13 and death that occurs during withdrawal from alcohol. Withdrawal is the brain's way of trying to get back to normal after prolonged or heavy drinking. It can leave the hands jittery, set off the classic headache, generate intense anxiety, and even provoke seizures, as neurons that had adjusted to the presence of alcohol try to adjust to its absence. Because alcohol slows down the transmission of nerve signals—in part by stopping glutamate from activating its NMDA receptors—nerve cells under the influence react by increasing the number and sensitivity of these receptors. When drinking stops, the brain is suddenly stuck with too many hyperactive receptors.

Mark Prendergast, a neuroscientist at the University of Kentucky, re-   14 cently revealed one way these hyperactive receptors kill brain cells. First, he exposed rat hippocampal slices to alcohol for 10 days, then removed the alcohol. Following withdrawal, he stained the tissue with a fluorescent dye that lit up dead and dying cells. When exposed to an alcohol concentration of about .08 percent, cell death increased some 25 percent above the baseline. When concentrations were two or three times higher, he wrote in a recent issue of *Alcoholism: Clinical and Experimental Research*, the number of dead cells shot up to 100 percent above the baseline.

Prendergast says that the younger brain tissue was far more sensi-   15 tive. Preadolescent tissue suffered four to five times more cell death than did adult tissue. In all cases, most of the death occurred in hippocampal cells that were packed with NMDA receptors. To home in on the cause, he treated another batch of brain slices with the drug MK–801, which blocks NMDA receptors. He reasoned that if overexcitability during alcohol withdrawal was causing cell death, blocking the receptors should minimize the carnage. It did, by about 75 percent.

Now Prendergast is examining what makes the receptors so lethal. By   16 tracking radioactive calcium, he found that the overexcited receptors open floodgates that allow calcium to swamp the cell. Too much calcium can turn on suicide genes that cause the neuron to break down its own membrane. Indeed, that is exactly what Prendergast observed during alcohol withdrawal: Overactive receptors opened wide, and the influx of calcium became a raging flood.

Prendergast says that four or five drinks may cause a mild with- 17 drawal. And, according to Harvard's Wechsler, 44 percent of college students binge in this manner. More alarming, 23 percent of them consume 72 percent of all the alcohol that college students drink.

Recent human studies support a conclusion Prendergast drew from his 18 molecular experiments: The greatest brain damage from alcohol occurs during withdrawal. At the University of California at San Diego and the VA San Diego Health Care System, Sandra Brown, Susan Tapert, and Gregory Brown have been following alcohol–dependent adolescents for eight years. Repeated testing shows that problem drinkers perform more poorly on tests of cognition and learning than do nondrinkers. Furthermore, "the single best predictor of neuropsychological deficits for adolescents is withdrawal symptoms," says principal investigator Sandra Brown.

The psychologists recruited a group of 33 teenagers aged 15 and 16, 19 all heavy drinkers. On average, each teen had used alcohol more than 750 times — the equivalent of drinking every day for two and a half years. Bingeing was common: The teens downed an average of eight drinks at each sitting. The researchers matched drinkers with nondrinkers of the same gender and similar age, IQ, socioeconomic background, and family history of alcohol use. Then, three weeks after the drinkers had their last drink, all the teens took a two–hour battery of tests.

The teens with alcohol problems had a harder time recalling infor- 20 mation, both verbal and nonverbal, that they had learned 20 minutes earlier. Words such as *apple* and *football* escaped them. The performance difference was about 10 percent. "It's not serious brain damage, but it's the difference of a grade, a pass or a fail," Tapert says. Other tests evaluated skills needed for map learning, geometry, or science. Again, there was a 10 percent difference in performance.

"The study shows that just several years of heavy alcohol use by 21 youth can adversely affect their brain functions in ways that are critical to learning," Sandra Brown says. She is following the group of teenagers until they reach age 30, and some have already passed 21. "Those who continue to use alcohol heavily are developing attentional deficits in addition to the memory and problem–solving deficits that showed up early on," Brown says. "In the past we thought of alcohol as a more benign drug. It's not included in the war on drugs. This study clearly demonstrates that the most popular drug is also an incredibly dangerous drug."

Brown's research team is also using functional magnetic resonance 22 imaging to compare the brain function of alcohol abusers and nondrinkers. Initial results show that brains of young adults with a history of alcohol dependence are less active than the brains of nondrinkers during tasks that require spatial working memory (comparable to the maze task that White conducted on rats). In addition, the adolescent drinkers seem to exhibit greater levels of brain activity when they are exposed to alcohol–related stimuli. For instance, when the drinkers read words such as *wasted* or *tequila* on a screen, the nucleus accumbens — a small section of the brain associated with craving — lights up.

The nucleus accumbens is integral to the brain's so–called pleasure 23 circuit, which scientists now believe undergoes major remodeling during adolescence. Underlying the pleasure circuit is the neurotransmitter dopamine. Sex, food, and many drugs, including alcohol, can all induce the release of dopamine, which creates feelings of pleasure and in turn encourages repetition of the original behavior. During adolescence, the balance of dopamine activity temporarily shifts away from the nucleus accumbens, the brain's key pleasure and reward center, to the prefrontal cortex. Linda Spear, a developmental psychobiologist at Binghamton University in New York, speculates that as a result of this shift in balance, teenagers may find drugs less rewarding than earlier or later in life. And if the drugs produce less of a kick, more will be needed for the same ef-fect. "In the case of alcohol, this may lead to binge drinking," she says.

During adolescence, the prefrontal cortex changes more than any other 24 part of the brain. At around age 11 or 12, its neurons branch out like crazy, only to be seriously pruned back in the years that follow. All this tumult is to good purpose. In the adult brain, the prefrontal cortex exe-cutes the thought processes adolescents struggle to master: the ability to plan ahead, think abstractly, and integrate information to make sound decisions.

Now there is evidence that the prefrontal cortex and associated areas 25 are among those most damaged in the brains of bingeing adolescents. Fulton Crews, director of the Center for Alcohol Studies at the University of North Carolina at Chapel Hill, has studied the patterns of cell death in the brains of adolescent and adult rats after four–day drinking bouts. While both groups showed damage in the back areas of the brain and in the frontally located olfactory bulb, used for smell, only the adolescents suffered brain damage in other frontal areas.

That youthful damage was severe. It extended from the rat's olfactory 26 bulb to the interconnected parts of the brain that process sensory infor-mation and memories to make associations, such as "this smell and the sight of that wall tell me I'm in a place where I previously faced down an enemy." The regions of cell death in the rat experiment corresponded to the human prefrontal cortex and to parts of the limbic system.

The limbic system, which includes the hippocampus, changes 27 throughout adolescence, according to recent work by Jay Giedd at the National Institute of Mental Health in Bethesda, Maryland. The limbic system not only encodes memory but is also mobilized when a person is hungry or frightened or angry; it helps the brain process survival impulses. The limbic system and the prefrontal cortex must work in concert for a person to make sound decisions.

Damage to the prefrontal cortex and the limbic system is especially   28 worrisome because they play an important role in the formation of an adult personality. "Binge drinking could be making permanent long–term changes in the final neural physiology, which is expressed as personality and behavior in the individual," Crew says. But he readily acknowledges that such conclusions are hypothetical. "It's very hard to prove this stuff. You can't do an experiment in which you change people's brains."

Nonetheless, evidence of the vulnerability of young people to alcohol   29 is mounting. A study by Bridget Grant of the National Institute on Alcohol Abuse and Alcoholism shows that the younger someone is when he begins to regularly drink alcohol, the more likely that individual will eventually become an alcoholic. Grant found that 40 percent of the drinkers who got started before age 15 were classified later in life as alcohol dependent, compared with only 10 percent of those who began drinking at age 21 or 22. Overall, beginning at age 15, the risk of future alcohol dependence decreased by 14 percent with each passing year of abstention.

The study leaves unanswered whether early regular drinking is merely   30 a marker of later abuse or whether it results in long–term changes in the brain that increase the later propensity for abuse. "It's got to be both," Crew says. For one thing, he points out that studies of rats and people have shown that repeated alcohol use makes it harder for a person — or a rat — to learn new ways of doing things, rather than repeating the same actions over and over again. In short, the way alcohol changes the brain makes it increasingly difficult over time to stop reaching for beer after beer after beer.

Ultimately, the collateral damage caused by having so many Ameri–   31 can adolescents reach for one drink after another may be incalculable. "People in their late teens have been drinking heavily for generations. We're not a society of idiots, but we're not a society of Einsteins either," says Swartzwelder. "What if you've compromised your function by 7 percent or 10 percent and never known the difference?"

Reading Closely

1. What details does Wuethrich include that reveal her expertise in science writing?

2. What are the steps of the process that Wuethrich is analyzing? Is hers a directional or informational process analysis?

3. How does the visual enhance (or why does it fail to enhance) Wuethrich's text?

Considering Larger Issues

1. What is Wuethrich's purpose? How do you know? What is her thesis statement?

2. Who is Wuethrich's audience? What specific information in the essay helps you determine that audience?

3. **Working with three or four classmates,** respond to the following questions: What big and small processes is Wuethrich analyzing? Which process is her main topic?

4. COMBINING METHODS. How does Wuethrich use *cause-and-consequence analysis* to explain the relationships between the bigger and smaller processes? between her main topic and the related smaller topics?

Thinking about Language

1. Using the context of the essay or your dictionary, define the following terms. Some of the technical terms are defined in the context. Be prepared to share your answers with the rest of the class.

binge–drink (1)	synapses (7)	socioeconomic
psychosis (3)	reverberations (7)	(19)
resilient (3)	maze–memory	benign (21)
hippocampus (4)	task (10)	tumult (24)
prefrontal cortex (4)	receptors (15)	integrate (24)
nerve cells (6)	cognition (18)	

2. List the technical terms or phrases that Wuethrich includes.

Writing Your Own Essays Using Process Analysis

1. Wuethrich's essay analyzes what happens when teenagers binge–drink. Although hers is a process analysis, it's also an analysis of causes and consequences. Do some research on a process with which you are unfamiliar, one that is connected with an occupation — farming, sewing, truck driving, birthing sheep, accounting, repairing machinery, merchandising, and so on. Using Wuethrich's essay as a starting point, draft a three- to four–page essay analyzing that occupational process, and extend your analysis to include consequences. Include some visuals to help readers follow the process. Refer to the guidelines for checking over the use of process analysis (p. 444) as you draft and revise.

2. Write about a process that you know well. Whether this process is related to a sport, hobby, pastime, or job, see if you can compare it to some other activity not usually linked with it. Then draft a three- to four–page essay in which you use an analogy to the secondary process to explain the primary process. **Consider working with three or four classmates** to discuss and review your essays while you draft. Refer to "Checking Over the Use of Process Analysis" (p. 444).

DAVID LIEBERMAN

Deal with Any Complaint Fast and Easy: Get Anyone to Stop Whining!

David Lieberman is the creator of neuro–dynamic analysis, a form of short–term therapy. A popular lecturer and television and radio guest, Lieberman holds a Ph.D. in psychology and is certified as a hypnotherapist with the American Board of Hypnotherapy. The following advice is from his book *Get Anyone to Do Anything: Never Feel Powerless Again — With Psychological Secrets to Control and Influence Every Situation* (2000). Lieberman is also the author of *Make Peace with Anyone: Breakthrough Strategies to Quickly End Any Conflict, Feud, or Estrangement* (2002).

Preview   What was the last complaint you registered — or handled? How did the process go?

Whether it's personal or professional, follow this list of tactics and you   1
can be sure to assuage anyone's complaints about anything.

First *listen*. Surprisingly most people don't know how to do this. To   2
listen you simply say nothing and do nothing other than listen. That means you don't agree, disagree, or argue. In the next step you're going to agree, but if you do it right away, you risk his thinking you're just placating or patronizing him. *So let him say everything he wants to say without any interruption* and *then* agree.

Sometimes people just need to get something off their chest. So let   3
them speak. Other times they're looking for a fight. If you don't interrupt, then they will eventually run out of things to say. If you interrupt you are going to give him more ammunition and risk a heated argument instead of a monologue.

Nobody wants to feel he's been manipulated or taken advantage of.   4
And that is 99.9 percent of the reason why he is so angry. His ego has been damaged. Somebody or something didn't respect him enough and he is hurting. When he is done speaking do the following.

First paraphrase back to him what he's said, so he knows that you've   5
been listening. Then build him up with phrases such as, "No one as important as you should have to go through this"; "I know you're not accustomed to being treated this way"; or "If I were you I would be just as upset." This completely takes the steam out of his tirade. The last thing you want is to be combative and with this first step you disarm him completely. You've made him feel important by listening, agreeing, and stroking his ego. Using this three–step process of listening, agreeing, and stroking will often defuse the situation. But if it doesn't continue with the following.

Now, ask him what he would like you to do. What he offers as a reso-   6
lution or solution is often much less than you would have given to compensate him for his troubles. In business situations we often make the

mistake of wanting to give the world to avoid a bigger problem. But hold off on your initial temptation and ask him what he would like you to do.

In personal situations, complaints may come the way of vague state- 7 ments, such as, "I'm not happy," or "You're driving me crazy." While there may be more serious relationship issues at hand, there is a specific way to help the situation. What you want to do is have him get as specific as possible about what is bothering him.

While you're doing the above, try to establish rapport to get him to like 8 you and to calm him down. The way you present yourself can greatly influence the attitude of the other person. If, while he's venting, your arms are crossed and your posture says, "When are you gonna shut up?" you're heading for a confrontation. That's why simple things such as unbuttoning your coat or uncrossing your arms can make the other person feel less defensive. When you have a rapport with someone, he is much more likely to feel comfortable and open up. Rapport creates trust, allowing you to build a psychological bridge to the person. The conversation is likely to be more positive and you will be much more persuasive. To review, here are a few powerful tips for establishing and building rapport:

> *Matching posture and movements:* If he has one hand in his pocket, you put your hand in yours. If he makes a gesture with his hand, after a moment, you casually make the same gesture.

> *Matching speech:* Try to match his rate of speech. If he's speaking in a slow, relaxed tone, you do the same. If he's speaking quickly, then you speak quickly.

> *Matching key words:* If she is prone to using certain words or phrases, employ them when you speak. For instance, if she says, "I was so uncomfortable with how I was treated," later in the conversation you might say something like, "I know you must have been so uncomfortable with that type of treatment." Make sure that you don't seem to be mimicking her. Obviously copying another's movements is unproductive. A simple reflection of aspects of the person's behavior or speech is enough. This can be a very powerful skill for you, once you become good at it.

Reading Closely

1. Is Lieberman's process analysis directional or informational, or both? What support can you provide for your answer?
2. What specific information does Lieberman include that helps readers avoid pitfalls in the process?

Considering Larger Issues

1. How is the purpose of this piece of writing affected by the audience, and vice versa? List the ways that purpose and audience intersect, citing evidence from the text.

2. What parts of Lieberman's advice seem to be easily replicable no matter what the rhetorical situation? What parts might depend on the setting, complainer, listener, or complaint? How?

3. If this essay is both directional and informational, which passages help fulfill each of those purposes? **Working with one or two classmates,** compare your responses and prepare a brief report for the rest of the class.

4. COMBINING METHODS. Mark the passages in which Lieberman uses *cause-and-consequence analysis* to enrich his process analysis. What effect does each of those passages have on the entire selection?

Thinking about Language

1. Use the context of the reading or your dictionary to define the following terms. Be prepared to share your answers with the rest of the class.

assuage (1)	monologue (3)	disarm (5)
placating (2)	paraphrase (5)	rapport (8)
patronizing (2)	tirade (5)	

2. What is the effect of the title, "Deal with Any Complaint Fast and Easy," and the subtitle, "Get Anyone to Stop Whining!"? How does the use of these two titles affect the overall tone of the essay?

3. Which passages specifically address the subtitle? What words, phrases, and examples does Lieberman include that relate to the subtitle?

4. Which passages indicate the complainer's point of view? the listener's point of view?

5. **Working with two or three classmates,** determine Lieberman's tone in this selection. What textual support can you find for your response? Be prepared to share your answers with the rest of the class.

Writing Your Own Essays Using Process Analysis

1. What's the closest you've ever come to disaster? How did you avoid or withstand it? Using your responses to these questions, draft a three- to four-page essay in which you describe a potential disaster and analyze the process of avoiding it. Try to include specific details that are both directional and informational. Refer to "Checking Over the Use of Process Analysis" (p. 444).

2. Think about your own experience or observation in registering or dealing with a complaint. If the process was successful, concentrate on a directional process analysis that could be replicated. If it was unsuccessful, analyze it in terms of the causes for its failure and the steps you could have taken to avoid failure. Draft a three- to four-page process analysis that concerns a complaint. **Consider working with another classmate.** Also, refer to the guidelines for checking over the use of process analysis (p. 444) as you draft and revise.

MALCOLM GLADWELL
The Trouble with Fries

Malcolm Gladwell (b. 1963) was born in England and educated in Canada, graduating with a degree in history from the University of Toronto in 1984. Since that time he's been a business writer and science writer for the *Washington Post* and then a regular contributor on a wide range of topics for the *New Yorker*, where the following essay first appeared in 2001. Besides writing essays and articles, Gladwell has published the book *The Tipping Point: How Little Things Can Make a Difference* (2000). "The Trouble with Fries" combines rhetorical methods: although its overall subject is the process by which French fries are made, much of the essay is developed using narration, description, comparison and contrast, and analysis of causes and consequences.

> **Preview**   What could possibly be the trouble with fries?

In 1954, a man named Ray Kroc, who made his living selling the five-spindle Multimixer milkshake machine, began hearing about a hamburger stand in San Bernardino, California. This particular restaurant, he was told, had no fewer than eight of his machines in operation, meaning that it could make forty shakes simultaneously. Kroc was astounded. He flew from Chicago to Los Angeles, and drove to San Bernardino, sixty miles away, where he found a small octagonal building on a corner lot. He sat in his car and watched as the workers showed up for the morning shift. They were in starched white shirts and paper hats, and moved with a purposeful discipline. As lunchtime approached, customers began streaming into the parking lot, lining up for bags of hamburgers. Kroc approached a strawberry blonde in a yellow convertible. 1

"How often do you come here?" he asked. 2

"Anytime I am in the neighborhood," she replied, and, Kroc would 3 say later, "it was not her sex appeal but the obvious relish with which she devoured the hamburger that made my pulse begin to hammer with excitement." He came back the next morning, and this time set up inside the kitchen, watching the griddle man, the food preparers, and, above all, the French-fry operation, because it was the French fries that truly captured his imagination. They were made from top-quality oblong Idaho russets, eight ounces apiece, deep-fried to a golden brown, and salted with a shaker that, as he put it, kept going like a Salvation Army girl's tambourine. They were crispy on the outside and buttery soft on the inside, and that day Kroc had a vision of a chain of restaurants, just like the one in San Bernardino, selling golden fries from one end of the country to the other. He asked the two brothers who owned the hamburger stand if he could buy their franchise rights. They said yes. Their names were Mac and Dick McDonald.

Ray Kroc was the great visionary of American fast food, the one who   4
brought the lessons of the manufacturing world to the restaurant business. Before the fifties, it was impossible, in most American towns, to buy
fries of consistent quality. Ray Kroc was the man who changed that. "The
french fry," he once wrote, "would become almost sacrosanct for me, its
preparation a ritual to be followed religiously." A potato that has too
great a percentage of water—and potatoes, even the standard Idaho russet burbank, vary widely in their water content—will come out soggy at
the end of the frying process. It was Kroc, back in the fifties, who sent out
field men, armed with hydrometers, to make sure that all his suppliers
were producing potatoes in the optimal solids range of twenty to
twenty-three per cent. Freshly harvested potatoes, furthermore, are rich
in sugars, and if you slice them up and deep-fry them the sugars will
caramelize and brown the outside of the fry long before the inside is
cooked. To make a crisp French fry, a potato has to be stored at a warm
temperature for several weeks in order to convert those sugars to starch.
Here Kroc led the way as well, mastering the art of "curing" potatoes by
storing them under a giant fan in the basement of his first restaurant,
outside Chicago.

Perhaps his most enduring achievement, though, was the so-called   5
potato computer—developed for McDonald's by a former electrical engineer for Motorola named Louis Martino—which precisely calibrated the
optimal cooking time for a batch of fries. (The key: when a batch of cold
raw potatoes is dumped into a vat of cooking oil, the temperature of the
fat will drop and then slowly rise. Once the oil has risen three degrees,
the fries are ready.) Previously, making high-quality French fries had
been an art. The potato computer, the hydrometer, and the curing bins
made it a science. By the time Kroc was finished, he had figured out how
to turn potatoes into an inexpensive snack that would always be hot,
salty, flavorful, and crisp, no matter where or when you bought it.

This was the first fast-food revolution—the mass production of food   6
that had reliable mass appeal. But today, as the McDonald's franchise approaches its fiftieth anniversary, it is clear that fast food needs a second
revolution. As many Americans now die every year from obesity-related
illnesses—heart disease and complications of diabetes—as from smoking, and the fast-food toll grows heavier every year. In the fine new book
Fast Food Nation, the journalist Eric Schlosser writes of McDonald's and
Burger King in the tone usually reserved for chemical companies, sweat-
shops, and arms dealers, and, as shocking as that seems at first, it is perfectly appropriate. Ray Kroc's French fries are killing us. Can fast food be
fixed?

Fast-food French fries are made from a baking potato like an Idaho russet,   7
or any other variety that is mealy, or starchy, rather than waxy. The potatoes are harvested, cured, washed, peeled, sliced, and then blanched—

cooked enough so that the insides have a fluffy texture but not so much that the fry gets soft and breaks. Blanching is followed by drying, and drying by a thirty-second deep fry, to give the potatoes a crisp shell. Then the fries are frozen until the moment of service, when they are deep-fried again, this time for somewhere around three minutes. Depending on the fast-food chain involved, there are other steps interspersed in this process. McDonald's fries, for example, are briefly dipped in a sugar solution, which gives them their golden-brown color; Burger King fries are dipped in a starch batter, which is what gives those fries their distinctive hard shell and audible crunch. But the result is similar. The potato that is first harvested in the field is roughly eighty per cent water. The process of creating a French fry consists, essentially, of removing as much of that water as possible—through blanching, drying, and deep-frying—and replacing it with fat.

Elisabeth Rozin, in her book *The Primal Cheeseburger*, points out that 8 the idea of enriching carbohydrates with fat is nothing new. It's a standard part of the cuisine of almost every culture. Bread is buttered; macaroni comes with cheese; dumplings are fried; potatoes are scalloped, baked with milk and cheese, cooked in the dripping of roasting meat, mixed with mayonnaise in a salad, or pan-fried in butterfat as latkes. But, as Rozin argues, deep-frying is in many ways the ideal method of adding fat to carbohydrates. If you put butter on a mashed potato, for instance, the result is texturally unexciting: it simply creates a mush. Pan-frying results in uneven browning and crispness. But when a potato is deep-fried the heat of the oil turns the water inside the potato into steam, which causes the hard granules of starch inside the potato to swell and soften: that's why the inside of the fry is fluffy and light. At the same time, the outward migration of the steam limits the amount of oil that seeps into the interior, preventing the fry from getting greasy and concentrating the oil on the surface, where it turns the outer layer of the potato brown and crisp. "What we have with the french fry," Rozin writes, "is a near perfect enactment of the enriching of a starch food with oil or fat."

This is the trouble with the French fry. The fact that it is cooked in fat 9 makes it unhealthy. But the contrast that deep-frying creates between its interior and its exterior—between the golden shell and the pillowy whiteness beneath—is what makes it so irresistible. The average American now eats a staggering thirty pounds of French fries a year, up from four pounds when Ray Kroc was first figuring out how to mass-produce a crisp fry. Meanwhile, fries themselves have become less healthful. Ray Kroc, in the early days of McDonald's, was a fan of a hot-dog stand on the North Side of Chicago called Sam's, which used what was then called the Chicago method of cooking fries. Sam's cooked its fries in animal fat, and Kroc followed suit, prescribing for his franchises a specially formulated beef tallow called Formula 47 (in reference to the forty-seven-cent

McDonald's "All–American meal" of the era: fifteen–cent hamburger, twelve–cent fries, twenty–cent shake). Among aficionados, there is general agreement that those early McDonald's fries were the finest mass–market fries ever made: the beef tallow gave them an unsurpassed rich, buttery taste. But in 1990, in the face of public concern about the health risks of cholesterol in animal–based cooking oil, McDonald's and the other major fast–food houses switched to vegetable oil. That wasn't an improvement, however. In the course of making vegetable oil suitable for deep frying, it is subjected to a chemical process called hydrogenation, which creates a new substance called a trans unsaturated fat. In the hierarchy of fats, polyunsaturated fats — the kind found in regular vegetable oils — are the good kind; they lower your cholesterol. Saturated fats are the bad kind. But trans fats are worse: they wreak havoc with the body's ability to regulate cholesterol. According to a recent study involving some eighty thousand women, for every five–per–cent increase in the amount of saturated fats that a woman consumes, her risk of heart disease increases by seventeen per cent. But only a two–per–cent increase in trans fats will increase her heart–disease risk by ninety–three per cent. Walter Willett, an epidemiologist at Harvard — who helped design the study — estimates that the consumption of trans fats in the United States probably causes about thirty thousand premature deaths a year.

McDonald's and the other fast–food houses aren't the only purveyors 10 of trans fats, of course; trans fats are in crackers and potato chips and cookies and any number of other processed foods. Still, a lot of us get a great deal of our trans fats from French fries, and to read the medical evidence on trans fats is to wonder at the odd selectivity of the outrage that consumers and the legal profession direct at corporate behavior. McDonald's and Burger King and Wendy's have switched to a product, without disclosing its risks, that may cost human lives. What is the difference between this and the kind of thing over which consumers sue companies every day?

The French–fry problem ought to have a simple solution: cook fries in oil 11 that isn't so dangerous. Oils that are rich in monounsaturated fats, like canola oil, aren't nearly as bad for you as saturated fats, and are generally stable enough for deep–frying. It's also possible to "fix" animal fats so that they aren't so problematic. For example, K. C. Hayes, a nutritionist at Brandeis University, has helped develop an oil called Appetize. It's largely beef tallow, which gives it a big taste advantage over vegetable shortening, and makes it stable enough for deep–frying. But it has been processed to remove the cholesterol, and has been blended with pure corn oil, in a combination that Hayes says removes much of the heart–disease risk.

Perhaps the most elegant solution would be for McDonald's and the 12 other chains to cook their fries in something like Olestra, a fat substitute developed by Procter & Gamble. Ordinary fats are built out of a molecular structure known as a triglyceride: it's a microscopic tree, with a trunk made of glycerol and three branches made of fatty acids. Our bodies can't absorb triglycerides, so in the digestive process each of the branches is broken off by enzymes and absorbed separately. In the production of Olestra, the glycerol trunk of a fat is replaced with a sugar, which has room for not three but eight fatty acids. And our enzymes are unable to break down a fat tree with eight branches—so the Olestra molecule can't be absorbed by the body at all. "Olestra" is as much a process as a compound: you can create an "Olestra" version of any given fat. Potato chips, for instance, tend to be fried in cottonseed oil, because of its distinctively clean taste. Frito-Lay's no-fat Wow! chips are made with an Olestra version of cottonseed oil, which behaves just like regular cottonseed oil except that it's never digested. A regular serving of potato chips has a hundred and fifty calories, ninety of which are fat calories from the cooking oil. A serving of Wow! chips has seventy-five calories and no fat. If Procter & Gamble were to seek F.D.A. approval for the use of Olestra in commercial deep-frying (which it has not yet done), it could make an Olestra version of the old McDonald's Formula 47, which would deliver every nuance of the old buttery, meaty tallow at a fraction of the calories.

Olestra, it must be said, does have some drawbacks—in particular, a   13 reputation for what is delicately called "gastrointestinal distress." The F.D.A. has required all Olestra products to carry a somewhat daunting label saying that they may cause "cramping and loose stools." Not surprisingly, sales have been disappointing, and Olestra has never won the full acceptance of the nutrition community. Most of this concern, however, appears to be overstated. Procter & Gamble has done randomized, double-blind studies—one of which involved more than three thousand people over six weeks—and found that people eating typical amounts of Olestra-based chips don't have significantly more gastrointestinal problems than people eating normal chips. Diarrhea is such a common problem in America—nearly a third of adults have at least one episode each month—that even F.D.A. regulators now appear to be convinced that in many of the complaints they received Olestra was unfairly blamed for a problem that was probably caused by something else. The agency has promised Procter & Gamble that the warning label will be reviewed.

Perhaps the best way to put the Olestra controversy into perspective   14 is to compare it to fibre. Fibre is vegetable matter that goes right through you: it's not absorbed by the gastrointestinal tract. Nutritionists tell us to eat it because it helps us lose weight and it lowers cholesterol—even though if you eat too many baked beans or too many bowls of oat bran you will suffer the consequences. Do we put warning labels on boxes of oat bran? No, because the benefits of fibre clearly outweigh its drawbacks. Research has suggested that Olestra, like fibre, helps people lose weight and lowers cholesterol; too much Olestra, like too much fibre, may cause problems. (Actually, too much Olestra may not be as troublesome as too much bran. According to Procter & Gamble, eating a large amount of Olestra — forty grams — causes no more problems than eating a small bowl — twenty grams — of wheat bran.) If we had Olestra fries, then, they shouldn't be eaten for breakfast, lunch, and dinner. In fact, fast-food houses probably shouldn't use hundred-per-cent Olestra; they should cook their fries in a blend, using the Olestra to displace the most dangerous trans and saturated fats. But these are minor details. The point is that it is entirely possible, right now, to make a delicious French fry that does not carry with it a death sentence. A French fry can be much more than a delivery vehicle for fat.

Reading Closely

1. Gladwell uses a great deal of technical information in his essay. Mark all the technical terms. What effect did these terms have on you?
2. What is the effect of the very last sentence?

Considering Larger Issues

1. Who is the audience for this essay? What is Gladwell's purpose for writing about French fries? How do his audience and purpose intersect? What textual support can you supply for each of your answers?
2. **Working with two or three classmates,** determine the main point of Gladwell's essay. Is his main point evident in his thesis statement?
3. How many processes does Gladwell analyze? Which ones are parts of larger processes? **Working with a classmate,** account for the relationships among the processes he analyzes.
4. COMBINING METHODS. Gladwell's essay is a process analysis, yet he spends a good deal of time accounting for the *causes and consequences* of the trouble with French fries. Mark the passages that explicitly analyze causes and consequences, and then explain their effect on the overall essay.

Thinking about Language

1. Using the context of the essay or your dictionary, define the following terms. Be prepared to share your answers with the rest of the class.

five-spindle (1)	hydrometers (4)	aficionados (9)
purposeful discipline (1)	calibrated (5)	purveyors (10)
relish (3)	blanched (7)	nuance (12)
franchise (3)	latkes (8)	gastrointestinal
sacrosanct (4)	beef tallow (9)	(13)

2. List the details, examples, and minor processes that Gladwell includes to support his thesis.

Writing Your Own Essays Using Process Analysis

1. Think of a process that's either unhealthy or dangerous. What steps could be taken to make this process healthier or safer? What pitfalls and opportunities does each step involve? In an essay of three to four pages, analyze the process necessary for positive change, doing some online research if necessary to gather information. Make sure that all the steps and details you include help develop a thesis statement about this process. If a visual would enhance your essay, include one. Refer to "Checking Over the Use of Process Analysis" (p. 444).

2. Using some of the ideas you developed in response to question 1, draft a three-page, tongue-in-cheek essay in which you tell the reader how to make a process more dangerous or less healthy or how to do it wrong, providing specific steps, explanations, causes, and consequences. **Consider working with three or four classmates** to make sure that you've chosen a promising topic and that you are developing it logically and precisely. Refer to "Checking Over the Use of Process Analysis" (p. 444).

AERO SAFETY GRAPHICS INC.

O_2

Every time we take an airplane trip, flight attendants ask for our attention so that they can review the airline emergency procedures with us. They enact what we're supposed to do in case of an emergency, while we follow along with the explanations provided on a card in the seat pocket in front of us. The following instructions come from a Continental Airlines flight on a Boeing 757 aircraft.

Preview How much attention do you pay to directions like these? Are they helpful?

- - - - - - ➤

Reading Closely

1. What strategy does the author use to organize the steps?

2. These instructions include mostly visuals and only a few numbers and abbreviations. **With a classmate,** discuss whether words would make the instructions easier to follow. What are the advantages of not using words?

Considering Larger Issues

1. Who is the audience for these instructions? How much does the author assume the audience knows about the process?

2. What is the purpose of these instructions?

3. COMBINING METHODS. This process analysis includes an implicit element of *cause-and-consequence analysis.* What causes go unmentioned in this visual? Explain the significance of those causes to the process analysis.

Thinking about Language

1. What point of view does the author use? Why?

2. Very quickly, jot down each basic step in the process of using airline oxygen. **Working with one or two classmates,** write out a verbal explanation of the process (with transitions and cautions) that helps explain how the steps work together.

3. Underline the words and phrases in your verbal explanation that indicate this process is replicable.

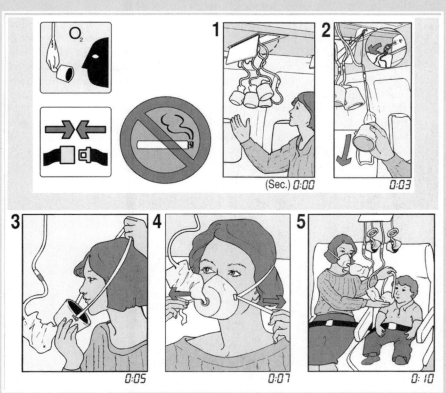

1 (Sec.) *0:00*

2 *0:03*

3 *0:05*

4 *0:07*

5 *0:10*

Writing Your Own Essays Using Process Analysis

1. Think of a process analysis that you routinely ignore—perhaps the in-structions on your shampoo bottle, or the ones that came with your hair dryer or cold medication. Drawing on your memory, draft a one- to two-page essay that explains the process your classmates should follow if they are using this product for the first time. Pay careful attention to the ways the steps are related to each other. Refer to the guidelines for checking over the use of process analysis on p. 444.

2. Locate a set of instructions that you have recently seen or tried to follow but found difficult or confusing. What details or steps were missing or hard to follow? Would visuals have helped, or were there visuals that were confusing or unhelpful? Draft a two-page essay in which you tell the author of these instructions how he or she should have written them for an audience of people like you. Remember to set up your own in-structions as a clear series of steps, and include visuals if you think they would be useful. Refer to the guidelines for checking over the use of process analysis (p. 444), and include a copy of the "bad" instructions when you submit your essay.

✳ Additional Suggestions for Writing

1. Identify a process of student life that is often troublesome: staying on a budget, negotiating living arrangements with a roommate, finding an honest and inexpensive car repair shop, registering for classes, getting good advice from a reliable adviser, and so on. Draft a three- to four-page directional process essay that will help your classmates with this problem. Refer to "Checking Over the Use of Process Analysis" (p. 444).

2. Ceremonies of all kinds are an important part of any culture: weddings, funerals, graduations, religious and political rites. Concentrate on one U.S. ceremony in particular and on the ways your own ethnicity, gender, or religion adds texture to the ceremony. Analyze the process of this ceremony, making sure that your three- to four-page essay has a thesis statement. Refer to "Checking Over the Use of Process Analysis" (p. 444).

3. Draft a three- to four-page essay in which you explain the process of enjoying a particular meal or of gaining someone's respect. Be sure to break the process down into steps in order to make it clear for your readers. Refer to "Checking Over the Use of Process Analysis" (p. 444).

4. **Working with one or two classmates,** discuss the processes you each know how to do on a computer—and the ones you do not. Think of a computer application or process that you know well, and break it down into a directional process essay for your classmates. You might consider how to research a topic on the World Wide Web, how to install a software application, how to run the defragmenter, how to check for viruses. Whichever process you choose, make sure that the members of your group can follow your process and replicate it, if necessary. Your final essay should be two to three pages. Refer to "Checking Over the Use of Process Analysis" (p. 444).

chapter

8

CAUSE-AND-CONSEQUENCE ANALYSIS

"*S*hape up, Texas"? The photo of Kenneth Cooper, M.D., suggests that he represents the Cooper Wellness Program perfectly: he's trim, energetic, and active. His running shoes look well worn, and his T-shirt attests to his dedication to wellness. In short, *he's* in shape, and he wants all of Texas to be in shape, too. Why do some people get in shape and stay that way whereas others don't? And what happens to a person who does—or doesn't—get in shape? **Cause-and-consequence analysis** helps you think critically about the answers to questions like these.

> **Looking at Your Own Literacy** Enumerate the causes as well as the consequences of your current physical condition. What information did you need in order to assess your condition? Where did you get this information?

What Is Cause-and-Consequence Analysis?

We think about causes and consequences constantly: when we worry about getting in shape, plan to lose weight, attempt to calm cranky children, try to make peace with our roommates or our partners, look for ways to succeed in school. We try to discover the reasons for a particular situation (flabbiness, too-tight jeans, crying, frustration, mediocre grades), and we determine or predict the consequences of that particular situation or action (our own unhappiness and dissatisfaction, a quieter child, a happier relationship, a better grade). Every day, we figure out *why* things occur and what happens as a result.

Like process analysis, cause-and-consequence analysis links events along a time line. But the purpose of process analysis is to explain *how* things happen, so readers can understand the process and, in many cases, repeat it if they want to. Cause-and-consequence analysis explains *why* things happen or predicts that certain events (or certain sets of events) will lead to particular consequences (or a particular set of consequences). Thus cause-and-consequence analysis can reveal a complex array of causes and predict a complex array of consequences. Whether it deals with single or multiple causes or consequences, the analysis generally uses a chronological pattern of organization, with causes usually preceding consequences (although analyses that deal with a past series of events sometimes use reverse chronological order to trace consequences back to their causes).

Whether we're enrolling in the Cooper Wellness Program, diagnosing a child's illness, researching the causes of divorce, collecting data on the effects of teen violence, or assessing a financial investment opportunity, we are analyzing causes or consequences. Many academic writing assignments call for such analysis. A typical writing assignment in a

history class is to ascertain the causes of a particular war or the consequences of an economic depression; in a chemistry lab, the instructor
may want a report on the consequences of a chemical interaction; in a
literature course, students might analyze the influence of one poet on
another.

The following advertisement for Toyota, which originally appeared in
October 2003, is based on a cause–and–consequence analysis aimed at an
audience of potential consumers.

Introducing
high performance technology that's also
good
for the environment. Now you can hug corners while you hug Mother Nature.

Toyota's revolutionary new Hybrid Synergy Drive* combines a gasoline engine with a powerful electric motor that never needs to be

plugged in. The result? Super-efficient, super-charged performance. This groundbreaking yet affordable technology has already hit the

roads in the all-new Prius. Prius achieves nearly 2.5 times the average fuel efficiency of conventional vehicles and close to 90% fewer

smog-forming emissions – all while accelerating from 0 to 60 mph in 20% less time than its competitor.*

Beyond Prius, Hybrid Synergy Drive will be available in more and more Toyota products – including SUVs.

With Hybrid Synergy Drive, we're helping save the planet. Faster.

toyota.com/tomorrow

*Based on 2004 EPA est. city & combined mpg. 0-60 mph for comparison only. Obtained with prototype vehicle by professional using special procedures. Do not attempt. ©2003

HYBRID SYNERGY DRIVE   TODAY   TOMORROW   **TOYOTA**

Thinking about Cause-and-Consequence Analysis

1. Look over the Toyota advertisement. What consequences does Toyota announce?
2. Why are these consequences possible? How does the advertisement explain these possibilities?
3. How does the ad take the audience into consideration? Who might that audience be?

Why Use Cause-and-Consequence Analysis?

Whether used as the primary or a secondary method in a piece of writing, a cause–and–consequence analysis can serve one or more of four main purposes: to entertain, to inform, to speculate, and to argue. For some analyses a writer might purposefully focus on just the causes of a situation (such as a disease, a natural disaster, or high school dropout rates), whereas in other cases a writer might concentrate on only the consequences of a situation (such as crime, epidemics, increasing longevity, or contentment). In this chapter you'll be asked to analyze causes and consequences separately as well as in combination.

Newspaper columnist Dave Barry is a prolific analyzer of causes and consequences. His purpose is almost always to entertain his loyal readers, as he does in the following excerpts from a column that first appeared in 1998:

> "These people are MORONS!" was their official report.
>
> That is the main cause of Road Rage: The realization that many of your fellow motorists have the same brain structure as a cashew. The most common example, of course, is the motorists who feel a need to drive in the left-hand, or passing lane, even though they are going slower than everybody else. Nobody knows why these motorists do this. Maybe they belong to some kind of religious cult that believes the right lane is sacred and must never come in direct contact with tires. Maybe one time, years ago, these motorists happened to be driving in the left lane when their favorite song came on the radio, so they've driven over there ever since, in hopes that the radio will play that song again.
>
> —Dave Barry, "When Roads Are All the Rage"

With his customary humor, Barry analyzes what he sees as the main cause of "road rage"—the stupidity of other motorists—and then goes on to speculate about absurdly unlikely causes for one example of this stupidity. Moving on to consider Parking Lot Rage, Shopping Cart Rage, and Automated Phone Answering System Rage, he pinpoints the causes of each kind of rage and teases out the consequences, using a narrative structure to make his point in an enjoyable—if somewhat exaggerated—way.

Barry doesn't get realistic about the causes of Shopping Cart Rage, for example, but he has a lot of fun as he portrays his fellow Floridians:

> When I finally get to the supermarket, I often experience Shopping Cart Rage. This is caused by the people — and you just KNOW these are the same people who always drive in the left-hand lane — who routinely manage, by careful placement, to block the entire aisle with a single shopping cart. If we really want to keep illegal immigrants from entering the United States, we should employ Mexican residents armed with shopping carts; we'd only need about two dozen to block the entire Mexican border.
>
> What makes the supermarket congestion even worse is that shoppers are taking longer and longer to decide what to buy, because every product in America now comes in an insane number of styles and sizes. For example, I recently went to the supermarket to get orange juice. For just one brand of orange juice, Tropicana, I had to decide whether I wanted Original, Homestyle, Pulp Plus, Double Vitamin C, Grovestand, Calcium or Old Fashioned; I also had to decide whether I wanted the 16-ounce, 32-ounce, 64-ounce, 96-ounce or six-pack size. This is WAY too many product choices. It caused me to experience Way Too Many Product Choices Rage. I would have called Tropicana and complained, but I probably would have wound up experiencing Automated Phone Answering System Rage (". . . For questions about Pulp Plus in the 32-ounce size, press 23. For questions about Pulp Plus in the 64-ounce size, press 24. For questions about . . .").

For Barry, one kind of rage leads to another; therefore, multiple rages are the causes of other rages — and the consequence.

Try Your Hand   Do you ever get frustrated while driving or shopping? Why? What kinds of incidents, events, or situations can lead to your frustration? Write out your responses.

In an article originally published in *Science* magazine in 2003, Jocelyn Kaiser writes an informative analysis of one cause of the decline in the number of migratory songbirds:

> Migratory songbirds have become scarcer in recent decades, in part because their tropical wintering grounds are being degraded and many birds don't survive the winter. A new study uses a chemical marker in birds' blood to suggest that this habitat loss has a ripple effect in surviving birds that extends well into the breeding season, when the birds may be a continent away.
>
> The American redstart, a warbler, spends winters in the Caribbean, Central America, and northern South America and summers in temperate forests in the United States and Canada. There the birds mate and pro-

duce up to five chicks. Redstarts that winter in poor habitat produce fewer chicks and their chicks fledge later, a team led by graduate student Ryan Norris of Queens University in Kingston, Ontario, reported here [Savannah, Georgia] earlier this month at the annual meeting of the Ecological Society of America.

The finding builds on earlier work linking winter habitat with a bird's health when it arrives to breed. But "nobody has demonstrated" a direct link between winter habitat and breeding success until now, says avian ecologist Susan Hannon of the University of Alberta in Edmonton. "This adds another potential problem [birds] have to deal with," along with threats such as fragmentation of northern forests, which attracts cowbirds that replace redstart eggs with their own.

A few years ago, Peter Marra of the Smithsonian Environmental Research Center in Edgewater, Maryland, and co-workers developed a chemical technique that can identify the kind of habitat in which a bird over-wintered. Because plants use different pathways for photosynthesis, those that grow in richer, wetter tropical habitats—such as mangroves and wet lowland forests—contain less of the carbon-13 isotope than do plants in drier areas, such as scrub. Insects eat the plants, birds eat the insects, and the habitat leaves a carbon-13 signature in the birds' blood. Marra's team used this marker to show that redstarts arrive up north sooner and in better physical condition when they have spent the winter in a richer habitat (*Science*, 4 December 1998, p. 1884).

In the new study, Norris, his adviser Marra, and co-workers show that better winter habitat translates into better breeding success. Norris spent two summers monitoring about 90 male and female redstarts nesting north of Lake Ontario. He found a striking correlation between carbon-13 levels in the birds' blood and breeding success: Males that had better winter diets not only arrived earlier at the breeding grounds but also sired slightly more young. Effects were even stronger for females: Those that arrived from better habitats produced up to two more chicks and fledged them up to a month earlier than did females that wintered in sparser grounds.

"Negative effects in one season can be negative again in another season," Norris says. He says this "carryover" effect underscores the fact that conserving migratory birds will require saving wet tropical forests and mangroves, which are rapidly being lost to logging and development.

– JOCELYN KAISER, "Lean Winters Hinder Birds' Summertime Breeding Efforts"

Kaiser's cause–and–consequence analysis explains all the reasons that winter habitats make a difference in the breeding habits of songbirds. She provides new scientific findings and includes quotes from experts to support her thesis, "migratory songbirds have become scarcer in recent decades, in part because their tropical wintering grounds are being degraded and many birds don't survive the winter." In addition to identifying one of the biological and environmental causes for this growing scarcity of songbirds, she also identifies a consequence of that scarcity: the need to stop the rapid loss of wet tropical forests and mangroves.

Try Your Hand   Do you accept Kaiser's explanation? Why or why not? What is her purpose? Who might be her audience?

What better way to illustrate speculative cause–and–consequence analysis than to consider the art — and science — of weather forecasting? In an essay first published in *Harper's* magazine in 1989, Jay Rosen writes about the effects on the weather of global warming, acid rain, the depletion of the ozone layer, ocean pollution, deforestation, and smog. He wryly speculates about some of the possible consequences of these conditions on television weather forecasts:

> The longest-running joke on television — that the weatherman is to be blamed for a forecast gone awry — will surely be dropped if "blame" for the weather begins to seem like a question of real importance.
> It will be interesting to see what television does as the weather loses its innocence. One possibility would be for the newscast to place more and more consequences of the social world under the heading of "nature," which is the direction marked out by the smog index. The comic persona of the weatherman might remain but it would become increasingly lurid, as various environmental hazards are ticked off in the same casual fashion as "our overnight low." The other possibility, unlikely as it seems, is for the newscast to politicize the weather, perhaps by making the weatherman into some kind of advocate for the Earth. Either way, the happy atmosphere of the weather report will be difficult for television to maintain, for the weather can no longer serve as a haven from history.
> —JAY ROSEN, "Don't Need a Weatherman"

When he wrote this essay, Rosen could not know for sure what the future of weather forecasting held, but he did know that the politicization of environmental conditions might eventually shift responsibility for the weather from "nature" to particular groups of people.

Try Your Hand   Given that Rosen's predictions are now more than fifteen years old, are they coming true? As you respond, consider where you get your weather information (from the newspaper, radio, television, or other sources).

In a column first published in *Newsweek* in 1994, George Dismukes writes from prison about the consequences of prison life. With ease and certainty, Dismukes enumerates the grim causes and consequences of an ever–expanding U.S. prison population. He opens his essay by describing the situation (doing prison time); then he lays out the causes that created the situations that led him and his fellow inmates to prison; then he circles back on the situation itself — all in order to argue a point:

> I speak to you from another world, that of the convicted criminal. I am in a minimum-security county holding unit. Do not be alarmed. Even were I not an innocent, 51-year-old grandfather jailed on circumstantial evidence, I'm in poor health and therefore not much of a threat. In addition, layers of steel and armed men separate you and me, not to mention time. My sentence is sixteen years for murder two, wrongly convicted of shooting a man I was trying to help. I have served five months. Unless I am released on appeal bond this summer, the earliest I'll be considered for parole is in four years.
>
> Many of my new colleagues are in here on minor charges such as petty theft or parole violation. There are a lot of small-time drug dealers who are repeat offenders. When I first arrived, I was placed in a cellblock that consisted of eight one-man night cells and a day room. There were a dozen of us altogether, meaning that those without seniority slept on the floor. The day room had a TV for our edification and amusement, two steel picnic tables with benches welded on the floor, a shower, a corner commode open to full view and a telephone. One wall of this place was bars, the others steel plates, as were the ceiling and floor. Here most of us watched the tube, read, played cards or squabbled about who would sit where and what shows we would watch.
>   — GEORGE DISMUKES, "Life on the Shelf: What It's Like to Live in Prison"

Dismukes's plainspoken analysis of why he and his fellow inmates are all in prison informs his readers that they are, to a man, a bunch of minor criminals ("wrongly convicted," "petty theft," "parole violation," "small-time drug dealers") living in barely tolerable (if not intolerable) conditions. Later he warns of the consequences of these conditions:

> The imprisoned are America's shame. The real crime here is that of your folly. . . . I say to you, the smug and contented: watch out. As one return for your indifference, our numbers are enlarging, our costs are rising swiftly. Building bigger and better or, alternatively, more degrading prisons does not begin to start resolving the reasons behind the problems and madness. It only makes the gibbering louder and the eventual consequences more awful for everyone when they finally occur. I find this situation to be humorous when I don't marvel.

Try Your Hand   Dismukes lays out the causes and conditions of his imprisonment. Given that information, what might be the "awful" eventual consequences he predicts? Why might he feel the way he does? Use evidence from the text to write a paragraph of response.

How Do You Read Cause-and-Consequence Analysis?

Knowing how to be a critical reader of examples of cause–and–consequence analysis will enable you to write your own with more skill and confidence. By looking closely at such an analysis, you can evaluate it in a number of ways. For example, do the causes or consequences, as presented by the author, seem plausible? If the analysis discusses multiple causes of something, is it clear how they're related, or which one is most important? And how well does the analysis achieve its specific purpose—to entertain, inform, speculate, or argue a point—for its specific audience? Writing a cause–and–consequence essay is a complex task, and taking a detailed look at how other writers deal with the distinctive challenges of such an essay will help you see both strategies to take advantage of and pitfalls to avoid.

Look, for instance, at the passage by Jocelyn Kaiser on p. 488. The title, "Lean Winters Hinder Birds' Summertime Breeding Efforts," alerts you that it's a causal analysis and suggests that the overall purpose of the essay is informative or argumentative, not humorous or speculative. Notice that the introduction consists of two sentences, a first sentence that introduces a cause—the loss of tropical winter habitat by migratory songbirds—and then a second sentence that states the effect or consequence of this cause: "this habitat loss has a ripple effect in surviving birds that extends well into the breeding season." The next paragraphs go on to explain the migration and breeding patterns of the American redstart, the specific consequences that the research team found were related to poor winter habitats, and the scientific significance of this finding. The rest of the passage explains the details of the research, including how the researchers measured the quality of the birds' habitat and how this quality is related to their success in breeding, and concludes with a statement from the research leader about the causes of the habitat loss and what he sees as the consequences of the scientific findings.

This is a fairly simple, straightforward causal analysis, which clearly presents just one cause (habitat loss) producing two consequences (fewer chicks and later fledging). As Kaiser explains in her final paragraph, however, the cause is also a consequence that can be traced back to its own causes—"wet tropical forests and mangroves . . . are rapidly being lost to logging and development"—which implies yet another cause–and–consequence relationship: conserving the birds requires saving the forests and mangroves. Often, a writer will present a much more complex web of causes and consequences than this one, requiring very careful thought and organization to be clear to readers. The most important cause won't always be the same as the most apparent one; in fact, they may not even be closely related. Seeing how—or whether—other writers make these distinctions clear will help you see how to clarify them in your own cause–and–consequence analyses.

In your critical reading, you also need to pay attention to the language the author uses. Notice that the language of this passage is not highly technical, but Kaiser does assume that her audience (readers of *Science* magazine) has some familiarity with scientific concepts and terminology like *degraded habitats, avian, photosynthesis, fledge,* and *fragmentation* of forests. When you write a cause–and–consequence analysis of your own, be sure to take your audience into account both in your language and in other ways, such as how much background information readers will need to understand the logical connections between particular causes and consequences. Notice also in the second sentence that Kaiser uses the word *suggest,* rather than *prove* or *establish,* to refer to what the study found. It's often difficult or impossible to prove beyond doubt that one thing is caused by another or will have certain consequences, so it's a good idea not to sound overconfident when making such a claim.

As you read an author's claims about causes or consequences, pay careful attention also to the supporting evidence that is provided—or to the lack of it. In Kaiser's analysis, she carefully sets out the evidence for the researchers' findings in her fourth and fifth paragraphs. Sometimes, though, authors assert causes or consequences without bothering to support those assertions. There might be plenty of supporting evidence, but the author didn't think or choose to use it. Other times, the author either hasn't done enough homework on the situation or wants you to believe there's a causal relationship when none exists.

In fact, one final important thing to consider in reading a cause–and–consequence analysis (or any other kind of writing) is what the author has left out. You'll need to think especially about whether the author has omitted not just evidence but entire causes or consequences altogether. In Kaiser's essay, for example, she doesn't mention whether there could be—or whether the researchers considered—possible causes other than tropical habitat loss for the finding that redstarts with more of the carbon–13 marker in their blood were less successful in breeding. Perhaps this case has no other plausible or likely explanation. But when you're writing such an analysis, always think carefully about what other causes or consequences the audience may expect you to mention; if you believe they're unlikely, you may need to explain why you think that, in addition to explaining the causes or consequences that you do believe are important.

How Do You Write Using Cause-and-Consequence Analysis?

Like any writing assignment, cause–and–consequence analysis demands that you pay careful attention to a number of concerns: your subject, purpose, audience, thesis statement, and method of organization. In addition, this method requires that you take particular care in figuring out and explaining relationships among the different causes and consequences you discuss and in choosing the language you use.

● Considering Your Subject

What event or situation are you analyzing? What causes or consequences of it can you think of immediately? Is it a subject that is complex or unfamiliar enough that you should consult sources to find other possible causes or consequences? You may find that discussing your subject with one or two classmates will help you answer these questions.

● Determining Your Purpose

What do you want your readers to do as a result of your analysis? Do you want them to laugh, understand your subject more fully, ponder the future, or change their behavior or way of thinking about the subject? As you determine which of the four purposes (to entertain, inform, speculate, or argue a point) your analysis will have, you'll also need to determine whether to concentrate on the *causes* of something, as Kaiser does when she accounts for one reason that some American redstarts are less successful at breeding than others (on p. 488), or on the *consequences* of something, as Rosen does when he speculates about how a "loss of innocence" about the weather might affect television weather forecasting (on p. 490). Keeping your purpose in mind will help you stay on course, concentrating on either causes or consequences—or perhaps finding a way to do both by establishing a causal chain, the way Barry does when he recounts how one rage causes another, which in turn causes yet another.

● Considering Your Audience

Who is your audience? Like every other kind of writing, cause-and-consequence analysis demands that you consider your purpose in light of your audience, and vice versa. Whether you are writing a causal or a consequence analysis, you'll want to consider specific characteristics of

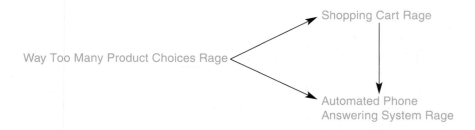

your audience: age, education, experience, attitudes, and so on. How informed are members of your audience about the event or situation that you are analyzing? What causes or consequences might they be expecting you to mention? Every audience has needs and expectations that you will want to address in terms of your overall purpose and the particular details you provide. For example, Dismukes, who knows that many *Newsweek* readers will be startled and perhaps "alarmed" to discover that they are reading an essay by a convict, begins by reassuring them with quiet sarcasm that he does not pose a physical danger to them—at least not now. He then goes on to attack them verbally ("you, the smug and contented") for their "folly" in ignoring the long–term consequences of imprisoning so many under such harsh conditions for such minor or questionable reasons.

Thinking Critically about Different Causes or Consequences

In every cause–and–consequence analysis, you'll discover a jumble of different causes. Your job is to untangle them, using two basic methods. For causes, you will need to distinguish (1) the **primary cause,** the most important one, from the **contributory causes,** and (2) the **immediate cause,** the one directly producing the event, from the **remote,** less obvious **causes.** In terms of consequences, you will want to distinguish (1) the **primary consequence** from the **secondary consequences** and (2) the **immediate consequence** from the **remote consequences.**

1. Let's say that you're exhausted. Sometimes you feel too tired to get out of bed and go to class. You've felt this way for several weeks now, and you're beginning to worry. Your mother says it's because you're studying too hard, working too many hours, and partying too much on the weekends. So you cut back on your studying (something's got to give, right?), but you're still pooped. You drag yourself over to the student health center and tell the doctor all the reasons you're tired. When she tells you that you have mononucleosis, you know immediately that mono is the primary cause of your exhaustion and that studying, working, and partying are only contributory causes. As you treat the primary cause—your illness—you will be treating the contributory causes as well. No more school or work or play for you—you're home on the sofa, recovering.

2. Or you could look at the situation in another way. You know you're tired on a Monday morning because you stayed out so late on Friday and Saturday nights. Indeed, partying (keeping late hours, eating junk food, and dancing) is the immediate cause of your malaise. But the remote causes are that you're not getting enough rest during the week because you attend classes, have a lot of homework, and work twenty hours a week as a cafeteria server. The most remote cause of all is your mono, a factor you never suspected.

Although often considered separately, these two types of causes are not mutually exclusive: sometimes you'll discover that the immediate cause is also the primary cause. If you are focusing on causes, you'll need to think critically about the various causes of an event or situation in order to arrive at a controlling idea that you can express in your thesis statement.

What about the consequences of having mononucleosis? The primary consequence is your exhaustion, but the secondary consequences could be that you must drop a course or two—or even leave school because you need time to rest and recover. The immediate consequence, again, is your exhaustion, but the remote consequences could be that your resistance to disease remains low for years to come, that you end up taking a year longer to finish your degree, that your time away from school gives you an opportunity to rethink and change your major.

To visualize these causes and consequences that are linked with mononucleosis, consider the following diagrams:

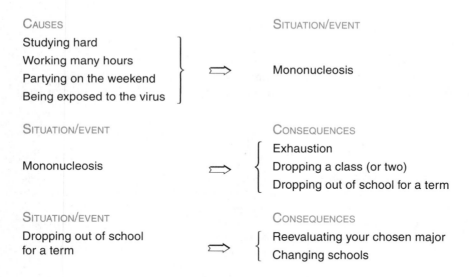

If your analysis reveals a series of related events, you may be uncovering a **causal chain,** in which one situation or event causes another situation or event which results in yet another situation or event. In this case you may find yourself analyzing both causes and consequences in your essay. For example, the causal chain of mononucleosis could look something like this:

Partying on the weekends →

    Exposure to the virus →

        Mononucleosis →

            Exhaustion →

                Sleeping →

                    Missing classes →

                        Failing classes →

                            Dropping out for a term →

                                Recovering at home →

                                    Reevaluating your plans →

                                        Changing your major

One particular pitfall in untangling causes and consequences is confusing them with chronology—that is, assuming that just because one event preceded another, the first caused the second (or, from another perspective, that the second was a consequence of the first). For example, to establish the first link in the casual chain illustrated here, you would have to establish clearly that your partying was indeed what exposed you to the mononucleosis virus. Certainly you could have been exposed at a party or a club, but you could also have been exposed in many other settings—the classroom, the dorm, the library, your job. If you went out partying several times with two people who came down with mono shortly before you did, that fact might enable you to say that your partying *probably* caused your exposure to the virus. In many cases, however, two events or situations that appear at first to have a cause–and–consequence relationship prove to be completely unrelated. So you will always need to (1) analyze each individual event or situation that could be understood as a cause or a consequence, and then (2) analyze its relationship to what precedes or follows it.

● Considering Your Thesis Statement

After considering your purpose, your audience, and the causes and/or consequences of the event or situation, what conclusions have you reached? Have you decided to concentrate on causes, consequences, or both? If you are focusing on causes, will you differentiate between primary and contributory causes or between immediate and remote causes? Or both? Whatever your focus, your thesis statement should introduce your subject, suggest the reason you're analyzing it, and state the idea about causes and/or consequences that you want your readers to accept. For example, you might write a thesis statement like one of the following:

1. I blamed myself for being lazy and stretched too thin with school, work, and play, but only when I went to the student health center did I discover I was suffering from an undiagnosed case of mononucleosis.

2. Because my mononucleosis went undiagnosed for too long, I was unable to remain in school.

3. Even though mononucleosis is a terrible disease, my bout with it provided me time to rethink my life's goals.

● Arranging All the Parts

How are you organizing your analysis? You might open your essay with a description of the event or situation you are analyzing and *then* introduce your thesis statement. For example, you might open with something like the following:

> I was constantly exhausted, often too tired to go to class, let alone do my homework. So during the week I rested up for my usual weekend of socializing. Only after collapsing at a dance club and being rushed to the hospital did I discover the cause of my weekday exhaustion: I had a severe case of mononucleosis.

After this introduction, however, you'll need to decide whether you should explain the causes or consequences of the event or situation in **chronological order** or **emphatic order.** Do you want to narrate the causes that led up to your illness in chronological order, almost like a process analysis? Or would it be more effective to order the causes emphatically, from least to most important?

In general, chronological order (or reverse chronological order) is most effective if you are focusing on the distinction between immediate and remote causes or consequences, because that distinction is related to time. Emphatic order (or reverse emphatic order) is most effective if you are focusing on the distinction between primary and contributory causes or between primary and secondary consequences, because those distinctions are related to importance. Whatever organizational pattern you decide on, however, remember to stay with that pattern throughout your analysis. Moving back and forth between the two patterns—or not following any pattern at all—will confuse your readers and weaken the impact of your analysis.

Considering Your Language

Cause–and–consequence analysis is often highly complex or highly controversial. To help readers follow your analysis and convince them to accept the causes or consequences you are presenting, you'll need to choose your words carefully. First, your thesis statement should clearly indicate whether you will focus on causes, consequences, or both. You might write something like, "I had always been a strong student, but when my grades began to fall, I had to find out the reasons why"; or "When I came down with mononucleosis my first term at college, the effects proved far–reaching"; or "Students should make every effort to avoid mononucleosis because the consequences are terrible."

Second, unless you're absolutely certain about the causes or conse- quences of an event or situation, using language such as *probably, most likely,* and *might well be* will enhance your credibility with readers, particu- larly if you're speculating about future consequences: "Although mono- nucleosis is a viral infection, it probably can be avoided if you follow some basic rules for good health."

Third, using clear transitional words or phrases will help your read- ers follow your line of thinking. Words and phrases such as *first of all* and *second; one cause, a contributing factor,* and *most important;* or *therefore, as a result,* and *brings about yet another* also help to indicate which cause you think is primary or immediate or what the consequences are. The best way to find out if your transitional language is working is to ask a classmate to read your draft and tell you where he or she had problems following your analysis.

Finally, your language signals your tone. If your goal is to entertain, you might want to include some Dave Barry–like exaggeration, making one sweeping assertion after another. If you are dead serious, then you will need to use an objective tone and include convincing facts, statistics, and other details. If you are working with a writing group, your fellow group members can help you calibrate your language to suit your purpose.

Considering Your Conclusion

Conclusions offer you an opportunity to push your own thinking as well as that of your audience a bit further than your thesis statement was able to do. What do you want your readers to take away with them? What did the analysis reveal to you, and what do you want it to reveal to them? What are its larger or long–term implications? Answering these questions will help you write a meaningful conclusion, one that goes be- yond a weary restatement of your introduction.

"Reading" and Using Visuals in Cause-and-Consequence Analysis

Visuals of various kinds can help clarify or breathe life into your cause–and–consequence analysis. If you think readers might have trouble following a complex chain of interrelated causes or consequences, for example, you might want to include a diagram like the ones on pp. 496 and 497.

More complex diagrams or other kinds of visuals can also be useful for cause-and-consequence analysis, but creating or choosing effective ones requires some thought and skill. To learn how to do this, make a habit of noticing visuals that illustrate cause–and–consequence relationships and then "reading" them critically in the same way you would a cause–and–consequence analysis in words. That is, consider how well the specific parts of the images work to-gether with the text to make clear relationships between causes and consequences that are effective for the writer's specific purpose and audience.

For example, look at the diagram shown here, developed by a group seeking to analyze and prevent domestic abuse in order to ex-

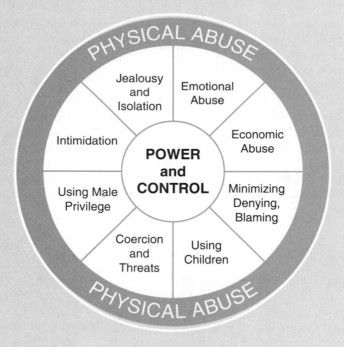

plain the causes and consequences of such abuse. Notice that instead of using arrows to show how one thing leads to another, as in the diagrams on pp. 496 and 497, this diagram places "POWER and CONTROL" in the center of a circle, as the root cause of all abuse. From this center — from the abuser's need for power and control — radiate the consequences: the immediate consequences of various kinds of nonphysical abuse and the more remote consequence of physical abuse. Using this circular arrangement keeps the focus on the root cause in the center and on the ultimate consequence on the rim, both of which are also emphasized by being set in larger type and in all capital letters. Various kinds of nonphysical abuse often precede physical abuse and may pave the way for it, this layout suggests. This diagram does not emphasize nonphysical abuse, however, or give any indication of whether some forms of it are more common than others or more likely to lead to physical abuse.

The visual qualities of the diagram suggest several things about its intended audience and purpose. Because it uses terms like "Economic Abuse" and "Using Male Privilege" without explaining them, it's apparently intended for readers who either already have some understanding of the dynamics of domestic abuse or are reading a verbal explanation of these dynamics along with the diagram. If you were using a similar diagram in your own cause–and–consequence analysis, in the text of your essay you would need to explain any terms like this that your readers aren't likely to be familiar with. Also notice that the diagram seems intended more to help people understand domestic abuse in a broad, abstract context rather than, say, to alert those women who are experiencing nonphysical abuse from their male partners that there is a risk that it may lead to physical abuse. For such women, a writer might instead choose a visual that highlighted the various kinds of nonphysical abuse under a heading like "Is He Going to Get Violent? Eight Danger Signs."

Although diagrams showing the relationships between causes and consequences can be especially useful in a cause–and–consequence analysis, other kinds of visuals — photographs, cartoons, graphs, and so on — can also help you illustrate your points. Always check with your instructor, though, before submitting visuals with an academic assignment. In addition, think about whether you need to add labels or captions to any visuals and whether you should refer to them in your written text or to let them stand on their own.

Understanding and Using Cause-and-Consequence Analysis

Analyzing Cause-and-Consequence Analysis

1. Reread George Dismukes's "Life on the Shelf" on p. 491. What cause is he analyzing? What are the consequences of that cause? **Working with two or three classmates,** read your responses aloud to determine where your answers overlap and diverge.

2. Look over your response to the previous question, and decide which cause is primary. Which one is immediate? Which causes are contributory or remote?

Planning and Writing Essays Using Cause-and-Consequence Analysis

1. Look at the excerpts from the Dave Barry article on pp. 487 and 488. What kinds of rage do you encounter or experience: Writing Rage? Computer Rage? Messy Roommate Rage? Dirty House Rage? **Working with two or three classmates,** come up with a list of causes or consequences of the particular rage on which you're concentrating. Choose the causes or consequences that best serve your purpose, ordering them chronologically or emphatically. Determine the primary and contributory causes or the immediate and remote consequences.

2. Think for a minute about a problem or a special talent you have. Maybe you're shy, behind in your classwork, overcommitted, out of shape, or out of money; maybe you're highly motivated, popular, or particularly witty. Make a list of both the causes and consequences of your problem or gift. Which list provides you with more information about your problem or talent?

   Concentrating on the richer list, begin planning an essay in which you develop the causes or consequences with specific examples. As you generate ideas for your essay, try to draft a purposeful thesis statement.

3. Drawing on your responses to either of the two previous questions, draft a three- to four–page essay in which you expand your analysis, focusing on the primary or immediate cause or consequence. Refer to the following guidelines for checking over the use of cause–and–consequence analysis.

4. If you're a sports fan, turn on your television set and watch a game, notebook in hand. Take careful notes so that you will be able to explain the causes of the outcome. Your notes will probably be descriptive and chronological. After the game is over, decide which of the causes is the most important (primary) one, which one might be immediate, and how you plan to arrange your information. Draft a three- to four–page essay in which you argue the causes of the outcome. Include specific examples from the game that help you make your points, and refer to "Checking Over the Use of Cause–and–Consequence Analysis".

✓ Checking Over the Use of Cause-and-Consequence Analysis

1. What event or situation are you analyzing? Are you concentrating on its causes, its consequences, or both? Identify your thesis statement. Does it clearly identify your focus?

2. Why are you writing about this event or situation? To entertain? To inform? To speculate? To argue a point? Does the thesis statement reflect this purpose? Does the rest of the essay?

3. Who is the audience for this analysis? Have you taken their needs and expectations into account throughout the essay?

4. What causes or consequences of the event or situation have you identified? Have you clearly connected each of the causes or consequences with the event or situation? Can you think of any additional causes or consequences you should include? Have you included language like *probably* or *most likely* where appropriate?

5. Have you identified specific causes as primary and contributory or as immediate and remote? Have you identified the consequences as primary and secondary or as immediate and remote? Do you have any second thoughts about your classifications? Have you included language like *probably* or *most likely* where appropriate?

6. In what order have you presented the causes or consequences: chronological or emphatic? Is this order effective, or would the other order work more effectively?

7. What transitional words or phrases have you included to help readers move from one cause or consequence to the next? Underline them. Are there other places where transitions are needed?

8. What point have you made in your conclusion? Do you move beyond your thesis statement by drawing larger or longer–term implications?

9. If you're using visuals, how do they support your thesis and purpose? Will your audience have any trouble understanding them? Do you need to add labels, captions, or references in the written text?

READINGS

TERRY McMILLAN
Easing My Heart Inside

Michigan native Terry McMillan (b. 1951) had little interest in writing as a child. Not until she began working at a library did she discover great writers and a love of literature — and the fact that African Americans like herself had written and published books. McMillan graduated in 1979 from the University of California at Berkeley, where she majored in journalism and published her first short story. She then moved to New York City, where she earned a master's degree in film studies at Columbia University. Since that time McMillan has published six novels, three of which have been made into movies or television movies: *Disappearing Acts* (1989), *Mama* (1991), *Waiting to Exhale* (1992), *How Stella Got Her Groove Back* (1996), *A Day Late and a Dollar Short* (2001), and *The Interruption of Everything* (2004). The following essay was written for *Why I Write: Thoughts on the Craft of Fiction* (1998), a collection of essays by American fiction writers.

> **Preview**   McMillan opens her essay with the statement "I never wanted to be a writer." How does that opening set up your expectations for what is to come?

I never wanted to be a writer. As a kid, all I ever dreamed of was living   1
in a house with central air and heat and a toilet that flushed. My mother
told me I was going to college — no ifs, ands, or buts about it — and that I
need not be concerned with "having anybody's babies" until after I had a
degree in my hand. As a result, I was too scared to have sex during high
school, when all my friends were having it, so I took to reading instead.
Got my first job shelving books at our local library and spent many
$1.25–per–hour hours hiding in the 700 and 900 sections.

This is where my dreams began to turn outward. I started traveling   2
all over the world. I flew with Amelia Earhart.* Sat with the Brontës.*
Rode in a sleigh in the snow with Robert Frost.* Touched and smelled
green with Thoreau.* John Steinbeck* fooled me with that story that
wasn't really about mice: I thought he could've been black. James
Baldwin* frightened me when I saw his dark face on his book jacket:
When did black people start writing books? I wondered. And then there
was *Bartlett's Quotations*, which blew my young mind because it was like
this dictionary of thought on all kinds of topics that I used to lie awake
at night and ponder but never had anybody to talk to about. I didn't
know then that I was already lonely. I couldn't share my feelings, and I
knew no one really cared what I felt or thought.

But then I went to college, and my reading became a little broader,   3
and one day this guy whose name I still can't remember broke a major
portion of my heart and I found myself sitting on my twin-size bed in
this tiny college apartment and I was in a coma for like four hours because I was unable to move (although I didn't try) and finally when I felt
the blood flowing through my body again something hit my brain and
exploded and I jumped up without knowing where I was going or what I
was about to do and I grabbed a pen and a steno pad and began to write
these words down one two three ten at a time and I wasn't even thinking
about what I was doing because it happened so fast and I didn't realize
until I was out of breath and four whole pages were filled with these
words and I exhaled a deep sigh of relief and exhaustion but I suddenly
felt better but then I panicked because when I looked at these words it
sounded and looked like a poem and I knew damn well I didn't write
this shit because I had never written anything before in my life.

And that's how it started.   4

This writing stuff saved me. It has become my way of responding to   5
and dealing with things I find too disturbing or distressing or painful to

----

* **Amelia Earhart** (1897–1937): first woman to fly solo across the Atlantic Ocean
and first person to fly solo across the Pacific Ocean; she disappeared during a flight to
circle the globe.

* **Brontës:** Emily, Anne, and Charlotte Brontë were nineteenth-century British sisters who became novelists: Emily wrote *Wuthering Heights*, and Charlotte wrote *Jane Eyre*.

* **Robert Frost** (1874–1963): American poet whose works include "Stopping by
Woods on a Snowy Evening."

* **Thoreau, Henry David** (1817–1862): American essayist, poet, and practical
philosopher, renowned for living the doctrine of transcendentalism (by living alone for
two years in a house he built in the woods) and for advocating civil disobedience.

* **John Steinbeck** (1902–1968): American novelist and Nobel Prize winner, best
known for *The Grapes of Wrath* and *Of Mice and Men.*

* **James Baldwin** (1924–1987): black novelist and essayist who was a prominent
U.S. literary voice during the era of civil rights activism in the 1950s and 1960s.

handle in any other way. It's safe. Writing is my shelter. I don't hide be–
hind the words; I use them to dig inside my heart to find the truth. I
guess I can say, honestly, that writing also offers me a kind of patience I
don't have in my ordinary day–to–day life. It makes me stop. It makes me
take note. It affords me a kind of sanctuary that I can't get in my hurried
and full–to–the–brim–with–activity life.

Besides that, I'm selfish. And self–absorbed. But I've discovered that 6
writing makes me less so. It has made me more compassionate. In fact,
that's what I've always prayed for: to have more compassion. For everybody. I've learned that every human being has feelings, despite the fact
that sometimes I have my doubts and people think no one understands
how they feel and that no one could possibly feel the same way. It's simply not true. Shock shock shock.

I'm also nosy. And I want to understand why I do some of the things 7
I do and why we're so stupid, and in order to come close to empathizing
I had to learn how to get under someone else's skin. Writing has become
my *under.*

If I understood half of what I did or felt, I probably wouldn't waste my 8
time writing. But I like the probing. I like being scared sometimes. I like
worrying about the folks I write about. I want to know if everything's
gonna turn out OK for them. I want to show what can happen when we err,
and when we "do the right thing," because as they say, no matter what you
do, sometimes, "shit happens." I like how we handle the shit when it does
hit the fan. Especially when we throw it in the blades ourselves.

I just want to pay attention. To the details of everyday life. I want to 9
be a better person. I want to feel good more often. I want to know, when
I don't, *why* I don't. Writing gives me this.

Chekhov* said, "Man will become better only when you make him see 10
what he is like." This is what I'm trying to do when I portray African–
American men and women behaving "badly." I'm not trying to "air dirty
laundry"; I'm just trying to get us to hold up a mirror and take a long look.
Most of us don't think about what we do, we just act and react. Many of
us don't reflect or wonder what larger issues are really at stake in our lives.

Writing is helping me mature. As long as I'm not bullshitting myself, 11
the act itself forces me to face and understand my flaws and weaknesses
and strengths, and if I'm honest—really fucking honest—then writing is
like a wake–up call. I become my own therapist. Because nobody knows
me better than me, and if I do my job, I can ease my heart inside another
character's until I feel what he or she feels and think the way he or she
thinks. When I'm able to become, say, a chronic liar—using lies as a way
to defend myself—then I know I'm on the right track because I can write
about someone whom I do not in real life respect or admire but whom
I've come to understand. Writing has taught me not to be so judgmental.
I usually write about people I don't necessarily favor, who do things I

* **Chekhov, Anton** (1860–1904): eminent Russian author of plays and short stories.

would never dream of doing, and therefore I sort of have to make myself undo my own sense of thinking and being. It can be exhilarating, freeing, a real eye–opener, and painful as hell.

Maybe I'm weird, but I want to know what it feels like to die. To 12 have your heart broken. Why people hurt each other intentionally. Why folks lie. And cheat. What kind of person can kill another person and sleep at night? What does a man feel when he beats his wife? How does she stay with him? How do children learn to hate? What is a good parent? What's it feel like to discover that you are gay when you're twelve? Why do some people not have the capacity to forgive? How long can I hold a grudge? And why are some people nicer and more likable, more responsible than others?

I could go on and on. But the bottom line is that I didn't make a 13 conscious decision to become a writer. I never did it for the money. I never did it for fame. Who knew? Who ever knows? I think somehow the craft chose me. The words have given me ownership and a sense of security. Writing is the only place I can be myself and not feel judged. And I like it there.

Reading Closely

1. What is McMillan analyzing? What were its causes? What are its consequences?
2. What examples does she supply for the causes and consequences?
3. How does the title, "Easing My Heart Inside," relate to the essay?

Considering Larger Issues

1. Who is the audience for this essay? How do you know?
2. How does McMillan's purpose for this essay intersect with her audience?
3. What is her thesis statement?
4. How does the concluding paragraph extend and enrich the thesis statement?
5. **COMBINING METHODS.** McMillan uses *exemplification* and *narration* within her cause–and–consequence analysis. **Working with a classmate,** mark the passages in which she uses one of these methods, and then discuss the effect of that specific method on the overall essay.

Thinking about Language

1. McMillan has earned great success by using casual language. Mark the passages in her essay that seem particularly casual to you, and be prepared to discuss those passages in terms of the overall essay.

2. **Work in groups of two or three,** with each group taking one or two paragraphs. Translate those paragraphs into more formal, "academic" language. Share your paragraphs with the rest of the class. What effect does academic language have on the tone of McMillan's essay?

Writing Your Own Essays Using Cause-and-Consequence Analysis

1. Many people who aren't writers are voracious readers. Draft a three- to four–page essay in which you recount some of your most memorable reading experiences — and the consequences of reading those books and authors. Be sure to consult the guidelines for checking over the use of cause–and–consequence analysis on p. 503.

2. Imagine that you always wanted to be a writer. Draft a three- to four–page essay in which you analyze the causes, consequences, or both of becoming a writer. You may want to draw on some of your earlier literacy experiences, those that propelled you toward this goal. As you draft and revise, **consider working with a classmate.** Remember to refer to "Checking Over the Use of Cause-and-Consequence Analysis" on p. 503.

ROBYN SYLVES

Credit Card Debt among College Students: Just What Does It Cost?

Robyn Sylves wrote this essay while she was an undergraduate at Penn State University. She has since graduated with a major in English, a minor in sociology, an emphasis in publishing, and a certificate through the university's World Campus in "Writing Social Commentary." Sylves worked her way through college at her family's restaurant, The Boalsburg Steakhouse, where she started as a dishwasher and worked her way up to management. She plans to continue her education sometime in the future. In the meantime, she continues to work at the restaurant and is also a freelance writer.

> **Preview**   As a student, what do you see as the causes and consequences of credit card debt? Be prepared to share your answers with the rest of the class.

College administrators like to say that alcohol is the number one vice of   1
their undergraduates. But in fact, an even bigger problem may be something that gets far less attention: credit card debt. Credit cards are dangled in front of undergraduates like free money, money that students do not actually have to earn or borrow or save. It's free—or at least that's how it seems. On their first trip to the campus bookstore, freshmen are bombarded by freebies—calling cards, water bottles, hats, the list goes on—that they can have "just for applying!" Representatives swarm the sidewalks with clipboards, applications, and sales pitches to provide new students with financial freedom. In all of the bustle, who really stops to read the fine print? Is it surprising to learn that credit card debt has led to health problems, conflicts with friends and family, long-term credit problems, academic failure, and, in extreme cases, to suicide?

Colleges and universities are like silent partners in the credit card busi-   2
ness. Many have multimillion-dollar deals with the credit card companies so that students can have their college logo embossed on their personal Visa or MasterCard. Does your school have a building adorned with the name of a credit card company, such as Penn State University's MBNA Career Center? It might: More than 700 colleges and universities have contracts with MBNA, the largest independent issuer of credit cards, under which they receive financial incentives in return for providing MBNA with information about students (Carlson). University officials are quick to preach about the sins of college that will haunt students for life, yet they say little about the damage that charging textbooks, late-night pizza, concert tickets, and spring break trips can do to a person's financial future.

Experts point to several factors for excessive credit card debt among   3
college students. High on the list is students' lack of financial literacy. The

credit card representatives on campus, the preapproved applications that arrive in the mail several times a week, and the incessant phone offers for credit cards tempt students into opening accounts before they really can understand what they are getting themselves into. The people marketing these cards depend on the fact that many students don't realize what an annual percentage rate is. Credit card companies count on applicants failing to read the fine print, which tells them how after an "introductory" period the interest rate on a given card can increase two to three times. The companies also don't want students to know that every year people send money (interest) to these companies that there is no need to send. That annual fee that credit card companies love to charge can be waived. I think that many people, students and nonstudents alike, might be surprised how often and easily it can disappear if people call the company to say they don't want to pay it.

Today's society, with its need for instant gratification, also pressures   4
young people to accumulate excessive credit card debt. No one wants to
wait in a world where the Internet and cells phones provide instant connection to anywhere. Even test scores arrive instantly: students can find
out their scores on the GRE (Graduate Record Examination) as soon as
they finish taking it. Why stand in line even when shopping? With a few
mouse clicks and a credit card, your purchase can arrive at your door as
soon as the next day. Like everyone else, students are more likely to buy
now and pay later than to save to afford purchases.

The third major contributor to high credit card debt among college   5
students, one that is more specific to students who say their cards are
"only for emergencies," is a student's overly broad definition of what constitutes an emergency — such as the need for that late night pizza. Steve
Bucci, a debt advisor for Bankrate.com and president of Consumer Credit
Counseling Service of Southern New England, has a rule of thumb for
people like this: "If you can eat it, drink it, or wear it, then it's not an
emergency" (qtd. in Lazarony). We can assume that spring break packages and DVDs are also included in that list.

In fact, students today "are being socialized to perceive consumer   6
credit as a generational entitlement rather than an earned privilege," according to a statement prepared for a U.S. Senate committee hearing in
2002 on "The Importance of Financial Literacy among College Students"
(Manning). Caught between the rising costs of higher education and outside pressures from peers, media, and marketing, students are turning to
"plastic" money more often and accruing higher amounts of personal
debt. In 2002, Penn State's *Daily Collegian* newspaper reported on a study
that found, that by 2001 more than three-fourths of all undergraduates
had at least one credit card, and almost a third of card holders had four
or more cards. "Nearly one in four students with credit debt owes more
than $3,000, and almost 10 percent owe $7,000 or more," the article noted
(Charsar). Unfortunately, it isn't as uncommon as one might think to find
undergraduates who have accumulated more than $20,000 in credit card
debt. Figure 1 illustrates the findings presented at the Senate committee
hearing, using data from a survey of students at George Mason University in April 2002.

When the U.S. financial services industry was deregulated in the   7
early 1980s, credit card companies changed their attitude towards young
people. Selling college students on credit cards went from a risky business to a marketing madhouse. In fact, teenagers are now the largest
marketing target for these companies, which recognize that teens and
college students are the group with the largest disposable income. Full-
time students are nearly always guaranteed approval of their credit card
applications because companies know that students can turn to their
parents or use student loans to pay balances. The George Mason Uni-

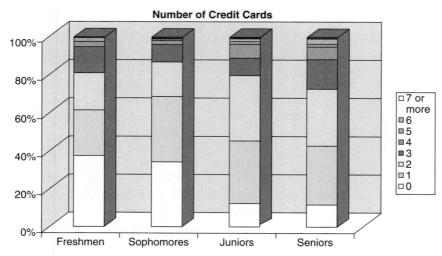

Fig. 1. As undergraduates obtain more credit cards, the amount of student debt climbs. From United States, Congress, Senate, Committee on Banking, Housing, and Urban Affairs, "Prepared Statement of Dr. Robert D. Manning," Table 1, by Robert D. Manning, *Hearing on "The Importance of Financial Literacy among College Students,"* 5 Sept. 2002, 21 May 2004 <http://banking.senate.gov/02_09hrg/090502/manning.htm>.

versity study backs up this belief, showing that many students are using student loans to pay their credit card bills (see Figure 2).

Today more than 20 percent of students open their credit card accounts while still in high school, compared to a mere 11 percent in 1994 (Manning). Data from the George Mason study shows a growing trend of young people opening credit card accounts at a younger age (see Figure 3). 8

Just as the reasons behind debt vary, so do the penalties. Lucky students might get a lecture and a strict budget enforced by parents. For others, the road is rougher. High debt may force them to cut back to part–time student status in order to have time for a job or even a second job. Of course, this drop in class time can translate into less financial aid, which means less money for rent, bills, and credit card payments. What can a student do? Take a semester off? Move home? Quit school altogether? Some students get into big trouble by sending each credit card company a few dollars "whenever," trying to pay—but not always succeeding in paying—the minimum monthly amount due on multiple cards. They think that once they graduate and get a good job, the money will come rolling in and their financial faults from student days will all be forgiven. It's not that simple. Instead of building their credit, they've turned something potentially positive into something as bad as, if not 9

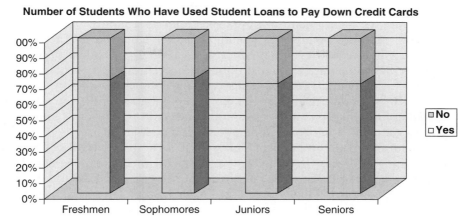

Number of Students Who Have Used Student Loans to Pay Down Credit Cards

Figure 2. Between 60 and 70 percent of college students have used student loans to help pay off their credit card debt. From United States, Congress, Senate, Committee on Banking, Housing, and Urban Affairs, "Prepared Statement of Dr. Robert D. Manning," Table 2, by Robert D. Manning, *Hearing on "The Importance of Financial Literacy among College Students*," 5 Sept. 2002, 21 May 2004 <http://banking .senate.gov/02_09hrg/090502/manning.htm>.

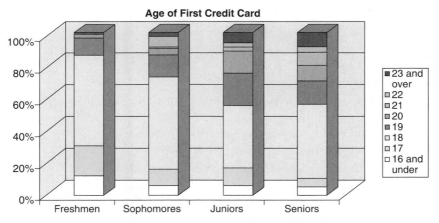

Age of First Credit Card

Figure 3. As with cell phones, today many students get their first credit card while still in high school. From United States, Congress, Senate, Committee on Banking, Housing, and Urban Affairs, "Prepared Statement of Dr. Robert D. Manning," Table 3, by Robert D. Manning, *Hearing on "The Importance of Financial Literacy among College Students*," 5 Sept. 2002, 21 May 2004 <http://banking.senate.gov/ 02_09hrg/090502/manning.htm>.

worse than, no credit at all—bad credit. When they reach this point, no bank will give them a loan to buy a car to get to school or work. They can't buy a house because no lending agency is going to give them a mortgage. They could even have trouble renting an apartment because many rental companies and most utilities run credit checks on potential customers. More than 800,000 Americans file for bankruptcy annually, and a growing number of the people who are filing are under the age of 25. Filing for bankruptcy can remain on your credit report for as long as 10 years, making it harder to build good credit as an adult.

So how does all this happen? How does it get to this point? It's as easy   10
to run into problems with credit cards as it is to use them. Not understanding penalties, fees, and interest rates can ruin people's credit just as fast as if they stopped paying their bills altogether. By not being responsible with credit, as well as not being informed and educated on the subject, young adults make mistakes that they will carry with them for years to come.

Many consumer credit experts have suggested that parents and edu-   11
cators should teach teens about safe credit just as they teach them about safe sex and safe driving. Knowing what an APR (annual percentage rate) is and what it means sounds like kid stuff, but that's exactly what it has to be. In an attempt to open students' eyes, Bankrate.com suggests cardholders get the answers to these simple questions before even considering applying for a credit card:

- Is there an introductory rate, what is it and how long does it last?
- After that, what will my rate be?
- Is there an application fee?
- Are there processing fees?
- Is there an annual fee?
- Is there a late fee?
- Is there an over–the–limit fee?
- Are there any other fees, like account termination fees or balance transfer fees?
- When and how can a variable rate be changed?
- When and how can a fixed rate be changed?
- What is the grace period before interest is applied?
- How will you inform me of any changes in my contract?
- Will the company inform me if I am about to go over my limit?
- If I go over my limit, what happens?
- What is the company policy if I have trouble paying my bill? ("Key Questions")

Many books and other resources are available to help students be-   12
come financially aware, but by asking these questions and reviewing ap-

plications with parents, students increase their chances for a successful financial future. A study of Penn State University's Erie campus showed that students who use credit cards co-signed or paid for by parents spend much less money than those who open and manage credit accounts on their own (Manning).

Whether or not parents, teachers, legislators, or even the credit card 13 companies make it a point to educate young people about using credit wisely, the choice to open an account is ultimately the student's. With the growing numbers of young adults holding credit cards and the increasing levels of debt among those under 25, the problem of student credit card debt is not one that will disappear overnight. An undergraduate quoted in the statement given at the Hearing on "The Importance of Financial Literacy among College Students" offered an insider's point of view:

> I believe credit card use by students is alarming. How do students who generally don't work pay back credit card bills ... [?] I think that there should be restrictions and legislation on credit card solicitations on college campus[es] — college administrators, student government council[,] et cetera have a responsibility to protect and educate students on the evils of credit card companies seeking student sign-ups. Also, I think credit card knowledge and awareness should be part of the College 101/1st year orientation class to help prevent this epidemic sweeping across college campuses. My mom was once a bank loan lender and she noted to me the sadness of the number of people who were denied loans because of poor credit ratings established as young college students. (qtd. in Manning)

No matter how students learn about building and maintaining healthy 14 credit, these may be among the more important lessons they learn, ones that can be useful in other aspects of life as well as beneficial to their credit report. Students must always read the fine print to know what they're getting into. They should learn as much as they can about the rules related to the credit card(s) they use. They need to be assertive in asking questions and doing research. Above all, students should think hard about how and when they use their credit. College is a place where young people should be able to make some mistakes, but accruing bad credit is a mistake that can and should be avoided at all costs. Much of what students learn in college will stick with them for life. What they learn about building credit — good or bad — will also stick with them for life.

WORKS CITED

Carlson, Michael. "Campus Rules Tightening." *Daily Lobo* 28 Aug. 2003. Pt. 1 of a series, Credit Card Companies Target Students. 17 May 2004 <http://www.lobolink .com/news/2003/08/28/News/Credit.Card.Companies.Target.Students.Pt.1-454172 .shtml>.

Charsar, Nicole. "Student Credit Card Debt Has Increased, Study Says." *Daily Collegian* 31 Oct. 2002. 20 May 2004 <www.collegian.psu.edu.archive>.

"Key Questions to Ask before You Sign Up." *Bankrate.com* 19 Mar. 2003. 16 May 2004 <http://www.bankrate.com/brm/green/cc/cc8.asp>.

Lazarony, Lucy, "College Students: Prepare for Credit Card Deluge." *Bankrate.com* 27 Aug. 1999. 17 May 2004 <http://www.bankrate.com/brm/news/cc/19980803.asp?prodtype=cc>.

United States. Congress. Senate. Committee on Banking, Housing, and Urban Affairs. "Prepared Statement of Dr. Robert D. Manning." By Robert D. Manning. *Hearing on "The Importance of Financial Literacy among College Students."* 5 Sept. 2002. 21 May 2004 <http://banking.senate.gov/02_09hrg/090502/manning.htm>.

Reading Closely

1. **Working with one or two classmates,** map out the various causes of student credit card debt: primary, contributory, immediate, and remote. Do any of the causes overlap? Which ones? Which causes stand alone? Prepare a group response that you can share with the rest of the class.

2. Now map out the consequences of student credit card debt: primary, secondary, immediate, and remote. Answer the same set of follow–up questions that you answered in the previous question, again preparing a group response for the class.

3. What specific information did you gain from each of the bar graphs? How did that information enhance or further explain the information in the verbal essay?

4. The photograph on p. 510 shows a man making an online purchase. What are some of the reasons people make online purchases? What is the primary reason? What are the primary and secondary consequences of online purchasing?

Considering Larger Issues

1. What is Sylves's purpose in writing this essay? Who is her audience? How do purpose and audience intersect in this essay?

2. After reading Sylves's essay, where do you think blame for student credit card debt should be assigned? Why? Be prepared to share your response with the rest of the class.

3. Judging from your own experience and that of your friends, in what ways do students follow or resist their parents' spending patterns? How do these patterns affect credit card debt for both parents and students?

4. COMBINING METHODS. Mark the places where Sylves uses *exemplification* to support her cause–and–consequence analysis. Do you think she provides enough examples to support her points? **Working with one or two classmates,** decide if there are any places where adding examples would have strengthened her essay, and report your findings to the class.

Thinking about Language

1. Using the context of the essay or a dictionary, define the following words and phrases. Be prepared to share your answers with the rest of the class.

incentives (2)	consumer credit (6)	deregulated (7)
preapproved applications (3)	generational entitlement (6)	the minimum (9) APR (11)
instant gratification (4)	accruing (6)	co-signed (12)

2. Define the term "financial literacy," using information from Sylves's essay, your own experience, and any research you care to do. Be prepared to share your definition with the rest of the class.

Writing Your Own Essays Using Cause-and-Consequence Analysis

1. Credit card debt is a big problem, and not just on college campuses or for young people. Draft a three- to four-page essay in which you explore the causes and consequences of someone's credit card or other financial decisions, good or bad. The person can be either yourself or someone you know well. Just be sure that you can supply enough detail to write an analysis that sets out clear causes and consequences and has a clear purpose (informative, entertaining, speculative, or argumentative). Be sure to refer to the guidelines for checking over a cause-and-consequence analysis on p. 503.

2. The author of this essay opens with examples of dire consequences: "health problems, conflicts with friends and family, long-term credit problems, academic failure, and, in extreme cases, ... suicide." Draft a three- to four-page essay in which you chart either the dire consequences of a bad set of decisions or actions or the positive consequences (the kind that too often go unnoticed) of good decisions. You can write about either yourself or someone else, as long as your essay is detailed, purposeful (informative, entertaining, speculative, or argumentative), and aimed at a specific audience. Refer to the guidelines for checking over a cause-and-consequence analysis on p. 503.

DAVID BROOKS

The Triumph of Hope over Self-Interest

David Brooks (b. 1961) is a senior editor at the conservative magazine *The Weekly Standard*, a contributing editor at *Newsweek* and the *Atlantic Monthly*, and a columnist for the *New York Times*, where this essay first appeared in 2003. Brooks is also a regular commentator on National Public Radio, *Late Edition* on CNN, and *The NewsHour with Jim Lehrer* on PBS. He is the author of two books, *Bobos in Paradise: The New Upper Class and How They Got There* (2000) and *On Paradise Drive: How We Live Now (and Always Have) in the Future Tense* (2004), and the editor of the anthology *Backward and Upward: The New Conservative Writing* (1996).

Preview   What does the title mean to you? Be prepared to share your responses with the rest of the class.

Why don't people vote their own self-interest? Every few years the Republicans propose a tax cut, and every few years the Democrats pull out their income distribution charts to show that much of the benefits of the Republican plan go to the richest 1 percent of Americans or thereabouts. And yet every few years a Republican plan wends its way through the legislative process and, with some trims and amendments, passes. 1

The Democrats couldn't even persuade people to oppose the repeal of the estate tax, which is explicitly for the mega-upper class. Al Gore, who ran a populist campaign, couldn't even win the votes of white males who didn't go to college, whose incomes have stagnated over the past decades and who were the explicit targets of his campaign. Why don't more Americans want to distribute more wealth down to people like themselves? 2

Well, as the academics would say, it's overdetermined. There are several reasons. 3

People vote their aspirations. 4

The most telling polling result from the 2000 election was from a *Time* magazine survey that asked people if they are in the top 1 percent of earners. Nineteen percent of Americans say they are in the richest 1 percent and a further 20 percent expect to be someday. So right away you have 39 percent of Americans who thought that when Mr. Gore savaged a plan that favored the top 1 percent, he was taking a direct shot at them. 5

It's not hard to see why they think this way. Americans live in a culture of abundance. They have always had a sense that great opportunities lie just over the horizon, in the next valley, with the next job or the next big thing. None of us is really poor, we're just pre-rich. 6

Americans read magazines for people more affluent than they are (*W, Cigar Aficionado, The New Yorker, Robb Report, Town and Country*) because 7

518

they think the someday they could be that guy with the tastefully appointed horse farm. Democratic politicians proposing to take from the rich are just bashing the dreams of our imminent selves.

Income resentment is not a strong emotion in much of America.   8

If you earn $125,000 a year and live in Manhattan, certainly, you are   9
surrounded by things you cannot afford. You have to walk by those buildings on Central Park West with the 2,500-square-foot apartments that are empty three-quarters of the year because their evil owners are mostly living at their other houses in L.A.

But if you are a middle-class person in most of America, you are not   10
brought into incessant contact with things you can't afford. There aren't Lexus dealerships on every comer. There are no snooty restaurants with water sommeliers to help you sort through the bottled *eau* selections. You can afford most of the things at Wal-Mart or Kohl's and the occasional meal at the Macaroni Grill. Moreover, it would be socially unacceptable for you to pull up to church in a Jaguar or to hire a caterer for your dinner party anyway. So you are not plagued by a nagging feeling of doing without.

Many Americans admire the rich.   11

They don't see society as a conflict zone between the rich and poor.   12
It's taboo to say in a democratic culture, but do you think a nation that watches Katie Couric in the morning, Tom Hanks in the evening and Michael Jordan on weekends harbors deep animosity toward the affluent?

On the contrary. I'm writing this from Nashville, where one of the   13
richest families, the Frists, is hugely admired for its entrepreneurial skill and community service. People don't want to tax the Frists—they want to elect them to the Senate. And they did.

Nor are Americans suffering from false consciousness. You go to a   14
town where the factories have closed and people who once earned $14 an hour now work for $8 an hour. They've taken their hits. But odds are you will find their faith in hard work and self-reliance undiminished, and their suspicion of Washington unchanged.

Americans resent social inequality more than income inequality.   15

As the sociologist Jennifer Lopez has observed: "Don't be fooled by   16
the rocks that I got, I'm just, I'm just Jenny from the block." As long as rich people "stay real," in Ms. Lopez's formulation, they are admired. Meanwhile, middle-class journalists and academics who seem to look down on megachurches, suburbia and hunters are resented. Americans see the tax debate as being waged between the economic elite, led by President Bush, and the cultural elite, led by Barbra Streisand, they are going to side with Mr. Bush, who could come to any suburban barbershop and fit right in.

Most Americans do not have Marxian categories in their heads.   17

This is the most important reason Americans resist wealth redistribu-   18
tion, the reason that subsumes all others. Americans do not see society as

a layer cake, with the rich on top, the middle class beneath them and the working class and underclass at the bottom. They see society as a high school cafeteria, with their community at one table and other communities at other tables. They are pretty sure that their community is the nicest, and filled with the best people, and they have a vague pity for all those poor souls who live New York City or California and have a lot of money but no true neighbors and no free time.

All of this adds up to a terrain incredibly inhospitable to class–based 19 politics. Every few years a group of millionaire Democratic presidential aspirants pretends to be the people's warriors against the overclass. They look inauthentic, combative rather than unifying. Worst of all, their basic message is not optimistic.

They haven't learned what Franklin and Teddy Roosevelt and even 20 Bill Clinton knew: that you can run against rich people, but only those who have betrayed the ideal of fair competition. You have to be more hopeful and growth–oriented than your opponent, and you cannot imply that we are a nation tragically and permanently divided by income. In the gospel of America, there are no permanent conflicts.

Reading Closely

1. Summarize this essay into one paragraph. **Working with one or two classmates**, share your summaries, discussing any inaccuracies or misunderstandings with regard to the essay itself. Then prepare a group summary that you'll share with the rest of the class.

2. Identify the primary, secondary, immediate, and remote causes Brooks cites for why nonwealthy Americans don't vote their own self–interest.

3. Make a list of all the times — and ways — the author refers to the hopes of Americans. What does he see as the connection between hopes and voting?

Considering Larger Issues

1. What are the primary, secondary, immediate, and remote consequences of Americans' not voting their own self–interest? Make a list of your answers. Then **discuss them with three or four classmates,** and report to the class about where you agreed and disagreed.

2. Who is the intended audience for this essay, and how does Brooks's attitude toward the topic relate to that of his audience? Be sure to refer to specific passages in the essay to support your answer. Prepare a response to share with the rest of the class.

3. What seems to be Brooks's purpose in writing this essay? What does he think readers should believe or do as a result of reading it?

4. **COMBINING METHODS.** Point out places where Brooks supports his cause–and–consequence analysis using *comparison and contrast* and *exemplification.* How effective are his uses of these methods?

Thinking about Language

1. Using the context of the essay of your dictionary, define the following terms and phrases. Be prepared to share your answers with the rest of the class.

self–interest (1)	income resentment (8)	waged (16)
income distribution charts (1)	incessant (10)	redistribution (18)
explicitly (2)	sommeliers (10)	terrain (19)
overdetermined (3)	conflict zone (12)	inauthentic (19)
aspirations (4)	affluent (12)	
	false consciousness (14)	

2. What words would you use to describe your own social or economic class? That of your grandparents? What words describe the social or economic dreams, if they had any, of your grandparents? Of yours?

Writing Your Own Essays Using Cause-and-Consequence Analysis

1. Consider your responses to question 2 under "Thinking about Language," and draft a three- to four-page essay in which you map out your future success, however you define success. What do you need to do now, what have you been doing, that will "cause" that success? Or to put it another way, what do you foresee as the consequences of your past and current actions? As you draft and revise, be sure to refer to the guidelines for checking over the use of cause–and–consequence analysis on p. 503. Also consider whether a visual might enliven your essay.

2. Draft a three- to four-page essay about an experience of your own that revealed something unexpected about the hopes and dreams of a familiar person. The person can be one of your parents or siblings, a partner, a friend, or your significant other. Decide whether you'll concentrate on the causes or the consequences of this unexpected discovery. Be sure to keep in mind the differences among primary, secondary, immediate, contributory, and remote causes or consequences. Refer to "Checking Over the Use of Cause–and–Consequence Analysis" on p. 503.

LINTON WEEKS

The No-Book Report:
Skim It and Weep

● Linton Weeks has worked since 1990 as a reporter and editor for the *Washing-ton Post*, where the following article appeared in May 2001. He is also the au-thor of *Memphis: A Folk History* (1985).

Preview   What does the author mean by "aliterate"? How do issues of aliteracy affect your life?

Jeremy Spreitzer probably wouldn't read this story if it weren't about   1
him.

He is an aliterate — someone who can read, but chooses not to.   2

A graduate student in public affairs at Park University in Kansas City,   3
Mo., Spreitzer, 25, gleans most of his news from TV. He skims required
texts, draws themes from dust jackets and, when he absolutely, positively
has to read something, reaches for the audiobook.

"I am fairly lazy when it comes to certain tasks," says Spreitzer, a   4
long-distance runner who hopes to compete in the 2004 Olympics.
"Reading is one of them."

As he grows older, Spreitzer finds he has less time to read. And less   5
inclination. In fact, he says, if he weren't in school, he probably wouldn't
read at all.

He's not alone. According to the survey firm NDP Group—which   6
tracked the everyday habits of thousands of people through the 1990s—
this country is reading printed versions of books, magazines and newspapers less and less. In 1991, more than half of all Americans read a half-
hour or more every day. By 1999, that had dropped to 45 percent.

A 1999 Gallup Poll found that only 7 percent of Americans were vo-   7
racious readers, reading more than a book a week, while some 59 percent said they had read fewer than 10 books in the previous year.
Though book clubs seem popular now, only 6 percent of those who read
belong to one. The number of people who don't read at all, the poll concluded, has been rising for the past 20 years.

The reports on changes in reading cut to the quick of American cul-   8
ture. We pride ourselves on being a largely literate First World country
while at the same time we rush to build a visually powerful environment
in which reading is not required.

The results are inevitable. Aliteracy is all around. Just ask: 9

• Internet developers. At the Terra Lycos portal design lab in Waltham,
Mass., researcher William Albert has noticed that the human guinea pigs
in his focus groups are too impatient to read much. When people look

up information on the Internet today, Albert explains, they are "basically scanning. There's very little actual comprehension that's going on." People, Albert adds, prefer to get info in short bursts, with bullets, rather than in large blocks of text.

- Transportation gurus. Chandra Clayton, who oversees the design of road signs and signals for the Virginia Department of Transportation, says, "Symbols can quickly give you a message that might take too long to read in text." The department is using logos and symbols more and more. When it comes to highway safety and getting lifesaving information quickly, she adds, "a picture *is* worth a thousand words."

- Packaging designers. "People don't take the time to read anything," explains Jim Peters, editor of BrandPackaging magazine. "Marketers and packagers are giving them colors and shapes as ways of communicating." For effective marketing, Peters says, "researchers tell us that the hierarchy is colors, shapes, icons and, dead last, words."

Some of this shift away from words—and toward images—can be 10 attributed to our ever-growing multilingual population. But for many people, reading is passe or impractical or, like, so totally unnecessary in this day and age.

To Jim Trelease, author of "The Read-Aloud Handbook," this trend 11 away from the written word is more than worrisome. It's wicked. It's tearing apart our culture. People who have stopped reading, he says, "base their future decisions on what they used to know.

"If you don't read much, you really don't know much," he says. 12 "You're dangerous."

LOSING A HERITAGE

"The man who does not read good books has no advantage over the man who cannot read them."   – MARK TWAIN

One thing you can say for illiteracy: It can be identified, nailed down. 13 And combated. Scores of programs such as the Greater Washington Literacy Council and the International Reading Association are geared toward fighting readinglessness in the home, the school and the workplace.

Aliteracy, on the other hand, is like an invisible liquid, seeping 14 through our culture, nigh impossible to pinpoint or defend against. It's the kid who spends hours and hours with video games instead of books, who knows Sim Cities better than "A Tale of Two Cities."

It's the thousands of business people who subscribe to executive book 15 summaries—for example, Soundview's easy-to-swallow eight-page pamphlets that take simply written management books such as "Secrets of Question-Based Selling" by Thomas A. Freese and make them even simpler.

It's the parent who pops the crummy movie of "Stuart Little" into a 16 machine for his kid instead of reading E. B. White's marvelous novel aloud. Or the teacher who assigns the made-for-TV movie "Gettysburg" instead of the book it was based on, "The Killer Angels" by Michael Shaara.

There may be untold collateral damage in a society that can read but 17 doesn't. "So much of our culture is embedded in literature," says Philip A. Thompsen, professor of communications at West Chester University in West Chester, Pa. Thompsen has been watching the rise of aliteracy in the classroom for 20 years, and "students today are less capable of getting full value from textbooks than they were 10 years ago."

He adds that these aliterate students are "missing out on our cultural 18 heritage."

That literature-based past included a reverence for reading, a cele- 19 bration of the works and a worshipful awe of those who wrote.

To draw you a picture: Where we once deified the lifestyles of writers 20 such as Ernest Hemingway and F. Scott Fitzgerald, we now fantasize about rock-and-roll gods, movie starlets or NBA super-studs (e.g. MTV's "Cribs"). The notion of writer-as-culture-hero is dead and gone. Comedic monologuists such as Jay Leno or David Letterman have more sex appeal than serious fiction writers. The grail quest for the Great American Novel has ended; it *was* a myth after all.

Where we once drew our mass-cult references from books ("He's a 21 veritable Simon Legree"*), we now allude to visual works—a Seinfeld episode (not there's anything *wrong* with that . . .) or "The Silence of the Lambs" (the movie, not the book). A recent story in *Salon** speaks of "learning to read a movie."

Where we once believed that a well-read populace leads to a healthy 22 democracy, many people now rely on whole TV broadcast operations built around politics and elections. Quick, name a Wolf Blitzer book.

Non-readers abound. Ask "Politically Incorrect" talk show host Bill 23 Maher, who once boasted in print that he hadn't read a book in years. Or Noel Gallagher of the rock band Oasis, who has been quoted as saying he'd *never* read a book. You can walk through whole neighborhoods of houses in the country that do not contain books or magazines—unless you count catalogues.

American historian Daniel Boorstin saw this coming. In 1984, while 24 Boorstin was serving as librarian of Congress, the library issued a land-mark report: "Books in Our Future." Citing recent statistics that only about half of all Americans read regularly every year, he referred to the "twin menaces" of illiteracy and aliteracy.

"In the United States today," Boorstin wrote, "aliteracy is widespread." 25

---

* **Simon Legree:** a cruel slave dealer in the novel *Uncle Tom's Cabin* by Harriet Beecher Stowe.

* ***Salon:*** an online news and entertainment magazine at <www.salon.com>.

Several of the articles in the report alluded to the growing number 26
of non–readers. In one essay, "The Computer and the Book," Edmund D.
Pellegrino, a former president of Catholic University who is now a
bioethicist at Georgetown University, observed: "The computer is simply
the most effective, efficient and attractive form for transmittal of
processed information. Added to the other nonbook devices like films,
tapes, television and the popular media, the computer accelerates the at–
rophy of the intellectual skills acquired for personally reading the books
from which the information is extracted."

READING FOR BLISS

Kylene Beers has talked about the evils of aliteracy for so long and so 27
loud, she's losing her voice. Today she's in the lecture hall of Oakton
High School bending the ears of 100 or so middle school teachers.

If someone graduates from high school and is aliterate, Beers be– 28
lieves, that person will probably never become a habitual reader.

One of the few academics who have written about the phenomenon, 29
Beers, a professor of reading at the University of Houston, says there are
two types of reading: efferent and aesthetic.

Efferent, which comes from the Latin word *efferre* (meaning to carry 30
away), is purposeful reading, the kind students are taught day after day
in schools. Efferent readers connect cognitively with the words and plan
to take something useful from it—such as answers for a test.

Aesthetic is reading for the sheer bliss of it, as when you dive deep 31
into Dostoevski or get lost in Louisa May Alcott. Aesthetic readers con–
nect emotionally to the story. Beers believes that more students must be
shown the marvels of reading for pleasure.

On this late afternoon, she is mapping out strategies for teachers 32
who hope to engage reluctant middle school readers. Teaching grammar
and parts of speech, such as dangling participles, is the kiss of death, she
says. "You don't want to talk about dangling anythings with middle–
schoolers," she says in her Texas drawl. And the room laughs.

Aliteracy, she continues, is no laughing matter. Using an overhead 33
projector, she explains that aliterate people just don't get it. Unlike ac–
complished readers, aliterates don't understand that sometimes you have
to read efferently and sometimes you have to read aesthetically; that
even the best readers occasionally read the same paragraph over and
over to understand it and that to be a good reader you have to visualize
the text.

To engage non–reading students—and adults—she proposes reading 34
strategies, such as turning a chapter of a hard book into a dramatic pro–
duction or relating tough words to easier-words.

She writes the word "tepid" on the acetate sheet. Then she asks the 35
audience to supply other words that describe water temperature. "Hot,"

someone calls out. "Freezing," somebody else says. Others suggest: cold, warm and boiling. Beers arranges the words in a linear fashion, from the coldest word, "freezing," to the hottest, "boiling." "Tepid" falls in the middle of the list. This method, she says, will help reluctant readers to connect words they don't know to words they do know. "Aliterates," she tells the teachers, "don't see relationships."

Apparently, teachers don't always see the relationships either. Jim 36 Trelease is concerned that teachers do not read. The aliteracy rate among teachers, he says, is about the same, 50 percent, as among the general public.

There is some good news on the reading front, according to Trelease 37 and others. The Harry Potter series has turned on a lot of young readers, and megabookstores, such as Barnes & Noble and Borders, are acrawl with people.

But there is plenty of bad news, too. Lots of aliterates, according to 38 Trelease, say they just don't have time to read anymore. "The time argument is the biggest hoax of all," he says. According to time studies, we have more leisure time than ever. "If people didn't have time, the malls would be empty, cable companies would be broke, video stores would go out of business. It's not a time problem, it's a value problem. You have 50 percent in the country who don't value reading."

Like Beers, Trelease believes that youngsters should be encouraged to 39 read aesthetically. Reading aloud to children, according to Trelease and other reading specialists, is the single best way to ensure that someone will become a lifelong reader.

"Even Daniel Boorstin wasn't born wanting to read," Trelease says. 40 "Michael Jordan wasn't born wanting to play basketball. The desire has to be planted."

SURFING THROUGH GRAD SCHOOL

Trelease and Beers and others are scrambling for ways to engage alit– 41 erates. For all kinds of reasons. "What aliteracy does is breed illiteracy," Beers explains. "If you go through school having learned to read and then you leave school not wanting to read, chances are you won't put your own children into a reading environment."

"What you have to do is play hardball," says Trelease. He suggests 42 running public awareness campaigns on TV. "That's where the aliterates are."

Trelease says we should try to eradicate aliteracy in the way we went 43 after tobacco. We should let people know, Trelease says, "what the consequences are to your family and children if you don't read."

"Aliteracy may be a significant problem today," says Philip 44 Thompsen. "But on the other hand, a narrow view of literacy—one that defines literacy as the ability to read verbal texts — may be a significant problem as well."

Many of the messages that we have to interpret in day-to-day life, 45 Thompsen says, "use multiple communication media. I think it is important to realize that as our society becomes more accustomed to using multimedia messages, we must also expand our thinking about what it means to be 'literate.'"

Olympic hopeful Jeremy Spreitzer plans to become a teacher and 46 maybe go into politics someday. For now, he's just trying to get through graduate school.

He watches a lot of television. "I'm a major surfer," he says. He 47 watches the History Channel, A&E, Turner Classic Movies and all of the news stations.

"I'm required to do a lot of reading," he says. "But I do a minimum of 48 what I need to do."

But how do you get through grad school without reading? Spreitzer 49 is asked.

He gives an example. One of his required texts is the recently pub- 50 lished "Bowling Alone: The Collapse and Revival of American Community" by Robert Putnam. In the book, Putnam argues, among other things, that television has fragmented our society.

Spreitzer thumbed through the book, dipped into a few chapters and 51 spent a while "skipping around" here and there.

He feels, however, that he understands Putnam and Putnam's theo- 52 ries as well as if he had read the book.

How is that? he is asked. 53

Putnam, he explains, has been on TV a lot. "He's on the news all the 54 time," Spreitzer says. "On MSNBC and other places. Those interviews with him are more invaluable than anything else."

Reading Closely

1. What are the reasons Weeks's provides for why people don't read?
2. **Working with a classmate,** discuss the consequences of aliteracy.

Considering Larger Issues

1. What is Weeks's purpose in writing about aliteracy?
2. Who is his intended audience?
3. What is Weeks's thesis statement? What information does he use to develop it?

4. Is Weeks concentrating on the causes or the consequences of aliteracy? Does he present them in primary/other or immediate/remote terms? **Working with one or two classmates,** discuss these questions and prepare a report for the rest of the class.

5. **COMBINING METHODS.** Weeks supports his assertions about the causes and consequences of aliteracy by using *exemplification.* Mark the passages of exemplification, and establish their importance to the overall essay.

Thinking about Language

1. Using the context of the essay or your dictionary, define the following terms. Be prepared to share your answers with the rest of the class.

bullets (9)	collateral (17)	efferent (30)
gurus (9)	deified (20)	aesthetic (31)
logos (9)	grail quest (20)	tepid (35)
icons (9)	atrophy (26)	acetate (35)
readinglessness (13)	phenomenon (29)	acrawl (37)

2. An author's choice of words surely affects the overall success of his essay. Does the lack of words carry the same importance? Consider the effects the bulleted list and short sentences and paragraphs have on this essay. How do they complement Weeks's information? Prepare to report to the rest of the class.

Writing Your Own Essays Using Cause-and-Consequence Analysis

1. Focus on the reading habits of your family members or a group of friends you know well. What, when, and how often does that group read? How would you define their reading habits? What are the causes and consequences of their habits? Do they organize their reading and meet to discuss it? Do they trade books and magazines? Or are they aliterate?

   Concentrate on the primary and other (contributory or secondary) causes or consequences of the group's reading habits, and draft a three- to four-page essay in which you analyze them. Refer to the guidelines for checking over the use of cause-and-consequence analysis on p. 503.

2. Go to a public place—a waiting room, dining hall, lounge, park, coffee bar, or library—and observe the kind of reading people are doing. You may have to walk around for a while to get the entire picture of how many people are reading and what exactly they are reading. How many are reading fiction, nonfiction, magazines, newspapers, e-mail, Web sites? Talk to as many readers as possible to ask why they are reading or what they think or hope will be the consequences of their reading. Draft a three- to four-page essay in which you analyze the causes or consequences of these public reading habits. Be sure to refer to the guidelines for checking over the use of cause-and-consequence analysis on p. 503.

STEPHEN JAY GOULD

Sex, Drugs, Disasters, and the Extinction of Dinosaurs

● Stephen Jay Gould (1941–2002), a professor of zoology and geology at Harvard University, was well known for his uncanny ability to write about science for a general audience. His numerous books include *Time's Arrow/Time's Cycle* (1988), *The Panda's Thumb* (1991), *The Mismeasure of Man* (1996), *Dinosaur in a Haystack* (1996), *Rock of Ages* (1999), *The Structure of Evolutionary Theory* (2002), *I Have Landed: The End of a Beginning in Natural History* (2002), *Triumph and Tragedy in Mudville* (2003), and *The Hedgehog, the Fox, and the Magister's Pox* (2003). In the following essay, taken from *The Flamingo's Smile* (1986) and first published in *Discover* magazine in 1984, he investigates the extinction of dinosaurs.

> **Preview**   As you read, consider Gould's emphases on causes as well as on consequences.

Science, in its most fundamental definition, is a fruitful mode of inquiry, not a list of enticing conclusions. The conclusions are the consequence, not the essence. 1

My greatest unhappiness with most popular presentations of science concerns their failure to separate fascinating claims from the methods that scientists use to establish the facts of nature. Journalists, and the public, thrive on controversial and stunning statements. But science is, basically, a way of knowing—in P. B. Medawar's apt words, "the art of the soluble." If the growing corps of popular science writers would focus on *how* scientists develop and defend those fascinating claims, they would make their greatest possible contribution to public understanding. 2

Consider three ideas, proposed in perfect seriousness to explain that greatest of all titillating puzzles—the extinction of dinosaurs. Since these three notions invoke the primarily fascinating themes of our culture—sex, drugs, and violence—they surely reside in the category of fascinating claims. I want to show why two of them rank as silly speculation, while the other represents science at its grandest and most useful. 3

Science works with testable proposals. If, after much compilation and scrutiny of data, new information continues to affirm a hypothesis, we may accept it provisionally and gain confidence as further evidence mounts. We can never be completely sure that a hypothesis is right, though we may be able to show with confidence that it is wrong. The best scientific hypotheses are also generous and expansive: They suggest extensions and implications that enlighten related, and even far distant, subjects. Simply consider how the idea of evolution has influenced virtually every intellectual field. 4

"I can't get over this . . . I thought you were extinct, too!"

Useless speculation, on the other hand, is restrictive. It generates no   5
testable hypothesis, and offers no way to obtain potentially refuting
evidence. Please note that I am not speaking of truth or falsity. The speculation may well be true; still, if it provides, in principle, no material for
affirmation or rejection, we can make nothing of it. It must simply stand
forever as an intriguing idea. Useless speculation turns in on itself and
leads nowhere; good science, containing both seeds for its potential
refutation and implications for more and different testable knowledge,
reaches out. But, enough preaching. Let's move on to dinosaurs, and the
three proposals for their extinction.

1. *Sex.* Testes function only in a narrow range of temperature (those of
   mammals hang externally in a scrotal sac because internal body temperatures are too high for their proper function). A worldwide rise in temperature at the close of the Cretaceous period caused the testes of dinosaurs to stop functioning and led to their extinction by sterilization of
   males.

2. *Drugs.* Angiosperms (flowering plants) first evolved toward the end of the
   dinosaurs' reign. Many of these plants contain psychoactive agents,
   avoided by mammals today as a result of their bitter taste. Dinosaurs
   had neither means to taste the bitterness nor livers effective enough to
   detoxify the substances. They died of massive overdoses.

3. *Disasters.* A large comet or asteroid struck the earth some 65 million years
   ago, lofting a cloud of dust into the sky and blocking sunlight, thereby
   suppressing photosynthesis and so drastically lowering world temperatures that dinosaurs and hosts of other creatures became extinct.

Before analyzing these three tantalizing statements, we must establish a basic ground rule often violated in proposals for the dinosaurs' demise. *There is no separate problem of the extinction of dinosaurs.* Too often we divorce specific events from their wider contexts and systems of cause and effect. The fundamental fact of dinosaur extinction is its synchrony with the demise of so many other groups across a wide range of habitats, from terrestrial to marine.

The history of life has been punctuated by brief episodes of mass ex-   6 tinction. A recent analysis by University of Chicago paleontologists Jack Sepkoski and Dave Raup, based on the best and most exhaustive tabulation of data ever assembled, shows clearly that five episodes of mass dying stand well above the "background" extinctions of normal times (when we consider all mass extinctions, large and small, they seem to fall in a regular 26–million–year cycle). The Cretaceous debacle, occurring 65 million years ago and separating the Mesozoic and Cenozoic eras of our geological time scale, ranks prominently among the five. Nearly all the marine plankton (single–celled floating creatures) died with geological suddenness; among marine invertebrates, nearly 15 percent of all families perished, including many previously dominant groups, especially the ammonites (relatives of squids in coiled shells). On land, the dinosaurs disappeared after more than 100 million years of unchallenged domination.

In this context, speculations limited to dinosaurs alone ignore the   7 larger phenomenon. We need a coordinated explanation for a system of events that includes the extinction of dinosaurs as one component. Thus it makes little sense, though it may fuel our desire to view mammals as inevitable inheritors of the earth, to guess that dinosaurs died because small mammals ate their eggs (a perennial favorite among untestable speculations). It seems most unlikely that some disaster peculiar to dinosaurs befell these massive beasts—and that the debacle happened to strike just when one of history's five great dyings had enveloped the earth for completely different reasons.

The testicular theory, an old favorite from the 1940s, had its root in an   8 interesting and thoroughly respectable study of temperature tolerances in the American alligator, published in the staid *Bulletin of the American Museum of Natural History* in 1946 by three experts on living and fossil reptiles—E. H. Colbert, my own first teacher in paleontology; R. B. Cowles; and C. M. Bogert.

The first sentence of their summary reveals a purpose beyond alliga-   9 tors: "This report describes an attempt to infer the reactions of extinct reptiles, especially the dinosaurs, to high temperatures as based upon reactions observed in the modern alligator." They studied, by rectal thermometry, the body temperatures of alligators under changing conditions of heating and cooling. (Well, let's face it, you wouldn't want to try sticking a thermometer under a 'gator's tongue.) The predictions under test go way back to an old theory first stated by Galileo in the 1630s — the unequal scaling of surfaces and volumes. As an animal, or any object, grows (provided its shape doesn't change), surface areas must increase more slowly than volumes — since surfaces get larger as length squared, while volumes increase much more rapidly, as length cubed. Therefore, small animals have high ratios of surface to volume, while large animals cover themselves with relatively little surface.

Among cold–blooded animals lacking any physiological mechanism   10
for keeping their temperatures constant, small creatures have a hell of a time keeping warm — because they lose so much heat through their relatively large surfaces. On the other hand, large animals, with their relatively small surfaces, may lose heat so slowly that, once warm, they may maintain effectively constant temperatures against ordinary fluctuations of climate. (In fact, the resolution of the "hot–blooded dinosaur" controversy that burned so brightly a few years back may simply be that, while large dinosaurs possessed no physiological mechanism for constant temperature, and were not therefore warm–blooded in the technical sense, their large size and relatively small surface area kept them warm.)

Colbert, Cowles, and Bogert compared the warming rates of small   11
and large alligators. As predicted, the small fellows heated up (and cooled down) more quickly. When exposed to a warm sun, a tiny 50–gram (1.76–ounce) alligator heated up one degree Celsius every minute and a half, while a large alligator, 260 times bigger at 13,000 grams (28.7 pounds), took seven and a half minutes to gain a degree. Extrapolating up to an adult 10–ton dinosaur, they concluded that a one-degree rise in body temperature would take eighty–six hours. If large animals absorb heat so slowly (through their relatively small surfaces), they will also be unable to shed any excess heat gained when temperatures rise above a favorable level.

The authors then guessed that large dinosaurs lived at or near their   12
optimum temperatures; Cowles suggested that a rise in global temperatures just before the Cretaceous extinction caused the dinosaurs to heat up beyond their optimal tolerance — and, being so large, they couldn't shed the unwanted heat. (In a most unusual statement within a scientific paper, Colbert and Bogert then explicitly disavowed this speculative extension of their empirical work on alligators.) Cowles conceded that this excess heat probably wasn't enough to kill or even to enervate the great beasts, but since testes often function only within a narrow range of temperature, he proposed that this global rise might have sterilized all the males, causing extinction by natural contraception.

The overdose theory has recently been supported by UCLA psychiatrist   13
Ronald K. Siegel. Siegel has gathered, he claims, more than 2,000 records of animals who, when given access, administer various drugs to them-

selves—from a mere swig of alcohol to massive doses of the big H.* Elephants will swill the equivalent of twenty beers at a time, but do not like alcohol in concentrations greater than 7 percent. In a silly bit of anthropocentric speculation, Siegel states that "elephants drink, perhaps, to forget . . . the anxiety produced by shrinking rangeland and the competition for food."

Since fertile imaginations can apply almost any hot idea to the ex- 14 tinction of dinosaurs, Siegel found a way. Flowering plants did not evolve until late in the dinosaurs' reign. These plants also produced an array of aromatic, amino–acid–based alkaloids—the major group of psychoactive agents. Most mammals are "smart" enough to avoid these potential poisons. The alkaloids simply don't taste good (they are bitter); in any case, we mammals have livers happily supplied with the capacity to detoxify them. But, Siegel speculates, perhaps dinosaurs could neither taste the bitterness nor detoxify the substances once ingested. He recently told members of the American Psychological Association: "I'm not suggesting that all dinosaurs OD'd on plant drugs, but it certainly was a factor." He also argued that death by overdose may help explain why so many dinosaur fossils are found in contorted positions. (Do not go gently into that good night.)

Extraterrestrial catastrophes have long pedigrees in the popular literature 15 of extinction, but the subject exploded again in 1979, after a long lull, when the father–son, physicist–geologist team of Luis and Walter Alvarez proposed that an asteroid, some 10 km in diameter, struck the earth 65 million years ago. (Comets, rather than asteroids, have since gained favor. Good science is self–corrective.)

The force of such a collision would be immense, greater by far than 16 the megatonnage of all the world's nuclear weapons. In trying to reconstruct a scenario that would explain the simultaneous dying of dinosaurs on land and so many creatures in the sea, the Alvarezes proposed that a gigantic dust cloud, generated by particles blown aloft in the impact, would so darken the earth that photosynthesis would cease and temperatures drop precipitously. (Rage, rage against the dying of the light.) The single–celled photosynthetic oceanic plankton, with life cycles measured in weeks, would perish outright, but land plants might survive through the dormancy of their seeds (land plants were not much affected by the Cretaceous extinction, and any adequate theory must account for the curious pattern of differential survival). Dinosaurs would die by starvation and freezing; small, warm–blooded mammals, with more modest requirements for food and better regulation of body temperature, would squeak through. "Let the bastards freeze in the dark," as bumper stickers

---

* **big H:** heroin.

of our chauvinistic neighbors in sunbelt states proclaimed several years ago during the Northeast's winter oil crisis.

All three theories, testicular malfunction, psychoactive overdosing, and asteroidal zapping, grab our attention mightily. As pure phenomenology, they rank about equally high on any hit parade of primal fascination. Yet one represents expansive science, the others restrictive and untestable speculation. The proper criterion lies in evidence and methodology; we must probe behind the superficial fascination of particular claims. 17

How could we possibly decide whether the hypothesis of testicular frying is right or wrong? We would have to know things that the fossil record cannot provide. What temperatures were optimal for dinosaurs? Could they avoid the absorption of excess heat by staying in the shade, or in caves? At what temperatures did their testicles cease to function? Were late Cretaceous climates ever warm enough to drive the internal temperatures of dinosaurs close to this ceiling? Testicles simply don't fossilize, and how could we infer their temperature tolerances even if they did? In short, Cowles's hypothesis is only an intriguing speculation leading nowhere. The most damning statement against it appeared right in the conclusion of Colbert, Cowles, and Bogert's paper, when they admitted: "It is difficult to advance any definite arguments against this hypothesis." My statement may seem paradoxical—isn't a hypothesis really good if you can't devise any arguments against it? Quite the contrary. It is simply untestable and unusable. 18

Siegel's overdosing has even less going for it. At least Cowles extrapolated his conclusion from some good data on alligators. And he didn't completely violate the primary guideline of siting dinosaur extinction in the context of a general mass dying—for rise in temperature could be the root cause of a general catastrophe, zapping dinosaurs by testicular malfunction and different groups for other reasons. But Siegel's speculation cannot touch the extinction of ammonites or oceanic plankton (diatoms make their own food with good sweet sunlight; they don't OD on the chemicals of terrestrial plants). It is simply a gratuitous, attention-grabbing guess. It cannot be tested, for how can we know what dinosaurs tasted and what their livers could do? Livers don't fossilize any better than testicles. 19

The hypothesis doesn't even make any sense in its own context. Angiosperms were in full flower ten million years before dinosaurs went the way of all flesh. Why did it take so long? As for the pains of a chemical death recorded in contortions of fossils, I regret to say (or rather I'm pleased to note for the dinosaurs' sake) that Siegel's knowledge of geology must be a bit deficient: Muscles contract after death and geological strata rise and fall with motions of the earth's crust after burial—more than enough reason to distort a fossil's pristine appearance. 20

The impact story, on the other hand, has a sound basis in evidence. It can be tested, extended, refined, and, if wrong, disproved. The Alvarezes 21 did not just construct an arresting guess for public consumption. They proposed their hypothesis after laborious geochemical studies with Frank Asaro and Helen Michael had revealed a massive increase of iridium in rocks deposited right at the time of extinction. Iridium, a rare metal of the platinum group, is virtually absent from indigenous rocks of the earth's crust; most of our iridium arrives on extraterrestrial objects that strike the earth.

The Alvarez hypothesis bore immediate fruit. Based originally on ev- 22 idence from two European localities, it led geochemists throughout the world to examine other sediments of the same age. They found abnormally high amounts of iridium everywhere—from continental rocks of the western United States to deep sea cores from the South Atlantic.

Cowles proposed his testicular hypothesis in the mid–1940s. Where 23 has it gone since then? Absolutely nowhere, because scientists can do nothing with it. The hypothesis must stand as a curious appendage to a solid study of alligators. Siegel's overdose scenario will also win a few press notices and fade into oblivion. The Alverezes' asteroid falls into a different category altogether, and much of the popular commentary has missed this essential distinction by focusing on the impact and its attendant results, and forgetting what really matters to a scientist—the iridium. If you talk just about asteroids, dust, and darkness, you tell stories no better and no more entertaining than fried testicles or terminal trips. It is the iridium—the source of testable evidence—that counts and forges the crucial distinction between speculation and science.

The proof, to twist a phrase, lies in the doing. Cowles's hypothesis 24 has generated nothing in thirty–five years. Since its proposal in 1979, the Alvarez hypothesis has spawned hundreds of studies, a major conference, and attendant publications. Geologists are fired up. They are looking for iridium at all other extinction boundaries. Every week exposes a new wrinkle in the scientific press. Further evidence that the Cretaceous iridium represents extraterrestrial impact and not indigenous volcanism continues to accumulate. As I revise this essay in November 1984 (this paragraph will be out of date when [it] is published), new data include chemical "signatures" of other isotopes indicating unearthly provenance, glass spherules of a size and sort produced by impact and not by volcanic eruptions, and high–pressure varieties of silica formed (so far as we know) only under the tremendous shock of impact.

My point is simply this: Whatever the eventual outcome (I suspect it 25 will be positive), the Alvarez hypothesis is exciting, fruitful science because it generates tests, provides us with things to do, and expands outward. We are having fun, battling back and forth, moving toward a resolution, and extending the hypothesis beyond its original scope.

As just one example of the unexpected, distant cross–fertilization that 26 good science engenders, the Alvarez hypothesis made a major contribution to a theme that has riveted public attention in the past few months—so-called nuclear winter. In a speech delivered in April 1982, Luis Alvarez calculated the energy that a ten–kilometer asteroid would release on impact. He compared such an explosion with a full nuclear exchange and implied that all-out atomic war might unleash similar consequences.

This theme of impact leading to massive dust clouds and falling tem- 27
peratures formed an important input to the decision of Carl Sagan and a group of colleagues to model the climatic consequences of nuclear holocaust. Full nuclear exchange would probably generate the same kind of dust cloud and darkening that may have wiped out the dinosaurs. Temperatures would drop precipitously and agriculture might become impossible. Avoidance of nuclear war is fundamentally an ethical and political imperative, but we must know the factual consequences to make firm judgments. I am heartened by a final link across disciplines and deep concerns—another criterion, by the way, of science at its best: A recognition of the very phenomenon that made our evolution possible by exterminating the previously dominant dinosaurs and clearing a way for the evolution of large mammals, including us, might actually help to save us from joining those magnificent beasts in contorted poses among the strata of the earth.

Reading Closely

1. List the information you did not know before you read this essay. What was most surprising? most puzzling? Share your responses with the rest of the class.

2. What are the three hypotheses for dinosaur extinction? List them, and provide a short explanation of each.

3. How does the title prepare you for the information in the body of the essay? What might Gould be trying to accomplish with this title?

Considering Larger Issues

1. Gould is well known for his ability to make scientific topics understandable for a general audience. What is his purpose in this essay? What evidence can you find in the essay for this purpose? Does Gould express his thesis in one specific statement? If so, what is his thesis statement? If not, what is his implied thesis?

2. **Working with three or four classmates,** list each of the three hypotheses and indicate how Gould tests each of them. What experiments, statistics, narratives, examples, and comparisons does he use to support or question each hypothesis? Share your responses with the rest of the class.

3. **COMBINING METHODS.** In which passages does Gould rely on *definition* to help expand his cause–and–consequence analysis? What is the overall effect of these definitions? Which ones are necessary? unnecessary (although maybe interesting)? Be prepared to share your responses with the rest of the class.

4. How does the cartoon on p. 530 affect the tone of Gould's text?

Thinking about Language

1. Using the context of the essay and your dictionary, define the following terms. Be prepared to share your answers with the rest of the class.

enticing (1)	terrestrial (5)	violate (19)
titillating (3)	debacle (7)	indigenous (21)
speculation (5)	resolution (10)	nuclear
implications (5)	anthropocentric (13)	holocaust (27)
synchrony (5)	scenario (16)	

2. What is the tone of this essay? How does the tone further the author's purpose? How does Gould's word choice help make his topic accessible to a popular audience? What other language strategies does he use?

3. **Working with one or two classmates,** examine the ways Gould establishes his authority and expertise on the subject (even while he's defining terms and replacing scientific terms with more common ones for his readers). Underline examples of these authority–establishing strategies, and share your answers with the rest of the class.

Writing Your Own Essays Using Cause-and-Consequence Analysis

1. Have a little fun with Gould's essay, modeling your own cause–and–consequence analysis on his. What might be the consequences if humans rather than dinosaurs had suffered extinction from one or all of the causes Gould examines? Draft a short essay (of three to four pages) in which you examine possible causes and consequences of the extinction of humans; use some of the causes Gould discusses as well as ones you come up with. Try using a visual or two to add interest. Refer to "Checking Over the Use of Cause–and–Consequence Analysis" on p. 503.

2. Work backwards from an event or situation, and trace its possible causes. You could write about a divorce, a marriage, a fire, an award or honor, or a larger topic such as the outcome of the 2004 presidential election, for which you might need to do some research. List the possible causes of the event or situation, and draft a three- to four-page essay in which you test each possibility. **Consider working with one or two classmates** to test your causes. Finally, decide on a primary cause and organize your essay emphatically. Refer to "Checking Over the Use of Cause–and–Consequence Analysis" on p. 503.

DOUGLAS FOSTER

The Disease Is Adolescence

Douglas Foster, a former editor of *Mother Jones* magazine, former John S. Knight Fellow at Stanford University, and former lecturer at the University of California at Berkeley, is currently a correspondent and producer for KQED, a public television station in San Francisco. His essays have appeared in *Harper's, Rolling Stone,* the *Los Angeles Times Sunday Magazine,* and the *New York Times Magazine.*

Numerous school shootings—particularly the tragedy that occurred in Littleton, Colorado, in 1999—have forced Americans to pay attention to the phenomenon of adolescent violence. In the following essay, which was first published in 1993 in *Rolling Stone* magazine, Foster notes that "three-quarters of the deaths of young people from ages 10 to 24—a total of 30,000 each year—occur not from disease but from preventable causes." He leads his readers through the many serious consequences of being in this age group. The lead-in to his article states that "if the symptoms are rapid increases in teen deaths from murder, suicide and car crashes, alcohol and drugs, . . . the disease is adolescence."

> **Preview** Judging from the title, do you think the author will concentrate mostly on causes or consequences? What might the causes and consequences of this "disease" be?

"This ankle is most assuredly broken," Dr. Barbara Staggers says, sounding almost gleeful.

Staggers is tall, 39 years old, African American, a physician. She smiles broadly and turns. Her 16-year-old Latino patient, laid out on a few chairs, narrows his eyes, perhaps startled by the pleasure he can hear in her voice. Staggers pats the boy's hand, surveys his pale face. Her eyes follow his long, muscled leg, stopping to study the spot where his foot draws down to the south. There, the bone takes a sharp detour east, its trajectory sketched by a plum-colored bruise, the fruit of basketball played too hard.

Staggers raises her arms in a *V* of triumph and grins. "Yep. Broken. Yes!"

After following Staggers on rounds—here in a clinic at Fremont High School and at the Teen Clinic of Children's Hospital in north Oakland, Calif.—even a casual observer might understand her glee. This is the first clean break of the day. The patient, suffering from the kind of injury doctors are trained to handle, will be treated and sent on his way. Within a few months, he will be playing ball too aggressively again.

Many of Staggers' other patients suffer far murkier ailments. So far today she has seen teenagers who are suicidal and homicidal; victims of sexual abuse; sufferers of serious diseases, from asthma to AIDS; and kids who are addicts to everything from alcohol to crack and junk. She has also seen teenagers who are pregnant or love starved and too many who have given up all hope.

The crisis among patients like Staggers' has been widely reported as 6 a tale of inner–city poverty and youth crime, but her weekly schedule is a rebuke to that simple notion. Many of her patients are poor, minority teenagers, but she also draws patients from more privileged neighbor-hoods. One kind of patient comes to her after taking a bullet in the belly during a downtown shootout. Another kind arrives bruised and broken, having drunk himself sick before wrecking his parents' luxury car in a high–speed crash.

"As a physician, I'm dealing with people who are incredibly resilient 7 physically," Staggers says in her cramped office at the school clinic, just before the injured athlete arrives. "Yet they still see their most positive option as being dead." In conversation, Staggers rolls her shoulders for-ward for emphasis and explains things in well–crafted bursts. "Guns and cars are different kinds of weapons. But they can be weapons all the same. Different presenting symptoms. The same disease."

What are the different presenting symptoms Staggers confronts? While 8 black teen–agers are far more likely to be shot to death, white teens are more likely to be injured or killed in an automobile crash—or to kill themselves. But both groups share this underlying condition: Three-quarters of the deaths of young people from ages 10 to 24—a total of 30,000 each year—occur not from disease but from preventable causes.

For most other age groups in the country, the risk of a violent death 9 or injury from these causes has leveled off or declined. Not so for adoles-cents—or for young people in their 20s, whose escalating risk of violent in-jury and death begins in their teens. Among youths from 15 to 19 years of age, the risk of being shot to death more than doubled in the last decade.

Consider this toll: 5,749 teens were killed—and tens of thousands in- 10 jured—in automobile crashes in 1991. Among youths 10 to 19, 3,398 were murdered, and 2,237 killed themselves in 1990. During the 1980s, 68,997 teen–agers died in car crashes, 19,346 were murdered, and 18,365 killed themselves. That added up to 106,718 for the decade. Today's teen-ager runs roughly twice the risk of being murdered or becoming a victim of suicide compared with teens during most years of the turbulent 1960s. (The risk of death from car crashes has declined, perhaps as a result of safety laws, public education and lower speed limits.) As if the old dangers were not threatening enough, HIV infection has begun to cut a wider swath.

Across lines of race and class among teen–agers, the number of pre- 11 ventable deaths is rising at an alarming rate. Adolescence has become a high–risk activity.

As the athlete with the broken ankle hobbles off to have his bone set, 12 Staggers tugs at the MD credentials hanging from a chain around her neck and surveys a waiting room full of difficult cases. Few of Staggers' patients readily reveal the underlying reasons for their visits. The receptionist's sign–in sheet contains a litany of mundane complaints—aching ears, persistent coughs, upset stomachs. Inside the examining room, the more serious business will tumble out if Staggers can find a way to dredge it up. On this morning, it turns out that the earache was caused by a beating, the cough by parental neglect and the stomachache by a suicide attempt.

Staggers sees several patients, including one young man, who are ex-   13
ploring their sexuality. "This school has a fair number of kids who openly identify [themselves] as gay or bisexual," she says. Staggers has double-barreled concerns about the boy: Does he know everything he needs to know about safer sex? Are the older men he has been staying with overnight—perhaps trading sex for shelter—taking advantage of his youth and naiveté?

The boy is handsome, soft-spoken, painfully shy. He has had several   14
near-fatal bouts of asthma, but his family is scattered, and nobody seems to be in charge of his care. Treating teens like this boy seems to require a kind of double vision: Staggers is treating the asthma but also trying to anticipate an underlying danger, counseling him to avoid exploitation, drug abuse, AIDS.

Next door, three young women have arrived—a few days after their   15
junior prom—for pregnancy tests. As she reads their names, Staggers raises her eyebrows in disappointment. There's a faint, nearly inaudible growl in her throat. These three girls know better. They've been taught how to protect themselves from sexually transmitted diseases and pregnancy.

Like these young women, teen-agers all over the country, most of   16
whom are sexually active, increasingly risk serious illness and death through sex. A recent report by the Centers for Disease Control found that among teens, new infections with HIV are occurring at a startlingly high rate.

Preparing to meet with the girls individually, Staggers suppresses an   17
exasperated scowl and replaces it with a stoic, neutral expression. This part of her practice—inspiring teens to make use of what they already know—is by far her biggest challenge. It demands the ability to hector and persuade without seeming to nag or lecture.

"It's hard when you're angry, but you have to take time with these   18
kids if you expect to make a difference," Staggers says outside the examining room. "To make an impact, you have to push past the facts. You have to press the girls for more information and look for the underlying causes. I ask them, 'Is an orgasm worth dying for?' and, 'Why do you want to be pregnant?' They'll tell you they want to get an education first. But then they'll go and have unprotected sex. Many of them don't think they have any control. The boys tell them they don't like the feel of a

condom. The boys say, 'Trust me.' And the girls desperately want to trust somebody."

Staggers is a vicious mimic, and she pauses to take on the role of a 19 teen-age boy, wheedling: "I just don't like how it feels. Please, baby. Trust me." She rolls her eyes and whirls. "Please, girls. Let's trust ourselves."

Staggers believes there's an "influential connection" between the 20 1 million teen-agers who get pregnant each year and the violence that pervades their lives. "Even though, in many ways, they don't want to get pregnant, they do it to replace some of the people they've lost," she says. At first blush, this sweeping statement seems hyperbolic, a shade New Age. To blame teen-age pregnancies on violence in the streets seems a bit of a stretch. But during her examination, one of the three prom revelers, a striking and articulate high-school senior, proves a spot-on example. This young woman can rattle off safe-sex guidelines so expertly that she could work for the CDC. Still, here she is waiting for the results of her preg- nancy test, having picked up a bad case of herpes after the big dance.

I ask if there's anything else bothering her. At that, the forthright 21 teen-ager becomes querulous. She hems and dodges. Finally, her hands flapping back and forth, she admits to having a hard time keeping a clear head ever since the recent murder of her 25-year-old cousin. The killing has left her feeling betrayed. Her cousin was called out of his home by his friends—among them people she knows from the neighborhood. Clearly, the young man was set up. She puffs big clouds of air through her cheeks. You learn not to trust anybody, she says.

Perhaps Staggers can chart the perils of adolescence so well because she 22 grew up in an upwardly mobile home that was thoroughly guarded against teen dangers. Her greatest influence was her father, one of the first African American doctors in a surgical subspecialty (urology) in the Navy. When Dr. Frank Staggers Sr. left military service, he moved the family to Castro Valley, an archetypal California suburb. The Staggers family settled above a sleepy commercial strip in one of the Eichler homes dotting the hills. Eichler's design, distinguished by expansive panes of glass and open redwood beams, was the architectural corollary to the family's upward arc.

Barbara Staggers' great-grandmother was born to a slave woman 23 and an Irish slaveholder. On her father's side, there was a railroad switchman and his wife, who never went to high school. Among her par- ents' generation, there were great social strides; all of her father's siblings and many of his 35 cousins have advanced degrees.

Under the watchful eye of two attentive parents, Staggers' younger 24 brother became an ordained minister and teacher and her elder brother a doctor specializing in the treatment of addiction. Staggers wobbled be- tween her desire to dance, her wish to pursue veterinary medicine and her ambition to become a doctor like her dad. At 18, she worked in a summer camp for inner–city Oakland teen–agers. There, she got hooked on the idea of doctoring teens. "Black physicians are social engineers," her father says. "I told her it was pretty hard to pursue a doctor's career as a dancer. But it would be possible to keep dancing if she trained to be a doctor."

For Barbara Staggers, being an upwardly mobile black in the 'burbs   25 was a sometimes mixed experience. Her junior–high–school counselor told her she would "never be able to achieve anything higher than a job washing dishes," she remembers, and she was tracked out of the class of high achievers she'd studied with until then. Her father intervened forcefully with school officials.

"What if my parents hadn't been watching out for me? I think about   26 that a lot," she muses. "Lots of kids just fall through the cracks because nobody is paying attention when they need it the most. It's in that moment when the crack is opening up for a kid that it's most important to intervene."

"Boy! Oh, my! No! Don't tell me!" Staggers hunches over the tele-   27 phone, as if the sheer weight of her concern can be brought to bear on her umpteenth case of life or death.

At the Teen Clinic of Children's Hospital in Oakland, she's packed   28 into her chair, surrounded by papers and correspondence and piles of telephone messages. Boxes of research files, speech materials and papers spill out of pink milk crates.

This is the first time I've heard Staggers stopped cold. She scuffs her   29 Reeboks beneath her chair and nestles the receiver against her cheek. A patient is nearing physical collapse from starving herself.

"Uh, oh! Anorexia and psychosis, too. She's hearing voices. Ah, man,"   30 Staggers says, frowning. "Do we know how much she weighs?"

"Excuse me. She weighs how much? Boy, oh, boy. Is she pale and   31 blue–looking? When anorectics need hospital care, we're talking cardio-vascular trouble. And so we're talking risk of instant death."

Staggers quickly refers the doctor to Lucile Salter Packard Children's   32 Hospital at Stanford, across the bay. Packard has a specialized eating-disorders clinic and in–patient psychiatric care. It's the appropriate place for this particular teen–ager. Swiveling in her chair, Staggers looks glum. "That was a tough one. You know, among anorectics, the odds aren't ter-rific. One–third of those who get treated get better, one–third or more stay the same — and up to a fifth die."

She's up and out before finishing the sentence, clearly discomfited by   33 the notion that there are cases even she can't get traction on. We've been talking about some of the others troubling her sleep. There's a 14–year-old female patient who lives with a 28–year–old pimp and drug dealer. So far, he's not sexually involved with the girl, and he doesn't show any signs of trying to pressure her into prostitution. "I've been watching to

see if he would try to pimp her out," Staggers says. "He seems to genuinely care for and protect her."

Staggers could turn the girl over to Child Protective Services. But that 34
public agency is overwhelmed with urgent cases, and the best they could
offer is foster care. Staggers still remembers, with a shiver of disgust, an
11-year-old girl with chronic illness turned over to the agency a few
years ago. The girl's parents were homeless, and CPS officials believed
she could not be adequately cared for on the street. So they separated
the girl from her parents.

"She ended up getting hospitalized as a psychiatric case," Staggers re- 35
members. "Her parents were good to her, and she missed them. What we
did initially, by referring the case, was take a tragedy and make it worse.
In the end, we got the parents jobs and a house. The kid is doing won-
derfully now." With that experience as a backdrop, Staggers calculates
that her current 14-year-old patient may be better off staying with the
one person who has cared for her, even if he's a pimp.

Staggers hurries off to meet with a middle-class teen-age girl, a run- 36
away from her suburban home. "I can't tell you how many middle-class
girls I have who get involved with the gangs at this age," she says. "This
girl was an A student. Now she's failing." Staggers sends two peer counselors, young women who have graduated from gang-involvement and
drug-treatment programs themselves, in for some straight talk with the
teen. Then the doctor follows up, both with the girl and with her parents — getting her to agree to go to family therapy and advising them to
lighten up once they get their daughter home.

As the parents and daughter file out, reunited, Staggers allows herself 37
a moment of relief. Her eyebrows bobble, and she grins. About her advice
to the parents, she explains, "We don't get very far by just telling teen-agers
not to take risks because it scares us. When we demand to know why
they've screwed up, the kid says, 'I had to. Everybody else was doing it.' The
adult replies, 'If everybody else jumped off the cliff, would you, too?'

"The honest answer to that question," continues Staggers, "is *yes*. It's 38
really, really important that we understand this. For the teen at that moment, being down at the bottom together feels better than being on the
edge of a cliff alone. What we need to engage our teens in discussing is
this question: What else can you do to be part of a group and still survive, while taking reasonable risks? If you've got to jump off the cliff,
can't you choose one that's not 50-feet high? Can you jump off the cliff
that's 2-feet high instead?"

Staggers' approach to treating teen-agers involves more engaged lis- 39
tening than most doctors or parents ever muster. Her method uncovers
underlying symptoms. She mentions a 16-year-old white boy who came
into the clinic for treatment of his swollen knees. By probing further, she
learned that he'd jumped from the second story of a building while high
on PCP and needed help with his drug habit. Another boy was in the

hospital recovering from injuries suffered in an automobile accident. Since his breath smelled as if he'd been drinking at the time of an accident, alcohol treatment was recommended. But nobody asked him why he'd crashed into the wall in the first place. Staggers did ask. "He told me, 'I've done this before. Several times,'" Staggers recalls. "And so we knew he needed suicide–prevention counseling, too. The experience left me wondering: How many suicides are really homicides? And how many homicides are really suicides?"

From experiences like these, Staggers first developed her theory 40 about the common problems of teen-agers. She believes a festering generational grievance cuts across differences of income, ethnic background or particular trauma.

But if adolescence itself has become a high–risk activity—a disease 41 to be treated with preventive therapy, as Staggers believes—what is the most effective treatment? Collecting her belongings at the end of the day, Staggers considers this question carefully and answers a bit haltingly. "With all the kids I know who make it, there's one thing in common: an individual contact with an adult who cared and who kept hanging in with the teen through his hardest moments," Staggers says. "People talk programs, and that's important. But when it comes down to it, individual, person–to–person connections make the difference. . . . Every kid I know who made it through the teen-age years had at least one adult in his life who made that effort."

When Staggers leaves work in downtown Oakland, she beats a retreat to 42 the suburbs where she was brought up—and where she presently lives with her second husband, 8–year-old son and 9–year-old stepson. Zipping along in her new Acura Integra at 75 mph, it's a short drive but a world away. The freeway slices around inner–city Oakland like a melon spoon, cutting southeast past a string of suburban villages, to Castro Valley.

"Notice anything?" Staggers laughs as we emerge from the car out- 43 side Castro Valley High School. At Fremont High, most of the school gates were chained shut, and security guards roamed the hallways, two-way radios at the ready. The average grade–point average is 1.7, and only a small fraction of the students will go on to college. At Castro Valley High, students wander freely. Most students come from two–parent families, and incomes are high. Almost all of them will go on to college.

"You're about to find out the problems for teens are similar even in 44 very different settings," Staggers insists, bustling down the hallway to the school's counseling office. "Sure, it looks better out here. It is better. But there are plenty of scary things happening here, too."

Just last spring, one Castro Valley teen-ager was killed with a base- 45 ball bat in a brawl after a Little League game. Although not reported at the time, tensions at the school had been fierce in the weeks before the brawl. The school's wrestling coach had been charged with making sexual advances to a boy on his team. That had led to gay–baiting teasing aimed at the wrestlers, some of whom were also baseball players. Then, ongoing racial skirmishes between Anglo and Latino students resulted in a series of confrontations.

Natalie Van Tassel, an ebullient white woman who has worked in 46 Castro Valley schools for 25 years, was Staggers' counselor during high school. She still treats Castro Valley's troubled teens. Within a minute of hitting the door of Van Tassel's office, the two are deep into cases.

The women compare notes about sexual activity among their pa- 47 tients. "I don't think I'm misrepresenting the past," Van Tassel says. "I mean, I came from a small Midwestern town where most of the girls got married the day after graduation because they were all pregnant. But what has happened is that the explosion of sexual activity moved down in the age groups — 12, 13, 14 . . ."

Staggers interrupts. "Among mine: 10, 11, 12 —"   48

"And the big difference," Van Tassel continues, "is, if you wanted to be 49 sexually active in your high–school years, you could do it without running the risk of dying because of it."

The risk of HIV infection is an increasing danger for all teen–agers. 50 Among the thorniest issues in prevention work is the ambiguous sexuality of many teen–agers — and the disdainful disapproval or loaded silence from adults concerning same–sex exploration. In this more privileged setting, oddly enough, there seems to be even less acceptance of gay teen–agers than at Fremont High. Only one young man is open about his homosexuality here.

Van Tassel finds it toughest of all to deal with teen–agers who have 51 no meaningful relationship with any adult. Suburban teen–agers are set loose to fend for themselves far too early, Van Tassel tells Staggers. "The parents here have a great capacity to give their kids things. Giving them so many material things masks what they're failing to give — time. What I see are kids without real parents."

Staggers is pounding the table. "See, it's the same disease, different 52 symptoms. Here the kids have economic opportunity, but no real family life." She's worked up now. "I'm tired of hearing people say, 'I'm too busy.' If you have kids — or you're related to kids — and they don't have adults in their lives, it's your job to either take care of them yourself or find some other grown–up who can do it for you. Either do it or find someone who can. But just throwing up your hands and saying, 'Time, time, there's no time' — that just doesn't cut it with me. How can we get that message through to the adults?"

Staggers doesn't wear a watch. Sometimes her schedule seems chaotic, 53 full of what appears — to some of her superiors, at any rate — to be

overly generous amounts of time for her patients. She has a way of locking on to whoever is in her presence and letting all the others wait. There
have been rumblings about her supposed failings as an administrator
and turf fights with the hospital administration. Staggers' department has
been hit with a series of cutbacks in staff and resources in a hospital-
wide restructuring.

In the midst of the cutbacks, even Staggers' clinic at Fremont High 54
may be in jeopardy. "That's where services should be—in the schools, in
the community," Staggers says firmly. "Can you imagine those kids turning up at a hospital clinic? With no insurance, no parent support, no information? Yet they're the kids who need treatment most."

But Staggers knows that her real beef is not with the budget–cutting 55
administrators at her hospital. She's at odds, fundamentally, with the way
medicine is currently organized. Staggers is trying to practice public-
health medicine in a fee–for–service world. No matter which proposal is
eventually adopted to reform the nation's health–care system, the underlying problem for doctors like Staggers will remain. Her focus on prevention, no matter how socially important, simply does not generate the fees
that would fund such a practice.

Preventive medicine is not rewarded under the current system. 56
Consider one example: While researching this story, I watched in the
emergency room of Oakland's Children's Hospital one Friday afternoon
as a 13–year–old gang member was treated for a gunshot wound suffered in a drive–by shooting. A 9mm slug was lodged in his thigh, and
like dozens of other teen–age shooting victims treated over the summer, his case generated a hefty bill. These kinds of bills are paid off either by a private insurance company or by the state.

By contrast, if Staggers succeeds as Doctor to the Teens—talking an 57
angry young man out of a gang, in one instance—her efforts often don't
generate a bill. Since her time isn't billable, she and her institution are
left holding the bag. Her model of health care makes sense, particularly
in treating teen–agers, but Staggers' efforts at prevention are never rewarded as well as the standard program of stitch–then–release.

When she gets agitated on this subject, Staggers sets her jaw and 58
waves her arms. Teen–agers are less likely to receive medical care than
any other age group in the country, she insists, and rarely do they get the
kind of care they need, even when they are treated. For all the hazy rhetoric floating around in Washington about the domestic agenda, Staggers
can't understand how anyone expects to make headway without taking
into account the special problems of teens.

Staggers often gives speeches around the country. She's a doctor 59
of publicity, too, turning out between appointments on one day, for
example, to support the efforts of community groups in Oakland trying
to shut down alcohol outlets. ("You put alcohol and firearms together,

and you account for 50 to 75 percent of all adolescent deaths," she says.) She's also a regular fixture in testimony before state legislative committees.

The uphill nature of her cause was evident at an afternoon hearing 60 last May in Sacramento, the state capital. With teens and their advocates from all over the state waiting and ready to testify about their problems, a special hearing about teen–age health was abruptly canceled because legislators were busy downstairs grappling with a state budget that was $9 billion from balancing. In times of such stark shortage, it's harder than ever to get teen–agers the attention they desperately need.

When Staggers was honored with the Lewis Hine Award in New York 61 this year for her service to young people, Hillary Rodham Clinton, a fellow honoree, asked for her advice. The first lady got an impassioned briefing about adolescent medicine.

"She listened carefully, and I hope it made a difference in her think- 62 ing," Staggers says. "If only the federal government could restructure health care so there's community–based operations and more school-based clinics, we might get a grip on some of these problems."

On my last day with Staggers at the school clinic, a tall, lively African 63 American teen–ager stops by to share the good news: She has been accepted at San Jose State University, and she'll be starting college in the fall. Dressed in a red blouse and stretch pants, Ebony Hawthorne acknowledges that her prospects seemed rather bleak not so long ago. She had gotten pregnant at 15, and she nearly decided to carry the baby to term. It was a dicey conflict. On the one hand, she would not have been likely to have gone on to college if she had had the baby. But her family was dead set against an abortion, and she felt a powerful need to "have somebody to call my own."

At home, it was difficult to find support. Ebony's father, estranged 64 from her mother, is a drug dealer who has been in and out of prison. Her mother is an addict. At the school clinic, she had opened up about her problems at home, her hopes and fears, and she ultimately decided to have an abortion.

As it turned out, her unwanted pregnancy was the prelude to a 65 period of raw travail, which hit during last year's holiday season. First, her stepfather died of a heart attack. Then, last November, Ebony and her mother were evicted from their home on Thanksgiving Day. Ebony was distracted, to say the least, from her schoolwork. She worried that notices from the colleges she'd applied to would never catch up with her.

On their way to a homeless shelter, mother and daughter stopped for 66 fuel. There, at the gas station, they bumped into Ebony's father, out of prison and back into business. He allowed them to stay for a week in an apartment he had rented nearby. Then he tossed them out, because he needed the apartment back "for work."

Ebony sets her chin, speaking crisply, as if she's desperately trying to distance herself from the bitterness she feels. "Does this make any sense to you? He told me he was throwing us out for my own good. For my own good! Why? Because he needed the apartment to sell his drugs from. And if he didn't make any money, he wouldn't be able to give me any Christmas money. Tell me, would you rather have a roof over your head—or Christmas money? That's when I decided: As far as I'm concerned, I have no father." 67

Luckily, Ebony salvaged a relationship with her mother, who is now in a drug treatment program in San Francisco. She has been clean for eight months. "She's trying to get my respect back," Ebony says, frowning. "I don't feel I lost my respect for her. Not at all. But she feels I have. She went through a hard task to get sober. And I'm proud of her." 68

Hawthorne betrays a hint of pride in herself as well. She has managed to finish high school in an environment of homelessness, drug addiction, violence and neglect. Most of her classmates are headed for the streets, while she is going off to college. From a deep reservoir of will and hope, Ebony Hawthorne has mustered a quality in scant supply among today's teen-agers. She has ambition. 69

"The difference between me and some of the others is that I push myself, because I've seen how my mother ended up," Hawthorne says. "And I have people here at the clinic who push me, too. 70

"I want to be a psychiatrist," she adds tentatively, as if ready to be challenged. "Because I want to really understand it all better. I want to understand myself—what happened to me and all the anger I have— much better. And then I want to be in a position to help people. I want to help the kind of people . . . who have problems like mine." 71

Outside the door, another set of patients is waiting. In one room, peer counselors are giving a lecture about safer sex, practicing rolling condoms onto rubber phalluses with their mouths. A couple of students need prescriptions. Another doctor is on the line. But Staggers has already moved on to the next examining room, her face upturned and open, anxious to dig out the essence of her next case. 72

Reading Closely

1. Describe what the essay labels "the disease called adolescence." List the symptoms of this disease, the causes, and the consequences. Provide examples for each of these categories to share with the rest of the class.
2. List all the preventable problems that the adolescents described in this essay are facing. What solutions does Barbara Staggers propose or imply for these problems?

Considering Larger Issues

1. Write out what you consider to be Foster's thesis. What situation is he describing, and how does he describe it? Enumerate the causes for the situation and the consequences of it. Prepare to share your answers with the rest of the class.

2. Who is the audience for this essay? What evidence can you find in the text for your answer?

3. In the essay, Staggers discusses all kinds of adolescents: rich and poor; black and white; homeless, neglected, and cared for. **Working with one or two classmates,** determine the overall effect of including experiences from such a wide range of adolescents. Provide evidence from the text for your answer. Prepare a group response for the rest of the class.

4. COMBINING METHODS. The author reveals very little about himself or his interest in the topic, but he reveals a good deal about Staggers. What effect does his use of *narration* (in the biographical information about Staggers) have on the essay? Prepare to share your response with the rest of the class.

Thinking about Language

1. Using the context and your dictionary, define the following terms. Be prepared to share your answers with the rest of the class.

trajectory (2)	mundane (12)	anorectics (31)
murkier (5)	exasperated (17)	discomfited (33)
rebuke (6)	hector (17)	festering (40)
resilient (7)	hyperbolic (20)	dicey (63)
escalating (9)	querulous (21)	travail (65)
litany (12)	archetypal (22)	

2. Using your answer for question 1 under "Reading Closely," discuss the use of the term *disease* to refer to adolescence. What does this term imply about teenagers? Is it fair?

3. Foster includes many quotes in his essay. One of the most familiar is "If everybody else jumped off the cliff, would you, too?" (paragraph 37). How does Staggers's analysis of this cliché help ground the essay? Write out your response. What other quotations seem particularly startling, moving, or overused to you? **Working with one or two classmates,** prepare a joint response to share with the rest of the class.

Writing Your Own Essays Using Cause-and-Consequence Analysis

1. Respond to Foster's essay by writing a few minutes on the consequences of your own adolescence (the symptoms you suffered or the pleasures you enjoyed, or the ones you have witnessed in other adolescents). How many of the consequences you suffered were similar to the ones Foster

mentions? What consequences does he mention that you didn't experi-ence? Use your responses as the basis for a three- to four-page essay on *one aspect* of adolescence. Refer to "Checking Over the Use of Cause–and–Consequence Analysis" (p. 503).

2. You probably know of a tragedy that happened to a teenage boy or girl; unfortunately, such stories are fairly common. Draft a three- to four-page essay in which you discuss the causes or the consequences of this tragedy. You may want to gather information by interviewing people; you may also want to consult print and online sources. Consider using a chronological structure to organize the causes or consequences and make your point. Refer to "Checking Over the Use of Cause–and–Consequence Analysis" on p. 503.

3. Draft an essay similar to Foster's, describing the problems of adolescence and untangling the causes or consequences of those problems. Don't hesitate to use anecdotes, as Foster does, to bring your essay to life. You might want to gather information by interviewing classmates, adolescents, and people who work with them as well as from other sources to supplement your own thinking on this subject. You may also need to conduct library or World Wide Web research. As you draft and revise, **consider working with a classmate.** Also, refer to the guidelines for checking over the use of cause–and–consequence analysis on p. 503.

SUSAN GLASPELL
A Jury of Her Peers

● Susan Glaspell (1882–1948) is best known as a dramatist. Her plays include *Trifles* (1916), *Inheritors* (1921), and *Alison's House* (1930), which is loosely based on the life of Emily Dickinson and won the Pulitzer Prize for drama in 1931. Glaspell and her husband, George Gig Cook, helped establish the Province-town Theatre Group, a famous theater company on Cape Cod, Massachusetts, for which she was an actor and producer as well as a playwright. Much of her work explores the idea of women's roles, and she adapted *Trifles*, perhaps her best-known play on the subject, into the short story "A Jury of Her Peers" (1927). Glaspell also wrote the novels *Brook Evans* (1928) and *The Fugitive's Return* (1929), as well as *The Road to Temple* (1926), a biography of Cook.

> **Preview** What information does the title, "A Jury of Her Peers," tell you about the story you're about to read?

When Martha Hale opened the storm–door and got a cut of the north 1
wind, she ran back for her big woolen scarf. As she hurriedly wound that round her head her eye made a scandalized sweep of her kitchen. It was no ordinary thing that called her away — it was probably farther from ordinary than anything that had ever happened in Dickson County. But what her eye took in was that her kitchen was in no shape for leaving; her bread all ready for mixing, half the flour sifted and half unsifted.

She hated to see things half done; but she had been at that when the 2
team from town stopped to get Mr. Hale, and then the sheriff came run-ning in to say his wife wished Mrs. Hale would come too. So she had dropped everything right where it was.

She again opened the storm–door, and this time joined the three 3
men and the one woman waiting for her in the big two–seated buggy. After she had the robes tucked around her she took another look at the woman who sat beside her on the back seat. She had met Mrs. Peters the year before at the county fair, and the thing she remembered about her was that she didn't seem like a sheriff's wife. She was small and thin and didn't have a strong voice. But if Mrs. Peters didn't look like a sheriff's wife, Peters made it up in looking like a sheriff. He was to a dot the kind of man who could get himself elected sheriff — a heavy man with a big voice, who was particularly genial with the law–abiding, as if to make it plain that he knew the difference between criminals and non–criminals. And right there it came into Mrs. Hale's mind, with a stab, that this was going to the Wrights' now as a sheriff.

They had gone up a little hill and could see the Wright place now. It 4
looked very lonesome this cold March morning. It had always been a lonesome–looking place. It was down in a hollow, and the poplar trees

around it were lonesome–looking trees. The men were looking at it and talking about what had happened. The county attorney was bending to one side of the buggy.

"I'm glad you came with me," Mrs. Peters said nervously.   5

Martha Hale had a moment of feeling she could not cross that   6
threshold, because she hadn't crossed it before. Time and time again it had been in her mind, "I ought to go over and see Minnie Foster"—she still thought of her as Minnie Foster, though for twenty years she had been Mrs. Wright. And then there was always something to do and Minnie Foster would go from her mind. But *now* she could come.

The men went over to the stove. The women stood close together by   7
the door, at first not even so much as looking around the kitchen.

Sheriff Peters stepped back from the stove, unbuttoned his outer   8
coat, and leaned his hands on the kitchen table in a way that seemed to mark the beginning of official business. "Now, Mr. Hale," he said in a sort of semi–official voice, "before we move things about, you tell Mr. Henderson just what it was you saw when you came here yesterday morning."

The county attorney was looking around the kitchen. "Are things just   9
as you left them yesterday?"

Peters looked from cupboard to sink; from that to a small worn   10
rocker a little to one side of the kitchen table.

"It's just the same."   11

"Well, Mr. Hale," said the county attorney, "tell just what happened   12
when you came here yesterday morning."

Mrs. Hale, still leaning against the door, had that sinking feeling of   13
the mother whose child is about to speak a piece. She hoped Lewis would tell this straight and plain, and not say unnecessary things that would just make things harder for Minnie Foster. He didn't begin at once, and she noticed that he looked queer—as if having to tell what he had seen there yesterday morning made him almost sick.

"Harry and I had started to town with a load of potatoes," Mrs. Hale's   14
husband began.

Harry was Mrs. Hale's oldest boy. He wasn't with them now, for the   15
very good reason that those potatoes never got to town yesterday and he was taking them this morning. With all Mrs. Hale's other emotions came the fear now that maybe Harry wasn't dressed warm enough—they hadn't any of them realized how that north wind did bite.

"We come along this road," Hale was going on, with a motion of his   16
hand to the road over which they had just come, "and as we got in sight of the house I says to Harry, 'I'm goin' to see if I can't get John Wright to take a telephone.' You see," he explained to Henderson, "unless I can get somebody to go in with me they won't come out this branch road except for a price I can't pay. I'd spoke to Wright about it once before; but he put me off, saying folks talked too much anyway. But I thought maybe if

I went to the house and talked about it before his wife, and said all the women-folks liked the telephones, and that in this lonesome stretch of road it would be a good thing — though I didn't know as what his wife wanted made much difference to John — "

Now, there he was! — saying things he didn't need to say. Mrs. Hale   17
tried to catch her husband's eye, but fortunately the county attorney interrupted with:

"Let's talk about that a little later, Mr. Hale. I'm anxious now to get   18
along to just what happened when you got here."

When he began this time, it was very deliberately and carefully: 19

"I didn't see or hear anything. I knocked at the door. And still it was   20
all quiet inside. So I knocked again, louder, and I thought I heard somebody say, 'Come in.' I wasn't sure — I'm not sure yet. But I opened the door — this door," jerking a hand toward the door by which the two women stood, "and there, in that rocker" — pointing to it — "sat Mrs. Wright."

Every one in the kitchen looked at the rocker. It came into Mrs.   21
Hale's mind that that rocker didn't look in the least like Minnie Foster — the Minnie Foster of twenty years before. It was a dingy red, with wooden rungs up the back, and the middle run was gone, and the chair sagged to one side.

"How did she — look?" the county attorney was inquiring.   22

"Well," said Hale, "she looked — queer."   23

"How do you mean — queer?"   24

As he asked it he took out a note-book and pencil. Mrs. Hale did not   25
like the sight of that pencil. She kept her eye fixed on her husband, as if to keep him from saying unnecessary things that would go into that notebook and make trouble.

Hale did speak guardedly, as if the pencil had affected him too.   26

"Well, as if she didn't know what she was going to do next. And kind   27
of — done up. I said, 'Ho' do, Mrs. Wright? It's cold, ain't it?' And she said, 'Is it?' — and went on pleatin' at her apron.

"Well, I was surprised. She didn't ask me to come up to the stove, or   28
to sit down, but just set there, not even lookin' at me. And so I said: 'I want to see John.'

"And then she — laughed. I guess you would call it a laugh.   29

"I thought of Harry and the team outside, so I said, a little sharp, 'Can   30
I see John?' 'No,' says she — kind of dull like. 'Ain't he home?' says I. Then she looked at me. 'Yes,' says she, 'he's home.' 'Then why can't I see him?' I asked her, out of patience with her now. 'Cause he's dead,' says she, just as quiet and dull — and fell to pleatin' her apron. 'Dead?' says I, like you do when you can't take in what you've heard.

"She just nodded her head, not getting a bit excited, but rockin' back   31
and forth.

"Why — where is he?' says I, not knowing *what* to say.   32

"She just pointed upstairs—like this"—pointing to the room above.   33

"I got up, with the idea of going up there myself. By this time I—   34
didn't know what to do. I walked from there to here; then I says: 'Why,
what did he die of?'

"'He died of a rope round his neck,' says she; and just went on   35
pleatin' at her apron."

Hale stopped speaking, and stood staring at the rocker.   36

"And what did you do then?" the county attorney at last broke the si-   37
lence.

"I went out and called Harry. I thought I might—need help. I got   38
Harry in, and we went upstairs." His voice fell almost to a whisper. "There
he was—lying over the—Well, my first thought was to get that rope off.
It looked—" He stopped, his face twitching. "But Harry, he went up to
him, and he said, 'No, he's dead all right, and we'd better not touch anything.' So we went downstairs.

"She was still sitting that same way. 'Has anybody been notified?' I   39
asked. 'No,' says she, unconcerned.

"'Who did this, Mrs. Wright?' said Harry. He said it businesslike, and   40
she stopped pleatin' at her apron. 'I don't know,' she says. 'You don't
know?' says Harry. 'Weren't you sleepin' in the bed with him?' 'Yes,' says
she, 'but I was on the inside.' 'Somebody slipped a rope round his neck
and strangled him, and you didn't wake up?' says Harry. 'I didn't wake
up,' she said. After a minute she said, 'I sleep sound.'

"Harry was going to ask her more questions, but I said maybe that   41
weren't our business; maybe we ought to let her tell her story first to
the coroner or the sheriff. So Harry went fast as he could over to High
Road—the Rivers' place, where there's a telephone. I got a feeling that I
ought to make some conversation, so I said I had come in to see if John
wanted to put in a telephone; and at that she started to laugh, and then
she stopped and looked at me—scared."

At sound of a moving pencil the man who was telling the story   42
looked up.

"I dunno—maybe it wasn't scared," he hastened; "I wouldn't like to   43
say it was. Soon Harry got back, and then Dr. Lloyd came, and you, Mr.
Peters, and so I guess that's all I know that you don't."

He said that last with relief, and moved a little, as if relaxing. Every   44
one moved a little. The county attorney walked toward the stair door.

"I guess we'll go upstairs first—then out to the barn and around there."   45

He paused and looked around the kitchen.   46

"You're convinced there was nothing important here?" he asked the   47
sheriff. "Nothing that would—point to any motive?"

"Nothing here but kitchen things," he said, with a little laugh for the   48
insignificance of kitchen things.

The county attorney was looking at the cupboard—a peculiar, un-   49
gainly structure, half closet and half cupboard, the upper part of it being

built in the wall, and the lower part just the old-fashioned kitchen cupboard. As if its queerness attracted him, he got a chair and opened the upper part and looked in. After a moment he drew his hand away sticky.

"Here's a nice mess," he said resentfully.   50

The two women had drawn nearer, and now the sheriff's wife spoke.   51

"Oh—her fruit," she said, looking to Mrs. Hale for sympathetic un-   52
derstanding. She turned back to the county attorney and explained: "She worried about that when it turned so cold last night. She said the fire would go out and her jars might burst."

Mrs. Peters' husband broke into a laugh.   53

"Well, can you beat the women! Held for murder, and worrying   54
about her preserves!"

"Oh, well," said Mrs. Hale's husband, with good-natured superiority,   55
"women are used to worrying over trifles."

The two women moved a little closer together. Neither of them   56
spoke. The county attorney went to the sink and began washing his hands. He turned to wipe them on the roller towel—whirled it for a cleaner place.

"Dirty towels! Not much of a housekeeper, would you say, ladies?"   57

He kicked his foot against some dirty pans under the sink.   58

"There's a great deal of work to be done on a farm," said Mrs. Hale   59
stiffly.

"To be sure. And yet"—with a little bow to her—"I know there are   60
some Dickson County farm-houses that do not have such roller towels." He gave it a pull to expose its full length again.

"Those towels get dirty awful quick. Men's hands aren't always as   61
clean as they might be."

"Ah, loyal to your sex, I see," he laughed. He stopped and gave her a   62
keen look. "But you and Mrs. Wright were neighbors. I suppose you were friends, too."

Martha Hale shook her head.   63

"I've seen little enough of her of late years. I've not been in this   64
house—it's more than a year. Farmers' wives have their hands full, Mr. Henderson. And then—" She looked around the kitchen. "It never seemed a very cheerful place," said she, more to herself than to him.

"No," he agreed; "I don't think any one would call it cheerful. I   65
shouldn't say she had the home-making instinct."

"Well, I don't know as Wright had, either," she muttered.   66

"You mean they didn't get on very well?" he was quick to ask.   67

"No; I don't mean anything," she answered, with decision. As she   68
turned a little away from him, she added: "But I don't think a place would be any the cheerfuler for John Wright's bein' in it."

"I'd like to talk to you about that a little later, Mrs. Hale," he said. He   69
moved toward the stair door, followed by the two men.

"I suppose anything Mrs. Peters does'll be all right?" the sheriff inquired. "She was to take in some clothes for her, you know — and a few little things. We left in such a hurry yesterday." 70

The county attorney looked at the two women. 71

"Of course Mrs. Peters is one of us," he said, in a manner of entrusting responsibility. "And keep your eye out, Mrs. Peters, for anything that might be of use. No telling; you women might come upon a clue to the motive — and that's the thing we need." 72

"But would the women know a clue if they did come upon it?" Mr. Hale said; and, having delivered himself of this, he followed the others through the stair door. 73

The women stood motionless and silent, listening to the footsteps, first upon the stairs, then in the room above them. 74

Then, as if releasing herself from something strange, Mrs. Hale began to arrange the dirty pans under the sink, which the county attorney's disdainful push of the foot had deranged. 75

"I'd hate to have men comin' into my kitchen," she said testily — "snoopin' round and criticizin'. Seems mean to talk about her for not having things slicked up, when she had to come away in such a hurry." 76

She looked around the kitchen. Certainly it was not "slicked up." Her eye was held by a bucket of sugar on a low shelf. The cover was off the wooden bucket, and beside it was a paper bag — half full. 77

She thought of the flour in her kitchen at home — half sifted, half not sifted. She had been interrupted, and had left things half done. What had interrupted Minnie Foster? She made a move as if to finish it, — unfinished things always bothered her, — and then she glanced around and saw that Mrs. Peters was watching her — and she didn't want Mrs. Peters to get that feeling she had got of work begun and then — for some reason — not finished. 78

"I must be getting those things from the front room closet." The sheriff's wife opened the door into the other room, started in, stepped back. "You coming with me, Mrs. Hale?" she asked nervously. "You — you could help me get them." 79

They were soon back — the stark coldness of that shut-up room was not a thing to linger in. 80

"My!" said Mrs. Peters, dropping the things on the table and hurrying to the stove. 81

Mrs. Hale stood examining the clothes the woman who was being detained in town had said she wanted. "Wright was close!" she exclaimed, holding up a shabby black skirt that bore the marks of much making over. "I think maybe that's why she kept so much to herself. I s'pose she felt she couldn't do her part; and then, you don't enjoy things when you feel shabby. She used to wear pretty clothes and be lively — when she was Minnie Foster, one of the town girls, singing in the choir. But that — oh, that was twenty years ago." 82

With a carefulness in which there was something tender, she folded 83
the shabby clothes and piled them at one corner of the table.

"This all you was to take in?" asked Mrs. Hale. 84

"No," said the sheriff's wife; "she said she wanted an apron. Funny 85
thing to want," she ventured in her nervous little way, "but I suppose just
to make her feel more natural. If you're used to wearing an apron—. She
said they were in the bottom drawer of this cupboard. Yes—here they
are. And then her little shawl that always hung on the stair door."

She took the small gray shawl from behind the door leading upstairs, 86
and stood a minute looking at it.

Suddenly Mrs. Hale took a quick step toward the other woman. 87

"Do you think she—did it?" 88

A frightened look blurred the other thing in Mrs. Peters' eyes. 89

"Oh, I don't know," she said, in a voice that seemed to shrink away 90
from the subject.

"Well, I don't think she did," affirmed Mrs. Hale stoutly. "Asking for an 91
apron, and her little shawl. Worryin' about her fruit."

"Mr. Peters says—it looks bad for her. Mr. Henderson is awful sarcas- 92
tic in a speech, and he's going to make fun of her saying she didn't—
wake up."

For a moment Mrs. Hale had no answer. Then, "Well, I guess John 93
Wright didn't wake up—when they was slippin' that rope under his
neck," she muttered.

"No, it's *strange*," breathed Mrs. Peters. "They think it was such a— 94
funny way to kill a man. Mr. Henderson said, coming out, that what was
needed for the case was a motive. Something to show anger—or sudden
feeling."

"Well, I don't see any signs of anger around here," said Mrs. Hale. "I 95
don't—"

She stopped. It was as if her mind tripped on something. Her eye 96
was caught by a dish-towel in the middle of the kitchen table. Slowly she
moved toward the table. One half of it was wiped clean, the other half
messy. Things begun—and not finished.

After a moment she stepped back, and said, in that manner of releas- 97
ing herself:

"Wonder how they're finding things upstairs? I hope she had it a 98
little more red up up there. You know,"—she paused, and feeling gathered,—"it seems kind of *sneaking*: locking her up in town and coming out
here to get her own house to turn against her!"

"But, Mrs. Hale," said the sheriff's wife, "the law is the law." 99

"I s'pose 'tis," answered Mrs. Hale shortly. She turned to the stove. 100
"The law is the law—and a bad stove is a bad stove. How'd you like to
cook on this?"—pointing with the poker to the broken lining. She was
swept into her own thoughts, thinking of what it would mean, year after
year, to have that stove to wrestle with. The thought of Minnie Foster

trying to bake in that oven — and the thought of her never going over to see Minnie Foster —.

She was startled by hearing Mrs. Peters say: "A person gets discour- 101 aged — and loses heart."

The sheriff's wife had looked from the stove to the sink — to the pail 102 of water which had been carried in from outside. The two women stood there silent, above them the footsteps of the men who were looking for evidence against the woman who had worked in that kitchen. A look of seeing into things, of seeing through a thing to something else, was in the eyes of the sheriff's wife now.

Mrs. Peters went to the back of the room to hang up the fur tippet 103 she was wearing. A moment later she exclaimed, "Why, she was piecing a quilt," and held up a large sewing basket piled high with quilt pieces.

Mrs. Hale spread some of the blocks out on the table. 104

"It's log-cabin pattern," she said, putting several of them together. 105 "Pretty, isn't it?"

They were so engaged with the quilt that they did not hear the foot- 106 steps on the stairs. Just as the stair door opened Mrs. Hale was saying:

"Do you suppose she was going to quilt it or just knot it?" 107

The sheriff threw up his hands. 108

"They wonder whether she was going to quilt it or just knot it!" 109

There was a laugh for the ways of women, a warming of hands over 110 the stove, and then the county attorney said briskly:

"Well, let's go right out to the barn and get that cleared up." 111

"I don't see as there's anything so strange," Mrs. Hale said resentfully, 112 after the outside door had closed on the three men — "our taking up our time with little things while we're waiting for them to get the evidence. I don't see as it's anything to laugh about."

"Of course they've got awful important things on their minds," said 113 the sheriff's wife apologetically.

They returned to an inspection of the block for the quilt. Mrs. Hale 114 was looking at the fine, even sewing, and preoccupied with thoughts of the woman who had done that sewing, when she heard the sheriff's wife say, in a queer tone:

"Why, look at this one." 115

She turned to take the block held out to her. 116

"The sewing," said Mrs. Peters, in a troubled way. "All the rest of them 117 have been so nice and even — but — this one. Why, it looks as if she didn't know what she was about!"

Their eyes met — something flashed to life, passed between them; 118 then, as if with an effort, they seemed to pull away from each other. A moment Mrs. Hale sat there, her hands folded over that sewing which was so unlike all the rest of the sewing. Then she had pulled a knot and drawn the threads.

"Oh, what are you doing, Mrs. Hale?" asked the sheriff's wife, startled. 119

"Just pulling out a stitch or two that's not sewed very good," said Mrs. 120
Hale mildly.

"I don't think we ought to touch things," Mrs. Peters said, a little 121
helplessly.

"I'll just finish up this end," answered Mrs. Hale, still in that mild, 122
matter-of-fact fashion.

She threaded a needle and started to replace bad sewing with good. 123
For a little while she sewed in silence. Then, in that thin, timid voice, she
heard:

"What do you suppose she was so—nervous about?" 124

"Oh, I don't know," said Mrs. Hale, as if dismissing a thing not impor- 125
tant enough to spend much time on. "I don't know as she was—nervous.
I sew awful queer sometimes when I'm just tired."

She cut a thread, and out of the corner of her eye looked up at Mrs. 126
Peters. The small, lean face of the sheriff's wife seemed to have tightened
up. Her eyes had that look of peering into something. But next moment
she moved, and said in her thin, indecisive way:

"Well, I must get those clothes wrapped. I wonder where I could find 127
a piece of paper—and string."

"In that cupboard, maybe," suggested Mrs. Hale, after a glance 128
around.

One piece of the crazy sewing remained unripped. Mrs. Peters' back 129
turned, Martha Hale now scrutinized that piece, compared it with the
dainty, accurate sewing of the other blocks. The difference was startling.
Holding this block made her feel queer, as if the distracted thoughts of
the woman who had perhaps turned to it to try and quiet herself were
communicating themselves to her.

Mrs. Peters' voice roused her. 130

"Here's a bird-cage," she said. "Did she have a bird, Mrs. Hale?" 131

"Why, I don't know whether she did or not." She turned to look at the 132
cage Mrs. Peter was holding up. She sighed. "There was a man round last
year selling canaries cheap—but I don't know as she took one. Maybe
she did. She used to sing real pretty herself."

Mrs. Peters looked around the kitchen. 133

"Seems kind of funny to think of a bird here." She half laughed—an 134
attempt to put up a barrier. "But she must have had one—or why would
she have a cage? I wonder what happened to it." Mrs. Peters examined
the bird-cage. "Look at this door," she said slowly. "It's broke. One hinge
has been pulled apart. Looks as if some one must have been—rough
with it."

Again their eyes met—startled, questioning, apprehensive. For a mo- 135
ment neither spoke nor stirred. Then Mrs. Hale, turning away, said
brusquely:

"If they're going to find any evidence, I wish they'd be about it. I 136
don't like this place." She had picked up the sewing, but now it dropped

in her lap, and she murmured in a different voice: "But I tell you what I
do wish, Mrs. Peters. I wish I had come over sometimes when she was
here. I wish—I had. I can see now—"

"Well, you mustn't reproach yourself," counseled Mrs. Peters. "Some- 137
how, we just don't see how it is with other folks till—something comes
up."

"Not having children makes less work," mused Mrs. Hale, after a si- 138
lence, "but it makes a quiet house—and Wright out to work all day—
and no company when he did come in. Did you know John Wright, Mrs.
Peters?"

"Not to know him. I've seen him in town. They say he was a good 139
man."

"Yes—good," conceded John Wright's neighbor grimly. "He didn't 140
drink, and kept his word as well as most, I guess, and paid his debts. But
he was a hard man, Mrs. Peters." She stopped, shivered a little. "Like a raw
wind that gets to the bone." Her eye fell upon the cage on the table before her, and she added, almost bitterly: "I should think she would've
wanted a bird!"

"You didn't know—her?" Mrs. Hale asked, a gentler note in her voice. 141

"Not till they brought her yesterday," said the sheriff's wife. 142

"She—come to think of it, she was kind of like a bird her- 143
self. Real sweet and pretty, but kind of timid and—fluttery. How—she—
did—change."

That held her for a long time. Finally, as if struck with a happy 144
thought and relieved to get back to everyday things, she exclaimed:

"Tell you what, Mrs. Peters, why don't you take the quilt in with you? 145
It might take up her mind."

"Why, I think that's a real nice idea, Mrs. Hale," agreed the sheriff's 146
wife, as if she too were glad to come into the atmosphere of a simple
kindness. "Now, just what will I take? I wonder if her patches are in
here—and her things."

They turned to the sewing basket. 147

"Here's some red," said Mrs. Hale, bringing out a roll of cloth. Under- 148
neath that was a box. "Here, maybe her scissors are in here—and her
things." She held it up. "What a pretty box! I'll warrant that was something she had a long time ago—when she was a girl."

She held it in her hand a moment; then, with a little sigh, opened it. 149
"There's something wrapped up in this piece of silk," faltered Mrs. Hale.
Her hand not steady, Mrs. Hale raised the piece of silk. "Oh, Mrs. Peters!"
she cried. "It's—"

Mrs. Peters bent closer. 150

"It's the bird," she whispered. 151

"But, Mrs. Peters!" cried Mrs. Hale. "*Look* at it! Its *neck*—look at 'its 152
neck! It's all—other side *too*."

The sheriff's wife again bent closer. 153

"Somebody wrung its neck," said she, in a voice that was slow and   154
deep.

And then again the eyes of the two women met—this time clung   155
together in a look of dawning comprehension, of growing horror.
Mrs. Peters looked from the dead bird to the broken door of the cage.
Again their eyes met. And just then there was a sound at the outside
door.

Mrs. Hale slipped the box under the quilt pieces in the basket, and   156
sank into the chair before it. Mrs. Peters stood holding to the table. The
county attorney and the sheriff came in from outside.

"Well, ladies," said the county attorney, as one turning from serious   157
things to little pleasantries, "have you decided whether she was going to
quilt it or knot it?"

"We think," began the sheriff's wife in a flurried voice, "that she was   158
going to—knot it."

He was too preoccupied to notice the change that came in her voice   159
on that last.

"Well, that's very interesting, I'm sure," he said tolerantly. He caught   160
sight of the bird–cage. "Has the bird flown?"

"We think the cat got it," said Mrs. Hale in a voice curiously even.   161

"Is there a cat?" he asked absently.   162

"Well, not *now*," said Mrs. Peters. "They're superstitious, you know;   163
they leave."

The county attorney did not heed her. "No sign at all of any one hav-   164
ing come in from the outside," he said to Peters, in the manner of continuing an interrupted conversation. "Their own rope. Now let's go upstairs
again and go over it, piece by piece. It would have to have been some
one who knew just the—"

The stair door closed behind them and their voices were lost.   165

The two women sat motionless, not looking at each other, but as if   166
peering into something and at the same time holding back. When they
spoke now it was as if they were afraid of what they were saying, but as
if they could not help saying it.

"She liked the bird," said Martha Hale, low and slowly. "She was   167
going to bury it in that pretty box."

"When I was a girl," said Mrs. Peters, under her breath, "my kitten—   168
there was a boy took a hatchet, and before my eyes—before I could get
there—" She covered her face an instant. "If they hadn't held me back I
would have"—she caught herself, looked upstairs where footsteps were
heard, and finished weakly—"hurt him."

Then they sat without speaking or moving.   169

"I wonder how it would seem," Mrs. Hale at last began, as if feeling   170
her way over strange ground—"never to have had any children around?"
Her eyes made a slow sweep of the kitchen, as if seeing what that kitchen
had meant through all the years. "No, Wright wouldn't like the bird," she

said after that—"a thing that sang. She used to sing. He killed that too."
Her voice tightened.

Mrs. Peters moved uneasily.   171

"Of course we don't know who killed the bird."   172

"I knew John Wright," was Mrs. Hale's answer.   173

"It was an awful thing was done in this house that night, Mrs. Hale,"   174
said the sheriff's wife. "Killing a man while he slept—slipping a thing
round his neck that choked the life out of him."

"We don't *know* who killed him," whispered Mrs. Peters wildly. "We   175
don't *know*."

Mrs. Hale had not moved. "If there had been years and years of—   176
nothing, then a bird to sing to you, it would be awful—still—after the
bird was still."

It was as if something within her not herself had spoken, and it   177
found in Mrs. Peters something she did not know as herself.

"I know what stillness is," she said, in a queer, monotonous voice.   178
"When we homesteaded in Dakota, and my first baby died—after he was
two years old—and me with no other then—"

Mrs. Hale stirred.   179

"How soon do you suppose they'll be through looking for the evi-   180
dence?"

"I know what stillness is," repeated Mrs. Peters, in just that same way.   181
Then she too pulled back. "The law has got to punish crime, Mrs. Hale,"
she said in her tight little way.

"I wish you'd seen Minnie Foster," was the answer, "when she wore   182
a white dress with blue ribbons, and stood up there in the choir and
sang."

The picture of that girl, the fact that she had lived neighbor to that   183
girl for twenty years, and had let her die for lack of life, was suddenly
more than she could bear.

"Oh, I *wish* I'd come over here once in a while!" she cried. "That was a 184
crime! That was a crime! Who's going to punish that? I might 'a' *known*
she needed help! I tell you, it's *queer*, Mrs. Peters. We live close together,
and we live far apart. We all go through the same things—it's all just a
different kind of the same thing! If it weren't—why do you and I *understand*? Why do we *know*—what we know this minute?"

She dashed her hand across her eyes.   185

"My!" Mrs. Peters began, in a high, false voice, "it's a good thing the   186
men couldn't hear us! Getting all stirred up over a little thing like a—
dead canary." She hurried over that. "As if that could have anything to do
with—with—My, wouldn't they *laugh*?"

Footsteps were heard on the stairs.   187

"Maybe they would," muttered Mrs. Hale—"maybe they wouldn't."   188

"No, Peters," said the county attorney incisively; "it's all perfectly   189
clear, except the reason for doing it. But you know juries when it comes

A drawing used for publicity from an independent film of *A Jury of Her Peers* that was made in 1980.

to women. If there was some definite thing—something to make a story about. A thing that would connect up with this clumsy way of doing it."

In a covert way Mrs. Hale looked at Mrs. Peters. Mrs. Peters was 190 looking at her. Quickly they looked away from each other.

"I'm going to stay here awhile by myself," the county attorney sud– 191 denly announced. "I want to go over everything. I'm not satisfied we can't do better."

Again, for one brief moment, the two women's eyes found one an– 192 other.

The sheriff came up to the table.   193

"Did you want to see what Mrs. Peters was going to take in?"   194

The county attorney picked up the apron. He laughed.   195

"Oh, I guess they're not very dangerous things the ladies have picked 196 out."

Mrs. Hale's hand was on the sewing basket in which the box was 197 concealed. She felt that she ought to take her hand off the basket. She did not seem able to. He picked up one of the quilt blocks which she had piled on to cover the box. Her eyes felt like fire. She had a feeling that if he took up the basket she would snatch it from him.

But he did not take it up. With another little laugh, he turned away, 198 saying:

"No; Mrs. Peters doesn't need supervising. For that matter, a sheriff's 199 wife is married to the law."

"Married to the law!" chuckled Mrs. Peters' husband. He moved to– 200 ward the door into the front room, and said to the county attorney: "We ought to take a look at these windows."

"Oh—windows," said the county attorney scoffingly.   201

The sheriff followed the county attorney into the other room. Again— 202 for one final moment—the two women were alone in that kitchen.

Martha Hale sprang up, her hands tight together, looking at that 203 other woman, with whom it rested. Slowly, unwillingly, Mrs. Peters turned her head until her eyes met the eyes of the other woman. There was a moment when they held each other in a steady, burning look in which there was no evasion nor flinching. Then Martha Hale's eyes pointed the way to the basket in which was hidden the thing that would make certain the conviction of the other woman—that woman who was not there and yet who had been there with them all through that hour.

For a moment Mrs. Peters did not move. And then she did it. With a 204 rush forward, she threw back the quilt pieces, got the box, tried to put it in her hand-bag. It was too big. Desperately she opened it, started to take the bird out. But there she broke—she could not touch the bird. She stood there helpless, foolish.

There was the sound of a knob turning in the inner door. Martha 205 Hale snatched the box from the sheriff's wife, and got it in the pocket of her big coat just as the sheriff and the county attorney came back into the kitchen.

"Well, Henry," said the county attorney facetiously, "at least we found   206 out that she was not going to quilt it. She was going to—what is it you call it, ladies?"

Mrs. Hale's hand was against the pocket of her coat.   207

"We call it—knot it, Mr. Henderson."   208

Reading Closely

1. Outline the sequence of events in this story. Who are the characters? How are they related to one another?

2. What are the causes of Minnie Wright's actions? What are the consequences of her husband's actions?

3. What are the causes of Martha Hale's and Mrs. Peters's actions? What are the consequences of their actions?

4. How far did you read before you realized what had actually taken place?

Considering Larger Issues

1. As the headnote to this story explains, it is an adaptation of a play with the title "Trifles." Mark all the mentions of trifles (things, activities, interests) that the men consider to be such. What is the overall effect of these mentions?

2. What are the attitudes of the men toward the women in this story? What about the attitudes of the women toward the men? Be sure to use specific examples from the story to support your answers.

3. Storytellers usually want to entertain. In what ways is "A Jury of Her Peers" entertaining? Does it fulfill any other purpose as well: Does it inform, speculate, or argue?

4. **Working with two or three classmates,** prepare answers to the following questions: What event or situation is the author concentrating on? Is she concentrating on the causes or the consequences of this event or situation? Can you determine the primary, the contributory or secondary, and the immediate and remote causes or consequences? Prepare to report your answers to the rest of the class.

5. COMBINING METHODS. This story analyzes causes and consequences by using *narration* and *description*. Point to specific sentences or passages where you find the narrative or the description especially effective in making the link between causes and consequences.

6. This story is set in the early twentieth century. Did any aspects of it seem surprising, dated, strange, or hard to understand from your contemporary perspective? If so, what were they? In the drawing on p. 563, do

the characters look the way you had imagined them from reading the text? If not, how did they differ from your expectations?

Thinking about Language

1. Using a dictionary or the context of the story, define the following terms and phrases. Be prepared to share your answers with the rest of the class.

to a dot (3)	pleatin' (27)	red up (98)
genial (3)	ungainly (49)	poker (100)
looked queer (13)	roller towel (56)	piecing a quilt
branch road (16)	disdainful (75)	(103)
dingy (21)	deranged (75)	scrutinized (129)

2. As noted earlier, this story was adapted from a play titled "Trifles." What does that title connote? How does the meaning of that title differ from "A Jury of Her Peers"?

Writing Your Own Essays Using Cause-and-Consequence Analysis

1. Draft a three- to four–page essay analyzing "A Jury of Her Peers" according to the chart that appears on p. 500, starting with the primary cause of an abuser's overpowering need for power and control. Use evidence from the story itself to support your analysis of what happens in it— and why. Be sure to refer to the guidelines for checking over a cause–and–consequence analysis on p. 503.

2. Draft a three- to four–page essay in which you analyze the causes and consequences of the situation from the women characters' point of view. Pay special attention to the details the women noticed (and the incidents they remembered) that they didn't mention to the male characters. Refer to the guidelines for using cause–and–consequence analysis on p. 503.

Annual Deaths from Smoking Compared with Selected Other Causes in the United States

Hospitals and health organizations of all kinds use charts and graphs to invigorate their instructional materials. The following chart, for example, uses words, numbers, and a bar graph to explain the numbers of deaths annually from smoking and various other causes in the United States. As you can see, this 1995 chart, which appears on the Web site of St. George's Hospital and Medical School in London, draws on information from several other sources, including the *Journal of the American Medical Association* (JAMA), the National Center of Health Statistics (NCHS), and Smoking–Attributable Mortality, Morbidity, and Economic Costs (SAMMEC).

Preview   With what kinds of charts or graphs are you familiar? How did you become familiar with them? What kinds of information do you get from them?

Reading Closely

1. What are the health–related issues that are featured in this chart?
2. What information have you learned about them in this chart?

Considering Larger Issues

1. Does this information seem reliable to you? What experience or specific knowledge do you have that confirms or questions the reliability of this chart?
2. How are these various causes of death related to one another? What causes of death are left unmentioned? Why do you think they are omitted?
3. Who might be the intended audience for this chart? How can you tell?
4. What is the author's purpose in putting together this chart? How can you tell?
5. What do you need to know about smoking in order to appreciate this chart?
6. **COMBINING METHODS.** How does the author incorporate other rhetorical methods of development in this chart? Why would he or she need to do so in order to fulfill the purpose of this chart?

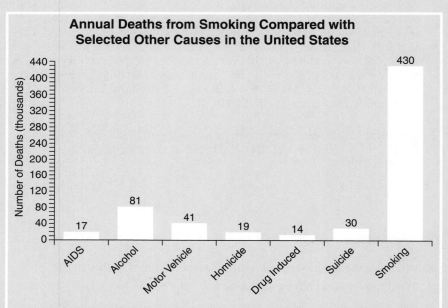

Annual Deaths from Smoking Compared with Selected Other Causes in the United States

Number of Deaths (thousands)

AIDS	17
Alcohol	81
Motor Vehicle	41
Homicide	19
Drug Induced	14
Suicide	30
Smoking	430

Sources: (AIDS) HIV/AIDS Surveillance Report, 1998; (Alcohol) McGinnis MJ, Foege WH. Review: Actual Causes of Death in the United States, JAMA 1993; 270: 2207-12; (Motor vehicle) National Highway Transportation Safety Administration, 1998, (Homicide, Suicide) NCHS, vital statistics, 1997, (Drug Induced) NCHS, vital statistics, 1996; (Smoking) SAMMEC, 1995

Writing Your Own Essays Using Cause-and-Consequence Analysis

1. By conducting a little online or library research, you should be able to come up with a cause–and–consequence analysis that you can illustrate with a chart, table, or other kind of visual. For instance, you might examine the connections between smoking and various kinds of diseases, from emphysema to cancer, or between the lower number of smokers in the United States and the rise in the number of smokers worldwide, especially in Southeast Asia. Or you might want to consider the financial consequences for actors who have lost weight, undergone plastic surgery, or taken singing/dancing/acting lessons. You might consider sports figures who have improved their performances with laser eye surgery or other kinds of physical improvements. Or you may want to consider the consequences of having a college degree. Draft a two–page essay analyzing the cause(s) and consequence(s) you are focusing on. Then compress your entire analysis into a visual. As you draft, refer to the guidelines for checking over a cause–and–consequence analysis on p. 503.

2. **Working with a classmate or two,** draft a two- to three-page essay in which you respond to the "Annual Deaths from Smoking Compared with Selected Other Causes in the United States" chart, determining remote consequences or secondary causes for the conclusions this chart tends to draw. Refer to the guidelines for checking over a cause–and–consequence analysis on p. 503.

✳ Additional Suggestions for Writing

1. Draft a three- to four-page essay in which you analyze the causes that led you to become a college student. **Working with one or two classmates,** decide how to rank your primary or immediate cause and contributory or remote causes. Refer to "Checking Over the Use of Cause-and-Consequence Analysis" on p. 503.

2. Look around you at the people in your classes, at your job, in your daily life. What kinds of judgments are you making about people on the basis of how they look? First make a list of the various "looks" you see every day, including clothing, hairstyle, grooming, footwear, coloring, and age, and of the accessories for each look. (See chapter 5 for help with classifying.) Then determine the consequences of these categories for yourself. What looks are you immediately attracted to? distrustful of? turned off by? Have you learned any important lessons about appearances being deceptive—or have your opinions about appearance been reinforced? Draft a three- to four-page essay in which you investigate the possible consequences of appearance. Refer to "Checking Over the Use of Cause-and-Consequence Analysis" on p. 503.

3. Define *success*, and then talk about the consequences of success. As evidence, you might want to use your own life or the life of someone you know well: a parent, for instance. Or you may turn to the popular media and examine one of the many examples of success they offer on a daily basis. Be sure to discuss immediate and more remote consequences. As you plan, draft, and revise your essay, be sure to use the guidelines for checking over the use of cause–and–consequence analysis (p. 503) to make sure that your essay has a clear purpose and carefully considered consequences.

4. Examine yourself—as a writer, a student, a worker, a friend, a spouse or partner. Open a four-page essay by describing yourself in one of these roles. How well do you fulfill your role? What are the causes of the success or failure you have had in this role? What are the consequences? Take some time to develop a list of both the causes and the consequences, and then choose one set of responses. Develop your essay by analyzing critically the causes or consequences as primary/other (contributory or secondary) or as immediate/remote. **Working with one or two classmates,** discuss your conclusion about yourself as well as the conclusion of your essay. Refer to "Checking Over the Use of Cause-and-Consequence Analysis" on p. 503.

5. Describe yourself as a college student, and chart the consequences of your decision to become one. What are the immediate consequences and the remote or long-term ones? Which is the primary consequence? Draft a two- to three-page speculative essay in which you analyze the consequences of your getting a college education. As you draft and revise, refer to the guidelines for checking over the use of cause-and-consequence analysis on p. 503.

chapter 9

DEFINITION

de•fine \di-ˈfīn\ *vb* **de•fined; de•fin•ing** [ME, fr. L *definire,* fr. *de-* + *finire* to limit, end, fr. *finis* boundary, end] *vt* (14c) **1 a :** to determine or identify the essential qualities or meaning of ⟨whatever ~*s* us as human⟩ **b :** to discover and set forth the meaning of (as a word) **c :** to create on a computer ⟨~ a window⟩ ⟨~ a procedure⟩ **2 a :** to fix or mark the limits of : DEMARCATE ⟨rigidly *defined* property lines⟩ **b :** to make distinct, clear, or detailed esp. in outline ⟨the issues aren't too well *defined*⟩ **3 :** CHARACTERIZE, DISTINGUISH ⟨you ~ yourself by the choices you make —*Denison Univ. Bull.*⟩ ~ *vi* **:** to make a definition — **de•fine•ment** \-ˈfīn-mənt\ *n* — **de•fin•er** \-ˈfī-nər\ *n*

de•fin•i•en•dum \di-ˌfi-nē-ˈen-dəm\ *n, pl* **-da** \-də\ [L, something to be defined, neut. of *definiendus,* gerundive of *definire*] (1871) **:** an expression that is being defined

de•fin•i•ens \di-ˈfi-nē-ˌenz\ *n, pl* **de•fin•i•en•tia** \di-ˌfi-nē-ˈen(t)-shē-ə\ [L, prp. of *definire*] (1838) **:** an expression that defines : DEFINITION

def•i•nite \ˈde-fə-nit, ˈdef-nət\ *adj* [L *definitus,* pp. of *definire*] (1553) **1 :** having distinct or certain limits ⟨set ~ standards for pupils to meet⟩ **2 a :** free of all ambiguity, uncertainty, or obscurity ⟨demanded a ~ answer⟩ **b :** UNQUESTIONABLE, DECIDED ⟨the quarterback was a ~ hero today⟩ **3 :** typically designating an identified or immediately identifiable person or thing ⟨the ~ article *the*⟩ **4 a** *of floral organs* **:** being constant in number, usu. less than 20, and occurring in multiples of the petal number ⟨stamens ~⟩ **b :** CYMOSE ⟨a ~ inflorescence⟩ *syn* see EXPLICIT — **def•i•nite•ly** *adv* — **def•i•nite•ness** *n*

definite integral *n* (1834) **:** the difference between the values of the integral of a given function *f(x)* for an upper value *b* and a lower value *a* of the independent variable *x*

def•i•ni•tion \ˌde-fə-ˈni-shən\ *n* [ME *diffinicioun,* fr. AF, fr. L *definition-, definitio,* fr. *definire*] (14c) **1 :** an act of determining; *specif* **:** the formal proclamation of a Roman Catholic dogma **2 a :** a statement expressing the essential nature of something **b :** a statement of the meaning of a word or word group or a sign or symbol ⟨dictionary ~*s*⟩ **c :** a product of defining **3 :** the action or process of defining **4 a :** the action or the power of describing, explaining, or making definite and clear ⟨the ~ of a telescope⟩ ⟨her comic genius is beyond ~⟩ **b** (1) **:** clarity of visual presentation : distinctness of outline or detail ⟨improve the ~ of an image⟩ (2) **:** clarity esp. of musical sound in reproduction **c :** sharp demarcation of outlines or limits ⟨a jacket with distinct waist ~⟩ — **def•i•ni•tion•al** \-ˈni-shə-nᵊl\ *adj*

¹de•fin•i•tive \di-ˈfi-nə-tiv\ *adj* [ME *diffinityf,* fr. AF *diffinitive,* fr. L *definitivus,* fr. *definitus*] (14c) **1 :** serving to provide a final solution or to end a situation ⟨a ~ victory⟩ **2 :** authoritative and apparently exhaustive ⟨a ~ edition⟩ **3 a :** serving to define or specify precisely ⟨~ laws⟩ **b :** serving as a perfect example : QUINTESSENTIAL ⟨a ~ bourgeois⟩ **4 :** fully differentiated or developed ⟨a ~ organ⟩ **5** *of a postage stamp* **:** issued as a regular stamp for the country or territory in which it is to be used *syn* see CONCLUSIVE — **de•fin•i•tive•ly** *adv* — **de•fin•i•tive•ness** *n*

²definitive *n* (1951) **:** a definitive postage stamp — compare PROVISIONAL

definitive host *n* (1901) **:** the host in which the sexual reproduction of a parasite takes place — compare INTERMEDIATE HOST 1

de•fi•ni•tize \ˈde-fə-nə-ˌtīz, di-ˈfi-\ *vt* **-tized; -tiz•ing** (1876) **:** to make definite

de•fi•ni•tude \di-ˈfi-nə-ˌtüd, -ˌtyüd\ *n* [irreg. fr. *definite*] (1836) **:** PRECISION, DEFINITENESS

def•la•grate \ˈdef-lə-ˌgrāt\ *vb* **-grat•ed; -grat•ing** [L *deflagratus,* pp. of *deflagrare* to burn down, fr. *de-* + *flagrare* to burn — more at BLACK] *vt* (ca. 1727) **:** to cause to deflagrate — compare DETONATE 1 ~ *vi* **:** to burn rapidly with intense heat and sparks being given off — **def•la•gra•tion** \ˌdef-lə-ˈgrā-shən\ *n*

de•flate \di-ˈflāt, ˌdē-\ *vb* **de•flat•ed; de•flat•ing** [*de-* + *-flate* (as in *inflate*)] *vt* (1891) **1 :** to release air or gas from ⟨~ a tire⟩ **2 :** to reduce in size, importance, or effectiveness ⟨~ his ego with cutting remarks⟩ **3 :** to reduce (a price level) or cause (a volume of credit) to contract ~ *vi* **:** to lose firmness through or as if through the escape of contained gas *syn* see CONTRACT — **de•fla•tor** *also* **de•fla•ter** \-ˈflā-tər\ *n*

de•fla•tion \di-ˈflā-shən, ˌdē-\ *n* (1891) **1 :** an act or instance of deflating : the state of being deflated **2 :** a contraction in the volume of available money or credit that results in a general decline in prices **3 :** the erosion of soil by the wind — **de•fla•tion•ary** \-shə-ˌner-ē\ *adj*

de•flect \di-ˈflekt, dē-\ *vb* [L *deflectere* to bend down, turn aside, fr. *de-* + *flectere* to bend] *vt* (ca. 1555) **:** to turn aside esp. from a straight course or fixed direction ~ *vi* **:** to turn aside : DEVIATE — **de•flect•able** \-ˈflek-tə-bəl\ *adj* — **de•flec•tive** \-tiv\ *adj* — **de•flec•tor** [illegible] *n*

de•flec•tion \di-ˈflek-shən, dē-\ *n* (1605) **1 :** a turning aside [illegible] off course : DEVIATION **2 :** the departure of an indicator or [illegible] from the zero reading on the scale of an instrument

de•flexed \ˈdē-ˌflekst, di-ˈ\ *adj* [L *deflexus,* pp. of *deflectere*] (1826) **:** turned abruptly downward ⟨a ~ [illegible]⟩

de•flo•ra•tion \ˌdef-lə-ˈrā-shən, ˌdē-flō-\ *n* [ME *defloracioun,* fr. MF & LL; MF *defloracion,* fr. LL *defloration-, defloratio,* fr. *deflorare*] (15c) **:** rupture of the hymen

de•flow•er \(ˌ)dē-ˈflau̇(-ə)r\ *vt* [ME *deflouren,* fr. MF or LL; OF *desflorer,* fr. LL *deflorare,* fr. L *de-* + *flor-, flos* flower — more at BLOW] (14c) **1 :** to deprive of virginity **2 :** to take away the prime beauty [illegible] — **de•flow•er•er** *n*

de•fog \(ˌ)dē-ˈfȯg, -ˈfäg\ *vt* (1904) **:** to remove fog or condensed moisture from ⟨~ a windshield⟩ — **de•fog•ger** *n*

de•fo•li•ant \(ˌ)dē-ˈfō-lē-ənt\ *n* (1943) **:** a chemical spray or dust applied to plants in order to cause the leaves to drop off prematurely

de•fo•li•ate \-lē-ˌāt\ *vt* [LL *defoliatus,* pp. of *defoliare,* fr. L *de-* + *folium* leaf — more at BLADE] (1791) **:** to deprive of leaves esp. prematurely — **de•fo•li•a•tion** \(ˌ)dē-ˌfō-lē-ˈā-shən\ *n* — **de•fo•li•a•tor** \(ˌ)dē-ˈfō-lē-ˌā-tər\ *n*

de•force \(ˌ)dē-ˈfȯrs\ *vt* [ME, fr. AF *deforcer,* fr. *de-* + *forcer* to force] (15c) **1 :** to keep (as lands) by force from the rightful owner **2 :** to eject (a person) from possession by force — **de•force•ment** \-ˈfȯrs-mənt\ *n*

de•for•es•ta•tion \(ˌ)dē-ˌfȯr-ə-ˈstā-shən, -ˌfär-\ *n* (1874) **:** the action or process of clearing of forests; *also* **:** the state of having been cleared of forests — **de•for•est** \(ˈ)dē-ˈfȯr-əst, -ˈfär-\ *vt*

de•form \di-ˈfȯrm, dē-\ *vb* [ME, fr. AF or L; AF *desfurmer,* fr. L *deformare,* fr. *de-* + *formare* to form, fr. *forma* form] *vt* (15c) **1 :** to spoil the form of **2 a :** to spoil the looks of : DISFIGURE ⟨a face ~*ed* by bitterness⟩ **b :** to mar the character of ⟨a marriage ~*ed* by jealousy⟩ **3 :** to alter the shape of by stress ~ *vi* **:** to become misshapen or changed in shape — **de•form•able** \-mə-bəl\ *adj*

syn DEFORM, DISTORT, CONTORT, WARP means to mar or spoil by or as if by twisting. DEFORM may imply a change of shape through stress, injury, or some accident of growth ⟨his face was *deformed* by hatred⟩. DISTORT and CONTORT both imply a wrenching from the natural, normal, or justly proportioned, but CONTORT suggests a more involved twisting and a more grotesque and painful result ⟨the odd camera angle *distorts* the figure in the photograph⟩ ⟨disease had painfully *contorted* her body⟩. WARP indicates physically an uneven shrinking that bends or twists out of a flat plane ⟨*warped* floorboards⟩.

de•for•mal•ize \(ˌ)dē-ˈfȯr-mə-ˌlīz\ *vt* (1880) **:** to make less formal

de•for•ma•tion \ˌdē-ˌfȯr-ˈmā-shən, ˌde-fər-\ *n* (15c) **1 :** alteration of form or shape; *also* **:** the product of such alteration **2 :** the action of deforming : the state of being deformed **3 :** change for the worse — **de•for•ma•tion•al** \-shə-nᵊl\ *adj*

de•for•ma•tive \di-ˈfȯr-mə-tiv, dē-\ *adj* (1641) **:** tending to deform

de•formed *adj* (15c) **:** distorted or unshapely in form : MISSHAPEN

de•for•mi•ty \di-ˈfȯr-mə-tē, dē-\ *n, pl* **-ties** [ME *deformite,* fr. MF *defformeteit,* fr. L *deformitat-, deformitas,* fr. *deformis* deformed, fr. *de-* + *forma*] (15c) **1 :** the state of being deformed **2 :** IMPERFECTION, BLEMISH: as **a :** a physical blemish or distortion : DISFIGUREMENT **b :** a moral or aesthetic flaw or defect

de•frag \dē-ˈfrag\ *vt* **defragged; defragging** (1988) **:** DEFRAGMENT

de•frag•ment \(ˌ)dē-ˈfrag-mənt\ *vt* (1985) **:** to reorganize separated fragments of related data on (a computer disk) into a contiguous arrangement — **de•frag•men•ta•tion** \-ˌfrag-mən-ˈtā-shən, -ˌmen-\ *n*

de•frag•ment•er \-ˈfrag-ˌmen-tər, -mən-\ *n* (1986) **:** software that defragments a computer disk

de•fraud \di-ˈfrȯd, dē-\ *vt* [ME, fr. AF *defrauder,* fr. L *defraudare,* fr. *de-* + *fraudare* to cheat, fr. *fraud-, fraus* fraud] (14c) **:** to deprive of something by deception or fraud *syn* see CHEAT — **de•fraud•er** \di-ˈfrȯ-dər\ *n*

de•fray \di-ˈfrā, dē-\ *vt* [MF *deffroyer,* fr. *des-* de- + *frayer* to expend, fr. OF, fr. *frais,* pl. of *fret, frait* expenditure, lit., damage by breaking, fr. L *fractum,* neut. of *fractus,* pp. of *frangere* to break — more at BREAK] (1536) **1 :** to provide for the payment of : PAY **2** *archaic* **:** to bear the expenses of — **de•fray•able** \-ə-bəl\ *adj* — **de•fray•al** \-ˈfrā(-ə)l\ *n*

de•frock \(ˌ)dē-ˈfräk\ *vt* (1581) **1 :** to deprive (as a priest) of the right to exercise the functions of office **2 :** to remove from a position of honor or privilege

de•frost \di-ˈfrȯst, ˈdē-ˌ\ *vt* (1895) **1 :** to release from a frozen state ⟨~ meat⟩ **2 :** to free from ice ⟨~ the refrigerator⟩; *also* **:** DEFOG ⟨~ the windshield⟩ ~ *vi* **:** to thaw out esp. from a deep-frozen state — **de•frost•er** *n*

deft \ˈdeft\ *adj* [ME *defte* gentle — more at DAFT] (15c) **:** characterized by facility and skill *syn* see DEXTEROUS — **deft•ly** *adv* — **deft•ness** \ˈdef(t)-nəs\ *n*

de•funct \di-ˈfəŋkt, dē-\ *adj* [L *defunctus,* fr. pp. of *defungi* to finish, die, fr. *de-* + *fungi* to perform — more at FUNCTION] (1599) **:** no longer living, existing, or functioning ⟨the committee is now ~⟩ *syn* see DEAD

de•fund \(ˌ)dē-ˈfənd\ *vt* (1948) **:** to withdraw funding from

de•fuse \(ˌ)dē-ˈfyüz\ *vt* (1943) **1 :** to remove the fuse from (as a mine or bomb) **2 :** to make less harmful, potent, or tense ⟨~ the crisis⟩

¹de•fy \di-ˈfī, dē-\ *vt* **de•fied; de•fy•ing** [ME, to renounce faith in, challenge, fr. AF *desfier, defier,* fr. *des-* de- + *fier* to entrust, fr. VL **fidare,* alter. of L *fidere* to trust — more at BIDE] (14c) **1** *archaic* **:** to challenge to combat **2 :** to challenge to do something considered impossible : DARE **3 :** to confront with assured power of resistance : DISREGARD ⟨~ public opinion⟩ **4 :** to resist attempts at : WITHSTAND ⟨the paintings ~ classification⟩

²de•fy \di-ˈfī, ˈdē-ˌ\ *n, pl* **defies** (1580) **:** CHALLENGE, DEFIANCE

deg *abbr* degree

dé•ga•gé \ˌdā-ˌgä-ˈzhā\ *adj* [F, fr. pp. of *dégager* to put at ease, fr. OF *desgagier* to redeem a pledge, free, fr. *des-* de- + *gage* pledge — more at GAGE] (1696) **1 :** free of constraint : NONCHALANT **2 :** being free and easy ⟨clothes with a ~ look⟩ **3 :** extended with toe pointed in preparation for a ballet step

de•gas \(ˌ)dē-ˈgas\ *vt* (1928) **:** to remove gas from ⟨~ an electron tube⟩

de Gaull•ism \di-ˈgō-ˌli-zəm, -ˈgȯ-\ *n* (1943) **:** GAULLISM — **de Gaull•ist** \-ləst\ *n*

de•gauss \(ˌ)dē-ˈgau̇s\ *vt* [*de-* + *gauss,* after Karl F. *Gauss*] (ca. 1940) **:** to remove or neutralize the magnetic field of ⟨~ a ship⟩ ⟨~ a magnetic tape⟩ — **de•gauss•er** *n*

de•gen•er•a•cy \di-ˈjen-rə-sē, -ˈje-nə-, dē-\ *n, pl* **-cies** (1664) **1 :** the state of being degenerate **2 :** the process of becoming degenerate **3 :** sexual perversion **4 :** the coding of an amino acid by more than one codon

¹de•gen•er•ate \di-ˈjen-rət, -ˈje-nə-, dē-\ *adj* [ME *degenerat,* fr. L *degeneratus,* pp. of *degenerare* to degenerate, fr. *de-* + *gener-, genus* race, kind — more at KIN] (15c) **1 a :** having declined or become less specialized [illegible] character, structure, or function) from an ancestral or [illegible] having sunk to a condition below that which is normal [illegible] having sunk to a lower and usu. corrupt and vicious state **c :** DEGRADED 2 **2 :** being mathematically simpler (as by having a factor or constant equal to zero) than the typical case ⟨a ~ hyperbola⟩ **3 :** characterized by atoms stripped of their electrons and by very great density ⟨~ matter⟩; *also* **:** consisting of degenerate matter ⟨a ~ star⟩ **4 :** having two or more states or subdivisions ⟨~ energy level⟩ **5 :** having more than one codon representing an amino acid; *also* **:** being such a codon *syn* see VICIOUS — **de•gen•er•ate•ly** *adv* — **de•gen•er•ate•ness** *n*

²de•gen•er•ate \di-ˈje-nə-ˌrāt, dē-\ *vi* (1545) **1 :** to pass from a higher to a lower type or condition : DETERIORATE **2 :** to sink into a low intel-

\ə\ abut \ᵊ\ kitten, F table \ər\ further \a\ ash \ā\ ace \ä\ mop, mar \au̇\ out \ch\ chin \e\ bet \ē\ easy \g\ go \i\ hit \ī\ ice \j\ job \ŋ\ sing \ō\ go \ȯ\ law \ȯi\ boy \th\ thin \t͟h\ the \ü\ loot \u̇\ foot \y\ yet \zh\ vision, beige \k, ⁿ, œ, ue, ʸ\ *see* Guide to Pronunciation

def·i·ni·tion (dĕf′ə-nĭsh′ən) *n. Abbr.* **def. 1.** The act of stating a precise meaning or significance, as of a word, phrase, or term. **2.** The statement of the meaning of a word, phrase, or term. **3.** The act of making clear and distinct: *a definition of one's intentions.* **4.** The state of being closely outlined or determined: *"A way of liberation can have no positive definition."* (Alan W. Watts). **5.** A determining of outline, extent, or limits: *the definition of a nation's authority.* **6.** *Telecommunications.* The degree of clarity with which a televised image is received or a radio receives a given station. **7.** *Optics.* The clarity of detail in an optically produced image, as in a photograph, produced by a combination of resolution and contrast. [Middle English *difinicioun*, from Old French *definition*, from Latin *dēfīnītiō*, from *dēfīnīre*, DEFINE.] —**def′i·ni′tion·al** *adj.*

"The act of stating a precise meaning or significance." "The statement of the meaning of a word." We rely on **definition** for successful, efficient communication; not only do we need to know what others mean when they speak or write to us, but we also want them to know exactly what we mean. When words have more than one meaning, we need to make sure that the intended meaning is clear. When a word or term may be unfamiliar to our audience, we need to take the time to define it. But definition is especially important when we use words that signify controversial or contested ideas. Terms such as *fairness, democracy, education,* and *human rights* have many different meanings to different people. Whenever we use such terms, we need to let listeners and readers know exactly how we are using them.

Looking at Your Own Literacy How do you define *literacy*? How can you measure it? How might your definition differ from that of your classmates?

What Is Definition?

The word *definition* implies a dictionary, a book filled with the specific meanings of particular words — like the *Merriam-Webster's Collegiate Dictionary,* where the definition on the previous page appears. But every day we need to know the meanings of words and the boundaries and relationships between one word and another; in other words, we define words constantly to ourselves and to others. If your instructor tells you that you write with *ingenuity,* you may wonder what that word means, exactly, and whether it is positive or negative. *Ingenuity,* with its "in" prefix, might have a negative sense — or does it? The *Merriam-Webster's Collegiate Dictionary* gives the following definitions of *ingenuity*:

> **in·ge·nu·i·ty** (ĭn′jə-nōō′ə-tē, -nyōō′ə-tē) *n., pl.* **-ties. 1.** Inventive skill or imagination; cleverness. **2.** The state of being ingeniously contrived. **3.** *Usually plural.* An ingenious or imaginative device. **4.** *Archaic.* Ingenuousness. [Latin *ingenuitās,* frankness, innocence (but influenced in meaning by INGENIOUS), from *ingenuus,* INGENUOUS.]

From this definition, with its use of **synonyms** (words that mean the same or nearly the same thing), you can tell that your instructor probably thinks your writing is skillful, imaginative, and clever — nothing negative. But you might also have picked up clues to your instructor's meaning from the way she spoke to you or the other comments written on your paper. If she says, "You write like an angel," she's using an **analogy** (a direct comparison between unlike things) to define your writing style.

Successful communication between instructors and students—or between friends, colleagues, or family members—is based on shared definitions of words. Even though we know that language naturally evolves and that the meanings of words change over time, as the *Oxford English Dictionary* (OED) so carefully demonstrates, the definition of words must be fairly stable or communication will break down. Unlike Humpty Dumpty, we can't have words mean whatever we want them to mean:

> "But 'glory' doesn't mean 'a nice knockdown argument,'" Alice objected.
> "When I use a word," Humpty Dumpty said, in rather a scornful tone, "it means just what I choose it to mean—neither more nor less."
> "The question is," said Alice, "whether you *can* make words mean so many different things." —LEWIS CARROLL, *Through the Looking Glass*

We *can* make words mean different things—but only if our **language community,** the people with whom we speak most frequently, agrees to share the meaning with us. Words mean what our community agrees that they mean; words enter our common vocabulary or acquire new meanings when the members of our community begin to use a new word or to use a word in a new way. Therefore we quickly catch on

"Instead of 'It sucks' you could say, 'It doesn't speak to me.'"

when we need to learn new words such as *netiquette, e-mail,* and *digerati* or when words such as *cool* and *bad* acquire new meanings. But we have trouble communicating when the way *we* define a word is markedly different from the way others in our community define it.

Thinking about Definition

1. Look over the cartoon on p. 574. How does the phrase "It sucks" differ from "It doesn't speak to me"? Would you define the two phrases the same way?
2. How does each phrase relate to the person who said it? What would be the effect of the woman saying "It sucks" or the boy saying "It doesn't speak to me?" Are these two people part of the same language community?

Why Use Definition?

Whether you are informing or arguing a point—the two general purposes of definition—definition is a powerful means of developing your ideas. First, when you define your terms, you immediately connect with your audience by clarifying for them exactly what you are—and are not—talking about. Second, by defining your terms, you filter out related ideas that you don't have the time or inclination to go into; instead, you focus on the concept or issue at hand. For instance, if you are talking with a sales clerk about buying a new coat, he or she will probably ask you to define the type of coat you need. Do you need a coat for winter or for cool summer nights? Do you need a rain–resistant coat or a warm coat? Do you need a long coat for walking to class or a shorter one for riding your bike? Definition can help you describe your needs or persuade yourself about them. It can also help you explain or understand an idea or a problem, compare and contrast, make choices, exemplify, or classify. ("I need a coat, but do I need a trench coat, a slicker, a parka, or a denim jacket? How badly do I need a coat?")

Every day we hear, read, and write definitions that are part of descriptions, arguments, comparisons and contrasts, and examples. Whether you are defining the concept of "good buy" when you're shopping for a new car, defining the perfect potential partner to a friend, defining the kind of apartment you need as you look through the real estate section of the local newspaper, or responding to a question that asks you "to define" on an essay exam, you are purposefully including—and excluding—information.

Most newspapers carry personal ads that define—by describing—the people who place the ads or their ideal potential partners. When you read these ads, you can usually tell who is included and excluded from the ad and what specific characteristics are sought—or rejected:

SWM, 25, 6'2", 190 lbs., blue eyes, enjoys horseback riding, hunting, housework, hiking, wishes to meet a slim, sassy, savvy, sentimental SWF 24–35, for friendship and fun.

SBF, 23, 5'4", smoker, student, enjoys playing tennis, poetry, the park, seeking medium-build SM, 21+.

Quiet and shy SWM, 20, 5'7", brown hair, blue eyes, smoker, employed, likes hiking, going out, seeking employed, slim SWM, 18–25.

By defining themselves or their ideal partner in terms of descriptive qualities — age, race, interests, goals, and sexual orientations and preferences — the people who place these ads are providing the information that they think (or hope) will yield a fruitful response.

Try Your Hand If you were looking for an ideal partner, how might you define yourself in a personal ad? How would you describe the person you were seeking?

Definitions also help us to learn about or explain situations, processes, and choices. If you are buying a house, you might ask your real estate agent to explain the roles of the various real estate and town professionals you need to deal with. The agent might give you a list that looks like this:

Appraiser An appraiser determines the fair market value of your property. Considering factors such as size, condition, and location, the appraiser compares your property with others in the area that have been sold in the past year and then establishes a competitive price. The buyer usually pays for this service, as most lenders require it for approval of a mortgage loan.

Attorney An attorney who specializes in real estate can assist you by reviewing aspects of the transaction and providing legal advice. If you want to hire an attorney, do so before you sign the real estate contracts.

Building Inspector Employed by the local government, a building inspector surveys new construction and remodeling to ensure that it meets basic requirements.

Home Inspector A home inspector assesses the quality of the property. By conducting a thorough examination, the inspector determines if the home's major systems are in good condition and if it is structurally sound. The buyer usually arranges and pays for this.

Settlement Agent Also known as an escrow agent, a settlement agent handles the paperwork of the transaction including the research to ensure the trouble–free transfer of the property's title. Both the seller and the buyer will pay the agent a fee.

This explanation of real estate and town professionals enables you to match their services to your needs by defining what each professional does. The list of definitions also compares and contrasts the services provided by each one.

> **Try Your Hand**   Consider a service that you use (a medical or dental office, a veterinarian's practice, or a school), and make a list of the people who work there. Define the responsibilities of each one.

Some definitions resonate with comparisons. *Love*, for instance, is a word with many definitions, each appropriate for a particular situation. If you were to ask a married couple why they married, for instance, they would probably say they were "in love." But what exactly is that feeling? As Henry A. Bowman and Graham B. Spanier point out, we use the term *love* in many ways, and without a great deal of precision. You might use the term in all the following ways: "I love my parents," "I love my partner," "I love God," "I love my country," "I love animals," "I love ice cream." But you don't love your mother in the same way you love ice cream. Nor do you have the same emotional experience with your country that you do with your partner.

Many of you may want to define *love* for one of your writing assignments. But to do so well, you'll need to compare situations and contexts for love. According to Bowman and Spanier, *love* has different meanings depending on the following factors:

- The background or experience of the person involved
- The nature of the love object (mother, partner, activity, object)
- The period in the individual's life
- The intensity of the individual's attraction to the love object
- The importance the individual places on being in love
  —HENRY A. BOWMAN AND GRAHAM B. SPANIER, *Modern Marriage*

If you compare these situations and contexts to find the definitions of *love*, you can use a specific definition that applies to a particular relationship or object.

> **Try Your Hand**   Jot down a list of five or more people whom you love, note your relationship to each of them, and list the ways you love them. For each person, write a sentence that defines the love you feel toward him or her.

Besides explaining and comparing, definitions like those of the different real estate professionals also exemplify when they include examples for a class or category. The following definition of vestigial organs from a zoology textbook uses exemplification:

> Structures seemingly without use and of reduced size are termed **vestigial organs.** They were at one time functional and necessary but appear to be in the process of disappearing. . . . The horse, rodents, and some other mammals have a large caecum or appendix as an accessory digestive chamber. In humans the appendix is a slender vestige about 6.5 cm long that seems to have little function and sometimes is a site of infection requiring surgical removal. The external ears of mammals are moved by special muscles; in humans, lacking need for such movement, the muscles are usually reduced and nonfunctional. In the inner angle of the human eye is a pinkish membrane . . . representing the transparent nictitating membrane, or third eyelid, to be seen in the cat, bird, frog, and other land vertebrates. The human "wisdom teeth," or posterior molars, are often smaller and more variable than the other molars and irregular as to time or manner of eruption; this suggests that they are becoming useless and may eventually disappear. A word of caution is necessary. An organ classed as vestigial and nonfunctional may, in fact, have an unknown, reduced, or changed function. The term, therefore, should be applied with reservation.
>
> —Tracy Storer, Robert Usinger, et al., *General Zoology*

Try Your Hand   Think of a technical term from your major or another course that you can define best by exemplifying. Compare your definition with that of a classmate to see if you both have made your meanings clear.

Definitions are a perfect way to classify, and classifying is a useful way to define a word. In the study of rhetoric, examples of persuasive language are classified into three categories: (1) legislators and other politicians use *deliberative rhetoric* to decide on the best course for the future, focusing on issues of expediency and inexpediency; (2) lawyers and judges use *judicial rhetoric* to make decisions about the past, focusing on issues of justice and injustice; and (3) speech writers and religious leaders use *epideictic rhetoric* to express their sense of the present occasion at a ceremony or memorial, focusing on issues of honor or dishonor. We can use these three kinds of rhetoric to classify any rhetorical event. Which kind of rhetoric is the president's annual State of the Union address? a knighting ceremony conducted by Great Britain's Queen Elizabeth? the indictment of Martha Stewart for violations of securities laws?

Try Your Hand   Provide one or more examples of each of the categories of rhetoric.

How Does Definition Work?

Usually you'll develop a definition in two steps. First you'll **classify** the term by placing it in a broader category. Then you'll **differentiate** it from other terms in the same category by stating its distinguishing characteristics.

Term	*Class*	*Differentiation*
Evolution	is a process	in which something changes into a significantly different form, especially one that is more complex or sophisticated.
Adolescence	is a process	of growth between childhood and maturity.
A beauty makeover	is a process	of aesthetic and cosmetic improvement.

For instance, if a question on an essay exam asks you to define *evolution*, you might start by classifying the term as a process. But then you'll need to differentiate *evolution* from other processes (*maturation; mitosis; revolution*) by focusing on evolution's distinguishing characteristics: "a process in which something changes into a significantly different form, especially one that is more complex or sophisticated." That **sentence definition** describes *evolution*, but it could also describe *adolescence* or even *beauty makeover*. To define this concept adequately, you need to develop an **extended definition** by introducing additional differentiating features:

> Evolution is a gradual process in which something changes into a significantly different form, especially one that is more complex or sophisticated. In biology, evolution is the theory that groups of organisms, such as species, may change with the passage of time so that descendants differ morphologically and physiologically from their ancestors.

You may also find yourself writing a **historical definition,** which is an extended definition that traces the different meanings a word has had over time. A historical definition shows when, where, and why the term was established and how it has been used. The *Oxford English Dictionary* (OED) is a reliable source of information about the history of words. The OED provides a long list of various definitions of *evolution*, including the relatively recent biological meanings that appear after five older meanings:

Evolution (evoliu· ʃən) . . .

6. *Biol.* **a.** Of animal and vegetable organisms or their parts: The process of developing from a rudimentary to a mature or complete state.

   1670 *Phil. Trans.* V 207[8] By the word Change [in Insects] is nothing else to be understood but a gradual and natural Evolution and Growth of the parts. **1745** NEEDHAM *Microsc. Disc.* Intro. I Nature . . ever exerting its Fecundity in a successive Evolution of organized Bodies. **1791** E. Darwin. *Bot. Gar.* II. 8 *note*, The gradual evolution of the young animal or plant from its egg or seed. **1801** *Med. Jrnl.* V. 588 A series of experiments on the evolution of the Chick. **1805** *Ibid.* XIV. 336 The formation and evolution of this part of the brain. **1859** JOHNSTON in *Proc. Berw. Nat. Club* I. 201 Masses of eggs, in different stages of their evolution, are met with in the same nest.

   b. *Theory of Evolution:* the hypothesis (first propounded under that name by Bonnet 1762) that the embryo or germ, instead of being brought into existence by the process of fecundation, is a development or expansion of a pre–existing form, which contains the rudiments of all the parts of the future organism. Also called 'the theory of Preformation'; the latter name is now preferred to avoid confusion with the following sense.

   1831 [see Epigensis]. **1877** HUXLEY *Encycl. Brit.* VIII. 745.

   c. The origination of species of animals and plants, as conceived by those who attribute it to a process of development from earlier forms, and not to a process of 'special creation'. Often in phrases *Doctrine, Theory of Evolution.*

   1832 PRINC. GEOL. II. II The testacea of the ocean existed first, until some of them by gradual evolution, were improved into those inhabiting land.

   1852 DARWIN *Orig. Spec.* vii (1873) 201 At the present day almost all naturalists admit evolution under some form. **1863** E. V. NEALE *Anal. Th. & Nat.* 185 The diversity of species has arisen by the evolution of one species out of another. **1881** SIR J. HOOKER in *Nature* No. 619. 446 The doctrine of the orderly evolution of species under known law.

Beginning in 1670, writers used the word *evolution* in a biological sense, and the meaning itself has evolved further since that time.

   Sometimes you'll need to write a **negative definition,** telling your readers not only what your word or term means but also what it does not mean. When someone says to you, "Success is not all it's cracked up to be," she is using a negative definition. *Success* does not mean many of the things you might think it means: an interesting job, prestige, money, leisure, connections. The speaker's own success might bring her plenty of money, but at the cost of too much work, responsibility, and worry; too many hours spent in hotels, airports, and restaurants; and incredible loneliness. A negative definition starts out by limiting the term to what it is not. A Lands' End catalogue offers such a definition: "Blazer Shirts are sized like dress shirts, but made in familiar, casual fabrics like twill and denim. You'll never struggle with too–short sleeves, never strangle or swim in the wrong size collar.... Blazer Shirts are a complete package, with both the fit and the tailoring of a fine dress shirt." The Lands' End copywriters make this negative definition work positively for them: as they distinguish their shirts from other shirts that are in the same class, they are making comparisons, always to the advantage of their own product.

Finally, in some situations you might need to write a **stipulative definition,** one in which you limit—or stipulate—the scope of your discussion by telling your readers how you'll be using a term. In some important ways a stipulative definition is both a sentence definition and a negative one. For example, in an article on Asian Americans in *Y* magazine, the editor–in–chief argues that "What does it mean to be Asian American?" is the most overused question in the Asian community, so she stipulates what she means when she uses the term *Asian American:* it's being "real to oneself." She writes that she's familiar with other ways the term is used: to describe a person's physical features; an inherited or a practiced culture of language, food, and religious customs; or "the pretentious attitude of those who consider themselves culturally superior while at the same time shunning their Asian traditions." But she can "do without" all those definitions, most of which carry an "undertoned social correctness," because she wants to concentrate on "being true to who you are."

The different kinds of definition all offer useful ways of thinking and writing about a given topic. Some definitions, like the ones you have already read in this chapter, are relatively short; they provide a quick idea of the boundaries of an individual concept, process, or object. These short definitions are the kind you'll often be expected to supply in your writing, especially when your audience is not as familiar with the subject as you are. If you're writing about funk music, for example, your instructor may not know what it is unless you insert a brief definition—or two: "FUNK MUSIC, *which has an identifiable beat and rhythm in the bass lines and chorus chants,* celebrates FUNK itself, *the life force in all its sweaty carnality.*"

But other definitions can be much longer and more detailed. Essays, chapters, entire books have been dedicated to defining one term or concept: *Modern Marriage; Heroines; Saints; Composition in the Twenty-first Century; Eloquence in an Electronic Age;* and *Chaucer's Danté.* Your instructors will certainly not ask you to write book–length definitions, but they will want you to develop paragraphs and essays that use definition to inform and persuade.

How Do You Read a Definition?

To learn how to write definitions that are clear and effective for their particular purpose and audience, it helps to learn how to read definitions critically, to analyze and evaluate ones that you encounter. If you develop the habit of looking closely at the definitions you read, you'll learn to pose the kinds of questions that will help you write your own. For example, does the definition clearly distinguish what's being defined from things that are similar to it? Will the intended readers understand the difference? Does the definition apply under all circumstances, or only at certain times or in certain places? Is it a definition that virtually everyone would agree on, or does it have an argumentative edge—and, if so, how convincing will it be to the intended audience? How is the definition organized and developed?

Look back at the definition *vestigial organs* on p. 578. Notice that it opens with a brief sentence definition giving the classification of these organs ("Structures") and the two essential characteristics that differentiate these organs from others ("seemingly without use and of reduced size"). The second sentence extends this definition by putting these characteristics in an evolutionary context: vestigial organs, now useless and small, were once useful and larger. Next, the definition is developed by exemplification, four examples of organs that are apparently vestigial in humans—the appendix, external ear muscles, nictitating membrane, and wisdom teeth—and that in some cases are compared with their functional counterparts in other animals. The definition ends with a stipulation, a "word of caution" against applying the term too broadly to organs that may in fact not possess the characteristic of "uselessness."

As you might expect of a definition that appears in a science textbook, this one is intended simply as informative; there is no disagreement among zoologists about how to define *vestigial organs*, although the writers do say that it's impossible to define particular organs as vestigial with absolute certainty. Notice also the language of this definition. In general, it's not difficult for the intended audience of college students to understand, but it's fairly formal and does include some terms that might confuse or puzzle readers. For example, in the first sentence it's not entirely clear what "of reduced size" refers to. Are vestigial human organs smaller than these organs used to be, smaller than comparable organs in other animals, or both? And what exactly does it mean that wisdom teeth are "often ... more variable than the other molars"? Asking questions like these will sharpen your ability to see both the strong and weak points in the definitions you read and thus to write your own definitions with more confidence and success.

One other point to think about as you read a definition critically is to consider not just what it says but also what it doesn't say—what it leaves out. Some definitions, especially those that are intended to make an argument, deliberately use terms in a biased way, without any stipulation by the writer that he or she is doing so. A reader who doesn't accept this definition will be unlikely to accept the argument that it's making. And even definitions that are intended to be neutral and objective may fail to take into account some meanings of a term. For example, the definition of the word *definition* that appears on p. 572 doesn't seem to include any meaning that covers the kind of "definition" you get from working out at a gym. Maybe this use of the word is too recent to have been reflected in a dictionary entry, or maybe those compiling the dictionary considered it too informal or temporary to include. When you write a definition, then, always try to think about whether your readers will be expecting a certain meaning and, if so, how you need to take their expectations into account.

How Do You Write Using Definition?

Whether you are writing a historical, negative, or stipulative definition, and whether it will be only a few sentences or paragraphs long or an entire essay, you will need to (1) consider your purpose and audience, and (2) decide on the details that will clarify the term for your readers. If you are writing an essay, you will also need to choose an effective organizational method for presenting details.

● Determining Your Purpose

Before you begin writing an extended definition or using a brief definition to develop your essay, consider your purpose. Do you want to inform your readers with an **objective definition,** which emphasizes the object itself and can be applied to various situations? Or do you want to persuade your readers to agree with your **subjective definition,** which emphasizes your own opinions and response and the way you want to define the term for this particular piece of writing? If you and students from other campuses are defining what it means to be *college educated,* then chances are your definitions will inform your readers, using classification and comparison. But if you are defining *college educated* for a lending or granting agency (whether it's your parents, a bank, a foundation, or a scholarship committee), then your definition will probably need to persuade your readers of the benefits of this education so that you will receive money.

● Considering Your Audience

As the previous example suggests, your purpose is often closely related to your audience. If you are writing your definition for a class, an instructor, or a supervisor, you will undoubtedly use different language and maybe even different examples and details from those you would use if you were writing a letter or an e-mail to a friend back home or across campus. When you consider audience, you need to think about what your readers may already know, or think they know, about your term or concept. You should also consider the tone you should take, the kinds of words you will use, and the information about the term or concept that you will include and exclude.

Considering What Kind of Definition to Use

Once you know the term or concept you are going to define, and why and for whom you are defining it, you will need to determine the kind of definition that will work best for your audience and purpose. Do you need to write only a sentence–length definition as part of a larger essay, or do you need to write an extended definition that shows readers a wide range of the subject at hand? If you need to chart the evolution of a word or idea, you may decide that a historical definition best suits your needs. If you need to define a term or concept in order to argue or explain your point, you may need to write a stipulative definition so that you can define how *you* will be using the word in your discussion. You may find that your definition merits further thought and study, so you may want to conduct research at the library or on the World Wide Web.

Considering Appropriate Examples and Details

In some ways, writing a definition can be easier than other kinds of writing for school or work; all you need to do is come up with the perfect examples and details (from your own experience and knowledge or from library or Web research) that will make the term or concept clear for your readers. For example, if you were defining *diabetes* for a general audience, you would first place the term in a class (physical disorders) and then provide the kind of information that distinguishes that disorder from other disorders in the class, as the following definition demonstrates:

> Diabetes is a disorder of the very engine of life, a subtle calamity at the molecular level. Its hallmark is a failure to metabolize glucose, the ubiquitous sugar molecule carried by the bloodstream to fuel every part of the body. Deprived of their prime energy supply, muscle and nerve cells slow their function, which is why early diabetes may manifest itself as lethargy and irritability. That was the experience of Maria DelMundo, 46, a Rochester, Minn., mother who weighed around 190 (she's 5 feet 2) when she stopped by her doctor's office for a checkup in 1991. "I just wasn't feeling good — tired and out of sorts, " she recalls; in effect, she was undernourished even while eating her fill of the "buttery icing and whipped cream, French pastries and Häagen-Dazs" she loves.
> —JERRY ADLER AND CLAUDIA KALB, "Diabetes: The Silent Killer"

This brief definition, excerpted from an extended–definition essay, shows how diabetes is a disease that deprives the body of energy by failing to metabolize glucose. As the writers continue, they extend the definition by including relevant details that describe the unique effects of the physical disorder called diabetes: "Deprived of their prime energy supply, muscle and nerve cells slow their function, which is why early diabetes may manifest itself as lethargy and irritability." Finally, the writers include a specific example of the disease in action: " 'I just wasn't feeling good—tired and out of sorts,'" Maria DelMundo recalls; "in effect, she was undernourished even while eating her fill of the 'buttery icing and whipped cream, French pastries and Häagen–Dazs' she loves."

Arranging All the Parts

There is no "right" way to organize a definition essay, but your organizational pattern should be linked to your purpose of either informing or persuading. Like all essays, a definition essay opens with an introduction that states (or implies) a thesis, moves into a well–developed body, and ends with a conclusion. To develop the body of your essay and fulfill either of the general purposes of informing or persuading, you might find yourself organizing information spatially or visually, chronologically, emphatically, or according to points of comparison. You can choose from a number of organizational patterns in order to define a term or concept. But regardless of the organizational pattern you choose, you'll need to establish your own definition for the term or concept and then support your definition by using examples, descriptions, comparison and contrast, narratives, or another method of development to expand the body of your essay.

If you are informing your audience about diabetes, you might want to provide an initial definition for the disease and then move into explaining its causes and consequences. For instance, in "Diabetes: The Silent Killer," Jerry Adler and Claudia Kalb explain the consequences of the disease:

> Something terrible was happening to Yolanda Benitez's eyes. They were being poisoned; the fragile capillaries of the retina attacked from within and were leaking blood. The first symptoms were red lines, appearing vertically across her field of vision; the lines multiplied and merged into a haze that shut out light entirely.

If the purpose of your definition essay is to argue that your diabetic audience should change their eating habits, then you may want to focus on talking about the preventive measures that can lessen the effects of the disease—as Adler and Kalb do:

> There's another surefire way [other than drugs] to control blood sugar and lessen the complications of diabetes; it calls for eating a healthy diet in the first place. A recurring theme in the conversations of diabetics is the foods they had to give up. Maria Menoza, a college janitor in Los

"Reading" and Using Visuals for Definition

When we think of a definition, we automatically think of using words to define something. But many definitions can be enhanced or need to be accompanied by a visual or visuals. For instance, guide–books for bird–watching or wildflower identification always include visuals, especially when they are differentiating a specific bird or flower from other members of its class. In the following visual, *wood–peckers* are defined as a genus verbally, and then three specific species of woodpecker are defined visually as well as in words.

Often only visuals can help you understand the differences among a class (or genus) of things, whether they're woodpeckers, flowers,

WOODPECKERS

Judy Loven, USDA-APHIS-Wildlife Services

IDENTIFICATION

There are 21 species of woodpeckers found in the United States, seven of which are present in Indiana. Year-round Indiana woodpeckers include the downy (63/4" in length), hairy (91/4"), red-headed (91/4"), red-bellied (91/4"), pileated (161/2") woodpeckers and the northern flicker (121/2"). The yellow-bellied sapsucker (73/4") is a resident of Indiana during the winter months.

Woodpeckers have short legs with two sharp-clawed toes forward and two backward-pointed toes. These toes, along with their stiff tail feathers, allow them to cling to trees, utility poles, or wood siding. Their strong, pointed beak is used for digging insects from trees, excavating nesting cavities, and for "drumming." Since woodpeckers do not have true "songs," they use sharp calls and perform rhythmic tapping (better known as drumming) with their beaks on surfaces such as dead tree limbs, metal poles, and building siding to attract a mate or announce their territorial boundaries. Both male and female woodpeckers drum. It is primarily this drumming behavior that may cause serious problems for homeowners.

The downy (Figure 1a) and the hairy (Figure 1b) woodpeckers cause the most damage in Indiana. Both are identified by their white backs and black and white striped wing feathers. The downy is sparrow-size and has a short bill. The hairy woodpecker is robin-size. The downy also has black and white bars on the outer tail feathers while the hairy has entirely white tail feathers. In both species, the male has a red spot on the back of the head.

Figure 1a.
**DOWNY
WOODPECKER**

Figure 1b.
**HAIRY
WOODPECKER**

Figure 1c.
**PILEATED
WOODPECKER**

paintings, buildings, cars, bicycles, or athletic shoes. We so depend on visuals to help us define and understand definitions that we may tend to take them for granted. To learn how to use visuals effectively for definition, though, it will help if you learn to "read" visual definitions closely and critically, the same way that you would read a definition in words, to see how well they succeed in expressing the meaning of a term for the writer's specific purpose and audience.

The woodpecker visual, for example, appeared on the Web site of the Department of Entomology at Purdue University, as one of a series of pages offering advice about how to deal with various animals that cause damage to homes, gardens, crops, and other things created or cultivated by humans. As the text suggests, the main intended audience for this advice are the residents of Indiana, where Purdue is a state university. The third paragraph of the text identifies the two species of woodpeckers that cause the most damage in Indiana, the downy and the hairy woodpeckers, and defines each one as it explains the similarities and differences between them in size, color pattern, and length of bill. The three images at the bottom of the page illustrate these two species as well as the pileated woodpecker, which is discussed on the next page of the Web site.

Notice how Figures 1a and 1b reflect the differences in size and in the shape of the bill that the text says differentiate the downy and hairy woodpeckers, as well as the white backs and striped wing feathers that make them alike. Placing the two drawings next to each other helps call attention to the differences and likenesses. But the two black-and-white figures don't (or can't) show the different coloration of the tail feathers or the similar red spots on the back of the head. In fact, the next page of the Web site advises that "[t]o accurately identify these and other woodpeckers, a field guide with color illustrations is recommended." When you use visuals as part of your own definitions, you will need to think about considerations like these—how large they need to be, whether they should be in color, whether to show what you're defining in relation to other things in the same category or classification—as you decide how best to achieve your purpose for your specific audience.

Remember that if you want to use visuals in writing for an academic assignment, it is a good idea to check with your instructor beforehand. You also need to consider whether to include labels or captions, like those in the woodpecker illustrations, if the visuals do not already include them, and whether to refer to the visuals in your written text or to let them stand on their own.

Angeles, cut down from "six or seven tortillas a day" to two, after she was diagnosed . . . and gave up "tacos, sweets, chocolates and *pan dulce* [sweet bread]. " "I can't eat what I want, and that makes me sad, " she says.

Regardless of your purpose in writing a definition, you can choose from a number of different methods of development and organization. Whatever method(s) you use, be sure to include clear transitions so that readers can follow your explanation or argument. You'll want your conclusion to move beyond your introduction, pushing forward the thinking of your readers, helping them decide what to do with the information you've provided.

Understanding and Using Definition

Analyzing Definition

1. Reread the personal ads on p. 576. How would you define *love* for each of the people who placed these ads? What are they looking for? What's their ideal partner like? Where are they now in their lives?

2. Reread the OED's historical definition of *evolution* on p. 580. What did you learn from the definition that you didn't know before? How has this word itself evolved? Which meanings are outdated?

3. As you read for school and other purposes this week, identify definitions used to inform and ones used to argue a point. You'll find definitions in sports, computer, and fashion magazines; in your school and local newspapers; and in the novels and textbooks you're reading. Classify the various kinds of definitions, and write out what you think the author wanted you as the reader to do with the information.

Planning and Writing Definitions

1. **Working with two or three classmates,** look carefully at the definitions of potential partners in the personal ads on p. 576. Rewrite one of those definitions in paragraph form, expanding on the telegraphic description that appeared in the newspaper to create an extended definition. Share your group response with the rest of the class.

2. Now rewrite your paragraph as a negative definition, one that defines not only who the right partner might be but, more important, who the right partner is not (who is excluded). Compare your original paragraphs and rewrites with the rest of the class.

3. If you were planning to buy a house, in what order would you use the services of the various real estate and town professionals listed on p. 576? Rewrite the explanatory list as a step–by–step process in which you define each step and each professional. Which professional seems most important to the real estate transaction? least important?

4. Take a few minutes to write your own definition of *love*, using your responses on p. 577 as a guide. After you've defined the term, take a few more minutes to consider your background or experience, the nature of your love object, the intensity of your feelings, and the importance of love in your life right now. Write out your responses to these factors, and then revise your definition of love accordingly.

5. A definition typically includes the class to which a term or concept belongs and the distinguishing characteristics that set it apart from other members of that class. **Working with two or three classmates,** select one or two of the following terms and briefly define them by determining their class and distinguishing characteristics. Try to be objective. As you develop your definition, think about the features of the term you want to explain for your readers:

   - education
   - love
   - family
   - middle age
   - responsibility
   - security
   - satisfaction
   - sin
   - character
   - loyalty
   - childhood
   - failure
   - success
   - happiness
   - bad words
   - another word or term of your choice

   Share your definitions with the rest of the class, and note your classmates' comments and suggestions. Then draft a two- to three–page essay defining one of your terms, using the guidelines for checking over the use of definition (p. 590). Ask a classmate to review your draft.

6. Choose one of the terms from the list in question 5 and write an extended, subjective definition essay, three to four pages long. Be sure to give your opinion on the meaning of the term, and try to persuade your reader to share that opinion. Use the guidelines for checking over the use of definition (p. 590), and **ask one or two classmates** to review your draft.

7. Building on your work for item 3 in "Analyzing Definition," **break into small groups** and compare your definitions and interpretations of those definitions with those of your classmates. Share with the rest of the class several definitions on which your group agrees or disagrees. Use the information you gleaned from this exercise as the basis for a two- to three–page comparison–and–contrast or classification–and–division essay on the ways writers use definition in writing intended for a mass audience. Refer to "Checking Over the Use of Definition" (p. 590).

8. Define yourself. But before you start, consider your audience. For whom do you want to define yourself? What part(s) of yourself do you want to define? What is your purpose in writing this definition? What character- istics will you definitely include — and exclude? Write a two- to three- page essay of self-definition. Refer to "Checking Over the Use of Defini- tion" below to decide how to revise your draft, and **ask one or two classmates** to give you feedback as well.

✓ Checking Over the Use of Definition

1. What is your purpose in writing this definition? Are you aiming to in- form or argue a point? What details did you include that helped make the definition objective or subjective? Label each detail objective (O) or subjective (S).

2. Who is your intended audience? How much do they know or think they know about the concept you're defining? What is their attitude toward it? Have you taken their knowledge and attitudes into account in writing the definition?

3. Which kind of definition are you using? Have you written a sentence definition or an extended definition? a historical definition, a negative definition, or a stipulative definition?

4. What words or phrases did you use to classify your term? to distinguish it from other terms in the same class? Underline them.

5. What is the thesis statement of your definition? Have you drawn clear boundaries around your term or concept? What exactly are you includ- ing in and excluding from your definition?

6. How do your details and examples support your definition? What meth- ods — description, comparison, classification, process analysis — did you use to develop and illustrate it? Do they help make your definition vivid and clear for your readers?

7. Did you consult any sources in writing your definition? If not, do you need to?

8. What organizational plan did you follow? Is it chronological, spatial, em- phatic, or something else? Does it seem to work effectively? Did you pro- vide clear transitions to help readers move from one part of your essay to the next?

9. What specific point does your conclusion make? How does it extend your thesis?

10. If you've used visuals, how do they enhance your definition and help to fulfill your purpose? Do you need to add labels, captions, or references to the visuals in the text? If you haven't used visuals, should you?

READINGS

JUDY BRADY
Why I Want a Wife

Judy Brady (b. 1937) earned a bachelor of fine arts degree from the University of Iowa and has published many articles and edited two books, *Women and Cancer* (1990) and *One in Three: Women with Cancer Confront an Epidemic* (1991). "Why I Want a Wife" first appeared in 1970 in *Motherload*, a feminist magazine, and reappeared in the premier issue of *Ms.* in 1972. Since then, this essay has been reprinted regularly in textbooks and anthologies. As you read it, notice how Brady uses irony as she extends and develops her definition of a wife.

Preview   How do you define *wife*? How do you define *husband? partner?*

I belong to that classification of people known as wives. I am A Wife. 1 And, not altogether incidentally, I am a mother.

Not too long ago a male friend of mine appeared on the scene fresh 2 from a recent divorce. He had one child, who is, of course, with his ex-wife. He is looking for another wife. As I thought about him while I was ironing one evening, it suddenly occurred to me that I, too, would like to have a wife. Why do I want a wife?

I would like to go back to school so that I can become economically 3 independent, support myself, and if need be, support those dependent upon me. I want a wife who will work and send me to school. And while I am going to school I want a wife to take care of my children. I want a wife to keep track of the children's doctor and dentist appointments. And to keep track of mine, too. I want a wife to make sure my children eat properly and are kept clean. I want a wife who will wash the children's clothes and keep them mended. I want a wife who is a good nurturant attendant to my children, who arranges for their schooling, makes sure that they have an adequate social life with their peers, takes them to the park, the zoo, etc. I want a wife who takes care of the children when they are sick, a wife who arranges to be around when the children need special care, because, of course, I cannot miss classes at school. My wife must arrange to lose time at work and not lose the job. It may mean a small cut in my wife's income from time to time, but I guess I can tolerate that. Needless to say, my wife will arrange and pay for the care of the children while my wife is working.

I want a wife who will take care of *my* physical needs. I want a wife   4
who will keep my house clean. A wife who will pick up after my children, a wife who will pick up after me. I want a wife who will keep my clothes clean, ironed, mended, replaced when need be, and who will see to it that my personal things are kept in their proper place so that I can find what I need the minute I need it. I want a wife who cooks the meals, a wife who is a *good* cook. I want a wife who will plan the menus, do the necessary grocery shopping, prepare the meals, serve them pleasantly, and then do the cleaning up while I do my studying. I want a wife who will care for me when I am sick and sympathize with my pain and loss of time from school. I want a wife to go along when our family takes a vacation so that someone can continue to care for me and my children when I need a rest and change of scene.

I want a wife who will not bother me with rambling complaints   5
about a wife's duties. But I want a wife who will listen to me when I feel the need to explain a rather difficult point I have come across in my course of studies. And I want a wife who will type my papers for me when I have written them.

I want a wife who will take care of the details of my social life. When   6
my wife and I are invited out by my friends, I want a wife who will take care of the babysitting arrangements. When I meet people at school that I like and want to entertain, I want a wife who will have the house clean, will prepare a special meal, serve it to me and my friends, and not interrupt when I talk about things that interest me and my friends. I want a wife who will have arranged that the children are fed and ready for bed before my guests arrive so that the children do not bother us. I want a wife who takes care of the needs of my guests so that they feel comfortable, who makes sure that they have an ashtray, that they are passed the hors d'oeuvres, that they are offered a second helping of the food, that their wine glasses are replenished when necessary, that their coffee is served to them as they like it. And I want a wife who knows that sometimes I need a night out by myself.

I want a wife who is sensitive to my sexual needs, a wife who makes   7
love passionately and eagerly when I feel like it, a wife who makes sure that I am satisfied. And, of course, I want a wife who will not demand sexual attention when I am not in the mood for it. I want a wife who assumes the complete responsibility for birth control, because I do not want more children. I want a wife who will remain sexually faithful to me so that I do not have to clutter up my intellectual life with jealousies. And I want a wife who understands that *my* sexual needs may entail

more than strict adherence to monogamy. I must, after all, be able to relate to people as fully as possible.

If, by chance, I find another person more suitable as a wife than the   8
wife I already have, I want the liberty to replace my present wife with
another one. Naturally, I will expect a fresh, new life; my wife will take
the children and be solely responsible for them so that I am left free.

When I am through with school and have a job, I want my wife to   9
quit working and remain at home so that my wife can more fully and
completely take care of a wife's duties.

My God, who *wouldn't* want a wife?   10

Reading Closely

1. In one sentence, define Brady's concept of *wife*. **Working with two or
   three classmates,** compare your definitions. How are they similar? dis-
   similar?

2. How does Brady also define the duties of the *mother* in the house? How are the duties of the wife and mother related?

3. Does the scene from the TV program *Everyone Loves Raymond* on p. 593 support Brady's definitions, or does it suggest that expectations for wives have changed since 1970, when her article was written? What details from the scene support your answer?

Considering Larger Issues

1. Reread the headnote on p. 591 to review the publication history of this essay. How does knowing that history help you establish the purpose and audience?

2. How does Brady develop her extended definition of *wife*? What distinguishing characteristics does she describe? What details, examples, or anecdotes does she use to bring these characteristics to life? Mark them in the text. Prepare to compare your responses and findings with the rest of the class.

3. **COMBINING METHODS.**   How does Brady use *comparison and contrast* to enrich her definition of *wife*? Specifically, what are the points of comparison between *husband* and *wife*? What is the effect of this comparison on her overall essay?

Thinking about Language

1. Using the context and your dictionary, define the following words. Be prepared to share your answers with the rest of the class.

   incidentally (1)   rambling (5)   entail (7)
   nurturant (3)   replenished (6)

2. Underline every use of the phrase *I want a wife*. How many times does Brady use that phrase in this relatively short essay? What is the effect of her refrain?

3. When writers use irony, they mean the opposite of what their words say. An author using irony often understates or exaggerates information in order to make a point. **Working with two or three classmates,** identify places in the essay where Brady understates or exaggerates. Prepare to present your group's findings to the rest of the class.

Writing Your Own Definitions

1. Write an essay *of no more than two pages* defining a type of person you encounter at school: professor, teaching assistant, secretary, cafeteria worker, janitor, and so on. You may draw on Brady's essay for examples of tone (irony) and supporting details (real–life examples), but embellish her style if you can, with ideas of your own, from your own experiences

and observations. Refer to "Checking Over the Use of Definition" on p. 590.

2. Prepare to write an essay that defines a word referring to a family member: *wife, husband, daughter, son, in-law, grandparent,* and so on. First jot down all the features of that role you can think of. Then list the three kinds of extended definitions: historical, negative, stipulative. For each type of definition, which of your details could you use? Match the details with the type of definition. For which type have you come up with the most details? Which kind of definition, then, are you prepared to write? What might your thesis statement be?

   Look over the details that you have gathered. How do those details define your conception of that role? **Consider working with one or two classmates** to determine how your definitions differ or overlap and how your own definition is unique. Will you arrange your information by describing, explaining, classifying, or comparing? As you draft and revise your two- to three-page essay, refer to the guidelines for checking over the use of definition on p. 590.

PAUL THEROUX

Being a Man

● Paul Theroux (b. 1941) was born and raised in Massachusetts and then left for Italy after his 1963 graduation from the University of Massachusetts at Amherst. For the next few years he taught English at the University of Urbino and then at Soche Hille College in Malawi. Later he joined the faculty at the University of Singapore, where he began establishing his reputation as an American novelist and travel writer. His numerous books include *Waldo* (1966), *The Great Railway Bazaar* (1975), *The Mosquito Coast* (1982), *Millroy the Magician* (1993), *Fresh Air Fiend* (2000), *Hotel Honolulu* (2001), *Dark Star Safari* (2003), and *The Stranger at the Palazzo d'Oro* (2004). The following essay, written in 1983, first appeared in his *Sunrise with Seamonsters* (1985).

> **Preview** What reasons might cause someone to feel the need to write an essay on being a man? What could possibly be complicated about being a man?

There is a pathetic sentence in the chapter "Fetishism" in Dr. Norman 1
Cameron's book *Personality Development and Psychopathology*. It goes, "Fetishists are nearly always men; and their commonest fetish is a woman's shoe." I cannot read that sentence without thinking that it is just one more awful thing about being a man — and perhaps it is an important thing to know about us.

I have always disliked being a man. The whole idea of manhood in 2
America is pitiful, in my opinion. This version of masculinity is a little like having to wear an ill-fitting coat for one's entire life (by contrast, I imagine femininity to be an oppressive sense of nakedness). Even the expression "Be a man!" strikes me as insulting and abusive. It means: Be stupid, be unfeeling, obedient, soldierly and stop thinking. Man means "manly" — how can one think about men without considering the terrible ambition of manliness? And yet it is part of every man's life. It is a hideous and crippling lie; it not only insists on difference and connives at superiority, it is also by its very nature destructive — emotionally damaging and socially harmful.

The youth who is subverted, as most are, into believing in the mas- 3
culine ideal is effectively separated from women and he spends the rest of his life finding women a riddle and a nuisance. Of course, there is a female version of this male affliction. It begins with mothers encouraging little girls to say (to other adults) "Do you like my new dress?" In a sense, little girls are traditionally urged to please adults with a kind of coquettishness, while boys are enjoined to behave like monkeys towards each other. The nine-year-old coquette proceeds to become womanish in a subtle power game in which she learns to be sexually indispensable, socially decorative and always alert to a man's sense of inadequacy.

Femininity—being lady-like—implies needing a man as witness and 4
seducer; but masculinity celebrates the exclusive company of men. That is
why it is so grotesque; and that is also why there is no manliness without
inadequacy—because it denies men the natural friendship of women.

It is very hard to imagine any concept of manliness that does not be- 5
little women, and it begins very early. At an age when I wanted to meet
girls—let's say the treacherous years of thirteen to sixteen—I was told to
take up a sport, get more fresh air, join the Boy Scouts, and I was urged
not to read so much. It was the 1950s and if you asked too many questions about sex you were sent to camp—boy's camp, of course: the
nightmare. Nothing is more unnatural or prison-like than a boy's camp,
but if it were not for them we would have no Elks' Lodges, no pool
rooms, no boxing matches, no Marines.

And perhaps no sports as we know them. Everyone is aware of how few 6
in number are the athletes who behave like gentlemen. Just as high school
basketball teaches you how to be a poor loser, the manly attitude towards
sports seems to be little more than a recipe for creating bad marriages, social misfits, moral degenerates, sadists, latent rapists and just plain louts. I
regard high school sports as a drug far worse than marijuana, and it is the
reason that the average tennis champion, say, is a pathetic oaf.

Any objective study would find the quest for manliness essentially 7
right-wing, puritanical, cowardly, neurotic and fueled largely by a fear of
women. It is also certainly philistine. There is no book-hater like a Little
League coach. But indeed all the creative arts are obnoxious to the manly
ideal, because at their best the arts are pursued by uncompetitive and
essentially solitary people. It makes it very hard for a creative youngster,
for any boy who expresses the desire to be alone seems to be saying that
there is something wrong with him.

It ought to be clear by now that I have something of an objection to 8
the way we turn boys into men. It does not surprise me that when the
President of the United States has his customary weekend off he dresses
like a cowboy—it is both a measure of his insecurity and his willingness
to please. In many ways, American culture does little more for a man
than prepare him for modeling clothes in the L. L. Bean catalogue. I take
this as a personal insult because for many years I found it impossible to
admit to myself that I wanted to be a writer. It was my guilty secret, because being a writer was incompatible with being a man.

There are people who might deny this, but that is because the Amer- 9
ican writer, typically, has been so at pains to prove his manliness that
we have come to see literariness and manliness as mingled qualities. But
first there was a fear that writing was not a manly profession—indeed,
not a profession at all. (The paradox in American letters is that it has always been easier for a woman to write and for a man to be published.)
Growing up, I had thought of sports as wasteful and humiliating, and the
idea of manliness was a bore. My wanting to become a writer was not a

"I'm tired of being sensitive. I want to be an oaf again."

flight from that oppressive role–playing, but I quickly saw that it was at odds with it. Everything in stereotyped manliness goes against the life of the mind. The Hemingway personality is too tedious to go into here, and in any case his exertions are well–known, but certainly it was not until this aberrant behavior was examined by feminists in the 1960s that any male writer dared question the pugnacity in Hemingway's fiction. All the bullfighting and arm wrestling and elephant shooting diminished Hemingway as a writer, but it is consistent with a prevailing attitude in American writing: one cannot be a male writer without first proving that one is a man.

It is normal in America for a man to be dismissive or even somewhat   10 apologetic about being a writer. Various factors make it easier. There is a heartiness about journalism that makes it acceptable—journalism is the manliest form of American writing and, therefore, the profession the most independent–minded women seek (yes, it is an illusion, but that is my point). Fiction–writing is equated with a kind of dispirited failure and is only manly when it produces wealth—money is masculinity. So is drinking. Being a drunkard is another assertion, if misplaced, of manliness. The American male writer is traditionally proud of his heavy drinking. But we are also a very literal-minded people. A man proves his manhood in America in old–fashioned ways. He kills lions, like Hemingway; or he hunts ducks, like Nathanael West; or he makes pronouncements like, "A man should carry enough knife to defend himself with," as James Jones once said to a *Life* interviewer. Or he says he can drink you under the table. But even tiny drunken William Faulkner loved to mount a horse and go fox hunting, and Jack Kerouac roistered up and down Manhattan in a lumberjack shirt (and spent every night of *The Subterraneans* with his mother in Queens). And we are familiar with the lengths to which Norman Mailer is prepared, in his endearing way, to prove that he is just as much a monster as the next man.

When the novelist John Irving was revealed as a wrestler, people 11 took him to be a very serious writer; and even a bubble reputation like Eric (*Love Story*) Segal's was enhanced by the news that he ran the marathon in a respectable time. How surprised we would be if Joyce Carol Oates were revealed as a sumo wrestler or Joan Didion active in pumping iron. "Lives in New York City with her three children" is the typical woman writer's biographical note, for just as the male writer must prove he has achieved a sort of muscular manhood, the woman writer— or rather her publicists—must prove her motherhood.

There would be no point in saying any of this if it were not gener- 12 ally accepted that to be a man is somehow—even now in feminist-influenced America—a privilege. It is on the contrary an unmerciful and punishing burden. Being a man is bad enough; being manly is appalling (in this sense, women's lib has done much more for men than for women). It is the sinister silliness of men's fashions, and a clubby attitude in the arts. It is the subversion of good students. It is the so–called "Dress Code" of the Ritz–Carlton Hotel in Boston, and it is the institutionalized cheating in college sports. It is the most primitive insecurity.

And this is also why men often object to feminism but are afraid to 13 explain why: of course women have a justified grievance, but most men believe—and with reason—that their lives are just as bad.

Reading Closely

1. What is this essay about? In a paragraph—no more—summarize it. Then summarize the essay in one sentence.

2. How does Theroux define *being a man*? Exchange your one–sentence definitions **with a classmate.** Ask your classmate to revise your

one–sentence definition while you edit the sentence that came your way. Share your sentences with the rest of the class.

3. How does the cartoon on p. 598 relate to Theroux's point?

Considering Larger Issues

1. What do you think Theroux's purpose is for writing this essay? Who do you see as his intended audience? How does his audience affect his over–all purpose, and vice versa?

2. What message do you think the author wants you to come away with?

3. What complications about being a man does Theroux enumerate? Do you agree with him? Which complications did he omit? Prepare to share your responses with the rest of the class.

4. **COMBINING METHODS.** In developing his definition of *being a man*, Theroux uses *cause-and-consequence analysis.* Mark the passages in which he uses this method, and then discuss the overall effect of these passages on his essay.

Thinking about Language

1. Using the context and your dictionary, define the following terms. Be prepared to share your answers with the rest of the class.

pathetic (1)	belittle (5)	publicists (11)
fetishists (1)	degenerates (6)	clubby (12)
manliness (2)	puritanical (7)	subversion (12)
connives (2)	philistine (7)	institutionalized
coquettishness (3)	mingled (9)	(12)
enjoined (3)	pugnacity (9)	
grotesque (4)	roistered (10)	

2. What is the effect of the last paragraph? Is it essential to the essay? Why or why not?

3. Unlike Brady's "Why I Want a Wife" (p. 591), there is nothing ironic in this essay. Theroux relates his experiences and observations in a straight–forward way, and with a measure of frustration. Mark all the places and list all the ways that Theroux's style expresses his disappointment and frustra–tion. **Working with two or three classmates,** compare your responses and prepare to present your group's findings to the rest of the class.

Writing Your Own Definitions

1. Take five minutes to write a short autobiography about "being a _____," filling in the blank with whatever role you identify with most: a man, a woman, a mother, a father, a laborer, a cook, a student, a leader, and so on. After you are finished writing, underline all the features of your role that have stayed the same over a period of time and circle the features

that have changed. Make two columns, one for each set of features. What did you learn about your role from this very short exercise? Has your definition of your role changed over time? Write a two- to three-page essay defining your identifying role over time. Refer to the guidelines for checking over the use of definition (p. 590).

2. Using Theroux's essay as a starting point, draft a three- to four-page essay in which you define being a man. You may want to consider that role in terms of religion, politics, marriage and family, the women's movement, social class, racial or ethnic identity, or work. **Consider working with a classmate** and including visuals as you draft and revise, and be sure to refer to the guidelines for checking over the use of definition (p. 590).

OMOTAYO BANJO
Personalizing Your College Education

Omotayo Banjo is a Nigerian American, born in Washington, D.C. She wrote the following essay as an undergraduate at Penn State University, where she majored in psychology, with a minor in English. Banjo is pursuing a career in communications, researching the psychological and social effects of media.

Preview   What does being college educated mean to you? How are you personalizing your college education?

Attending college is an experience that some forfeit. As a graduating sen-   1
ior, I've learned a few things about college and my education, and I would like to challenge you, as first–year students, to consider what it means to be college educated. What makes us different from those who have chosen to take other routes in their lives? While we have this op-portunity, it is to our advantage to learn the importance of having an ed-ucation. If we don't learn it early, we may graduate without reaping the full benefit of our college experience. By personalizing our education, we are able to get more out of school than mere book knowledge. Instead, we gain valuable experiences that help in developing our thinking abili-ties and building our character.

Getting a college education means more than passing classes and ob-   2
taining a degree. Adrienne Rich makes a distinction between "receiving" an education and "claiming" or personalizing one (231). She charges us to be eager to grasp our education, to take control of it and make it our own. By not settling for mere grades, we realize that college is more than just ad-vanced job training. By taking advantage of interpersonal resources, we find complements to our academic resources. If we don't personalize our education, we waste valuable time and money memorizing material for tests as opposed to applying what we learn in class and what we learn from others to our personal growth and betterment. I know some people — and you may also — who have completed four years of college but do not re-member anything they learned there. If this is what it means to be college educated, then our college education is pointless.

While thinking about the meaning of being college educated, I asked   3
my friends what they thought. Some defined it as a way to acquire wealth. Others said it enhances our intellectual ability, making us "more marketable" than people without a college education. However, these definitions do not suit people like Bill Gates, Frank Sinatra, Magic John-son, and a host of others who haven't finished or even attended college, yet have achieved material success. Dissatisfied with my friends' interpre-tations, I sought a more meaningful definition. I began with what being college educated is not.

Attaining a college education is not the only path to material success   4
or even to knowledge. It is possible to be successful and live a happy life
without a bachelor's degree. One can gain knowledge by reading, asking
questions, or experiencing the world. Many people's grandparents
haven't attended college but have a lot to teach us. Therefore, college
doesn't teach us everything. It may aid our quest for material success and
open doors for knowledge, but our justification for higher education
cannot be limited to those two factors only.

How we define a college education depends on how we define educa-   5
tion. First, the classroom experience is crucial. Aside from all of the knowledge offered in our textbooks, we also learn from our interactions in the
classroom. Without teachers, we wouldn't learn as much. Because they
have committed themselves to studying a particular subject, they are able
to expand our knowledge beyond what we read. Teachers make complex
ideas clearer; they make dead texts come to life for us. By asking questions
or meeting with our professors, we develop relationships that open doors
of information, which benefit us in the future. Our relationships with our
professors also help direct us in our career decision making. For instance,
professors often are able to help us network with people who can help us
in our endeavors to get a job or go to graduate school.

Social psychologists have demonstrated that we learn best from our   6
environment and our experiences; therefore, an important part of our
college education happens in our interactions with people outside of the
classroom. When we enter the college world, we become much more
aware that everybody is not like us nor does everyone believe what we
believe. Outside the college community, we probably meet mostly people
who look like us and share the same interests. For instance, if I worked at
Joe's Company eight hours a day, five days a week, I would spend a majority of my time with my co-workers. Because we would share the same
occupation, we would probably share similar interests. Therefore, our influence on one another might be limited to the culture and values of the
job. However, in college I am more likely to be exposed to many people
of diverse skills, interests, and values.

For instance, I have read a few articles on Indians' attitudes about   7
women, but not until I became friends in college with an Indian woman
did these values become tangible to me. My friend Stutee told me that
young Indian women are generally discouraged from pursuing education or working outside the home. They are expected to be housewives.
Obviously, however, not all Indians share these sentiments. Stutee had
come to the United States to study pre-med with her father's blessing.

I also had an in-depth conversation with a Taiwanese friend, Wan Yi,   8
who told me the history of China during the Qin dynasty and its influence on the Taiwanese people. And I learned from my Chinese friend
Selena that during an invasion in the 1930s, Japanese soldiers raped and
killed many Chinese, so now wearing Japanese clothes is taboo among

the Chinese people. Though I had heard these stories in high school, they seemed more meaningful when I heard them from people I knew.

Diversity in college isn't limited to people's race and ethnicity. I've 9 had many conversations with engineering majors about kinetic energy, thermodynamics, ergonomics, and the difference between mechanical engineering and engineering mechanics. I've spoken with pre–med students about the controversies surrounding health policies in the United States compared to those in other countries. Speaking with students in liberal arts, I've obtained a less narrow view of life and have come to understand that everybody's path is different. From these various interactions, I've learned to value life and respect other people's choices.

These experiences have personalized my education and taught me that 10 college offers many sources of knowledge, but we won't learn from them unless we study and discuss issues with people different from us. Higher education provides the key, but what we do with the key is up to us. When professors encourage discussion and interaction, we must make an effort to engage in conversation with them. We must also take advantage of the diverse types of people we meet in our different courses. Although engineers may be friends with engineers and English majors may socialize with English majors, there are many others we need to meet as well.

So what does it mean to be college educated? Even though each per– 11 son's experiences may be quite different, getting an education means that we have seized the opportunity to learn from our classes, our professors, and our peers. A college–educated person has learned how to appreciate and adjust to others, to test her interests and apply herself, to explore his purpose in life. All the mansions and cars and all the intellectual knowledge in the world, could never compare in value to what college has to offer — if we claim our education for ourselves.

WORK CITED

Rich, Adrienne. "Claiming an Education." *On Lies, Secrets, and Silence.* 1979. New York: Norton, 1995. 231–5.

Reading Closely

1. What are the characteristics and attitudes of those who have personalized their college educations in the way Banjo recommends?
2. According to Banjo, what does being "college educated" mean? What does it *not* mean?

Considering Larger Issues

1. How do you respond to Banjo's opening sentence? Do you believe that some people "forfeit" college, or might other issues be involved?

2. What role do teachers play in a college education, according to Banjo? Do you agree? What role do you think teachers play or should play? Be prepared to share your answer with the rest of the class.

3. How many kinds of definitions does Banjo include in her essay: sentence, extended, historical, negative, stipulative? **Working with another classmate or two,** mark each kind in the text. Then note which ones are objective and which ones are subjective. What kind does Banjo use most? least? To what overall effect? Prepare a group response that you can share with the rest of the class.

4. Who is the audience for Banjo's essay? What is her overall purpose in writing this essay to that audience? In other words, how do issues of audience and purpose come together for Banjo in this essay?

5. **COMBINING METHODS.** Mark places where Banjo uses *exemplification* as part of her definition essay. How effective do you find her examples?

Thinking about Language

1. Using the context and your dictionary, define the following terms. Be prepared to share your answers with the rest of the class.

forfeit (1)	material success (3)	tangible (7)
complements (2)	justification (4)	kinetic energy (9)
marketable (3)	endeavors (5)	

2. Reread Banjo's essay to determine how many definitions she provides for "college educated." Compile her definitions and summarize them into one that you think exemplifies her points and then share that definition with the rest of the class.

Writing Your Own Definitions

1. Draft a three– to four–page essay in response to Banjo's. She will serve as your audience as you explain what being college educated means to you — as well as what personalizing your college education will mean to you. Be sure to look over the guidelines for using definition on p. 590 as you draft and revise.

2. Banjo's essay responds to many of the issues that Michael Eric Dyson brings up in his (see p. 615), particularly in terms of obligations. Using both of these essays as a resource, draft a three– to four–page essay in which you define the obligations of being smart, intellectual, and/or well educated. Refer to the guidelines for using definition on p. 590.

KRUTI TRIVEDI

A Big Push for Learning "Differences," Not Disabilities

● Kruti Trivedi (b. 1978), who graduated from Princeton University in 2000, has written for the *New York Times*, the *Wall Street Journal*, and *On the [Princeton] Campus, Online*. In the following article, which first appeared in the *New York Times* in August 2000, Trivedi writes about the endowment that billionaire businessman Charles Schwab has given to groups who use the term *learning differences* rather than *learning disabilities*.

> **Preview** What do you imagine to be the difference between learning *differences* and learning *disabilities*?

Charles Schwab, the billionaire businessman who runs one of the world's most successful brokerage firms, is dyslexic. But, he insists, that does not mean he is disabled. "I look at it as a difference," he said.

At a time when school districts are moving to standardize curriculum and districts are placing a heavier emphasis on state tests, Mr. Schwab is spending the equivalent of hundreds of millions of dollars leading a campaign of Americans who refer to themselves as having "learning differences" rather than learning disabilities.

To some, Mr. Schwab is on a quixotic semantic quest, something like making sure the bald are called "follically challenged." But to others, he is using his name and fortune to undermine a delicate and vital financing structure it has taken years to erect.

Mr. Schwab said his main purpose was to encourage schools to see all children as distinct learners who need individualized attention.

"What you're trying to do with all this definitional stuff is to make sure you don't beat the kids down and make them think they're fully defective," he said. "My fundamental belief is that you want to emphasize the kids' strengths."

Mr. Schwab's initiative makes the Learning Disabilities Association of America, the most powerful advocacy group for the learning disabled, nervous. It is concerned that children with learning disabilities will not get the services they need if they are redefined under the broader term "learning differences." What's more, the group is worried that the federal financing for which it has fought for years will decline or even disappear if "learning differences" comes into favor with legislators.

"The danger, and where the controversy comes from, is that there are some parents who would not like to have their child called disabled," said Ann Kornblet, executive director of the Learning Disabilities Association of America.

"The reality is that a true learning disability is a handicapping condi-   8
tion. Without understanding that, you're not prepared to help them prepare for a life of advocating for themselves."

The Individuals with Disabilities in Education Act of 1975 uses the   9
term "learning disability" to classify children with "a disorder in one or
more of the basic psychological processes involved in understanding or
in using language, spoken or written."

A learning disability may show up as an imperfect ability to listen,   10
think, speak, read, write, spell, or do mathematical calculations, according to the federal definition. Education officials say that 12 percent of all
school-aged children are now classified as learning disabled.

Mr. Schwab is not alone in his opposition to the term. An increasing   11
number of parents seem to be referring to their learning disabled children as "learning different" and teachers are starting to use the term in
the classroom.

He and his wife founded the Charles and Helen Schwab Foundation,   12
now called the Schwab Foundation for Learning, in 1988 to address the
needs of such families.

Along with his own foundation, he is the co-chairman of All Kinds of   13
Minds, an iconoclastic organization that looks at every child — disabled
or not — in terms of strengths and weaknesses.

"Our model is one where we refuse to label anybody, so we have no   14
'learning disabilities,'" said Mel Levine, co-chairman of the organization
with Mr. Schwab.

The group has already trained 5,000 teachers around the country to   15
speak the language of learning differences at several regional training
centers, including one program run by The Bank Street College of Education in Manhattan. Plans are in the works to open a chain of consultation
centers where parents can take their children to be evaluated.

Eventually, Dr. Levine hopes that every school in the country will   16
follow his model.

"We are determined to start a national movement," he said. "As of   17
now, we're swimming upstream in many respects because people love to
label kids, people love to medicate kids and people love to test kids."

Some of the strongest voices in the learning-disabled community —   18
which includes researchers, lawyers, and the advocacy group — say the
term "disabled" may have a negative connotation to some but is still the
most accurate. They worry that Mr. Schwab's opposition to the term
could unravel an identity it has taken years to weave.

"We're stuck with the term partly because we need to because of ad-   19
vocacy and partly because it's true," said Larry Silver, president of the
disabilities association.

"You empower your kids by helping them understand themselves: 20
'learning differences' suggest that you're just like everyone else, except if
they add with their fingers, you add with your toes."

Mr. Schwab's pronouncements bear a special weight in the learning– 21
disabled community, because he is its largest benefactor.

To date, he has endowed what amounts to $280 million in Schwab 22
stock to the groups that use the term "learning difference."

Mr. Schwab said that he first discovered his dyslexia as an adult, 23
when listening to a psychologist explain why his eight–year–old son was
having problems reading. As he sat in the office, Mr. Schwab said, he re–
alized that many of his own problems with language had the same
cause.

"You need a few people to step out and say there is an issue, there's a 24
stigma," Mr. Schwab said.

"I need to say, 'I've dealt with it and it's not going to be the worst 25
thing in the world.' "

Reading Closely

1. According to Trivedi, what is the difference between a learning *difference* and a learning *disability*?

2. Write for a few minutes about the definitions this essay provides. **Working with one or two classmates,** compare your terms and definitions and then prepare a group response to share with the rest of the class.

Considering Larger Issues

1. What is the author's purpose in explaining the differences between the two terms?

2. Who is her audience?

3. How does the author's purpose affect her audience, and vice versa?

4. **COMBINING METHODS.**   Make a list of all the consequences of using one term (*learning difference*) or another (*learning disability*). Then consider how Trivedi uses comparison and contrast in this essay. Prepare a response to share with the rest of the class that explains the effect of Trivedi's use of *consequence analysis* and *comparison and contrast* on her overall essay.

Thinking about Language

1. Using the context or your dictionary, define the following terms or phrases. Be prepared to share your answers with the rest of the class.

dyslexic (1)	iconoclastic (13)	pronouncements
quixotic semantic	advocacy group (18)	(21)
quest (3)	unravel (18)	benefactor (21)

2. How exactly are *learning difference* and *learning disability* defined? What other terms does Trivedi define in this essay?

3. **Working with one or two classmates,** make a list of all the words, phrases, and examples that define *learning difference*. Make another list of all the words, phrases, and examples that define *learning disability*. Work with your classmates to determine the specific ways these definitions overlap and/or diverge. What is the overall effect of any overlap and any divergence?

Writing Your Own Definitions

1. "A Big Push . . ." compares the definitions of *learning difference* and *learning disability*. Using your lists from question 3 under "Thinking about Language," begin drafting a three- to four-page essay that compares the definitions of the terms. Before you start drafting, however, enumerate the points of comparison that you plan to use. Each point should include the ways that the meanings of the terms are alike and the ways they are different. Refer to "Checking Over the Use of Definition" (p. 590) as you draft and revise. (For more on comparison and contrast, see chapter 6.)

2. "A Big Push . . ." compares the definitions of the two terms, and the essay also compares the consequences of using one term or another. Using your responses from question 4 under "Considering Larger Issues," draft a three- to four-page essay in which you chart the consequences of using one term or the other. You may want to explore relevant sources on the World Wide Web or at your campus library in order to locate even more information that will help you develop your essay. Refer to "Checking Over the Use of Definition" (p. 590) as you draft and revise. (For more on cause–and–consequence analysis, see chapter 8.)

3. Define two groups or kinds of people. You might be able to rely on your own knowledge of or experience with people representing different religious groups, ethnic groups, nationalities, ages, physical characteristics, or talents; or you may want to conduct research on the World Wide Web or at the library to enhance your own understanding.

   As you develop your definition of each group or type, make note of your points of comparison. **Consider working with two or three classmates** to judge what details can best help you develop these points of comparison as well as your purpose in defining these groups or types and then in comparing them. Make sure that your purpose is reflected in the thesis statement of your three- to four-page essay. Refer to "Checking Over the Use of Definition" (p. 590) as you draft and revise. (For more on comparison and contrast, see chapter 6.)

RANDY OLSON

Shifting Baselines: Slow-Motion Disaster below the Waves

Randy Olson holds a Ph.D. in marine biology as well as an M.F.A. in cinema; currently he teaches biology at the University of Southern California. He has produced various science films and serves as director of the Shifting Baselines Campaign, which seeks to educate the public about the ecological decline of the world's oceans. The following essay, which helped to launch the campaign, was published in 2002 in the *Los Angeles Times*. Olson also directed and coproduced a public service announcement for the campaign, and in 2004 he joined efforts with the improvisational comedy group The Groundlings to create four short films that premiered at the Shifting Baselines Hollywood Ocean Night.

> **Preview** What does the term *baseline* suggest to you? Do you associate it with baseball? finances? something else? How might it be related to ocean ecology?

There is a new term in the environmental movement. It sounds esoteric, like the kind of thing you don't really need to understand, something you can leave to the more technical types.

The term is "shifting baselines," and you do need to know it, because shifting baselines affect the quality-of-life decisions you face daily. Shifting baselines are the chronic, slow, hard-to-notice changes in things, from the disappearance of birds and frogs in the countryside to the increased drive time from L.A. to San Diego. If your ideal weight used to be 150 pounds and now it's 160, your baseline — as well as your waistline — has shifted.

The term was coined by fisheries biologist Daniel Pauly in 1995. It was a term we'd apparently been needing, because it quickly spread to a variety of disciplines. It's been applied to analysis of everything from deteriorating cities to declining quality of entertainment.

Among environmentalists, a baseline is an important reference point for measuring the health of ecosystems. It provides information against which to evaluate change. It's how things used to be. It is the tall grass prairies filled with buffalo, the swamps of Florida teeming with bird life, and the rivers of the Northwest packed with salmon. In an ideal world, the baseline for any given habitat would be what was there before humans had much impact.

If we know the baseline for a degraded ecosystem, we can work to restore it. But if the baseline shifted before we really had a chance to chart it, then we can end up accepting a degraded state as normal — or even as an improvement.

The number of salmon in the Pacific Northwest's Columbia River today is twice what it was in the 1930s. That sounds great — if the 1930s are your baseline. But salmon in the Columbia River in the 1930s were only 10% of what they were in the 1800s. The 1930s numbers reflect a baseline that had already shifted.

This is what most environmental groups are now struggling with. They are trying to decide: What do we want nature to look like in the future? And more important: What did nature look like in the past?

These questions are particularly important to ask about oceans, my main research interest. Last year Jeremy Jackson of the Scripps Institution of Oceanography brought the problem into focus with a cover article in *Science* that was chosen by *Discover* magazine as the most important discovery of the year.

Jackson and his 18 co-authors pulled together data from around the world to make the case that overfishing had been the most important alteration to the oceans over the past millennium. Furthermore, humans have had such a strong effect on the oceans for so long that, in many locations, it is difficult to even imagine how full of life the oceans used to be.

One of scientists' biggest concerns is that the baselines have shifted for many ocean ecosystems. What this means is that people are now visiting degraded coastal environments and calling them beautiful, unaware of how they used to look.

People go diving today in California kelp beds that are devoid of the large black sea bass, broomtailed groupers, and sheephead that used to fill them. And they surface with big smiles on their faces because it is still a visually stunning experience to dive in a kelp bed. But all the veterans can think is, "You should have seen it in the old days."

Without the old-timers' knowledge, it's easy for each new generation to accept baselines that have shifted and make peace with empty kelp beds and coral reefs. Which is why it's so important to document how things are—and how they used to be.

For the oceans, there is disagreement on what the future holds. Some marine biologists argue that, as the desirable species are stripped out, we will be left with the hardiest, most undesirable species—most likely jellyfish and bacteria, in effect the rats and roaches of the sea. They point to the world's most degraded coastal ecosystems—places like the Black Sea, the Caspian Sea, even parts of the Chesapeake Bay. That's about all you find: jellyfish and bacteria.

We have already become comfortable with a new term, "jellyfish blooms," which is used to describe sudden upticks in the number of jellyfish in an area. The phenomenon has become sufficiently common that an international symposium was held on the subject in 2000. Meanwhile, other types of world fisheries are in steep decline.

It is easy to miss changes in the ocean. It's big and deep. But sometimes, if people have studied the same oceanic trends over time, we get a glimpse of a highly disturbing picture. The Scripps Institution's Jackson,

for example, has documented the nearly complete disappearance of the ecosystem he built his career studying: the coral reefs of Jamaica. "Virtually nothing remains of the vibrant, diverse coral reef communities I helped describe in the 1970s," Jackson says. "Between overfishing, coastal development, and coral bleaching, the ecosystem has been degraded into mounds of dead corals covered by algae in murky water." Nothing you would want to make into a postcard.

Next year two major reports will be released on the state of the 16 oceans: the Oceans Report from the Pew Charitable Trusts, and the report of the U.S. Oceans Commission. The advance word on both is that the news will not be good.

The last major U.S. report on the oceans was 30 years ago. That re- 17 port warned that "there may be a risk some day of severely declining oceans." The inside word on the upcoming reports is that they will conclude that the oceans are today in severe decline.

The Ocean Conservancy, Scripps Institution, and the Surfrider Foun- 18 dation are mounting a major media campaign for early next year to call attention to the overall fate of the oceans and the problem of shifting baselines. The solutions are already known: We must care more about the environment and work to prevent its decline. Hundreds of environmental groups have action plans to help achieve such goals. The only thing they are lacking is mass support.

The oceans are our collective responsibility. We all have to ask the 19 questions: What did they used to look like? What are we putting into

them? Where did these fish we are eating come from? Are my food preferences jeopardizing the health of the oceans?

And, in a more philosophical vein, we should consider the shifting 20
baselines in our own lives, examining how and where have we lowered
our standards to the point that we accept things that once would have
been unacceptable. Our environment has clearly suffered from our increasing comfort with shifting baselines. I suspect our lives have suffered
in other ways as well.

Reading Closely

1. How does Olson define the phrase "shifting baselines"? Mark all the passages in the essay that extend his definition into various areas of study.
2. Enumerate the features of slow–motion disaster that Olson outlines in
   his essay.

Considering Larger Issues

1. What are the causes of underwater baseline shifts, according to Olson's
   article? What are their consequences? Have you witnessed (or heard or
   read about) any of the changes that Olson mentions or other changes of
   the same kind? Be prepared to share your answers with the rest of the
   class.
2. What does Olson state or imply that we should do — or not do — to prevent further shifts in underwater baselines? Have you participated in (or
   heard or read about) any of these efforts?
3. What is your response to Olson's assertion that you need to know about
   the term "shifting baselines" because these baselines "affect the quality–
   of–life decisions you face daily"? What "quality–of–life decisions" might
   he be alluding to? Be prepared to share your answers with the rest of the
   class.
4. **COMBINING METHODS.**   Olson uses *exemplification* to help define the concept of shifting baselines in the oceans. Which of his examples do you
   find the most dramatic and compelling? Why?
5. Does the photograph on p. 612 heighten the effect of Olson's essay, helping to make the concept he's defining less abstract? Or does it just seem
   decorative? **Discuss your response with two or three classmates,**
   and be prepared to share your answer with the rest of the class.

Thinking about Language

1. Using the context or your dictionary, define the following terms and
   phrases. Be prepared to share your answers with the rest of the class.

esoteric (1)	habitat (4)	veterans (11)
chronic (2)	degraded (5)	symposium (14)
deteriorating (3)	millennium (9)	murky (15)
ecosystems (4)	devoid (11)	jeopardizing (19)

2. **With another classmate or two,** identify and mark all the specific words and phrases Olson uses that refer to undersea life. Which of these terms do you need to know the meaning of in order to understand Olson's argument? Which ones serve mostly as background material, as part of the context? What effect does Olson's defining some terms and skimming over others have on your reading comprehension and pleasure? Prepare a brief group report to share with the rest of the class.

Writing Your Own Definitions

1. Using Olson's essay as a model, draft a three- to four–page essay in which you define a shifting baseline or group of baselines in your own life. You might see the shift(s) as contributing to a slow–motion disaster, a slow–motion success, or something else altogether. **Consult with another classmate or two** as you draft and revise. Be sure to refer to the guidelines for checking over the use of definition on p. 590.

2. Draft a three- to four–page essay in which you stipulate and argue for your own definition of "quality of life" or "quality-of–life decisions." Refer to the guidelines for checking over the use of definition on p. 590.

MICHAEL ERIC DYSON

The Public Obligations of Intellectuals

Michael Eric Dyson is an ordained Baptist minister and the Avalon Professor of Religious and African Studies at the University of Pennsylvania. He has contributed to magazines that include *Christian Century, Savoy,* and *Vibe;* is a regular media commentator on *The Tavis Smiley Show;* and has received awards from the National Association of Black Journalists and the NAACP. Dyson's books include the bestseller *Holler If You Hear Me: Searching for Tupac Shakur* (2002), *Why I Love Black Women* (2003), and *Mercy, Mercy Me: The Art, Loves, and Demons of Marvin Gaye* (2004). "The Public Obligations of Intellectuals" was originally published in the *Chronicle of Higher Education* in 2003 and was reprinted in *The Michael Eric Dyson Reader* (2004).

Preview   How do you define the term "intellectual"? Do you know any such people? Do you believe they have "public obligations"? If so, what might they be? Be prepared to share your responses with the rest of the class.

My religious background has a lot to do with how I see the life of the 1
mind: not as career but vocation, and not as a pursuit isolated from the joy and grief of ordinary folk, but as a calling to help hurting humanity. I suppose it would be fair to say that one of the reasons I became an intellectual was to talk back to suffering—and if possible, to relieve it. I wanted to be as smart as I could be about the pain and heartache of people I knew were unjustly oppressed.

First off, there were the poor, working poor, and working–class black 2
folk I saw in my own tribe and in the ghetto neighborhoods I lived in. Later, as I matured and traveled around the country, there were the people who suffered because of the skin or class into which they were born, or the way they had sex, or thought about it. And finally, as I have learned about the world, there are the folk on whom brutality descends because of their color, their native tongue, their religion, or the region of land to which their lives are staked.

Of course, these might be good reasons for becoming a minister, that 3
is, if you embrace a social gospel, one that cares about people's bodies and health and housing as much as it attends to their souls. But to many, these are poor grounds to stand an intellectual life on. For me they spring from the same soil. The intellectuals I admire most are just as eager to preach resistance to ignorance, pain, and yes, evil as evangelists are to promulgate spiritual salvation.

Intellectuals have an obligation to be as smart as we can possibly 4
be, but we have an even greater obligation to be good with the smarts we possess. We don't have to apologize for not being factory laborers, sanitation workers, or even politicians. There's no shame in thinking well about the mathematics of black holes or the theory of

615

social privilege, about the biology of evolution or the chemistry of genetic inheritance, about the philosophy of gender or the psychology of
race, since they contribute to the knowledge of ourselves and the world
we inhabit. But as for me and my house—those whose intellectual work
takes a public bent, and whose knowledge can combat the plagues on
our social and moral lives, and on our physical existence, too—we must
consider the plight of factory laborers and sanitation workers.

If the goal is to do more than recite a laundry list of oppression, then   5
intellectuals must join the struggle to aid the vulnerable. I got the notion
that struggle is key to the intellectual's vocation from the communities I
grew up in. In the fifth grade, I was transformed by the teaching of Mrs.
James, mostly because she helped her students see themselves in a fresh
and powerful racial light. My birth certificate says I'm a Negro, like all birth
certificates of colored children born as I was in the late '50s. But Mrs. James
helped us to shed old definitions and to embrace a new grammar of self-
respect tied to what soul singer Curtis Mayfield called "a choice of colors."
She convinced us that we were black, not colored or Negro. In unfolding
her lesson plan, Mrs. James persuaded me that my skills and talents, like
those of our leaders, must help the struggle for black freedom.

As long as I have understood what an intellectual is—especially one   6
who rises from a people for whom history is not a blackboard, like it is for
those with power, but a scuzzy washrag with grime and stains—I have believed that she should combat half-truths about the people she loves. To
skeptics, that smacks of provincialism, propaganda, and the hijacking of
knowledge for ethnic therapy and consolation. To be sure, if that's what we
end up with, we're mere replicas of the very forces we decry as inexorably
biased. But such fear is relieved when we consider the context in which our
intellectual lives play out. The life of the mind is tied to the public good,
and unavoidably, at least initially, the promise of this good is defined by the
well-being of *my* tribe and kin. If there are insuperable barriers to our getting a fair share of what everyone deserves, the public good is diminished.
Under these circumstances, it is, at best, a disappointing abstraction of a social ideal that is placed unjustly beyond our reach.

The identification of the public good with what's good for my group   7
has limits and dangers, of course, since at times the public good may run
counter to my group's benefit. In fact, in many instances—say, when the
Voting Rights Act undercut the monopoly on political power for Southern whites, or when the Equal Rights Amendment gave women the
chance to compete with men for jobs—the public good was served by
cutting off an unjust group privilege. We have to be willing to wish for
every other group what we wish for our own if we are to make the identification of the public good with the good of our group work. The public
good is hampered when we idolize our slice of the social welfare and el-
evate our group above all others in the political order. Such a thing is
bad enough if groups simply aspire to unjust social dominance, but if
they've got the power to pull it off, it greatly harms the commonweal.

The struggle to specify the complex character of black life—how it is   8
far more flexible, durable, and intricate, and contradictory and elusive
too, than is usually acknowledged, even among some blacks—is part of
the black freedom struggle too. Protest marches were crucial to our liberation; sit-ins and boycotts were fundamental to our freedom; and the
court brief was decisive in striking down legal barriers to our social
flourishing. But the will to clarify our aims and examine our identity is,
in its own way, just as important to our freedom as the blows struck in
our defense by revolutionary stalwarts. Neither does love cancel out criticism; nor should it prevent black intellectuals from publicly discussing
hard truths about black life that might embarrass or anger us. The role of
the black intellectual is to discover, uncover, and recover truth as best we
can, and to subject our efforts to healthy debate and examination.
I learned from Malcolm X in particular that the black freedom struggle
is no good without self-criticism and holding each other morally
accountable.

It must be admitted that the black intellectual is sometimes wary of   9
being candid about our blemishes because the nation is in chronic denial about its flaws, even as it can't seem to get enough of cataloging
black failure. That's why the black intellectual's desire to tell the truth is
seen by many blacks as naïve and traitorous. To make matters worse,
some mainstream critics argue that black intellectuals pollute the quest
for truth and knowledge when they use it to fight oppression. But if
we're honest, we'll admit that the quest for truth and knowledge is never
free of social and cultural intrusions. Knowledge and truth are never di-
vorced from the ends for which they exist. Even those drunk on a belief
in objectivity must acknowledge that culture and custom are at war with
the idea of an unchanging reality that transcends our means to know it.
That doesn't mean that anything goes, that there are no moral landmarks
to which we can point, that tradition must be jettisoned and history ar-
bitrarily revised, that truth is up for grabs to the highest intellectual bid-
der, or that knowledge is hostage to emotion.

Of course, the sheer pleasure of knowledge, of engaging great ideas   10
and wrestling with great thinkers, is not in dispute—Socrates' dialogues,
Shakespeare's sonnets, Beethoven's concertos, Newton's calculus, Dou-
glass's autobiographies, all have great intrinsic worth. I am not arguing
for a crude instrumentalism to every bit of knowledge; nor am I saying
that every fact has to fit in place and serve a concrete function. That
sort of thinking suits a mechanical view of the world long since demolished by science and common sense. There is something ennobling
about reading lovely sentences that hang together because of poetry and
penetrating thought. There is, too, genuine joy in noting the elegance of
a mathematical equation. All of these good things need no justification
outside of the fact of their existence; their goodness is the reason for
their existence, and vice versa. But the pursuit of knowledge for its own
sake can only be a good thing when it is a possibility for everyone.

Knowledge, after all, is not neutral, neither the getting of it nor the keeping of it, or even the uses of it.

The pursuit of knowledge for its own sake can only make sense in a   11
society where knowledge, at least the ownership of it, makes no moral
difference, and where learning and thinking lack political value. I'm not
saying that we live in an Orwellian nightmare where free thought is corrupted and suppressed. Neither am I saying that we live in a nation
where thinking is only politically useful if it supports the interests of the
state. But the liberty to think out loud as one wishes to, without qualification or permission, is pretty rare, even in our society, and where such
freedom exists, it's the result of vigilant effort to unmask the official story,
the enshrined truth. The freedom to pursue truth wherever it leads, at
least in social and political terms, depends on where you stand in the
culture and how much clout you have.

A real freethinker can be shunned or silenced for straying too far   12
from the nation's political consensus. If, for example, one runs afoul of
the attorney general's pulverizing views of how terror should be defined
and fought, he might be harassed, stigmatized, or arrested. Knowledge is
never just knowledge, it can never simply be pursued without regard to
context, and its results are just as likely to upset as to unify us. All of
which is to say that the black intellectual, without even trying, is a threat
to a society that subordinates his people. There is little choice as to
whether the black intellectual is involved in the struggle of black folk; to
be alive and black makes one a potential candidate for social animus,
and thus, a player in the theater of race.

I learned this lesson in Mrs. James's classroom and in the factories   13
where I worked before eventually going to college when I was 21. My
longest tenure came in the wheel–brake–and–drum factory where my father labored for more than 30 years before being laid off and forced into
maintenance work and odd jobs, from painting houses to cutting grass
and laying sod, all of which his five sons joined him in. Taking note of,
but not completely understanding, and hence, not unqualifiedly supporting, my intellectual bent, my father nevertheless brought home encouragement in the form of factory laborers he discovered were also attending college or liked books like me. They were usually young, black
(sometimes African) male workers who saw the factory as a means to a
larger end: enjoying upward mobility, bettering the lot of their families,
financing college, and, in some cases, bringing the worker's revolution
closer to fulfillment. These men were usually active in the same United
Auto Workers (UAW) union where my father was a member.

Later, when I went to work in the factory as a teen father fending off   14
welfare, and with the hope of saving money for college, I got provocative
instruction from workers who drilled the point in my head: Learning is
for liberation, and knowledge must be turned to social benefit if we are
to justify the faith placed in us by our forebears. In between unloading
brake drums, and welding and balancing them, I got a strong dose of

Marxism, but a homegrown version attuned to the gritty particularities of black working life. That didn't mean there wasn't high theory; there was theory aplenty, though it was tailored to our needs and driven by our aspirations as a degraded and oppressed people—but a people who resolved to rise up from their suffering through self-determining struggle. I was awed by these grass-roots intellectuals who stood their ground and defended their lives with their brains and words. There wasn't even a hint of anti-intellectualism among them. They didn't pooh-pooh self-criticism like some do in the highest rungs of government, saloons, malls, some sidewalk streets—and in parts of the media.

The factory wasn't the only place I got a sense of intellectual voca-   15
tion. I absorbed it in the sanctuary as well. My pastor, Frederick G. Sampson, was an American original, a tall, commanding, impossibly literate dark brown prince of the pulpit who lived up to that title when it still resonated in the world of homiletics. It was Sampson, more than any figure in my life, who convinced me of the service that intellectuals must render. Sampson believed that those who breathed the life of the mind must serve the people in whose womb they came to exist. His thinking made sense to me because of how faithfully he adhered to his own principle. He wasn't a preacher who festooned his pulpit oratory with violent grunts or theatrical posing, though he was a verbal master with dramatic flair. Sampson unabashedly laced his rhetoric with the theology and poetry and philosophy he ardently consumed.

It is because of Sampson that I believe that intellectuals must serve   16
the communities we live and work in. We've got to look beyond a comfortable career, a safe niche behind academe's protective walls, and a serene existence removed from cultural and political battles that shape the nation's fate. We must be willing to shirk the contemptuous pose of distant observer—undoubtedly, we still need observation, and it mustn't be fatally intertwined in the events or ideas we're called on to examine, but intellectuals must at some point get our hands dirty as we help our world become more just. We must even be willing to give up one of academe's most self-serving bombasts: that "serious" thinkers stand apart from the seductions of pop culture to dig into archives and render compelling histories of events long before our time.

That's all good, but it's surely not all-knowing about what intellectu-   17
als are good for. In a show of remarkable adolescence, and obsolescence too, there are many academics who believe that speaking in the tongue of the common person betrays the profession. Well, perhaps that's so, but it's a betrayal we should be proud of, and one that should spur us to resist the tedious professionalism that has noisily ripped through the academy's upper ranks. (That's largely not the case for the thousands upon thousands of part-time teachers whose plight is barely distinguishable from any group of maligned workers, and the battalion of nonunionized graduate students who are depended on to teach vast numbers of American undergraduates.)

It was Jesse Jackson who once remarked to me, "If you say something   18
I can't understand, that's a failure of *your* education, not mine," and he
was right. No sloppy thinker or lazy rhetorician himself, Jackson knows
the intellectual effort it takes to understand an idea so well that one can
explain it to the learned and the layman alike. To paraphrase Ecclesiastes,
there is a time and place for every academic language under the sun —
and for the jargons, obscurantisms, esoterica, dialects, glosses, and inside
meanings that attend their path. But there is also the need to write and
speak clearly about important matters for the masses of folk who will
never make it to class.

There is in the academy today something akin to hip–hop's vexing   19
quest for the rapper who can "keep it real," that is, the rapper who best
matches his lyrics with a life of crime or ghetto glory, depending on which
version of reality wins the day. Many academics are caught up in trying to
prove who's more authentic, who's more academically hard–core, who's
the realest smart person around. That usually ends up being the scholar
who is most "rigorous," and in academic circles that's often the thinker who
is least accessible or who eschews "public" scholarship. But these debates
break down on their own logic: Academics and scholars who are rigorous
don't have to do work that panders to the mainstream in order to be effective (after all, devoted students can carry their former professors, or their
work, with them to the State Department or to *Newsweek*). Work that can be
widely understood or that is relevant to current affairs shouldn't be automatically suspect or seen as second rate. As Jackson understood, our failure
to make our work accessible may be as much the fault of intellectuals as it
is the problem of a society that has dumbed down.

These are the beliefs that guide my vision of the intellectual — the   20
American intellectual, the black intellectual, the engaged intellectual, the
public intellectual (and in a way, aren't all of us intellectuals in the academy *public* intellectuals, since universities are among the biggest public
spheres in the country?). Relieving suffering, reinforcing struggle, and
rendering service are not bad ways to live the life of the mind.

Reading Closely

1. How does Dyson define the term "intellectual"? Mark all the passages in
    the essay that contribute to his definition.
2. Explain the "public obligations" of intellectuals, according to Dyson.
    Refer to the essay to support your answer.

Considering Larger Issues

1. What are the causes and consequences of being a public intellectual, ac-
    cording to Dyson? Do you agree? Why or why not? Be prepared to share
    your answers with the rest of the class.

2. How does Dyson connect the dream of upward mobility with wanting to be an intellectual?

3. What is your response to Jesse Jackson's assertion, "if you say something I can't understand, that's a failure of *your* education, not mine"? What experiences have you had that support your response? Be prepared to share your answers with the rest of the class.

4. COMBINING METHODS.   In a number of places in his essay, Dyson uses *comparison and contrast* to make points about the public obligations of intellectuals. Find and mark these places. How do these comparisons and contrasts help him to define what he thinks an intellectual should be?

Thinking about Language

1. Using the context or your dictionary, define the following terms and phrases. You may want to **work with another classmate.**

genetic inheritance (4)	hampered (7)	vigilant (11)
philosophy of gender (4)	elusive (8)	pulverizing (12)
psychology of race (4)	wary (9)	stigmatized (12)
public bent (4)	mainstream (9)	fending off (14)
plight (4)	arbitrarily (9)	niche (16)
skeptics (6)	ennobling (10)	obsolescence
provincialism (6)	Orwellian nightmare	(17)
insuperable (6)	(11)	vexing (19)
public good (6)		

2. Dyson uses a number of words for color to refer to himself and the people who influenced him. Mark all these words and account for their denotative and connotative meanings. Be prepared to share your answers with the rest of the class.

Writing Your Own Definitions

1. In "The Triumph of Hope over Self-Interest" in chapter 8, David Brooks speaks to some of the same issues that Dyson covers in his essay. Referring to both of these essays for ideas and responses, draft a three- to four-page essay in which you define upward mobility, equal opportunity, the public good, or some other term or phrase that you consider appropriate. **Consult with another classmate or two** as you draft and revise. Be sure to refer to the guidelines for using definition on p. 590.

2. Using your own experiences or those of someone you know well (or know a good deal about), draft a three- to four-page essay in which you define what you consider to be the public obligations of any specific group of people, such as intellectuals, Christians, scientists, political activists, or adults in general. Refer to the guidelines for using definition on p. 590.

DAVID PLOTZ

The American Teen-ager

David Plotz (b. 1970) has been Washington bureau chief and deputy editor of the online magazine *Slate,* in which the following article first appeared in September 1999. Plotz has also written for the *New York Times Magazine, Harper's, Rolling Stone, GQ,* the *New Republic,* and the *Washington Post.*

Preview   How would you define the typical U.S. teenager? How would you define *Generation X? Generation Y?*

They are ardent environmentalists. They adore technology and under-   1
stand it as no generation before them did. They practically invented the Internet. They don't vote: They distrust politics and prefer voluntarism. They're skeptical of corporations and impervious to traditional advertising. They're less racist and more multiracial than any group of Americans in history.

They are, of course, Generation Y, as trend–mongers describe them   2
today. But they are also Generation X, as trend–mongers described them six years ago. And no doubt they are Generation Z, as trend–mongers will describe them in 2015. Generalizing about a generation is always bogus, especially when most of its members aren't out of short pants yet. But no matter. Fifty–five million Gen Xers, once hailed for their iconoclasm, have been discarded as "cynical" and "sour." Supplanting them are the 77 million sunny children of Gen Y. (Generation Y — a ridiculous name — includes those born since 1981.) Gen Xers were in their 20s when they became media darlings. The oldest members of Gen Y have just entered college, which means that for the first time since the baby boom, America is obsessed with teen–agers.

Teens (and 25–year–olds masquerading as teens) have kidnapped pop   3
culture. Their movies — from *Titanic* to *Scream* to *Cruel Intentions* — have swallowed multiplexes. Their melodramas own the networks and have turned their nymphs — *Dawson's Creek's* Katie Holmes, *Party of Five's* Jennifer Love Hewitt, *Felicity's* Keri Russell — into superstars. Their music rules, from Kid Rock to Eminem to Backstreet Boys. Even adults have been bewitched by the teen invasion. The *New York Times Magazine* is fretting about teen–age boys' body image problems. *U.S. News* just ran a cover story on "The Teen Brain." (Why are your teen–agers sullen and irrational? Because the parts of the brain that develop last are those that regulate judgment and emotion. Also because they hate you.)

The United States is global HQ for teendom, but Americans have not al-   4
ways fixated on teens or even been aware of them. As Thomas Hine reports in his new book, *The Rise and Fall of the American Teenager,* the teen

"Take a load off, Leonard—we're watching
Generations X and Y duke it out."

was invented in the 20th century. For most of American history, adoles-cents (also a modern creation) inhabited the adult world as laborers and apprentices. No one claimed that teens were incapacitated by raging hormones or needed an eight-year respite to find themselves. The Great Depression minted the American teen by exiling kids from the labor force to high schools. Only after World War II did high school become the universal, defining experience of youth. For the first time, adoles-cents were artificially segregated from adults, and developed their own culture of cars, dating, and rock 'n' roll. America was fascinated by teen-age boomers not only because there were so many of them, but also because they were so alien: The country had never seen teen-agers before.

We, however, have seen and been teen-agers. So what explains our tyromania? Demography is part of it. Generation Y is huge, 50 percent larger than Generation X. By 2010, 35 million teen-agers will haunt malls and chat rooms, more teens than there ever were during the baby boom. The media cycle has also boosted Generation Y. Trend-spotters need trends. Yuppies were the stereotype of the '80s. The bleak early '90s were defined by the allegedly darker and less materialistic Gen Xers. Now the media need a new plot line, and Gen Y is providing it.

Generation Y is also booming because it is a cheerful story for a cheerful   6
age. Just as the slump of the '90s has been replaced by the eternal boom, the cynical pessimists of Gen X have been vanquished by the cheery Ys. In the '80s, writing about teen–agers meant writing about rising pregnancy rates, drug use, and crime. Today, teen pregnancy, drug use, crime, dropout rates, and sexual activity are down. Church–going is up. Racism is out. The "New Earnestness" and the "New Familism" are in. Rebellion is passé. At last, commentators gloat, kids are having real childhoods again. The school massacres in Littleton, Colo., and Jonesboro, Ark., have barely soured the mood. The media have focused on kids' passionate, unified response to the killings.

This incessant cheer is inspiring inane predictions about what magnif   7
icent adults these Gen Yers will be. Commentators opine that their childhood prosperity will make them generous and idealistic. According to polls, teens are optimistic. Pop prophets William Strauss and Neil Howe call them a "Hero" generation. But young people, especially teens, have always registered optimism. Even Gen Xers were optimistic when they were polled five years ago. Of course Gen Yers are peppy now: Who wouldn't be? Let's see what they say when the economy dives the year they graduate from college. And let's wait until most Gen Yers are capable of rational thought. Most of them haven't reached puberty yet, and many are in diapers.

The most important reason for today's tyromania is economic. America   8
seems obsessed with youth because corporations are obsessed with youth: If they catch kids early enough, they can cement their brand preferences for life. Networks are producing teen dramas so that their advertisers can reach this impressionable audience. Movies are pitched to teen–age sensibilities because only teen–agers go to movies again and again and again. As far as marketers are concerned, Gen X is over: It has aged out of the consumption game. But Generation Y kids are up for grabs: They are young, they have monstrous amounts of cash to spend — the average teen has $94 a week of disposable income! — and they'll be even richer when they grow up.

It's unsurprising, therefore, that the people pushing the Gen Y boom   9
hardest are not sociologists, journalists, or activists but market researchers. The most quoted Gen Y pundits are folks who work at companies such as Youth Information Network and Teenage Research Unlimited, which collect data on trendy brands. (TRU is the Ford Foundation of Gen Y analysis.) Stories about Gen Y tend to shortchange kids' views on family, school, and politics, and dwell instead on their favorite clothing stores.

(To cynical Gen Xers such as myself, this marketing talk seems both   10
contradictory and fatuous. The market researchers instruct that Gen Yers

are brand-conscious yet skeptical of established brands, independent-minded yet conformist. They say things like "This is the coolest generation ever." If you can use "viral marketing" and "Abercrombie & Fitch" in the same sentence, you too can be a Gen Y pundit. Then again, if you could use "grunge" and "Social Security reform" in the same sentence, you could have been a Gen X pundit.)

The final reason for the teen renaissance is boomer self-obsession. A pervasive theme of Generation Y is that it is growing up just as the boomers did: prosperous, happy, well-adjusted. If you consume teen culture at all, you have surely noticed the remarkable number of sympathetic parents around. Today's TV parents are wisdom figures, not the adult buffoons we have grown accustomed to. Similarly, articles about Gen Y—many written by boomer parents—are fulsome about how well boomers are raising their tots, how intimately parents and kids communicate, and how much kids admire mom and dad. The "surprising fact" that pops up in almost every Gen Y story is a survey in which teens named parents as their favorite role models. (I would bet that every survey of teens taken since Cain and Abel found that they named parents as their favorite role models.) 11

Boomers, whose self-absorption has long been ridiculed, have finally managed to get over themselves. They have found a new object of their affection. They don't need self-love anymore. They've got Mini-Me.* 12

1. How exactly does Plotz define the American teenager?
2. List the assertions Plotz makes that support his definition. **Working with two or three classmates,** compare your definitions and assertions. Prepare to report to the rest of the class.
3. How does Plotz arrange his information? his assertions? Does he follow a chronological, spatial, or emphatic pattern of arrangement? What textual evidence can you provide for your answer?
4. How—if at all—does the cartoon on p. 623 support Plotz's assertions?

1. This essay appeared online, posted on <www.slate.msn.com>. Who are the readers for online magazines? for *Slate*? Who might be especially interested in an essay on the American teenager? Write a brief profile of these readers in terms of age, gender, and interests.

---

* **Mini-Me:** a small-scale version of another; the Mini-Dr. Evil first appeared in the box-office hit *The Spy Who Shagged Me,* an Austin Powers movie.

2. What is the purpose of this essay?

3. **COMBINING METHODS.** "The American Teen–ager" reads like a definition essay, yet Plotz depends on the use of *cause-and-consequence analysis.* **Working with a classmate,** mark the passages in which he clarifies the causes and the consequences of being in Generation Y. Prepare a short report for the rest of the class.

Thinking about Language

1. Using the context and your dictionary, define the following terms. Be prepared to share your answers with the rest of the class.

ardent (1)	nymphs (3)	opine (7)
voluntarism (1)	global HQ (4)	fatuous (10)
impervious (1)	incapacitated (4)	pundit (10)
trend–mongers (2)	tyromania (5)	buffoons (11)
bogus (2)	inane (7)	fulsome (11)
iconoclasm (2)		

2. What is the overall tone of the essay — sympathy, understanding, admiration, confusion, disapproval, or something else? Choose one term that you think describes the tone, and mark all words, phrases, and passages that support your choice. Be prepared to share your answers with the rest of the class.

Writing Your Own Definitions

1. Take a few minutes to write about your generation, your children's generation, or your parents' generation. How would you define that generation? How would you differentiate it from other generations?

    Draft a two- to three–page essay in which you explore and extend the definition of that particular generation; you might write an extended, stipulative, negative, or historical definition essay. You might also include ideas you've gathered from your classmates. Refer to "Checking Over the Use of Definition" (p. 590) as you draft and revise.

2. If you have a collection of any kind, write one sentence that defines it. What is it that you collect? How wide is the range of your collection? Write another sentence that defines your collection in terms of what it is *not.*

    Now **work with two or three classmates** and share your definitions of your collections. What questions do you have for the other collectors in your group? Why do they collect the things they do? Where do they get individual pieces for their collections? How long have they been collecting?

    Using the information you've gathered from the preceding exercises, draft a three- to four–page definition essay that describes, classifies, or provides explanatory examples of your collection. Refer to "Checking Over the Use of Definition" (p. 590) as you draft and revise. (For more on description, classification, or exemplification, see chapters 2, 5, or 4.)

GENERAL MOTORS CORPORATION

Mr. Goodwrench

Mr. Goodwrench is a trademarked name for a range of services offered by General Motors, including diagnostics, alignments, lube and brake jobs, vehicle inspections and safety checks, collision repairs, and service reminders. Mr. Goodwrench also represents GM–trained technicians and repair people, GM-specific advanced diagnostic equipment, and genuine GM parts—at more than 7,000 locations nationwide.

> **Preview**   What does the name "Mr. Goodwrench" mean to you?

- - - - - - ➤

Reading Closely

1. What are the specific features of Mr. Goodwrench?
2. What is the overall purpose of this definition?

Considering Larger Issues

1. How does the visual itself—the man and the uniform—create a definition of a repairman who is "much more than just a name"?
2. What kind of definition is this? Is it objective, subjective, or a mixture of the two? Be prepared to share your responses with the rest of the class.
3. **COMBINING METHODS.**   How does the advertisement imply *comparison and contrast?* use *exemplification? cause-and-consequence analysis?*

Thinking about Language

1. What specific words or phrases in this advertisement suggest that Mr. Goodwrench is an essential?
2. What might be the purpose of introducing this ad with the sentence "Mr. Goodwrench is much more than just a name"?

Writing Your Own Definitions

1. Using this advertisement as a model, put together a two- to three–page essay composed of text and visuals that delivers a positive definition of something that can be represented by someone like Mr. Goodwrench. Or you may choose one of the following concepts: what it means to be college educated, what it means to be talented, what it means to be

Mr. Goodwrench
IS MUCH MORE THAN JUST A NAME
THE FACE OF A GM-TRAINED TECHNICIAN
A GOOD LISTENER
KNOWS GM VEHICLE DIAGNOSTICS LIKE THE BACK OF HIS HAND
THIS UNIFORM IS SYNONYMOUS WITH GM EXPERTISE
USES GENUINE GM PARTS
HAS OVER ONE MILLION HOURS OF GM TRAINING UNDER HIS BELT
CAN BE FOUND AT OVER 7,000 DEALERSHIPS
HAS AN EXCLUSIVE LINK DIRECTLY TO GM
CHEVROLET PONTIAC OLDSMOBILE BUICK CADILLAC GMC HUMMER
1-800-GM USE US
Goodwrench.com
©2004 GM Corp. All rights reserved.
GM Goodwrench
MR. GOODWRENCH. THE ONE AND ONLY GM EXPERT.

intelligent. Be ready to share your essay with the rest of the class. Refer to the guidelines for checking over the use of definition on p. 590.

2. Do some research if necessary, and prepare a historical definition of one of the concepts mentioned in the previous question or a term of your own choosing. Your finished essay should be three or four pages long. As you draft and revise, be sure to refer to the guidelines for checking over the use of definition on p. 590.

✷ Additional Suggestions for Writing

1. Consider writing an essay about a disease, disability, or other physical difference with which you are familiar. Begin by writing a one-sentence definition of that condition. Then write another sentence that states what the condition is *not*. Draft a three-page essay about this condition, defining it with a history, a set of causes, or a set of consequences. You might use the World Wide Web or the library to research the history of the condition in terms of its being understood or misunderstood, diagnosed or misdiagnosed. You might research the causes of the condition or its consequences. Refer to "Checking Over the Use of Definition" on p. 590 as you draft and revise.

2. Jot down a word that is painful for you, a word you would not want to be called, maybe a word you have been called. Write a few sentences about a situation where its use was or could be painful for you. Now consider what you might do or say to respond to this word.

    Draft a three- to four-page essay in which you develop your definition of that word, based on actual or hypothetical situations. **Ask a classmate** to review your draft to ensure that you've defined the terms of your discussion, developed a thesis statement, and carried out your purpose. As you draft and revise, refer to the guidelines for checking over the use of definition on p. 590.

3. Watch television for at least 30 minutes, being on the lookout for different types of definitions. Listen carefully, and take notes about each example of a sentence definition, negative definition, historical definition, or stipulative definition that you see and/or hear.

    When and how do the words and visuals work together? What terms seem most successfully or accurately defined? Are any terms defined persuasively yet inaccurately? **Work with one or two classmates** to compare your findings before drafting a three- to four-page essay based on your findings. Ask someone in your writing group to give you comments as you draft and revise your essay. Be sure to refer to the guidelines for checking over the use of definition on p. 590.

chapter **10**
···•

ARGUMENT

Stop the Music!

I like ice cream. I like children. Years ago, I used to drive a truck for a plumbing company, so I guess I like trucks well enough, too. But it's hard to like an ice cream truck.

In my Hicksville neighborhood, on any given night, three different ice cream trucks drive through, stopping within half a block of my house. One truck plays "Camptown Races" over and over and over. Another plays a tune and then, after a pause, a recorded female voice shouts "Hello!"

Whether it's dinner hour or after, these trucks are a noise-menace to any neighborhood.

I appreciate the need to earn a living, but I propose that, at the very least, trucks be required to shut off their sounds whenever they are not moving.

I wonder how many others just grit their teeth at this summer-time nuisance.

Michael Blitz
Hicksville

"**S**top the music!" argues a frustrated man in Hicksville. Oh, he likes ice cream, and he likes children, but he's had it with the nonstop music of the ice cream trucks that circulate through his neighborhood. What should he do? Write a letter to the editor of his local newspaper, expressing his opinion.

Argument is the very essence of opinion, such as this man's. Argument surrounds us; it's the essence of many intellectual, political, and financial discussions; it's also the essence of advertising. Every day, each of us is bombarded with arguments that range from which candidate to vote for or which school to attend, to how to invest our money or how loud to play our favorite music. We are encouraged to read important books, see particular movies, sign up for a certain class, take better care of ourselves, and accept ourselves just the way we are. Sometimes argument is quarrelsome, even unpleasant, but on the whole it merely demonstrates a "certainty" of opinion with regard to a disputable statement.

In the course of our daily lives, we argue with ourselves to accept or reject disputable statements: "I should not be expected to pick up my boss's dry cleaning"; "My car insurance is too high"; "I can save money if I do my own taxes instead of using a CPA"; or "My relationship with my partner will never improve." These are the kinds of disputable statements we consider on a regular basis. And we constantly advance our own arguments to others. It's important, then, to keep in mind that argument is not reserved for law courts or legislatures; it is used everywhere, every day.

> **Looking at Your Own Literacy**   Think about the last important issue you argued about. What was it? Why was it important to you? With whom were you arguing? What did you want that person to do? What was the result? Where did you learn how to argue? How would you like to improve your skills at arguing?

What Is Argument?

Although a distinction is sometimes made between *argument* and *persuasion*, in fact the two terms are often used interchangeably. When the distinction is made, **argument** usually refers to expressing a point of view and then using logical reasoning to try to get an audience to accept that point of view as true or valid. **Persuasion,** on the other hand, is usually defined as using emotion as well as reasoning to *change* an audience's point of view and often to move them to action. But because writing almost any extended expression of a point of view involves using both reason and emotion—and might change readers' minds or move them to action—in this chapter and this book *argument* is used to cover all meanings of both terms.

Now, successful argument often does change a point of view, that's for sure, but its purpose is not always victory over an opponent. Rather, argument often invites exchange, cooperation, mutually beneficial decisions. The best arguments make points openly and honestly, addressing any opposition straight on and working for clarity and understanding all around. We use argument to help an audience understand our point of view. Whether or not we have anything to "win," we want to be heard and understood. And we want to understand others' points of view as well.

The letter to the editor that opens this chapter argues that because their music and other sound effects are repetitive and annoying, the ice cream trucks should turn off the sound while they're stopped. The writer brings attention to the problem and offers what seems to be a sensible solution. He doesn't argue that the trucks should stay away from his neighborhood or that they should keep their music turned off all the time. He understands that folks love ice cream and that the music is necessary to attract the children. So he offers a solution that he feels is beneficial to him and not harmful to the ice cream dealer.

We ourselves use these techniques every day to bring attention to and sell *our* ideas, opinions, and decisions to friends and colleagues. If we perceive a problem, we employ these techniques to explore and analyze complicated issues, to provide information that might eventually change someone's mind (say, about where to eat, whom to date, where to vacation), and to invite and consider additional information. Whether you are watching an NBA game with friends, phoning in to a radio station, writing e-mail, completing a written assignment, or reading the letters to the editor, chances are you're encountering argument.

Thinking about Argument

1. Read through the advertisement on the facing page. What is the problem that needs a solution?
2. What argument is the ad making about a solution?
3. Underline the words that appeal, positively or negatively, to readers' emotions. What emotional appeal does the image make?

Why Argue?

Whether you're describing an architectural style for your art history professor, comparing and contrasting two military leaders of the Vietnam War for your political science professor, or analyzing the benefits of the

Photo: Roslyn Dickens

Without someone to share it, dinner is always a cold meal.

Close relatives move far away. Old friends become increasingly frail and homebound. For some seniors, loneliness and isolation erode all of life's joys.

With your help, UJA-Federation is there — providing community centers and programs where the elderly can find warmth, companionship, and a renewed appetite for life.

Give to UJA-Federation of New York.

New York • Long Island • Westchester • Israel • Around the Globe • **1.212.836.1880** • **www.ujafedny.org/give**

euro currency for your economics professor, chances are you're also using elements of argument. As a writer you will use argument for three general, and often overlapping, purposes: to *express* or *defend* your own position or opinion; to *question* or *argue against* an established belief or course of action; or to *invite* or *convince* readers to change their position.

See how Robert Sapolsky argues to defend his position that there's a direct link between wealth and health:

> Modern science has finally provided some information that should aid everyone in making lifestyle decisions. If you wish to live a long and healthy life, it is advisable to be wealthy. More specifically: Try not to be born into poverty, and if you have inadvertently made that mistake, change your station in life ASAP.
>
> People have long known about what is called the socioeconomic status (SES) gradient in health. For example, in the United States the poorer you are, the more likely you are to contract and succumb to heart disease, respiratory disorders, ulcers, rheumatoid disorders, psychiatric disease, or a number of types of cancer. And this is a whopper of an effect: In some cases disease or mortality risk increases more than fivefold as you go from the wealthiest to the poorest segments of our society, with things worsening each step of the way.
>
> —ROBERT SAPOLSKY, "How the Other Half Heals"

Sapolsky gets readers' attention with his initial assertion that modern science has discovered the connection between wealth and good health. He argues this point with additional information about who is most likely to contract various illnesses or disorders.

Try Your Hand   If Sapolsky is correct, we should all try to change our socioeconomic status as soon as possible. But such a grand claim demands support. List some specific ways that having more money could lead to an improvement in a person's health. It might help to consider a specific case—the health of your parents or grandparents, perhaps.

Now look at an example of argument used to raise questions about an established belief. In the following passage Sallie Tisdale takes on the question of what's "wrong" with high schools in the United States. Going beyond blaming students or teachers, she questions the very idea of high school, arguing that as a system it has few if any redeeming qualities:

> Much of the commentary on what's wrong with high school today is framed as what's wrong with high school students, who are blamed for drop-out rates, low attendance, declining test scores, crime, pregnancy and everything from litter to vandalism. The sad fact is that almost everything about high school fails to work — yet the system itself, the very idea of high school, is rarely blamed.

. . . [H]igh school as we conceive it now is fundamentally bad —
not a flawed system needing to be fixed, but a bureaucracy of the
worst kind, directly counterproductive to education, made up of a
million pieces of glue and tape, without a core. It can't simply be
"fixed."

High school is chaos mixed with boredom — much of it thoughtless, a
matter of many tiny decisions made over time. It is, I think, the only
world that can be made by people who have not known other worlds; it
is made up of piecemeal solutions that present themselves to people
who have seen only similar solutions. It is so big, entrenched and familiar that real change will always seem radically amiss to a lot of people
inside it. Real change here will be met with alarm by people who are utterly convinced nothing else would work but have never tried any other
way.   —Sallie Tisdale, "Second Thoughts"

Tisdale continues her essay by enumerating some specific problems high
school students face: boredom, noise, frustration, and so on. In each case
she traces the cause not to the students but to the structure of high
school itself.

> **Try Your Hand**   Try extending Tisdale's argument to consider some
> possible solutions to the problems she raises. List three ways that high
> school could be improved. Share your suggestions with one or two
> classmates, and then present the group's responses to the rest of the
> class.

Finally, argument is often used to invite or convince readers to reconsider or even change their position on an issue. One controversial
issue in U.S. education today is linguistic diversity: What languages and
dialects should students use at school? What languages and dialects
should be taught? Or should all students in U.S. schools use and learn
only "standard" English? In the following excerpt, stage and film critic
John Simon invites readers to consider (and perhaps be convinced of)
his opinion that "Good English Is Good for You":

The usual basic defense of good English (and here, again, let us not
worry about nomenclature — for all I care, you may call it "Standard
English," "correct American," or anything else) is that it helps communication, that it is perhaps even a *sine qua non** of mutual understanding. Although this is a crude truth of sorts, it strikes me as, in some
ways, both more and less than a truth. Suppose you say, "Everyone in
their right mind would cross on the green light" or "Hopefully, it won't
rain tomorrow"; chances are very good that the person you say this to

---

* **sine qua non:** a necessity.

will understand you, even though you are committing obvious sole-cisms* or creating needless ambiguities. Similarly, if you write in a let-ter, "The baby has finally ceased it's howling" (spelling *its* as *it's*), the recipient will be able to figure out what was meant. But "figuring out" is precisely what a listener or reader should not have to do. There is, of course, the fundamental matter of courtesy to the other person, but it goes beyond that: why waste time on unscrambling simple meaning when there are more complex questions that should receive our undi-vided attention? If the many cooks had to worry first about which out of a large number of pots had no leak in it, the broth, whether spoiled or not, would take forever to be ready.

Simon writes widely—and "correctly"—about English usage, and this essay is no exception. He spends the rest of the piece trying to convince his readers that the *only* good American language is "good English"; no other dialects, languages, or usages will do.

Try Your Hand   What is your position on "correct" English? What di-alects, languages, or usages do you feel are useful, even valuable, in America? How does your position overlap with or diverge from Simon's? Write out your position, and then write three reasons you hold that position.

How Do You Read an Argument?

In some ways, all spoken and written language is an argument. Every time a meaningful transaction occurs between a writer (or speaker) and reader (or listener), every time one person has successfully conveyed meaning to another person, a kind of argument takes place—to the ex-tent that everything or almost everything is an argument, to some de-gree. Whether you're listening to your friend's description of her wed-ding gown, reading about someone's battle with leukemia, watching a television news report about the torture of Iraqi prisoners, or listening to a radio ad enumerating all the reasons you should vote for a specific candidate in the next election, you're experiencing argument. Each of these speakers or writers is trying to express a point of view in such a way that you accept it. Because arguments are so prevalent, it's obviously important that you know how to read them closely and critically, to evaluate how strong an argument is and decide to what extent you are persuaded by it. Close critical reading of arguments is also important for another reason—seeing the ways that others succeed (or don't succeed)

---

* **solecisms:** violations of accepted language use or grammar.

in making their case will help you learn how to write your own arguments more effectively.

For example, look again at the letter to the editor about ice cream trucks on p. 632. The title and thesis statement of an argument — if they appear at all — will help orient you to the subject of the argument, the author's purpose for writing, and the intended audience. And the opening section of the argument will also often tell you how successfully the author connects with the audience. In "Stop the Music!" the title informs you right away about the general subject of the argument, although you have to read on to learn that it's about ice cream trucks. Notice that the writer begins by asserting that he likes ice cream and he likes children. He doesn't want readers to think he's nothing more than a neighborhood grouch, and so starting the letter by joining in these opinions that his readers are likely to share is a good way to gain their sympathy. Even when he moves on to a kind of preliminary thesis statement, it's phrased in a mild, not strongly negative way: "But it's hard to like an ice cream truck."

As you read the body of an argument, try to trace the progress of the author's reasoning to see if it makes good sense. In the case of the ice cream trucks, the reasoning is simple and straightforward. The man who likes ice cream and children doesn't like these trucks — and for what most readers would see as a good logical reason: they play obnoxious music when they tour his neighborhood each night. In the body of his argument, he details the situation that he's complaining about, but notice again that he describes the details in strictly neutral language. In fact, the harshest language he eventually uses about it is "a noise-menace to any neighborhood" and "this summer-time nuisance."

Finally, when reading an argument, you'll want to determine if the author has recommended any specific belief or course of action — appreciate the wedding gown, empathize with the leukemia patient, complain to officials about the treatment of prisoners, vote for Candidate Smith. The man who likes ice cream and children is arguing against an existing course of action: he wants ("I propose") to require the ice cream trucks to turn off their music whenever they are not moving. Even as he makes this proposal, he presents himself once more as a fair-minded person who's aware of all the implications of his argument: "I appreciate the need to earn a living." And he ends by directly inviting his readers to identify with him: surely many of them, who read the same newspaper and therefore live in the same general area, are suffering through the same experience as his. He's managed to make himself and his request sound reasonable and generous. Sometimes you'll want to make an argument in a more forceful, aggressive way than he has, but you'll still need to think carefully about how your audience feels about the subject and what they'll expect and accept in order to appeal to them successfully.

One last thing to be aware of as you analyze an argument critically is what it does *not* say. In "Stop the Music!" for example, the writer doesn't say anything about how loud the music from each truck is or how long it continues before the truck moves on to a new location. Nor does he mention that some readers may like the music from ice cream trucks, maybe because they associate it with summer or their childhood. These issues may not be essential to his argument, since most readers can agree that repeated music can be annoying no matter how briefly or softly it's played or how nostalgic it makes them feel. But often the things a writer leaves unmentioned *are* central to the effectiveness of an argument—and leaving out details or objections that readers need or expect to find may fatally weaken it. Think about this issue both when you're reading an argument and when you're writing one of your own.

How Do You Write an Argument?

When you argue a point in writing, you need to be concerned with a number of important issues that are generally more complex than issues related to any of the rhetorical methods discussed in earlier chapters. So, if you can, work with a classmate or two as you write. You and your classmates can help each other stay on track and remain alert to problems and weaknesses in your arguments.

Making a Claim

Once you decide what you're writing about, you'll need to consider your opinion on or belief about that subject and the **claim** you want to make about it—the position you want to take. The claim you make must necessarily be one of several claims that *could* be made with regard to this subject, and you should be aware of—and perhaps respond to—those other perspectives as you form your claim. In other words, your claim, which will become the basis of your **thesis statement,** must be **arguable.** In the readings that follow (pp. 654–73), James L. Shulman and William G. Bowen argue that athletes should not receive such preferential treatment in college admissions as they now do. Lynda Rush claims that Shulman and Bowen base their argument on sloppy science. Michael Webber argues that college athletics are a positive influence, both on campus and off. And William F. Shughart II argues that colleges and universities should create four-year degree programs in football and basketball, just like the degree programs in art, drama, and music. Of course, there are other perspectives for each of these claims, and the writers knew that when they made their arguments. None of them made claims that were not arguable: for instance, a claim like "college athletes have many boosters" or "some college athletes are also scholars."

Determining Your Purpose

What is at stake? What are the possible consequences of your argument? Are you writing to express or defend your own beliefs? to question or argue against something? or to invite or convince someone to reconsider a position? For instance, you might write a letter to the editor of your school newspaper expressing your belief that the student union should stay open longer on the weekends. Or you might question your instructor's assumption that careful planning is essential to success in writing, especially in your case. You might even write to the chair of the English Department in an attempt to convince her to drop attendance requirements from the department's grading policy; in your view, undergraduate students are old enough to monitor their own academic progress. Any of these arguments might be successful; in other words, your belief might prevail.

On the other hand, if you assert that having multiple romantic partners can be physically safe, your purpose might be to open up a lively discussion, given the pressure in America to practice monogamy and safe sex. In this case you probably shouldn't expect to convince all your readers to accept your argument, but you might succeed in being heard and understood.

Considering Your Audience

Who will be reading your argument? Whose opinion would you like to influence or change? How do your readers feel—and how much do they know—about the issue you are addressing?

In argument even more than in other kinds of writing, your audience is almost inseparable from your purpose. In fact, your audience may even shape your purpose, depending on whether its members (1) already agree with you and want their beliefs to be confirmed (look back at the Sapolsky excerpt on p. 636); (2) are willing to consider opinions, beliefs, or practices that differ from their own, but will need to be convinced (Tisdale is counting on readers to do just that in the excerpt on p. 636); or (3) are hostile or deaf to your opinion and will be looking for faults in it (consider Simon's excerpt on p. 637). Regardless of how you imagine your audience's response to your argument, you'll need to establish **common ground** with them, stating a goal toward which you both want to work or a belief, assumption, or value that you both share.

With college writing, it is sometimes hard to decide what audience to address your argument to, because your instructor may seem to be your only audience—as well as your judge. But once you decide on a subject that you feel strongly about, you need to imagine the person you need to convince, the person whose actions or opinions you'd like to influence. You can address this imagined audience as you write, even if you suspect that your instructor is your only flesh–and–blood reader. If you address a specific audience, the instructor can assume that position. After all, you need to determine this specific audience in order to write your thesis statement and choose your supporting arguments, according to what that audience knows and how they feel about your subject. For instance, educator Etta Kralovec imagines an audience already interested in homework and the issues surrounding it when she writes

> The problem isn't homework per se, it's that homework is unfair. It plays on social inequities. Consider the differences between families: One kid goes home to two well-educated parents, a home library and computer access to massive databases. Another kid goes home to parents who work at night, have no computer and no books. Which kid is going to handle homework better and do better in school?
>   — ETTA KRALOVEC, "Give Me a Break"

Kralovec establishes common ground immediately when she assures her readers that she is not objecting to homework in itself. As she continues, she explains that the problem is the implementation of homework, which has become a burden to families and the cheapest of school reforms:

> It's school reform on the cheap. It doesn't cost anything for educators and politicians seeking to please parents to say, "Let's raise academic standards by increasing the amount of homework." Many parents believe the more homework a school gives, the better it must be.

Even though Kralovec imagines an audience willing to listen to her argument, she still addresses another claim that could be made for homework — that it teaches good study habits:

> There is no reason to believe that having kids go home after sports and activities and sit down at 8 P.M. — after 13 hours of school — teaches good study habits. Good study habits are taught by teachers who can help kids learn how to structure their time.
>   It's a chicken-and-egg problem. If kids had more after-school programs and more time to take advantage of them, they might spend their time differently. One reason there aren't more opportunities for kids is homework consumes so much of their time. Actually, statistics show that kids watch less TV in the summer.

Convincing readers to agree completely with her is not Kralovec's purpose; rather, she wants the audience to reconsider their own ideas about homework:

> [I recommend] the end of homework as we know it. The school day needs to be restructured, probably lengthened, so homework can be done at school, under the direction of professionals, where students have

equal access to educational resources. What is currently called homework would not be done at home at all.

Kralovec makes her claim—that "homework" should be reconceived—to
the broad readership of *People* magazine. As she attends to her purpose
(questioning the value of homework as we know it) and to her audience
(*People* readers), she also attends to three other essential features of argument that all writers must address: (1) the ways you appeal to your audience; (2) the way you arrange your material; and (3) your pattern of reasoning. There are also several common errors of logic you'll want to take
care to avoid.

● Making Rhetorical Appeals

Just as you'll need to establish common ground with your audience,
you'll need to use other strategies as well in order to appeal to them. The
three basic kinds of strategies, called **rhetorical appeals,** are (1) the appeal of your own trustworthiness, or **ethos;** (2) the appeal of the reasoning in your argument, or **logos;** and (3) the appeal to the audience's
emotions, or **pathos.**

The first of these appeals, the **ethical appeal,** demonstrates your
character, credibility, and integrity as a writer and thinker, so that your
audience will continue listening to you. Establishing common ground
with the audience is one important part of the ethical appeal. You'll also
need to show how knowledgeable you are about the issue you're discussing and to represent opposing viewpoints accurately and fairly even
while disagreeing with them.

In an essay questioning the push to computerize classrooms, the author uses her introductory paragraphs to establish her ethos:

> . . . Today's children are the subjects of a vast and optimistic experi-
> ment. It is well financed and enthusiastically supported by major corpo-
> rations, the public at large, and government officials around the world. If
> it is successful, our youngsters' minds and lives will be enriched, society
> will benefit, and education will be permanently changed for the better.
> But there is no proof—or even convincing evidence—that it will work.
>
> The experiment, of course, involves getting kids "on computers" at
> school and at home in hopes that technology will improve the quality of
> learning and prepare our young for the future. But will it? Are the new
> technologies a magic bullet aimed straight at success and power? Or are
> we simply grasping at a technocentric "quick fix" for a multitude of prob-
> lems we have failed to address?
>
> I have spent hundreds of hours in classrooms, labs, and homes,
> watching kids using new technologies, picking the brains of leaders in
> the field, and researching both off- and on-line. As a longtime enthusiast
> for and user of educational computing, I found this journey sometimes
> shocking, often disheartening, and occasionally inspiring. While some

very exciting and potentially valuable things are happening between children and computers, we are currently spending far too much money with too little thought. It is past time to pause, reflect, and ask some probing questions.   —JANE M. HEALY, "Blundering into the Future: Hype or Hope?"

The second category, the **logical appeals,** are the reasons and evidence—facts, statistics, comparisons, anecdotes, expert opinions, personal experiences and observations—that illustrate or support your claim fairly, accurately, and knowledgeably. In another essay on classroom computerization, the authors write the following:

> Most schools have installed computers (the latest figures from Market Data Retrieval show the ratio of students to computers has fallen below 5 to 1). Most schools are wired and about 98 percent have internet access; more than half have a home page on the web, and about 70 percent of teachers claim regular use of computers. eLearning tools and the internet are opening windows to the world for most pupils.
> —WILLIAM G. ZIMMERMAN JR. AND RICHARD H. GOODMAN, "Thinking Differently about Technology in Our Schools"

Finally, the **pathetic appeals** are the emotional appeals that clarify the issue by touching its human elements. Appealing to an audience's emotions is one of the most effective ways to move that audience toward your own feelings about an issue. For example, in a report to the president and Congress about expanding the use of the Internet for education, the authors use pathos to argue their thesis:

> . . . Millions still cannot access the Internet and do not understand how to use it to harness the global web of knowledge.
> They do not know how to deal in information, the basic currency of the knowledge economy. They do not know how to find information, how to handle it, how to trade in it, how to invest it for their futures.
> —WEB-BASED EDUCATION COMMISSION, "The Power of the Internet for Learning"

Naturally, your choice of logical and pathetic appeals can enhance—or detract from—your ethos, so you'll want to choose reasons, evidence, and emotional appeals that not only are effective in their own right but also support your credibility as a fair-minded writer. For example, personal anecdotes can be powerful evidence, but if your own problems in, say, getting a student loan are the *only* evidence you cite for your argument that such loans are too hard to get, your audience may suspect that you are overgeneralizing from your own experience. On the other hand, citing statistic after statistic about loans without giving any individual examples may convince your readers, but at the cost of having them lose interest in your argument. In the same way, you'll need to judge emotional appeals carefully. If the audience feels that you're relying on emotion to make up for a weakness in your logical case—or if you've misjudged their own feelings about the issue—such appeals can back-fire.

Arranging All the Parts

Argument also requires that you pay careful attention to the arrangement of your essay, the ordering of your material. Every essay, of course, has an introduction, a body, and a conclusion, but an argumentative essay imposes special requirements for each section.

In your introduction, you'll want to orient your reader to your topic and, at the same time, establish it as worthy of consideration and yourself as a trustworthy writer. To get your reader's attention, you might open with a dramatic anecdote, a startling fact or statistic, or a brief historical overview. Your introduction should also establish your ethos in three ways: it should provide evidence of your goodwill, your good sense, and your good character. You may want to close your introduction with your thesis statement, the belief or opinion that you are arguing, as Lynda Rush does in the last sentence of her introduction (p. 661). (Using another organizational pattern, as discussed in the next section, you might save your thesis statement for the conclusion of your argument.)

Following the introduction is the body, in which you present the argument itself, providing reasons for your belief or opinion. Each reason must be supported with clear, relevant, and representative evidence that enhances the logic of your argument. Either before or after framing your opinion, you'll also need to mention and refute, or disprove, any opposing views—or admit their strong points—so that your audience knows that you are arguing from a basis of knowledge and understanding. As you move from one piece of evidence to the next, and between your own views and opposing ones, you'll need to use transitional words and phrases to help your readers follow your argument.

By the time you arrive at the conclusion of your argument, you will have laid out the importance of your subject, your own credibility as a thinker and writer, and a series of logical arguments. In your conclusion, then, you might want to use emotional appeals in order to connect—person to person—with your audience. (Of course, you may have included such appeals in earlier parts of the argument as well.) If you foresee potentially harmful or dangerous—or potentially beneficial or wonderful—consequences of a belief or an activity, now is the time to describe those consequences in a last attempt to encourage your readers to consider (if not commit to) a course of action. If you have not stated your thesis explicitly in your introduction—and perhaps even if you have—you will want to do so in your conclusion. Notice how Shulman and Bowen conclude their essay about preferential admissions for college athletes with an explicit statement of the proposal they are making for change, a proposal they have only implied up to that point:

> It seems clear that consideration should be given to changing the way in which at least some admissions offices approach the athletics side of the process of selecting a class. The admissions process should rely much less heavily on the coaches' lists, and less weight should be given to raw athletic talent and single-minded commitment to a sport—or what we can only call athletic "purposiveness." Rather, admissions staffs could be encouraged to revert to the practices of earlier days, when more weight was given to athletic talent seen in combination with other qualifications that made the applicant attractive to the institution—including a commitment to the educational purposes of the institution. The exceptional records achieved both in college and after graduation by the male athletes who entered in 1951 and the female athletes who entered in 1976 reflect the presence of the admissions approach we are advocating.
>
> In sum, intercollegiate athletics has come to have too pronounced an effect on colleges and universities—and on society—to be treated with benign neglect. Failure to see where the intensification of athletics programs is taking us, and to adjust expectations, could have the unintended consequence of allowing intercollegiate athletics to become less and less relevant to the educational experiences of most students, and more and more at odds with the core missions of the institutions themselves. The objective should be to strengthen the links between athletics and educational missions—and to reinvigorate an aspect of college life so that it can be celebrated for its positive contributions, not condemned for its excesses or criticized for its conflicts with educational values.
> —JAMES L. SHULMAN AND WILLIAM G. BOWEN, "How the Playing Field Is Encroaching on the Admissions Office"

● Considering Patterns of Reasoning

There are two basic ways to frame an argument: deductively and inductively. Deductive arguments move from a generalized claim to a series of supporting examples, and inductive arguments move in the opposite direction, from a limited number of specific cases to a generalization. Sociolinguist Deborah Tannen uses a deductive pattern of reasoning to argue that men talk more than women, supporting her claim with specific examples:

> Women are believed to talk too much. Yet study after study finds that it is men who talk more—at meetings, in mixed-group discussions, and in classrooms where girls or young women sit next to boys or young men. For example, communications researchers Barbara and Gene Eakins tape-recorded and studied seven university faculty meetings. They found that, with one exception, men spoke more often and, without exception,

> spoke for a longer time. The men's turns ranged from 10.66 to 17.07 seconds, while the women's turns ranged from 3 to 10 seconds. In other words, the women's longest turns were still shorter than the men's shortest turns.   —DEBORAH TANNEN, *You Just Don't Understand*

Tannen goes on to support her generalization with even more examples and studies of men talking more than women. But she doesn't always use deductive arguments; often she uses inductive ones, providing a series of examples or cases that lead readers to her general claim. Likewise, in the following excerpt, sportswriter Alexander Wolff provides a series of vignettes that illustrate the questionable values of many college athletes:

> Last week *The Miami Herald* reported that for several years University of Miami football players routinely took money, including incentive bonuses for hits and maimings, from former Hurricane players and Luther Campbell, the leader of the rap group 2 Live Crew. The players' attitude toward accepting this prohibited largess? Decidedly guilt-free. "They want us to be like regular students . . . but regular students don't generate revenue like we do. I don't remember the last time 70,000 people packed into the Orange Bowl to watch a chemistry experiment."
>
> Only a week earlier *SI [Sports Illustrated]* reported that seven Florida State football players had gone on an agent-funded shopping spree worth thousands of dollars at a Foot Locker store last season, and that six of them had also pocketed improper payments (*SI*, May 16 [1993]). "You work so hard to give to that program and get nothing out of it. . . . The most you can get out of it is a trip to the NFL. I felt entitled to money or clothing.   —ALEXANDER WOLFF, "An Honest Wage"

These examples work inductively toward Wolff's general claim, which appears at the very end of his essay: "So long as sports are conducted on college campuses, let the payoff for playing be something so valuable that no sleazy booster or agent could possibly slip it into an envelope and palm it off. Let it be a degree."

Avoiding Logical Fallacies

Throughout your essay you will want to use sound reasoning, avoiding errors of logic. If you use such **logical fallacies** (faulty reasoning), however innocently, you are sending up a warning flag to your readers that your thinking is not entirely trustworthy. Some of the most common logical fallacies are the following:

> The *ad hominem* fallacy (a personal attack) targets the actual person who holds an opinion rather than the opinion itself. For example: "I won't vote for any politician that Rush Limbaugh supports"; "I won't vote for any Democrats after the way Bill Clinton behaved with Monica Lewinsky."

"Reading" and Using Visuals in Argument

As you compose your essay, consider whether particular kinds of visuals—photographs, for instance—might enhance the pathetic appeal of your argument, just as diagrams, charts, and graphs might enhance its logical appeal. Politicians are well known for staging and distributing photos of themselves in military uniform, at military gatherings, and so on as a way to enhance their ethical appeal as strong, fearless leaders. And all the photographs of the late Princess Diana visiting the elderly, the infirm, and the diseased did more than any news story to enhance her ethos as a beautiful humanitarian.

To learn to use visuals effectively as a tool for argument, make a habit of examining visuals you encounter to see how they go about making their point and how effective they are at doing so. That is, learn to "read" visual arguments with a critical eye, the same way you would written arguments, to judge how well they achieve their purpose for their intended audience.

Look, for example, at the computer screen shot on p. 649, which shows the beginning of the "Education" page of the official White House Web site, www.whitehouse.gov, as it appeared on August 24, 2004. Notice that the main heading on the page—which is even larger than "The White House" at the top—calls attention to President George W. Bush's education reform initiative, No Child Left Behind. And the main focus of the page is an argument on behalf of this initiative, which is given a visual focus by a large photograph of the president with a group of elementary school children. The photograph starts the argument off with a strong ethical appeal—the most powerful man in the world makes time to visit a school and spend time with children, suggesting that his support for education reform is not just an abstract interest but a personal commitment. Depicting young children as opposed to high school seniors also gives the argument the maximum possible pathetic appeal, since most people are more sympathetic to arguments on behalf of younger children.

Following the photo, the main text of the page makes a logical appeal by emphasizing the connections between school preparation and future economic success. Notice that this text is placed in the center of the page and is in larger type than the lists in the left and right margins, which are mostly links to news stories and speeches with smaller pictures of Bush in various education-related settings. And the parts of the text that focus on the president's proposals and the benefits that are claimed for them are emphasized by boldface type, whereas the background information about graduation rates and the growing requirements for post-secondary education is in regular type.

Transforming the Federal Role in Education - Microsoft Internet Explorer

File   Edit   View   Favorites   Tools   Help

Back · · x · · Search · Favorites · Media · · · · · ·

Address · http://www.whitehouse.gov/infocus/education/   · Go   Links

President · News · Vice President · History & Tours · First Lady · Mrs. Cheney

YOUR GOVERNMENT   KIDS   ESPAÑOL   CONTACT   PRIVACY POLICY   SITE MAP   SEARCH

The White House
PRESIDENT GEORGE W. BUSH

HOME

EMAIL UPDATES [   ]   SEARCH

Issues
· Economy
· Iraq
· Education
· National Security
· Homeland Security
· More Issues
· En Español

News
· Current News
· Press Briefings
· Proclamations
· Executive Orders
· Radio

News by Date
· July 2004
· June 2004
· May 2004
· April 2004
· March 2004
· February 2004
· January 2004
· December 2003
· November 2003
· October 2003
· September 2003
· August 2003
· July 2003
· June 2003
· May 2003
· April 2003
· March 2003
· February 2003
· January 2003
· December 2002
· November 2002
· October 2002
· September 2002
· August 2002
· July 2002
· June 2002
· May 2002
· April 2002
· March 2002
· February 2002
· January 2002
· December 2001
· November 2001
· October 2001
· September 2001
· August 2001
· July 2001
· June 2001
· May 2001
· April 2001
· March 2001
· February 2001
· January 2001

Appointments
· Nominations
· Application

Home > News & Policies > Policies in Focus > Education   · Email This Page

EDUCATION REFORM
No Child left Behind

No Child Left Behind

Celebrating the second anniversary of the No Child Left Behind Act, President
George W. Bush visits with students at West View Elementary School in Knoxville,
Tenn., Jan. 8, 2004. White House photo by Paul Morse.

**President Bush is helping to expand opportunities for American students
and workers. His proposals will help more Americans graduate from
high school prepared for college or the workforce, access post-
secondary education, and get the job training and skills to compete in a
changing and dynamic economy and fill jobs in emerging industries.**

Students who fall behind in reading have a greater chance of dropping out
of high school altogether. Nationally, of 100 ninth-graders, only 68 will
graduate from high school on time, only 38 will directly enter college, only
26 are still enrolled their sophomore year, and only 18 will end up
graduating from college. The rates for minority students are even lower.
Only one-third of America.s workforce has any post-secondary education,
yet 60% of new jobs in the 21st century require post-secondary education.

**The President has set a new national goal: to ensure that every high
school student graduates and is ready for the workplace or college.**

High School Education: Through No Child Left Behind, President Bush has
already made the commitment to make a real difference in America.s
schools. While No Child Left Behind will prepare a new generation of
students with the knowledge they need to succeed, more can be done to
improve our Nation's high schools to meet the needs of the 21st Century
workforce. President Bush has proposed initiatives to ensure that every
student graduates from high school prepared to enter college or the
workforce with the skills needed to succeed, including:

- **Striving Readers:** The Striving Readers Initiative will provide
  competitive grants to schools to give extra help to middle and high
  school students who fall behind in reading. The President's FY
  2005 budget provides $100 million for the Striving Readers Initiative.
- **Mathematics and Science Partnership Program:** Increased
  funding for the Mathematics and Science Partnership Program
  authorized in No Child Left Behind will provide extra help to middle
  and high school students who fall behind in math. The President's
  FY 2005 budget provides an additional $120 million for this
  Department of Education program.

Speeches & News Releases

June 21, 2004
President's Education Policies
Discussed on "Ask the White
House"

May 12, 2004
President Bush Discusses No
Child Left Behind & "Reading
First"

May 11, 2004
President Bush Visits
Butterfield Junior High in Van
Buren, Arkansas

May 4, 2004
Charter Schools Discussed
on Ask the White House

April 30, 2004
President Bush Signs Indian
Education Executive Order

April 21, 2004
President Bush Announces
2004 National/State Teachers
of the Year

April 6, 2004
President Announces New
Education Initiatives for
Stronger Workforce

March 5, 2004
Education Discussed on Ask
the White House

February 13, 2004
President Meets with Parents,
Teachers on School
Choice/Parental Options

February 12, 2004
President Visits PA School to
Discuss Education &

This Web page uses visual and verbal elements to pull together all the rhetorical appeals (ethos, logos, and pathos) into a clear argument on behalf of the No Child Left Behind initiative. Taking into account the wide range of people who visit the White House Web site, it makes a broad-based appeal on the basis of widely shared values: concern for children and the desire to improve one's economic prospects. But notice that it does not address charges made by critics of the initiative, notably that Bush did not provide enough funding for his proposals and that they rely too heavily on standardized testing. (These criticisms would be difficult to address using visuals, other than perhaps charts or graphs about funding levels.) So the argument is likely to be effective mostly for those visitors to the site who are already favorably inclined or at least neutral toward the Bush administration.

If you are thinking of using visuals in an academic writing assignment, it's a good idea to check with your instructor beforehand. Also consider whether the visuals can stand on their own or whether you need to include captions, labels, or references to the visuals in the written text.

Begging the question (what is true is true) asks the audience simply to accept a statement as the truth when in actuality it is controversial. For example: "You and I both know that all lawyers are crooked"; "Of course, all interior walls should be painted off-white"; "All pornography is protected by the U.S. Constitution." Sometimes the logic is circular. The writer supports the supposedly controversial claim by restating the same claim in different words: "He is guilty of murdering his wife because he killed her"; "I am a Republican/Democrat because it is the best political party"; "Penn State lost the game because the other team kept scoring."

The *post hoc, ergo propter hoc* (after this, therefore because of this) fallacy assumes a cause-and-consequence relationship just because one event happened after another. If you argue that your grandmother broke her hip because she fell, you might be ignoring the possibility that her hip had been weakened by osteoporosis and that in fact she fell because her hip gave way. If you argue that Oregon State had a winning football season because of its new coach, you may be overlooking the fact that some of the star players are juniors and seniors who were trained for several years by the former coach.

The *non sequitur* (it does not follow) fallacy, like the preceding one, is also an error in cause-and-consequence analysis. Non sequiturs are faulty conclusions about consequences: "Because more retired people are moving to this area, we need to build another hospital"; "I'm related to the mayor; vote for me for city council"; "The war in Iraq was very divisive politically, so we shouldn't intervene elsewhere."

Sweeping generalizations (jumping to conclusions) are the kind of overstatements almost everyone resorts to when they have not thought through an issue or action. For example: "AIDS is a gay disease"; "Welfare recipients don't want to work"; "The United States is being overrun by illegal immigrants."

The *false dilemma* (either–or) fallacy, imagining only and no more than two sides or solutions to an issue, might be the most common kind of illogical thinking. Controversial issues such as abortion, same-sex marriage, welfare, euthanasia, and affirmative action may seem to have only two sides, pro and con. But in every case the issues are complicated in terms of their causes and possible solutions.

In fact, few of the issues you will argue offer easy answers or solutions. As you write arguments, you will want to take care to move your readers ethically and logically toward your careful and possibly tentative conclusion.

Understanding and Using Argument

Analyzing Argument

1. **Working with two or three classmates,** come up with two examples of each of the logical fallacies on pp. 647 and 650–51. Share your list with the rest of the class.

2. Reread the excerpt from John Simon's "Good English Is Good for You" on p. 637. Determine (1) if he uses deductive or inductive argument; (2) how he uses ethical, logical, and emotional rhetorical appeals; and (3) if he slips into any logical fallacies.

3. Refer back to the excerpts from Etta Kralovec's "Give Me a Break" (pp. 642–43). List as many reasons for having students do homework as you can think of. Given her position on the subject, how might she respond to each of your reasons?

Planning and Writing an Argument

1. Complete this statement: "One thing I believe in strongly is _____." Now list every reason you can think of to support your view.

2. Who — what groups or individuals — might agree with you?

3. Now complete this statement: "Mine is not the only opinion on this subject, though, because other people believe _____ or _____."

4. List all the reasons you can think of that these people might hold these opinions.

5. **Share your list with a classmate** to see whether he or she can suggest any other opinions you've not thought of. These might be views you
would need to acknowledge and perhaps refute in a written argument
on this topic.

6. Draft a three- to four-page argument essay, using as your topic the idea
you tried out in question 1. On a separate sheet of paper, describe your
audience, naming them if possible. List the views you think they hold
that are different from yours, and be sure to address them head-on in
your essay. Assume that this audience is willing to listen to, maybe even
consider seriously, your point of view. Refer to "Checking Over an Argument," below, as you draft and revise.

7. Look at the advertisement on p. 635 (or locate another advertisement
that you think offers a clear argument) and analyze it, evaluating its
power and noting its weaknesses. Draft a two- to three-page essay
in which you discuss the audience, purpose, rhetorical appeals, and
arrangement of this advertisement. Point out any logical fallacies that
you notice. Your thesis statement should make an argument about the
overall effectiveness of the ad. Refer to the following guidelines for
checking over an argument as you draft and revise.

✓ Checking Over an Argument

1. What is the topic or issue? How is it arguable? What claim does the essay
make about this topic? Underline the thesis statement of the argument.

2. Who is the audience for this argument? What do you think their attitude
is toward the issue? toward the essay's position? Does the argument take
their attitudes into account?

3. Given the audience, what is the argument's purpose? Write out the purpose in one sentence. Does the argument reflect this purpose?

4. Does the introduction establish goodwill, good sense, and good character? Does it establish common ground with the audience? How, exactly?

5. What specific support is provided for the claim? Number the supporting
points in the order that they are introduced. Are they all accurate? relevant? representative? In other words, are they used to best advantage?
After each number, write the kind of support it is: statistic, fact, personal
experience or observation, comparison, and so on. What other kinds of
support are needed?

6. Does the argument proceed deductively or inductively? Is this arrangement successful — or not?

7. Can you identify any logical fallacies in the argument?

8. Does the essay acknowledge and respond to opposing viewpoints?

9. Circle all transitional words or phrases that move the reader from one
point to the next. Are there other places where transitions are needed?

10. How does the conclusion appeal to the audience? What does it do to get readers to be sympathetic to the argument? How else could the conclusion establish an emotional link between you and the audience?

11. Do the visuals enhance the argument itself? How, specifically? Are captions, labels, or references to the visuals needed in the written text? If there are no visuals, should there be?

READINGS

Casebook:
College Athletics

JAMES L. SHULMAN AND WILLIAM G. BOWEN
How the Playing Field Is
Encroaching on the Admissions Office

James L. Shulman (b. 1965) is executive director of ARTstor, a project of the Andrew W. Mellon Foundation, which makes grants to institutions in education, cultural affairs, the performing arts, and environmental and public affairs. William G. Bowen (b. 1933) has been the president of the foundation since 1988 and was president of Princeton University from 1972 to 1988. He has written extensively on issues in higher education, especially affirmative action. The following article, which appeared in the *Chronicle of Higher Education* in January 2001, is excerpted from Shulman and Bowen's book *The Game of Life: College Sports and Educational Values* (2001).

> **Preview**   How do you imagine college athletics encroaches on college admissions?

Faculty members often remark that the most discouraging aspect of   1
teaching is encountering a student who just does not seem to care, who
has to be cajoled into thinking about the reading, who is obviously
bored in class, or who resists rewriting a paper that is passable but not
very good. Such students are failing to take full advantage of the educational opportunities that colleges and universities are there to provide.

Uninspired students come in all sizes and shapes, and no one would   2
suggest that athletes are uniformly different from other students in this

regard. But the evidence presented does demonstrate a consistent tendency for athletes to do less well academically than their classmates —
and, even more troubling, a consistent tendency for athletes to under-
perform academically not just relative to other students, but relative to
how they themselves might have been expected to perform. Those tendencies have become more pronounced over time, and all-pervasive:
Academic underperformance is now found among female athletes as well
as male, among those who play the lower-profile sports as well as those
on football and basketball teams, and among athletes playing at the Division III level as well as those playing in bowl games and competing for
national championships.

In our research, we studied 30 academically selective colleges and   3
universities. Being selective means that they receive many more applications from well-qualified students than they have places in their entering
classes, and thus must pick and choose among applicants on a variety of
criteria, including athletic talent. By national standards, the freshman
classes that they admit have very strong academic qualifications — with
SAT scores, for example, that are well above national norms, and with
large numbers of high-school valedictorians and National Merit Scholarship winners.

The institutions included Ivy League members — Columbia, Prince-   4
ton, and Yale Universities, and the University of Pennsylvania — and
women's colleges — Barnard, Bryn Mawr, Smith, and Wellesley. We also
studied coed liberal-arts institutions: Denison and Wesleyan Universities,
and Hamilton, Kenyon, Oberlin, Swarthmore, and Williams Colleges.
Some of the others that we reviewed were private universities in the Na-
tional Collegiate Athletic Association's Division I-A: Duke, Georgetown,
Northwestern, Rice, Stanford, Tulane, and Vanderbilt Universities, and the
University of Notre Dame. Others were Division I-A public institutions:
Miami University of Ohio, Pennsylvania State University at University
Park, the University of Michigan at Ann Arbor, and the University of
North Carolina at Chapel Hill. In addition, we looked at Emory, Tufts, and
Washington (Mo.) Universities.

What did we find? Athletes who are recruited, and who end up on   5
the carefully winnowed lists of desired candidates submitted by coaches
to the admissions offices of those selective institutions, now enjoy a very
substantial statistical "advantage" in the admissions process. That advantage — for both male and female athletes — is much greater than that enjoyed by other targeted groups, such as underrepresented minority students and alumni children.

For example, at a representative nonscholarship institution for which   6
we have complete data on all applicants, recruited male athletes who applied to enter with the fall-1999 class had a 48-percent greater chance of
being admitted than did male students at large, after taking differences
in SAT scores into account. The corresponding admissions advantage en-

joyed by recruited female athletes in 1999 was 53 percent. The admissions advantages enjoyed by minority students and legacies were in the range of 18 to 24 percent.

When recruited athletes make up such a substantial fraction of the   7
entering class in at least some colleges, is there a risk that there will be too few places for other students, who want to become poets, scientists, or leaders of civic causes? Is there a possibility that, without realizing what is leading to what, the institutions themselves will become unbalanced in various ways? For example, will they feel a need to devote more and more of their teaching resources to fields like business and economics — which are disproportionately elected by athletes — in lieu of investing more heavily in less "practical" fields, such as classics, physics, and language study? Similarly, as one commentator put the question, what are the effects on those students interested in fields like philosophy? Could they feel at risk of being devalued?

In an ideal world, institutions would like to see a diversity of majors,   8
values, and career choices among all subgroups of students. Society is best served when the financial-services sector "inherits" some students who have a deep commitment to understanding history and culture, rather than mainly those with a narrower focus on earning a great deal of money as an end in itself. In the same way, academe benefits when some of those who pursue Ph.D.'s include students who also have learned some of the lessons about life that are gained on the playing field, rather than just students with a narrower focus on an arcane, if not obscure, realm of academic research. In short, the heavy concentration of male athletes, in particular, in certain fields of study raises real questions of institutional priorities and balance.

Moreover, high-school students, their parents, and their schools   9
watch attentively for the signals that colleges send. The more that leading institutions signal *through their actions* how much they value athletic prowess, the greater the emphasis that potential applicants will place on those activities. The issuing of rewards based on sports accomplishments supports — and, in fact, makes real — the message that sports is the road to opportunity.

As a result, young people in schools of all kinds — from prep schools   10
to inner-city schools — are less likely to get a message that the way upward is to learn to write computer code or take chemistry seriously when it is not only the big-time-sports institutions but also the Ivies and the most selective liberal-arts colleges that place a large premium on athletic prowess, focus, and specialization. Athletics scholarships and tickets of admission to nonscholarship institutions provide a more powerful incentive than the promises contained in high-minded proclamations.

Taken together, such a signaling process has a powerful impact. We   11
were told of one situation in which almost half of the students from a leading prep school who had been admitted to an Ivy League university

*"I'm glad we won, and I hope that someday we'll have a
university that our football team can be proud of."*

were either outstanding hockey or lacrosse players, and not particularly noteworthy students. When asked at a recruiting session in a large city about the success of his prep school in placing its students in the most prestigious colleges, the school's representative gave the absolute number of students admitted to that Ivy League institution, hoped that no one would ask him how many of the admittees had been athletes, and went home with mixed feelings about his presentation. The real issue, however, is not about how forthcoming the prep-school representative was in explaining his school's success in placing students, but the nature of the reality that underlies that "success."

In fact, the changes in the face of athletics between the 1950's and 12 today can be related to a still broader shift in admissions philosophies. In the 1950's, much was said about the desirability of enrolling "well-rounded students." One consequence, among many others, was that athletes needed to have other attributes—to be ready to take advantage of the broad range of the institution's academic offerings, or to be interested in being part of the larger campus community, for example. Many of them were class officers, not just team captains. We suspect that the subsequent success of a number of the athletes of this era in gaining leadership positions, including positions as chief executive officers, owes something to their having had a strong combination of attributes.

Sometime in the late 1960's or the 1970's, that admissions philosophy 13 was altered in major ways. At some of the institutions with which we are familiar, the attack on the desirability of the well-rounded individual came from faculty members. One group of mathematicians objected vehemently to the rejection of candidates who had extremely high math aptitude scores but were not impressive in other respects. A new admissions mantra was coined; the search was on to enroll the "well-rounded class," rather than the well-rounded individual. The idea was that the super-mathematician should definitely be admitted, along with the super-musician and maybe even the super-gymnast. It was argued that, taken together, such an array of talented individuals would create an attractively diverse community of learners. For some years now, most admissions officers at academically selective institutions have talked in terms of the well-rounded class.

The mathematicians who lobbied for the admission of high-school 14 students with off-the-scale mathematical potential were absolutely right. "Spiky" students of that kind belong in a great university with a great mathematics department. We are much more skeptical, however, that "spikiness" can be used to justify the admission of a bone-crushing fullback whose high-school grades are over the academic threshold but who otherwise does not seem a particularly good fit for the academic values that a college espouses. There are many types of spikiness, and the objective should be to assemble a well-rounded class with a range of attributes that resonate with the academic and service missions of the institution. Looked at from that perspective, the arguments for spiky mathematicians and for spiky golfers seem quite different.

We also wonder how well some of the increasingly spiky athletes 15 who entered the colleges that we studied in 1989 (and those who entered later) will do in the long run. Not as well, we suspect, as their male predecessors who entered in the fall of 1951, and the female athletes who entered in 1976—and who appear to have had, as the saying goes, "more arrows in their quivers."

It seems clear that consideration should be given to changing the 16 way in which at least some admissions offices approach the athletics side of the process of selecting a class. The admissions process should rely much less heavily on the coaches' lists, and less weight should be given to raw athletic talent and single-minded commitment to a sport—or what we can only call athletic "purposiveness." Rather, admissions staffs could be encouraged to revert to the practices of earlier days, when more weight was given to athletic talent seen in combination with other qualifications that made the applicant attractive to the institution—including a commitment to the educational purposes of the institution. The exceptional records achieved both in college and after graduation by the male athletes who entered in 1951 and the female athletes who entered in 1976 reflect the presence of the admissions approach we are advocating.

In sum, intercollegiate athletics has come to have too pronounced an 17 effect on colleges and universities—and on society—to be treated with benign neglect. Failure to see where the intensification of athletics programs is taking us, and to adjust expectations, could have the unintended consequence of allowing intercollegiate athletics to become less and less relevant to the educational experiences of most students, and more and more at odds with the core missions of the institutions themselves. The objective should be to strengthen the links between athletics and educational missions—and to reinvigorate an aspect of college life so that it can be celebrated for its positive contributions, not condemned for its excesses or criticized for its conflicts with educational values.

Reading Closely

1. What specific information in this essay surprised you? Did any of the information alarm you?

2. What is your reaction to the following passage: "Athletes who are recruited ... enjoy a very substantial statistical 'advantage' in the admissions process. That advantage—for both male and female athletes—is much greater than that enjoyed by other targeted groups, such as underrepresented minority students and alumni children" (paragraph 5)? What is the basis for your reaction? Be prepared to share it with the rest of the class.

3. **Working with a classmate,** list all the examples and anecdotes the authors provide to support each of their assertions. Discuss your list to determine which examples do and do not work successfully to advance the authors' argument.

4. What is your reaction to the cartoon on p. 657? What argument is it making? How does it relate to Shulman and Bowen's thesis?

Considering Larger Issues

1. "How the Playing Field Is Encroaching on the Admissions Office" first appeared in the *Chronicle of Higher Education*. Who are the readers of that journal? Describe them.

2. What is Shulman and Bowen's purpose for this essay, particularly in terms of their *Chronicle* audience? What passages support your answer?

3. What is Shulman and Bowen's thesis? List the reasons they give to support their thesis? Why do you think they develop their argument inductively, waiting until their conclusion to state the thesis?

4. **COMBINING METHODS.** In order to advance their argument, Shulman and Bowen use *cause-and-consequence analysis.* Mark the passages that analyze consequence, identifying the consequences and explaining their effect on the overall essay.

Thinking about Language

1. Use the context of the essay or your dictionary to define the following words and phrases. Be prepared to share your definitions with the rest of the class.

cajoled (1)	arcane (8)	"spiky" (14)
underperform (2)	obscure (8)	benign neglect
winnowed (5)	mantra (13)	(17)
legacies (6)		

2. What one word would you use to describe Shulman and Bowen's attitude toward their subject in this essay? What specific phrases, passages, and examples develop and extend their attitude?

Writing Your Own Arguments

1. Whether or not you're a college athlete, you might be offended by Shulman and Bowen's essay. Draft a two- to three-page argument essay that defends an actual or hypothetical college admissions policy that favors athletes. Use as much specific information and support for your thesis as possible, and refer to the guidelines for checking over an argument on p. 652.

2. **Working with one or two classmates,** gather material for a short (two- to three-page) essay in response to Shulman and Bowen's. You might decide to divide up the research necessary to prove their argument wrong or to support them. Possible supporting or opposing information could include recruiting rules and violations, graduation rates of athletes in various programs, percentage of athletes given an admissions advantage in comparison to other targeted groups, and so on. You might focus on admissions at your own school or broaden your research to include the schools in your league, state, or region. You might then write individual essays or a coauthored group essay. Remember to use the guidelines for checking over an argument on p. 652.

LYNDA RUSH

Assessing a Study of College Athletes

● Lynda Rush (b. 1953), a professor and chair of the Department of Economics at California State Polytechnic University, Pomona, wrote a letter to the editor of the *Chronicle of Higher Education* in response to the previous essay, addressing head-on Shulman and Bowen's findings that athletes are favored in college admissions. Rush specializes in the economics of poverty and discrimination with an emphasis on gender issues.

> **Preview**   What do you imagine a professor of economics might have to say about the previous essay?

To the Editor:

James L. Shulman and William G. Bowen's *The Game of Life: College Sports and Educational Values* will certainly stimulate a storm of activity in college admissions offices and high–school advising offices throughout the country. The authors attempt to make the case that student athletes are taking the place of more deserving students. Their nostalgia for the good old days of the gentleman athlete pursuing a liberal arts education in the 1950s has certainly colored their analysis. While their story may be cloaked in statistics and elaborate charts, it's an example of very sloppy social science.

The authors appear to discount the contributions and accomplishments of student–athletes. The most egregious omission is the impact on socioeconomic diversity that I suspect that athletes bring to the elite institutions included in the study. Today's student athletes may bear little resemblance to the gentlemen athletes of the fifties and the authors appear to be blind to the fact that this may be a benefit. Student athletes attending these elite institutions in the fifties were typically white, upper class, and male.

Over the last 50 years, intercollegiate athletic programs have opened the doors of our elite colleges and universities to people of color, the working class, and women. The Civil Rights Movement and the passage of Title IX of the Education Amendments in 1972 broke down the barriers for minority and female athletes. Minorities were barely accepted in professional sports during the 1950's and were rarely if ever admitted to elite colleges and universities. Opportunities for women athletes to compete at the intercollegiate level did not even begin to percolate until the mid 1980's. The benefits of diversity are not easily calculated and are virtually ignored by the authors.

Shulman and Bowen include pages and pages of charts on mean G.P.A.'s, SAT scores, etc. to support their hypothesis, but they generally

1

2

3

4

fail to include even the most basic statistical significance tests. Their conclusions are based on the mean values of the performance indictors, and they fail to discuss the distribution of the values (the standard deviations) or even basic test of significance (*t*-values). An exception to this practice is their reported finding that athletes tend to earn higher wages after college. The authors did mention that the statistical significance of these findings was marginal. Mean values are only a piece of the story, because extreme high or low values can skew the mean up or down. For example, a closer look at individual SAT scores may have shown that most athlete SAT scores were comparable to the general student population with the exception of a few very low scores.

Shulman and Bowen write disdainfully about the athlete's typical   5
major (economics or political science) and their financial success later in life. Athletes' GPA's are probably lower due to the hours allocated to athletic competition. The authors make an interesting comparison to grades of students active in other extracurricular activities. Students involved in non-athletic extracurricular activities have higher grades according to their analysis. However, the authors did not directly compare the actual time commitment of the two groups. The spillover benefits of athletic competition are less likely to be direct and are more likely to accrue over time. The study did not attempt to address these indirect benefits.

The Game of Life appears to be an exercise in elitism designed to stir up   6
controversy in the hallowed halls of some of our most prestigious insti-

tutions of higher learning. I would hope that its intended audience sees through the foggy lens of the authors. Their nostalgia for a time when student athletes with large trust funds competed on verdant lawns surrounded by walls of ivy is just that, nostalgia.

Lynda Rush
Chair
Department of Economics
Professor of Economics
California State Polytechnic University
Pomona, Calif.

Reading Closely

1. Why does Rush feel she must respond to Shulman and Bowen?
2. What is your initial response to Rush's argument? How much do you care about college admissions, particularly in terms of college athletes?
3. On what grounds does Rush criticize the findings of Shulman and Bowen? Do you think her grounds are valid? Why or why not?
4. How exactly does the visual enhance Rush's argument?
5. **Working with a classmate,** determine the basic issue that Shulman and Bowen and Rush set out in each of their essays. What solution does each of these essays propose? Be prepared to share your response with the rest of the class.

Considering Larger Issues

1. What is Rush's thesis? What assertions does she make to support or extend her thesis?
2. Who is her intended audience? What might she want the readers to do in terms of her argument?
3. COMBINING METHODS. Although hers is an argumentative essay, Rush uses *causal analysis* throughout. How successful is her causal analysis? Why do you think she uses it?

Thinking about Language

1. Use the context of the essay or your dictionary to define the following words and phrases. Be prepared to share your definitions with the rest of the class.

student athletes (1)	socioeconomic (2)	allocated (5)
nostalgia (1)	hypothesis (4)	spillover (5)
gentleman athlete (1)	mean values (4)	elitism (6)
cloaked (1)	skew (4)	prestigious (6)
egregious (2)	disdainfully (5)	foggy lens (6)

2. What is Rush's attitude toward her subject? What specific words, phrases, passages, and examples demonstrate her attitude?

Writing Your Own Arguments

1. If you are a sports fan, you might be interested in drafting a three- to four–page essay in which you argue for the importance of intercollegiate athletics. You might argue for the value of intercollegiate athletics to the school, the student body, the alumni, and/or the athletes themselves. (Your argument might be strengthened by factual information regarding attendance records, box–office receipts, and income from memorabilia.) You might want to consider directing your argument to an audience of readers who want to de–emphasize intercollegiate athletics or abolish them altogether in order to emphasize academics. Refer to the guidelines for checking over an argument on p. 652.

2. Take another side on the issue of college sports. Draft a three- to four–page essay in which you argue that intercollegiate athletics should be re–placed with organized intramural sports in which all students would be required to participate or that women's sports should be given equal financial support and news coverage with men's sports. Whatever your argument, be sure to explain the advantages of your position. Refer to the guidelines for checking over an argument on p. 652.

MICHAEL WEBBER
Athletics Provide Positive Influence

Michael Webber was a Michigan State University student when he wrote the following column for the school newspaper, the *State News Loop*, in 2001.

> **Preview**   How might a sportswriter argue that athletics provide a "positive influence"?

Last Sunday during halftime of the men's basketball game at Breslin Student Events Center, the 1951 men's tennis team was awarded for its efforts of a half-century ago.

The team was the first outfit to win a Big Ten championship for MSU, shortly after joining the conference. The ceremony was symbolic of what is good about sports, and in particular college athletics.

Recently the drum beat has grown louder, as it does every few years, that higher education has lost its focus and that college athletics are destroying the American university.

"Sports Illustrated" recently wrote an article on the subject, citing two new books written by former university presidents.

The basic argument is that universities are so wrapped up in big-time college athletics they can't see straight. College athletics are not a

university need, but an unnecessary excess, one that is "losing relevance to the rest of university life," writes former U–M President James Duderstadt in his book "Intercollegiate Athletics and the American University: A University President's Perspective."

. . . College athletics are not losing their relevance to the rest of university life, at least not on campuses where the basketball student section doesn't call for the coach's head after every game. . . .   6

Proponents of Duderstadt's argument cite facts and figures which suggest college athletics have no bearing on either alumni contributions or admissions applications to the school.   7

In addition, the enrollment of college athletes with potentially lower academic achievements leaves other potentially more qualified students out in the cold.   8

However, numbers can often be manipulated to serve an argument's interest. And even if they are accurate, maybe the relevancy of and necessity for college athletics cannot be measured in mere numbers.   9

At MSU, we have a self–sustaining athletics program that is built on event revenues and alumni contributions. Our student athletes have the same graduation rate as the general student population. With class, practice and travel, their days are often longer than the average student's.   10

Like any other extracurricular activity, athletics are a part of a well–rounded education. People who criticize big–time college athletics fail to see that, while only looking at television and sneaker contracts as proof that higher education has sold out.   11

Though I do not think athletics should run a university, they should be a part of it. The end of big–time college athletics would inevitably mean the end of all other college sports, which would be a shame.   12

Not only are sports teams our university's most recognized ambassadors, but our athletic achievements bring a spirit and a glow that cannot come through other means.   13

Everyone is talking about MSU nowadays, and it is no small coincidence that we are coming off our first NCAA Men's Basketball Championship in 21 years.   14

It is hard to believe this exposure does not translate into a higher number of admissions applications or alumni contributions. However, I don't think these need to be the measurements of relevancy. Maybe an alumnus taking his family to a Spartan football game and teaching his young son or daughter the MSU Fight Song is a measurement of relevancy.   15

Maybe a national championship team that brings a community of students and residents closer together is a measurement of relevancy. Maybe a 1951 men's tennis team that can still command a standing ovation a half–century later is a measurement of relevancy.   16

For the future of college athletics, let's hope it is.   17

Reading Closely

1. What is the occasion for Webber to write this essay?

2. What arguments does Webber advance and what evidence does he provide that echo those of Shulman and Bowen? of Rush?

3. How does the visual support each of the arguments you've read (Shulman and Bowen's, Rush's, and Webber's)?

Considering Larger Issues

1. Who is Webber's intended audience? What does he want them to do with the information he's providing?

2. What is Webber's thesis? What reasons does he give to support it?

3. What might Webber's argument be were he discussing minor sports (soccer, lacrosse, diving) or women's athletics at Michigan State? How would he change his thesis, his examples, his purpose?

4. **COMBINING METHODS.** To support his argument, Webber analyzes both *causes* and *consequences*. Mark the passages in which he uses each kind of analysis. Why does he choose to use such analysis?

Thinking about Language

1. Use the context of the essay or your dictionary to define the following terms. Be prepared to share your definitions with the rest of the class.

   outfit (2)   bearing (7)   revenues (10)
   symbolic (2)   self-sustaining (10)   inevitably (12)

2. Unlike the authors of the previous essays in this casebook, Webber did not yet have a college degree when he wrote this essay. What specific terms, passages, or examples alert you to the fact that this essay was written by a younger person?

3. Which passages in this essay support the title "Athletics Provide Positive Influence"?

Writing Your Own Arguments

1. Webber doesn't mention the positive influence of women's college athletics. Draft a three- to four-page essay in which you argue for the value of women's athletics, using information from the federal policy enacted in 1972 known as Title IX, which states, "No person in the United States shall, on the basis of sex, be excluded from participation in, be denied benefits of, or be subjected to discrimination under any education program or activity receiving Federal assistance." Refer to the guidelines for checking over an argument on p. 652.

2. Using Webber's column as a basis, expand—and improve—his argument into a three- to four-page essay about the importance of another university program, such as debate, drama, marching band, or choir. Use your own experience, observation, and research to establish a thesis and to support it with reasons and evidence. As you draft and revise, refer to the guidelines for checking over an argument on p. 652.

WILLIAM F. SHUGHART II

Why Not a Football Degree?

William F. Shughart II (b. 1947) is F. A. P. Barnard Distinguished Professor of Economics and holder of the Robert M. Hearin Chair in Business Administration at the University of Mississippi. He has published numerous books, including *Modern Managerial Economics: Economic Theory for Business Decisions* (1994), *The Political Economy of the New Deal* (1998), and *Economics of Budget Deficits* (2002). Given his economic expertise, it is no wonder that he sees college football from a financial perspective. "Why Not a Football Degree?" first appeared in the *Wall Street Journal* in 1990; it offers yet another solution to the problems generated by college athletics.

> **Preview**   As you read the essay, consider the effectiveness of Shughart's use of logos—his logical reasoning.

Clemson University's football program was placed on probation last 1 spring for the second time in six years, and the coach who guided the team to a national championship in 1981 quit or was forced to resign. Last season's Heisman Trophy winner played at the University of Houston, a school banned from TV and postseason bowl appearances by the National Collegiate Athletic Association; Southern Methodist University fields a team barely resurrected last fall from the "death penalty" it received three years ago; and scandals have rocked the basketball programs at Kansas, Kentucky, Memphis State and North Carolina State.

Each of these events, which are only the latest in a series of NCAA 2 rules violations, has generated the usual amount of hand-wringing about the apparent loss of amateurism in college sports. Nostalgia for supposedly simpler times when love of the game and not money was the driving force in college sports has led to all sorts of reform proposals. The NCAA's decision to require its member institutions to make public athletes' graduation rates is perhaps the least controversial example. Proposition 48's mandate that freshman athletes must meet more stringent test score and grade point requirements to participate in intercollegiate sports has been criticized as a naked attempt to discriminate against disadvantaged (and mostly minority) high-school graduates who see athletics as a way out of poverty.

HALF-MEASURES

But whether or not one supports any particular reform proposal, 3 there seems to be a general consensus that something must be done. If so, why stop at half-measures? I hereby offer three suggestions for solving the crisis in college athletics.

1. *Create four-year degree programs in football and basketball.* Many colleges 4
and universities grant bachelor's degrees in vocational subjects. Art,
drama and music are a few examples, but there are others. Undergraduates who major in these areas are typically required to spend only about
one of their four years in basic English, math, history and science
courses; the remainder of their time is spent in the studio, the theater or
the practice hall honing the creative talents they will later sell as professionals.

Although a college education is no more necessary for success in the 5
art world than it is in the world of sports, no similar option is available
for students whose talents lie on the athletic field or in the gym. Majoring in physical education is a possibility, of course, but while PE is hardly
a rigorous, demanding discipline, undergraduates pursuing a degree in
that major normally must spend many more hours in the classroom
than their counterparts who are preparing for careers on the stage. While
the music major is receiving academic credit for practice sessions and
recitals, the PE major is studying and taking exams in kinesiology, exercise physiology and nutrition. Why should academic credit be given for
practicing the violin, but not for practicing a three–point shot?

2. *Extend the time limit on athletic scholarships by two years.* In addition to 6
practicing and playing during the regular football or basketball season,
college athletes must continue to work to improve their skills and keep
in shape during the off-season. For football players, these off–season activities include several weeks of organized spring practice as well as
year–round exercise programs in the weight room and on the running
track. Basketball players participate in summer leagues and practice with
their teams during the fall. In effect, college athletes are required to work
at their sport for as much as 10 months a year.

These time–consuming extracurricular activities make it extremely 7
difficult for college athletes to devote more than minimal effort to the
studies required for maintaining their academic eligibility. They miss lectures and exams when their teams travel and the extra tutoring they
receive at athletic department expense often fails to make up the difference.

If the NCAA and its member schools are truly concerned about the 8
academic side of the college athletic experience, let them put money
where their collective mouth is. The period of an athlete's eligibility to
participate in intercollegiate sports would remain four years, but the two
additional years of scholarship support could be exercised at any time
during the athlete's lifetime. Athletes who use up their college eligibility
and do not choose a career in professional sports would be guaranteed
financial backing to remain in school and finish their undergraduate degrees. Athletes who have the talent to turn pro could complete their degrees when their playing days are over.

3. *Allow the competitive marketplace to determine the compensation of college* 9
athletics. Football and basketball players at the top NCAA institutions pro-

vide millions of dollars in benefits for their respective institutions. Successful college athletic programs draw more fans to the football stadium and to the basketball arena. They generate revenues for the school from regular season television appearances and from invitations to participate in postseason play. There is evidence that schools receive increased financial support from public and private sources—both for their athletic and academic programs—if their teams win national ranking. There is even evidence that the quality of students who apply for admission to institutions of higher learning may improve following a successful football or basketball season.

Despite the considerable contributions made to the wealth and welfare of his or her institution, however, the compensation payable to a college athlete is limited by the NCAA to a scholarship that includes tuition, books, room and board, and a nominal expense allowance. Any payment above and beyond this amount subjects the offending athletic program to NCAA sanctions. In-kind payments to players and recruits in the form of free tickets to athletic contests, T-shirts, transportation and accommodations are also limited. These restrictions apply to alumni and fans as well as to the institutions themselves. The NCAA also limits the amount of money athletes may earn outside of school by curtailing the use of summer jobs as a means by which coaches and team supporters can offer higher wages to athletes.

The illegal financial inducements reported to be widespread in collegiate football and basketball represent conclusive evidence that many college athletes are now underpaid. The relevant question is whether the current system of compensation ought to remain in place. Allowing it to do so will preserve the illusion of amateurism in college sports and permit coaches, athletic departments and college administrators to continue to benefit financially at the expense of the players. On the other hand, shifting to a market-based system of compensation would transfer some of the wealth created by big-time college athletic programs to the individuals whose talents are key ingredients in the success of those programs.

It would also cause a sea change in the distribution of power among the top NCAA institutions. Under current NCAA rules, some of the major college athletic programs, such as those of Alabama, Notre Dame and Penn State in football, and North Carolina and Indiana in basketball, have developed such strong winning traditions over the years that they can maintain their dominant positions without cheating.

These schools are able to attract superior high school athletes season after season at the mandated NCAA wage with the offer of a package of non-monetary benefits (well-equipped training facilities, quality coaching staff, talented teammates, national exposure and so on) that increases the present value of an amateur athlete's future professional income relative to the value added by historically weaker athletic programs. Given this factor, along with NCAA rules that mandate uniform compensation across member schools, these top institutions have a built–in competitive advantage in recruiting the best and brightest athletes.

ILLEGAL INDUCEMENTS

It follows that under the current system, the weaker programs are 14 virtually compelled to offer illegal financial inducements to players and recruits if they wish to compete successfully with the traditional powers. It also follows that shifting to a market–based system of compensation would remove some of the built–in advantages now enjoyed by the top athletic programs. It is surely this effect, along with the reduction in the incomes of coaches and the "fat" in athletic departments to be expected once a competitive marketplace is permitted to work, that is the cause of the objection to paying student–athletes, not the rhetoric about the re-pugnance of professionalism.

It is a fight over the distribution of the college sports revenue pie 15 that lies at the bottom of the debate about reforming NCAA rules. And despite the high moral principles and concern for players usually ex-pressed by the debaters on all sides of the issue, the interests of the ath-lete are in fact often the last to be considered.

Reading Closely

1. What background information does Shughart supply that explains his solution?
2. **Working with two classmates,** discuss the arrangement of Shughart's argument. What information does he include in his introduction, his thesis statement, his supporting argument, his attention to opposing views, and his conclusion? Mark the specific passages that compose each of those sections. Share your group's findings with the rest of the class.

Considering Larger Issues

1. What is Shughart's purpose? How does it differ from the purposes of each of the preceding essays, particularly in terms of his *Wall Street Journal* audience?
2. What is Shughart's thesis statement? What reasons does he provide to support or extend his thesis statement?
3. **Working with a classmate,** mark the specific passages that support each of Shughart's reasons. Be prepared to share your findings with the rest of the class.
4. Which kind of rhetorical appeal does Shughart rely on most heavily: ethos, logos, or pathos? Identify words, phrases, or passages that support your answer.

5. **COMBINING METHODS.** On what other rhetorical method does Shughart rely as he develops his argument? Mark the passages using that other method. Why do you suppose Shughart used it?

Thinking about Language

1. Use the context of the essay or your dictionary to define the following terms or phrases. Be prepared to share your definitions with the rest of the class.

"death penalty" (1)	respective (9)	sea change (12)
amateurism (2)	compensation (10)	mandated (13)
stringent (2)	inducements (11)	non–monetary
counterparts (5)	market–based	(13)
kinesiology (5)	system (11)	repugnance (14)

2. When Shughart mentions "half–measures," what is he referring to? How do the half-measures compare with his suggestions, which might be called "full-measures"?

3. **Working with a classmate,** determine Shughart's attitude toward the subject of college sports. What specific words, phrases, or passages demonstrate his attitude? Share your group's response with the rest of the class.

Writing Your Own Arguments

1. Draft a two- to three–page essay in which you address each of Shughart's assertions. You may want to develop his argument and assertions further, or you may want to develop an argument that opposes his, perhaps point by point. In either case you'll need to do some research about college sports, on your campus, your school's athletic league, or your area of the country. Be sure to organize your argument so that it has an introduction, a thesis statement, supporting arguments, recognition of opposing arguments, and a conclusion. Refer to the guidelines for checking over an argument on p. 652.

2. **Consider working with two or three classmates** to discuss various new degrees that colleges might offer based on student interest or experience and moneymaking potential. You may have to study college catalogues in order to see what degrees are already in place. Draft a three- to four–page essay in which you argue for one such degree. You may want to arrange your essay like Shughart's, introducing the background information necessary to help you establish your argument. Work with your group as you each draft and revise your essays, referring to the guidelines for checking over an argument on p. 652.

Casebook:
Vegetarianism

ANDY KERR
On Eating Meat

Andy Kerr (b. 1955) is a self-proclaimed "conservationist, writer, analyst, political operative, inside/outside agitator, public speaker, strategist, tactician, foot
soldier, schmoozer, and raconteur." A well-known leader in environmental
causes in his native Oregon, especially for the preservation of old-growth
forests, he is the owner of The Larch Company, which carries out conservation projects; director of the National Public Lands Grazing Campaign, which
seeks a federal buyout of permits for grazing livestock on government land;
and founder and president of Alternatives to Growth Oregon, which seeks to
limit the state's population growth and resource consumption. Kerr is the author of the *Oregon Desert Guide: 70 Hikes* and has also written numerous articles
and a biweekly newspaper column. The following essay was published on his
Web site, <www.andykerr.net>, in 2001.

Preview   Do you have any opinions about eating meat? Do you eat
meat? Do you eat only certain kinds of meat?

Why, on this lovely but cold day, am I carrying this very high-powered   1
weapon? It's a crisp November morn in Oregon's Blue Mountains. The
light of first dawn is creeping down the opposite canyon wall and will
soon reach me. It's about time. I warm at the sight of the sun-struck old
growth ponderosa pine. If they have taken several centuries of cold
mornings worse than this, I guess I can take this morning.

Not yet fully awake and still tired from a long night in a down   2
sleeping bag whose loft is as down and out as they come, I walked with
James up the river trail well before sunrise to meet the other four members of our hunting party. A more hardy lot than James or I (maybe just
better sleeping bags), they camped last night with light rations and no tent.

The bivouac was our latest theory on how best to kill a Rocky   3
Mountain bull elk. We rationalized that by being "out there" before
dawn, before the animals were stirred up would provide the best opportunity to provide some meat for winter.

I am standing in a half-foot of snow at the mouth of a creek that   4
pours into the river. I stop and wait since I believe this is where the others will eventually arrive. A more energetic James has taken a mid-slope
sojourn through the pines now in full sun. Not only will they come

through here I reason, but most importantly I won't have to get my feet wet crossing the stream.

Why am I here? Oh yes, to kill an elk. Not a pleasant assignment, but   5
since I choose—for now at least—to eat flesh, I should at least attempt to personally acquire some of it each year. Since I currently eat and enjoy eating what once very much breathed such as I, should I not take the moral responsibility for the slaughtering and butchering?

As I prepared for "elk camp," several of my liberal friends and associ-   6
ates, when informed of my pending absence, said in effect, "have a good time and I hope you don't get anything."

I would smile and repress my urge to shout "You hypocritical bas-   7
tards! Where in hell do you think meat comes from? Not the goddamn supermarket all neatly sliced on Styrofoam and encased in cellophane. No, it comes from living animals who *died* by human hands to bring it to you. Now, if you haven't got the gonads to do it, that's one thing, but don't give me shit for taking direct responsibility for it."

Like I said, I suppressed those thoughts.   8

During the same period, I also encountered vegetarians who said the   9
same thing. That I could better tolerate.

I shuffle around, taking a quick tour of my stand. The river flows   10
below, snow mounds on the exposed rocks. The clouds tumble past quickly overhead, evidence of the high winds aloft. A noisy raven glides high to the south. I stare at a melting icicle, timing in my mind the drips.

Suddenly I get the feeling that I'm being watched. That hard to de-   11
scribe creepy feeling of being watched. Perhaps my paranoia, but just be- cause you are paranoid doesn't mean you are not being followed. I slowly turn and confirm my feeling. It's Tim, 30 yards up the trail with one of his near continuous cigarettes hanging out of his mouth. I now catch the smell of the smoke on the wind.

He stands there with his Nordic complexion, with hair more white   12
than blonde and his moustache submerging in four days worth of beard. I nod and he proceeds quietly. We meet. No blood on his hands. The elk are safe again. We chat in whispers and take nips from his whiskey flask. I don't care much for the stuff, but it tastes good now. We shift positions to better utilize the warmth of the sun. He relates his bivouac tale.

"Didn't see a thing. Fresh tracks everywhere, but not an animal in   13
sight. I know they are in there. Heard some shots. I was hoping they were you guys. Where's Jim?"

"You know how he is," I whispered.   14

"Yeah . . . , maybe the shots were Tommy. Heard one shot, followed   15
by three in rapid succession."

We chat on quietly waiting for the others. Soon, Tommy shows up.   16
Just as Nordic as Tim and a half–foot shorter, Tommy skips up to us with a big shit–eatin' grin on his face. No blood on his hands either. He *always* has that shit–eatin' grin. We repeat our earlier chat, this time not quite as

quietly. Tommy throws in lewd and obscene comments at every available opportunity. He's the horniest man in Oregon and makes no pretenses about it. Rumor has it that he has a closet full of negligees in all colors and sizes for whomever may be at his cabin. It is further rumored that he has a complete set of diaphragms ("You look like about a 48") in case his woman friend didn't bring hers.

The flask passes again and our conversation is at a near normal level. 17 Out of the corner of my eye, I see another walking body. We turn to see a lanky, tall man of 24 who acts a rightful 30, lumbering toward us with his rifle strung over his shoulder. A large pinch of Copenhagen serves to give the effect of a fat lip. No blood on his hands either. Again, we repeat our tales to Steve, who adds a few of his own. Our talk is now at a roar and is liberally aided by Steve's George Dickel "sippin' whiskey."

"Who the hell fired those shots?" roared Steve. "I thought it was you," 18 as he points with his whiskey bottle to Tommy.

"I wish," grins Tommy.   19

"Our only hope is Marty. And where *is* Jim?" says Tim.   20

"We'll find him on the way out," I offered.   21

The conversation is now at a full tavern roar. We finally hear a wild 22 whoop down by the creek. Our eyes turn and it is Marty saluting us with an upraised fist. The other hand holds a yellow government–issue plastic litterbag. A chorus of cheers commences, for we all know what's in the bag. The heart and the liver of a bull elk.

"Fresh meat in camp," shouts Tommy. Marty wearily stalks up the 23 slope to our caucus site. He sets his big frame on the log. He looks tired, and before he speaks he takes an offered cigarette. Another round of the flasks before we get down to the bloody details.

"It wasn't a half an hour after I left you guys. The snow was so damn 24 crunchy that rather than walking slow and quiet, I just bulled through the stuff for a while, and then I'd sit real quiet until I got cold.

"So I was sitting looking across this meadow at this badger. The little 25 sucker was playing in the snow, trying to get over this log. Hell, I must of watched him for 20 minutes. Finally I got cold, so I get up and start rolling up my sleeping pad that I'm sitting on. I see something out of the corner of my eye. I turn my head and there is the big bull elk standing right in the middle of the meadow. I just about shit. I reach down for my rifle, raise, aim, and fire. He goes down."

"But I heard four shots," interrupted Tim.   26

"Yeah. I shot him three more times. He was laying there flopping 27 around. It was making me sick. I couldn't stand it."

"He was probably dead. It was just reflexes," says Steve, who knows 28 all about that kind of stuff.

"Shit, I don't know. I just couldn't stand it. So, anyway, it's time to gut 29 it. God, I cut him open from bow to stern. I never seen such a big paunch. It was huge. The gut pile must be three feet high."

My paunch, still well attached, gets a bit queasy by the details. But 30
dammit, I think, this is what being a carnivore is all about. The story and
backslapping ceases and we start our long trek back to the rig.

That night in camp, all of us with Marty's wife, Catherine, ate heart, 31
liver, and gonads for dinner. Some of us passed on the "oysters," since
there were only two to go around. Since there wasn't enough ketchup in
camp (or the county for that matter), I passed on the liver as well. I con–
centrated on the heart, while Steve waxed eloquent about the ventricle
and aorta.

Around the fire in the teepee, Marty explains the gutting in even 32
more detail. "Shit, I never gutted anything before. Seen and read about it
a bit. After it finally stops flailing around, I roll it over as best I can and
pull my knife. I slit its belly from prick to neck. Out comes that *huge*
paunch. I thought it would never end."

There it goes with the paunch stuff again.   33

"So I get that out. But I knew you had to cut its throat to disconnect 34
the heart and lungs from the windpipe. I cut out the heart and liver and
set them aside. I know you have to be careful about the bladder, but I
had a hard time finding it. Finally I get all the stuff detached. I tried to
maneuver him for a better position, but he's so damn heavy. I didn't

want the meat to get tainted, so I must of washed the chest cavity out
with snow about six times."

"Christ, it will be shining," says Jim.   35

"Did you have any trouble skinning it?" asks Steve.   36

"Skin it," says Marty. "I was supposed to skin it there? Oh shit, I hope   37
I didn't blow it."

"No big deal," assured our resident anatomist. "It's just that tomorrow   38
morning the whole thing will be frozen solid. Tough skinning is all. In
warmer weather, you should skin right away to make sure the meat cools
properly."

More eating, drinking and finally sleep.   39

It was up at the crack of midmorning for the big pack out. Marty   40
managed to slew the beast in the wilderness as far from a road as possible. We loaded pack frames, lunches and beer into Tim's father's 1954
Willys four wheel drive station wagon and drove to the nearest road's
end. It was two steep downhill miles to the kill.

We are in excellent spirits on the way down. All seven of us headed   41
out choosing to discuss the lovely day rather than the torturous loads we
would carry on the way out. Steve carried the lone rifle in case we saw
something else.

It was indeed a glorious day. A few clouds drifted by to the northeast.   42
The snow was powdery and knee–deep as we headed down the slope. We
were soon all strung out, with Marty leading and I bringing up the rear. No
chance of getting lost, since I have six sets of tracks to choose from.

I am not looking forward to the quartering and boning. I actually   43
prefer to think of the killer pack. But, I reason, it's only right to have
blood on your hands if it's going to be in your mouth.

My thoughts turn to my youth and my first big kill. Hunting was se-   44
rious business in my family. My mother wasn't keen on it, but I grew up
mainly on venison and elk supplied by my father. If not wild game, it
was mostly beef or chicken for dinner. My grandmother shot her last
deer when she was in her seventh decade. Before I carried a gun at 13, I
always clamored to accompany my father on his hunting trips.

With a rifle in hand, however, I was confronted with the stark reality.   45
Yes, the goal was to shoot that very beautiful and very living mule deer.
After that, one had to gut it, skin it, cut and wrap it, and of course eat it. I
always was grossed out when I had to assist in the family gutting. Up to
your armpits in hot, still living guts, blood, hair, and other indescribable
tissues and liquids.

But what really bothered me was the killing. Put the defenseless ani-   46
mal in the sights and blast it to death with a .30 caliber bullet. Would I
have the "guts" to do it? It bothered me greatly, since I could detect no
such reluctance from my fellow hunters and role models.

Due to fortunate circumstances for me and the deer, I never had to   47
confront my cowardice for the first two seasons. My reluctant cowardice

was two-fold. The inability to shoot the animal and the fear of telling my father of my fears.

In my 15th year, I came up with what I thought was the perfect solu- 48 tion: I'd just shoot and miss. Embarrassing, but face-saving. Rather a bad shot than a pansy. Then I'd phase myself slowly out of the hunting religion.

However, it didn't work out as planned. About 20 miles south of 49 where I now stand on the bank of the North Fork of the Malheur River is Antelope Mountain. My father and I had dropped off some fellow hunters and were driving the rig around to meet them on a "stand." Stands are great. You can sit against a tree and pretend to be seriously looking for the mere movement of a deer. I usually contemplated more serious matters, such as the jigsaw pattern of ponderosa pine bark or my budding sexuality. Come to think of it, I still think a lot about sex on the stand.

We are cruising along and a forked horn buck runs across the road. 50 My father hits the brakes and looks over to me and says to go it. I jump out and run behind the vehicle. Although I intend to shoot to miss, I nonetheless am very excited. I raise my Remington 760 "Gamemaster" and peer through the 3 to 9 power variable scope.

The primeval instinct took over. The prey was trying to escape me, 51 the predator. Kill! Kill! I had the blood lust. I squeezed the trigger. Nothing happened. Forgot to release the safety catch. I squeeze again. I feel the recoil, but don't hear anything. I focus again. The buck turns and looks toward me and drops to the ground. It's still moving. I shoot (unnecessarily) again. It doesn't move anymore. We run up to it. I stand staring with both pride and revulsion. My first shot was right out of the textbook. Right through the shoulder. The second, however, was a gut shot. Very messy. As a result, my father gutted it to make sure the meat didn't get tainted. Fortunately, I missed my full immersion baptism in guts.

The deed done, I placed my duly authorized State of Oregon deer tag 52 number 144328 on the animal. We carted it to the rig and drove off. The magpies already eyeing the gut pile. Later my grandfather mounted the tiny antlers, and they hang still as a reminder in my front room.

The canyon narrows, and it's necessary to cross the stream several 53 times. I hear voices and know I'm near the kill. I sit to rest, out of sight of the others.

That didn't end my hunting. It took a more spiritual experience 54 while hunting chuckars on the east side of Steens Mountain. The following Christmas vacation was a time to slew this exotic Asian bird. The chuckar is fair eating if you shoot enough. The little devils were tough hunting, since they always flew uphill. I am again walking along with my father, this time on foot through the sagebrush. The old man notices that I'm not into it and proceeds to chew me out.

So I take the long route back to camp. I sit down on a big boulder 55
covered with orange lichen and have a talk with myself. It was a beautiful day. The Alvord Desert, a barren alkali flat to the east, framed cloud
shadows on its white canvas with ease. The sun was warm, the air cool
and crisp.

But I was just pissed. Mad at my father, mad at myself, and mad at 56
the world. Just then a jackrabbit hopped by, and I simply blasted it with
my .20 gauge double–barreled shotgun. Both barrels. For no other reason
than I was pissed off. The rabbit was just in the wrong place at the wrong
moment. I walked over to it, kicked it over and then started crying.

Oh well, I can't avoid it any longer. I walked around the bend in the 57
creek with my comrades in the meadow. They were rolling up their
sleeves. We discussed the task. Steve assumed the unspoken command,
since he was the anatomical fanatic. He directed work crews top and bottom.

Catherine built a fire, more for atmosphere rather than any needed 58
heat value. We named him Herman. I quickly volunteer to be the sawyer.
Less chance of touching blood and flesh, I figured.

There was a short silence where I and, I suspect, the others said a 59
short prayer of thanks in our own religion for Herman's sacrifice. I am
standing over this recently living elk. Its rich golden brown fur coat hides
a third of a ton of blood and guts and brains and brawn. "Let's go," someone said softly.

I was directed to saw off the horns. Tommy held while I hacked first 60
through hair then skull and then brain. My stomach was slightly queasy.
Not too bad, though, since Herman was stone cold dead. I sawed incor-
rectly, and the rack of antlers broke in two.

Soon the hide was off. As we cut and hacked, Herman gradually 61
turned from a once–living being to pieces of meat. Tommy stripped off
the meat from the ribs. Tim, Marty, and Steve wrestled with the massive
hindquarters. Then the front quarters. Jim cut at various parts, more like
a surgeon than a butcher. Catherine shuttled between creek and fire,
washing and bagging meat.

Finally, it is all cut up. The sun is getting a bit low in the southwest- 62
ern sky. Herman isn't Herman anymore. It's just piles and piles of meat,
bones, hide and, oh yes, let us not forget, guts. As I stare at the bare rib
cage, I realize why it got progressively easier for me to handle the meat
as we went along. It wasn't that I got used to it in the sense of becoming
callous to it, but rather that the animal turned progressively from a
once–living being to simply cuts of meat. With some Styrofoam and cellophane and some rose–colored glasses, we could be at Safeway.

But we aren't. We are two miles down in this deep canyon and it is 63
getting dark. To a chorus of groans, we lift our 100–pound packs. One
step at a time. No problem. Just take it easy. As we trudge up the snow
slippery slope, the rest stops become more frequent. Each step is becom-

ing a serious chore. Damn this pack aches. I am relishing each brief rest and every flat spot in the trial is a brief paradise.

I suggest that Steve pass that gun around so we may take turns 64 holding it on each other, so we may force each other up the hill. The sun is down now and it's getting cold, but the pouring sweat insulates me well. Left foot, right foot. Ah, the last stretch. I hear the others. By their boisterous yells, I know they are at the Willys. Someone touches off a rifle shot in a one–gun salute.

Reading Closely

1. What is Kerr's thesis? List the assertions he makes to support his thesis.

2. **Together with a classmate,** list all the examples and anecdotes the author provides to support each of his assertions. Discuss your list to determine which examples do and don't work successfully to advance the argument.

3. What specific information in this essay surprised you? Did any of the information alarm you?

Considering Larger Issues

1. Kerr's essay first appeared on his pro–conservation Web site. Who reads such Web sites? Who might comprise the reading audience of this particular essay? Who might Kerr have been considering as his audience when he wrote this essay? Describe them.

2. What is Kerr's purpose for this essay, particularly in terms of a potential audience? What specific passages support your answer?

3. What is your reaction to the following passage?

> Where in hell do you think meat comes from? Not the goddamn supermarket all neatly sliced on Styrofoam and encased in cellophane. No, it comes from living animals who *died* by human hands to bring it to you. Now, if you haven't got the gonads to do it, that's one thing, but don't give me shit for taking direct responsibility for it.

What is the basis for your reaction? Be prepared to share it with the rest of the class.

4. **COMBINING METHODS.**   In order to advance his argument, Kerr uses *narration.* Mark the passages that display narrative elements — setting, characters, dialogue, sequence of events, and so on — and explain their effect on the overall essay.

5. How does the visual on p. 677 enhance or complement Kerr's argument? Be prepared to share your answer with the rest of the class.

Thinking about Language

1. **With another student,** use the context of the essay or your dictionary to define the following words and phrases. Be prepared to share your definitions with the rest of the class.

high–powered weapon (1)	suppressed (8)	paunch (29)
old growth (1)	negligees (16)	queasy (30)
hardy (2)	Copenhagen (17)	slew (40)
bivouac (3)	"sippin' whiskey" (17)	torturous (41)
sojourn (4)	full tavern (22)	strung out (42)
pending (6)	stalks (23)	clamored (44)

2. What words, phrases, or passages suggest and develop the metaphor of hunting as a kind of war? How does this war metaphor enhance Kerr's attitude toward his subject in this essay? What additional phrases, passages, and examples develop and extend this attitude?

3. What specific descriptive details does Kerr include to create images of members of his hunting party? What words or phrases help create a positive, negative, or neutral overall image of each member?

Writing Your Own Arguments

1. **With one or two classmates,** research material for a three- to four-page essay in response to Kerr's argument, either agreeing that meat eaters should experience killing their own meat or arguing that there's no logical reason they should do so. You may decide to divide up the research in various ways, such as according to which side each of you supports. Possible supporting or opposing information could be government limits on slaughter and hunting, health and safety regulations for slaughter houses and hunting, the levels of expertise necessary for successful hunting and butchering, and so on. You may find yourselves relying on comparison and contrast analysis or on an in–depth look at one method of meat preparation in particular. Depending on the extent to which your group agrees and the preferences of your instructor, you might then write individual essays or a group, coauthored essay. Remember to use the guidelines for checking over an argument on p. 652.

2. Whether you're a carnivore, vegetarian, hunter, or grocery–store shopper, you might be offended by Kerr's essay. Draft a two- to three–page argumentative essay that defends your eating habits or method of procuring food. Use as much specific information and support for your thesis as possible, and refer to the guidelines for checking over an argument on p. 652.

ALISON GREEN

Living in Harmony with Vegetarians

The following essay originally appeared in the *Washington Post* in 1995. It has since been widely republished on various pro-vegetarian Web sites, such as vegweb.com.

Preview   Have you ever had trouble living in harmony with vegetarians — or, if you are a vegetarian, living in harmony with nonvegetarians?

I concluded, after careful consideration, that eating meat was incompatible with my values, even though I loved meat and didn't care much for vegetables. I was sure my tastebuds would rebel, perhaps hold a beansprout or two hostage in my mouth until I paid a ransom of a burger or strip of bacon.

Happily, it didn't work out quite the way I expected; my biggest problem as a vegetarian has not been the food — which I've found to be delicious and every bit as satisfying as meat — but the bewildering attitudes of my family and friends. Other vegetarians have the same complaints: the weird looks, the silly questions, the hostile interrogations. It seems vegetarians — 12 million of us in the U.S. and growing daily — are a sadly misunderstood minority indeed. Thus, I've devised ten simple edicts for meat-eaters in their dealings with vegetarians:

Rid yourself of the idea that vegetarians are spartans who subsist on raw carrots and bean sprouts. The question I hear more than anything else is "What do you eat?" This one baffles me; how would anyone with a reasonably varied diet answer that? I eat spaghetti, stir-fry, hummus, stew, raspberry sorbet, minestrone soup, salads, bean burritos, gingerbread, lentil chili, lasagna, tofu kabobs, waffles, veggie burgers, artichokes, tacos, bagels, saffron rice, lime mousseline, wild mushroom risotto — what do you eat?

Learn some biology. I'm still not sure what to do with otherwise intelligent people who think a chicken is not an animal. For the record, vegetarianism means no red meat, poultry, or fish — nobody with a face. I can't count the number of times waiters have suggested the seafood platter as a "vegetarian" entree.

Especially if someone is a vegetarian for ethical reasons, don't assume they won't object to "just a little" meat in their meal. Would you accept "just a bit" of your cat, or "just a little" of Uncle Jim in your soup?

Quit lobbying for the meat industry. Carnivores seem to think that vegetarians are like dieters and that we want to cheat a little now and then. My father is convinced that if he can convince me of how good his corned beef and cabbage tastes, I'll give in and eat it. Friends try to get me to try "just a bite" of whatever meat product they're eating, on the premise that it's so good, I couldn't possibly pass it up. I sometimes think meat–eaters took their lessons in peer pressure from the bad kids in the anti–drug movies we used to watch in high school. Listen up: no matter how "good" you insist it is, we're not going to eat it.

When a vegetarian gets sick, don't tell him or her it's because of mal-   7
nourishment. From the comments I hear when I have the flu, you'd think meat–eaters never get sick. When I get sick, there's always someone waiting to tell me it's because of my diet. In actuality, just as there are healthy and unhealthy meat–eaters, there are healthy and unhealthy vegetarians. (And by the way, studies have shown that vegetarians have stronger immune systems than meat–eaters.)

When you're in a restaurant with a vegetarian, have patience—eat-   8
ing out can be a challenge for even seasoned vegetarians. Despite the acceptance into the mainstream of a veggie diet, most restaurant menus are still cluttered with animal products. Some restaurants seem to have nothing but meat on their menus; even the salads have eggs or chicken in them! Don't complain if our attempts at ascertaining the exact ingredients in the minestrone seem like paranoia; experience has taught us these tableside inquisitions are warranted. After years of quizzing waiters and waitresses, I've found that items described as vegetarian often contain chicken broth, lard, eggs, or other animal ingredients.

Don't make faces at our food. Before you scrunch up your face at my   9
soy hot dog or tofu, think about what you're eating. Just because eating animals is widely accepted doesn't mean it's not gross.

Realize we've probably heard it before. One of the funniest things   10
about being veg is the person who is positive that he has the argument that is going to change my mind. It's almost invariably one of these gems:
(a) "Animals eat other animals, so why shouldn't humans?" (Answer: Most animals who kill for food couldn't survive if they didn't do so. That's obviously not the case with humans. And since when have we looked to animals for our standards of behavior?)
(b) "Our ancestors ate meat." (Answer: Perhaps—but they also lived in caves, conversed in grunts, and had very limited choices of lifestyle. Supposedly, we've evolved since then.)

Despite popular opinion, you do not have the right to expect vege-   11
tarians to compromise personal beliefs for the sake of "politeness." People who would never dream of asking a recovered alcoholic to try their favorite vodka, or demand that someone who kept kosher have some bacon still think it perfectly reasonable to expect me to eat Aunt Sue's meatloaf because I adored it as a child and she would be ever so insulted if I didn't have some now.

Stop telling us humans "have to" eat meat; we're living proof they   12
don't. People who otherwise respect my ability to take care of myself refuse to trust that I did not make the decision to become a vegetarian rashly. I've done plenty of research on vegetarianism—probably more

than you've done on diet and nutrition—and I'm confident in the choice I've made. Are you aware of the studies showing meat–eaters are almost twice as likely to die from heart disease, 60% more likely to die from cancer, and 30% more likely to die from other diseases? I wouldn't be eating this way if extensive research hadn't convinced me that vegetarianism is healthier and more ethical than eating meat; a more appropriate question might be whether you can back up your diet.

Now go forth and exult in your smooth dealings with vegetarians. 13 You might find things so harmonious that you'll want to try vegetarianism yourself.

Reading Closely

1. Why does Green feel she needs to defend her eating habits?
2. What is your initial response to the points she makes in her argument? How much do you care about someone else's eating habits?
3. **With a classmate,** determine the basic problem that Green sets out in this essay. What solutions does she propose? How would you summarize her solutions in one sentence? Be prepared to share your responses with the rest of the class.

Considering Larger Issues

1. What is Green's thesis? Does she state it explicitly?
2. Who is her intended audience? What might she want her readers to do in terms of her argument? How does her intended audience differ (or not) from the readers of the *Washington Post,* where her essay originally appeared? How does it differ (or not) from the online readers of vegweb.com?
3. **COMBINING METHODS.** Although hers is an argumentative essay, Green depends on *comparison and contrast* analysis throughout. How successful is her comparison and contrast analysis? Why do you think she uses it in this essay?

Thinking about Language

1. **Together with a classmate,** use the context of the essay or your dictionary to define the following words and phrases. Be prepared to share your definitions with the rest of the class.

incompatible (1)	ethical (5)	warranted (8)
bewildering (2)	lobbying (6)	invariably (10)
interrogations (2)	malnourishment (7)	kosher (11)
spartans (3)	ascertaining (8)	exult (13)
baffles (3)	inquisitions (8)	harmonious (13)

2. What is Green's attitude toward her subject? What specific words and phrases demonstrate her attitude?

3. Green says she is providing "ten simple edicts" for meat–eaters, and most of her ten points begin with short, blunt commands: "Learn some biology." "Quit lobbying for the meat industry." "Don't make faces at our food." What is the effect of giving her advice this way? Why might she have chosen to do so? Would a less direct approach be more successful with her meat–eating readers or less so?

Writing Your Own Arguments

1. If you are careful about what you eat, you might be interested in drafting a three– to four–page essay in which you argue for the importance of a healthful or an ethical diet. You might argue for the value of vegetarianism for global ecology, for your health, or for animal rights. You might argue for a diet balanced in meats, vegetables, and starches. Or you might argue for a low–carbohydrate diet for reasons of weight or cholesterol control. Your argument can be strengthened by factual and personal information regarding the health consequences of any of these diets. You might want to consider directing your argument to an audience of readers who want to reconsider their own eating habits. Refer to the guidelines for checking over an argument on p. 652.

2. Take another side to the issue of eating habits. Draft a three– to four–page essay in which you argue for improving (in some way) the food available on your campus. You might discuss the food service in the dorms, the restaurants available on and off campus, your grocery–store options, or (on a smaller scale) the eating habits of you and your friends. Whatever your argument, be sure to explain the advantages of your position. Refer to the guidelines for checking over an argument on p. 652.

LAURA FRASER

Why I Stopped Being a Vegetarian

Laura Fraser (b. 1961) is author of *Losing It: False Hopes and Fat Profits in the Diet Industry* (1997) and the travel memoir *An Italian Affair* (2001). She has written for numerous magazines, including *Vogue, Mother Jones, Gourmet,* and the *New York Times Magazine.* "Why I Stopped Being a Vegetarian" originally appeared in the online magazine salon.com and was published in print in the collection *Best American Food Writing* (2001).

Preview   What eating or drinking habits have you started — and then stopped?

1   Until a few months ago, I had been a vegetarian for 15 years. Like most people who call themselves vegetarians (somewhere between 4 and 10 percent of us, depending on the definition; only 1 percent of Americans are vegans, eating no animal products at all), I wasn't strict about it. I ate dairy products and eggs, as well as fish. That made me a pesco-ovo-lacto–vegetarian, which isn't a category you can choose for special meals on airlines.

2   About a year ago, in Italy, it dawned on me that a little pancetta was really good in pasta, too. After failing to convince myself that pancetta was a vegetable, I became a pesco–ovo–lacto–pancetta–vegetarian, with a "Don't Ask, Don't Tell" policy about chicken broth. It was a slippery slope from there.

3   Nevertheless, for most of those 15 years, hardly a piece of animal flesh crossed my lips. Over the course of that time, many people asked me why I became a vegetarian. I came up with vague answers: my health, the environment, the impracticality and heartlessness of killing animals for food when we can survive perfectly well on soy burgers. It was political, it was emotional and it made me special, not to mention slightly morally superior to all those bloodthirsty carnivores out there.

4   The truth is, I became a vegetarian in college for two reasons. One was that meat was more expensive than lentils, and I was broke, or broke enough to choose to spend my limited budget on other classes of ingestibles. The other was that I was not a lesbian.

5   This is not to say that all lesbians are carnivores; in fact, there's probably a higher percentage of vegetarians among lesbians than most other groups. But there was a fair amount of political pressure to be something in those days. Since, as a privileged white girl from suburban Denver, I couldn't really identify with any oppressed minority group, I was faced with becoming a lesbian in order to prove my political mettle. I had to decide between meat and men, and for better or worse, I became a vegetarian.

The identity stuck, even though the political imperative for my label   6
faded. It wasn't an identity that ever really fit: My friends thought it odd
that such an otherwise hedonistic woman should have that one ascetic
streak. It was against my nature, they said. But by then, I'd started to believe the other arguments about vegetarianism.

First was health. There's a lot of evidence that vegetarians live longer,   7
have lower cholesterol levels and are thinner than meat–eaters. This is somewhat hard to believe, since for the first few years of not eating meat, I was
basically a cheesetarian. Try leafing through some of those vegetarian recipe
books from the early '80s: You added three cups of grated cheddar to everything but the granola. Then vegetarianism went through that mathematical
phase where you had to figure out which proteins you had to combine with
which in order to get a complete protein. Since many nutritionists will tell
you people don't need that much protein anyway, I gave up, going for days
and days without so much as contemplating beans or tofu.

For whatever haphazard combination of proteins I ate, being a vege-   8
tarian did seem to have a stunning effect on my cholesterol level. This, of
course, could be genetic. But when I had a very involved physical exam
once at the Cooper Institute for Aerobic Fitness in Dallas, my total cholesterol level was a super–low 135, and my ratio of HDL (good) cholesterol to LDL (evil) was so impressive that the doctor drawled, "Even if you
had heart disease, you would be reversing it." This good news, far from
reassuring me that I could well afford a few barbecued ribs now and
then, spurred me on in my vegetarianism, mainly because my cholesterol
numbers effectively inoculated me against the doctor's advice that I also
needed to lose 15 pounds.

"Why?" I asked. "Don't you lose weight to lower your cholesterol?"   9

He couldn't argue with that. Whether or not most vegetarians are   10
leaner than carnivores, in my case I was happy to more than make up
the calories with carbohydrates, which, perhaps not coincidentally, I always craved.

After the health rationale came the animal rights one. Like most veg-   11
etarians, I cracked Peter Singer's philosophical treatise on animal rights,
and bought his utilitarian line that if you don't have to kill animals, and
it potentially causes suffering, you shouldn't do it. (Singer, now at Princeton, has recently come under attack for saying that if a human being's
incapacitated life causes more suffering than good, it is OK to kill him.)

It's hard to know where to stop with utilitarianism. Do I need a cash-   12
mere sweater more than those little shorn goats need to be warm themselves? Do animals really suffer if they have happy, frolicking lives before
a quick and painless end? Won't free–range do?

My animal rights philosophy had a lot of holes from the start. First of   13
all, I excluded fish from the animal kingdom—not only because fish
taste delicious grilled with a little butter and garlic, but also because they
make it a lot easier to be a vegetarian when you go out to restaurants.
Now that's utilitarian. Besides, as soon as you start spending your time

*"I started my vegetarianism for health reasons, then it became
a moral choice, and now it's just to annoy people."*

fretting about the arguments that crowd the inner pens of animal rights
philosophy—do fish think?—then you know you're experiencing a real
protein deficiency.

I rationalized the fish thing by telling myself I would eat anything I 14
would kill myself. I had been fly-fishing with my dad and figured a few
seconds of flopping around was outweighed by the merits of trout al-
mondine. (Notice that I, not the fish, was doing the figuring.) But who
was I kidding? If I were hungry enough, I'd kill a cow in a heartbeat. I'd
practically kill a cow just for a great pair of shoes.

Which brings me to the leather exception. As long as other people 15
are eating cow, I decided, I might as well recycle the byproducts and di-
minish the harm by wearing leather jackets and shoes. When everyone
stopped eating meat, I'd stop buying leather jackets and shoes. In the
meantime, better stock up.

Then there's the environmental rationale. There is no doubt, as 16
Frances Moore Lappe first pointed out in her 1971 book *Food First*, that
there is a huge loss of protein resources going from grain to meat, and
that some animals, especially cattle and Americans, use up piggish
amounts of water, grain and crop land.

But the problem really isn't meat, but too much meat — over-grazing, 17
over-fishing and over-consumption. If Americans just ate less meat — like
driving cars less often — the problem could be alleviated without giving
up meat entirely. That approach has worked for centuries, and continues
to work in Europe.

All my deep vegetarian questioning was silenced one day when a 18
friend ordered roasted rosemary chicken for two. I thought I'd try "just a
bite," and then I was ripping into it like a starving hyena. Roasted
chicken, I realized, is wonderful. Meat is good.

From a culinary point of view, that's obvious. Consider that most veg- 19
etarians live in America and England, places tourists do not visit for the
food. You don't find vegetarians in France, and rarely in Italy. Enough said.

As for health, if nutritionists are always telling you to "listen to your 20
body," mine was definitely shouting for more meat. One roasted bird unleashed 15 years' worth of cravings. All of a sudden I felt like I had a bass
note playing in my body to balance out all those soprano carbohydrates.
Forget about winning the low-cholesterol Olympics. For the first time in
a long time, I felt satisfied.

As a vegetarian, not only had I denied myself something I truly en- 21
joyed, I had been anti-social. How many times had I made a hostess uncomfortable by refusing the main course at a dinner party, lamely saying
I'd "eat around it"? How often did my vegetarianism cause other people to
go to extra trouble to make something special for me to eat, and why did
it never occur to me that that was selfish? How about the time, in a small
town in Italy, when the chef had presented me with a plate of very special
local sausage, since I was the American guest — and I had refused it, to the
mortification of my Italian friends? Or when a then-boyfriend, standing in
the meat section of the grocery store, forlornly told a friend, "If only I had
a girlfriend who ate meat"? If eating is a socially conscious act, you have to
be conscious of the society of your fellow homo sapiens along with the animals. And we humans, as it happens, are omnivores.

Reading Closely

1. What is the occasion for Fraser to write this essay?

2. What arguments does Fraser advance for becoming a vegetarian in the
   first place?

3. What specific information suggests that she was never very strongly
   committed to vegetarianism?

Considering Larger Issues

1. Who is Fraser's intended audience at salon.com? What does she want
   that audience to do with the information she's providing?

2. How does Fraser's basic argument run counter to Green's "Living in Harmony with Vegetarians"? What do the two essays have in common?

3. What might Fraser's argument be were she discussing why she stopped being a meat eater? How would she change her thesis, her examples, her purpose, her intended audience?

4. **COMBINING METHODS.**   To support her argument, Fraser analyzes both causes and consequences of being a vegetarian. Mark the passages in which she uses each kind of analysis. What is the overall effect of such analysis? What other methods of development does she use? Where and to what effect?

5. How does the visual on p. 689 relate to arguments you hear about vegetarianism—or about vegetarians?

Thinking about Language

1. Use the context of the essay or your dictionary to define the following terms and phrases. Be prepared to share your definitions with the rest of the class.

vegans (1)	imperative (6)	treatise (11)
pesco–ovo–lacto (1)	hedonistic (6)	incapacitated (11)
pancetta (2)	cheesetarian (7)	utilitarianism (12)
slippery slope (2)	contemplating (7)	fretting (13)
lentils (4)	inoculated (8)	deficiency (13)
ingestibles (4)	carnivores (10)	culinary (19)
mettle (5)	rationale (11)	mortification (21)

2. What tone does Fraser take toward her subject, that of becoming and then ceasing to be a vegetarian? What words or phrases support your answer?

Writing Your Own Arguments

1. Fraser mentions both the positive and the negative consequences of being a vegetarian. Draft a three- to four-page essay in which you argue for or against using diet as a way to assert one's identity and beliefs. Refer to the guidelines for checking over an argument on p. 652.

2. Write a three- to four-page essay arguing for the importance of consistently standing by a specific ethical decision one has made, whether it has to do with diet, war and peace, loyalty to friends or family, avoidance of plagiarism, women's rights, animal rights, or some other issue. Or, if you prefer, argue for the importance of being flexible and the dangers or drawbacks of being rigid about a particular ethical stance. Use your own experience, observation, and (if necessary) research to establish a thesis and reasons and to support your argument. As you draft and revise, refer to the guidelines for checking over an argument on p. 652.

MICHAL POLLAN

An Animal's Place

Michael Pollan is a contributing writer to the *New York Times Magazine*, where this essay originally appeared in 2002, and writes a column on architecture for *House & Garden*. He has also served as executive editor of *Harper's* magazine and has been a guest lecturer at the University of California, Berkeley. Pollan's books include *A Place of My Own: The Education of an Amateur Builder* (1997), *Second Nature: A Gardener's Education* (1991), and *The Botany of Desire* (2001). He received the 1992 QPB New Vision Award for *Second Nature*, the John Burroughs prize for the best natural history essay in 1997, the 2000 Reuters-World Conservation Union Global Award for Environmental Journalism for reporting on genetic engineering, and the Borders Original Voice Award for the best nonfiction work of 2001.

> **Preview**   What do you consider to be the place of domestic, farm, household, or wild animals in the world, particularly in relation to humans?

The first time I opened Peter Singer's "Animal Liberation," I was dining 1
alone at the Palm, trying to enjoy a rib–eye steak cooked medium–rare. If this sounds like a good recipe for cognitive dissonance (if not indigestion), that was sort of the idea. Preposterous as it might seem, to supporters of animal rights, what I was doing was tantamount to reading "Uncle Tom's Cabin" on a plantation in the Deep South in 1852.

Singer and the swelling ranks of his followers ask us to imagine a fu- 2
ture in which people will look back on my meal, and this steakhouse, as relics of an equally backward age. Eating animals, wearing animals, experimenting on animals, killing animals for sport: all these practices, so resolutely normal to us, will be seen as the barbarities they are, and we will come to view "speciesism"—a neologism I had encountered before only in jokes—as a form of discrimination as indefensible as racism or anti-Semitism.

Even in 1975, when "Animal Liberation" was first published, Singer, 3
an Australian philosopher now teaching at Princeton, was confident that he had the wind of history at his back. The recent civil rights past was prologue, as one liberation movement followed on the heels of another. Slowly but surely, the white man's circle of moral consideration was expanded to admit first blacks, then women, then homosexuals. In each case, a group once thought to be so different from the prevailing "we" as to be undeserving of civil rights was, after a struggle, admitted to the club. Now it was animals' turn.

That animal liberation is the logical next step in the forward march 4
of moral progress is no longer the fringe idea it was back in 1975. A growing and increasingly influential movement of philosophers, ethicists,

law professors and activists are convinced that the great moral struggle of our time will be for the rights of animals.

So far the movement has scored some of its biggest victories in Europe. Earlier this year, Germany became the first nation to grant animals a constitutional right: the words "and animals" were added to a provision obliging the state to respect and protect the dignity of human beings. The farming of animals for fur was recently banned in England. In several European nations, sows may no longer be confined to crates nor laying hens to "battery cages"—stacked wired cages so small the birds cannot stretch their wings. The Swiss are amending their laws to change the status of animals from "things" to "beings."

Though animals are still very much "things" in the eyes of American law, change is in the air. Thirty-seven states have recently passed laws making some forms of animal cruelty a crime, 21 of them by ballot initiative. Following protests by activists, McDonald's and Burger King forced significant improvements in the way the U.S. meat industry slaughters animals. Agribusiness and the cosmetics and apparel industries are all struggling to defuse mounting public concerns over animal welfare.

Once thought of as a left-wing concern, the movement now cuts across ideological lines. Perhaps the most eloquent recent plea on behalf of animals, a new book called "Dominion," was written by a former speechwriter for President Bush. And once outlandish ideas are finding their way into mainstream opinion. A recent Zogby poll found that 51 percent of Americans believe that primates are entitled to the same rights as human children.

What is going on here? A certain amount of cultural confusion, for one thing. For at the same time many people seem eager to extend the circle of our moral consideration to animals, in our factory farms and laboratories we are inflicting more suffering on more animals than at any time in history. One by one, science is dismantling our claims to uniqueness as a species, discovering that such things as culture, tool making, language and even possibly self-consciousness are not the exclusive domain of Homo sapiens. Yet most of the animals we kill lead lives organized very much in the spirit of Descartes, who famously claimed that animals were mere machines, incapable of thought or feeling. There's a schizoid quality to our relationship with animals, in which sentiment and brutality exist side by side. Half the dogs in America will receive Christmas presents this year, yet few of us pause to consider the miserable life of the pig—an animal easily as intelligent as a dog—that becomes the Christmas ham.

We tolerate this disconnect because the life of the pig has moved out of view. When's the last time you saw a pig? (Babe doesn't count.) Except for our pets, real animals—animals living and dying—no longer figure in our everyday lives. Meat comes from the grocery store, where it is cut

and packaged to look as little like parts of animals as possible. The disappearance of animals from our lives has opened a space in which there's
no reality check, either on the sentiment or the brutality. This is pretty
much where we live now, with respect to animals, and it is a space in
which the Peter Singers and Frank Perdues of the world can evidently
thrive equally well.

Several years ago, the English critic John Berger wrote an essay, "Why 10
Look at Animals?" in which he suggested that the loss of everyday contact between ourselves and animals—and specifically the loss of eye
contact—has left us deeply confused about the terms of our relationship
to other species. That eye contact, always slightly uncanny, had provided
a vivid daily reminder that animals were at once crucially like and unlike us; in their eyes we glimpsed something unmistakably familiar (pain,
fear, tenderness) and something irretrievably alien. Upon this paradox
people built a relationship in which they felt they could both honor and
eat animals without looking away. But that accommodation has pretty
much broken down; nowadays, it seems, we either look away or become
vegetarians. For my own part, neither option seemed especially appetiz-
ing. Which might explain how I found myself reading "Animal Liberation" in a steakhouse.

This is not something I'd recommend if you're determined to con- 11
tinue eating meat. Combining rigorous philosophical argument with
journalistic description, "Animal Liberation" is one of those rare books
that demand that you either defend the way you live or change it. Because Singer is so skilled in argument, for many readers it is easier to
change. His book has converted countless thousands to vegetarianism,
and it didn't take long for me to see why: within a few pages, he had
succeeded in throwing me on the defensive.

Singer's argument is disarmingly simple and, if you accept its prem- 12
ises, difficult to refute. Take the premise of equality, which most people
readily accept. Yet what do we really mean by it? People are not, as a
matter of fact, equal at all—some are smarter than others, better looking,
more gifted. "Equality is a moral idea," Singer, points out, "not an assertion of fact." The moral idea is that everyone's interests ought to receive
equal consideration, regardless of "what abilities they may possess." Fair
enough; many philosophers have gone this far. But fewer have taken the
next logical step. "If possessing a higher degree of intelligence does not
entitle one human to use another for his or her own ends, how can it entitle humans to exploit nonhumans for the same purpose?"

This is the nub of Singer's argument, and right around here I began 13
scribbling objections in the margin. But humans differ from animals in
morally significant ways. Yes they do, Singer acknowledges, which is why
we shouldn't treat pigs and children alike. Equal consideration of interests is not the same as equal treatment, he points out: children have an
interest in being educated; pigs, in rooting around in the dirt. But where

their interests are the same, the principle of equality demands they receive the same consideration. And the one all–important interest that we
share with pigs, as with all sentient creatures, is an interest in avoiding
pain.

· · ·

I have yet to find anyone who still subscribes to Descartes's belief that 14
animals cannot feel pain because they lack a soul. The general consensus
among scientists and philosophers is that when it comes to pain, the
higher animals are wired much like we are for the same evolutionary
reasons, so we should take the writhings of the kicked dog at face value.
Indeed, the very premise of a great deal of animal testing — the reason it
has value — is that animals' experience of physical and even some psychological pain closely resembles our own. Otherwise, why would cosmetics testers drip chemicals into the eyes of rabbits to see if they sting?
Why would researchers study head trauma by traumatizing chimpanzee
heads? Why would psychologists attempt to induce depression and
"learned helplessness" in dogs by exposing them to ceaseless random
patterns of electrical shock?

　　That said, it can be argued that human pain differs from animal pain 15
by an order of magnitude. This qualitative difference is largely the result
of our possession of language and, by virtue of language, an ability to
have thoughts about thoughts and to imagine alternatives to our current
reality. The philosopher Daniel C. Dennett suggests that we would do
well to draw a distinction between pain, which a great many animals experience, and suffering, which depends on a degree of self-consciousness
only a few animals appear to command. Suffering in this view is not just
lots of pain but pain intensified by human emotions like loss, sadness,
worry, regret, self-pity, shame, humiliation and dread. . . .

　　Which brings us — reluctantly, necessarily — to the American factory 16
farm, the place where all such distinctions turn to dust. It's not easy to
draw lines between pain and suffering in a modern egg or confinement
hog operation. These are places where the subtleties of moral philosophy
and animal cognition mean less than nothing, where everything we've
learned about animals at least since Darwin has been simply . . . set aside.
To visit a modern CAFO (Confined Animal Feeding Operation) is to enter
a world that, for all its technological sophistication, is still designed according to Cartesian principles: animals are machines incapable of feeling pain. Since no thinking person can possibly believe this any more,
industrial animal agriculture depends on a suspension of disbelief on the
part of the people who operate it and a willingness to avert your eyes on
the part of everyone else.

　　From everything I've read, egg and hog operations are the worst. 17
Beef cattle in America at least still live outdoors, albeit standing ankle
deep in their own waste eating a diet that makes them sick. And broiler

chickens, although they do get their beaks snipped off with a hot knife to keep them from cannibalizing one another under the stress of their con-finement, at least don't spend their eight-week lives in cages too small to ever stretch a wing. That fate is reserved for the American laying hen, who passes her brief span piled together with a half-dozen other hens in a wire cage whose floor a single page of this magazine could carpet. Every natural instinct of this animal is thwarted, leading to a range of behavioral "vices" that can include cannibalizing her cagemates and rub-bing her body against the wire mesh until it is featherless and bleeding. Pain? Suffering? Madness? The operative suspension of disbelief depends on more neutral descriptors, like "vices" and "stress." Whatever you want to call what's going on in those cages, the 10 percent or so of hens that

can't bear it and simply die is built into the cost of production. And when the output of the others begins to ebb, the hens will be "force-molted" — starved of food and water and light for several days in order to stimulate a final bout of egg laying before their life's work is done.

Simply reciting these facts, most of which are drawn from poultry- 18 trade magazines, makes me sound like one of those animal people, doesn't it? I don't mean to, but this is what can happen when . . . you look. It certainly wasn't my intention to ruin anyone's breakfast. But now that I probably have spoiled the eggs, I do want to say one thing about the bacon, mention a single practice (by no means the worst) in modern hog production that points to the compound madness of an impeccable industrial logic.

Piglets in confinement operations are weaned from their mothers 10 19 days after birth (compared with 13 weeks in nature) because they gain weight faster on their hormone- and antibiotic-fortified feed. This premature weaning leaves the pigs with a lifelong craving to suck and chew, a desire they gratify in confinement by biting the tail of the animal in front of them. A normal pig would fight off his molester, but a demoralized pig has stopped caring. "Learned helplessness" is the psychological term, and it's not uncommon in confinement operations, where tens of thousands of hogs spend their entire lives ignorant of sunshine or earth or straw, crowded together beneath a metal roof upon metal slats suspended over a manure pit. So it's not surprising that an animal as sensitive and intelligent as a pig would get depressed, and a depressed pig will allow his tail to be chewed on to the point of infection. Sick pigs, being underperforming "production units," are clubbed to death on the spot. The U.S.D.A.'s recommended solution to the problem is called "tail docking." Using a pair of pliers (and no anesthetic), most but not all of the tail is snipped off. Why the little stump? Because the whole point of the exercise is not to remove the object of tail-biting so much as to render it more sensitive. Now, a bite on the tail is so painful that even the most demoralized pig will mount a struggle to avoid it.

Much of this description is drawn from "Dominion," Matthew Scully's 20 recent book in which he offers a harrowing description of a North Carolina hog operation. Scully, a Christian conservative, has no patience for lefty rights talk, arguing instead that while God did give man "dominion" over animals ("Every moving thing that liveth shall be meat for you"), he also admonished us to show them mercy. "We are called to treat them with kindness, not because they have rights or power or some claim to equality but . . . because they stand unequal and powerless before us."

Scully calls the contemporary factory farm "our own worst night- 21 mare" and, to his credit, doesn't shrink from naming the root cause of this evil: unfettered capitalism. (Perhaps this explains why he resigned from the Bush administration just before his book's publication.) A tension has always existed between the capitalist imperative to maximize efficiency and the moral imperatives of religion or community, which have historically served as a counterweight to the moral blindness of the market. This is one of "the cultural contradictions of capitalism"—the tendency of the economic impulse to erode the moral underpinnings of society. Mercy toward animals is one such casualty.

More than any other institution, the American industrial animal 22 farm offers a nightmarish glimpse of what capitalism can look like in the absence of moral or regulatory constraint. Here in these places life itself is redefined—as protein production—and with it suffering. That venerable word becomes "stress," an economic problem in search of a cost-effective solution, like tail-docking or beak-clipping or, in the industry's latest plan, by simply engineering the "stress gene" out of pigs and chickens. "Our own worst nightmare" such a place may well be; it is also real life for the billions of animals unlucky enough to have been born beneath these grim steel roofs, into the brief, pitiless life of a "production unit" in the days before the suffering gene was found.

Vegetarianism doesn't seem an unreasonable response to such an 23 evil. Who would want to be made complicit in the agony of these animals by eating them? You want to throw something against the walls of those infernal sheds, whether it's the Bible, a new constitutional right or a whole platoon of animal rightists bent on breaking in and liberating the inmates. In the shadow of these factory farms, Coetzee's notion of a "stupefying crime" doesn't seem far-fetched at all.

But before you swear off meat entirely, let me describe a very differ- 24 ent sort of animal farm. It is typical of nothing, and yet its very existence puts the whole moral question of animal animal agriculture in a different light. Polyface Farm occupies 550 acres of rolling grassland and forest in the Shenandoah valley of Virginia. Here, Joel Salatin and his family raise six different food animals—cattle, pigs, chickens, rabbits, turkeys and sheep—in an intricate dance of symbiosis designed to allow each species, in Salatin's words, "to fully express its physiological distinctiveness."

What this means in practice is that Salatin's chickens live like chick- 25 ens; his cows, like cows; pigs, pigs. As in nature, where birds tend to follow herbivores, once Salatin's cows have finished grazing a pasture, he moves them out and tows in his "eggmobile," a portable chicken coop that houses several hundred laying hens—roughly the natural size of a flock. The hens fan out over the pasture, eating the short grass and picking insect larvae out of the cowpats—all the while spreading the cow manure and eliminating the farm's parasite problem. A diet of grubs and grass makes for exceptionally tasty eggs and contented chickens, and their nitrogenous manure feeds the pasture. A few weeks later, the chickens move out, and the sheep come in, dining on the lush new growth, as well as on the weed species (nettles, nightshade) that the cattle and chickens won't touch.

Meanwhile, the pigs are in the barn turning the compost. All winter 26 long, while the cattle were indoors, Salatin layered their manure with straw, wood chips—and corn. By March, this steaming compost layer cake stands three feet high, and the pigs, whose powerful snouts can sniff out and retrieve the fermented corn at the bottom, get to spend a few happy weeks rooting through the pile, aerating it as they work. All you can see of these pigs, intently nosing out the tasty alcoholic morsels, are their upturned pink hams and corkscrew tails churning the air. The finished compost will go to feed the grass; the grass, the cattle; the cattle, the chickens; and eventually all of these animals will feed us.

I thought a lot about vegetarianism and animal rights during the 27 day I spent on Joel Salatin's extraordinary farm. So much of what I'd read, so much of what I'd accepted, looked very different from here. To many animal rightists, even Polyface Farm is a death camp. But to look at these animals is to see this for the sentimental conceit it is. In the same way that we can probably recognize animal suffering when we see it, animal happiness is unmistakable, too, and here I was seeing it in abundance.

For any animal, happiness seems to consist in the opportunity to ex- 28 press its creaturely character—its essential pigness or wolfness or chickenness. Aristotle speaks of each creature's "characteristic form of life." For domesticated species, the good life, if we can call it that, cannot be achieved apart from humans—apart from our farms and, therefore, our meat eating. This, it seems to me, is where animal rightists betray a profound ignorance about the workings of nature. To think of domestication as a form of enslavement or even exploitation is to misconstrue the whole relationship, to project a human idea of power onto what is, in fact, an instance of mutualism between species. Domestication is an evolutionary, rather than a political, development. It is certainly not a regime humans imposed on animals some 10,000 years ago.

Rather, domestication happened when a small handful of especially 29 opportunistic species discovered through Darwinian trial and error that they were more likely to survive and prosper in an alliance with humans than on their own. Humans provided the animals with food and protection, in exchange for which the animals provided the humans their milk and eggs and—yes—their flesh. Both parties were transformed by the relationship: animals grew tame and lost their ability to fend for themselves (evolution tends to edit out unneeded traits), and the humans gave up their hunter–gatherer ways for the settled life of agriculturists. (Humans changed biologically, too, evolving such new traits as a tolerance for lactose as adults.) . . .

There is, too, the fact that we humans have been eating animals as 30 long as we have lived on this earth. Humans may not need to eat meat in order to survive, yet doing so is part of our evolutionary heritage, reflected in the design of our teeth and the structure of our digestion. Eating meat helped make us what we are, in a social and biological sense.

Under the pressure of the hunt, the human brain grew in size and complexity, and around the fire where the meat was cooked, human culture
first flourished. Granting rights to animals may lift us up from the brutal
world of predation, but it will entail the sacrifice of part of our identity —
our own animality.

Surely this is one of the odder paradoxes of animal rights doctrine. It 31
asks us to recognize all that we share with animals and then demands
that we act toward them in a most unanimalistic way. Whether or not
this is a good idea, we should at least acknowledge that our desire to eat
meat is not a trivial matter, no mere "gastronomic preference." We might
as well call sex — also now technically unnecessary — a mere "recreational
preference." Whatever else it is, our meat eating is something very deep
indeed.

Are any of these good enough reasons to eat animals? I'm mindful of 32
Ben Franklin's definition of the reasonable creature as one who can come
up with reasons for whatever he wants to do . . . .

• • •

During my visit to Polyface Farm, I asked Salatin where his animals were 33
slaughtered. He does the chickens and rabbits right on the farm, and
would do the cattle, pigs and sheep there too if only the U.S.D.A. would
let him. Salatin showed me the open-air abattoir he built behind the
farmhouse — a sort of outdoor kitchen on a concrete slab, with stainless-
steel sinks, scalding tanks, a feather-plucking machine and metal cones
to hold the birds upside down while they're being bled. Processing
chickens is not a pleasant job, but Salatin insists on doing it himself because he's convinced he can do it more humanely and cleanly than any
processing plant. He slaughters every other Saturday through the summer. Anyone's welcome to watch.

I asked Salatin how he could bring himself to kill a chicken.   34

"People have a soul; animals don't," he said. "It's a bedrock belief of 35
mine." Salatin is a devout Christian. "Unlike us, animals are not created in
God's image, so when they die, they just die."

The notion that only in modern times have people grown uneasy 36
about killing animals is a flattering conceit. Taking a life is momentous,
and people have been working to justify the slaughter of animals for
thousands of years. Religion and especially ritual has played a crucial
part in helping us reckon the moral costs. Native Americans and other
hunter-gathers would give thanks to their prey for giving up its life so
the eater might live (sort of like saying grace). Many cultures have offered sacrificial animals to the gods, perhaps as a way to convince themselves that it was the gods' desires that demanded the slaughter, not
their own. In ancient Greece, the priests responsible for the slaughter
(priests! — now we entrust the job to minimum-wage workers) would
sprinkle holy water on the sacrificial animal's brow. The beast would
promptly shake its head, and this was taken as a sign of assent. Slaughter

doesn't necessarily preclude respect. For all these people, it was the ceremony that allowed them to look, then to eat.

Apart from a few surviving religious practices, we no longer have 37 any rituals governing the slaughter or eating of animals, which perhaps helps to explain why we find ourselves where we do, feeling that our only choice is to either look away or give up meat. Frank Perdue is happy to serve the first customer; Peter Singer, the second.

Until my visit to Polyface Farm, I had assumed these were the only 38 two options. But on Salatin's farm, the eye contact between people and animals whose loss John Berger mourned is still a fact of life — and of death, for neither the lives nor the deaths of these animals have been secreted behind steel walls. "Food with a face," Salatin likes to call what he's selling, a slogan that probably scares off some customers. People see very different things when they look into the eyes of a pig or a chicken or a steer — a being without a soul, a "subject of a life" entitled to rights, a link in a food chain, a vessel for pain and pleasure, a tasty lunch. But figuring out what we do think, and what we can eat, might begin with the looking.

We certainly won't philosophize our way to an answer. Salatin told 39 me the story of a man who showed up at the farm one Saturday morning. When Salatin noticed a PETA bumper sticker on the man's car, he figured he was in for it. But the man had a different agenda. He explained that after 16 years as a vegetarian, he had decided that the only way he could ever eat meat again was if he killed the animal himself. He had come to look.

"Ten minutes later we were in the processing shed with a chicken," 40 Salatin recalled. "He slit the bird's throat and watched it die. He saw that the animal did not look at him accusingly, didn't do a Disney double take. The animal had been treated with respect when it was alive, and he saw that it could also have a respectful death — that it wasn't being treated as a pile of protoplasm."

Salatin's open-air abattoir is a morally powerful idea. Someone 41 slaughtering a chicken in a place where he can be watched is apt to do it scrupulously, with consideration for the animal as well as for the eater. This is going to sound quixotic, but maybe all we need to do to redeem industrial animal agriculture in this country is to pass a law requiring that the steel and concrete walls of the CAFO's and slaughterhouses be replaced with . . . glass. If there's any new "right" we need to establish, maybe it's this one: the right to look.

No doubt the sight of some of these places would turn many people 42 into vegetarians. Many others would look elsewhere for their meat, to farmers like Salatin. There are more of them than I would have imagined. Despite the relentless consolidation of the American meat industry, there has been a revival of small farms where animals still live their "characteristic form of life." I'm thinking of the ranches where cattle still spend their lives on grass, the poultry farms where chickens still go outside and the hog farms where pigs live as they did 50 years ago—in contact with the sun, the earth and the gaze of a farmer.

For my own part, I've discovered that if you're willing to make the 43 effort, it's entirely possible to limit the meat you eat to nonindustrial animals. I'm tempted to think that we need a new dietary category, to go with the vegan and lactovegetarian and piscatorian. I don't have a catchy name for it yet (humanocarnivore?), but this is the only sort of meat eating I feel comfortable with these days. I've become the sort of shopper who looks for labels indicating that his meat and eggs have been humanely grown (the American Humane Association's new "Free Farmed" label seems to be catching on), who visits the farms where his chicken and pork come from and who asks kinky-sounding questions about touring slaughterhouses. I've actually found a couple of small processing plants willing to let a customer onto the kill floor, including one, in Cannon Falls, Minn., with a glass abattoir.

The industrialization—and dehumanization—of American animal 44 farming is a relatively new, evitable and local phenomenon: no other country raises and slaughters its food animals quite as intensively or as brutally as we do. Were the walls of our meat industry to become transparent, literally or even figuratively, we would not long continue to do it this way. Tail-docking and sow crates and beak-clipping would disappear overnight, and the days of slaughtering 400 head of cattle an hour would come to an end. For who could stand the sight? Yes, meat would get more expensive. We'd probably eat less of it, too, but maybe when we did eat animals, we'd eat them with the consciousness, ceremony and respect they deserve.

Reading Closely

1. What different ethical stances toward animals does Pollan discuss?
2. What specific examples does he provide to support each of those stances?
3. **Together with a classmate,** discuss the arrangement of Pollan's overall argument, paying close attention to each strand of supporting arguments. What information does he include in his introduction, his thesis statement, his supporting arguments, his attention to opposing views, and his conclusion? Mark the specific passages that make up each of those sections. Share your findings with the rest of the class.

Considering Larger Issues

1. What is Pollan's purpose? How does it differ from the purposes of each of the preceding essays—the Kerr, Green, and Fraser essays? How does his purpose relate to his *New York Times* audience?

2. What is Pollan's thesis statement? What reasons does he provide to support or extend his thesis statement?

3. **Working with two classmates,** mark the specific passages that support each of his reasons. Be prepared to share your findings with the rest of the class.

4. COMBINING METHODS.   To make his argument, Pollan resorts to several methods of rhetorical development: *comparison and contrast, cause-and-consequence analysis,* and *narration,* for example. Mark the passages in which he uses various methods and account for the way each of those passages contribute to the essay. Be prepared to share your answers with the rest of the class.

5. **Working with two classmates,** discuss how appropriate the visuals on pp. 696 and 697 are as illustrations for Pollan's essay, and prepare a short statement to share with the rest of the class.

Thinking about Language

1. **Together with another classmate,** use the context of the essay or a dictionary to define the following terms or phrases. Be prepared to share your definitions with the rest of the class.

cognitive dissonance (1)	ideological (7)	consensus (14)
preposterous (1)	eloquent (7)	traumatizing (14)
tantamount (1)	dismantling (8)	magnitude (15)
barbarities (2)	uniqueness (8)	CAFO (16)
"speciesism" (2)	schizoid (8)	albeit (17)
neologism (2)	disconnect (9)	operative (17)
fringe idea (4)	thrive (9)	ebb (17)
ethicists (4)	uncanny (10)	counterweight
provision (5)	irretrievably (10)	(21)
obliging (5)	alien (10)	venerable (22)
amending (5)	paradox (10)	morsels (26)
agribusiness (6)	accommodation (10)	mutualism (28)
defuse (6)	disarmingly (12)	

2. **Together with another classmate,** determine Pollan's attitude toward animals. What specific words and phrases demonstrate his attitude? Share your response with the rest of the class.

3. When Pollan mentions the paradoxes of animal rights doctrine, what exactly is he referring to? How might these paradoxes be addressed, according to his observations and suggestions?

Writing Your Own Arguments

1. **In a group of two or three students,** discuss various positions on animal rights. You may want to research the writings of Peter Singer, John Berger, the American Beef/Pork/Chicken Producers, Matthew Scully,

and other writers or organizations to see what attitudes are already in circulation. Then draft a three- to four-page essay in which you argue for a specific position. You may want to arrange your essay like Pollan's, introducing the background information necessary to help you establish your argument. You may want to find one or more visuals to include as well. Work with your small group as you each draft and revise your essays, referring to the guidelines for checking over an argument on p. 652.

2. Draft a two- to three-page essay in which you either further develop Pollan's argument about factory farming or develop an argument that opposes his, perhaps point by point (or almost point by point). In either case, you'll need to do some research about the range of ways that meat is produced for human consumption. Be sure to organize your argument so that it has an introduction, a thesis statement, supporting arguments, recognition of opposing arguments, and a conclusion. Refer to the guidelines for checking over an argument on p. 652.

THE POST HOUSE
Horrifying Vegetarians since 1980

The Post House restaurant in New York City is owned by the Smith & Wollensky Restaurant Group, widely known for its steakhouses across the country. This ad appeared in the *New York Times* in 2004.

> **Preview** What, exactly, might horrify a vegetarian?

· · · · · · ➤

Reading Closely

1. What specific information is conveyed by the visual part of this advertisement?
2. How do the verbal parts enhance the visual part?

Considering Larger Issues

1. What is the overall purpose of this advertisement? And how does it fulfill its purpose?
2. Who is the audience for this ad?
3. Which kind of rhetorical appeal does the ad most rely on — ethos, logos, or pathos? Identify words, phrases, or visual details that support your answer.
4. **COMBINING METHODS.** How does the ad use *comparison and contrast* to extend its argument?

Thinking about Language

1. What words or phrases in the ad support the concept of "horrifying vegetarians"?
2. How do the endorsements support the ad in terms of who is making them and what exactly the endorsers say?

Writing Your Own Arguments

1. Locate a food or restaurant advertisement that uses both visual and verbal argument. Write a two- to three-page essay evaluating the advertisement in terms of its audience, purpose (stated or implied), thesis statement, and rhetorical appeals. Account for the success or lack thereof of

Horrifying Vegetarians Since 1980.

The Post House
New York City

"The restaurant remains a haunt of dedicated carnivores and lobster-grapplers..."
— *Gourmet*

"All that a steakhouse should be..."
— **ZAGAT**SURVEY

"One of the Ten Best Steakhouses in America."
— *Wine Spectator*

the advertisement in fulfilling its overall purpose. Be sure to consider its original place of publication, whether in a magazine, a billboard, or a newspaper. Include a copy of the ad with your essay. Refer to the guidelines for checking over an argument on p. 652.

2. Create a visual–verbal combination that argues for a specific diet or eating habit. As you draft and revise, refer to the guidelines for checking over an argument on p. 652.

Casebook:
The Draft and National Service

CHARLES B. RANGEL
Bring Back the Draft

Charles B. Rangel (b. 1930) has been a Democratic member of the House of Representatives from New York since 1970, representing the Upper West Side and Harlem neighborhoods of New York City. His political career has focused on revitalizing poor neighborhoods and giving opportunities to the under-privileged. Rangel is the ranking Democratic member of the House Ways and Means Committee, chairman of the board of the Democratic Congressional Campaign Committee, and the senior member (in length of service) of the New York State Congressional delegation.

A combat veteran of the Korean War, Rangel was a vocal critic of President George W. Bush's decision to go to war with Iraq; and in early 2003, shortly before the war began, he introduced a bill in Congress to resume the military draft. The following essay, explaining his reasons for doing so, was published in the *New York Times* on December 31, 2002. In May 2004, after revelations of abuse of Iraqi prisoners, he introduced articles of impeachment against Defense Secretary Donald Rumsfeld.

Preview   What are your feelings about reinstating the draft?

WASHINGTON | President Bush and his administration have declared a   1
war against terrorism that may soon involve sending thousands of American troops into combat in Iraq. I voted against the Congressional resolution giving the president authority to carry out this war — an engagement that would dwarf our military efforts to find Osama bin Laden and bring him to justice.

But as a combat veteran of the Korean conflict, I believe that if we   2
are going to send our children to war, the governing principle must be that of shared sacrifice. Throughout much of our history, Americans have been asked to shoulder the burden of war equally.

That's why I will ask Congress next week to consider and support   3
legislation I will introduce to resume the military draft.

Carrying out the administration's policy toward Iraq will require   4
long-term sacrifices by the American people, particularly those who have sons and daughters in the military. Yet the Congress that voted overwhelmingly to allow the use of force in Iraq includes only one member who has a child in the enlisted ranks of the military — just a few more have children who are officers.

I believe that if those calling for war knew that their children were 5
likely to be required to serve—and to be placed in harm's way—there
would be more caution and a greater willingness to work with the international community in dealing with Iraq. A renewed draft will help
bring a greater appreciation of the consequences of decisions to go to
war.

Service in our nation's armed forces is no longer a common experi- 6
ence. A disproportionate number of the poor and members of minority
groups make up the enlisted ranks of the military, while the most privileged Americans are underrepresented or absent.

We need to return to the tradition of the citizen soldier—with alter- 7
native national service required for those who cannot serve because of
physical limitations or reasons of conscience.

There is no doubt that going to war against Iraq will severely strain 8
military resources already burdened by a growing number of obligations.
There are daunting challenges facing the 1.4 million men and women in
active military service and those in our National Guard and Reserve. The
Pentagon has said that up to 250,000 troops may be mobilized for the invasion of Iraq. An additional 265,000 members of the National Guard and
Reserve, roughly as many as were called up during the Persian Gulf War
in 1991, may also be activated.

Already, we have long–term troop commitments in Europe and the 9
Pacific, with an estimated 116,000 troops in Europe, 90,000 in the Pacific
(nearly 40,000 in Japan and 38,000 in Korea) and additional troop commitments to operations in Afghanistan, Bosnia, Kosovo and elsewhere.
There are also military trainers in countries across the world, including
the Philippines, Colombia and Yemen.

We can expect the evolving global war on terrorism to drain our 10
military resources even more, stretching them to the limit.

The administration has yet to address the question of whether our 11
military is of sufficient strength and size to meet present and future commitments. Those who would lead us into war have the obligation to support an all–out mobilization of Americans for the war effort, including
mandatory national service that asks something of us all.

Reading Closely

1. What is your response to Rangel's argument? On what do you base your
   response?
2. How does Rangel establish his ethos in this essay? How does he use
   logos? pathos? Mark the passages that best establish those three appeals.

Considering Larger Issues

1. **Together with a classmate,** define Rangel's intended audience for this essay. What information in the essay itself helps you to define the audience?

2. What is Rangel's purpose in writing this essay? What does he want his audience to do with his argument?

3. COMBINING METHODS. To develop his argument, Rangel uses *cause-and-consequence analysis.* Concentrate on his use of cause and consequence analysis and account for its effect in terms of supporting the argument, fulfilling the rhetorical appeals, and reaching the intended audience.

4. What questions did you have after reading this essay? In other words, what specifics about national service does the author leave unspoken? **Working with a classmate,** list all the places that Rangel talks about national service but doesn't mention who exactly should serve, where, and how. How might you and your classmate fill in the blanks? Be prepared to share your answers with the rest of the class.

Thinking about Language

1. **With a classmate,** use the context of the essay and a dictionary to define the following words and phrases. You'll see that some familiar words are being used in unfamiliar ways. Be prepared to share your definitions with the rest of the class.

terrorism (1)	shared sacrifice (2)	daunting (8)
engagement (1)	force (4)	mobilized (8)
dwarf (1)	disproportionate (6)	commitments (9)
governing principle (2)	citizen soldier (7)	mandatory (11)

2. What is the author's attitude toward war? What words and phrases express his attitude?

Writing Your Own Arguments

1. In a three- to four-page essay, respond to Rangel. You might argue that it's impossible, unnecessary, or unwise to reinstate the draft and develop a list of good reasons for your assertion. Or you might flesh out his argument, such as by arguing that the concept of national service needs to be broadened to include men and women of all social classes, physical abilities, religious convictions, and age. You'll need to conduct library and online research in order to supply convincing logical appeals. Be sure to refer to the guidelines for checking over an argument on p. 652, as you draft and revise.

2. In an essay of three to four pages, argue for various ways that Americans should be allowed to accomplish their national service if it becomes a requirement. Such a paper will entail research on your part because

you'll want to incorporate statistics, facts, experiences, and observations that support your argument. You'll also want to be sure to establish goodwill and common ground with readers, to enhance your credibility as a writer. You should assume an audience of traditional college–age young people for this essay. Refer to the guidelines for checking over an argument on p. 652.

CHARLES MOSKOS AND PAUL GLASTRIS
Now Do You Believe We Need a Draft?

Charles Moskos (b. 1934) is professor emeritus of sociology at Northwestern University. The *Wall Street Journal* has dubbed him the country's "most influential military sociologist," a scholar who studies the military as a social structure and its relationship to the larger society. A peacetime draftee who served in the U.S. Army Combat Engineers in Vietnam, Moskos was the author of the "don't ask, don't tell" policy for gay and lesbian military personnel that was adopted in 1993. Paul Glastris is editor in chief of the liberal political magazine the *Washington Monthly*. He was previously a correspondent and editor at *U.S. News and World Report* for ten years and a special assistant and senior speechwriter to President Bill Clinton. The following essay was originally published in the November 2001 issue of the *Washington Monthly*.

Preview   What specific knowledge do you have of the draft?

President Bush has said that the new war against terrorism will be "a different kind of conflict." He is more right than he knows. Not only are we facing a uniquely shadowy enemy, one committed to inflicting mass civilian casualties on U.S. soil. But for the first time in our history we are entering a war of significant size and probable duration (administration officials have said it may last for "years") without drafting young men to fight the threat.

Not only are we not drafting our young men. We are not even planning to draft them. Elected leaders are not even talking about the possibility of drafting them. That terrorists might poison municipal water supplies, spray anthrax from crop dusters, or suicidally infect themselves with small pox and stroll through busy city streets, is no longer considered farfetched. That we might need to draft some of our people to counter these threats—now that's considered farfetched, to the extent that it's considered at all.

America needs to wake up. We're at war. We need a draft. But because this is a new kind of conflict, we need a new kind of draft. A 21st century draft would be less focused on preparing men for conventional combat—which probably won't be that extensive in this war—than on the arguably more daunting task of guarding against and responding to terrorism at home and abroad. If structured right, this new draft might not be as tough to sell as you would think.

Churchill famously said that America could be counted on to do the right thing, after exhausting all other possibilities. On the subject of the draft, we are rapidly reaching that point of exhaustion. A draft might be avoidable if enough Americans were volunteering to serve. But we're not. Soon after the events of September 11, newspapers reported that the

1

2

3

4

phones in military recruitment offices were ringing off the hook. Follow up with stories showed that all that clamor had brought virtually no new recruits. So far, our patriotism, though sincerely felt, has largely amounted to flag–waving and coat holding.

Perhaps we could get by without a draft if our all–volunteer military had more than enough troops on hand. But it doesn't. The actions so far taken in Afghanistan, and the buildup to support those actions, have been relatively modest. Yet with personnel cut by a third since the end of the Cold War, the services were hard–pressed to meet ongoing missions even before September 11. There is already talk of pulling U.S. forces out of the Balkans, something the Bush administration wanted to do anyway. But it will not please our NATO allies, whose long–term support we will need in the fight against terrorism, and who will have to fill the gap with more troops of their own. 5

We are calling up large numbers of reservists, but because so many of them work as police officers, firefighters, and emergency medical tech- nicians, our municipalities are being drained of precisely the people we will need if (when) the terrorists return. 6

Indeed, it seems clear that we are going to need thousands more men and women in uniform to deal with terrorist threats here at home. The president has appointed former Pennsylvania Governor Tom Ridge 7

Young men burning their draft cards during a protest against the Vietnam War.

as his new homeland security "czar." The federal government will be taking over airport security, either providing the services directly or supervising private firms providing it. However the restructuring shakes out, we are clearly going to need more federal armed personnel to guard dams, nuclear power plants, sports complexes, and U.S. embassies abroad; more border patrol and customs agents to keep terrorists and their weapons from entering the country; more INS agents track down immigrants who have overstayed their visas; more coast guard personnel to inspect ships; more air marshals to ride on passenger jets; and more FBI agents to uncover terrorist cells still operating within and outside our borders.

Where are all these brave men and women going to come from? Certainly, America is rich enough, and the need vital enough, that we could afford to offer significant salaries to lure candidates. But even in a weak economy, there is a finite number of competent people willing to choose a career that requires wearing a uniform, performing often dull work, such as guard duty, with alertness, and being ready at any moment to risk one's life for others. A whole range of government agencies and private firms, from the U.S. Army to Brinks to local police departments, must compete for this limited labor pool. And the pool is probably not expanding. 8

Consider this: Between 1980 and 2000, surveys showed that the number of young people saying they would definitely not serve in the military rose from 40 to 64 percent. The only reason this change of attitude did not destroy military recruiting efforts is that the need for new recruits plummeted with the end of the Cold War. But the military is feeling the pinch nonetheless. The armed services have had to double starting pay to recruit half as many enlistees, and the quality of new recruits is not what it should be. The number of enlistees scoring in the top half of the armed forces qualification tests has dropped by a third since the mid–1990s. In fiscal year 2000, the Army took in some 380 recruits with felony arrest records, double the number in 1998. Desertions are also on the rise. Most telling, over one–third of those entering the military fail to complete their enlistments. Contrast this with the one in ten of draftees who did not complete his two–year obligation during the Cold War. Much better to have a soldier serve a short term honorably than to be discharged for cause. 9

NO PEELING POTATOES

Reinstituting the draft is the obvious way to meet the suddenly increased manpower needs for military and homeland security. This fact would have seemed obvious to previous generations of Americans. That today we aren't even talking about a draft is a measure of the deep psychological resistance Americans have developed to anything that smacks 10 of the state compelling anyone to do anything. Ideology plays a role here. In general, the left doesn't like the military, and the right doesn't like anything that interferes with the marketplace. When it comes to national needs, the left believes in something for nothing, the right in every man for himself.

The psychological resistance also gains comfort from arguments 11 made by the opponents of the draft and by the military hierarchy, which also resists a return to conscription. (The military resists the draft largely because it resists all change; it opposed ending the draft in 1973).

One argument is that today's military requires professional soldiers, 12 especially for overseas mission. Let's leave aside the fact that in World War II, Korea, and Vietnam, most combat soldiers had only six months of training before being sent to war. Let's also grant that because of today's high-tech weapons and complex war–fighting strategies, the actual combat must be left to professional soldiers (though there is some reason for skepticism here). Still, there are hundreds of thousands of vital military jobs—not peeling potatoes—that could be filled with short–term draftees.

One example is peacekeeping. From experience with U.S. deploy- 13 ments in Bosnia and Kosovo, we know that combat troops tend to chafe at peacekeeping duty when they are stuck on bases with nothing to do and little opportunity to train with their weapons. But it's also clear that military police thrive on such assignments, because they get to perform the jobs they are trained for—patrolling neighborhoods, arresting troublemakers, intervening in disputes with a minimum of force. Military police work doesn't require that many special skills. After two months of basic and four months of special police training, new recruits are shipped off to places like Tuzla, and they do just fine. The average tour of duty in Bosnia or Kosovo: about 6 months. Short–term draftees, in other words, could easily do these M.P. jobs, and many others besides. This would free up more professional soldiers to fight the war on terrorism without requiring that the U.S. to abandon other commitments.

Draftees would not have to be offered the relatively high wages and 14 benefits that it takes to lure voluntary recruits (an increasing number of whom are married with families). This would leave more funds available to raise pay for the kinds of personnel that the military is having a terribly hard time holding on to, such as computer specialists, mid–level officers, and master sergeants. To put it baldly, we now have overpaid recruits and underpaid sergeants. In the draft era, the pay ratio between a master sergeant and a private was seven to one; today it is less than three to one. Restoring something like the old balance is the best way to upgrade retention in hard–to–fill skills and leadership positions.

All these arguments apply equally to the homeland security front. 15 There is no reason why conscripts, with professional supervision, can't work as border guards, customs agents, anthrax inoculators, or disaster-relief specialists. Federal law enforcement agencies and unions will deny this with all their bureaucratic might, but it's true. It takes less than five months to train someone to be a border guard. The FBI turns applicants with law or accounting degrees into fully–fledged agents after only four months of training.

Other developed nations that have retained the draft typically use 16 conscripts for homeland security. In Israel, draftees serve in both the regular military and as as lightly armed "guard police" along the Gaza Strip. They also man the "home command," which provides security and other services in the country's cities during emergencies, such as the scud missile attacks during the Gulf War. In France, which finally abandoned its draft last year (believing that threats to its security had diminished), conscripts worked alongside professional police in the Gendarmerie and provided emergency airport security when terrorists set off bombs in the Paris Metro in 1995. In Germany, most draft–age men choose to serve either in the military or in some form of civilian service, such as working with the elderly. But about one in ten chooses to work in a state or federal police force, providing such things as border security, or they train as volunteer firefighters and serve part–time for seven years.

One can imagine a similar three–tiered system of youth service in 17 America, with 18–month terms of duty for all citizens age 18 to 25. In this

Supporters of AmeriCorps demonstrate in 2003 against funding cuts for the volunteer national service program.

new-style draft, conscripts would have what all Americans now demand: choice. They could choose to serve in the military, in homeland security, or in a civilian national service program like AmeriCorps (there's no reason women couldn't be drafted for the latter two categories). In return, draftees would get GI-bill-style college scholarships, with higher awards for those who accept more dangerous duty.

Back in Vietnam days, opting to fulfill your draft requirement state- 18 side in, say, the National Guard, was considered a way to save your skin. That won't be so true in the new war on terrorism. As we saw with the deaths of firefighters in New York, homeland security duty can be dangerous.

THE SUCKER FACTOR

That brings up the second argument against the draft: that the sons 19 of the elite will find ways to avoid service. Of course, that's even truer in an age of all-volunteer forces. But it's fair to ask: How can a draft be made equitable?

The best way would be to require all young people to serve. One 20 reason more young people don't serve now is the fear that while they're wearing the uniform, their peers will be out having fun and getting a leg up in their careers. If everyone were required to serve, no one would feel like a sucker. They might even enjoy the experience; surveys show that most former draftees look back on their time in the service with fondness and pride.

It's possible, however, that the country won't have the need for every 21 eligible young person to serve. What then? One answer is a lottery with no student deferments. (Under Selective Service rules established after Vietnam, college deferments are no longer allowed.)

Part of what makes Americans dubious of conscription is our mem- 22 ory of how the class-biased draft of the Vietnam War-era helped drive America apart. We tend to forget that the more equitable draft that existed during World War II and for 20 years afterwards helped bring the country together. During the peaceful years of the 1950s—a time not unlike our own, when the threat of mass destruction hung in the air—most Ivy League men had to spend two years in uniform, before or after college, working and bunking with others of very different backgrounds and races (the military, remember, was about the only racially integrated institution at the time).

This shared experience helped instill in those who served, as in the 23 national culture generally, a sense of unity and moral seriousness that we would not see again—until after September 11, 2001. It's a shame that it has taken terrorist attacks to awaken us to the reality of our shared national fate. We should use this moment to rebuild institutions like the draft that will keep us awake to this reality even as the memory of the attacks fade.

A 21st century draft might be more welcome than most of us realize, 24 especially among young people whose lives will be affected by it. While national leaders and pundits have avoided the subject, a potential return of the draft has been a hot topic of conversation among young people since September 11. "If it's something they want us to do for our country to keep us safe, then go for it," Ryan Aaron, a senior at U.S. Grant High School in Oklahoma City, told *National Journal.* Another young man, Julian Medina, a day laborer cleaning up office buildings near the still-smoldering World Trade Center, told *The Washington Post:* "If I have to, I'd fight to catch the man who did this." Not all young people are so gung ho; many, in fact, hate the idea. But at least they're talking about it. If their views can move from news pages to the editorial pages, and ultimately to the floors of Congress, then we could be on our way to a more secure and more unified America.

Reading Closely

1. What did you learn about the armed forces that you didn't know before reading this essay? Write out three things you've learned and one thing you'd like to know more about.

2. Map out the overall organization of the argument in terms of the introduction, the thesis statement, the supporting arguments, recognition of the opposition, and the conclusion. Which passages make up each of these organizational parts? Prepare to share your response with the rest of the class.

Considering Larger Issues

1. What is the thesis for this essay? Is it explicitly stated or only implied? What reasons do the authors give to support their thesis? What specific evidence do they provide to support each of their reasons? (You may find yourself drawing upon your responses to question 2 under "Reading Closely.")

2. Who is the audience for this essay? What words, passages, or examples help you establish the audience? How does knowing that this essay first appeared in the *Washington Monthly* affect your answer?

3. Which passages and examples fulfill the rhetorical appeals of logos, pathos, and logos?

4. **COMBINING METHODS.** The authors rely on *cause-and-consequence analysis* to build their assertion that we need to reinstate the draft. Mark the passages that analyze causes and those that analyze consequences, and explain why the authors chose to use them.

5. What specific information did you obtain from the visuals on pp. 714 and 717 that enhanced or complicated the information in the essay?

Thinking about Language

1. **With a classmate,** use the context of the essay or your dictionary to define the following terms. Be prepared to share your definitions with the rest of the class.

uniquely (1)	cells (7)	chafe (13)
casualties (1)	lure (8)	intervening (13)
municipal (2)	finite (8)	baldly (14)
crop dusters (2)	pinch (9)	conscripts (15)
daunting (3)	enlistees (9)	inoculators (15)
clamor (4)	reinstituting (10)	leg up (20)
recruits (4)	ideology (10)	class–biased (22)
hard–pressed (5)	conscription (11)	bunking (22)
reservists (6)	skepticism (12)	

2. **With another classmate or two,** write a short paragraph that summarizes all the ways the authors support the opening sentence: "The new war against terrorism will be 'a different kind of conflict.' " What words, phrases, and passages illustrate this assertion? Share your paragraph with the rest of the class. Now condense your paragraph into a single sentence. Be prepared to share your group's sentence with the rest of the class. Also be prepared to discuss the language you marked that illustrates the assertion.

Writing Your Own Arguments

1. How can a U.S. college student connect with the idea of "a different kind of conflict"? How might this essay be an inspiration to you—or just the opposite? **With one or two classmates,** discuss possible responses to these questions. Then draft a three- to four–page essay in which you argue either for or against the importance of reinstating the draft for reasons of national security. Pay careful attention to the organization of your argument as well as to your use of the rhetorical appeals. Work with the guidelines for checking over an argument on p. 652 as you and your classmates plan, draft, revise, and respond to each other's drafts.

2. The authors suggest a three–tiered system of national service, one limited to citizens 18 to 25 years old. Evaluate this suggestion by considering the following issues: whether short–term training could be enough to teach any job well (or make any job interesting), whether the choice among the three tiers would be fair to those in each tier, and whether you or anyone you know aged 18 to 25 would be interested in any of these tiers and why. In order to make a fair comparison, you'll want to conduct research into the current programs of voluntary U.S. national service, such as AmeriCorps and Teach for America. In addition, you'll want to re-

search the experiences and actions (both positive and negative) of military personnel stationed in the Middle East, the Balkans, and elsewhere, as well as in the United States. (Consider, for example, whether a draft would have had any effect on the treatment of prisoners in the Iraq war.) You may also want to research compulsory national service programs in other countries, including those mentioned by the authors. Write a three- to four-page essay in which you evaluate Moskos and Glastris's recommendations. Refer to the guidelines for checking over an argument on p. 652 as you draft and revise.

WALTER Y. OI

The Virtue of an All-Volunteer Force

Walter Y. Oi (b. 1929) is the Elmer B. Milliman Professor of Economics at the University of Rochester, a Fellow of the American Academy of Arts and Sciences, and a Distinguished Fellow of the American Economics Association. Oi, who was sent to an internment camp for Japanese Americans during World War II, served as staff economist for President Richard Nixon's Commission on the All-Volunteer Force, which developed the plan to end the U.S. military draft in the early 1970s. This essay first appeared in 2003 in *Regulation,* a magazine published by the Cato Institute, a libertarian research foundation.

Preview   What situation might provoke this author to link "virtue" with "all-volunteer"?

Last January, as Congress and the public grappled with the possibility   1
of U.S. military action in Iraq, war opponent Rep. Charles B. Rangel (D–N.Y.) introduced "The National Service Act of 2003" to reinstate compulsory service for U.S. citizens and permanent residents between the ages of 18 and 26. According to a statement his office released on January 7, the nation's defense should not be "the sole responsibility of paid volunteers."

"If our great nation becomes involved in an all–out war, the sacrifice   2
must be equally shared," Rangel said. "We must return to the tradition of the citizen soldier."

The congressman admitted that the legislation was intended in part   3
to disrupt the push for war. But, putting that aside, is it true that the nation's defense is better provided through compulsory service or by an all–volunteer force?

Raising an army. For most of U.S. history, volunteers have sup–   4
plied the manpower for the nation's defense. There have been only four departures from that tradition, and each of those occurred in times of significant perceived threat to the survival of the nation.

The first U.S. draft bill was passed in March of 1863, nearly two years   5
after the outbreak of the Civil War. It was met with riots in New York City and was temporarily suspended. The second draft bill passed Congress on May 18, 1917, six weeks after the United States formally entered the Great War. Draft calls were stopped fully three months before the end of hostilities. The third episode was the nation's first peacetime draft, enacted on September 16, 1940. It supplied more than 10 of the 15 million persons who served during World War II, and continued on until March 31, 1947. Then, for 15 months, the nation returned to an all–volunteer force. But the military failed to meet recruitment goals and, with the Cold War emerging, Congress established the Selective Service System on July

1, 1948. Under that law, compulsory service would affect the lives of young American men for a quarter of a century.

Questioning the draft. Selective Service increasingly elicited chal- 6 lenge and outright opposition. One challenger was John Kenneth Galbraith who criticized compulsory service from a market perspective:

> The draft survives principally as a device by which we use compulsion to get young men to serve at less than the market rate of pay. We shift the cost of military service from the well-to-do taxpayer who benefits by lower taxes to the impecunious young draftee. This is a highly regressive arrangement that we would not tolerate in any other area. Presumably, freedom of choice here as elsewhere is worth paying for.

The size of the tax—the difference between the wage needed to attract soldiers on a voluntary basis and the "below market rate of pay" of the draftee—was substantial. Further, the cost of collecting this hidden tax was more than the administrative costs of the Selective Service System; it also included the costs borne by young men trying to evade the tax. Some youths enrolled in college just to escape being drafted; others became fathers or ministers who were exempted; some feigned disabilities or fled to Canada or Europe. Lawrence Sjaastad and Ronald W. Hansen, in their influential 1970 study "The Conscription Tax: An Empirical Analysis," calculated that the full cost of the conscription tax, including the evasion costs, was higher than any other tax levied by the federal government.

The inequity of the arrangement led to the establishment in 1967 of a 7 presidential commission, headed by Burke Marshall, to examine the issue. The commission's report, "In Pursuit of Equity, Who Serves When Not All Serve," led to the lottery draft. But the lottery failed to achieve equity and resentment of compulsory service grew.

Ending the draft. In 1968, respected free-market economist and 8 University of Rochester president W. Allen Wallis presented a speech to the Rochester chapter of the American Legion in which he argued that the draft was both ethically and practically unjustifiable. Wallis summarized the speech, which would be reprinted as the influential essay "Abolish the Draft," as follows:

> My objections to the draft are of two kinds. First, it is immutably immoral in principle and inevitably inequitable in practice. Second, it is ineffective, inefficient, and detrimental to national security.

Wallis's comments resonated with policymakers across the political spectrum, and he helped to persuade President Richard Nixon to establish the President's Commission on the All-Volunteer Force, better known as the Gates Commission. The commission developed a plan: If the entry level pay of enlisted men could be raised, the recruiting organization expanded, and the conditions of service life improved, the Armed Services could attract enough volunteers to staff the active duty strength objectives. The report of the Gates Commission was unanimously approved by its members and presented to President Nixon on February 20, 1970.

Congress took the first step toward implementing the plan in 1972   9
when lawmakers raised the pay of first-term enlisted men by 61.2 percent. Congress also refused to extend the draft authority, which expired on June 30, 1973. With more recruiters and a larger advertising budget, Secretary of the Army Howard H. Callaway announced a year later that the recruitment goals had been met. The nation's defense was in the hands of an all-volunteer force.

The quality of volunteers. Unfortunately, over the first five years   10
of the new all-volunteer force, military pay did not keep pace with civilian wages. In order to meet recruiting goals, the Army accepted lower quality recruits, some with police records. Attrition rates from training bases were found to be substantially higher for men with low mental test scores. An Army study found that to have 100 soldiers on board at the end of two years, it had to recruit, enlist, and train 131 high school graduates or 188 men who did not complete high school.

Gen. Maxwell Thurman established a high-quality personnel policy   11
wherein recruiters were instructed to seek youths with a high school diploma and a score on the Armed Forces Qualification Test of 50 or higher (i.e., from the top half of the mental distribution). The higher-quality recruits allowed the Army to cut the size of its entry-level training bases by 27 percent and provided the military with soldiers who learned faster, could master sophisticated weapon systems, and were more likely to qualify for promotion.

Because labor became more expensive, the Pentagon shifted to a   12
leaner, more capital-intensive force. There was a smaller fraction of the force in the combat arms (infantry, armor, airborne, and special forces) and a longer, more professional support tail.

Soldiers in the all-volunteer force can enroll in demanding individ-   13
ual training courses to learn how to operate and maintain advanced weapons. Such training courses would not have been effective in a conscript force with its high personnel turnover rates. For instance, by the time a conscripted sailor completed his training to be a submariner, he would only have two to three months to serve before his term of service was completed. In the all-volunteer force, capital and training are substituted for raw untrained labor to economize not only on the cost of producing "defense" but also on the loss of life. A dozen years ago, the Gulf War was waged with a total of 147 battlefield deaths. At the time this article goes to press, the American military has experienced 79 deaths in Afghanistan's Operation Enduring Freedom and 177 deaths in Operation Iraqi Freedom. In comparison, during the Selective Service era, the U.S. military experienced 33,741 deaths in Korea and 47,414 in Vietnam.

Shared burden. Rep. Rangel claims that the U.S. military's all- 14
volunteer force is unacceptable because its demographics are not representative of the U.S. population. "It is apparent, however, that service in
the armed forces is not a common experience and that disproportionate
numbers of the poor and members of minority groups compose the enlisted ranks of the military," he said late last December. "We must be certain that the sacrifices we will be asking our armed forces to make are
shared by the rest of us."

But history shows compulsory service does not produce a fair shar- 15
ing of the burden of national defense. When the draft existed, many
youths failed to satisfy the mental and physical qualification standards
for induction and were rejected by their draft boards; in 1964, 35.6 percent of draft-eligible young men were exempted for those reasons. Under
the draft, women made up only four percent of the active duty forces,
but that number grew to 12 percent in 1990 and 15 percent in 2000.
African American college graduates comprise some 12 percent of the officer corps in the all-volunteer force, yet only 7.6 percent of all college

graduates are Black. Should we insist on a representative force by placing a cap on the number of African American officers?

Black enlisted men in the all–volunteer Army are under–represented 16 in the infantry and special forces, and over–represented in logistical support and administrative occupations—positions that they can serve to retirement. For the sake of shared sacrifice, would Rep. Rangel require more African Americans to serve on the front lines?

The draft is a poor way to provide an effective common defense—it can 17 raise a sufficient number of bodies to put in uniform, but it cannot guarantee the quality of the recruits. It discourages the adoption of military technologies that can reduce the loss of life during military operations. It increases the full economic cost of producing defense capability. And it does not make the military more representative. In a free society, individuals who serve by choice and not by compulsion should meet the call to arms.

Reading Closely

1. **Working with another classmate or two,** list of all the things that surprised you as you read this piece. Put a star beside each item that is based on Oi's research, not just on his opinion. Be prepared to share your group's list with the rest of the class.

2. What parts of this essay rang true to you? Which incidents, facts, or statistics have you experienced or observed? Share your responses with the rest of the class.

3. List all of the opinions or speculations that Oi includes in his essay to help him argue his points. What effect does speculation have on his argument?

Considering Larger Issues

1. What is the thesis statement of this essay? How does the author expand or support that thesis statement?

2. Who is the intended audience for this essay? What does Oi want the audience to do in response to his argument?

3. **Working with one or two other classmates,** discuss Oi's ethos in this essay. How successfully does he establish his goodwill, good sense, and good moral character? Mark the passages that emphasize logos. How successful are the logical appeals? Where does the author demonstrate pathos? How successful are the emotional appeals to Oi's particular readers?

4. COMBINING METHODS.   Oi uses both *cause-and-consequence analysis* and *narration* to bolster his argument. Find the specific passages that reflect these methods, and explain the ways that these passages advance or otherwise enhance his argument. What other methods does Oi use and to what overall effect?

5. The cartoon on p. 725 was published with Oi's essay. What role does it play in the overall effect of the essay? What is it emphasizing? Why?

Thinking about Language

1. **Together with one or two classmates,** define the following terms, some of which will be familiar to you but take on different meaning in this military context. If you cannot define them from experience or the context of the essay, use your dictionary. Be prepared to share your definitions with the rest of the class.

grappled (1)	feigned (6)	attrition (10)
compulsory (1)	conscription (6)	capital-intensive
citizen soldier (2)	immutably (8)	(12)
Cold War (5)	inevitably (8)	raw (13)
elicited (6)	inequitable (8)	demographics
regressive (6)	detrimental (8)	(14)
borne (6)	policymakers (8)	

2. Oi is an economics professor as well as a former government adviser. What terms and phrases does he use that reveal his professional experience? What terms and examples does he use that demonstrate his expertise as a researcher?

Writing Your Own Arguments

1. **Together with a classmate,** draft an evaluation of "The Virtue of an All-Volunteer Force," using the same techniques for analysis that you would use for producing your own argumentative essay. First, determine the purpose of the piece, then the audience. What is Oi's thesis statement? How clear is it? What reasons does Oi use to support his thesis statement? How valid are his reasons? What makes them valid, invalid, or altogether ineffective? How well does Oi establish the rhetorical appeals — successfully or only moderately so? Is his an inductive or deductive argument? What logical fallacies, if any, can you locate in his argument? As you move through the steps of evaluating this essay and drafting and revising your own two- to three-page essay, be sure to refer to the guidelines for checking over an argument on page 652.

2. What underlying beliefs does Oi have in common with Rangel and with Moskos and Glastris? How do their beliefs differ? What historical consequences have these common and differing beliefs had on the U.S. military, do you think? Draft a three- to four-page essay in which you argue that the model of national service that one (or one pair) of these people represents is the most beneficial to the United States. You may want to go beyond the information in these essays and, in addition, go to the library or the World Wide Web to better understand the historical background to this issue or locate additional supporting materials for your argument. Remember to refer to the guidelines for checking over an argument on p. 652.

MAGGIE KOERTH

Women in Draft Necessary Part of Quest to End Discrimination

● Maggie Koerth (b. 1981) wrote the following essay when she was a senior at the University of Kansas, majoring in journalism and anthropology. It was originally published in the *University Daily Kansan*, the student newspaper of the University of Kansas, in February 2003.

> **Preview**   What's your opinion on women in the draft? Do you think it's necessary for ending gender discrimination?

Women, what are you willing to do to gain gender equality? Stage a   1
protest? Lobby your congressman? How about go to war?

Chances are, most women on this campus would tell you they are in   2
favor of gender equality. We want all the beneficial effects that true
equality will bring. Unfortunately, while we have been busy fighting for
equal education and job opportunities, we have forgotten that true
equality does not always equal fun.

On Jan. 7, U.S. Representative Charles Rangel proposed that the draft   3
be reinstated if our country goes to war with Iraq. When he did not propose that women be included in the draft, the most common reaction I
heard from my peers was a sigh of relief.

In a way, this is understandable. Few people desperately want to risk   4
death on a battlefield, and the draft itself is not a popular institution.
However, the draft is also one of the most glaring examples of state-
sanctioned sexual discrimination in our country.

Every argument made by the Selective Service (www.sss.gov/   5
wmbkgr.htm) and by the Supreme Court (Rostker v. Goldberg, 453 U.S.
57) against the inclusion of women in the draft is based on the assumptions that women do not belong on the battlefield and that the military
has no use for anyone who is not on the front lines. Both are untrue.

The Israeli armed forces have drafted both men and women since   6
1948 without any detriment to their ability to fight and win. For decades,
those women aided their country by serving in technology, intelligence
and other behind-the-scenes positions crucial to the military effort. Their
work allowed more men to be moved to frontline positions.

According to the Israeli Defense Forces Web site, www.idf.il/english/   7
organization/chen/chen.stm, drafted women have been serving as paramilitary border police in combat positions since 1995. This is the equivalent of serving on the front lines.

Are Israeli women really that much more useful and capable than   8
American women? I doubt it.

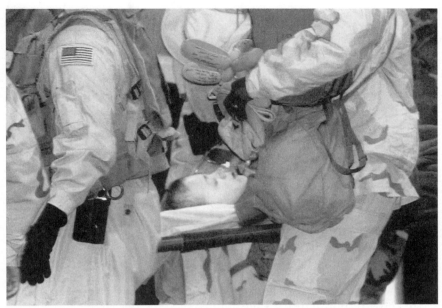

Jessica Lynch and Shoshana Johnson became symbols of the role of women soldiers in the Iraq war. Both were wounded and captured in the early weeks of combat before being rescued by U.S. troops; in the photo above, Lynch is carried off a military plane on a stretcher. Seven months later (in the photo below), she and Johnson were honored at *Glamour* magazine's Women of the Year awards ceremony.

So why have so many women ignored this issue? Why are there not   9
daily protests on Wescoe Beach demanding the military respect the
equality of the sexes?

It can't be because it's a hard point to argue.   10

Even those people who will never be convinced that women can   11
fight in a war must see how useful women can be to the support services
of the military, especially now that the military is so understaffed.

I am not asking women to believe the draft is a good thing. I am not   12
asking them to want to fight and die.

What I am telling women is that we cannot pick and choose what   13
equalities we want.

This is not a new problem. Gloria Steinem addressed the same issues   14
in 1970 in a *Washington Post* article called "Women's Liberation Aims to
Free Men Too."

To her, accepting all parts of equality would ultimately help both   15
sexes by equally distributing the pressure of traditionally sex-related
roles like military service.

"We want to liberate men from those inhuman roles as well," she   16
wrote. "We want to share the work and responsibility, and to have men
share equal responsibility for the children."

If we accept the discrimination of the draft, we accept the chauvinis-   17
tic images of an unreliable, delicate womanhood and a macho, war-
loving manhood. No amount of protesting for more "fun" rights will
erase that acceptance.

So ladies, stand up and fight for all your rights, even the unpopular   18
ones. Like the Selective Service ad says, "You can handle this."

Reading Closely

1. How does Koerth define "gender equality"?
2. How does she link gender equality with the draft?
3. What are three things you understand in her argument? What's one
   thing you want to know more about? Be prepared to share your question with the rest of the class.

Considering Larger Issues

1. Who is Koerth's audience for this essay? What does she want the audience to do?
2. **Working with a classmate,** identify the passages in which Koerth uses
   ethos, pathos, and logos. Be prepared to discuss the effectiveness of each
   of these passages with the rest of the class.

3. In making her logical appeals, Koerth refers to other sources of information. What are some of these sources? Explore them in order to evaluate their validity and relevance to her argument. Be prepared to share your answers with the rest of the class.

4. **COMBINING METHODS.**   How does Koerth use *cause-and-consequence analysis* to help shape her argument?

5. Which rhetorical methods other than argument do the photographs on p. 729 feature? to what effect?

Thinking about Language

1. Use your dictionary or the context of the essay to define the following terms. Be prepared to share your definitions with the rest of the class.

gender equality (1)	discrimination (4)	support services
lobby (1)	detriment (6)	(11)
reinstated (3)	paramilitary (7)	chauvinistic (17)
state–sanctioned (4)		

2. Mark all the words and phrases that Koerth uses to emphasize the concept of "equality." What is the overall effect of her word choices? Could they have been more subtle? more explicit?

Writing Your Own Arguments

1. In a two- to three–page response to Koerth, engage each of her assertions. You'll need to consult the citations she mentions (the Web sites, court cases, and articles) in order to understand the supporting materials to which she refers. Your response could be the basis for a longer argument paper. Refer to the guidelines for checking over an argument on p. 652.

2. If the United States required military or civilian national service of all 18- to 25–year–olds, what would you choose to do? Write a three- to four–page essay in which you argue for your personal plan and the reasons for it. You may find that you'll have to conduct Web–based or library research in order to come up with a plan, although the previous essays in this section may help you get started. If you are older than 25, write your essay in the form of advice to a specific younger person you know. Refer to the guidelines for checking over an argument on p. 652.

Classic Arguments

MARTIN LUTHER KING JR.

Letter from Birmingham Jail

Martin Luther King Jr. (1929–1968), the Baptist minister who led the campaign against racial discrimination in the United States in the 1950s and 1960s, won the Nobel Peace Prize in 1964, four years before he was assassinated. King's accomplishments are many, but he is most remembered for his advocacy of nonviolent civil disobedience and his inspiring eloquence as a speaker and writer. His best-known works include the "I Have a Dream" speech, delivered at the March on Washington for civil rights in 1963, and the following letter to white clergymen in Birmingham, Alabama, where he had been arrested later in 1963 while protesting unfair hiring practices. "Letter from Birmingham Jail" was first published in King's book *Why We Can't Wait* (1964).

Preview What do you know about Dr. Martin Luther King Jr.?

April 16, 1963

My Dear Fellow Clergymen:

While confined here in the Birmingham city jail, I came across your recent statement calling my present activities "unwise and untimely." Seldom do I pause to answer criticism of my work and ideas. If I sought to answer all the criticisms that cross my desk, my secretaries would have little time for anything other than such correspondence in the course of the day, and I would have no time for constructive work. But since I feel that you are men of genuine good will and that your criticisms are sincerely set forth, I want to try to answer your statement in what I hope will be patient and reasonable terms. 1

I think I should indicate why I am here in Birmingham, since you have been influenced by the view which argues against "outsiders coming in." I have the honor of serving as president of the Southern Christian Leadership Conference, an organization operating in every southern state, with headquarters in Atlanta, Georgia. We have some eighty-five affiliated organizations across the South, and one of them is the Alabama Christian Movement for Human Rights. Frequently we share staff, educational, and financial resources with our affiliates. Several months ago the affiliate here in Birmingham asked us to be on call to engage in a nonviolent direct-action program if such were deemed necessary. We readily consented, and when the hour came we lived up to our promise. So I, along with several members of my staff, am here because I was invited here. I am here because I have organizational ties here. 2

But more basically, I am in Birmingham because injustice is here. Just ₃ as the prophets of the eighth century B.C. left their villages and carried their "thus saith the Lord" far beyond the boundaries of their home towns, and just as the Apostle Paul left his village of Tarsus and carried the gospel of Jesus Christ to the far corners of the Greco–Roman world, so am I compelled to carry the gospel of freedom beyond my own home town. Like Paul, I must constantly respond to the Macedonian call for aid.

Moreover, I am cognizant of the interrelatedness of all communities ₄ and states. I cannot sit idly by in Atlanta and not be concerned about what happens in Birmingham. Injustice anywhere is a threat to justice everywhere. We are caught in an inescapable network of mutuality, tied in a single garment of destiny. Whatever affects one directly, affects all indirectly. Never again can we afford to live with the narrow, provincial, "outside agitator" idea. Anyone who lives inside the United States can never be considered an outsider anywhere within its bounds.

You deplore the demonstrations taking place in Birmingham. But ₅ your statement, I am sorry to say, fails to express a similar concern for the conditions that brought about the demonstrations. I am sure that none of you would want to rest content with the superficial kind of social analysis that deals merely with effects and does not grapple with underlying causes. It is unfortunate that demonstrations are taking place in Birmingham, but it is even more unfortunate that the city's white power structure left the Negro community with no alternative.

In any nonviolent campaign there are four basic steps: collection of the ₆ facts to determine whether injustices exist; negotiation; self–purification; and direct action. We have gone through all these steps in Birmingham. There can be no gainsaying the fact that racial injustice engulfs this community. Birmingham is probably the most thoroughly segregated city in the United States. Its ugly record of brutality is widely known. Negroes have experienced grossly unjust treatment in courts. There have been more unsolved bombings of Negro homes and churches in Birmingham than in any other city in the nation. These are the hard, brutal facts of the case. On the basis of these conditions, Negro leaders sought to negotiate with the city fathers. But the latter consistently refused to engage in good–faith negotiation.

Then, last September, came the opportunity to talk with leaders of ₇ Birmingham's economic community. In the course of the negotiations, certain promises were made by the merchants—for example, to remove the stores' humiliating racial signs. On the basis of these promises, the Reverend Fred Shuttlesworth and the leaders of the Alabama Christian Movement for Human Rights agreed to a moratorium on all demonstrations. As the weeks and months went by, we realized that we were the victims of a broken promise. A few signs, briefly removed, returned; the others remained.

As in so many past experiences, our hopes had been blasted, and the   8
shadow of deep disappointment settled upon us. We had no alternative
except to prepare for direct action, whereby we would present our very
bodies as means of laying our case before the conscience of the local and
the national community. Mindful of the difficulties involved, we decided
to undertake a process of self-purification. We began a series of work-
shops on nonviolence, and we repeatedly asked ourselves: "Are you able
to accept blows without retaliating?" "Are you able to endure the ordeal
of jail?" We decided to schedule our direct-action program for the Easter
season, realizing that except for Christmas, this is the main shopping period of the year. Knowing that a strong economic-withdrawal program
would be the by-product of direct action, we felt that this would be the
best time to bring pressure to bear on the merchants for the needed
change.

Then it occurred to us that Birmingham's mayoral election was coming   9
up in March, and we speedily decided to postpone action until after election day. When we discovered that the Commissioner of Public Safety,
Eugene "Bull" Connor, had piled up enough votes to be in the run-off, we
decided again to postpone action until the day after the run-off so that the
demonstrations could not be used to cloud the issues. Like many others,
we waited to see Mr. Connor defeated, and to this end we endured postponement after postponement. Having aided in this community need, we
felt that our direct-action program could be delayed no longer.

You may well ask, "Why direct action? Why sit-ins, marches, and so   10
forth? Isn't negotiation a better path?" You are quite right in calling for
negotiation. Indeed, this is the very purpose of direct action. Nonviolent
direct action seeks to create such a crisis and foster such a tension that a
community which has constantly refused to negotiate is forced to confront the issue. It seeks so to dramatize the issue that it can no longer be
ignored. My citing the creation of tension as part of the work of the
nonviolent-resistor may sound rather shocking. But I must confess that I
am not afraid of the word "tension." I have earnestly opposed violent
tension, but there is a type of constructive, nonviolent tension which is
necessary for growth. Just as Socrates felt that it was necessary to create a
tension in the mind so that individuals could rise from the bondage of
myths and half-truths to the unfettered realm of creative analysis and
objective appraisal, so must we see the need for nonviolent gadflies to
create the kind of tension in society that will help men rise from the dark
depths of prejudice and racism to the majestic heights of understanding
and brotherhood.

The purpose of our direct-action program is to create a situation so   11
crisis-packed that it will inevitably open the door to negotiation. I therefore concur with you in your call for negotiation. Too long has our
beloved Southland been bogged down in a tragic effort to live in monologue rather than dialogue.

One of the basic points in your statement is that the action that I and   12
my associates have taken in Birmingham is untimely. Some have asked:
"Why didn't you give the new city administration time to act?" The only
answer that I can give to this query is that the new Birmingham administration must be prodded about as much as the outgoing one, before it
will act. We are sadly mistaken if we feel that the election of Albert
Boutwell as mayor will bring the millennium to Birmingham. While Mr.
Boutwell is a much more gentle person than Mr. Connor, they are both
segregationists, dedicated to maintenance of the status quo. I have hoped
that Mr. Boutwell will be reasonable enough to see the futility of massive
resistance to desegregation. But he will not see this without pressure
from devotees of civil rights. My friends, I must say to you that we have
not made a single gain in civil rights without determined legal and nonviolent pressure. Lamentably, it is an historical fact that privileged groups
seldom give up their privileges voluntarily. Individuals may see the
moral light and voluntarily give up their unjust posture; but, as Reinhold
Niebuhr* has reminded us, groups tend to be more immoral than individuals.

We know through painful experience that freedom is never volun-   13
tarily given by the oppressor; it must be demanded by the oppressed.
Frankly, I have yet to engage in a direct–action campaign that was "well
timed" in the view of those who have not suffered unduly from the disease of segregation. For years now I have heard the word "Wait!" It rings
in the ear of every Negro with piercing familiarity. This "Wait" has almost
always meant "Never." We must come to see, with one of our distinguished jurists, that "justice too long delayed is justice denied."

We have waited for more than 340 years for our constitutional and   14
God–given rights. The nations of Asia and Africa are moving with jetlike
speed toward gaining political independence, but we still creep at horse-
and–buggy pace toward gaining a cup of coffee at a lunch counter.
Perhaps it is easy for those who have never felt the stinging darts of segregation to say, "Wait." But when you have seen vicious mobs lynch your
mothers and fathers at will and drown your sisters and brothers at
whim; when you have seen hate–filled policemen curse, kick, and even
kill your black brothers and sisters; when you see the vast majority of
your twenty million Negro brothers smothering in an airtight cage of
poverty in the midst of an affluent society; when you suddenly find your
tongue twisted and your speech stammering as you seek to explain to
your six–year–old daughter why she can't go to the public amusement
park that has just been advertised on television, and see tears welling up
in her eyes when she is told that Funtown is closed to colored children,
and see ominous clouds of inferiority beginning to form in her little

---

* **Reinhold Niebuhr** (1892–1971): American social and religious thinker.

mental sky, and see her beginning to distort her personality by developing an unconscious bitterness toward white people; when you have to
concoct an answer for a five–year–old son who is asking, "Daddy, why do
white people treat colored people so mean?"; when you take a cross-
country drive and find it necessary to sleep night after night in the uncomfortable corners of your automobile because no motel will accept
you; when you are humiliated day in and day out by nagging signs reading "white" and "colored"; when your first name becomes "nigger," your
middle name becomes "boy" (however old you are) and your last name
becomes "John," and your wife and mother are never given the respected
title "Mrs."; when you are harried by day and haunted at night by the fact
that you are a Negro, living constantly at tiptoe stance, never quite
knowing what to expect next, and are plagued with inner fears and outer
resentments; when you are forever fighting a degenerating sense of "no-
bodiness"—then you will understand why we find it difficult to wait.
There comes a time when the cup of endurance runs over, and men are
no longer willing to be plunged into the abyss of despair. I hope, sirs,
you can understand our legitimate and unavoidable impatience.

You express a great deal of anxiety over our willingness to break   15
laws. This is certainly a legitimate concern. Since we so diligently urge
people to obey the Supreme Court's decision of 1954 outlawing segregation in the public schools, at first glance it may seem rather paradoxical
for us consciously to break laws. One may well ask: "How can you advocate breaking some laws and obeying others?" The answer lies in the fact
that there are two types of laws: just and unjust. I would be the first to
advocate obeying just laws. One has not only a legal but a moral responsibility to obey just laws. Conversely, one has a moral responsibility
to disobey unjust laws. I would agree with St. Augustine* that "an unjust
law is no law at all."

Now, what is the difference between the two? How does one deter-   16
mine whether a law is just or unjust? A just law is a man–made code that
squares with the moral law or the law of God. An unjust law is a code
that is out of harmony with the moral law. To put it in the terms of St.
Thomas Aquinas:* An unjust law is a human law that is not rooted in
eternal law and natural law. Any law that uplifts human personality is
just. Any law that degrades human personality is unjust. All segregation
statutes are unjust because segregation distorts the soul and damages the
personality. It gives the segregator a false sense of superiority and the
segregated a false sense of inferiority. Segregation, to use the terminology
of the Jewish philosopher Martin Buber, substitutes an "I–it" relationship
for an "I–thou" relationship and ends up relegating persons to the status

---

* **St. Augustine** (354–430): theologian and philosopher of the early Christian
church.

* **St. Thomas Aquinas** (1225–1274): Italian theologian and philosopher.

of things. Hence segregation is not only politically, economically, and sociologically unsound, it is morally wrong and sinful. Paul Tillich* has said that sin is separation. Is not segregation an existential expression of man's tragic separation, his awful estrangement, his terrible sinfulness? Thus it is that I can urge men to obey the 1954 decision of the Supreme Court, for it is morally right; and I can urge them to disobey segregation ordinances, for they are morally wrong.

Let us consider a more concrete example of just and unjust laws. An 17 unjust law is a code that a numerical or power majority group compels a minority group to obey but does not make binding on itself. This is *difference* made legal. By the same token, a just law is a code that a majority compels a minority to follow and that it is willing to follow itself. This is *sameness* made legal.

Let me give another explanation. A law is unjust if it is inflicted on a 18 minority that, as a result of being denied the right to vote, had no part in enacting or devising the law. Who can say that the legislature of Alabama which set up that state's segregation laws was democratically elected? Throughout Alabama all sorts of devious methods are used to prevent Negroes from becoming registered voters, and there are some counties in which, even though Negroes constitute a majority of the population, not a single Negro is registered. Can any law enacted under such circumstances be considered democratically structured?

Sometimes a law is just on its face and unjust in its application. For 19 instance, I have been arrested on a charge of parading without a permit. Now, there is nothing wrong in having an ordinance which requires a permit for a parade. But such an ordinance becomes unjust when it is used to maintain segregation and to deny citizens the First-Amendment privilege of peaceful assembly and protest.

I hope you are able to see the distinction I am trying to point out. In 20 no sense do I advocate evading or defying the law, as would the rabid segregationist. That would lead to anarchy. One who breaks an unjust law must do so openly, lovingly, and with a willingness to accept the penalty. I submit that an individual who breaks a law that conscience tells him is unjust, and who willingly accepts the penalty of imprisonment in order to arouse the conscience of the community over its injustice, is in reality expressing the highest respect for law.

Of course, there is nothing new about this kind of civil disobedience. 21 It was evidenced sublimely in the refusal of Shadrach, Meshach, and Abednego* to obey the laws of Nebuchadnezzar, on the ground that a

---

* **Paul Tillich** (1886–1965): U.S. Protestant theologian and philosopher.
* **Shadrach, Meshach, and Abednego:** three Jewish men who were thrown into a fire by the Babylonian king Nebuchadnezzar for refusing to worship a golden statue, according to the biblical Book of Daniel; the fire miraculously failed to burn them.

higher moral law was at stake. It was practiced superbly by the early Christians, who were willing to face hungry lions and the excruciating pain of chopping blocks rather than submit to certain unjust laws of the Roman Empire. To a degree, academic freedom is a reality today because Socrates practiced civil disobedience. In our own nation, the Boston Tea Party represented a massive act of civil disobedience.

We should never forget that everything Adolph Hitler did in Ger- 22 many was "legal" and everything the Hungarian freedom fighters did in Hungary was "illegal." It was "illegal" to aid and comfort a Jew in Hitler's Germany. Even so, I am sure that, had I lived in Germany at the time, I would have aided and comforted my Jewish brothers. If today I lived in a Communist country where certain principles dear to the Christian faith are suppressed, I would openly advocate disobeying that country's anti-religious laws.

I must make two honest confessions to you, my Christian and Jewish 23 brothers. First, I must confess that over the past few years I have been gravely disappointed with the white moderate. I have almost reached the regrettable conclusion that the Negro's great stumbling block in his stride toward freedom is not the White Citizens Counciler or the Ku Klux Klanner, but the white moderate, who is more devoted to "order" than to justice; who prefers a negative peace which is the absence of tension to a positive peace which is the presence of justice; who constantly says, "I agree with you in the goal you seek, but I cannot agree with your methods of direct action"; who paternalistically believes he can set the timetable for another man's freedom; who lives by a mythical concept of time and who constantly advised the Negro to wait for a "more convenient season." Shallow understanding from people of good will is more frustrating than absolute misunderstanding from people of ill will. Lukewarm acceptance is much more bewildering than outright rejection.

I had hoped that the white moderate would understand that law and 24 order exist for the purpose of establishing justice and that when they fail in this purpose they become the dangerously structured dams that block the flow of social progress. I had hoped that the white moderate would understand that the present tension in the South is a necessary phase of the transition from an obnoxious negative peace, in which the Negro passively accepted his unjust plight, to a substantive and positive peace, in which all men will respect the dignity and worth of human personality. Actually, we who engage in nonviolent direct action are not the creators of tension. We merely bring to the surface the hidden tension that is already alive. We bring it out in the open, where it can be seen and dealt with. Like a boil that can never be cured so long as it is covered up but must be opened with all its ugliness to the natural medicines of air and light, injustice must be exposed, with all the tension its exposure creates, to the light of human conscience and the air of national opinion, before it can be cured.

In your statement you assert that our actions, even though peaceful,   25
must be condemned because they precipitate violence. But is this a logical assertion? Isn't this like condemning a robbed man because his possession of money precipitated the evil act of robbery? Isn't this like condemning Socrates because his unswerving commitment to truth and his
philosophical inquiries precipitated the act by the misguided populace in
which they made him drink hemlock? Isn't this like condemning Jesus
because his unique God–consciousness and never–ceasing devotion to
God's will precipitated the evil act of crucifixion? We must come to see
that, as the federal courts have consistently affirmed, it is wrong to urge
an individual to cease his efforts to gain his basic constitutional rights
because the quest may precipitate violence. Society must protect the
robbed and punish the robber.

I had also hoped that the white moderate would reject the myth   26
concerning time in relation to the struggle for freedom. I have just received a letter from a white brother in Texas. He writes: "All Christians
know that the colored people will receive equal rights eventually, but it
is possible that you are in too great a religious hurry. It has taken Christianity almost two thousand years to accomplish what it has. The teachings of Christ take time to come to earth." Such an attitude stems from a
tragic misconception of time, from the strangely irrational notion that
there is something in the very flow of time that will inevitably cure all
ills. Actually, time itself is neutral; it can be used either destructively or
constructively. More and more I feel that the people of ill will have used
time much more effectively than have the people of good will. We will
have to repent in this generation not merely for the hateful words and
actions of the bad people, but for the appalling silence of the good
people. Human progress never rolls in on wheels of inevitability; it
comes through the tireless efforts of men willing to be co–workers with
God, and without this hard work, time itself becomes an ally of the
forces of social stagnation. We must use time creatively, in the knowledge
that the time is always ripe to do right. Now is the time to make real the
promise of democracy and transform our pending national elegy into a
creative psalm of brotherhood. Now is the time to lift our national policy
from the quicksand of racial injustice to the solid rock of human dignity.

You speak of our activity in Birmingham as extreme. At first I was   27
rather disappointed that fellow clergymen would see my nonviolent efforts as those of an extremist. I began thinking about the fact that I stand
in the middle of two opposing forces in the Negro community. One is a
force of complacency, made up in part of Negroes who, as a result of
long years of oppression, are so drained of self-respect and a sense of
"somebodiness" that they have adjusted to segregation; and in part of a
few middle–class Negroes who, because of a degree of academic and economic security and because in some ways they profit by segregation,
have become insensitive to the problems of the masses. The other force is

one of bitterness and hatred, and it comes perilously close to advocating violence. It is expressed in the various black nationalist groups that are springing up across the nation, the largest and best-known being Elijah Muhammad's Muslim movement. Nourished by the Negro's frustration over the continued existence of racial discrimination, this movement is made up of people who have lost faith in America, who have absolutely repudiated Christianity, and who have concluded that the white man is an incorrigible "devil."

I have tried to stand between these two forces, saying that we need 28 emulate neither the "do-nothingism" of the complacent nor the hatred and despair of the black nationalist. For there is the more excellent way of love and nonviolent protest. I am grateful to God that, through the influence of the Negro church, the way of nonviolence became an integral part of our struggle.

If this philosophy had not emerged, by now many streets of the 29 South would, I am convinced, be flowing with blood. And I am further convinced that if our white brothers dismiss as "rabble-rousers" and "outside agitators" those of us who employ nonviolent direct action, and if they refuse to support our nonviolent efforts, millions of Negroes will, out of frustration and despair, seek solace and security in black-nationalist ideologies — a development that would inevitably lead to a frightening racial nightmare.

Oppressed people cannot remain oppressed forever. The yearning for 30 freedom eventually manifests itself, and that is what has happened to the American Negro. Something within has reminded him of his birthright of freedom, and something without has reminded him that it can be gained. Consciously or unconsciously, he has been caught up by the *Zeitgeist*, and with his black brothers of Africa and his brown and yellow brothers of Asia, South America, and the Caribbean, the United States Negro is moving with a sense of great urgency toward the promised land of racial justice. If one recognizes this vital urge that has engulfed the Negro community, one should readily understand why public demonstrations are taking place. The Negro has many pent-up resentments and latent frustrations, and he must release them. So let him march; let him make prayer pilgrimages to the city hall; let him go on freedom rides — and try to understand why he must do so. If his repressed emotions are not released in nonviolent ways, they will seek expression through violence; this is not a threat but a fact of history. So I have not said to my people, "Get rid of your discontent." Rather, I have tried to say that this normal and healthy discontent can be channeled into the creative outlet of nonviolent direct action. And now this approach is being termed extremist.

But though I was initially disappointed at being categorized as an 31 extremist, as I continued to think about the matter I gradually gained a measure of satisfaction from the label. Was not Jesus an extremist for love: "Love your enemies, bless them that curse you, do good to them that hate you, and pray for them which despitefully use you, and persecute you." Was not Amos an extremist for justice: "let justice roll down like waters and righteousness like an everflowing stream." Was not Paul an extremist for the Christian gospel: "I bear in my body the marks of the Lord Jesus." Was not Martin Luther an extremist: "Here I stand; I cannot do otherwise, so help me God." And John Bunyan: "I will stay in jail to the end of my days before I make a butchery of my conscience." And Abraham Lincoln: "This nation cannot survive half slave and half free." And Thomas Jefferson: "We hold these truths to be self-evident, that all men are created equal. . . ." So the question is not whether we will be extremists, but what kind of extremists we will be. Will we be extremists for hate or for love? Will we be extremists for the preservation of injustice or for the extension of justice? In that dramatic scene of Calvary's hill three men were crucified. We must never forget that all three were crucified for the same crime — the crime of extremism. Two were extremists for immorality, and thus fell below their environment. The other, Jesus Christ, was an extremist for love, truth, and goodness, and thereby rose above his environment. Perhaps the South, the nation, and the world are in dire need of creative extremists.

I hoped that the white moderate would see this need. Perhaps I was 32 too optimistic; perhaps I expected too much. I suppose I should have realized that few members of the oppressor race can understand the deep groans and passionate yearnings of the oppressed race, and still fewer have the vision to see that injustice must be rooted out by strong, persistent, and determined action. I am thankful, however, that some of our white brothers in the South have grasped the meaning of this social revolution and committed themselves to it. They are still all too few in quantity, but they are big in quality. Some — such as Ralph McGill, Lillian Smith, Harry Golden, James McBride Dabbs, Ann Braden, and Sarah Patton Boyle — have written about our struggle in eloquent and prophetic terms. Others have marched with us down nameless streets of the South. They have languished in filthy, roach-infested jails, suffering the abuse and brutality of policemen who view them as "dirty nigger-lovers." Unlike so many of their moderate brothers and sisters, they have recognized the urgency of the movement and sensed the need for powerful "action" antidotes to combat the disease of segregation.

Let me take note of my other major disappointment. I have been so 33 greatly disappointed with the white church and its leadership. Of course, there are some notable exceptions. I am not unmindful of the fact that each of you has taken some significant stands on this issue. I commend you, Reverend Stallings, for your Christian stand on this past Sunday, in welcoming Negroes to your worship service on a nonsegregated basis. I commend the Catholic leaders of this state for integrating Spring Hill College several years ago.

But despite these notable exceptions, I must honestly reiterate that I 34
have been disappointed with the church. I do not say this as one of those
negative critics who can always find something wrong with the church. I
say this as a minister of the gospel, who loves the church; who was nur–
tured in its bosom; who has been sustained by its spiritual blessings and
who will remain true to it as long as the cord of life shall lengthen.

When I was suddenly catapulted into the leadership of the bus 35
protest* in Montgomery, Alabama, a few years ago, I felt we would be
supported by the white church. I felt that the white ministers, priests, and
rabbis of the South would be among our strongest allies. Instead, some
have been outright opponents, refusing to understand the freedom
movement and misrepresenting its leaders; all too many others have
been more cautious than courageous and have remained silent behind
the anesthetizing security of stained–glass windows.

In spite of my shattered dreams, I came to Birmingham with the 36
hope that the white religious leadership of this community would see
the justice of our cause and, with deep moral concern, would serve as
the channel through which our just grievances could reach the power
structure. I had hoped that each of you would understand. But again I
have been disappointed.

There was a time when the church was very powerful—in the time when 37
the early Christians rejoiced at being deemed worthy to suffer for what
they believed. In those days the church was not merely a thermometer
that recorded the ideas and principles of popular opinion; it was a ther–
mostat that transformed the mores of society. Whenever the early Chris–
tians entered a town, the people in power became disturbed and imme–
diately sought to convict the Christians for being "disturbers of the
peace" and "outside agitators." But the Christians pressed on, in the con–
viction that they were "a colony of heaven," called to obey God rather
than man. Small in number, they were big in commitment. They were
too God–intoxicated to be "astronomically intimidated." By their effort
and example they brought an end to such ancient evils as infanticide
and gladiatorial contests.

Things are different now. So often the contemporary church is a 38
weak, ineffectual voice with an uncertain sound. So often it is an arch–
defender of the status quo. Far from being disturbed by the presence of
the church, the power structure of the average community is consoled by
the church's silent—and often even vocal—sanction of things as they are.

But the judgment of God is upon the church as never before. If 39
today's church does not recapture the sacrificial spirit of the early church,
it will lose its authenticity, forfeit the loyalty of millions, and be dis–

* **the bus protest:** King had first gained national prominence by leading a boycott
of the Montgomery bus system, starting in 1955, that succeeded in ending the requirement that black people sit in the back of buses.

missed as an irrelevant social club with no meaning for the twentieth century. Every day I meet young people whose disappointment with the church has turned into outright disgust.

Perhaps I have once again been too optimistic. Is organized religion 40 too inextricably bound to the status quo to save our nation and the world? Perhaps I must turn my faith to the inner spiritual church, the church within the church, as the true *ekklesia** and the hope of the world. But again I am thankful to God that some noble souls from the ranks of organized religion have broken loose from the paralyzing chains of conformity and joined us as active partners in the struggle for freedom. They have left their secure congregations and walked the streets of Albany, Georgia, with us. They have gone down the highways of the South on torturous rides for freedom. Yes, they have gone to jail with us. Some have been dismissed from their churches, have lost the support of their bishops and fellow ministers. But they have acted in the faith that right defeated is stronger than evil triumphant. Their witness has been the spiritual salt that has preserved the true meaning of the gospel in these troubled times. They have carved a tunnel of hope through the dark mountain of disappointment.

I hope the church as a whole will meet the challenge of this decisive 41 hour. But even if the church does not come to the aid of justice, I have no despair about the future. I have no fear about the outcome of our struggle in Birmingham, even if our motives are at present misunderstood. We will reach the goal of freedom in Birmingham and all over the nation, because the goal of America is freedom. Abused and scorned though we may be, our destiny is tied up with America's destiny. Before the pilgrims landed at Plymouth, we were here. Before the pen of Jefferson etched the majestic words of the Declaration of Independence across the pages of history, we were here. For more than two centuries our forebears labored in this country without wages; they made cotton king; they built the homes of their masters while suffering gross injustice and shameful humiliation — and yet out of a bottomless vitality they continued to thrive and develop. If the inexpressible cruelties of slavery could not stop us, the opposition we now face will surely fail. We will win our freedom because the sacred heritage of our nation and the eternal will of God are embodied in our echoing demands.

Before closing I feel impelled to mention one other point in your 42 statement that has troubled me profoundly. You warmly commended the Birmingham police for keeping "order" and "preventing violence." I doubt that you would have so warmly commended the police force if you had seen its dogs sinking their teeth into unarmed, nonviolent Negroes. I doubt that you would so quickly commend the policemen if you were to observe their ugly and inhumane treatment of Negroes here in the city jail; if you were to watch them push and curse old Negro women and

---

* *ekklesia:* Greek word for the early Christian church.

Firefighters in Birmingham turn their hoses on civil rights demonstrators in July 1963.

young Negro girls; if you were to see them slap and kick old Negro men and young boys; if you were to observe them, as they did on two occasions, refuse to give us food because we wanted to sing our grace together. I cannot join you in your praise of the Birmingham police department.

It is true that the police have exercised a degree of discipline in han- 45 dling the demonstrators. In this sense they have conducted themselves rather "nonviolently" in public. But for what purpose? To preserve the vile system of segregation. Over the past few years I have consistently preached that nonviolence demands that the means we use must be as pure as the ends we seek. I have tried to make clear that it is wrong to use immoral means to attain moral ends. But now I must affirm that it is just as wrong, or perhaps even more so, to use moral means to preserve immoral ends. Perhaps Mr. Connor and his policemen have been rather nonviolent in public, as was Chief Pritchett in Albany, Georgia, but they have used the moral means of nonviolence to maintain the immoral end of racial injustice. As T. S. Eliot has said, "The last temptation is the greatest treason: To do the right deed for the wrong reason."

I wish you had commended the Negro sit-inners and demonstrators 44 of Birmingham for their sublime courage, their willingness to suffer, and their amazing discipline in the midst of great provocation. One day the South will recognize its real heroes. They will be the James Merediths,* with the noble sense of purpose that enables them to face jeering and hostile mobs, and with the agonizing loneliness that characterizes the life of the pioneer. They will be old, oppressed, battered Negro women, symbolized in a seventy-two-year old woman in Montgomery, Alabama, who rose up with a sense of dignity and with her people decided not to ride segregated buses, and who responded with ungrammatical profundity to one who inquired about her weariness: "My feets is tired, but my soul is at rest." They will be the young high school and college students, the young ministers of the gospel and a host of their elders, courageously and nonviolently sitting in at lunch counters and willingly going to jail for conscience's sake. One day the South will know that when these disinherited children of God sat down at lunch counters, they were in reality standing up for what is best in the American dream and for the most sacred values in our Judaeo-Christian heritage, thereby bringing our nation back to those great wells of democracy which were dug deeply by the founding fathers in their formulation of the Constitution and the Declaration of Independence.

Never before have I written so long a letter. I'm afraid it is much too 45 long to take your precious time. I can assure that it would have been much shorter if I had been writing from a comfortable desk, but what else can one do when he is alone in a narrow jail cell, other than write long letters, think long thoughts, and pray long prayers?

If I have said anything in this letter that overstates the truth and in- 46 dicates an unreasonable impatience, I beg you to forgive me. If I have said anything that understates the truth and indicates my having a patience that allows me to settle for anything less than brotherhood, I beg God to forgive me.

I hope this letter finds you strong in the faith. I also hope that cir- 47 cumstances will soon make it possible for me to meet each of you, not as an integrationist or a civil-rights leader but as a fellow clergyman and a Christian brother. Let us all hope that the dark clouds of racial prejudice will soon pass away and the deep fog of misunderstanding will be lifted from our fear-drenched communities, and in some not too distant tomorrow the radiant stars of love and brotherhood will shine over our great nation with all their scintillating beauty.

Yours for the cause of Peace and Brotherhood,
Martin Luther King Jr.

* **James Meredith:** the first African American student to enroll (in 1962) at the all-white University of Mississippi.

Reading Closely

1. What is the thesis of this letter? What specific arguments does King use to support this thesis?

2. **Together with a classmate,** mark all the passages that date this letter. What anecdotes, practices, terms, or phrases indicate that this letter was written in 1963? Prepare a response to share with the rest of the class.

3. What did you learn from this letter that you didn't know before about U.S. life and race relations in 1963?

Considering Larger Issues

1. Who is the audience for this letter? What does King want his audience to do with the information in his letter?

2. What is the purpose of his letter? How, specifically, does this letter fulfill its overall purpose?

3. How does King establish his ethos? Which passages support his good–will, good sense, and good moral character? Which passages help him create common ground with his readers?

4. **COMBINING METHODS.**   King relies on *cause-and-consequence analysis, comparison and contrast, narration,* and *exemplification* to develop his argument. Trace King's use of one of those methods in this essay. Be prepared to share with the rest of the class the reasons King may have used that method and the specific reasons that method enhances King's argument.

5. What do you learn from the visual on p. 744 that you don't learn from the essay?

Thinking about Language

1. **With another classmate (or two),** use the context of this essay and a dictionary to define the following words or phrases. Be prepared to share your responses with the rest of the class.

affiliated (2)	retaliating (8)	advocate (20)
nonviolent (2)	cloud the issues (9)	arouse (20)
direct–action (2)	gadflies (10)	excruciating (21)
prophets (3)	bogged down (11)	paternalistically
cognizant (4)	monologue (11)	(23)
interrelatedness (4)	prodded (12)	precipitate (25)
deplore (5)	devotees (12)	quest (25)
superficial (5)	ominous (14)	stagnation (26)
grapple (5)	plagued (14)	extremist (27)
gainsaying (6)	diligently (15)	complacency (27)
engulfs (6)	paradoxical (15)	*Zeitgeist* (30)
segregated (6)	existential (16)	
moratorium (7)	estrangement (16)	

2. **Working with two other classmates,** locate some of the sentences that you find most beautiful or poetic, such as "Injustice anywhere is a threat to justice everywhere." Account for the overall effect of your sentences in terms of the rhetorical appeals, the attention to audience, and the purpose. Be prepared to share your response with the rest of the class.

Writing Your Own Arguments

1. In many ways, King's letter is a historical document, more than forty years old. In other ways, the problems of inequality have accompanied us into the twenty–first century. Draft a three– to four–page letter in response to King's, one that argues that racial equality is much closer, somewhat closer, or not much closer than it was when he was alive. Address your letter to King. Be sure to employ the rhetorical appeals as you write an introduction, thesis statement, supporting argument, response to opposing views, and conclusion. You may find that library and Web research is the best way to find the necessary support you need. As you revise your essay for submission, refer to the guidelines for checking over an argument on p. 652.

2. Follow your local or school newspaper for several days (the past week, too, if you'd like) and locate an interesting controversial issue that is receiving a good deal of press. As you read and collect all the articles (and related articles on Web sites and in other publications), come up with a position on the issue that you can support in an essay of three to four pages. Be sure to refer to the guidelines on p. 652 for checking over an argument as you draft and revise.

THOMAS JEFFERSON

The Declaration of Independence

Thomas Jefferson (1743–1826) started his career as a lawyer and served as governor of Virginia, a diplomat to France, and vice president to John Adams before becoming the third president of the United States in 1801. A "Renaissance man" who was, among other talents, a speaker of several languages, a musician, an inventor, a farmer, an architect, and the founder of the University of Virginia, Jefferson is perhaps most famous for crafting one of the most influential political documents of all time: the Declaration of Independence.

> **Preview**   Can you recite any of the Declaration of Independence by heart? Even if you cannot, what do you remember about it?

When in the course of human events, it becomes necessary for one 1 people to dissolve the political bonds which have connected them with another, and to assume among the powers of the earth, the separate and equal station to which the Laws of Nature and of Nature's God entitle them, a decent respect to the opinions of mankind requires that they should declare the causes which impel them to the separation.

We hold these truths to be self–evident, that all men are created 2 equal, that they are endowed by their Creator with certain unalienable rights, that among these are life, liberty and the pursuit of happiness. That to secure these rights, governments are instituted among men, deriving their just powers from the consent of the governed. That whenever any form of government becomes destructive to these ends, it is the right of the people to alter or to abolish it, and to institute new government, laying its foundation on such principles and organizing its powers in such form, as to them shall seem most likely to effect their safety and happiness. Prudence, indeed, will dictate that governments long established should not be changed for light and transient causes; and accordingly all experience hath shown, that mankind are more disposed to suffer, while evils are sufferable, than to right themselves by abolishing the forms to which they are accustomed. But when a long rain of abuses and usurpations, pursuing invariably the same object, evinces a design to reduce them under absolute despotism, it is their right, it is their duty, to throw off such government, and to provide new guards for their future security. Such has been the patient sufferance of these Colonies; and such is now the necessity which constrains them to alter their former systems of government. This history of the present king of Great Britain is a history of repeated injuries and usurpations, all having in direct object the establishment of an absolute tyranny over these States. To prove this, let facts be submitted to a candid world.

He has refused his assent to laws, the most wholesome and necessary 3
for the public good.

He has forbidden his Governors to pass laws of immediate and 4
pressing importance, unless suspended in their operation till his assent
should be obtained; and when so suspended, he has utterly neglected to
attend to them.

He has refused to pass other laws for the accommodation of large 5
districts of people, unless those people would relinquish the right of representation in the legislature, a right inestimable to them and formidable
to tyrants only.

He has called together legislative bodies at places unusual, un- 6
comfortable, and distant from the depository of their public records,
for the sole purpose of fatiguing them into compliance with his measure.

He has dissolved representative houses repeatedly, for opposing with 7
manly firmness his invasions on the rights of people.

He has refused for a long time, after such dissolutions, to cause oth- 8
ers to be elected; whereby the legislative powers, incapable of annihila-
tion, have returned to the people at large for their exercise; the State remaining in the meantime exposed to all the dangers of invasion from
without and convulsions within.

He has endeavoured to prevent the population of these states; for 9
that purpose obstructing the laws for naturalization of foreigners; refusing to pass others to encourage their migration hither, and raising the
conditions of new appropriations of lands.

He has obstructed the administration of justice, by refusing his as- 10
sent to laws for establishing judiciary powers.

He has made judges dependent on his will alone, for the tenure of 11
their offices, and the amount and payment of their salaries.

He has erected a multitude of new offices, and sent hither swarms of 12
officers to harass our people, and eat out their substance.

He has kept among us, in times of peace, standing armies without 13
the consent of our legislatures.

He has affected to render the military independent of and superior 14
to the civil power.

He has combined with others to subject us to a jurisdiction foreign 15
to our constitution, and unacknowledged by our laws; giving his assent
to their acts of pretended legislation:

For quartering large bodies of troops among us: 16

For protecting them, by a mock trial, from punishment for any mur- 17
ders which they should commit on the inhabitants of these States:

For cutting off our trade with all parts of the world: 18

For imposing taxes on us without our consent: 19

For depriving us in many cases of the benefits of trial by jury: 20

For transporting us beyond seas to be tried for pretended offences: 21

For abolishing the free system of English laws in a neighbouring 22
Province, establishing therein an arbitrary government, and enlarging its
boundaries so as to render it at once an example and fit instrument for
introducing the same absolute rule into these Colonies:

For taking away our Charters, abolishing our most valuable laws, 23
and altering fundamentally the forms of our governments:

For suspending our own legislatures, and declaring themselves in- 24
vested with power to legislate for us in all cases whatsoever.

He has abdicated government here, by declaring us out of his pro- 25
tection and waging war against us.

He has plundered our seas, ravaged our coasts, burnt our towns, and 26
destroyed the lives of our people.

He is at this time transporting large armies of foreign mercenaries to 27
complete the works of death, desolation and tyranny, already begun with
circumstances of cruelty and perfidy scarcely paralleled in the most bar-
barous ages, and totally unworthy the head of a civilized nation.

He has constrained our fellow citizens taken captive on the high seas 28
to bear arms against their country, to become the executioners of their
friends and brethren, or to fall themselves by their hands.

He has excited domestic insurrections amongst us, and has endeav- 29
oured to bring on the inhabitants of our frontiers, the merciless Indian
savages, whose known rule of warfare, is an undistinguished destruction
of all ages, sexes, and conditions.

In every stage of these oppressions we have petitioned for redress in 30
the most humble terms: our repeated petitions have been answered only
by repeated injury. A prince whose character is thus marked by every act
which may define a tyrant is unfit to be the ruler of a free people.

Nor have we been wanting in attention to our British brethren. We 31
have warned them from time to time of attempts by their legislature to extend an unwarrantable jurisdiction over us. We have reminded them of the
circumstances of our emigration and settlement here. We have appealed to
their native justice and magnanimity, and we have conjured them by the
ties of our common kindred to disavow these usurpations, which would inevitably interrupt our connections and correspondence. They too have
been deaf to the voice of justice and of consanguinity. We must, therefore,
acquiesce in the necessity, which denounces our separation, and hold them,
as we hold the rest of mankind, enemies in war, in peace friends.

We, therefore, the Representatives of the United States of America, in 32
General Congress assembled, appealing to the Supreme Judge of the world
for the rectitude of our intentions, do, in the name, and by authority of the
good people of these Colonies, solemnly publish and declare, That these
United Colonies are, and of right ought to be, Free and Independent States;
that they are absolved from all allegiance to the British Crown, and that all
political connection between them and the state of Great Britain, is and
ought to be totally dissolved; and that as Free and Independent States,

they have full power to levy war, conclude peace, contract alliances, establish commerce, and to do all other acts and things which Independent States may of right do. And for the support of this declaration, with a firm reliance on the protection of Divine Providence, we mutually pledge to each other our lives, our fortunes, and our sacred honor.

Reading Closely

1. What truths are self-evident, according to this document?
2. List ten of the reasons Jefferson gives for declaring independence from England.
3. What reasons does Jefferson supply for declaring independence rather than working toward a more productive relationship with England?
4. What did you learn about England's colonial rule during this period that you didn't know before?

Considering Larger Issues

1. Overall, what do you think is the purpose of Jefferson's argument: to express or defend his ideas, to question an idea, or to invite or convince his readers to change their point of view? What audience does he have in mind, and what does he want his readers to do with his argument? How successfully does the declaration fulfill its purpose? What specific passages help support your answers?
2. What is Jefferson's thesis? Where is it located in the declaration? Why do you think he placed it where he did?
3. **Together with a classmate or two,** determine the ways Jefferson establishes his ethos (goodwill, good sense, good character) in the introduction. What specific logical (or reasonable) support does Jefferson offer in the body of his argument? Is it all reasonable? Is his argument arranged deductively or inductively? How does he use emotion to connect with his readers in the conclusion? Write out your answers, and prepare to share them with the rest of the class.
4. COMBINING METHODS. In order to fulfill the purpose of his argument, Jefferson relies on *cause-and-consequence analysis*. Outline the progression of his analysis. What information does he include for its logical appeal? its emotional appeal? What kinds of information might he be omitting?

Thinking about Language

1. Use the context of the declaration or a dictionary to define the following terms or phrases. Be prepared to share your definitions with the rest of the class.

impel (1)	sufferance (2)	obstructed (10)
self-evident (2)	assent (4)	swarms (12)
unalienable (2)	relinquish (5)	mercenaries (27)
deriving (2)	inestimable (5)	redress (30)
prudence (2)	formidable (5)	magnanimity (31)
transient (2)	annihilation (8)	conjured (31)
disposed (2)	endeavoured (9)	disavow (31)
usurpations (2)	hither (9)	consanguinity
evinces (2)	appropriations (9)	(31)
despotism (2)		

2. Select one of the longer paragraphs (or a series of short paragraphs) and rewrite it, using more contemporary language. If your class can divide up the entire declaration, then you can all combine your translations, providing a paragraph-by-paragraph Declaration of Independence for the twenty-first century.

Writing Your Own Arguments

1. Draft a three- to four-page essay in which you declare your independence from something (school, job, drugs, junk food, e-mail) or someone (parents, family, partner, friend). Use either the original declaration or your class's update of the declaration as your model. Be sure to employ the rhetorical appeals, spending a good deal of time working on the logical appeals of your declaration. Argue for the reasons that you should be independent and that the thing or person should agree with your decision. Your challenge will be in determining your audience as well as in establishing goodwill and common ground in your introduction. Be sure to refer to the guidelines for checking over an argument on p. 652.

2. Consider a grievance that you (or you and your friends) have. Write a two- to three-page essay in which you state your grievance and then argue for the way it should be resolved. Be sure to articulate your audience and purpose as you develop the ethos, pathos, and logos of your essay. Refer to the guidelines for checking over an argument on p. 652 as you draft and revise.

JONATHAN SWIFT

A Modest Proposal

● Jonathan Swift (1667–1745) was born in Dublin, Ireland, and is perhaps best known as the author of *Gulliver's Travels* (1726). He was ordained to the Anglican clergy and served as dean of St. Patrick's Cathedral in Dublin from 1714 until his death, but he spent much of his time writing bitter political critiques and satires, usually taking aim at England and its oppressive treatment of the Irish. His political writings include "Irish Manufacture" (1720), "The Drapier Letters" (1724), and "A Modest Proposal" (1729), which was written during a severe famine in Ireland.

> **Preview** If you're not already familiar with this essay, what does the title suggest to you?

It is a melancholy object to those who walk through this great town* or   1
travel in the country, when they see the streets, the roads, and cabin doors, crowded with beggars of the female sex, followed by three, four, or six children, all in rags and importuning every passenger for an alms. These mothers, instead of being able to work for their honest livelihood, are forced to employ all their time in strolling to beg sustenance for their helpless infants, who, as they grow up, either turn thieves for want of work, or leave their dear native country to fight for the Pretender in Spain, or sell themselves to the Barbadoes.*

I think it is agreed by all parties that this prodigious number of chil-   2
dren in the arms, or on the backs, or at the heels of their mothers, and frequently of their fathers, is in the present deplorable state of the kingdom a very great additional grievance; and therefore whoever could find out a fair, cheap, and easy method of making these children sound, useful members of the commonwealth would deserve so well of the public as to have his statue set up for a preserver of the nation.

But my intention is very far from being confined to provide only for   3
the children of professed beggars; it is of a much greater extent, and shall take in the whole number of infants at a certain age who are born of parents in effect as little able to support them as those who demand our charity in the streets.

As to my own part, having turned my thoughts for many years upon   4
this important subject, and maturely weighed the several schemes of the other projectors, I have always found them grossly mistaken in their computation. It is true, a child just dropped from its dam may be

---

* **this great town:** Dublin.
* **Pretender . . . Barbadoes:** Many Irish people went to fight as mercenaries in Spain or to work as indentured servants in the West Indies.

753

supported by her milk for a solar year, with little other nourishment; at most not above the value of two shillings, which the mother may certainly get, or the value in scraps, by her lawful occupation of begging; and it is exactly at one year old that I propose to provide for them in such a manner as instead of being a charge upon their parents or the parish, or wanting food and raiment for the rest of their lives, they shall on the contrary contribute to the feeding, and partly to the clothing, of many thousands.

There is likewise another great advantage in my scheme, that it will prevent those involuntary abortions, and that horrid practice of women murdering their bastard children, alas, too frequent among us, sacrificing the poor innocent babies, I doubt, more to avoid the expense than the shame, which would move tears and pity in the most savage and inhuman breast. 5

The number of souls in this kingdom being usually reckoned one 6 million and a half, of these I calculate there may be about two hundred thousand couples whose wives are breeders, from which number I subtract thirty thousand couples who are able to maintain their own children, although I apprehend there cannot be so many under the present distress of the kingdom; but this being granted, there will remain an hundred and seventy thousand breeders. I again subtract fifty thousand for those women who miscarry, or whose children die by accident or disease within the year. There only remain an hundred and twenty thousand children of poor parents annually born. The question therefore is, how this number shall be reared and provided for, which, as I have already said, under the present situation of affairs, is utterly impossible by all the methods hitherto proposed. For we can neither employ them in handicraft nor agriculture; we neither build houses (I mean in the country) nor cultivate land. They can very seldom pick up livelihood by stealing till they arrive at six years old, except where they are of towardly parts,* although I confess they learn the rudiments much earlier, during which time they can however be looked upon only as probationers, as I have been informed by a principal gentleman in the country of Cavan, who protested to me that he never knew above one or two instances under the age of six, even in a part of the kingdom so renowned for the quickest proficiency in that art.

I am assured by our merchants that a boy or a girl before twelve 7 years old is no salable commodity; and even when they come to this age, they will not yield above three pounds, or three pounds and half a crown at most on the Exchange; which cannot turn to account either to the parents or the kingdom, the charge of nutriment and rags having been at least four times that value.

I shall now therefore humbly propose my own thoughts, which I 8 hope will not be liable to the least objection.

---

* **of towardly parts:** precocious.

I have been assured by a very knowing American of my acquain- 9
tance in London, that a young healthy child well nursed is at a year old a
most delicious, nourishing, and wholesome food, whether stewed,
roasted, baked, or boiled; and I make no doubt that it will equally serve
in fricasee or a ragout.

I do therefore humbly offer it to public consideration that of the 10
hundred and twenty thousand children, already computed, twenty thousand may be reserved for breed, whereof only one fourth part to be
males, which is more than we allow to sheep, black cattle, or swine; and
my reason is that these children are seldom the fruits of marriage, a cir-
cumstance not much regarded by our savages, therefore one male will be
sufficient to serve four females. That the remaining hundred thousand
may at a year old be offered in sale to the persons of quality and fortune
through the kingdom, always advising the mother to let them suck plen-
tifully in the last month, so as to render them plump and fat for a good
table. A child will make two dishes at an entertainment for friends; and
when the family dines alone, the fore or hind quarter will make a reasonable dish, and seasoned with a little pepper or salt, will be very good
boiled on the fourth day, especially in winter.

I have reckoned upon a medium that a child just born will weigh 11
twelve pounds, and in a solar year if tolerably nursed increaseth to
twenty–eight pounds.

I grant this food will be somewhat dear, and therefore very proper 12
for landlords, who, as they have already devoured most of the parents,
seem to have the best title to the children.

Infant's flesh will be in season throughout the year, but more plenti- 13
ful in March, and a little before and after. For we are told by a grave author, an eminent French physician,* that fish being a prolific diet, there
are more children born in Roman Catholic countries about nine months
after Lent, than at any other season; therefore, reckoning a year after
Lent, the markets will be more glutted than usual, because the number
of popish infants is at least three to one in this kingdom; and therefore it
will have one other collateral advantage, by lessening the number of Papists* among us.

I have already computed the charge of nursing a beggar's child (in 14
which list I reckon all cottagers, laborers, and four fifths of the farmers)
to be about two shillings per annum, rags included; and I believe no
gentleman would repine to give ten shillings for the carcass of a good fat
child, which, as I have said, will make four dishes of excellent nutritive
meat, when he hath only some particular friend or his own family to
dine with him. Thus the squire will learn to be a good landlord, and

---

* **French physician:** François Rabelais, a sixteenth–century satirical writer.
* **Papists:** followers of the Pope, i.e., Roman Catholics.

grow popular among the tenants; the mother will have eight shillings net profit, and be fit for work till she produces another child.

Those who are more thrifty (as I must confess the times require) may 15 flay the carcass; the skin of which artificially* dressed will make admirable gloves for ladies, and summer boots for fine gentlemen.

As to our city of Dublin, shambles* may be appointed for this pur– 16 pose in the most convenient parts of it, and butchers we may be assured will not be wanting; although I rather recommend buying the children alive, and dressing them hot from the knife as we do roasting pigs.

A very worthy person, a true lover of his country, and whose virtues 17 I highly esteem, was lately pleased in discoursing on this matter to offer a refinement upon my scheme. He said that many gentlemen of his kingdom, having of late destroyed their deer, he conceived that the want of venison might be well supplied by the bodies of young lads and maidens, not exceeding fourteen years of age nor under twelve, so great a number of both sexes in every county being now ready to starve for want of work and service; and these to be disposed of by their parents, if alive, or otherwise by their nearest relations. But with due deference to so excellent a friend and so deserving a patriot I cannot be altogether in his sentiments; for as to the males, my American acquaintance assured me from frequent experience that their flesh was generally tough and lean, like that of our schoolboys, by continual exercise, and their taste disagreeable; and to fatten them would not answer the charge. Then as to the females, it would, I think with humble submission, be a loss to the public, because they soon would become breeders themselves; and besides, it is not improbable that some scrupulous people might be apt to censure such a practice (although indeed very unjustly) as a little bordering upon cruelty; which, I confess, hath always been with me the strongest objection against any project, how well soever intended.

But in order to justify my friend, he confessed that this expedient 18 was put into his head by the famous Psalmanazar,* a native of the island Formosa, who came from thence to London above twenty years ago, and in conversation told my friend that in his country when any young person happened to be put to death, the executioner sold the carcass to the persons of quality as a prime dainty; and that in his time the body of a plump girl of fifteen, who was crucified for an attempt to poison the emperor, was sold to the Imperial Majesty's prime minister of state, and other great mandarins of the court, in joints from the gibbet, at four hundred crowns. Neither indeed can I deny that if the same use were made of several plump young girls in this town, who without one single

---

* **artificially:** skillfully.
* **shambles:** slaughterhouse or meat market.
* **Psalmanazar:** Frenchman who pretended to be a native of Formosa (present–day Taiwan).

groat to their fortunes cannot stir abroad without a chair,* and appear at the playhouse and assemblies in foreign fineries which they never will pay for, the kingdom would not be the worse.

Some persons of a desponding spirit are in great concern about the   19 vast number of poor people who are aged, diseased, or maimed, and I have been desired to employ my thoughts what course may be taken to ease the nation of so grievous an encumbrance. But I am not in the least pain upon that matter, because it is very well known that they are every day dying and rotting by cold and famine, and filth and vermin, as fast as can be rea– sonably expected. And as to the younger laborers, they are now in almost as hopeful a condition. They cannot get work, and consequently pine away for want of nourishment to a degree that if any time they are accidentally hired to common labor, they have not strength to perform it; and thus the country and themselves are happily delivered from the evils to come.

I have too long digressed, and therefore shall return to my subject. I   20 think the advantages by the proposal which I have made are obvious and many, as well as of the highest importance.

For first, as I have already observed, it would greatly lessen the num–   21 ber of Papists, with whom we are yearly overrun, being the principal breeders of the nation as well as our most dangerous enemies; and who stay at home on purpose to deliver the kingdom to the Pretender, hoping to take their advantage by the absence of so many good Protestants, who have chosen rather to leave their country than to stay at home and pay tithes against their conscience to an Episcopal curate.

Secondly, the poorer tenants will have something valuable of their   22 own, which by law may be made liable to distress,* and help to pay their landlord's rent, their corn and cattle being already seized and money a thing unknown.

Thirdly, whereas the maintenance of an hundred thousand children,   23 from two years old and upwards, cannot be computed at less than ten shillings a piece per annum, the nation's stock will be thereby increased fifty thousand pounds per annum, besides the profit of a new dish intro– duced to the tables of all gentlemen of fortune in the kingdom who have any refinement in taste. And the money will circulate among ourselves, the goods being entirely of our own growth and manufacture.

Fourthly, the constant breeders, besides the gain of eight shillings   24 sterling per annum by the sale of their children, will be rid of the charge for maintaining them after the first year.

Fifthly, this food would likewise bring great custom to taverns, where   25 the vintners will certainly be so prudent as to procure the best receipts* for dressing it to perfection, and consequently have their houses frequented

---

   * **chair:** a portable, covered chair designed to seat one person and then carried by two men; a sedan chair.
   * **liable to distress:** able to be seized by creditors.
   * **receipts:** recipes.

by all the fine gentlemen, who justly value themselves upon their knowledge in good eating; and a skillful cook, who understands how to oblige
his guests, will contrive to make it as expensive as they please.

Sixthly, this would be a great inducement to marriage, after which all 26
wise nations have either encouraged by rewards or enforced by laws and
penalties. It would increase the care and tenderness of mothers toward
their children, when they were sure of a settlement for life to the poor
babes, provided in some sort by the public, to their annual profit instead
of expense. We should see an honest emulation among the married
women, which of them could bring the fattest child to the market. Men
would become as fond of their wives during the time of pregnancy as
they are now of their mares in foal, their cows in calf, or sows when they
are ready to farrow; nor offer to beat or kick them (as is too frequent a
practice) for fear of miscarriage.

Many other advantages might be enumerated. For instance, the addi- 27
tion of some thousand carcasses in our exportation of barreled beef, the
propagation of swine's flesh, and improvements in the art of making
good bacon, so much wanted among us by the great destruction of pigs,
too frequent at our tables, which are no way comparable in taste or mag-
nificence to a well–grown, fat, yearling child, which roasted whole will
make a considerable figure at a lord mayor's feast or other public entertainment. But this and many others I omit, being studious of brevity.

Supposing that one thousand families in this city would be constant 28
customers for infants' flesh, besides others who might have it at merry
meetings, particularly weddings and christenings, I compute that Dublin
would take off annually about twenty thousand carcasses, and the rest of
the kingdom (where probably they will be sold somewhat cheaper) the
remaining eighty thousand.

I can think of no one objection that will possibly be raised against 29
this proposal, unless it should be urged that the number of people will
be thereby much lessened in the kingdom. This I freely own, and it was
indeed one principal design in offering it to the world. I desire the reader
will observe; that I calculate my remedy for this one individual kingdom
of Ireland and for no other that ever was, is, or I think ever can be upon
earth. Therefore, let no man talk to me of other expedients: of taxing our
absentees at five shillings a pound: of using neither clothes nor household furniture except what is of our own growth and manufacture: of
utterly rejecting the materials and instruments that promote foreign luxury: of curing the expensiveness of pride, vanity, idleness, and gaming in
our women: of introducing a vein of parsimony, prudence, and temper-
ance: of learning to love our country, in the want of which we differ even
from Lowlanders* and the inhabitants of Topinamboo:* of quitting our

---

* **Lowlanders:** the Dutch.
* **Topinamboo:** in the Brazilian jungle.

animosities and factions, nor acting any longer like the Jews,* who were murdering one another at the very moment their city was taken: of being a little cautious not to sell our country and conscience for nothing: of teaching landlords to have at least one degree of mercy toward their tenants: lastly, of putting a spirit of honesty, industry, and skill into our shopkeepers; who, if a resolution could now be taken to buy only our native goods, would immediately unite to cheat and exact upon us in the price, the measure, and the goodness, nor could ever yet be brought to make one fair proposal of just dealing, though often and earnestly invited to it.

Therefore, I repeat, let no man talk to me of these and the like expe- 30 dients, till he hath at least some glimpse of hope that there will ever be some hearty and sincere attempt to put them in practice.

But as to myself, having been wearied out for many years with offer- 31 ing vain, idle, visionary thoughts, and at length utterly despairing of success, I fortunately fell upon this proposal, which, as it is wholly new, so it hath something solid and real, of no expense and little trouble, full in our own power, and whereby we can incur no danger in disobliging England. For this kind of commodity will not bear exploration, the flesh being of too tender a consistence to admit a long continuance in salt, although perhaps I could name a country which would be glad to eat up our whole nation without it.

After all, I am not so violently bent upon my own opinion as to re- 32 ject any offer proposed by wise men, which shall be found equally innocent, cheap, easy, and effectual. But before something of that kind shall be advanced in contradiction to my scheme, and offering a better, I desire the author or authors will be pleased maturely to consider two points. First, as things now stand, how they will be able to find food and raiment for an hundred thousand useless mouths and backs. And secondly, there being a round million of creatures in human figure throughout this kingdom, whose sole subsistence put into a common stock would leave them in debt two million of pounds sterling, adding those who are beggars by profession to the bulk of farmers, cottagers, and laborers, with their wives and children who are beggars in effect; I desire those politicians who dislike my overture, and may perhaps be so bold to attempt an answer, that they will first ask the parents of these mortals whether they would not at this day think it a great happiness to have been sold for food at a year old in this manner I prescribe, and thereby have avoided such a perpetual scene of misfortunes as they have since gone through by the oppression of landlords, the impossibility of paying rent without money or trade, the want of common sustenance, with neither house nor clothes to cover them from the inclemencies of

---

* **like the Jews:** the Roman general Pompey was able to conquer Jerusalem in the first century B.C., in part because the population was divided among rival factions.

the weather, and the most inevitable prospect of entailing the like or greater miseries upon their breed forever.

I profess, in the sincerity of my heart, that I have not the least per-   33 sonal interest in endeavoring to promote this necessary work, having no other motive than the public good of my country, by advancing our trade, providing for infants, relieving the poor, and giving some pleasure to the rich. I have no children by which I can propose to get a single penny; the youngest being nine years old, and my wife past child-bearing.

Reading Closely

1. What is the problem that Swift identifies? What is his solution for the problem?
2. **Together with a classmate,** brainstorm a list of your immediate responses to this essay. What passages help explain your response? Be prepared to share your small group's response with the rest of the class.
3. What information surprised you? What did you learn that you didn't know before you read this essay?

Considering Larger Issues

1. In what ways does Swift's essay remain relevant to our own society? What solutions do we currently offer to the problem?
2. What is Swift's thesis? Where is it located?
3. Who is his audience? What does he expect his audience to do with the suggestions he's offering? Might he have more than one audience in mind? Might they have different responses to and opportunities to resolve the problem? If so, list them.
4. **In a group of two or three classmates,** divide this argument into sections: introduction, thesis statement, supporting argument, consideration of opposing argument, and conclusion. Be prepared to report your group's findings to the rest of the class.
5. COMBINING METHODS.   To develop this argument, Swift uses *cause-and-consequence* and *process analyses*. What is the effect of using these other rhetorical methods? Where are they located? How essential are they to the overall argument?

Thinking about Language

1. **Together with one or two other students,** use the context of the essay or a dictionary to define the following words or phrases. Be prepared to share your definitions with the rest of the class.

melancholy (1)

importuning (1)

alms (1)

sustenance (1)

prodigious (2)

grievance (2)

projectors (4)

raiment (4)

reckoned (6)

rudiments (6)

commodity (7)

eminent (13)

popish (13)

collateral (13)

carcass (14)

flay (15)

esteem (17)

discoursing (17)

prime dainty

　(18)

mandarins (18)

desponding (19)

encumbrance

　(19)

enumerated (27)

2. Some writers depend on one rhetorical appeal more than the other two. Which of the appeals (ethos, logos, pathos) does this writer use the most frequently? What words, phrases, or passages provide support for your answer?

3. How serious is Swift? Is there any gap between the seriousness of the problem and that of his proposed solutions? What specific words, phrases, or passages alert you to his attitude toward his subject and his recommendations? Be prepared to share your answers with the rest of the class.

Writing Your Own Arguments

1. Draft a three- to four-page argumentative essay in which you argue for a "modest proposal" that will resolve a problem in your home, school, family, church, or other setting. If you can, use Swift's proposal as your model. Like Swift, you may need to research the subject in order to support your thesis. You may also want to find or create a visual or two to bolster your case. Use the guidelines for checking over an argument on p. 652 as you draft and revise.

2. **Together with a small group of classmates,** discuss the hardships or punishments you've endured, particularly in terms of your college education. What ones do you all share? Which ones are unique to each of you? Draft a three- to four-page essay in which you argue for the ways school-related burdens could be lifted, offering a modest—or not so modest—proposal of some kind. You want to convince your audience that you deserve to be in college and invite them to consider your belief that you could do even better if you had the necessary encouragement or material support. Be sure to refer to the guidelines for checking over an argument on p. 652 as you draft, revise, and respond to one another's work.

H. L. MENCKEN

The Penalty of Death

● Henry Louis Mencken (1880–1956) was born in Baltimore and worked there
for many years as a newspaper reporter, editor, and columnist. Mencken
began writing for the *Baltimore Herald Tribune* and *Baltimore Sun* and then broadened his career to become a freelance writer and editor of his own magazine,
the *American Mercury*. Throughout his career Mencken was known for his social criticism and satiric wit in commentaries on everything from the Scopes
Trial to the Ku Klux Klan. The following essay is taken from his book *Preju-
dices, Fifth Series* (1926).

> **Preview**   What's the difference between Mencken's title, "The Penalty of
> Death," and the phrase we usually use, "the death penalty"?

Of the arguments against capital punishment that issue from uplifters, 1
two are commonly heard most often, to wit:

1. That hanging a man (or frying him or gassing him) is a dreadful business, degrading to those who have to do it and revolting to those who
   have to witness it.

2. That it is useless, for it does not deter others from the same crime.

The first of these arguments, it seems to me, is plainly too weak to 2
need serious refutation. All it says, in brief, is that the work of the hangman is unpleasant. Granted. But suppose it is? It may be quite necessary
to society for all that. There are, indeed, many other jobs that are unpleasant, and yet no one thinks of abolishing them — that of the plumber,
that of the soldier, that of the garbageman, that of the priest hearing confessions, that of the sandhog, and so on. Moreover, what evidence is there
that any actual hangman complains of his work? I have heard none. On
the contrary, I have known many who delighted in their ancient art, and
practiced it proudly.

In the second argument of the abolitionists there is rather more 3
force, but even here, I believe, the ground under them is shaky. Their
fundamental error consists in assuming that the whole aim of punishing
criminals is to deter other (potential) criminals — that we hang or electro-
cute A simply in order to so alarm B that he will not kill C. This, I believe,
is an assumption which confuses a part with the whole. Deterrence,
obviously, is *one* of the aims of punishment, but it is surely not the only
one. On the contrary, there are at least a half dozen, and some are probably quite as important. At least one of them, practically considered, is
more important. Commonly, it is described as revenge, but revenge is really not the word for it. I borrow a better term from the late Aristotle:
katharsis. Katharsis, so used, means a salubrious discharge of emotions, a

Supporters of the death penalty, mostly members of the Young Republicans at Sam Houston State University, demonstrate outside a Texas prison on the day Karla Faye Tucker was executed there in 1998. The case of Tucker, who had helped to murder two people with a pick-axe, drew national attention when then-governor George W. Bush declined to commute her sentence.

healthy letting off of steam. A schoolboy, disliking his teacher, deposits a tack upon the pedagogical chair; the teacher jumps and the boy laughs. This is *katharsis*. What I contend is that one of the prime objects of all judicial punishments is to afford the same grateful relief (*a*) to the immediate victims of the criminal punished, and (*b*) to the general body of moral and timorous men.

These persons, and particularly the first group, are concerned only   4 indirectly with deterring other criminals. The thing they crave primarily is the satisfaction of seeing the criminal actually before them suffer as he made them suffer. What they want is the peace of mind that goes with the feeling that accounts are squared. Until they get that satisfaction they are in a state of emotional tension, and hence unhappy. The instant they get it they are comfortable. I do not argue that this yearning is noble; I simply argue that it is almost universal among human beings. In the face of injuries that are unimportant and can be borne without damage it may yield to higher impulses; that is to say, it may yield to what is called Christian charity. But when the injury is serious Christianity is adjourned, and even saints reach for their sidearms. It is plainly asking too much of human nature to expect it to conquer so natural an impulse. A keeps a store and has a bookkeeper, B. B steals $700, employs it in playing at dice or bingo, and is cleaned out. What is A to do? Let B go? If he does so he will be unable to sleep at night. The sense of injury, of injustice, of frustration will haunt him like pruritus. So he turns B over to the police, and they hustle B to prison. Thereafter A can sleep. More, he has pleasant dreams. He pictures B chained to the wall of a dungeon a hundred feet underground, devoured by rats and scorpions. It is so agreeable that it makes him forget his $700. He has got his *katharsis*.

The same thing precisely takes place on a larger scale when there is a   5 crime which destroys a whole community's sense of security. Every law-abiding citizen feels menaced and frustrated until the criminals have been struck down—until the communal capacity to get even with them, and more than even, has been dramatically demonstrated. Here, manifestly, the business of deterring others is no more than an afterthought. The main thing is to destroy the concrete scoundrels whose act has alarmed everyone, and thus made everyone unhappy. Until they are brought to book that unhappiness continues; when the law has been executed upon them there is a sigh of relief. In other words, there is *katharsis*.

I know of no public demand for the death penalty for ordinary   6 crimes, even for ordinary homicides. Its infliction would shock all men of normal decency of feeling. But for crimes involving the deliberate and inexcusable taking of human life, by men openly defiant of all civilized order—for such crimes it seems, to nine men out of ten, a just and proper punishment. Any lesser penalty leaves them feeling that the criminal has got the better of society—that he is free to add insult to injury by laughing. That feeling can be dissipated only by a recourse to *katharsis*,

the invention of the aforesaid Aristotle. It is more effectively and economically achieved, as human nature now is, by wafting the criminal to
realms of bliss.

The real objection to capital punishment doesn't lie against the ac-   7
tual extermination of the condemned, but against our brutal American
habit of putting it off so long. After all, every one of us must die soon or
later, and a murderer, it must be assumed, is one who makes that sad fact
the cornerstone of his metaphysic. But it is one thing to die, and quite
another thing to lie for long months and even years under the shadow of
death. No sane man would choose such a finish. All of us, despite the
Prayer Book, long for a swift and unexpected end. Unhappily, a murderer,
under the irrational American system, is tortured for what, to him, must
seem a whole series of eternities. For months on end he sits in prison
while his lawyers carry on their idiotic buffoonery with writs, injunc-
tions, mandamuses, and appeals. In order to get his money (or that of his
friends) they have to feed him with hope. Now and then, by the imbecil-
ity of a judge or some trick of juridic science, they actually justify it. But
let us say that, his money all gone, they finally throw up their hands.
Their client is now ready for the rope or the chair. But he must still wait
for months before it fetches him.

That wait, I believe, is horribly cruel. I have seen more than one man   8
sitting in the death-house, and I don't want to see any more. Worse, it is
wholly useless. Why should he wait at all? Why not hang him the day
after the last court dissipates his last hope? Why torture him as not even
cannibals would torture their victims? The common answer is that he
must have time to make his peace with God. But how long does that
take? It may be accomplished, I believe, in two hours quite as comfort-
ably as in two years. There are, indeed, no temporal limitations upon
God. He could forgive a whole herd of murderers in a millionth of a second. More, it has been done.

Reading Closely

1. What information surprised you the most in this essay? Why?

2. How does Mencken establish his ethos in this essay? How does he use
   logos and pathos to his advantage?

3. Overall, how convincing is Mencken's argument? Whether you support,
   don't support, or are unsure about your attitude toward the death
   penalty, what parts of his argument (which specific passages) supported
   your thinking? If you changed your mind, what specific passages helped
   you do so?

4. What arguments are evident in and implied by the photograph on p. 763?
   Are they the same as or different from the arguments Mencken is making?

Considering Larger Issues

1. What is Mencken's thesis? What assertions does he make to expand or support that thesis?

2. Who is Mencken's audience? What information does he include in his essay that alerts you to his intended audience? What does Mencken want his audience to do with his argument?

3. Menken's essay was published in 1926. How much of his evidence and support is outdated? How much seems to be timeless?

4. How does Mencken address and then avoid logical fallacies? Which passages support your response?

5. **Working with two or three classmates,** consider how Mencken's argument is shaped in terms of the introduction, thesis statement, supporting argument, response to opposing views, and conclusion. What sentences, paragraphs, or ideas form each of these sections?

6. COMBINING METHODS.   Mencken relies on several other rhetorical methods to develop his argument: *definition, consequence analysis,* and *narration.* How does he use each of these methods to strengthen his argument?

Thinking about Language

1. Use the context of the essay or your dictionary to define the following terms or phrases. Be prepared to share your definitions with the rest of the class.

uplifters (1)	pruritus (4)	metaphysic (7)
refutation (2)	menaced (5)	buffoonery (7)
sandhog (2)	communal capacity (5)	writs,
salubrious (3)	brought to book (5)	injunctions,
timorous (3)	infliction (6)	mandamuses,
yearning (4)	dissipated (6)	and appeals (7)
Christian charity (4)	recourse (6)	imbecility (7)
adjourned (4)	cornerstone (7)	juridic science (7)

2. Mencken's argument is richly satirical in that he exposes and attacks the follies and stupidities of others, often humorously. Which passages do you find particularly sarcastic? humorous? How do his sarcasm and humor affect you as a reader? How do they affect the success of his overall argument?

3. What is the effect of beginning with "Of the arguments against capital punishment that issue from uplifters, two are commonly heard most often"? How does that opening affect the reader? affect the tone of the argument?

Writing Your Own Arguments

1. Argue against the death penalty from the point of view of someone who is facing it. You might do what Mencken did and imagine the torture of

awaiting execution. Or you might write about how life imprisonment would provide an almost equally severe punishment while forcing you to come to terms with your moral responsibility for your crime. This three- to four-page argument essay might rely on your research findings (from the library, World Wide Web, or interviews) as well as on your own experience and observation. As you draft and revise, keep in mind your audience and purpose as well as your use of reason and rhetorical appeals. Refer to the guidelines for checking over an argument on p. 652.

2. In paragraph 3, Mencken asserts that there are at least half a dozen reasons for punishing offenders, but he supplies only two: deterrence and revenge. **Consider working with a classmate** to discuss other reasons that someone should or does receive the death penalty. Feel free to share your findings with other classmates. Then write an individual three- to four-page essay in which you argue a number of good reasons that a person should face the death penalty. Be attentive to your use of the rhetorical appeals as you draft and revise. Remember that guidelines for checking over an argument can be found on p. 652.

✱ Additional Suggestions for Writing

1. Think back to a time when you were treated unfairly, maybe by a police officer, a professor, a boss, or a relative. Write a two- to three-page letter to that person in which you argue your point of view, taking special care to establish common ground and your goodwill, good sense, and good character. Refer to the guidelines on p. 652 for checking over an argument.

2. Think of a movie that you like but that others are criticizing, maybe on the grounds of sentimentality, violence, artificiality, or predictability. Argue for reconsideration of that movie, demonstrating its positive qualities and addressing each of the criticisms of it. Be sure to imagine a particular audience, in this case an almost hostile one. You may want to research reviews or talk with your friends about their opinions before you begin writing your argument. You'll certainly want to watch the movie again before you start. As you draft and revise, refer to the guidelines on p. 652 for checking over an argument.

3. Draft a three- to four-page essay in which you make an argument about the role of alcohol in your life. For example, you may want to defend its role in your life, argue that you should change that role, or make a factual argument that alcohol is more—or less—important to you than it is to other students. Before you begin writing, though, imagine an audience for such an essay: your parents, your partner, your roommate, your children. List all the reasons you have for holding your opinion, particularly in terms of your audience, and refer to the guidelines for checking over an argument.

4. Draft a three- to four-page argument essay in which you argue for better health care. Your essay could focus on the practices of the student health center, your family doctor, or your local hospital. What is the situation now, and how could it be improved, with or without additional funding? In addition to evidence from your personal experience, this topic will probably require research at the library, on the World Wide Web, or at specific health services. Rely on the guidelines on p. 652 for checking over an argument as you draft and revise this essay.

appendix

· ●

Using and Documenting Sources

The quality of your writing will often depend on how well you use and document the intellectual work of others. In many cases, you will decide to limit your sources to firsthand evidence — your own observations and experiences. Often, however, you will want or need to balance such firsthand evidence with secondhand evidence — library research, online research, or maybe interviews you conduct or questionnaires you administer.

The purpose of this appendix is twofold: first, to help you learn how to use sources to your advantage in the text of your essays; and second, to help you learn how to document clearly the sources you are using, both in your text and in your Works Cited list. All of the examples follow the style recommended by the Modern Language Association (MLA). If you find that you need additional information, refer to the sixth edition of the *MLA Handbook for Writers of Research Papers*, edited by Joseph Gibaldi (New York: MLA, 2003).

Summarizing and Paraphrasing

Summarizing and paraphrasing are two common ways of referring to the intellectual work of others without directly quoting the entire work. When you summarize a text, you condense that work or a substantial passage of it (which can be anything from a paragraph to several chapters) into a much shorter piece of writing within your own writing. For instance, if you need to refer to the plot of *Romeo and Juliet*, you might write a summary like the following:

> Summary: Many of the most romantic love stories, whether true or fiction, are based on the plot of William Shakespeare's late sixteenth-century play Romeo and Juliet, a story of young lovers from feuding families. Romeo and Juliet manage to elope and hatch a plan for their life together, but through a series of unfortunate coincidences they both die at the end of the play, to the sorrow of their reconciled families.

A summary should be as short as possible — a sentence or a couple of sentences. Within the summary, you should identify the author of the source and, if you are citing more than one work by that author in your essay, the title as well. If you are summarizing a specific passage, you will need to list the page number(s) (or, in the case of Shakespeare, the act and scene) of the part being summarized.

Another common way to use someone else's ideas or research is to paraphrase. Paraphrasing deals with a much shorter passage in the original work — a few sentences at most — and restates it in about the same number of words as the original. Though you rephrase the idea in your own words, you still need to give credit to the original source. Here is an example of a paraphrased idea from Bruce Catton's "Grant and Lee: A Study in Contrasts":

> Quotation: "Thousands of tired, underfed, poorly clothed Confederate soldiers, long-since past the simple enthusiasm of the early days of the struggle, somehow considered Lee the symbol of everything for which they had been willing to die" (194).

> Paraphrase: Catton shows that the Confederate troops, despite physical disadvantages that were increasingly discouraging, still found the inspiration and purpose to fight for the South through the figure of their General Lee (194).

Using and Integrating Quotations

In general, try to summarize and paraphrase most of the materials that you take from other sources, saving only the most compelling passages or bits of material to use as direct quotations. When you do use a quotation, the first rule is to be sure that you've copied it out correctly, which is harder to do than you might think. All of us become familiar with the outside sources we are using—so familiar that we begin to leave out, add, or change words within the original quotation. The second rule of using quotations is to weave the quotation smoothly into the fabric of the sentence or paragraph. Rather than dropping the quotation into your work abruptly, introduce it with your own words. For instance, if you are arguing that allegiance to the cause represented by the figure of Robert E. Lee was the only reason the Confederate soldiers continued fighting a losing Civil War, you might write something like this:

> The Confederate soldiers continued fighting a losing battle because they "considered Lee the symbol of everything for which they had been willing to die" (Catton 194).

Avoiding Plagiarism

Good writers use the work of others to their own advantage. But you cannot simply take another's words and ideas and put them into your own essay; you must be sure to document the source—to give that other writer credit for his or her thoughts and language. Plagiarism, the use of someone else's words or ideas without acknowledgment, is the theft of someone else's intellectual work; it does not matter if the theft is intentional or unintentional—the consequences for you are the same, from failing the essay or the course to being expelled from school. Therefore it is important that you acquaint yourself with the distinction between appropriate paraphrasing and quoting on the one hand and plagiarizing on the other. If you use an author's words or ideas without crediting him or her, the plagiarism is obvious. More subtle, however, would be if you credited the author but neither paraphrased his or her language nor enclosed it in quotation marks.

If you decided to paraphrase the Bruce Catton quotation, for example, you would need to go far beyond the following:

> Catton shows that thousands of tired, underfed, poorly clothed Confederate soldiers, long-since past the simple enthusiasm of the early days of the struggle, found in Lee the inspiration to fight on (194).

The language of this sentence is mostly that of the original Catton quote; it is not original language from you, the writer. As a result, a good deal of it would need to be enclosed in quotation marks. As it stands, the sentence above constitutes plagiarism.

Ideas that are considered common knowledge do not need to be credited to a particular author or source. For example, you may have learned that former president Bill Clinton was born on August 19, 1946, from reading a biography of him, but that information is available in many sources and is not in dispute. Facts that could not be argued with are considered common knowledge.

MLA Style for Source Citations in the Text

The most common way of citing sources in the humanities is the style recommended by the Modern Language Association (MLA). The following examples explain the variety of ways you can use MLA style to cite the sources you are using. Remember, if you need further reference, consult the *MLA Handbook for Writers of Research Papers*.

In MLA style, citations in the text provide the reader with just enough information to find the source in a Works Cited list at the end of the essay or research paper. Unless you are referring to an entire work, these citations are placed in parentheses immediately following the source information they refer to. A parenthetical citation includes the page number(s) of the information and sometimes the author and the title of the source as well. The following examples demonstrate the ways to use text citations for various kinds of sources.

A Work with One Author

If you have not mentioned the author in your sentence, list the author's last name and the page number(s) of the material you are citing in parentheses.

> The police of Beverly Hills have won awards for
> their fashionable uniforms four times since 1989
> (Steinmetz 129).

If you do name the author in your sentence, you only need to include the page number(s) in the parenthetical citation.

> Steinmetz claims that in the real-life zip code
> 90210 area, "perception truly is reality" and "wealth
> is not displayed with more exuberance anywhere else"
> (128, 129).

A Work with Two or Three Authors

Use *and* before the name of the last author, and use commas after the names of the first and second authors if there are three.

> David Snowdon studied the autobiographies of 200
> nuns and found that those whose emotions were most
> positive and detailed in their writing ended up living
> the longest and were the least likely to suffer from
> Alzheimer's later in life (Lemonick and Park 56).

A Work with More Than Three Authors

List either the names of all the authors or the name of the first author followed by *et al.* ("and others").

> "Conscription without representation" became a
> rallying cry in the 1960s, when the voting age was 21
> but a young man could be drafted into the army at 18
> (Wayne, Mackenzie, O'Brien, and Cole 316).

> Despite the tragic cause that brought about the
> lowering of the voting age to 18, few 18- to 21-year-
> olds today actually vote (Wayne et al. 316).

An Entire Work

If you are referring to an entire work, you do not need to include page numbers.

> The Solace of Open Spaces paints a picture of the
> West that contains more complicated characters than
> those Americans have met in John Wayne films and Little
> House on the Prairie reruns.

> In "About Men," Gretel Ehrlich shows us both the
> limitations and the almost feminine humanity of the
> modern-day cowboy.

A Work in More Than One Volume

List the volume number before the page number, and separate the two with a colon and a space.

> Fields, Barber, and Riggs show that half of
> Cambodia's population died or fled the country within
> three years in the 1970s and that the Cambodian case is
> representative of several violent population dislocations
> that have occurred since World War II (2: 1041).

Two or More Works by the Same Author

If you do not name the author in your own text, in the parenthetical citation put a comma and the title of the work, or a shortened version of it, after the author's name and before the page number. If you do name the author in your own text, include just the title and the page number in the parenthetical citation.

> The Pima became the most obese group of people in
> the world after they were forced off of their land in
> central Arizona and their traditional diet changed
> markedly (Gladwell, "Pima Paradox" 36).

> The fast food industry, Gladwell argues, once
> designed to make people's lives more convenient and,
> hence, better, now plays a major role in the high death
> rate of Americans due to obesity ("Trouble" 24).

An Unsigned Work

If the title is not mentioned in your own text, include it or a shortened version of it in the parenthetical citation.

> Sheldrick experimented for 28 years to find a
> formula that a baby elephant could digest as easily as
> its mother's milk ("Caring Hands" xv).

An Indirect Source

Use the abbreviation *qtd. in* before the author of the indirect source.

> In preparing for the Louisiana Purchase expedition,
> Thomas Jefferson instructed Lewis and Clark to treat the
> Native Americans they met "in the most friendly and
> conciliatory manner which their own conduct will admit
> [and] allay all jealousies as to the object of your
> journey" (qtd. in Deverell and Hyde 163).

A Literary Work

Your reader will need to be able to find your source in any edition of the work, not just the one you are using. Therefore, for novels, list the chapter number after the page number and separate the two with a semicolon. For a play or poem, list the line number instead of the page number. If the play contains parts or acts, list those and the line number, if given.

> Maggie, a girl who seemed to have "none of the dirt of Rum Alley . . . in her veins," is a classic Naturalist character, doomed to desperation and failure in a hostile urban environment (<u>Maggie</u> 49; ch. 5).

> In one of the most famous poems of the Harlem Renaissance, Langston Hughes writes, "I've known rivers ancient as the world and older than the flow of / human blood in human veins. / My soul has grown deep like the rivers" ("The Negro Speaks of Rivers," lines 2-4).

> Shepard suggests that his play is going to be an exploration of personal identity when the troubled and unstable Lee tells his recluse brother, Austin, "I always wondered what'd be like to be you" (<u>True West</u>, 1.4).

More Than One Work

Cite both works in the order in which they appear in your text (if pertinent), and separate them with a semicolon.

> In the 1990s a third of all children were born to unmarried mothers, suggesting not only that women are increasingly choosing to become single parents but that women who have not traditionally chosen this life course, including single, middle-class, educated women, are no longer willing to sacrifice their desire to parent (Kantrowitz and Wingert 48; Davis 72).

MLA List of Works Cited

Whenever you have cited the work of someone else in your text, you will need to provide a list of works cited at the end of your essay or re-search project. The following examples provide guidelines for listing your sources correctly. Besides following the guidelines for each kind of source, remember that the list of works cited should be arranged alpha-betically, according to the last names of the authors (or editors). When a work has neither an author nor an editor, alphabetize by the first word of the title other than *A, An,* or *The.*

Your works cited page(s) should be double-spaced throughout, just like the rest of your essay or research project, with the same margins (format) as your essay. If a citation is longer than one line, then indent the subsequent line(s) 0.5 inch.

Books

The basic entry for a book looks like this:

```
Author's last name, author's first name [and middle
     initial, if any]. Title of the Book: Subtitle of
     the Book. Place of publication: Publisher, year
     of publication.
```

If several places or years of publication are listed, use the first city or the most recent year. In general, use a shortened form of the publisher's name, such as "St. Martin's" for "St. Martin's Press" or "Random" for "Random House." For university presses, abbreviate "University" as "U" and "Press" as "P."

A Book with One Author

```
Dillard, Annie. Teaching a Stone to Talk. New York:
     Harper, 1982.
```

A Book with Two or Three Authors

List authors in the order they appear on the title page. (Notice that the first author is listed last name first, but the second author is listed first name first.)

```
Hall, John A., and Charles Lindholm. Is America Breaking
     Apart? Princeton: Princeton UP, 1999.
```

A Book with More Than Three Authors

You may either list all of the authors in the order they appear on the title page, or list the first author named and *et al.* ("and others"), not italicized. If you list all the others, you give them equal credit for their work. Notice that only the first author is listed last name first.

```
Gould, Eric, Robert DiYanni, William Smith, and Judith
     Stanford. The Art of Reading. 2nd ed. New York:
     McGraw, 1990.

Gould, Eric, et al. The Art of Reading. 2nd ed. New
     York: McGraw, 1990.
```

More Than One Work by the Same Author(s)

List the works alphabetically by title, and list the author's name only in the first entry. In subsequent entries, substitute three hyphens for the name.

> Tannen, Deborah. <u>The Argument Culture: Moving from</u>
>   <u>Debate to Dialogue</u>. New York: Random, 1998.
>
> ---. <u>You Just Don't Understand</u>. New York: Morrow, 1990.

A Book with an Editor

List the editor as you would an author, followed by *ed.* (which is not italicized).

> Varenne, Herve, ed. <u>Symbolizing America</u>. Lincoln: U of
>   Nebraska P, 1986.

A Book with an Author and an Editor

List the author first, and give the editor's name, preceded by *Ed.*, after the title.

> Catton, Bruce. <u>Reflections on the Civil War</u>. Ed. John
>   Leekley. Garden City: Doubleday, 1981.

A Later Edition

Cite the edition number after the title.

> Zinsser, William. <u>On Writing Well: An Informal Guide to</u>
>   <u>Writing Nonfiction</u>. 2nd ed. New York: Harper, 1980.

A Work in a Series

List the series title before the publication information. Do not punctuate or underline the series title.

> McKay, Nellie, and Kathryn Earle, eds. <u>Approaches to</u>
>   <u>Teaching the Novels of Toni Morrison</u>. Approaches to
>   Teaching World Lit. New York: MLA, 1997.

An Anthology

List the editor of the anthology as you would an author, followed by *ed.* (not italicized).

> Reed, Ishmael, ed. <u>MultiAmerica: Essays on Cultural Wars</u>
>   <u>and Cultural Peace</u>. New York: Viking Penguin, 1997.

A Selection from an Anthology

Follow the author, title of the selection, title of the anthology, editor, and publication information with the page numbers of the selection.

```
Ozick, Cynthia. "A Drugstore in Winter." Eight Modern
    Essayists. Ed. William Smart. 6th ed. New York: St.
    Martin's, 1995. 249-54.
```

An Article in a Reference Work

Well–known reference works do not require publication information. If the article has an author, begin your citation with the author's name. In all other cases, list the title of the article, the title of the work, the edition, and the date.

```
"Smith." Encyclopedia of American Family Names. 1st ed.
    1995.
```

Periodicals

The basic entry for a periodical looks like this:

```
Author's last name, author's first name [and middle
    initial, if any]. "Title of the Article." Name of
    the Periodical Other publication information [such
    as volume and issue numbers, edition, date]: page
    numbers of the article.
```

If an article is not printed on consecutive pages (for example, if it skips from page 3 to page 14), list only the first page number followed by a plus sign: 3+.

An Article in a Journal with Continuous Pagination throughout the Annual Volume

Follow the author's name, title of the article, title of the journal, volume number, and date with a colon and the page numbers of the article.

```
Helmer, Marguerite. "Media, Discourse, and the Public
    Sphere: Electronic Memorials to Diana, Princess of
    Wales." College English 63 (2001): 437-56.
```

An Article in a Journal That Paginates Issues Separately

Add a period and the issue number after the volume number.

```
Green-Anderson, Gail. "Writing in the World: Teaching
    about HIV/AIDS in English 101." Teaching English in
    the Two-Year College 28.1 (2000): 44-51.
```

An Article in a Monthly or Bimonthly Magazine

List the month and year of the issue after the title of the magazine. Do not include volume or issue numbers. Abbreviate all months except May, June, and July.

Wuethrich, Bernice. "Getting Stupid." <u>Discover</u> Mar.
    2001: 56-63.

An Article in a Weekly or Biweekly Magazine

List the date of the issue after the title of the magazine.

Surowiecki, James. "Farewell to Mr. Fix-It." <u>New Yorker</u>
    5 Mar. 2001: 41.

An Article in a Newspaper

Day, Sherri. "Two Groups Are at Odds over the Proper Way
    to Observe Malcolm X's Birthday." <u>New York Times</u> 17
    May 2001, late ed.: B9.

An Unsigned Article

Begin the entry with the title of the article. Ignore *A*, *An*, or *The* at the beginning of the title when alphabetizing the entry.

"Open Up and Say 'Blaaaahhh.'" <u>Newsweek</u> 16 Apr. 2001: 10.

A Review

List the reviewer's name first. Follow the title of the review with *Rev. of* (not italicized), the title of the work reviewed, and the name of the author, editor, director, or other creator of the work.

Lane, Anthony. "The Devil and Miss Jones." Rev. of
    <u>Bridget Jones's Diary</u>, dir. Sharon Maguire. <u>New</u>
    <u>Yorker</u> 16 Apr. 2001: 90-91.

Nonperiodical Publications on CD-ROM, Diskette, or Magnetic Tape

For publications in those media that are published like books rather than as periodically revised databases, list the author and title of the selection; the title of the CD-ROM, diskette, or magnetic tape; the medium of the publication; and the publication information. If the publication exists in multiple editions, list the edition after the medium type.

Frost, Robert. "The Road Not Taken." <u>American Poetry</u>.
    CD-ROM. Alexandria: Chadwyk-Healey, 1995.

Online Sources

Because online sources do not exist in the stable and predictable forms that most print sources do, they can be particularly difficult to cite in an accurate and useful way. The two general guidelines you should keep in mind are as follows: (1) if you can't find some of the information for a citation, cite what is available to you, and (2) if an online source also appears in print, list the information for the print source first, followed by the information for the electronic version. For sources from the World Wide Web, this information should include all of the following items that are relevant to the particular kind of source you are citing:

- The version number of the site, preceded by *Vers.* (not italicized).
- The date of electronic publication of the source or the most recent update
- The sponsor of the site, if it is an institution or organization
- The most recent date you accessed the source
- The URL, in angle brackets. If the URL for the specific page you are citing is very long or not provided, give the URL for the search page; if there is no search page, list the home page of the site. If a URL will not fit on one line, break it only after a slash. Do not add a hyphen at the break; if your computer adds a hyphen, delete it.

An Entire Web Site

Unless the site has an overall author, begin with the title of the site, underlined. If the site is sponsored by an organization and does not appear to have its own title, list the organization as both the title and the sponsor.

```
Common Cause. 2004. Common Cause. 6 Aug. 2004
        <www.commoncause.org>.
```

A Document from a Web Site

Begin with the author of the document, if given, followed by its title, in quotation marks.

```
"Fox News Channel: Fair and Balanced?" Common Cause. 21
        July 2004. Common Cause. 6 Aug. 2004
        <www.commoncause.org>.
```

A Home Page for a Course

Begin with the name of the instructor, the title of the course, a description of the site, the course dates, and the department and school.

```
Wilkins, John. Writing and Speaking in Physics and
        Astronomy. Course home page. Mar.-June 2001. Dept.
        of Physics, Ohio State U. 3 Nov. 2003 <http://
        www.physics.ohio-state.edu/~wilkins/writing/>.
```

A Home Page for an Academic Department

Begin with the department, a description of the site, and the school.

Mass Communications. Dept. home page. Shaw University.
    23 Apr. 2004 <http://www.shawuniversity.edu/
    ap_cas_dept_mass_communications.htm>.

A Personal Site

Begin with the name of the person who created the site, its title, underlined (or, if there is no title, the description "Home page"), and the date the site was published or last updated (if given).

Fulton, Alice. Home page. 14 May 2004. 11 July 2004 <http://
    www.people.cornell.edu/pages/af89/afhome.html>.

A Scholarly Project

Begin with the name of the project, underlined, and include the names of the editor and the sponsoring institution. If you are citing a specific document, begin with its author and title, in quotation marks.

Voices from the Gaps: Women Writers of Color. Ed. Kim
    Surkan. 2001. Dept. of English, U of Minnesota. 14
    May 2001 <http://voices.cla.umn.edu>.

A Book

For a book that is published as part of a scholarly project, include the editor's name (if any). To cite part of an online book, begin with the part you are citing.

Cather, Willa. My Antonia. Ed. Charles Mignon. Lincoln:
    U of Nebraska P, 1994. The Willa Cather Electronic
    Archive. U of Nebraska. 14 May 2004 <http://
    www.people.cornell.edu/pages/af89/afhome.html>.

Lowell, Amy. "A Lady." The New Poetry: An Anthology. Ed.
    Harriet Monroe. New York: Macmillan, 1917.
    Bartleby.com: Great Books Online. 7 Nov. 2003
    <http://www.bartleby.com/265/199.html>.

An Online Government Publication

Cite this as you would a print publication, ending with the date of access and the URL.

United States Food and Drug Administration. Center for
    Food Safety and Applied Nutrition. Guidance on How
    to Understand and Use the Nutrition Facts Panel on
    Food Labels. July 2003. 29 Aug. 2004 <http://
    www.cfsan.fda.gov/~dms/foodlab.html>.

An Article in a Journal

Include the range or total number of pages, paragraphs, or other sections if they are numbered.

Moore, Randy. "Writing about Biology: How Rhetorical
      Choices Can Influence the Impact of a Scientific
      Paper." <u>Bioscene: Journal of College Biology
      Teaching</u> 26 (2000): 23-25. 14 Sept. 2003 <http://
      papa.indstate.edu/amcbt/volume_26-123-25.pdf>.

An Article in a Newspaper

Chass, Murray. "Bonds Hits 70th to Tie Home Run Record."
      <u>New York Times on the Web</u> 5 Oct. 2001. 12 Oct. 2001
      <http://www.nytimes.com/2001/10/05/sports/baseball/
      05BARR.html?searchpv=past7days>.

An Article in a Magazine

Last, Jonathan. "How to Market <u>Pearl Harbor</u> in Japan."
      <u>Slate</u> 11 May 2001. 16 May 2001 <http://
      slate.msn.com/culturebox/entries/01-05-11_105878.asp>.

A Review

Conquest, Robert. "The Terror." Rev. of <u>Stalin: The
      Court of the Red Tsar</u> by Simon Sebag Montefiore.
      <u>Atlantic Online</u> July/Aug. 2004. 15 July 2004
      <http://www.theatlantic.com/issues/2004/07/
      conquest.htm>.

An Editorial

"AIDS in Africa." Editorial. <u>New York Times on the Web</u>
      14 July 2004. 17 July 2004 <http://www.nytimes.com/
      2004/07/14WED2.html>.

A Letter to the Editor

Tucker, David. Letter. <u>Newsweek</u> 19 July 2004. 1 Aug. 2004
      <http://www.msnbc.com/id/5304753/site/newsweek/>.

A Work Accessed through a Library Subscription Service

If only the first page number for the print version of the article is given, follow that number with a hyphen and a space. Then give the name of the database, underlined; the name of the service; and the name of the library, followed by the access date. End with the URL of the home page of the service, if available.

Ruskin, Gary. "The Fast Food Trap: How Commercialism
      Creates Overweight Kids." <u>Mothering</u> Nov./Dec.
      2003: 34- . <u>Infotrac OneFile</u>. Gale Group Databases.

Florida Division of Library and Information
Services. 3 May 2004 <http://
web4.infotrac.galegroup.com/>.

An E-mail Message

List the author of the message followed by the subject line, if any, in quotation marks. Include a description of the message that mentions the recipient, and end with the date of the message.

Rezny, Jane. "Re: Writing on the Edge." E-mail to the
author. 3 Dec. 2003.

Other Sources

A Film or Video Recording

Begin with the title of the work unless you are citing the contribution of a specific person, such as a director, performer, producer, or screenwriter. In that case, begin with the person's name. If you do not start with the director's name, include it after the title, where you may also include the names of other contributors. End with the name of the distributor and the year of release. For a recording, indicate the film's original release date and the recording format.

Lee, Spike, dir. She Hate Me. Perf. Kerry Washington and
Anthony Mackie. Sony Pictures Classics, 2004.

Malcolm X. Dir. Spike Lee. Perf. Denzel Washington.
1992. DVD. Warner Studios, 2000.

A Television or Radio Program

List the episode title, the title of the program, the name of the network, the call letters and city of the local station, and the broadcast date.

"The One with the Cheap Wedding Dress." Friends. NBC.
WNBC, New York. 15 Mar. 2001.

A Sound Recording on Compact Disc

Lopez, Jennifer. "I'm Real." J. Lo. Sony, 2001.

Bach, Johann Sebastian. Goldberg Variations. Perf.
Murray Perahia. Sony, 2000.

A Letter

Frost, Robert. "Letter to Editor of the Independent." 28
Mar. 1894. Selected Letters of Robert Frost. Ed.
Lawrance Thompson. New York: Holt, 1964. 19.

Quillen, Anna. Letter to the author. 25 Sept. 2001.

An Interview

Angelou, Maya. Interview with Terri Gross. <u>Fresh Air</u>.
    Natl. Public Radio. WWNY, New York. 5 July 1993.

Clinton, William Jefferson. "Bill Clinton: The <u>Rolling
    Stone</u> Interview." <u>Rolling Stone</u> 4 Jan. 2001:
    84-128.

Shiflett, Mary. Personal interview. 8 Oct. 2001.

Glossary of Terms

analogy   a direct comparison of the similarities between two unlike things, one of which is usually more familiar or less abstract

anecdote   a short narrative that helps make a point within another kind of writing or speech

arguable   the quality of a statement that makes it open for discussion and debate

argument   a rhetorical method that expresses a point of view and then uses logical reasoning to attempt to get an audience to accept the point of view as true or valid; often defined more broadly to include the use of both logical and emotional appeals and the effort to change the audience's point of view and move them to action

basis for comparison   the shared aspect of two or more things being compared; what the things have in common

causal chain   the idea that one situation or event causes another, which then causes another, and so on

cause–and–consequence analysis   a rhetorical method that explains why certain events happen or predicts that certain events will lead to particular consequences

chronological order   the order in which events occurred over time

chronological organization   the arrangement of parts of an essay in order of the time period they refer to

claim   a statement that asserts the writer's opinion on or belief about a subject, or the position the writer wants to take

classification   a rhetorical method that involves sorting specific things into more general categories

climax   the highest point or turning point in a narrative

common ground   the beliefs or values shared between the writer or speaker and the audience

comparison   a rhetorical method that shows how two or more things are alike

connotative language   words that suggest evaluations and emotional responses

contrast   a rhetorical method that shows how two or more things are different

contributory cause   a cause that contributes to an event but that does not directly cause it

deductive arguments   arguments that move from a general claim to a specific statement or example

definition   a rhetorical method that states what a word or term means

deliberative rhetoric   legislative rhetoric used in deciding on the best course for the future, focusing on issues of expediency and inexpediency

denotative language   words that sound neutral and do not carry any emotional associations

description   a rhetorical method that depicts in words the details of what we see, hear, smell, taste, touch, or sense in some less physical way — or in our imagination

directive process analysis   a set of step-by-step instructions for a reader to follow

division   a rhetorical method that involves breaking a general whole into more specific parts

dominant impression   the quality of a subject that a writer wants to convey to readers, or the attitude toward a subject that a writer wants the readers to share

editing   checking a draft and making changes as necessary for such issues as the length, structure, and variety of paragraphs and sentences; the choice of words; the transitions between ideas; and the effectiveness and accuracy of the punctuation

emphatic order   an order based on relative importance

emphatic organization   the arrangement of parts of an essay in a sequence from the least to the most important

epideictic rhetoric   rhetoric used to express a sense of the occasion at a ceremony or memorial, focusing on issues of honor or dishonor

ethos   a rhetorical appeal that relies on the writer's or speaker's character and credibility to persuade an audience

exemplification   a rhetorical method that provides concrete examples— such as stories, expert opinions, or facts—to support a generalization

extended definition   a definition that expands on a sentence definition by differentiating the word or term from others and introducing additional features

figurative language   a type of subjective language that departs from the denotative meaning of a word or phrase for the sake of emphasis; involves the comparison of two unlike things by means of simile and metaphor

flashback   a stylistic technique in narration that gives the reader a glimpse of the past to illuminate the present

flashforward   a stylistic technique in narration that quickly takes readers to future events

historical definition   a definition that states where, when, why, and how a term came into being

immediate cause   the cause directly preceding an event

immediate consequence   the consequence that follows directly from an event

implied thesis   a thesis that conveys the writer's mood or overall impression, as well as purpose, but not directly; the implied thesis is suggested by means of the selection, organization, focus, and force of the details in the writing

inductive arguments   arguments that move from specific examples to a generalization

informative process analysis   a process analysis that explains how something works, is done, or has happened; readers do not necessarily follow the steps of the process themselves

judicial rhetoric   rhetoric that makes decisions about the past and focuses on issues of justice and injustice

language community   the people with whom one speaks most frequently

literacy   on a basic level, the ability to read and write; more broadly, how a person reacts to and interprets language in particular ways and produces and uses language to achieve certain goals

logical fallacies   arguments that are based on faulty reasoning or an error in judgment

logos   a rhetorical appeal that relies on reason or logic to persuade an audience, using facts, statistics, comparisons, narrative examples, documentation, personal experience, and observation

metaphor   an indirect comparison of one thing to another, such as "the snow covered the hills with a white blanket"

narration   a rhetorical method that tells a story

negative definition   a definition that distinguishes the meaning of a word or term by telling readers what it is not

objective definition   a definition that emphasizes the object being defined instead of the writer's feelings, opinions, or perspectives toward the object

objective description   a method of description that tells about a subject without evaluating it

pathos   a rhetorical appeal to the emotions, values, and attitudes of an audience

persuasion   a form of communication that relies on emotion as well as reasoning to change the audience's point of view and move them to action

point(s) of comparison   the aspect(s) of two or more things that are being compared and contrasted (When comparing two movies, points of comparison might be: which movie is funnier? more intellectual? more romantic? more action-packed?)

point of view   the assumed perspective from the mind and eye of the writer

primary cause   the most important cause

primary consequence   the most important consequence

process   a series of actions that always leads to the same result, no matter how many times it's repeated

process analysis   a rhetorical method that explains a process by breaking it down into a fixed order of steps that produces a result

proofreading   checking a draft and changing it as necessary for surface-level problems like typos and misspellings

relevant   specifically supporting or illustrating an aspect of a generalization; examples must be relevant in order to be effective

remote cause   a cause that is not as close in time to the event it causes as the immediate cause is

remote consequence   a consequence that does not occur immediately after an event but does eventually occur because of it

representative   typical of the whole group of items covered by a generalization; examples used to argue a point must be representative in order to be effective

revising   the step of the writing process in which the writer looks at a draft and makes changes as necessary in light of the following: how well it achieves its purpose; how successfully the writing addresses the specific audience; how clear the thesis is; whether the writer has met the requirements of the particular rhetorical method; how effective the organization, introduction, and conclusion are; whether there is too little or too much information

rhetoric   language used for a specific purpose that leads to the creation of knowledge

rhetorical   making use of language for a specific purpose in a way that leads to the creation of knowledge

rhetorical appeals   strategies a writer or speaker uses to make an argument, including ethos, logos, and pathos

rhetorical method   any of the nine types of discourse described in the book, including narration, description, and exemplification

rhetorical situation   the conditions in which language is used, including the intended audience, purpose, topic, medium (oral, written, electronic), time, and place

ruling principle   the basis or criterion used to group items in a classification or division; the ruling principle must group items consistently (all items must be grouped accordingly), exclusively (there cannot be overlap in the grouping), and completely (no items can be omitted)

secondary consequences   consequences that occur because of an event but are less important than the primary consequence

sensibilities   a person's ethical, moral, and ideological inclinations, such as prudence, nostalgia, empathy, kindness, and aesthetic taste

sensory details   descriptions that appeal to a reader's physical senses (sight, hearing, taste, touch, smell)

sentence definition   a definition in one complete sentence that defines a term clearly and concisely

simile   a direct comparison connecting two unlike things with *like, as,* or *than,* such as "her voice was like honey"

spatial organization   the arrangement of information within an essay in an order related to its physical location

stipulative definition   a definition in which the writer specifies how a term will and will not be used

subjective definition   a definition that emphasizes the writer's opinions and responses and the way he or she wants to define the term for this particular occasion

subjective description   a method of description that emphasizes the writer's perspective, personal reactions, and responses to the object described

synonym   a word that has nearly the same meaning as another word

thesis   the main idea developed in a piece of writing

thesis statement   an explicit declaration (usually in one sentence) of the main idea of a piece of writing

topic sentence   a sentence within a paragraph, usually the first sentence, that states the main idea of the paragraph; it usually reflects the thesis statement of the piece of writing and also previews the message of the sentences to follow

transitions   words or phrases that indicate to the reader a logical connection or change of direction between parts of a discussion; examples are *however, similarly, in contrast to, in other words, first, second, third,* and *next*

Acknowledgments

Picture Credits

Page 13, AP/WIDE WORLD PHOTOS; **30–37,** Photofest; **45,** permission of BELO INTERAC-
TIVE; **48,** courtesy of Colgate–Palmolive Company; **58,** reprinted from the SANTA FEAN Magazine;
75, J. B. Grant/ESTOCK Photo; **87,** Bob Daemmrich/THE IMAGE WORKS; **101,** Matt Rainey, The
Star–Ledger (Newark, NJ); **109,** John Kobal Foundation (1930)/Getty Images; **127,** courtesy of Steve
Brenkwitz; **131,** Joel Axelrad/Retna; **135,** AccuWeather, Inc.; **152,** AP/WIDE WORLD PHOTOS;
170, Larry Mulvehill/Photo Researchers; **177,** Photofest; **182,** AP/WIDE WORLD PHOTOS; **191,**
Michael Newman/PhotoEdit; **200,** courtesy of GOLF Monthly © 2003; **203,** reprinted by permission
of Scribner, an imprint of Simon & Schuster Adult Publishing Group, Cover of ON WRITING: A
MEMOIR OF THE CRAFT by Stephen King. Copyright © 2000 by Simon & Schuster, Inc.; **219,** ©
LATINA Magazine; **225,** John Eastcott & Yva Momatiuk/Stock, Boston; **235,** Margaret Miller/Photo
Researchers; **238,** Cannonieri & Fortis; Chris Edwards and Biondi Productions/Getty Images;
264–5, illustrations by Tim Bower; **269–70,** courtesy of the author; **274–5,** © 2004 by Consumers
Union of US, Inc., Yonkers, NY, a non–profit organization. Reprinted by permission from the April
2004 issue of CONSUMER REPORTS® for educational purposes only. No commercial use or reproduction permitted; **288,** © 2003, LATINA Magazine; **313,** Photofest; **336** (top) William
Philpott/Reuters; (inset) Pam Francis/Getty Images; **347,** courtesy of NATURE Magazine, © 2003;
351, Joel Gordon; **352,** courtesy of DeVito/Verdi, New York; **355,** UNILEVER USA; **358,** courtesy
of Santa Fe Stages; **378,** Geri Engberg/Stock, Boston; **379,** Catrina Genovese/Omni Photo Communications; **394,** "Surrender of General Lee to General Grant" (1867) by Louis M. Guillaume, courtesy
of Appomattox Court House, NHP, Appomattox, Va.; **415,** photo by Carl Van Vechten, by permission
of the Van Vechten Trust; photo courtesy of the James Weldon Johnson Memorial Collection, Bei-
necke Library, Yale U.; **427,** Larry Crowe/AP/WIDE WORLD PHOTOS; **430,** Bayer HealthCare, LLC;
431, Atkins Nutritionals, Inc.; **439,** Shutterfly.com; **441,** courtesy of Sylvia Acevedo, COMMUNI-
CARD, LLC: **456,** Custom Medical Stock; **462,** Andrew Lichtenstein/THE IMAGE WORKS; **479,** Aero
Safety Graphics, Inc.; **483,** Joel Gordon; **484,** courtesy, Cooper Aerobics Center; **486,** Toyota Motor
North America, Inc.; **510,** Bob Daemmrich; **530,** drawing by Veley; **563,** drawing by Randy Jones
for the film "A Jury of Her Peers," directed by Sally Heckel; **571,** from *Merriam-Webster's Collegiate®* Dic-
tionary, Eleventh Edition © 2004 by Merriam–Webster, Inc. (www.Merriam–Webster.com); **593,**
Photofest; **612,** Secret Sea Visions/Peter Arnold, Inc.; **628,** General Motors Corp. Used with permis-
sion, GM Media Archives; **631,** Yolanda Perez/Omni Photo Communications; **635,** reproduced with
permission from United Jewish Appeal-Federation of Jewish Philanthropies of New York, Inc.; **662,**
Bob Daemmrich Photography; **665,** Jonathan Daniel/Getty Sports Images; **677,** Michigan Tourist
Council; **696,** Arthur C. Smith III/Grant Heilman Photography; **697,** Douglas Pizac/AP/WIDE
WORLD PHOTOS; **707,** courtesy of Smith & Wollensky Restaurant Group; **714,** Burt Glinn/MAG-
NUM Photos; **717,** Steven Senne/AP/WIDE WORLD PHOTOS; **729** (top), Michael Probst/AP/WIDE
WORLD PHOTOS; (bottom), Jennifer Graylock/AP/WIDE WORLD PHOTOS; **744,** Bill Hudson/
AP/WIDE WORLD PHOTOS; **763,** Bob Daemmrich/THE IMAGE WORKS.

Text

Ted Allen. "The Laws of Fashion." From *Esquire*, March 2003. Copyright © 2003 by Ted Allen.
Reprinted by permission of William Morris Agency, Inc., on behalf of the author.

Julia Alvarez. "Snow." From *How the Garcia Girls Lost Their Accents* by Julia Alvarez. Copyright ©
1991 by Julia Alvarez. Published by Plume, an imprint of Penguin Group USA and originally in
hardcover by Algonquin Books of Chapel Hill. Reprinted by permission of Susan Bergholz Literary
Services, New York. All rights reserved.

Amnesty International On–Line. "The Death Penalty: Questions and Answers." Copyright © Amnesty International. www.amnesty.org. Reprinted by permission.

Maya Angelou. "Finishing School." From *I Know Why the Caged Bird Sings* by Maya Angelou.
Copyright © 1969 and renewed 1997 by Maya Angelou. Used by permission of Random House, Inc.

Kathy Antoniotti. "Marshmallow Mayhem." From the *Centre Daily Times*, January 20, 2004,
pp. C25–26. © 2004 Knight Ridder/Tribune Media Services. Text is reprinted by permission of the author.

Dave Barry. "Guys vs. Men." From *Dave Barry's Complete Guide to Guys* by Dave Barry. Copyright © 1995 by Dave Barry. Used by permission of Random House, Inc.

Barrie Jean Borich. "What Kind of King." From *My Lesbian Husband* by Barrie Jean Borich. © 1999 by Barrie Jean Borich. Reprinted by permission of Graywolf Press, Saint Paul, Minnesota.

Judy Brady. "I Want a Wife." Originally published in *Ms. Magazine*. Reprinted by permission of the author.

Suzanne Britt. "Neat People vs. Sloppy People." From *Show & Tell* by Suzanne Britt. Reprinted with permission of the author.

David Brooks. "The Triumph of Hope over Self-Interest." From *The New York Times*, January 12, 2003. Copyright © 2003 The New York Times. Reprinted with permission.

Bruce Catton. "Grant and Lee: A Study in Contrasts." From *The American Song* by Earl Schenck, editor. Reprinted by permission of the U.S. Capitol Historical Society.

Bob Costas. "Ali & Jordan." From *Rolling Stone*, May 15, 2003. © 2003 Rolling Stone LLC 2003. All Rights Reserved. Reprinted by permission.

Meghan Daum. "Music Is My Bag." From *My Misspent Youth* by Meghan Daum. Copyright © 2001 by Meghan Daum. Used by permission of Open City, Inc.

"Definition" and "Ingenuity." From *Merriam-Webster's Collegiate Dictionary*, Eleventh Edition. Copyright © 2003 by Merriam-Webster, Incorporated. Reprinted by permission.

Annie Dillard. "The Deer at Providencia." From *Teaching a Stone to Talk: Expeditions and Encounters* by Annie Dillard. © 1982 by Annie Dillard. Reprinted by permission of HarperCollins Publishers, Inc.

Jeff Drayer. "Bedside Terror." From www.salon.com. June 5, 2000. Reprinted by permission.

Steve Earle. "A Death in Texas." From *Tikkun*, September/October 2000. Reprinted in the January/February 2001 issue of *Utne Reader*. Reprinted by permission.

Gretel Ehrlich. "About Men." From *The Solace of Open Spaces* by Gretel Ehrlich. Copyright © 1985 by Gretel Ehrlich. Used by permission of Viking Penguin, a division of Penguin Putnam Group (USA), Inc.

Stephanie Ericsson. "The Ways We Lie." Originally published by *The Utne Reader*. Copyright © 1992 by Stephanie Ericsson. Reprinted by the permission of Dunham Literary as agents for the author.

"Evolution." From *The Oxford English Dictionary*, 22nd printing (1982). © 1971 Oxford University Press. Reprinted by permission of Oxford University Press.

Douglas Foster. "The Disease Is Adolescence." Published in *Rolling Stone*, December 9, 1993. © Rolling Stone LLC 1993. All Rights Reserved. Reprinted by permission.

Laura Fraser. "Why I Stopped Being a Vegetarian." From *Best Food Writing*. Copyright © 2000. Reprinted by permission of the author.

Malcolm Gladwell. "The Trouble with Fries." Originally published in *The New Yorker*, March 5, 2000, pp. 52–55. Copyright © 2000. Reprinted by permission of the author.

Stephen Jay Gould. "Sex, Drugs, Disasters, and the Extinction of Dinosaurs." From *The Flamingo's Smile: Reflections in Natural History* by Stephen Jay Gould. Copyright © 1984 by Stephen Jay Gould. Used by permission of W.W. Norton & Company, Inc.

Alison Green. "Living in Harmony, with Vegetarians." From *The Washington Post*, August 25, 1995. Copyright © 1995 The Washington Post.com. Reprinted with permission.

Zora Neale Hurston. "How It Feels to Be Colored Me." Used with the permission of the Zora Neale Hurston Trust.

Andy Kerr. "On Eating Meat." © Andy Kerr 2001. All Rights Reserved. Reprinted by Permission of the author. www.andykerr.net.

Martin Luther King Jr. "Letter From a Birmingham Jail." Reprinted by arrangement with the Estate of Martin Letter King Jr., c/o Writers House as agent for the proprietor, New York, NY. Copyright © 1963 Martin Luther King Jr. Copyright renewed 1991 Coretta Scott King.

Jonathan Kozol. "The Human Cost of an Illiterate Society." From *Illiterate America* by Jonathan Kozol. Copyright © 1985 by Jonathan Kozol. Used by permission of Doubleday, a division of Random House, Inc.

David Lieberman. "Deal with Any Complaint Fast and Easy." From *Get Anyone to Do Anything:*

Brent Staples. "Just Walk On By." Originally titled "Black Men and Public Space" from the December 1986 issue of *Harper's Magazine*. Reprinted by permission of the author.

Laura Sessions Stepp. "Alpha Girl." From *The Washington Post*, February 23, 2002. Copyright © 2002 The Washington Post. Reprinted with permission.

Amy Tan. "Mother Tongue." First appeared in *The Threepenny Review*. Copyright © 1990 by Amy Tan. Reprinted by permission of the author and the Sandra Dijkstra Literary Agency.

Deborah Tannen. "Cross Talk." From *You Just Don't Understand* by Deborah Tannen. Copyright © 1990 by Deborah Tannen. Reprinted by permission of HarperCollins Publishers, Inc.

Paul Theroux. "Being a Man." From *Sunrise with Seamonsters* by Paul Theroux. Copyright © 1985 by Cape Cod Scriveners Company. Reprinted by permission of Houghton Mifflin Company. All rights reserved.

Kruti Trivedi. "A Big Push for Learning 'Differences' Not Disabilities." From *The New York Times*, August 8, 2000. Copyright © 2000 by The New York Times Company. Reprinted with permission.

Michael Webber. "Athletics Provide Positive Influence." From www.statenews.com. Reprinted by permission of the author.

Linton Weeks. "The No-Book Report: Skim It and Weep." From *The Washington Post*, May 14, 2001, p. C1. Copyright © 2001 The Washington Post. Reprinted with permission.

E. B. White. "Once More to the Lake." From *One Man's Meat*. Text copyright © 1941 by E. B. White. Copyright renewed. Reprinted by permission of Tilbury House, Publishers, Gardiner, Maine.

Bernice Wuethrich. "Getting Stupid." From *Discover Magazine*. Reprinted by permission.

William Zinsser. "College Pressures." From *Blair and Ketchum's Country Journal*, Vol. VI., No. 4, April 1979. © 1979 by William Zinsser. Reprinted by permission of the author.

Art Credits

Amazon.com. screen shot. Copyright © 2004. Reprinted by permission. All Rights Reserved.

AP/Wide World Photos. Death-row inmate, Jonathan Nobles. © AP/Wide World Photos.

Istvan Banyai. Caricature of 4 couples. First published in *The New Yorker*, March 8, 2004. Reproduced by permission of 1st-1, Inc.

Cannoniere & Fortis; Chris Edwards and Biondi Productions/Getty Images. "Size Matters" food chart.

Christian Clayton. "Ali & Jordan" illustration. From *Rolling Stone*, May 15, 2003. By permission of Christian Clayton.

Robin Tinay Sallie. "Marshmallow Blaster" photo. KRT photo published in *Centre Daily Times*, January 30, 2004, p. C25. Reproduced by permission of Knight Ridder/Tribune.

Index

Where can you find more help?
At bedfordstmartins.com.

We have a wide variety of Web sites designed to help students with their most common writing concerns. You'll find advice from experts, models you can rely on, and exercises that will tell you right away how you're doing. And it's all free and available any hour of the day.

Need help with tricky grammar problems?
Exercise Central
bedfordstmartins.com/exercisecentral

Want to see what other papers for your course look like?
Model Documents Gallery
bedfordstmartins.com/modeldocs

Stuck somewhere in the research process? (Maybe at the beginning?)
The Bedford Research Room
bedfordstmartins.com/researchroom

Wondering whether a Web site is good enough to use in your paper?
Tutorial for Evaluating Online Sources
bedfordstmartins.com/onlinesourcetutorial

Having trouble figuring out how to cite a source?
Research and Documentation Online
bedfordstmartins.com/resdoc

Confused about plagiarism?
The St. Martin's Tutorial on Avoiding Plagiarism
bedfordstmartins.com/plagiarismtutorial

Want to learn more features of your word processor?
Using Your Word Processor
bedfordstmartins.com/wordprocessor

Trying to improve the look of your paper?
Using Your Word Processor to Design Documents
bedfordstmartins.com/docdesigntutorial

Need to create slides for a presentation?
Preparing Presentation Slides Tutorial
bedfordstmartins.com/presentationslidetutorial

Interested in creating a Web site?
Web Design Tutorial
bedfordstmartins.com/webdesigntutorial